THE GOVERNANCE OF CLOSE CORPORATIONS AND PARTNERSHIPS
US AND EUROPEAN PERSPECTIVES

The Governance of Close Corporations and Partnerships
US *and European Perspectives*

Edited by
JOSEPH A. McCAHERY
THEO RAAIJMAKERS
and
ERIK P. M. VERMEULEN

OXFORD
UNIVERSITY PRESS

OXFORD

UNIVERSITY PRESS

Great Clarendon Street, Oxford OX2 6DP

Oxford University Press is a department of the University of Oxford.
It furthers the University's objective of excellence in research, scholarship,
and education by publishing worldwide in

Oxford New York

Auckland Bangkok Buenos Aires Cape Town Chennai
Dar es Salaam Delhi Hong Kong Istanbul Karachi Kolkata
Kuala Lumpur Madrid Melbourne Mexico City Mumbai Nairobi
São Paulo Shanghai Taipei Tokyo Toronto

Oxford is a registered trade mark of Oxford University Press
in the UK and in certain other countries

Published in the United States
by Oxford University Press Inc., New York

British Library Cataloguing in Publication Data

Data available

Library of Congress Cataloging in Publication Data

Data available

ISBN 0–19–926435–X

1 3 5 7 9 10 8 6 4 2

Typeset by Hope Services (Abingdon) Ltd.
Printed in Great Britain
on acid-free paper by
Biddles Ltd., King's Lynn

Preface

This collection of essays arose out of a May 2001 Conference on Close Corporation and Partnership Law Reform in Europe and the United States, organized by the Faculty of Law and the Center for Company Law, at Tilburg University in May 2001. We are grateful to the Anton Philips Fund for their generous support of our investigation into the reform of unincorporated business forms. We were also fortunate to have the generous financial assistance of Linklaters & Alliance, the Center for Company Law, and the Schoordijk Institute of the Faculty of Law.

The Conference brought together a large number of the leading judges, policymakers, and lawyers from England, Europe, and the United States to participate in a debate on the appropriate course of partnership law reform in Europe. Conference participants addressed questions, from a range of diverse standpoints, about the essential role of organizational law, the role of standards of performance in limiting agency costs and creating a level playing field, the effect that horizontal jurisdictional competition has on the evolution and variety of business entity laws in Europe and the United States, the architectural features of English and US partnership law, the suitability of the LLP in the United Kingdom for small firms, the reform experience in business organization law in the United States, and the spread of new partnership-type business forms in continental Europe. The collection benefited from the comments and insights from Conference participants, many of which are reflected in the essays in this volume.

We decided to divide the essays into four parts, corresponding to the themes explored at the Conference: (i) theory: close corporation and partnership law, (ii) regulatory competition and the evolution of partnership law, (iii) partnership law reform in United Kingdom and United States, and (iv) unincorporated business entities in Europe. The chapters in this collection should appeal to entrepreneurs, policymakers, and lawyers working in the fields of business organization law and entrepreneurial finance.

We would like to thank the many individuals who have provided us with helpful comments and encouragement. We would particularly like to thank John Armour, Bill Bratton, Mic van Bremen, Bill Callison, The Rt Hon Lord Justice Carnwath, Eric van Damme, Claire Dickerson, Peter Essers, Gerard Meussen, Larry Ribstein, Jay Soled, Allan Vestal, and Reinout Vriesendorp. We would also wish to acknowledge our gratitude to Marjolijn Verhoeven for assisting us in organizing the Conference. We are also grateful for the administrative support provided by the Center for Company Law. We would like to thank the speakers, commentators, and chairs of sessions for the contributions at the Conference. We are particularly grateful for the contributions of John

Armour, William Callison, Deborah DeMott, Clair Moore Dickerson, Robert Drury, Peter Essers, Judith Freedman, Henry Hannsman, Reinier Kraakman, Gerard Meussen, Geoffrey Morse, Larry Ribstein, Edward Rock, Allan Vestal, Michael Wachter, Donald Weidner, and Michael Whincop.

While this volume was going to press, we learned of the untimely death of one of our key contributors to this project, Dr Michael Whincop of Griffith University Law School. We will miss Michael's distinctive approach to law and economics, but expect that his work will continue to stimulate creative developments in the field of business organization law.

We would like to thank those who have helped us in preparing the volume. The European Private Company Draft Regulation (in Appendixes 1 and 2) is reproduced by kind permission of the Chambre de Commerce et d'Industrie (CREDA). We are grateful to James J. Risser for his expert assistance in preparing the final manuscript for submission to the Press. We thank Barbara Gabor for able research assistance. We owe special thanks to our editor at Oxford University Press, John Louth, and Gwen Booth for their support and professionalism. Finally, we thank the Center for Company Law and the Tilburg Law and Economics Center for the stimulating research environments that they provide.

Contents

PART IV. THE EUROPEAN PRIVATE COMPANY AND PARTNERSHIP LAW REFORM IN THE EUROPEAN UNION

Tables of Cases

US CASES

EU CASES

UK AND COMMONWEALTH CASES

Lists of Authorities

US Legislation

US State Legislation

EU LEGISLATION

UK LEGISLATION

France Legislation

Australia Legislation

Institutional References

Jersey Statutes

List of Contributors

John Armour, B.A., B.C.L. (Oxon.), LL.M. (Yale) is University Lecturer and Fellow in Law, Trinity Hall and Fellow at the Centre for Business Studies Research at Cambridge University. He is interested in the economic analysis of corporate law and finance, with particular reference to insolvency. His work includes empirical and theoretical studies of the law and practice of corporate insolvency, the role of commercial norms in resolving financial distress, the effects of insolvency upon environmental liabilities, and the theory of secured credit.

J. William Callison is a Partner at Faegre and Benson, LLP in Denver, Colorado, where he specializes in corporate finance and securities, entity structuring, federal income taxation and litigation, mergers and acquisitions, partnerships, real estate, and tax planning. He earned his J.D. from the University of Colorado School of Law (Order of the Coif), and an LL.M. from Yale University School of Law. He also graduated from Oberlin College. He is the author of *Limited Liability Companies: A State-by-State Guide to Law and Practice* (West Publishing Company, 1994) (annual supplementation) and *Partnership Law and Practice: General and Limited Partnerships* (Clark Boardman Callaghan, 1992) (annual supplementation). He has written numerous professional articles on corporate law, partnership law, and venture capital.

Deborah A. DeMott is David F. Cavers Professor of Law at Duke University School of Law. She earned a B.A. from Swarthmore College and her J.D. from New York University School of Law, where she served as articles editor of the *New York University Law Review*. She began her professional career with a judicial clerkship in a federal court in New York City, and later practised with a large firm in that city, until she joined the Duke Law Faculty in 1975. Since 1995 Professor DeMott has served as Reporter for the American Law Institute's Restatement (Third) of Agency. From 2000–02, she held a secondary appointment as Centennial Visiting Professor in the Law Department of the London School of Economics. She has also taught at the Universities of Melbourne, Texas, Colorado, San Diego, the Hastings College of Law of the University of California, and the Osgoode Hall Law School, York University, Toronto. She is the author of a treatise, *Shareholder Derivative Actions*, published in 1987 and a casebook, *Fiduciary Obligation, Agency and Partnership*, published in 1991. Her other writing concerns corporate law, takeovers and acquisitions, and fiduciary obligation.

Claire Moore Dickerson is Professor of Law and Arthur L. Dickson Scholar at the Rutgers School of Law, Newark. Professor Dickerson earned her J.D. from

Columbia School of Law, where she was a Stone Scholar, and an LL.M. in taxation from New York University School of Law. She also graduated from Wellesley College, where she was a Durant Scholar. She began her career in New York City at the international law firm of Coudert Brothers, where she became a partner specializing in international transactions and worked principally with French multinationals. In recognition of this service, the French Republic's Centre Français du Commerce Exterieur awarded her its Medaille d'Honneur. Following twelve years at Coudert, she became partner of, and later counsel to, Schnader Harrison Segal & Lewis, a Philadelphia-based firm. In 1986 Professor Dickerson began her teaching career at St. John's University School of Law. Her research has applied socio-economic principles to business-related areas of law. She has written extensively on corporate governance, corporate law, and partnership law.

Robert R. Drury LL.B. Newcastle, Solicitor, is Senior Lecturer in Law at the University of Exeter. He has written extensively in the fields of company law, contract, European company law, comparative commercial laws, and commercial law. He is the co-editor of *International Corporate Procedures*, Vols. I–III (Jordans, 1992). He is the European Chairholder, European Studies Program, Chulalongkorn University, Bangkok, Thailand, and serves as a Specialist Assessor in Law, HEFCE.

Peter Essers studied fiscal economics at Tilburg University, the Netherlands, where he graduated in 1982. After graduation, he was employed as deputy-inspector of taxes at the Ministry of Finance in The Hague. In 1984 he was appointed lecturer in tax law at Tilburg University, where he received his Ph.D. in 1989. Since 1991 he has been Professor of Tax Law, specializing in national, European, and international personal and corporate income tax at Tilburg University. From September 1998 until December 2001 he was Dean of the Law Faculty of Tilburg University. He is also director of the European Tax College in Leuven (providing an LL.M. in European and International taxation), coordinator of EUCOTAX (European Universities Cooperating on Taxes) which is responsible for the organization of the yearly EUCOTAX Wintercourse, sponsored by the European Commission, and editor and contributor of various national and international reviews and book series (i.e. the Kluwer Law International EUCOTAX Series on European Taxation). He has been a visiting professor at the Université Panthéon-Sorbonne, the University of Barcelona, LUISS University Rome, the University of Bologna, the University of Osnabruck, and the Vienna University of Economics and Business Administration. He is also technical adviser of PricewaterhouseCoopers.

Judith Freedman B.A., M.A. (Oxon.), Solicitor, is KPMG Professor of Taxation Law and Fellow of Worcester College. She was Lecturer, Senior Lecturer, Reader, and finally a Professor in the Law Department of the London School of

Economics (1982–2001), with a secondment to the Institute of Advanced Legal Studies as Senior Research Fellow in Contemporary and Commercial Law from 1989–1992. Previously, she lectured in law at Surrey University (1980–82) after qualifying as a solicitor and working in the corporate tax department of Freshfields, a London law firm. She was a member of the Company Law Review's working party on small companies. Her research interests are taxation law, particularly corporate and company taxation, company law, and the interaction between law and accounting. She has written numerous articles on company law, partnership law, and taxation. She is one of the editors of the *British Tax Review*, European editor of *Palmer's Company Law*, a member of the editorial committee of the *Modern Law Review* and a member of the Tax Research Network steering group.

Henry Hansmann is George T. Lowy Professor of Law at New York University School of Law. Trained as both an economist and legal scholar, Professor Hansmann has focused his research primarily on the law and economics of enterprise organization. He has written extensively on non-profit firms, cooperatives, mutual companies, employee-owned firms, condominiums, trusts, and public enterprises, as well as conventional investor-owned business organanizations.

Reinier Kraakman is Erza Ripley Thayer Professor of Law at Harvard University School of Law. He was previously Professor of Law at Yale Law School and Visiting Professor of Law at both Georgetown University Law Center and New York University Law School. He received his J.D. degree from Harvard Law School and an A.B. degree from Harvard College. He also completed three years as a graduate student in sociology (ABD) at Harvard. He was also a law clerk for Judge Henry J. Friendly of the US Court of Appeals for the Second Circuit. He has been an adviser on company law reform in Russia and Vietnam. Currently, he teaches corporate law, corporate finance, and conducts seminars devoted to theoretical issues in organizational law. He has written numerous professional articles in corporate law, corporate governance, and liability strategies for controlling corporate behaviour.

Joseph A. McCahery is Professor of International Business Law at Tilburg University Faculty of Law, Research Fellow at the Tilburg Law and Economics Center, and Research Associate at the European Corporate Governance Institute (Brussels). He holds a visiting appointment at the Leiden University Faculty of Law. Previously, he held an appointment at Warwick University, where he also received a Ph.D. degree. He was also a law clerk for Judge Nathaniel R. Jones of the US Court of Appeals for the Sixth Circuit. His research interests are corporate control, corporate finance, European corporate law, the political economy of federalism, and international banking and securities regulation. He has written extensively on corporate law, corporate governance, securities, and regulation.

Gerard T. K. Meussen is Professor of Tax Law at the Law Department of the University of Nijmegen (the Netherlands). He is a technical adviser (of counsel) to Ernst & Young Tax Advisers in Rotterdam (the Netherlands). He acts as a judge at the lower tax courts of Amsterdam and Arnhem (The Netherlands). He is a member of the editorial board of the EUCOTAX Series on European Taxation, published by Kluwer Law International in London. He teaches and acts as a tutor at the European Tax College in Leuven (Belgium)/Tilburg (the Netherlands), an advanced master programme in international and European taxation. International publications by his hand appeared in *EC Tax Review*, *European Taxation*, and *Steuer und Wirtschaft*. He wrote the 2002 national report on The Netherlands for the conference of the European Association of Tax Law Professors (EATLP) in Lausanne (Switzerland) on 'The Concept of Harmful Tax Competition in the European Union'. Recently he gave guest lectures on European tax law issues in Lodz (Poland), Riga (Latvia), and Trier (Germany).

Geoffrey Morse is currently the Professor of Company Law at the University of Nottingham, a post which he has held since 1988, having previously also taught at the Universities of East Anglia and Liverpool. He was head of the law school at Nottingham University from 1994 to 1999. From September 2004 he will be taking up a post as Professor of Corporate and Tax Law at the University of Birmingham. He has held a number of visiting posts abroad, most recently as the David Marshall Professor of Law at the National University of Singapore (2002). He is also a member of the European Association of Tax Law Professors. He is the principal editor of *Palmer's Company Law* and editor of *Charlesworth and Morse: Company Law* (Sweet & Maxwell) and has written extensively on company law, the law of partnership and tax law. In particular his book on *Partnership Law* (OUP) is currently in its 5th edition. He is also one of the editors and coordinating editor of *Palmer's Limited Liability Partnerships Law* (Sweet & Maxwell) and an editor of *Davies: Principles of Tax Law* (Sweet & Maxwell). He also writes regularly on UK takeovers regulation in the *Journal of Business Law*.

M. J. G. C. (Theo) Raaijmakers is Professor of Corporate Law at Tilburg University Faculty of Law, Former Legal Adviser to Royal Philips Electronics, Justice of the Court of Appeals (Arnhem, The Netherlands), and a Member of the Social and Economic Council's Committee on Mergers. He is the author of a number of books including *Herziening van de Fusiecode* (Tjeenk Willink, 1994) and *Rechtspersonnen-en Vennootschapsrecht* (Gouda Quint, 2000). His areas of research include corporate law, securities, partnership law, corporate finance, group of companies, and corporate reorganizations.

Larry E. Ribstein is Richard W. and Marie L. Corman Professor of Law at the University of Illinois College of Law, Champaign-Urbana. He received his J.D. degree from the University of Chicago Law School and a B.A. from Johns

Hopkins University. Professor Ribstein, who works in the areas of choice of law, ethical rules and uniform laws, was instrumental in shaping the curriculum and programs of George Mason University School of Law during his fifteen-year tenure there. He is the author of *Unincorporated Business Entities* (Anderson Publishing, 2nd edn., 2000) and *Business Associations* (Matthew Bender, 3rd edn., with Letsou 1996) used by law schools throughout the United States. He is the co-author of the leading multivolume treatises on partnership law and on limited liability companies. He also wrote *The Constitution and the Corporation* (American Enterprise Institute, 1995). He served as an editor of the *Supreme Court Economic Review* from 1998 to 2001 and as an official adviser to the Drafting Committee to Revise the Uniform Partnership Act for the National Conference of Commissioners on Uniform State Laws. He has presented papers and testimony, among other places, at the American Law & Economics Association and the Federal Trade Commission.

Edward B. Rock is the Saul A. Fox Distinguished Professor of Business Law at the University of Pennsylvania Law School. He also serves as co-director of the Institute for Law and Economics and has written widely in corporate law: on the role of institutional investors in corporate governance; close corporations, the overlap between corporate and antitrust; the overlap between corporate and labour law; comparative corporate governance; and the regulation of mutual funds. In 1994 he was a Visiting Professor of International Banking and Capital Markets at the Goethe Universität (Frankfurt) and in 1995–6, he was a Fulbright Senior Scholar at the Hebrew University (Jerusalem). His current research focuses on mergers and acquisitions and corporate constitutionalism.

Erik P. M. Vermeulen is Assistant Professor at Tilburg University Faculty of Law and Research Fellow at the Tilburg Center of Law and Economics. He is also a corporate lawyer in the Legal Department of Philips International, N.V. He received a Ph.D. degree in law at Tilburg University in 2003, where he graduated cum laude. He has published articles on corporate law, partnership law, venture capital, and regulatory competition and is author of *The Evolution of Legal Business Form in Europe and the United States* (Kluwer Law International, 2003). He has been a Visiting Research Fellow at the Centre for Business Research at Cambridge University and the University of Connecticut Law School. He is currently working on a study on private equity funds and limited partnerships.

Allan Walker Vestal is Dean and Professor of Law at the University of Kentucky College of Law. Prior to joining the College of Law Faculty, he was on the faculty of the Washington and Lee School of Law from 1989 to 2000, where he taught in the areas of partnership and corporation law, commercial law, and real estate. Prior to teaching, he practised law in Wisconsin and Iowa for a total of ten years. He received his B.A. in 1976 and his J.D. in 1979, both from Yale University. He is the author of a treatise on the Revised Uniform Partnership Act (with Professor Hillman and Dean Weidner) and has published numerous articles on a wide variety of subjects in partnership and commercial law. He is a member of the American Law Institute.

Michael L. Wachter is William B. Johnson Professor of Law and Economics and Co-Director of the Institute for Law and Economics at the University of Pennsylvania Faculty of Law. Since 1970, when he joined the Penn faculty, he has held full professorships in three of Penn's schools: Arts and Sciences, where he has been full professor since 1976; the Wharton School, where he was professor of management, 1980–92; and the Law School, where he became professor of Law and Economics. Professor Wachter has also served at the University of Pennsylvania as Interim Provost (1988); Deputy Provost (1995–8); and Faculty Assistant to the President (1975–9). He has written numerous articles in the fields of law and economics, with his current research focusing on topics of corporate law, labour law, and economics.

Donald J. Weidner has written numerous law review articles on partnerships, fiduciary duties and real estate finance, and is co-author of *The Revised Uniform Partnership Act* (West Group, 2002) (with R. Hillman and A. Vestal). He also has recently written on the use of special purpose entities by large corporations to keep debt off their books. He teaches property, agency and partnership, and real estate finance. A member of the American Law Institute who also was the Reporter for the Revised Uniform Partnership Act, he has also served as a Visiting Professor at Stanford Law School, the University of Texas, the University of New Mexico, and the University of North Carolina. He began his legal career at the New York law firm of Willkie Farr & Gallagher. Dean Weidner is a graduate of Fordham University and an honors graduate of University of Texas Law School, where he was project editor of the *Texas Law Review*. He served as Dean of Florida State University College of Law from 1991 to 1997, as Interim Dean from 1998 to 2000, and as Dean from 2000 to the present.

Michael J. Whincop was Deputy Head of the Griffith University Law School and Director of the Business Regulation Program prior to his death in June of 2003. He was an Associate Professor at Griffith University Law School and was Visiting Professor of Law at the University of Pennsylvania Law School in 2003. His research interests concerned corporate law, contract law, venture capital and small and medium-sized enterprises, the economics of privatization, and law and economics. He received a Ph.D. degree from Griffith University and an LL.B. from Queensland University. Professor Whincop was the author of many books including most recently, *An Economic and Jurisprudential Genealogy of Corporate Law* (Ashgate, 2001).

Abbreviations

AAP	affirmative asset partitioning
BV	besloten vennootschap
CLRSG	Company Law Review Steering Group
CREDA	Centre de recherche sur le droit des affaires
DAP	defensive asset partitioning
EEIG	European Economic Interest Groupings
EPC	European Private Company
ESOP	employment stock option plan
GAAP	generally accepted accounting principles
IPO	initial public offering
ITF	institutional theory of the firm
LLC	limited liability company
LLLP	limited liability limited partnership
LLP	limited liability partnership
LLPA	Limited Liability Partnerships Act
MEDEF	Mouvement des Entreprises de France
NBER	National Bureau of Economic Research
NCCUSL	National Conference of Commissioners on Uniform State Laws
NTF	neoclassical theory of the firm
PRTF	property rights theory of the firm
RMBCA	Revised Model Business Corporation Act
RULPA	Revised Uniform Limited Partnership Act
RUPA	Revised Uniform Partnership Act
SAS	société par actions simplifiée
SMEs	small and medium-sized enterprises
SORP	statement of recommended practice
UCC	Uniform Commercial Code
ULLCA	Uniform Limited Liability Company Act
UPA	Uniform Partnership Act
VC	venture capitalists

1

Introduction: Governance in Partnership and Close Corporation Law in Europe and the United States

JOSEPH A. McCAHERY

1.1. INTRODUCTION

An expansion of the menu of business forms is essential to meet the complex needs of all types of firms. It has been clear for some time that a single business association form, which offers firms a shield of limited liability, is unlikely to maximize the interests of investors. The choice of business entity decision has, until recently, been constrained by legal and regulatory impediments. The interest in there being a variety of legal rules available to meet the needs of businesses at all levels has become an influential theme in corporate law due to the development of new organizational business forms such as the Limited Liability Company (LLC) and the Limited Liability Partnership (LLP).

In recent years, a rapid succession of statutory innovations of partnership forms has transformed business organization law in the United States. Since the IRS approved tax treatment of the limited liability companies (LLCs) in 1988,[1] LLC provisions have been approved in all 50 states and the District of Columbia. The emergence of the LLC improved the menu of business forms in several ways by, for example, bundling together limited liability, a flexible governance structure, and preferential tax treatment. The choice available to firms was expanded further in 1991 when Texas developed the Limited Liability Partnership (LLP), which allows general partners in professional firms to avoid joint and several malpractice liabilities. Thereafter, the LLP spread rapidly from two states in 1992 to all 50 jurisdictions and the District of Columbia in 2001. As the LLP evolved, most states expanded the scope of the LLP by allowing non-professional firms to use the statute, and in some jurisdictions lawmakers extended the concept to include limited liability limited partnerships (LLLPs) (Callison, Chapter 8, this volume). At the same time, business lawyers figured importantly in partnership law reform (Weidner, Chapter 13, this volume). The

---

[1] See Rev. Rul. 88-76 1988-2 C.B. 360.

promulgation in 1994 of the Revised Uniform Partnership Act, the first comprehensive revision of the Uniform Partnership Act by the National Conference of Commissioners on Uniform State Laws (NCCUSL), reinforced the changes occurring in partnership law generally. Moreover, the success of the LLP triggered the subsequent adoption of LLP provisions to the Revised Uniform Partnership Act (RUPA) in 1997.[2] In the light of the cumulative success of partnership reforms in recent years, states today are continuing to experiment and develop new forms, a number of which are likely to emerge shortly (Vestal, Chapter 12, this volume).

Similar processes can also be identified as taking place internationally. The growth in new business organization forms is evident in the United Kingdom and many other developed countries (Morse, Chapter 11, this volume). The issue of closely held firms has also drawn the attention of policymakers across the European Union and over the past several years conferences have been arranged on the subject at research institutes and international organizations. Indeed, the importance of creating business organization forms tailored to meet the needs of the closely held firm is now receiving worldwide attention as a major policy issue facing market economies. What forces explain the emergence of these reform efforts? Over the last decade, small and medium-sized enterprises (SMEs) have come into the spotlight because of the considerable impact they have on the business environment (OECD 1998). In particular, venture capital-backed firms have, until the recent economic downturn, stimulated product and labour market development (Gompers and Lerner 1999). Even though the traditional close corporation is particularly well suited to enterprises with a high proportion of 'match-specific assets', it is argued that it does not meet the needs of the typical small firm (Rock and Wachter, Chapter 4, this volume).[3] From an efficiency perspective, it may be clear that closely held firms would be more productive if there were governance arrangements that limit intra-firm opportunism and provide adequate incentives for the firm's participants (Talley 1999). In turn this requires a menu of coherent legal forms available to closely held firms to select legal rules that suit their organizational needs. The US experience underscores that some countries have, in order to encourage entrepreneurship, sought to expand the vertical choices of business forms (Ribstein, Chapter 6, this volume).

Until recently, European countries were not eager or even likely to adopt statutory innovations to their corporate law regimes. Despite the increased pressures from SME organizations, corporate law reform efforts tended to be piecemeal and reactionary due to the absence of incentives, which has led to the creation of inefficient legal codes and a paucity of limited liability business

---

[2] See Rev. Unif. P'ship Act, 6 U.L.A. 6 (Supp. 2001) (prefatory note explaining the process of authorizing the incorporation of LLP provisions in RUPA).

[3] See e.g. Hampe and Steininger (2001) (arguing that German high-tech firms that employed the Gesellschaft mit beschränkter Haftung (GmbH) form between 1985 and 1989 had a higher probability of survival compared with businesses that selected partnership forms).

vehicles (McCahery and Vermeulen, Chapter 7, this volume). Nevertheless, it appears that the pattern of lawmaking may be evolving slowly. What forces explain the changes occurring in business organization law? One critical factor is the advent of competition pressures from offshore jurisdictions that have created incentives for national governments to generate new statutory measures. A recent example is the United Kingdom's decision to adopt an LLP statute, in order to stem the outflow of professional firms to Jersey, which created an LLP statute in 1996 (Freedman, Chapter 10, this volume). A further manifestation of this new pattern in regulatory policymaking is the adoption by a number of European states of new flexible business organization statutes, such as the French société par actions simplifiée, designed to stimulate the formation of joint venture enterprises. A second factor, coinciding with these changes, is the renewed debate within the European Community (EC) about the merits of regulatory competition, which could give rise eventually to a market for corporate charters. Consequently, if Europe succeeds in creating the conditions more conducive to regulatory competition, one could then expect more states to be involved in increasing a variety of legal rules that are beneficial to different types of firms.

The evolution of the new business organization forms has tended naturally to awakened scholarly interest. Within the United States the growing acceptance of the new business forms is reflected in the high-profile debates emerging from the conferences at Washington, Colorado, Washington and Lee, and Maryland universities. Thinking about these innovations has generated much research on the relationship between fiduciary duties and governance structure, partners' property rights, and dissociation and dissolution. The sudden development of the LLC and LLP and the rapid adoption of these new business vehicles for conducting business activities would be reason enough to justify the considerable research interest. Yet, in some ways, the interest in the unincorporated firm has been propelled further by the focus of several prominent scholars on the relation between the evolution of legal rules and the incentives created by regulatory competitive pressures that work in favour of creating bundles of legal rules that are attractive to investors. In terms of the research agenda on the unincorporated firm, it seems that the initial stages of development have been driven, in large part, by questions about whether the new business forms are efficient (Ribstein 1995), and the role of competitive lawmaking in encouraging innovation (Ribstein, Chapter 6, this volume; McCahery and Vermeulen, Chapter 7, this volume; Callison, Chapter 8, this volume; Vestal, Chapter 12, this volume). What studies tended to confirm is that the new business forms clearly have advantages over earlier partnership forms. To start, the LLC and LLP, which combine a menu of limited liability, a flexibility respecting governance terms, and a choice of tax treatments, allow firms to select legal forms that are compatible with their organizational features. It is often claimed, moreover, that these off-the-rack standard legal forms provide an efficient, low-cost solution to the governance problems of closely held firms. Despite the rich and extensive literature on the beneficial aspects of these new forms, there have been few attempts to specify empirically the efficiency characteristics of these statutes.[4] Consequently, there is a tendency by some to challenge the efficiency aspects of the legal forms. For others, the analytical tools of public choice theory have been deployed to show that the new statutes are the logical result of a policymaking process shaped largely by influential and well-organized pressure groups (Levmore 1992). Seen in this light, the contours of the new business statutes reflect the preferences of the groups that had the strongest incentive to organize to influence legislative outcomes (Macey 1995).

In the case of Europe, a slightly different analysis, albeit bereft of law and economics understandings of organization forms, which is explicitly focused on the form and character of the statutory instruments has emerged to address the key legal problems of closely held firms (Lutter 1998). Much of the scholarly interest lies in determining whether lawmakers should create a limited liability vehicle tailored for small businesses (Rider and Andenas 1999). For those writers sceptical of the efficiency justification for extending limited liability to small firms, issues about the degree it is possible for closely held firms to select an optimal business statute arise (Freedman 2000: 325). A recurring theme in the literature concerns the role of mandatory rules in statutory standard forms. In contrast with the United States, the trend in European corporate law has been to dismiss the benefits associated with the enabling approach too quickly, relying on a narrow range of techniques and mandatory rules to balance the interests of the various parties. In the meantime, the US debates on economic analysis of the firm and their implications for corporate law appear to be influencing a variety of European-wide debates on the governance of the closely held firm (McCahery and Vermeulen, Chapter 7, this volume).

Entering into the US debate, European scholars have been forced to confront the prevailing view concerning the desirable scope of limited liability (Alexander 1992; Easterbrook and Fischel 2000; Grundfest 1992; Hansmann and Kraakman 1991). The law and economics rationale for limited liability is that it reduces the need for shareholders to monitor managers and other shareholders, it encourages public trading in shares, and it facilitates diversification. This discussion of limited liability, as it arises in the closely held firm context, emphasizes the diversification benefits and monitoring cost savings of negotiating into limited liability (Ribstein 1995: 101–5; Macey 1995: 449). More recent analysis in the United States has questioned the efficiency presumption of limited liability for closely held firms (Callison, Chapter 8, this volume). The problems start first with underlying assumptions of the advantages of limited liability in the closely held firm context. The basic argument here is that limited liability is thought to have little impact on monitoring costs, liquidity, and risk diversification in the small-firm context (Bratton and McCahery 1997: 638–40).

---

[4] Unlike the debate on the efficiency for corporate charters, partnership law scholars have limited means to measure the productivity effects of the new legislation.

Under this approach, limited liability is particularly harmful because it creates moral hazard problems for third parties (Freedman 2000: 331–2). In addition, some law and economics scholars have been forced to conclude that since limited liability for corporate torts is inefficient it should not be considered as part of the essential role of organization law (Hansmann and Kraakman, Chapter 2, this volume). For similar reasons, European scholars find that costs outweigh the benefits of extending limited liability to small firms. These considerations in turn help support national lawmakers' continued reliance on signalling devices, such as minimum capital requirements, and other techniques to balance the levels of risk taking (Armour 2000). Inevitably, these legal rules also maintain their usefulness for blocking the development of new business organization statutes. Clearly, the notion that European lawmakers will eventually adjust their legal frameworks to facilitate companies to opt out of mandatory minimum capital restrictions is naïve. Sometimes, however, the effects of the competition between states may lead lawmakers to abandon the limitations on limited liability, even in the face of intense interest group lobbying, when competitive pressures are introduced (Lutter 1995: 203–5). In this view, the new British LLP and the current reforms to the UK company law regime may serve to introduce new incentives that could foster a pattern of corporate lawmaking that leads ultimately to the unlocking of limitations on limited liability across continental Europe (Bachmann 2001).

Having described the tensions over extending limited liability to small firms, we now turn to the equally complex problem of determining whether to modify fiduciary prohibitions in closely held firms. Differences between the corporation and unincorporated firm have also featured in the US debate about the appropriate role of fiduciary duties in limiting overreaching behaviour (Talley 1999; O'Neil 1998). Many economists think that the role of fiduciary duties should vary across the type of organizational form. In the context of closely held firms, strict fiduciary duties are justified, given the organizational characteristics, to prevent the greater threat of opportunistic behaviour. While some (including William Callison, Claire Moore Dickerson, Deborah DeMott, and Allan Vestal) develop or defend this kind of approach to fiduciary duties in closely held firms, others (especially Larry E. Ribstein, Eric Talley, and to some extent, Edward Rock and Michael Wachter) resist this view of fiduciary duties. For these scholars, strict fiduciary duties are counterproductive in closely held firms, encouraging parties to engage in over-monitoring at the expense of productivity. Indeed, some argue that an obvious alternative to strict fiduciary duties in partnership-type firms is the contractual tailoring of obligations. Accordingly, allowing firms to waive partnership-type fiduciary duties would constitute a signal of their governance preference. Scholars who have expressed concern about allowing firms to opt out of their obligations claim that this trend will eventually undermine the function of fiduciary duties (Blair and Stout 2001). The first steps in this direction appear to have emerged. That is, the provisions in Delaware's LLC, general partnership and limited partnership act that provide the freedom to contract out of fiduciary duties, gives credence to the argument that partnership law may be unravelling to the lowest possible level (Dickerson 1997). Moreover, it seems that norm entrepreneurs have influenced successfully the dynamics of norm-following behaviour applicable to the unincorporated business by reducing the standards of performance relating to the fiduciary standards of a partner's duty of loyalty and good faith and fair dealing within the RUPA (RUPA § 404(b)(1)–(3); § 404(d)). Yet it is worth pointing out that the lowering of minimum level of fiduciary duties is occurring gradually and the process is punctuated by numerous reversions back to the higher standard elaborated in *Meinhard v. Salmon* (164 N.E. 545 (1928), see Talley (1999)). Nevertheless, it would appear that the statutory and doctrinal changes under-way have contributed in the short run to norm erosion and may induce a norm change in the long run. Undoubtedly, this highly relevant and not wholly uncontroversial debate can be expected to migrate to the European unincorporated firms context where many of the same conflicts and situations have arisen.[5]

In Europe, the introduction of new legal entities figures highly on the policy agenda. Given the similarities between European and US partnership law, the conference organizers set out to focus on the reform efforts of various governments to create new business organization statutes. In the United States the evolution of new forms has become the backbone of the law of unincorporated business forms. The last few years have witnessed a lively debate about the apparent success of the new vehicles and the forces that have produced partnership forms that are suited to business needs. Although the US business organization forms were created in a different institutional and political environment, the debate has resonated among European corporate law scholars, with a number of them arguing that national governments should emulate the US reforms. Despite the attractions of the LLC and LLP, the conference provided an opportunity to understand not only the difficulties of formulating new policies but also the results and performance of the legislation. Other approaches to reform of legal business forms brought attention to the hazards of poorly conceived regulation, which is likely to evolve in the direction of greater stringency and more costs for closely held firms.

1.2. Issue Coverage

The book is organized in four parts. Part I addresses the recent theoretical debates on the nature of the unincorporated firm. The first chapter by Henry Hansmann and Reinier Kraakman examines the legal and institutional framework required for affirmative asset partitioning and its economic role in organization enterprise. The next chapter by John Armour and Michael Whincop

---

[5] While European and US partnership law differs in some respects, there are important similarities. For instance, there are broad fiduciary duties in partnerships in Europe and the United States. See Heenen (1975); Miller (1997).

describes the main functions of affirmative asset partitioning and explains how changing proprietary entitlements can be efficiency enhancing. In their chapter, Edward Rock and Michael Wachter show how the close corporation, with its limitations on exit and the general prohibition of non pro rata distributions, appears to offer a general framework for start-up firms that protects business participants from the opportunistic conduct of fellow participants. Claire Moore Dickerson, starting from the view that standards of performance are under siege in the United States, argues in Chapter 5 that the standards such as good faith and fiduciary duty can substantially reduce agency costs while levelling the playing field.

Part II begins with an essay by Larry Ribstein in which he shows that the recent history of US partnership forms strongly supports the efficient evolution through horizontal and vertical choice. In Chapter 7, Erik Vermeulen and I analyse the development of new legal organization forms and the constraints on the efficient evolution of legal rules in Europe. William Callison evaluates in Chapter 8 how the US federal tax law changes instigated the rapid state adoption of limited liability alternatives to the corporation.

Part III shifts the emphasis from the theoretical and doctrinal debates on the law of business organizations to analyses of partnership law developments in England and the United States. In Chapter 9, Deborah DeMott focuses on the common starting point of US partnership law, which is based on the Uniform Partnership Act (UPA) and English partnership law and the subsequent developments, which has led to different elements dominating partnership law in England compared with the United States. Judith Freedman studies in Chapter 10 the emergence of a new legal form, the LLP in the United Kingdom. Geoffrey Morse sets out in Chapter 11 to examine some of the proposals in the Law Commission's joint consultation paper on Partnership Reform in the United Kingdom. In Chapter 12, Allan Walker Vestal focuses on the accomplishments of the decade-long reform of unincorporated law, arguing that most of the law reforms proceeded without an underlying theory to structure and support the experimentation. Donald Weidner studies, in Chapter 13, the RUPA's extensive new provisions that treat partnerships as entities, define relations among partners, clarify the law of partnership breakups, and provide for limited liability partnerships.

The chapters in Part IV provide an up-to-date account of the closely held company reforms underway in Europe and assess the important tax issues involving hybrid entities. In Chapter 14, Robert Drury explores the genesis and development of the European Private Company Regulation. In his contribution, Theo Raaijmakers offers a critical account of the partnership law reform agenda in the Netherlands, noting that Dutch lawmakers have failed to adequately embrace a modern approach to partnerships. In Chapter 16, Peter Essers and Gerard Meussen examine the Dutch approach to partnerships and offer a critical evaluation of the tax treatment of the US LLC in the Netherlands.

1.3. OVERVIEW

The collection opens with the essay by Henry Hansmann and Reinier Kraakman on 'The Essential Role of Organizational Law'. As the theory's leading proponents, the authors advance the argument that the essential role of organizational law is to define the property rights over which the participants in the firm can contract. The separation of the firm's assets and its participants is designated 'affirmative asset partitioning'. This form of asset partitioning assigns to the firm's creditors a prior claim on the firm's assets, which is the core characteristic of the corporate form. In this view, affirmative asset partitioning reduces firm risk substantially by allowing creditors and others to deal with the firm as a unit rather than with the individual members. As a consequence, it protects the firm and its creditors from the possibility of partial or complete liquidation of the firm's assets by the owner's creditors. Affirmative asset partitioning also promotes the efficient apportionment of risk among owners and creditors.

Hansmann and Kraakman also focus on the second form of asset partitioning, 'negative asset partitioning' or limited liability. It functions to protect owners by limiting creditors of the entity to pursue claims on shareholders' separate assets. Limited liability, in turn, promotes efficiency by limiting monitoring costs, externalizing risk, enabling the transfer of securities, and facilitating diversification. Despite the key role of limited liability in facilitating a more productive investment policy for the firm, Hansmann and Kraakman insist that negative asset partitioning plays a secondary role to affirmative asset partitioning. In the absence of affirmative asset partitioning, it would be practically impossible to establish limited liability. Are there other essential functions of organizational law? Whilst there are a number of important features of organizational law that appear to perform an 'essential' role—such as rules governing the relations between the firm's owners and the firm's creditors, the relationships among the firm's owners and between the firm's owners and managers, and relationships between the firm and non-owner patrons—they cannot be justified as 'essential', since these functions are typically performed by contract law. Hansmann and Kraakman conclude that affirmative asset partitioning played a central role in enhancing the development of modern business activity.

John Armour and Michael Whincop's essay, 'An Economic Analysis of Shared Property in Partnership and Close Corporations Law', provides an analytic framework for thinking about the role of property rights in firms. The starting point for their chapter is the theory of the firm. Recent work on incomplete contracts, according to Armour and Whincop, has challenged the 'nexus of contracts' view of the firm by showing that the allocation of property rights—residual entitlements to control over access to physical and intangible assets—is crucial to the design of efficient governance structures. Yet doubts arise about the implications of the property rights theory for corporate law. Some recognize however that since contracts are not comprehensive and are often revised, it is the allocation of residual rights of control that determine the *ex post* distribution of the firm's surplus.[6] Hence it is possible to argue that governance consists of no more than the allocation of rights to control assets. Yet corporate law, Armour and Whincop argue, does more than this. They share with Hansmann and Kraakman the view that corporate law generates entitlements that are valid not only against a counterparty, but against an indefinite number of potential parties. Not only does law provide such frameworks, but to a significant extent it allows insiders to specify their contents. In other words, the law gives 'multital' effect to the contracts parties write about allocations of control of assets. Armour and Whincop think that without this, such governance arrangements would not be credible. While the flexibility this provides has obvious efficiency advantages, the fact that insiders determine relations with third parties creates opportunities for rent-seeking behaviour. But the contractibility of such multital relations is tempered by general restrictions designed to protect third parties. It is crucial, on this view, that the law must trade-off facilitating *ex ante* optimal arrangements between insiders and limiting the costs to outsiders. To the extent that outsiders' costs are endogenous to the range of terms on offer, the law limits the flexibility insiders have to determining their proprietary entitlements, which accounts for the partitioning of organizational terms into forms. After explaining the functions of organizational law in general, the authors turn to the unique asset partitioning features in both partnerships and close corporations. They show how the proprietary entitlements are differentiated across the available menu of English business law forms.

The next chapter by Edward Rock and Michael Wachter focuses on the persistent features of the close corporation that serve to protect participants from the misconduct by fellow participants. The early literature on close corporations assumed that close corporations and partnerships are functionally equivalent business forms with the same organizational needs. This approach is based on the assumption that business participants choose only the corporate form over the partnership to take advantage of limited liability and tax benefits. Advocates proposed modifications of the exit rules of close corporations so that business participants would enjoy the same exit options as partners in a partnership. Agency theory rebuts the functional equivalence approach by showing that business participants choose the close corporation structure to maximize the return on their low agency costs. As a result, agency theory holds that the optimal close corporation form is one that provides no additional protections to reduce the risk of majority opportunism and majority shareholders should be held to the same strict standards of fiduciary duty as managers of publicly held firms.

Building on the agency cost assumption, Rock and Wachter move this literature forward a step to show that, where there is an intensity of match-specific

---

[6] See e.g. Hart and Moore (2000).

assets in which all the participants invest, the close corporation is best served by rules that lock-in the majority and minority participants by giving them a limited right to dissociate. This view is more in line with the experiences of high-tech start-ups where a rule against opportunistic exit serves to protect the initial investments of human and physical capital made by the participants in the development stage. Rock and Wachter's theory relies on extra-legal mechanisms, such as self-enforcing norms of trust and reputation, to constrain opportunistic behaviour. For instance, the informal enforcement mechanisms found in a long-term employment relationship form an essential component in deterring defection and inducing cooperation among the participants. In this model, there are a number of incentive devices and mechanisms that can be adapted to unforeseen contingencies that resist contractual treatment *ex ante*. As a consequence, there is a strong case for relying on credible self-regulation strategies without reference to legal mandate. Where does this leave the judicial role on minority shareholder protection? Rock and Wachter explain that the advantages of the lock-in do not, of course, apply across the board. For example, judicial intervention may be justified to prevent non pro rata distributions. In so far as this principle is crucial to the strategy of allowing majority shareholders to manage the firm in the general shareholder interest, it is necessary to strictly enforce this principle. But any enthusiasm this mechanism generates in preventing non pro rata distributions needs to be quelled in the cases involving the protection of minority shareholders' employment in the firm. The evidence suggest that judicial intervention in these kind of conflicts is far too complex and could undermine the self-regulatory mechanisms required for stable, cooperative relationships in the firm.

Claire Moore Dickerson's essay, 'Bracketed Flexibility: Standards of Performance Level the Playing Field', explores the role of fiduciary duties in limiting opportunism in closely held businesses. In a closely held firm, high standards of performance are thought to be necessary to constrain opportunism. Yet, it is widely recognized that there has been considerable pressure in the United States to de-emphasize standards of performance, such as fiduciary duty or heightened good faith, for unincorporated business forms. There is evidence of similar pressure in Europe. The reason typically given for opposing standards of performance is that they impede the parties' ability to bargain freely. However, the standards actually are designed to level the playing field and thus to enhance the possibility of meaningful bargaining. The standards accomplish this goal by being flexible and rising in relation to the transactor's power and conflict.

Dickerson speculates that the real reason behind the hostility to the standards is the perception that the standards are uncertain. Because past discussion has focused only on the floor—the minimum legal behaviour—the generally unarticulated concern is that, in order to avoid falling through the floor, the transactor must act very cautiously, even generously. In fact, she argues that standards are sufficiently precise to have a ceiling as well as a floor. Both this floor and ceiling are socially constructed: the law supports only the floor directly, although it does support the ceiling indirectly. However, the principle and direct constraint on excessively generous behaviour is the other party's non-cooperative reaction. Naturally, behaviour so generous as to hit the ceiling is self-limiting. Nevertheless, because the standards of performance are designed to level the playing field, and because they are effective due to their flexibility and precision, parties should not be permitted to opt out of their fiduciary duties. The evidence further suggests that fiduciary duties are effective in influencing firms' managers because they both reflect and reinforce the standards applicable in the larger society.

In Part II, Larry Ribstein's chapter, 'The Evolving Partnership', introduces a theme that, as noted earlier, occupies many of the contributions: whether partnership law particularly as it developed in the United States has evolved to efficiency as a consequence of regulatory competition. He sees the development of new limited liability statutes as benefiting from the pressures of state competition, which stimulated lawmakers to supply an efficient bundle of legal rules that benefit investors. In so far as competition produces a race to the top, Ribstein points out there is a body of evidence that supports the rationale that permitting horizontal and vertical choice of business forms produces value-enhancing outcomes. If society were to rely on a centralized regulator, it is almost certain moreover that the legal regime would have produced suboptimal business forms. This provides an important lesson for Europe in the wake of the European Court of Justice's decision in the *Centros* case.[7] He argues that regulatory competition creates a dynamic law that is responsive to the varied needs of modern firms. This is preferable to uniform lawmaking that erroneously assumes that lawmakers can anticipate what optimal rules should be across time and across different firms. He then goes on to analyse the specific effects of the process of horizontal and vertical choice. Having reviewed the developments and changes within the different business forms, Ribstein contends the basic issue remains how to balance the benefits of legal evolution against the needs of the parties who are implicated by the changes. He concludes that the benefits of horizontal jurisdictional competition to facilitate market testing, variety, and evolution of law are significant and accordingly this approach is the best model to facilitate the development of European business organization law.

In my essay with Erik Vermeulen, we show that close corporations have become the preferred vehicle for small and medium-sized enterprises in Europe. While scholars have debated the advantages of close corporation statutes for more than a decade, some who favour reform suggest that lawmakers should devise new business organization statutes that are varied, less complex, and can potentially enhance efficient outcomes. Indeed, since in most jurisdictions close corporations are a mirror image of their publicly held counterpart, small and medium enterprises are burdened by a number of regulatory requirements,

---

[7] Case C-212/97, *Centros Ltd. v. Erhvervs- og Selskabsstyrelsen* [1999] E.C.R. I-1459.

which cause them to incur substantial costs in carrying out their normal business activities. In particular, the imposition of many of the European Community's harmonized corporate law provisions on smaller firms is viewed as disproportionate and over-regulatory, and tends to impede the development of an efficient supply of legal rules.

Reform-minded scholars, supported by product and capital market pressures to supply the most competitive business statute for small and medium-sized enterprises, point to the success of the US LLC. We argue that making new business forms available, such as the LLC, will likely lead to an increase in the number of start-up firms while also satisfying the needs of a range of closely held firms. However we note that the combination of organized interest group pressure and the significant switching costs are important barriers to the creation of new business organization statutes. Hence, an important question is whether the introduction of competitive pressures could limit the difficulties encountered in creating a flexible business form with few mandatory rules. From our perspective, we observe that the combination of the ECJ's recent judgment in *Centros* and the legislative inertia in the European Community's harmonization law programme has stimulated considerable interest in the competition between states. We believe however that there are significant legal and cultural barriers to near term development of a market for business forms. Consequently, despite the pent-up demand for low-cost business forms across Europe, it is difficult to predict with certitude the circumstances that would lead to the development of regulatory competition within the LLC context. Finally, we believe that a model statute could be a contributing factor in the introduction of an LLC-type business form within the European Community.

J. William Callison's essay, 'Federalism, Regulatory Competition, and the Limited Liability Movement: The Coyote Howled and the Herd Stampeded', offers both an account of the rapid diffusion of the LLC in the United States and a substantive defence of judicial veil-piercing mechanisms for looking through limited liability. Callison begins his essay by exploring the gradual erosion over the last decade or so of the US law dichotomy between corporations, which provided shareholders with limited liability protection at the expense of double taxation, and partnerships, which provided partners with favourable tax treatment at the expense of limited liability. In the meantime, the introduction of the LLC legislation by Wyoming led to increased stress on the federal government's tax classification rules. The Internal Revenue Service's 1988 determination to accord flow-through tax treatment for the LLC triggered the spontaneous expansion of LLC legislation in the 1990s. Thereafter, the IRS finally abandoned the business classification regulations and issued new rules permitting most unincorporated firms to be classified as partnerships without regard to the absence of corporate characteristics. After explaining the long and complex route from rules connecting aggregate partnership tax treatment to aggregate organizational characteristics to rules disconnecting partnership tax treatment from business characteristics, Callison goes on to show that the rapid development of the LLC is due to two factors, notably the de-linking of limited liability from tax classification and the influence of organized interests that persuaded state lawmakers to enact the statutes.

Limited liability, Callison argues, is not on the whole efficient. Consequently, a variety of legal restraints are necessary to avoid adverse consequences of extending limited liability to closely held businesses. Mandatory insurance and a minimum capital requirement may limit the consequences of increased risk to certain groups. Similarly, it may be necessary for lawmakers, particularly where there are large costs involved, to establish guidelines where, at least in some contexts, limited liability should be set aside. In addition to these suggestions, Callison concludes that a theoretically informed analysis of limited liability might guide the courts in developing a coherent set of principles to guide judicial veil piercing, which could in certain instances limit the effects of excessive risk-taking.

Part III commences with Deborah DeMott's chapter, 'Transatlantic Perspectives on Partnership Law: Risk and Instability'. In this chapter, she explains that English and US law relating to partnership cover the same subject matter and have similar general principles and laws. For instance, partners in both countries have individual liability as a consequence of the obligations incurred by the partnership. Notice that the high initial uniformity between England and the US partnership law was due to William Draper Lewis and James Burr Ames grafting the main provisions of the English Partnership Act (1890) onto the UPA. Despite the common provisions, DeMott asks us to look at the different elements that dominate partnership law in England compared with the United States. The fact that the United States did not follow the 1890 Act on the grounds to dissolve a partnership resulted in the subsequent divergent development of US partnership law, which persists in RUPA. This divergence was significant, DeMott argues, since a general partnership is a relatively fragile business organization form due to many circumstances that permit dissolution. By contrast, English partnership law, which reflects the dominance of contract, is more stable and thus is more beneficial to partners. The United States, DeMott shows, is dominated by agency elements in partnership, which recognize the effect of revocation and renunciation even when they contravene a contract between principal and agent. In general, the effect of agency principles has been to allow both principal and agent to effectively protect their expectations while facilitating the development of the business.

Yet central to her essay is the claim that the general architectural features of partnership law in the United States and England involve a basic design choice—which may entail harsh consequences—and are in turn offset by a variety of statutory provisions. As it turns out, there are a number of doctrinal and statutory provisions in UPA and RUPA that serve to mitigate the risk of wrongful dissolution and dissociation. However, these mitigating elements are far from efficient, and most agree that parties should be permitted to create a binding agreement that reflects accurately the risks and benefits of the partnership.

DeMott warns, however, that this proposed alternative depends on the ability of the parties to specify *ex ante* the risks created by the agency of the partnership. The danger is that complex or abnormal risk often proves difficult to quantify. Similarly, English law also contains statutory provisions that allow a court to dissolve a partnership. DeMott concludes by showing how the basic differences in general partnership law, which carry important implications, can be productively extended to other contexts, including the new legislation for limited liability partnerships.

Judith Freedman's contribution to the collection, 'Limited Liability Partnerships in the United Kingdom: Do They Have a Role for Small Firms?', begins by noting that small businesses require a vehicle that combines the flexible organization structure of a partnership and the benefits of limited liability. Since the middle of the nineteenth century there have been pressures to relax the provisions surrounding the limited company form. The private company is a flexible form, and with the encouragement of Company Law Review Steering Group (CLRSG) is likely to be further simplified. Despite the proposed reforms, there is continuing pressure to introduce a new corporate structure for small firms. Nevertheless, the CLRSG has concluded recently that no new limited liability business forms are needed, particularly in the light of the adoption of the LLP.

Freedman emphasizes that the introduction of a new limited liability vehicle, while significant, is unlikely to serve the business needs of small firms and consequently the overall impact of the statute is probably going to be small. She focuses on how the LLP is likely to give rise to significant costs. Despite its internal flexibility, the form will prove difficult for small firms to use because the general governing law is borrowed from company law. Another obstacle with using the LLP relates to the extensive disclosure and auditing requirements, which include the filing of accounts. One additional obstacle that will undermine its impact significantly is the tax problem. Unlike the United States, there are few tax advantages for firms to select the LLP over incorporation. She concludes that LLP, which was designed to meet the needs of large professional firms, is fraught with difficulties and it remains to be seen whether the targeted beneficiary firms will find it an efficient vehicle for their business.

Geoffrey Morse's chapter on 'Limited Liability Partnerships and Partnership Law Reform in the United Kingdom' evaluates the recent proposals of the Law Commission's joint consultation paper on Partnership Law Reform. He begins by considering the development and introduction of the LLP and whether it will provide effective limited liability for the professions. The essay then considers three general themes in the proposals of the Law Commissions' joint consultation paper on partnership law reform: (1) the introduction of automatic and continuing legal personality; (2) the continuation of the association after a change in partners; and (3) the remodelling of dissolution and winding up. Morse examines some of the specific areas for reform, distinguishing between those that are acceptable as they stand and those that may require further consideration. The former include: the definition of partnership; the abolition of numerical limits; and joint and several liability. The latter entail: contemplated partnerships; the effect of repudiatory breach by one partner; the rights of an ongoing partner to a share of the profits pending final accounts; and, most importantly, the issue of competing or complementary fiduciary duties as between the partners and the firm and each other. Finally, Morse evaluates two important areas for reform that are not addressed by the Law Commissions: (1) the problem of agency and the undisclosed principal; and (2) partnership liability for breaches of express and constructive trusts.

Turning to legal developments in the United States, Allan Walker Vestal's chapter provides a probing and critical account of the reforms and accomplishments of last decade's experimentation in business organization law. Vestal's judgement is that the US experience involved three essential features. First, norm entrepreneurs proceeded without a coherent, underlying theory to guide their experimentation. They acted because it was in their power to do so and not because of any consensus-based justifications. To reach this conclusion, Vestal argues, for example, that there is no convincing underlying theory yet to justify having either LLPs or LLCs or both forms. In practice, the absence of a theory to lend support to law reform is ordinarily unproblematic. However, Vestal submits, the reforms involved more than adjusting technical rules. Consequently, it was a mistake to proceed along a course of creating new forms of organization without *ex ante* forging an appropriate theory to guide and justify these changes.

Having shown the hazards of unreflective law reform, he offers a number of examples that arise from the reform process that begin to confirm his judgement. For instance, RUPA's approval of partner self-interest is confusing because it permits two conflicting interpretations: (1) it is a technical rule; or (2) the provision provides an endorsement of a partner's pursuit of self-interest. This and other inconsistencies or mistakes reinforce the call for a robust theory to guide the practice of law reform. While these concerns are surely matters of interpretation, Vestal argues that there were indeed deeper problems associated with the reform process. That is, because lawmakers borrowed and reshaped statutory provisions without inspection of the implications, the resulting legislation is a confused and often duplicative mosaic of legal business forms. He notes that even the higher level reform efforts, such as RUPA, often ended up with some problematic and uncertain provisions. Perhaps the most disappointing aspect of the reform exercise was the absence of substantive policy debate over the social costs of creating new limited liability statutes. Such a social exchange, Vestal concludes, may have contributed substantively to the adoption of a coherent set of reforms.

Donald Weidner, the Reporter for RUPA between 1987 and 1994, supplies a vivid first-hand assessment, for the benefit of European lawmakers, of the vagaries of the US unincorporated law reform process in his essay, 'Pitfalls in Partnership Law Reform: Some US Experience'. Weidner offers a substantive account of earlier, failed efforts at partnership reform and argues sensibly that the processes of creating improved statutes should include the articulation of concise and coherent principles. One such situation is where US reformers, at the beginning of last century, attempted to capture the meaning of the term 'dissolution' by emulating English partnership law (Partnership Act 1890). Despite these efforts to establish a coherent and comprehensive definition of dissolution, the Uniform Partnership Act 1914 provision met with little long-run success. More than three-quarters of a century later, the RUPA project overcame the long-standing problem with statutory provisions that clarified the distinction between buyouts and wind-ups. Initially, officials were optimistic that the term 'dissolution' could be dropped, but they were forced ultimately, in order to circumvent political opposition, to save the term 'dissolution'.

Another issue relates to problems that stem from the extension of limited liability for professional partners. When should limited liability be made available? What is the default rule concerning limited liability? From an efficiency perspective, perhaps efforts should be made to improve access to limited liability making it available without filing. Correspondingly, even though reform efforts have not yet reached the point of recommending a limited liability default rule for general partners in limited partnerships, placing the issue on the agenda is necessary to catch up with developments in practice. The fact that unresolved issues complicate the reform process is not the only problem. The trend towards increasing complexity has not helped to make the statutory changes particularly clear. For instance, RUPA's statutory provision on joint and several liability for partners conflicts with the provisions that require both contract and tort creditors to exhaust partnership assets before pursuing the separate assets of partners. Weidner devotes the remainder of his essay to discussing the different approaches of the American Law Institute and the NCCUSL to the composition of Drafting Committees and the substantive process of statutory revision.

Part IV considers the development of new business forms in continental Europe. This part begins with Robert T. Drury's essay on 'Private Companies in Europe and the European Private Company', which argues that a new business form for Europe may now finally be on its way, but it will certainly not suit every type of business. He shows that small and medium-sized enterprises may also have the need of a transnational European structure, and the European Private Company Project seeks to provide a possible format. The chapter explains how this project came about, and then seeks to outline the structure of the Regulation that was drafted to effect it. The Regulation covers the basic features of such a company, who can form it and how they can do so. Freedom of choice is an important guiding factor, especially in the organization and management of such an entity, but protection of third parties dealing with it requires greater constraints. Protection of minority shareholders is an essential requirement in systems of company law, but in the Regulation it is balanced with the needs of those who remain in the company and continue to run it. Engendering economic credibility for the European Private Company is a major concern and the parts played by capital and accounting requirements are examined. Employee participation raises its own problems as does insolvency, but the latter issue has been contracted out as it were and referred to the law applicable to companies of parallel type in the Member States. The hierarchy of rules governing the European Private Company is explored in the context of the need to avoid using national laws as subsidiary laws and winding up with fifteen different versions of the EPC. The chapter concludes with an exposition of the thinking behind the drafting of the model forms of articles of association and a critical appraisal of the recent Winter Report's discussion of the role of the European Private Company in the EC company law reform process.

In his chapter, Theo Raaijmakers suggests that Dutch lawmakers should, in the light of the EU policy to create one of the most competitive economies in Europe, be encouraged to contribute to the attractiveness of the business environment by taking steps to modernize the partnership law regime in the Netherlands. Having analysed the difficulties in changing the national business organization law regime, Raaijmakers goes on to offer an account of the recent Dutch Partnership Bill. He shows that the proposed legislation is primarily designed to dispose of the obsolete distinction between civil and commercial partnerships. It is clear, however, that the Dutch reform strategy is cumbersome and inefficient and unlikely to establish productive arrangements for a large class of entrepreneurs and professionals. In particular, he notes that, under the new regime professional partners will be jointly and severally liable for wrongful acts, breaches of trust and other obligations. As a consequence, there will be additional monitoring costs and few benefits. Thus, having identified a number of shortcomings in the Dutch partnership bill, Raaijmakers advocates, in contrast, adopting reforms that would promote greater contractual flexibility. Following insights from the US debate on the design of limited liability vehicles, he concludes by recommending the introduction of a variety of limited liability forms (LLC and LLP) so as to provide efficient choice for a large group of entrepreneurs. In this view, the introduction of new vehicles will promote a more competitive economy.

Peter Essers and Gerard T. K. Meussen argue, in 'Taxation of Partnerships/Hybrid Entities' that the taxation of partnerships in cross-border situations remains a complex issue for European tax lawyers. Fortunately, there have been recent attempts to address the policy issues regarding qualified partnerships. In this regard, Essers and Meussen critically assess the OECD (1999) partnership report that deals with the application of tax conventions to partnerships. The report and commentary attempt to offer a solution for the so-called qualification conflicts, which may arise as a result of differences in law of the source state and the resident state. For instance, a qualification conflict may arise if the Netherlands chooses not to recognize a loan between a Netherlands company and a US domestic reverse hybrid entity. In this context, because of differences in domestic law, the Netherlands and the United States will apply different provisions of the treaty, which means that the payments from the US structure to the Dutch company will avoid double taxation.

Against this background, they explore a range of complex tax problems of the hybrid form through the lens of Dutch law and consider thereafter the implications for fiscal transparency. The logic of revenue classifications of foreign entities is assessed critically. In contrast to the US approach, they note that the Dutch approach has yet to adopt the so-called 'check the box' system. Consequently, Dutch entities cannot be treated as fiscally transparent or as a corporation. Rather, the Netherlands employs a six-factor test, which appears slightly cumbersome, compared with the US approach. Essers and Meussen then move on to take a closer look at the treatment of the US LLC in the Netherlands. They conclude by assessing the recent proposed changes in Dutch partnership law, arguing that reforms within partnership law will arguably produce a suboptimal mix of rules unless tax considerations are taken into account.

1.4. CONCLUSION

As this introduction suggests, a comparative approach provides a basis for analysis, generating insights about the efficiency of alternative legal regimes in producing new business forms. The chapters in this collection offer a variety of insights, from distinct perspectives, into the inevitable trade-off between stability and risk for the unincorporated firm. It is hoped that the important issues explored in this volume will improve further our understanding of the evolution of the unincorporated firm.

REFERENCES

Alexander, J. C. (1992), 'Unlimited Shareholder Liability through a Procedural Lens', *Harvard Law Review* 106: 387.

Armour, J. (2000), 'Share Capital and Creditor Protection: Efficient Rules for a Modern Company Law', *Modern Law Review* 63: 355.

Bachmann, Gregor (2001), 'Grundtendenzen der Reform geschlossener Gesellschaften in Europa Dargestellt am Beispiel des britischen Reformprozesses und der Europaischen Privatgesellschaft', *Zeitschrift für Gesellschafts Recht* (ZDF) 351.

Blair, M., and Stout, L. (2001), 'Trust, Trustworthiness, and the Behavioral Foundations of Corporate Law', *University of Pennsylvania Law Review* 149: 1735.

Bratton, W. W., and McCahery, J. A. (1997), 'An Inquiry into the Efficiency of the Limited Liability Company: Of Theory of the Firm and Regulatory Competition', *Washington and Lee Law Review* 54: 629.

Dickerson, C. M. (1997), 'Cycles and Pendulums: Good Faith, Norms, and the Commons', *Washington and Lee Law Review* 54: 399.

Easterbrook, F., and Fischel, D. (1985), 'Limited Liability and the Corporation', *University of Chicago Law Review* 52: 89.

—— ——(2000), *The Economic Structure of Corporate Law*, Cambridge, Mass.: Harvard University Press.

Freedman, J. (1999), 'The Quest for an Ideal Legal Form for Small Businesses—A Misconceived Enterprise?', in B. Rider and M. Adenas (eds.), *The Quest for an Ideal Legal Form for Small Businesses*, London: Kluwer.

—— (2000), 'Limited Liability: Large Company Theory and Small Firms', *Modern Law Review* 63: 317.

Gompers, P. A., and Lerner, J. (1999), *The Venture Capital Cycle*, Cambridge, Mass.: MIT Press.

Grundfest, J. A. (1992), 'The Limited Future of Unlimited Liability: A Capital Markets Perspective', *Yale Law Journal* 102: 387.

Hampe, J., and Steininger, M. (2001), 'Survival, Growth and Interfirm Collaboration of Start-up Companies in High Tech Industries: A Case Study of Upper Bavaria', University of Bonn, Working Paper.

Hansmann, H., and Kraakman, R. (1991), 'Toward Unlimited Liability for Corporate Torts', *Yale Law Journal* 100: 1879.

Hart, O., and Moore, J. (2000), 'Property Rights in the Theory of the Firm', *Journal of Political Economy* 98: 1119.

Heenen, J. (1975), 'Partnerships and Other Personal Associations for Profit', in *International Encyclopedia of Comparative Law*, ch. 1.

Levmore, S. (1992), 'Partnerships, Limited Liability Companies and Taxes: A Comment on the Survival of Organizational Forms', *Washington University Law Quarterly* 70: 489.

Lutter, M. (1995), 'A Mini-Directive on Capital', in H.-J. de Kluiver and W. van Gerven (eds.), *The European Private Company*, Antwerpen: MAKLU.

—— (1998), 'Limited Liability Companies and Private Companies', in D. Vagts (ed.), *International Encyclopedia of Comparative Law*, Vol. 13, Tübingen: Mohr Siebeck, ch. 2.

Macey, J. R. (1995), 'The Limited Liability Company: Lessons for Corporate Law', *Washington University Law Quarterly* 73: 433.

Miller, S. K. (1997), 'Minority Shareholder Oppression in the Private Company in the European Community: A Comparative Analysis of German, United Kingdom and French "Close Corporation Problem"', *Cornell International Law Journal* 30: 381.

OECD (1998), *Fostering Entrepreneurship*, Paris: OECD.

—— (1999), *OECD Partnership Report*, Paris: OECD.

O'Neil, T. A. (1998), 'Reasonable Expectations in Family Businesses, and the Family Business: A Comment on Rollock', *Indiana Law Journal* 73: 589.

Ribstein, L. E. (1995), 'Limited Liability and Theories of the Corporation', *Maryland Law Review* 50: 80.

Rider, B. A. K., and Andenas, M. (eds.) (1999), *Developments in European Company Law*, Vol. 2/1997: *The Quest for an Ideal Legal Form for Small Businesses*, London: Kluwer Law International.

Talley, E. (1999), 'Taking the "I" Out of the "Team": Intra-Firm Monitoring and the Content of Fiduciary Duties', *Journal of Corporation Law* 24: 1001.

PART I
THEORY: PARTNERSHIP LAW
AND CLOSE CORPORATIONS

2

The Essential Role of Organizational Law

HENRY HANSMANN and REINIER KRAAKMAN*

2.1. INTRODUCTION

In every developed market economy, the law provides for a set of standard-form legal entities. In the United States, these entities include, among others, the business corporation, the cooperative corporation, the non-profit corporation, the municipal corporation, the limited liability company, the general partnership, the limited partnership, the private trust, the charitable trust, and marriage. To an important degree, these legal entities are simply standard-form contracts among the parties who participate in an enterprise—including, in particular, the organization's owners, managers, and creditors. It is therefore natural to ask what more, if anything, these entities offer. Do they—as the current literature increasingly implies—play essentially the same role performed by privately supplied standard-form contracts, just providing off-the-rack terms that simplify negotiation and drafting of routine agreements (Easterbrook and Fischel 1991: 24–5; Posner 1992: 396)?[1] Or do the various legal entities provided by organizational law permit the creation of relationships that could not practicably be formed by contract alone? In short, what, if any, essential role does organizational law play in modern society?

We offer an answer to that question here. In essence, we argue that the essential role of all forms of organizational law is to provide for the creation of a pattern of creditors' rights—a form of 'asset partitioning'—that could not

* For helpful discussions and comments we would particularly like to thank Barry Adler, John Armour, Lucian Bebchuk, John Coates, Marcus Cole, Richard Craswell, Robert Ellickson, Wolfgang Fikentscher, Jesse Fried, Antonio Gambaro, Zohar Goshen, Christopher Harrison, Louis Kaplow, Paul Mahoney, Ronald Mann, Yoshiro Miwa, Peter Muelbert, Larry Ribstein, Roberta Romano, the Roundtable Conference on Team Production and Business Organizations at Georgetown University Law Center, and participants in faculty workshops at Berkeley, Harvard, Michigan, NYU, Stanford, USC, Virginia, and Yale. We also wish to thank the NYU School of Law and its Dean, John Sexton, for important logistical and material support throughout this project. Professor Kraakman's research was supported in part by the Harvard Law School Faculty Summer Research Program and the Harvard Law School Program in Law, Economics, and Business, which is funded by the John M. Olin Foundation.

[1] See Section 2.8.1.

practicably be established otherwise.[2] One aspect of this asset partitioning is the delimitation of the extent to which creditors of an entity can have recourse against the personal assets of the owners or other beneficiaries of the entity. But this function of organizational law—which includes the limited liability that is a familiar characteristic of most corporate entities—is, we argue, of distinctly secondary importance. The truly essential aspect of asset partitioning is, in effect, the reverse of limited liability—namely, the shielding of the assets of the entity from claims of the creditors of the entity's owners or managers. This means that organizational law is much more important as property law than as contract law. Surprisingly, this crucial function of organizational law has rarely been the explicit focus of commentary or analysis.[3]

2.2. Firms and Legal Entities

There are a variety of ways to coordinate the economic activity of two or more persons. One common approach is to have each of those persons enter into a contract with a third party who undertakes the coordination through design of the separate contracts and, most importantly, through exercise of the discretion given the third party by those contracts. A third party that serves this coordination function is what we commonly call a firm. The firm therefore serves—not just metaphorically, but quite literally—as the requisite 'nexus of contracts' for the persons whose activity is to be coordinated: it is the common party with whom each of those persons has an individual contract.[4]

Economic theory does not offer a completely satisfactory explanation for the fact that productive activity is commonly organized in the form of large nexuses of contracts, in which a single central actor contracts simultaneously with employees, suppliers, and customers who may number in the thousands or even millions. Why, for example, are organizational employment relationships not constructed in the form of contractual cascades, in which each employee contracts, not directly with the firm, but rather with his or her immediate superior, so that the pattern of contracts corresponds to the authority relationships we see in a standard pyramidal organization chart? Although this subject is interesting, we will not delve into it here. Rather, we will simply take it for granted that it is

---

[2] A preliminary version of the economic argument developed here was presented at the European Economic Association meeting in Santiago, Spain, September 1999, and published as Hansmann and Kraakman (2000a).

[3] Since we offered our initial paper on this issue, Hansmann and Kraakman (2000a), Paul Mahoney (2000), building on that analysis, has written a short but informative essay exploring the historical roots of asset partitioning in organizational law. We say a few more words on these historical issues in Section 2.9.

[4] The now-familiar economic concept of the firm as a 'nexus of contracts' derives from Jensen and Meckling (1976), and Alchian and Demsetz (1972).

essential, in modern market economies, that such large nexuses of contracts can be constructed.[5]

To serve effectively as a nexus of contracts, a firm must generally have two attributes. The first is well-defined decision-making authority. More particularly, there must be one or more persons who have ultimate authority to commit the firm to contracts. We will term those persons the managers of the firm. In a corporation, the managers (as we use the term here) are the members of the firm's board of directors; in a partnership, they are the firm's general partners.[6] The firm's managers may or may not be distinct from the persons for whose benefit the managers are charged to act—namely, the firm's owners or, in the case of non-proprietary organizations, the firm's beneficial owners or beneficiaries. (For simplicity, we will generally use the simple term 'owners', rather loosely, to refer to all of these persons: the partners in a general partnership, the shareholders of a business corporation, and the members of a cooperative, as well as the limited partners in a limited partnership, the beneficial owners of a private trust, the beneficiaries of a non-profit corporation, and the residents of a municipal corporation.)

The second attribute a firm must have, if it is to serve effectively as a locus of contracts, is the ability to bond its contracts credibly—that is, to provide assurance that the firm will perform its contractual obligations. Bonding generally requires that there exist a pool of assets that the firm's managers can offer as satisfaction for the firm's obligations.[7] We term this pool of assets the firm's bonding assets.

A natural person has the two attributes just described, and hence can—and very frequently does—serve as a firm, in the form of a sole proprietorship. In this case, the single individual is both manager and owner, and the bonding assets consist of all of the assets owned by that individual. Note, however, that individuals have these attributes because the law provides them. In particular, the law gives an individual the authority to enter into contracts that will bind

---

[5] The literature that focuses on asset specificity to explain vertical integration is of course important here, e.g. Williamson (1985), and Klein et al. (1978), as is the 'property rights' approach to the theory of the firm that has evolved out of that work, most conspicuously in the work of Hart and Moore (Hart 1995; Hart and Moore 1990).

A related but somewhat different reason for large centralized nexuses (as opposed, e.g., to more decentralized structures) may be the need to avoid opportunistic threats to disassemble a set of transactional relationships that has been costly to assemble, or to expropriate an entrepreneur's or organization's accumulated experience with working procedures and forms of organization. See Rajan and Zingales (1998). All of this literature, however, seems to leave important things unexplained. See e.g. Hansmann (1996).

[6] In large partnerships, authority is sometimes delegated to designated managing partners. In those cases, only the latter partners would constitute managers in our sense of the term.

[7] There are alternative means of bonding performance. The most obvious is to expose the firm's managers or owners to personal sanctions such as (publicly enforced) criminal penalties or (privately enforced) reputational penalties, including personal shaming and refusals to deal with them in the future. These are poor substitutes for bonding assets, however, particularly when—as with the shareholders in publicly held business corporations—the firm's owners are numerous and constantly changing.

him in most future states, and the law also provides that, if the individual defaults on a contract, the other party will have (unless waived) the right to levy on all assets owned by that individual (which is to say that the law provides that all assets owned by an individual serve as bonding assets).

Legal entities, like individuals, are legal (or 'juridical') persons in the sense that they also have the two attributes described above: (1) a well-defined ability to contract through designated managers, and (2) a designated pool of assets that are available to satisfy claims by the firm's creditors. Legal entities are distinct from natural persons, however, in that their bonding assets are, at least in part, distinct from assets owned by the firm's owners or managers, in the sense that the firm's creditors have a claim on those assets that is prior to that of the personal creditors of the firm's owners or managers.

In our view, this latter feature—the separation between the firm's bonding assets and the personal assets of the firm's owners and managers—is the core defining characteristic of a legal entity, and establishing this separation is the principal role that organizational law plays in the organization of enterprise. More particularly, our argument has four elements: (1) that a characteristic of all legal entities, and hence of organizational law in general, is the partitioning off of a separate set of assets in which creditors of the firm itself have a prior security interest; (2) that this partitioning offers important efficiency advantages in the creation of large firms; (3) that it would generally be infeasible to establish this form of asset partitioning without organizational law; and (4) that this attribute—essentially a property attribute—is the only essential contribution that organizational law makes to commercial activity, in the sense that it is the only basic attribute of a firm that could not feasibly be established by contractual means alone.

2.3. Forms of Asset Partitioning

There are two components to asset partitioning. The first is the designation of a separate pool of assets that are associated with the firm, and that are distinct from the personal assets of the firm's owners and managers. In essence, this is done by recognizing juridical persons (or, as we will usually say here, 'legal entities') that are distinct from individual human beings and that can own assets in their own name. When a firm is organized as such an entity, the assets owned by that entity in its own name become the designated separate pool of firm assets.

The second component of asset partitioning is the assignment to creditors of priorities in the distinct pools of assets that result from the formation of a legal entity. This assignment of priorities takes two forms. The first assigns to the firm's creditors a claim on the assets associated with the firm's operations that is prior to the claims of the personal creditors of the firm's owners. We term this *affirmative* asset partitioning, to reflect the notion that it sets forth a distinct pool of firm assets as bonding assets for all the firm's contracts. The second form of asset partitioning is just the opposite, granting to the owners' personal creditors a claim on the owners' separate personal assets that is prior to the claims of the firm's creditors. We term this *defensive* asset partitioning, to reflect the common perception that it serves to shield the owners' assets from the creditors of the firm.

Both forms are clearly illustrated by the typical business corporation. Under the default rules established by corporate law, a corporation's creditors have first claim on the corporation's assets—which is to say, their claims must be satisfied before the corporation's assets become available to satisfy any claims made against the corporation's shareholders by the shareholders' personal creditors. This is affirmative asset partitioning. Defensive asset partitioning, in turn, is found in the rule of limited liability that bars the corporation's creditors from levying on the shareholders' personal assets.

We should emphasize that, throughout our discussions of asset partitioning, we use the term 'creditors' quite broadly to include all persons to whom there is owed a contractual obligation that has not yet been fulfilled.

2.3.1. Affirmative Asset Partitioning

The type of affirmative asset partitioning that we see in the business corporation can be termed 'priority with liquidation protection'. It not only assigns to the corporation's creditors a prior claim on corporate assets, but also provides that, if a shareholder becomes insolvent, the shareholder's personal creditors cannot, upon exhausting the shareholder's personal assets, force liquidation of corporate assets to satisfy their claims. Rather, a shareholder's creditors can at most step into the shareholder's role as an owner of shares—a role that generally offers the power to seek liquidation only when at least a majority of the firm's shareholders agree. This type of affirmative asset partitioning is found not only in business corporations but also, for example, in cooperative corporations and limited liability companies, and for the limited partners in a limited partnership.[8]

A weaker type of asset partitioning, priority without liquidation protection, is afforded by the partnership-at-will, in which creditors of a bankrupt partner generally have the power to force liquidation of the partnership by foreclosing on the partner's interest in the partnership—though if the partnership assets are insufficient to satisfy both individual and partnership creditors, then the creditors of the partnership itself have priority over the partner's creditors in the assets of the partnership (Bromberg and Ribstein 1988: § 3.05(d)(3)(v), § 7.06(f); Revised Uniform Partnership Act (RUPA): § 801(6); Uniform Partnership Act (UPA): § 32(2)).

A stronger type of affirmative asset partitioning is found among firms that are managed on behalf of beneficiaries who lack the complete earning and control

---

[8] A limited partner's personal creditors generally cannot force dissolution of the partnership or otherwise levy directly on partnership property, but can only accede to the bankrupt partner's rights in distributions made by the partnership. See *Baybank v. Catamount Construction, Inc.*, 141 N.H. 780, 693 A.2d 1163 (1997); Bromberg and Ribstein (1988: § 13.07(b)(2)).

rights of full owners, including non-profit corporations, municipal corporations, charitable trusts, and spendthrift trusts. This form gives to a firm's creditors not just a prior but (among creditors) an exclusive claim on the entity's assets, in the sense that the creditors of a beneficiary have no claim even to the beneficiary's interest in the firm. The beneficiaries can continue to be beneficiaries even after they have gone through personal bankruptcy, without passing to their creditors any portion of their expected benefits from the firm.

Legal entities in which affirmative asset partitioning takes the form of priority for business creditors without liquidation protection we will term, for convenience, weak form legal entities. Entities exhibiting both priority and liquidation protection we will term strong form legal entities. Strong form legal entities in which entity creditors get an exclusive claim to the entities' assets we will term super-strong form legal entities.

2.3.2. Defensive Asset Partitioning

There are various degrees of defensive asset partitioning, just as there are degrees of affirmative asset partitioning. Indeed, the range and variety we observe among forms of defensive asset partitioning is far greater than what we observe in affirmative asset partitioning.

The strongest type of defensive asset partitioning is that found in the standard business corporation, in which creditors of the firm have no claim at all upon the personal assets of the firm's shareholders, which are pledged exclusively as security to the personal creditors of the individual shareholders. This exclusive type of defensive asset partitioning, generally referred to simply as 'limited liability', also characterizes other standard types of corporations—non-profit, cooperative, and municipal—as well as limited liability companies.

At the other extreme lies the contemporary US general partnership,[9] in which there is no defensive asset partitioning at all: partnership creditors share equally with the creditors of individual partners in distributing the separate assets of partners when both the partnership and its partners are insolvent. Indeed, as the latter example indicates, defensive partitioning is not requisite for the formation of a legal entity.

Between these two extremes lie a variety of intermediate degrees of defensive asset partitioning that are, or once were, in common use. One of these is illustrated by the traditional approach to partnerships prior to the 1978 Bankruptcy Reform Act. Under that approach, partnership creditors could levy on the assets of individual partners, but their claims were subordinated to the claims of the partners' personal creditors.[10] A second is a rule of pro rata

---

[9] That is, the modern general partnership under the Bankruptcy Reform Act of 1978 and the Revised Uniform Partnership Act.

[10] This approach applies even today for the liquidation outside of bankruptcy of partnerships still governed by the old Uniform Partnership Act.

personal liability, under which owners are liable without limit for the debts of the firm, but bear this liability in proportion to their claims on the firm's distributions. This rule—which was in fact applied to all corporations in California from 1849 until 1931 (Blumberg 1995: 42–6; Weinstein 2000)—implies, for example, that a 5 per cent shareholder is personally liable, without limit, for 5 per cent of any corporate debts that cannot be satisfied out of the corporation's own assets. A third intermediate form is a rule of multiple liability, exemplified by the rules of double- and triple-liability that were applied to many US banks in the late nineteenth and early twentieth centuries, under which the personal assets of a shareholder are exposed to liability for the firm's unpaid obligations up to a limit equal to the par value (or, in the case of triple liability, twice the par value) of the shareholder's stock in the firm (Macey and Miller 1992). A fourth alternative, illustrated by the 'companies limited by guarantee' provided for in the law of the United Kingdom and some other Commonwealth countries, permits individual owners to make specific pledges of the amount for which they will be personally liable for a firm's unpaid debts (Davies 1997: 10–11).

2.3.3. Patterns of Partitioning

The standard-form legal entities that we observe today involve different combinations of affirmative and defensive asset partitioning. Table 2.1 categorizes a few of the most common types of legal entities in these terms, and also includes, for comparison, the sole proprietorship, where the firm is not a separate legal entity.

TABLE 2.1. ORGANIZATIONAL FORMS AND CREDITORS' PRIORITIES

Type of legal identity	Affirmative partitioning: firm creditors' claim on firm's assets	Defensive partitioning: owner's creditors' claim on owner's assets
Non-profit corporation Municipal corporation Spendthrift trust	Exclusive	Exclusive
Business corporation Cooperative corporation Limited liability company Limited partnership	Prior with liquidation protection	Exclusive
Partnership for a term	Prior with liquidation protection	Prior (pre-1978) Shared (post-1978)
Partnership-at-will	Prior with liquidation protection	Prior (pre-1978) Shared (post-1978)
Sole proprietorship	Shared without liquidation protection	Shared

Various other patterns of affirmative and defensive asset partitioning, beyond those included in Table 2.1, can also be found. Interesting examples are provided, for example, by the law of marriage, where the pattern of partitioning differs substantially from state to state.[11]

2.3.4. Partitioning with Respect to a Firm's Managers

The preceding discussion has focused on partitioning between the assets of a firm and the assets of the firm's owners. Partitioning between the assets of the firm and the assets of the firm's managers is also important, however. Here the pattern established by organizational law is quite uniform. In nearly all standard-form legal entities, both affirmative and defensive asset partitioning with respect to managers follows a rule of exclusivity: the firm's assets are not available to satisfy the manager's personal obligations, and the manager's personal assets are not available to satisfy the firm's obligations. While we generally take this rule for granted, the importance that organizational law plays in establishing this pattern will become evident when we discuss the law of trusts below.

---

[11] Among states that have adopted the community property approach to marital property law, there are a variety of different patterns of partitioning between the property of the marriage and the separate property of the individual spouses (Thomas 1994: §§ 37.13(b)(4)–(b)(5)). The following table offers illustrations, based largely on Thompson's. Among the states in the table, Wisconsin and Arizona clearly establish marriage as a legal entity, in the sense that they give marriage creditors priority (indeed, an exclusive claim) on marital assets. California, conversely, actually gives marital property less protection from the separate creditors of the individual spouses than would be available to property owned jointly by the spouses if they were not married, since it grants a separate creditor of an individual spouse the right to proceed against all of the marital property, and not just the individual spouse's share. Thus, in California, marriage might be considered an 'anti-entity'.

Table 2.2. MARITAL ASSET PARTITIONING IN SELECTED COMMUNITY PROPERTY STATES

State of marriage	Affirmative partitioning: claim of marriage creditors on marital assets	Defensive partitioning: claim of spouse's separate creditors on spouse's separate assets
Wisconsin	Exclusive	Exclusive
Arizona	Exclusive	Shared
New Mexico	Shared without liquidation protection	Shared
California	Shared (with respect to *entirety* of marital property) without liquidation protection	Exclusive?

Another common organizational form whose status as a legal entity has varied over time and from state to state is the unincorporated association, discussed in note 28.

2.4. BENEFITS OF AFFIRMATIVE ASSET PARTITIONING

Asset partitioning plays several distinct roles in the functioning of legal entities that are critical to the interests of both the creditors and the owners of these entities. We examine those roles here, with special focus on the functional contributions made by affirmative asset partitioning. In particular, we consider how affirmative asset partitioning reduces the cost of credit for legal entities by reducing monitoring costs, protecting against premature liquidation of assets, and permitting efficient allocation of risk.

In important respects, defensive asset partitioning is just the mirror image of affirmative asset partitioning: defensive partitioning with respect to claims by the firm's creditors is effectively affirmative partitioning with respect to claims by the owners' creditors. Consequently, the efficiency advantages of affirmative asset partitioning described here also apply in large part to defensive asset partitioning. But the symmetry is not perfect. Defensive asset partitioning serves some special purposes of its own, which we will examine separately in section 2.6.

2.4.1. Reducing Monitoring Costs

The potential economies offered by asset partitioning are most clearly seen by considering subpartitioning of assets within a single firm. Consequently, we begin with that case. We then turn to the more important and familiar use of affirmative asset partitioning, namely to partition the business assets of a firm from the personal assets of the firm's multiple owners.

2.4.1.1. *Subpartitioning Assets within a Single Firm: Corporate Subsidiaries*

Imagine a company that is engaged in two distinct lines of business: ownership and management of a chain of hotels and ownership and management of oil fields and refineries. Then consider two distinct ways in which these entities could be structured: (1) as a single corporation with two operating divisions, one for the hotel business and one for the oil business; (2) as two distinct corporations, one for the hotel business and one for the oil business, both of which are wholly owned by a single parent holding company that has no separate assets of its own, but simply holds all of the stock of the two subsidiary corporations. In terms of decision-making authority, the two structures are essentially identical: in each, the board of directors of the parent firm has complete control over both the oil business and the hotel business. Likewise, the company's aggregate assets are the same in both cases. Yet the choice between these two structures may have a large effect on overall costs. In particular, the structure in which the two operating divisions are separately incorporated may face a substantially lower cost of credit.

The reason is that the two lines of business are likely to depend, to a significant degree, on two distinct classes of creditors. (Again, we use the term 'creditor' here and throughout to refer not just to persons to whom the firm is indebted in monetary terms, but to any person to whom the firm has an outstanding contractual obligation.) This is most obvious with respect to trade creditors. A lessor of real estate or a supplier of linens to the hotel business, for example, is likely to be in a relatively good position to judge the financial viability of the hotel operation. To begin with, the supplier may also deal with other hotel chains, and thus be continually well informed about the overall prospects of the hotel industry. In addition, through its repeated dealings with the particular hotel chain in question, the supplier is likely to know a great deal about how sound that chain is financially and how well it is managed. Such a supplier to the hotel business is not likely, however, to know much about the oil industry, either in general or as administered by the particular company that also owns and operates the hotel chain.

If the hotel business is operated as a separately incorporated subsidiary, then the hotel supplier need not be much concerned about the prospects of the oil business. Even if the company's oil operation becomes insolvent, there will be little effect on the ability of the hotel subsidiary to pay its debts. The same, conversely, is true for suppliers to the oil operation: they need not concern themselves with screening and monitoring the fortunes of the hotel operation. Indeed, this is also true for customers of the oil business who hold long-term supply contracts and consequently have a strong interest in the business's continued solvency.

If the hotel and oil operations are conducted as part of a single corporate entity, however, then suppliers to the hotel business will always run the risk that unexpected developments in the oil business will impair the security of their credit, and vice versa for suppliers (and some customers) of the oil operation. It follows that both sets of suppliers are likely to extend credit on more favourable terms if the hotel and oil operations are separately incorporated, so that the suppliers are spared the costs of monitoring business activities with which they are unfamiliar.[12]

There are, of course, costs to partitioning the assets of a single firm by subincorporation. One is that formal bankruptcy proceedings, and the transaction costs associated with them, are more likely to arise as asset pools become smaller and more homogeneous. Both the hotel operation and the oil operation in our example are more likely to become the subject of bankruptcy proceedings if they are separately incorporated than if they are organized simply as divisions within a single conglomerate corporate shell. The latter form of organization offers the advantage of diversification as a bankruptcy-prevention device.[13]

Another potential cost of asset partitioning is the increased risk of opportunism by the debtor. For example, if insolvency should threaten the hotel

[12] The same logic applies if the hotel and oil businesses are simply spun off as separate companies with different sets of stockholders rather than held by a single parent company.

[13] This rationale for the conglomerate form is well known from the finance literature: Gahlon and Stover (1979); Levy and Sarnat (1970); Lewellen (1971); Melicher and Rush (1974).

subsidiary in our example, the holding company might be tempted to drain assets from that subsidiary to the parent corporation or to the oil subsidiary, hence effectively expropriating the creditors of the hotel business. Various legal doctrines—including fraudulent conveyance, veil-piercing, minimum legal capital, and equitable subordination—are designed to reduce the potential for this kind of opportunism. Nevertheless, these protections are by no means perfectly effective, and they bring administrative and incentive costs of their own.

Asset partitioning will reduce the overall costs of credit only when its benefits outweigh such disadvantages. In general, it appears that the more distinct the business operations involved, the more likely it is that partitioning will be efficient.

The idea that partitioning a fixed pool of assets can reduce overall costs of credit by reducing monitoring costs is already familiar (Jackson and Kronman 1979; Levmore 1982; Posner 1976). In large part, however, the existing literature on this subject focuses on devices for asset partitioning other than organizational law (e.g. security interests) (Jackson and Kronman 1979) or, when it does look at organizational law, focuses just on the law's role in establishing defensive asset partitioning—i.e. limited liability for a firm's owners vis-à-vis a firm's business creditors.[14] Our principal objective here is to demonstrate the critical role played by organizational law in establishing affirmative asset partitioning as a means of reducing the costs of business contracting. The importance of that role becomes even clearer when we examine firms with multiple owners.

2.4.1.2. *Partitioning between a Firm and Its Individual Owners*

The hotel and oil example is useful because it illustrates in reasonably clear isolation the potential monitoring cost advantages of asset partitioning. Since the assets in the example are under the same common management and ownership with or without partitioning, other incentive issues are largely unaffected. This simple common ownership structure, however, also makes the potential efficiency advantages of partitioning relatively modest; such partitioning by subincorporation will be cost-effective only in particular circumstances.[15]

---

[14] See e.g. Posner (1976) who offers an example very much like our oil and hotel business but employs it only to illustrate the utility of respecting limited liability among affiliated corporations.

[15] One such circumstance involves large-scale capital development projects of the type that have commonly been organized under the increasingly popular 'project finance' approach. The projects involved are, for example, capital infrastructure projects in developing countries that involve construction and operation of facilities such as telecommunications networks, railroads, or toll roads. Equity financing and management of the project is provided by a sponsoring corporation with relevant expertise that also operates other projects or businesses and may have its principal operations outside the country where the project is located. Most financing for the project is provided by loans from one or more public or private lending institutions. The project is organized through the formation of a separate corporation—a subsidiary of the sponsoring corporation—that owns the project assets and receives the project revenues. The loans that finance the project are obligations of the latter corporation and not of the parent sponsoring corporation. This arrangement is chosen self-consciously to permit the project lenders to confine their evaluation and monitoring to the project in question, free of credit risks from the sponsor's other obligations, and conversely to keep the project from affecting directly the creditworthiness of the sponsor. See Buljevich and Park (1999: 87–95, 121–9).

The advantages of asset partitioning, and particularly of affirmative asset partitioning, are far more obvious in the case of a business firm that has numerous individuals as owners. In the absence of affirmative asset partitioning, creditors of any single owner would have the right to proceed against that owner's share of the firm's assets in case of the individual's insolvency. As a consequence, potential creditors of the firm itself would have difficulty determining the appropriate terms on which to extend credit. Intimate familiarity with the firm's own assets and business affairs would not suffice to determine the firm's creditworthiness; knowledge of the personal creditworthiness of each of the firm's owners would be necessary as well. Moreover, if a creditor's relationship with the firm were to extend over any considerable period of time, the creditor would need to keep monitoring the creditworthiness, not only of the firm itself, but also of all of its individual owners. And, if the nature and number of the firm's owners were to change over time—as they commonly do with business corporations—the creditor would need to keep assessing the creditworthiness of the new owners.

Clearly the costs of such monitoring would often be enormously high—so high, presumably, that creditors would frequently be unwilling to incur them. Rather, potential creditors of the firm would simply increase the cost of credit to compensate for the high uncertainty they must face, or just deny credit entirely.

This becomes all the more obvious when one considers that it is not just the personal financial affairs of the individual owners that would be relevant to a potential firm creditor, but also the affairs of any other businesses in which the owners had an equity investment. Thus, suppose that—in a firm without asset partitioning—firm A were to have among its owners individual X, who also had an ownership stake in firms B, C, and D. Someone considering doing business with firm A would need to consider, not only the probability that X would mismanage his personal finances in a fashion that would render him insolvent, but also that any of firms B, C, or D might for any reason fail, with the result that the creditors of the failed firm would seek to foreclose, via their claims against X, on X's share in A.

Nor is it just potential creditors of the firm that would have an interest in the status of each owner's personal and other business affairs. All owners of the firm would have a similar interest, since they will bear the consequences in terms of the firm's cost of credit. Mutual monitoring among the individual owners of a firm may make sense in a small partnership with stable membership, but it is obviously less efficient in firms that, as with much medium and large-scale enterprise today, have a numerous and constantly changing class of owners.[16]

---

[16] Easterbrook and Fischel (1985) emphasized some time ago that limited liability—a form of defensive asset partitioning—has the benefit of reducing the need for a corporation's shareholders to monitor the finances of their fellow shareholders. What we wish to point out here is that similar monitoring economies result from affirmative asset partitioning as well.

Affirmative asset partitioning eliminates much of the risk that a firm's finances will be affected by unrelated changes in the personal and business affairs of its owners. It assures that the creditors of a firm will have first right to the assets of that firm against any personal creditors, or other business creditors, of the firm's owners. *Defensive* asset partitioning, such as the limited liability of the type we see in the modern business corporation, is neither necessary nor sufficient for this form of partitioning. Even if organizational law offered only the contemporary partnership, which offers affirmative asset partitioning but no defensive asset partitioning, first priority claim on any firm's assets could easily be pledged to that firm's creditors alone.

2.4.1.3. Protecting the Firm's Going Concern Value

As the last statement suggests, many of the monitoring cost advantages of affirmative asset partitioning can be obtained simply with the weak form of affirmative asset partitioning found in partnerships, which grants to creditors of the firm priority of claims but no liquidation protection vis-à-vis the owners' personal creditors. So long as a firm's own creditors have a prior claim on firm assets, there is a substantial limit to the threat that can be presented to them by any effort of the owners' personal creditors to liquidate firm assets. Nevertheless, absent liquidation protection, some threat still remains.

That threat lies, principally, in the possibility that partial or complete liquidation of the firm's assets could destroy some or all of the firm's going concern value, with the result that, even if the firm were to remain solvent after a partial liquidation, the net value left to the firm's owners, and available as security for the firm's creditors, might well be reduced. If this loss of firm value would exceed the value of the foreclosing personal creditor's claim, then it would of course be open to the firm to buy out that claim. But this would require that the firm be sufficiently liquid. Moreover, a personal creditor with a right to foreclose on firm assets might well threaten to exercise that right and destroy substantial going concern value—even if he could realize little or nothing thereby because the firm lacks sufficient net worth—simply to hold up the firm (or its owners or creditors) for a sum larger than his claim on the firm would receive if he actually foreclosed.[17]

For these reasons, even with the weak form of asset partitioning that offers priority of claims but no liquidation protection, both the firm's creditors and its owners would be at the mercy of, and have an incentive to seek to monitor, the personal and other business affairs of all of the firm's owners—a burden that would often be inefficient for them to bear. It is understandable, then, that the dominant form of affirmative asset partitioning among legal entities today is the

---

[17] This point is well understood in partnership law where liquidation by creditors is possible. See Bromberg and Ribstein (1988: § 6.02(c)).

strong form in which firm creditors are given not just priority in firm assets but also liquidation protection.[18]

2.4.1.4. Risk Sharing

The foregoing discussion has focused largely on monitoring—that is, efficient incentives for gathering and using information. But asset partitioning can also be used to apportion risk among owners and creditors in various patterns according to their relative costs of bearing that risk—costs that will be affected by factors such as liquidity and diversification. This is a familiar benefit of limited liability and other forms of defensive asset partitioning. It is also an important benefit, however, of affirmative asset partitioning, which substantially isolates a firm's creditors from risks not associated with the fortunes of the firm.

2.4.1.5. The Corporation Sole

As the oil and hotel example illustrates, efficient asset partitioning may often involve formation of a corporation with a sole shareholder—a 'corporation sole'. That single shareholder may be another corporation, as in the example. But use of the corporation sole for asset partitioning may also be efficient where the shareholder is an individual, and the individual (and her personal creditors) find it most convenient to segregate her personal assets from her business assets for purposes of pledging those assets as credit. Opposition to the 'corporation sole' as an acceptable legal form—an opposition that has largely died out in the United States of America[19] but continues in some civil law jurisdictions—stems from a failure to appreciate this important asset partitioning function of the corporate form. Although the term 'corporation' may suggest a collective entity, the rationale for the form of asset partitioning established by the business corporation does not depend on collective ownership of the firm, and there is no reason to insist on collective ownership when employing that form.

2.4.2. Preserving the Assets of Beneficiaries

As we noted in section 2.3, a few legal entities deploy a form of affirmative asset partitioning even stronger than priority with liquidation protection—namely, exclusive partitioning that denies the separate creditors of a firm's owners (or, more accurately for the firms involved, the firm's beneficiaries) any claim on the assets of the firm. Principal examples of these legal entities are non-profit corporations, municipal corporations, charitable trusts, and spendthrift trusts.

---

[18] Even in general partnerships-at-will, which as a general rule lack liquidation protection, the courts are sensitive to the desirability of preserving going concern value, and for this reason will generally decree foreclosure on an interest in a partnership only as a last resort. See Bromberg and Ribstein (1988: § 3.05(d)(3)(v)); *91st St. Joint Venture v. Goldstein*, 691 A.2d 272 (Md. 1997).

[19] This opposition continues with respect to the 'LLC Sole', as reflected in the recent Massachusetts legislative debate on the subject.

One rationale for exclusivity is paternalism, as the example of the spendthrift trust suggests. The settlor of the trust, while giving up all claims on the trust assets for himself and his own creditors, wishes to protect the trust's assets from the possibly reckless spending habits of the beneficiary, and thus provides that trust assets are unavailable to the beneficiary's creditors. A similar paternalistic rationale may be present in charitable trusts and, to the extent they are redistributive, municipal corporations. A second rationale for refusing personal creditors any claim on the assets of these entities is that in many cases the beneficiaries' expected benefits from the firm would be extremely difficult to value and virtually impossible to levy on as a practical matter. What is the value of municipal services to a given resident, for example, and how might that value be monetized to repay a debt?

Exclusivity is a far more common rule in defensive asset partitioning than it is in affirmative asset partitioning, as Table 2.1 illustrates. We explore the reasons for this in section 2.6, when we discuss defensive asset partitioning more thoroughly.

2.5. CONSTRUCTING ENTITIES WITHOUT ORGANIZATIONAL LAW

In the absence of organizational law, it would effectively be impossible to create the affirmative asset partitioning that is the core characteristic of a legal entity. While in theory the pattern of rights that constitute affirmative asset partitioning might still be established through contracting, the transaction costs necessary to accomplish this would be prohibitive.

To understand these transaction costs, we will explore here the methods that might be employed to create the functional equivalent of a legal entity using only the basic tools of property law, contract law, and agency law.[20] That is, we will ask how difficult it would be to establish affirmative asset partitioning if society lacked those special bodies of statutory and decisional law that constitute the separate law of partnerships, business corporations, private trusts, and so forth. By this means, we can see more clearly what makes organizational law distinctive and important.

2.5.1. Single-Owner Enterprise

It is easiest and most instructive to begin with the simplest possible case, in which a single individual owns and operates a business as a sole proprietor.

---

[20] The concept of agency, in which a principal can authorize an agent to bind the principal to contracts with third parties, is crucial to the construction of a nexus of contracts with any appreciable scope, whether the juridical person that is the central node of that nexus is an individual human being, a group of individuals, or an organization. It is interesting to ask whether the legal doctrine of agency is primitive, or whether it would be feasible to construct the functional equivalent of agency using other, more basic elements of contract doctrine. We will not explore that question here, however, but rather will take it for granted that agency doctrine is in place.

Suppose that this entrepreneur wishes to partition off the assets associated with the business into a separate pool in which his business creditors will be given a prior claim over his personal creditors—that is, he wishes to undertake affirmative asset partitioning. If the law of business corporations were available, this could of course be accomplished easily: the entrepreneur would simply incorporate his business, transferring to the corporation his title to the business assets in exchange for the corporation's stock. This would result in the desired asset partitioning without interfering with the entrepreneur's control over the business, which, as sole shareholder in the corporation, he would continue to exercise as before.

It would not be practicable, however, to accomplish the same result without incorporating the business or otherwise relying upon organizational law. We can see this by considering how our hypothetical entrepreneur might try to establish affirmative asset partitioning simply by contract. (Since our focus for the moment is on affirmative rather than defensive asset partitioning, we will assume that the entrepreneur is not concerned about shielding his personal assets from his business creditors. We explore contractual approaches to defensive asset partitioning in section 2.7.)

2.5.1.1. *Establishing Priority by Contract*

The default rules of property and contract law in effect provide that, absent contractual agreement to the contrary, each of the entrepreneur's creditors has an equal-priority floating lien upon the entrepreneur's entire pool of assets as a guarantee of performance. That is, the creditors each have a shared property right of sorts in the entrepreneur's assets—a contingent claim on the assets that can be exercised in case of the entrepreneur's non-performance.[21] If we ignore the possibility of using security interests—a topic we return to below—the entrepreneur cannot alter these rights simply by putting a term in his contracts with his business creditors that promises them a prior claim, over his other creditors, on the subset of the entrepreneur's assets that he uses in his business. The entrepreneur's existing personal creditors already have a claim on those assets that cannot be subordinated without those creditors' consent. Moreover, so far as the entrepreneur's future non-business creditors are concerned, the law will also, absent explicit agreement to the contrary, impose a default term in their contracts with the entrepreneur that gives them, likewise, an equal-priority claim on the entrepreneur's assets in case of default—a contractual commitment that is inconsistent with any prior claim that the entrepreneur previously gave to his business creditors.

Consequently, to assure his business creditors a prior claim on his business assets, the entrepreneur would need to promise them credibly that he would

---

[21] To be more precise, the creditors have a right to levy on the assets so long as they remain in the pool of assets belonging to the entrepreneur: the claim floats in the sense that assets are subjected to the claim when they become property of the entrepreneur and are released from the claim when they are no longer his property.

obtain from all of his personal creditors, both past and future, agreements subordinating their claims on the entrepreneur's business assets to those of the entrepreneur's business creditors. Absent organizational law, an entrepreneur would generally be both unwilling and unable to make a credible promise of this sort. He would be unwilling because the costs of obtaining the necessary subordination agreements would be prohibitive in virtually any practical situation. He would be unable because his compliance could not be monitored or bonded.

Consider first the simple transaction costs that the contracting in question would involve. These would include the expense of drafting and inserting appropriate provisions in all contracts between the entrepreneur and his personal creditors on one side, and in all contracts between the entrepreneur and his business creditors on the other. Those provisions would not be simple. They would need to be crafted with sufficient detail and precision to distinguish clearly the entrepreneur's business assets from his personal assets and to distinguish his business creditors—those entitled to a prior claim on the business assets—from his personal creditors. In this connection, we must remember that the business assets are likely to be a large and shifting pool of tangible and intangible items, including equipment, supplies, inventory, accounts receivable, supply contracts, credit agreements, and trade marks. Moreover, beyond these drafting costs, there would be the costs of bargaining with all of the entrepreneur's personal creditors to secure their agreement and to determine, among other things, the consideration necessary to offset those creditors' loss of security.

Even if the costs of obtaining the requisite subordination agreements were worth incurring, however, the entrepreneur would find it virtually impossible to assure his business creditors that he would in fact obtain them. Although each of the entrepreneur's business creditors would have a contractual right to insist that the entrepreneur obtain those agreements, that right would generally be enforceable only against the entrepreneur—and not against his personal creditors—in the event that the entrepreneur failed to negotiate the requisite subordination term.

Thus, the entrepreneur and his business creditors would face an enormous problem of moral hazard. The entrepreneur would have a strong incentive to neglect to obtain the necessary subordination agreements, particularly in the circumstances in which they would be most important to the business creditors—namely, when the entrepreneur is facing a substantial risk of insolvency and hence both (a) in strong need of further credit, and (b) in a poor position to obtain credit that is subordinated. By failing to obtain a subordination agreement with a personal creditor, the entrepreneur and the personal creditor can externalize to the entrepreneur's business creditors a larger portion of the potential costs of the entrepreneur's insolvency than the business creditors had bargained for. For these reasons, for the entrepreneur's business creditors to have faith in the entrepreneur's compliance with his promise to give them priority in his business assets, they would have to engage in continuous monitoring of the entrepreneur's contracts with all of his individual creditors—a task that would generally be infeasible.

Organizational law eliminates the need for such elaborate contracting, and thereby avoids the transaction costs and moral hazard it involves. First, by permitting the firm itself to be an owner of assets, organizational law provides a simple means for identifying which assets are to be considered personal assets as opposed to business assets: the latter are simply the assets to which an appropriately organized firm holds title.[22] Second, organizational law provides a simple means for distinguishing the individual's personal creditors from his business creditors: the latter are simply those whose contracts are with an appropriately organized firm rather than with the individual directly. Third, and most importantly, organizational law alters the default rules of contract law by imposing a special term in every contract that a person enters into with a personal creditor. That term provides, in effect, that if (a) that person transfers assets to an appropriately organized firm owned by that person, or (b) that person purchases assets in the name of an appropriately organized firm that he owns, rather than in his own name, then his personal creditor's claim on those assets will be subordinated to the claims of the business creditors with whom he has contracted in the name of the firm.

This special contractual term that organizational law imposes is, moreover, a mandatory term. If it were just a default term, waivable by the parties, then the problems of moral hazard discussed above would return. A business creditor would have difficulty assuring that his claim is in fact prior to those of all of the personal creditors of the firm's owner, since the owner might have waived the term in question for the benefit of some or all of that owner's personal creditors.

2.5.1.2. *Efficiency Concerns*

This altered pattern of contractual rights that organizational law establishes would not be useful, of course, if it were not efficient—that is, if it did not lead to an increase in the aggregate value of the contractual rights held by all parties concerned. In general, however, one can expect not only that it will be efficient, but also that the individual transactions that it facilitates will be to the advantage of all the contracting parties involved.

Consider, again, our hypothetical entrepreneur. Suppose that he has already incorporated his business and now wishes to transfer to the business a piece of equipment that was previously his personal property. In exchange, he will receive additional shares in the corporation (or perhaps, if he is the sole shareholder, simply an increase in the value of his existing shares). His personal creditors will, as a consequence of this transaction, lose the right to levy directly on the equipment and will receive, in place of that right, an increase in the value of the entrepreneur's shares upon which they can levy. The creditor-monitoring

---

[22] Of course, in the case of small, informal entities such as general partnerships, there may still be ambiguity on the margin as to which property belongs to the firm and which belongs to individual partners. See Bromberg and Ribstein (1988: §§ 3.02–3.03).

economies and other advantages of affirmative asset partitioning, however, should render that increase in share value greater than the value that the equipment had when it was owned personally by the entrepreneur. If it were otherwise, the entrepreneur would have had little incentive to transfer the equipment to the corporation.

Thus, the transaction should redound to the benefit of all involved—the entrepreneur's personal creditors, the entrepreneur himself, and the entrepreneur's business creditors. The same logic applies, moreover, when an entrepreneur originally incorporates a business that was previously operated as a sole proprietorship. In sum, affirmative asset partitioning is a bonding mechanism—a means of pledging assets to business creditors—that the entrepreneur generally has an incentive to use only when its benefits exceed its costs, from both an individual and a social point of view.

2.5.2. Multiple-Owner Enterprise

When a business has multiple owners, the costs of establishing affirmative asset partitioning by simple contracting—already prohibitive in the case of a single owner—grow exponentially, while at the same time the benefits of affirmative asset partitioning also increase dramatically. This becomes clear when we imagine how a group of numerous individuals might try to create a jointly-owned business with affirmative asset partitioning—the sort of firm that could be formed using partnership law or corporate law—if partnership law, corporate law, and other forms of organizational law did not exist.

Basic property law would permit these individuals to purchase and own the property used in the business jointly, as tenants-in-common. Basic agency law would permit the co-owners to delegate to managers well-defined authority to act on behalf of the owners and to commit, as security for performance of the business's contracts, both the jointly-owned assets used in the business and the individual owners' personal assets. And basic contract law would permit the co-owners to commit themselves both to their chosen methods for apportioning among themselves the earnings of the enterprise, and to the voting rules or other mechanisms they will use to make those decisions that are not delegated to the managers. Consequently, using just these basic legal tools, the individuals could create a nexus of contracts with many of the attributes of a partnership. What these individuals could not practicably do is establish either of the two basic elements of affirmative asset partitioning: priority of claims or liquidation protection.

2.5.2.1. Establishing Priority

Consider first the problem of giving creditors of the business a prior claim on the jointly-owned assets used in the business. Under the background rules of contract and property law, the personal creditors of an individual co-owner would (in the event of the individual's non-performance) be able to levy on all of the individual's assets, including his share in the co-owned business property. And their claim on the latter property would be equal in priority with that of the business creditors. Any effort to change this pattern of creditors' rights would run into problems of the same kinds explored above in the case of a single-owner enterprise, though exponentially greater in magnitude.

In particular, to give the business creditors a prior claim to the assets used in the business would require that each of the co-owners pledge, in each contract with a business creditor, that they will extract from each of their personal creditors—both those already existing as well as all future personal creditors—a waiver of claims against the co-owners' share of the business assets. These pledges might be made easily enough by the managers, acting as their agent, via standard-form contracting. But the transaction costs to the co-owners of complying with these pledges would be immense—roughly the same as for the single owner we discussed previously, but multiplied by the number of co-owners involved. Moreover, the problems of moral hazard and monitoring involved in enforcing these pledges would increase much more than proportionately to the number of co-owners. The reason is that, with multiple co-owners, there arises a free-rider problem. Each co-owner has a stronger incentive than would a single owner-entrepreneur to neglect to extract the promised waiver from one or more of his personal creditors, and thus effectively pledge to them his share of the commonly-owned assets, since—holding the actions of the other co-owners constant—he bears only part of the costs that such action imposes on the creditworthiness of the business. Further, as the number of co-owners increases, it becomes more difficult for co-owners themselves to control this problem by monitoring each other's private debts.

2.5.2.2. *Liquidation Protection*

In addition to the problem of establishing priority in business assets for business creditors, there is the problem of liquidation protection. With only basic property law to work with, liquidation protection would be difficult to obtain. Each co-tenant of property held as tenancy-in-common has a right to force partition of the property, either through physical partition (nominally the law's preferred method) or through sale of the property and division of the proceeds.[23] Creditors of a bankrupt tenant-in-common step into the bankrupt person's shoes as tenant-in-common,[24] and therefore presumably have the same right to force partition. Although tenants-in-common can enter into a contractual agreement among themselves not to partition the property, such an agreement

---

[23] e.g. *Delfino v. Vealencis*, 436 A.2d 27 (Conn. 1980); *Johnson v. Hendrickson*, 24 N.W.2d 914 (S.D. 1946). Statutory law in most states includes provisions allowing this forced partition. Restatement (Second) of Property (1983: § 4.5 cmt. a); Cribbet (1975: 106). See Cardozo Law Review (1986) (surveying and criticizing the law's preference for partition in kind).

[24] 20 Am. Jur. 2d Cotenancy and Joint Ownership (1995: § 38) (citing *New Haven Trolley & Bus Employees Credit Union v. Hill*, 142 A.2d. 730 (Conn. 1958); *First Fed. Sav. & Loan Ass'n v. Lewis*, 14 A.D.2d 150 (N.Y. App. Div. 1961); *Sipes v. Sanders*, 66 S.W.2d 261 (Tenn. Ct. App. 1933)). See also 86 C.J.S. Tenancy in Common (1997: § 13) (sale or conveyance of common property to a third person).

must be limited in duration.[25] Moreover, it is doubtful whether an agreement not to partition, whatever its duration, would bind the co-tenants' creditors.[26]

2.5.2.3. *Partnership as Partitioning*

The law of partnership solves the problem of granting creditors a prior claim on the assets of the firm, and hence permits the weak form of affirmative asset partitioning, by creating a special form of concurrent tenancy for all assets held in partnership name. (A partner is said to hold partnership assets as a 'tenant-in-partnership' under the old Uniform Partnership Act. UPA § 25.) The rules of creditors' rights and bankruptcy applied to partnership provide that creditors of the partnership have a claim on these partnership assets, in case of the partnership's insolvency, that is prior to the claims of the partners' personal creditors.[27]

From the functional view of legal entities that we take here, it is this feature of partnership law that makes the partnership a legal entity rather than a mere common agency, and thus makes partnership law part of organizational law. There has long been debate in the legal literature as to whether the partnership, at one or another point in its historical evolution, should properly be considered to have attained legal personality. Those who have argued to the contrary have pointed, for example, to the fact that until relatively recently it was necessary to name all of a firm's individual partners in a lawsuit to enforce a claim against the partnership, or to the traditional rule that a change in the membership of the partnership leads to a dissolution of the partnership. While such elements of the traditional law of partnership are inconveniences for a smoothly functioning firm, however, they are only that; in general, they can be avoided by contractual means. The priority of claims that partnership law establishes for the firm's creditors is of a different character, since it could not, as a practical matter, be established by contract.[28]

---

[25] An agreement not to partition is unenforceable as an invalid restraint on alienation unless it is for a reasonable time only. Restatement (Second) of Property (1983: Donative Transfers § 4.5, reporter's note 2(c)); *Raisch v. Schuster*, 352 N.E.2d 657, 659–60 (Ohio Ct. App. 1975). See also Cribbet (1975: 106) (citing *Michalski v. Michalski*, 142 A.2d 645 (N.J. Super. Ct. App. Div. 1958)).

[26] The Bankruptcy Code permits a trustee in bankruptcy to sell both the interest of a bankrupt debtor and the interest of a co-owner in property that the parties held as tenants in common. 11 U.S.C. § 363(h). This provision of the Code makes no reference to agreements not to partition, and it seems implausible that they would be considered relevant. The same Code provision, for example, applies to property held as tenancy by the entirety, in which by law, and not just as a contractual option, an individual co-owner lacks the right to compel partition.

[27] The rule is stated quite explicitly, for example, in UPA § 40(h).

[28] Like the partnership, the unincorporated association has long been the subject of debate as to its status as a legal entity. In the case of the unincorporated association, however, there has been more reason for debate.

The traditional common law rule was that an unincorporated association could not hold assets in its own name. As a result, there existed no separate pool of association assets against which creditors of the association could proceed. Creditors of the association who sought satisfaction of their claims were consequently permitted to bring suit against members and other persons acting on behalf of the association. An unincorporated association was therefore not a legal entity as we use that term here.

Beginning in the early twentieth century, many states adopted 'sue and be sued' statutes recognizing the capacity of an unincorporated association to hold assets and incur debts in its own

If the owners of a firm want liquidation protection, the general partnership-at-will, of course, will not suffice. Rather, the owners will need to use a strong-form legal entity, such as the business corporation.

2.5.3. An Aside on the 'Partnership Sole'

Once this last point is recognized, we see that it would make sense for partnership law to recognize the 'partnership sole'—that is, a partnership with only a single partner—just as corporation law has come to recognize the corporation sole. With the ability to establish a business as a partnership sole, an individual entrepreneur could give all of her business creditors a prior claim on her business assets while also offering them a claim against her personal assets for any business debts that could not be satisfied out of business assets. This form of affirmative asset partitioning without defensive asset partitioning would have the same advantages for a small business with a single owner as it does for one with two or more owners. The fact that partnership law requires, instead, at least two partners[29] is perhaps explainable in part, like early resistance to the corporation sole, by conceptual confusion: 'Partnership', even more than 'corporation', seems to connote multiple owners. Another explanation may be that, at least today, roughly the same result can be obtained by incorporating the business and having its sole shareholder assume personal liability by co-signing contracts between the corporation and its most important creditors.

2.5.4. Agency with Title

In the preceding discussion, we assumed that the individuals investing in the business would remain co-owners of the specific assets used in the business. An alternative approach to establishing affirmative asset partitioning without

name, with the result that creditors of the association could reach the assets of the association to satisfy unpaid debts. Those statutes consequently established affirmative asset partitioning, and thus made unincorporated associations legal entities in the sense used here. To be sure, affirmative asset partitioning requires not only demarcation of the firm's assets, but also creation of a priority claim on those assets for firm creditors. The statutes in question do not expressly address the latter question of priority. Nevertheless, priority for association creditors is the logical consequence of the statutes: assets held by the association are presumably not also to be considered personal property of the members, and thus cannot be levied upon directly by creditors of the individual members.

The sue and be sued statutes did not, however, establish defensive asset partitioning. Members, as well as others acting on behalf of the association, remained personally liable, jointly and severally, for the association's debts. *Karl Rove & Co. v. Thornburgh*, 39 F.3d 1273, 1285–86 (5th Cir. 1994); see Davison (1994: 235–6). It was largely this issue that prompted the promulgation, in 1992, of the Uniform Unincorporated Nonprofit Association Act, which has now been adopted in a number of states. That Act roughly replicates the affirmative asset partitioning provisions of the sue and be sued statutes but goes further by establishing a substantial, though ambiguous, degree of defensive asset partitioning, stating that a person is not personally liable for an unincorporated association's debts 'merely' because that person is a member of the association or participates in its management. Davison (1994: 254–6).

[29] At present, formation of a partnership requires 'an association of two or more persons'. UPA § 6; RUPA § 202(a).

organizational law might be to transfer ownership of those assets to the manager(s) of the business, subject to a contractual commitment by the manager, acting as agent for the owners, to manage the assets for the exclusive benefit of the owners and to reconvey the assets to the owners under appropriate circumstances.

This approach would provide a relatively workable means of granting business creditors a claim in the business assets that is prior to the claims of the owners' personal creditors. Since title to the business assets would not be in the hands of the owners, the owners' personal creditors would have no right to levy on those assets. At most the owners' creditors could succeed to the owners' contractual claims against the agent. But those claims, being contractual, would be limited to the terms of the contracts. And the contracts between the owners and the manager serving as their agent could provide that claims of the owners against the assets held by the manager would be subordinate to the claims of the business creditors with whom the manager contracts.

Consequently, separate waivers from all the personal creditors of the owners would not be necessary, thus avoiding the prohibitive transaction costs and moral hazard that such waivers would involve. To make the business creditors' priority credible to them, it would be sufficient to show them the waivers in the agency contracts between the owners and the manager.

Liquidation protection from the owners' personal creditors might also be established through this approach. In case of an owner's personal bankruptcy, his creditors could seek to realize the value of his contractual commitments from the manager of the business, but presumably—at least so long as the agency is not revocable[30]—could pursue only a monetary claim against the manager and could not seek to levy directly on the business assets whose title is held by the manager.

This approach may therefore succeed in insulating the pledged assets from the creditors of the co-owners.[31] The reason it succeeds is that the owners are, in fact, employing a separate legal person to serve as the firm. That person, however, is a real individual—the agent/manager—rather than an artificial legal person. And therein lies the problem with this approach. By borrowing the legal personality of the manager to form the firm, the business assets held by the manager become indistinct from the manager's personal property. The result is that

---

[30] The general rule is that an agency cannot be made non-revocable. There is an exception, however, if the agency 'is coupled with an interest'. Presumably the transfer of title in the pledged assets to the agent gives the agent the requisite interest (from the law's point of view). To be sure, the agency contract employed here seeks to deprive the manager of any equitable interest in the assets, leaving him only with formal legal title. On the other hand, as the following discussion shows, there may be no way to prevent those assets from serving as security for the manager's personal creditors, and thus the manager does, in fact, have a substantial equitable interest in the assets.

[31] As a bonus, this approach may also provide limited liability for the owners, in the sense that their exposure to the creditors of the firm may be limited to the assets whose title they have transferred to the manager. This will not be the case, however, if the owners retain sufficient control over the manager that the law of agency makes them personally responsible for contracts entered into by the agent on their behalf.

the business assets, while insulated from the creditors of the owners, are not insulated from the creditors of the manager. Absent organizational law, the business assets would, as a default rule, be available to the manager's personal creditors unless the manager secured explicit agreement from those creditors that the assets are not available to them.

The agency contract between the owners and the manager could, to be sure, require that the manager obtain such an agreement from each of his personal creditors. But the resulting transaction costs—which would resemble those we surveyed when considering the possibility that a single owner of a business could affirmatively partition off the assets of that business—would commonly make such agreements impracticable. Moreover, not only the creditors of the business but also the owners would run the substantial risk that the manager would fail to obtain such an agreement from one or more of his creditors, whether from opportunism or mere inattention. In that case, while the owners (and perhaps the business creditors) would retain contractual claims against the manager, those claims would be parallel with, rather than superior to, the claims of the manager's personal creditors. As a result, in the absence of organizational law, this approach fails to establish affirmative asset partitioning, just as do the other two approaches we have examined.

The common law trust solves this problem of insulating the business assets from the personal creditors of the manager by permitting the manager to be designated a 'trustee' whose assets—that is, assets to which he holds legal title—are effectively partitioned into two sets: his personal assets and the assets he holds in trust for designated beneficiaries. Further, trust law provides that, as a general rule, the latter assets are not available to satisfy the claims of the trustee's personal creditors. Thus, the law of trusts makes the trustee, vis-à-vis creditors with whom he contracts, two distinct legal persons: a natural person contracting on behalf of himself, and an artificial person acting on behalf of the beneficiaries.

This insulation of assets held in trust from the personal creditors of the trustee is the essential contribution of trust law. Its importance can be seen by examining the use of trust-like relationships in civil law countries where the law of trusts is lacking. While it is not uncommon in those jurisdictions for individuals to proceed in the manner described above, transferring to an agent the title to assets that the agent is to manage on the individuals' behalf, the persons chosen as agents are almost invariably banks or other institutions with sufficient safe assets to effectively eliminate the risk of the agent's insolvency. This is in contrast to common law jurisdictions where, as a consequence of the law of trusts, individuals have long been commonly used as trustees (Hansmann and Mattei 1998). While it is sometimes said that the common law trust lacks legal personality, in our view it is, on the contrary, quite clearly a legal entity, and trust law is consequently a form of organizational law.

Indeed, one might go further. We have taken it for granted that, even in the absence of trust law, the agency-with-title arrangement described here would at least succeed in partitioning off the business assets held by the manager from the personal assets of the owners. But that assumption is based on legal rules that might themselves be considered to have the character of organizational law. After all, the law might quite reasonably say, instead, that an effort to transfer formal title in an asset from a principal to an agent, when that agent remains subject to the control of the principal and to a promise ultimately to reconvey the asset and the title to the principal, does not succeed in changing the legal character of that asset as property of the principal rather than of the agent, at least for purposes of creditors' rights. Thus, the asset would remain available to the principal's personal creditors just like other assets owned directly by the principal. Viewed this way, the law of trusts is important not only for permitting affirmative partitioning of trust assets with respect to the personal assets of the trustee, but also—like corporation law and partnership law—for permitting affirmative partitioning with respect to the personal assets of the owners.

2.5.5. Security Interests

It remains to ask whether affirmative asset partitioning might be accomplished through contracting, without resort to organizational law, if we supplement contract law rules with the modern law of secured transactions, such as that found in Article 9 of the Uniform Commercial Code (UCC).

Of the two principal components of affirmative asset partitioning—priority of claims and liquidation protection—security interests offer a potential substitute only for the first. They provide a mechanism for assigning different priorities to the claims that different creditors hold on a given set of assets, but they do not, in their contemporary form, offer a means of preventing one or another class of creditors from forcing liquidation of the assets in satisfaction of their claim. Consequently, security interests can at most serve as an alternative to organizational law in forming weak form legal entities such as partnerships; they cannot suffice for the construction of strong form entities such as corporations. Moreover, even with respect to priority of claims, security interests do not today offer an effective substitute for organizational law.

2.5.5.1. *Establishing Priority*

To see the possibilities for using security interests to establish a priority of claims, let us return to the case of a group of individuals who wish to create a business that they will jointly own, and whose creditors will have a prior claim, over those individuals' personal creditors, on assets associated with the business. And let us suppose that the owners have at their disposal the contemporary US commercial law of security interests, but no organizational law such as the law of partnership or the law of business corporations (thus forcing the owners to employ a non-entity form of joint ownership, such as tenancy-in-common).

To achieve their purposes using only the law of secured transactions, our hypothetical owners might seek to draft and register a financing agreement assigning to all business creditors an undivided security interest in all present and future business assets, with the creditors' claims to be satisfied out of the security pro rata according to the amount owed them. This would require a reduction to writing of (1) a description of all of the assets to be pledged, and (2) a listing of all of the present and future creditors to which these assets can be pledged. A statement pledging these assets as security would then need to be included in the individual contracts between the firm and each of its creditors. To be comprehensive, this class of creditors would have to include all of the firm's suppliers, employees, and customers. The essential question is whether the transaction costs of accomplishing this would be prohibitive.

The current law of secured transactions permits the pledge of both present and future ('after-acquired') assets by type. Consequently, it offers a relatively simple method of establishing a broad floating lien over assets held by a given debtor. To be sure, the most recent revisions to the UCC specifically forbid debtors from offering, in a security agreement, a blanket pledge of all assets of any description, requiring instead more specific description of the particular assets that are covered by the agreement.[32] Consequently, using just the law of secured transactions, business creditors could not be given priority over the business owners' personal creditors in assets of a type not specifically described. This clearly makes a security agreement a relatively awkward means for affirmative asset partitioning. Since, however, most business assets of consequence can be described and pledged effectively under current law, this problem is not a fundamental obstacle to substantially effective asset partitioning via secured transactions.

In contrast to the flexibility it offers in describing pledged assets, however, current commercial law creates severe difficulties in describing the creditors to whom those assets are to be pledged. A financing agreement must list the name and address of each creditor who is secured by the agreement.[33] This means that a secured financing agreement cannot be extended to include unnamed future business creditors without requiring a new filing each time the firm deals with a new creditor. As one court has put it, 'the UCC clearly contemplates and sanctions floating collateral (after-acquired property of the debtor) and floating debt (future advances [from already-existing creditors]). However, the UCC does not . . . contemplate floating secured parties.'[34] Undertaking a new filing with each new creditor—which means, to match the consequences of organizational law, virtually every time that the firm contracts with someone new—would obviously be an infeasible burden in a business of any complexity.

---

[32] In a new version of Uniform Commercial Code (UCC) art. 9, recently drafted by NCUSL, § 9-108 explicitly disallows such pledges in security agreements (though the new § 9-504 specifically allows such a description in a financing statement).

[33] UCC § 9-402. Although the new § 9-502 dispenses with the requirement that a financing statement include the creditor's address, 'the name of the secured party' is still required.

[34] *Republic Nat'l Bank v. Fitzgerald (In re E. A. Fretz Co.)*, 565 F.2d 366, 369 (5th Cir. 1978) (internal citation omitted).

Consequently, security interests fall far short of offering a workable substitute for establishing the pattern of priorities that is involved in the affirmative asset partitioning offered by organizational law.

It might be argued that, while security interests cannot suffice to provide priority of claims for all of the creditors of a business, this is not really necessary to create a viable firm. Rather, it is sufficient if the business simply obtains all of its credit from one big creditor rather than from many small ones. In fact, small businesses commonly follow this path today in any event, obtaining most or all of their financing from a single creditor such as a bank that takes a security interest in all of the business's assets.[35] If the business goes bankrupt, the single secured creditor commonly gets paid nearly in full, while the other, smaller creditors get little or nothing (Bebchuk and Fried 1996: 862). Realizing this, the unsecured creditors can adjust their terms of credit accordingly.

But this one-big-secured-creditor approach to creating a viable firm suffers from two serious problems. First, it is not the case that, if a business relies upon a single secured creditor for its principal financing, it is irrelevant to other parties who contract with the firm whether the firm is formed as a legal entity—that is, whether the business as a whole exhibits affirmative asset partitioning. Other persons who contract with the business (customers, suppliers, workers, etc.) will still need to assess the likelihood that the firm will keep its contractual promises to them, so that they can determine the terms on which they are willing to deal with the business. This requires, in particular, an ability to predict the likelihood with which the business will go bankrupt. For, even if (or especially if) it is clear to the firm's customers and suppliers that they will get nothing from the firm in the case of its bankruptcy, owing to the presence of the one, big secured creditor, the probability of non-performance (and non-payment of damages) remains important when deciding whether and on what terms to contract with the business. And, in the absence of affirmative asset partitioning, it will be very much harder than it otherwise would be for the firm's customers and suppliers to predict the likelihood of the business's bankruptcy, since that will depend on the probability that each of the business's owners will become insolvent, and not just on the probability that the business itself will become unprofitable. In short, the monitoring cost advantages of affirmative asset partitioning do not disappear when a firm depends principally on one large secured creditor for financial credit.

Second, there is the problem of how the business's one large creditor will obtain its own financing in the absence of organizational law. Suppose, for example, that—as is common for small businesses today—the one large creditor is a bank that obtains the funds it lends by taking deposits from numerous small depositors. In the absence of organizational law, and of the affirmative asset partitioning it affords, the bank's depositors run the risk that the bank will be thrown into bankruptcy by creditors of the bank's owners even if the bank's

---

[35] See Scott (1986: 948–50) (discussing single creditor 'relational' lending to small firms).

own operations are highly profitable. Thus, to an important degree the one-big-secured-creditor approach just shifts the problem of creditors' monitoring costs from the creditors of the business itself to the creditors of the business's single secured creditor.

2.5.5.2. Respecting Priority

Beyond the problem of determining the pattern of priorities among a business's creditors and the creditors of the business's owners, there is the problem of determining how closely those priorities, once established, will be respected. Here, too, there is a difference between what can be accomplished with organizational law and what can be accomplished with the law of secured interests. Organizational law offers stronger respect for these priorities.

Bankruptcy law in the United States sometimes fails, in practice, to give full respect to the relative priorities among the creditors of a business, advantaging junior creditors and equityholders at the expense of senior creditors.[36] To avoid this problem, some companies obtain debt financing through the use of a separate entity. This approach is typified by the asset securitization transactions that have become commonplace in recent years.[37]

In a typical asset securitization transaction, a corporation transfers some of its assets (say, its accounts receivable) to a wholly-owned subsidiary corporation created just for purposes of the transaction. The subsidiary in turn issues bonds backed by the accounts receivable, paying the receipts from the bond issue to the parent corporation as compensation for those assets.[38] In economic effect, the parent corporation is just borrowing against its accounts receivable. Those assets are usually well within the categories of assets in which security interests can easily be created. Consequently, the same basic secured borrowing transaction might be undertaken without use of the subsidiary by having the corporation itself issue the bonds and back them with a security interest in the corporation's accounts receivable. The advantage of using the subsidiary—which, though nominally a distinct legal entity, typically performs no significant operational functions—is that it serves as a 'bankruptcy remote vehicle': if the parent corporation should ever fall into bankruptcy, the trust assets will remain

[36] Undercompensation of secured creditors relative to general creditors and equity is, for example, a direct consequence of the doctrine established in the Supreme Court's ruling in *United Savings Association v. Timbers of Inwood Forest Associates*, 484 U.S. 365 (1988), which disallows interest on secured creditors' unpaid claims during bankruptcy proceedings. For discussion, see Baird, Jackson, and Adler (2000: 381–3).

For a general analysis of absolute priority valuations, as well as the direct costs of bankruptcy reorganization, see Weiss (1990). See also Lopucki and Whitford (1990) (offering an empirical estimate of deviations from absolute priority). See generally Adler (1997) (collecting sources on the theory and empirical evidence of absolute-priority violations and the costs of reorganization).

[37] On the popularity of these transactions, see Smith and Walter (1997: 201, fig. 7-6); Langbein (1997).

[38] See Schwarcz (1993: 16–36) (describing the structure and motivation of typical securitization transactions); Committee on Bankruptcy and Corporate Reorganization of the Association of the Bar of the City of New York (1995: 538, 569) (describing vendor and lessor financing through separate entities such as General Motors Acceptance Corporation).

completely insulated from the bankruptcy proceedings, reducing the risk that the priority of the bondholders' claim on the pledged assets will be compromised (Committee on Bankruptcy and Corporate Reorganization of the Association of the Bar of the City of New York 1995: 553–67; Hill 1996: 1090–3; Schwarcz 1993: 16–36; Schwarcz 1994: 135; Tracht 1997: 310–11). Even greater bankruptcy remoteness can be obtained through a common variant on such transactions in which the pledged assets are transferred, not to a wholly-owned subsidiary, but to a legal entity such as a trust that is, at least nominally, completely separate from the corporation for whose benefit the transaction is undertaken (Schwarcz 1993: 21–36).

The great popularity of these types of 'structured finance' transactions reflects the widespread belief that legal entities provide greater protection than do security interests against the tendency of bankruptcy law to compromise priorities among creditors and hence frustrate efficient asset partitioning. To be sure, this advantage of legal entities over security interests is arguably a relatively modest one. Moreover, it is in part just an artefact of the weakness of US bankruptcy law in respecting priorities—a weakness not generally shared by other legal systems. The critical advantage of legal entities over security interests today does not lie in the degree of protection that they offer for established priorities, but rather, as described in the preceding subsection, in the greater facility that entities offer to establish priorities in the first place.

2.5.5.3. Adding Flexibility to Property Law

If the law of security interests were substantially more flexible, and permitted the creation of floating liens with the appropriate scope and force, and with substantial flexibility in accommodating shifting creditors, then that body of law might provide a workable substitute for organizational law at least so far as establishing priority of claims is involved (though it still would not provide liquidation protection).[39] The reason for this is that both organizational law and the law of security interests are, in essence, forms of property law: they define the types of property interests that can be created and made binding against third parties.

The underlying law of property rights in all economies places strong limitations on the ways in which transferable property rights in any given asset can be divided up among two or more persons (Hansmann and Kraakman 2002). Both the law of security interests and organizational law create exceptions to these limitations. They permit the grant of a contingent ownership right—a right to take possession of the asset in case of contractual default—and make that right

---

[39] As a historical matter, it should be kept in mind that the law of secured interests is relatively recent and localized law. In the United States of America, where that body of law appears most advanced, it expanded to something approximating its current scope only with the advent, in the mid-twentieth century, of the Uniform Commercial Code (UCC). Most contemporary forms of organizational law are substantially older, having arisen when even the law of security interests was much less well developed, and hence even less useful than it is now as an alternative approach to asset partitioning.

enforceable against third parties, including in particular other creditors who also have a contingent claim on the assets in question. An important consideration in permitting creation of these rights is that third parties who might be affected by the rights—such as other creditors whose interests might be subordinated by them—have some form of notice. The law of security interests provides for notice through means such as filing. Organizational law provides for notice by permitting assignment of rights only to assets held by a legal entity. When assets are held in the name of a legal entity, the owners of that entity effectively give notice to personal creditors that a prior contingent claim on those assets may well be held by other persons—namely, creditors who have contracted with the entity itself.

2.5.5.4. *Historical Evolution*

The law of security interests, in its modern general form, is a relatively recent innovation. Until well into the twentieth century, that body of law was much less suited than it is now to creating broad floating liens of a type that offer a partial substitute for organizational law.

It is possible that the law of security interests will continue to evolve, so that it provides not only for floating assets and floating debt, but also for floating secured parties. Perhaps, too, it will at some point come to offer a form of liquidation protection. If so, the line between organizational law and the law of secured interests may become quite indistinct—particularly given the tendency of organizational law to develop forms like the business trust, discussed below, that can effectively be employed as pure asset partitioning devices.

2.6. Benefits of Defensive Asset Partitioning

Defensive asset partitioning limits the exposure of the personal assets of a firm's owners to the claims of business creditors. In contrast to affirmative asset partitioning, which by and large takes a single form, we observe many degrees of defensive asset partitioning. These range, as we noted in section 2.3, from none whatsoever in the contemporary general partnership to complete claim exclusion (conventional 'limited liability') in most corporate forms, with various intermediate forms between these extremes (and even more in the past). As this variety suggests, defensive asset partitioning has costs as well as benefits, and those costs and benefits are sometimes in close balance. In this respect defensive asset partitioning contrasts with affirmative asset partitioning, the net benefits of which are so decisive that it is today an element of all of the law's standard forms for enterprise organization.

The costs of defensive asset partitioning, which are conspicuous, derive principally from the possibilities it creates for the firm's owners to act opportunistically toward business creditors. If the credit required for the business substantially exceeds the value of the assets held by the firm, then limited liability creates an inducement for the owners of the firm to divert value from the firm's creditors by any of a variety of means, such as shirking with respect to their own promised effort, investing in excessively risky projects, or simply withdrawing assets from the firm in anticipation of insolvency.

The benefits of defensive asset partitioning, on the other hand, are various. Some of those benefits have been well explored in the existing literature, while others have not (Easterbrook and Fischel 1985: 93–101; Halpern et al. 1980: 147–9; Ribstein 1991: 99–107; Woodward 1985: 601–2). We briefly survey here the most important of these benefits.

2.6.1. Monitoring Economies

To begin with, limits on liability create monitoring economies much like those generated by affirmative asset partitioning. Just as affirmative asset partitioning permits firm creditors to focus their attention principally on the firm's assets, defensive asset partitioning permits the personal creditors of the firm's owners to focus principally on the personal assets of owners. From the perspective of the two sets of creditors, defensive and affirmative asset partitioning are largely symmetric: affirmative asset partitioning is 'defensive' with respect to the claims of personal creditors, and defensive asset partitioning is 'affirmative' with respect to the claims of personal creditors.

Defensive asset partitioning also generates potential monitoring economies for the firm's owners. As others have observed, in the absence of limited liability, each of a firm's owners would have an interest in continually monitoring not only the assets and liabilities of their jointly-owned business, but also the personal assets and liabilities of their fellow owners (Easterbrook and Fischel 1985). It is not only conventional limited liability that generates these monitoring economies. They are also offered by weaker forms of defensive asset partitioning—such as multiple personal liability or pro rata personal liability[40]—though in lesser degree.

2.6.2. Decision-Making Economies

Defensive asset partitioning also performs functions that have no parallel in the context of affirmative asset partitioning. Chief among these is reducing the costs of firm governance.

One way in which defensive asset partitioning can reduce governance costs is by lowering the decision-making costs of a firm—such as a corporation—in which multiple owners share in the legal right to control the firm's policies or select its managers. Limited liability ensures that all owners in such a firm experience the same proportional gains and losses from the firm's policies, regardless of their identities or assets. Consequently, limited liability gives these owners a

---

[40] See generally Hansmann and Kraakman (1991) (exploring a rule of pro rata liability).

homogeneous economic interest in the firm's decisions, which greatly facilitates collective decision-making.[41] Weaker forms of defensive asset partitioning can be expected to reduce governance costs in much the same way. For example, pro rata shareholder liability homogenizes the preferences of shareholders as effectively as full limited liability so long as all shareholders are able to cover their share of the firm's liabilities. In the complete absence of defensive asset partitioning, on the other hand, owners—such as partners in a general partnership— must select fellow owners with similar assets and risk preferences or face significant negotiating costs.

2.6.3. Enhanced Creditor Monitoring

A second way in which defensive asset partitioning can reduce governance costs is by shifting some of the burden of monitoring the firm's managers from the firm's owners to its creditors. This is a particularly conspicuous advantage of full limited liability in firms that, like most public corporations, are managed by professional managers.

In effect, limited liability permits the firm to enlist creditors as monitors. If creditors know that they have recourse only to assets held by the firm, they are more likely than otherwise to scrutinize closely—both before and after extending credit—the likely fortunes of the firm and the behaviour of the firm's managers. The resulting creditor monitoring may often be a useful complement to monitoring by the firm's owners, even when these owners themselves can monitor with fair competence. Creditors may have access to different types of information than do owners, and they may also have different means for influencing managers. But creditor monitoring of managers may have particularly strong efficiencies when a firm's owners are poorly situated to monitor the organization's managers for themselves, as with corporations that have numerous dispersed shareholders. In firms of the latter type, important creditors may sometimes be even better overall monitors of management than are the firm's owners. Limited liability gives creditors the incentive to make use of their monitoring abilities—for which, of course, they will extract a price from the firm's owners in the cost they charge for credit.

In contrast to other benefits from defensive asset partitioning, the strength of partitioning matters a great deal here. Full limited liability is a credible incentive for creditors; weaker forms, such as double liability and pro rata liability, give creditors a much weaker monitoring incentive as long as a firm's owners are solvent. The same is true of the next benefit we examine.

---

[41] For a related argument concerning the virtues of having a corporate income tax that is strongly separated from the personal tax liability of the corporation's shareholders, see Kanda and Levmore (1991: 229–34). On the importance of homogeneity of interest among those who share ownership in firms generally, see Hansmann (1996).

2.6.4. Collection Economies

A third benefit of defensive asset partitioning, often given as a justification for limited liability in publicly held business corporations, is that the costs of securing and collecting personal judgments against the personal assets of the firm's owners would consume a large fraction of the amount collected—so large as to render personal liability inefficient, in the sense that shareholders would be better off *ex ante* paying more for credit in return for a pledge from creditors not to collect from them personally.

There is undoubtedly some truth to this, though it has perhaps been exaggerated. Corporations with numerous shareholders that bore personal liability for the firm's unpaid debts were relatively common in the nineteenth and early twentieth centuries, and procedures for collecting personal judgments against their owners were, at least in some contexts, developed to the point where the transaction costs of collecting were evidently quite manageable (Macey and Miller 1992: 55–7).

2.6.5. Economies of Transfer

Limited liability is also commonly said to facilitate the transferability of ownership shares in an organization such as a business corporation. This point, which is undoubtedly correct, is closely related to the monitoring and governance economies considered above. As a practical matter, markets for ownership interests are unlikely to form unless traders can separate the value of these shares from their own personal assets and the personal assets of other owners. Limited liability obviously permits such a separation. Weaker forms of defensive asset partitioning can, however, effect the same separation in varying degrees, as evidenced by historical examples of business corporations whose shares have traded freely under regimes of multiple or pro rata shareholder liability (Grossman 1995: 72–5; Hansmann and Kraakman 1991: 1923–5; Macey and Miller 1992: 35–9; Weinstein 2000: 7–9).

2.6.6. Risk-Bearing Economies

Finally, risk sharing provides a potential rationale for defensive asset partitioning. It is important here to distinguish between two forms of risk sharing. The first is risk sharing between a firm's creditors and its owners. Limited liability, the most extreme form of defensive asset partitioning, has the important advantage here that, by putting a greater or lesser amount of equity in the firm, the balance between risk borne by owners and that borne by the firm's creditors can be modulated over a wide range. Weaker forms of defensive partitioning, in turn, provide for even greater risk bearing by owners.

The second form of risk sharing is among the owners themselves. A background rule of joint and several liability, i.e. no defensive asset partitioning, gives the owners little control over their relative exposure to risk. The degree of control available then increases progressively as increasingly stronger forms of defensive partitioning are employed.

2.6.7. The Evolution of Defensive Asset Partitioning

As the previous discussion indicates, defensive asset partitioning can offer various efficiencies, only one of which—the reduction of monitoring costs—directly parallels an efficiency of affirmative asset partitioning. Many of these efficiencies can be realized with weaker limitations on the liability of owners, such as multiple liability and pro rata liability. This may explain the complex pattern of evolution that defensive asset partitioning has followed over the past two centuries.

In the late nineteenth century, a variety of intermediate forms of defensive asset partitioning were in common use, including all of the forms described in Part 2.3—pro rata liability, multiple liability, and liability limited by guarantee. Today these intermediate forms have largely fallen into disuse,[42] leaving only the two extreme rules—full limited liability, on the one hand, and unlimited joint and several personal liability, on the other hand. Moreover, the gap between these two extreme forms has widened, as a result of recent changes in US bankruptcy and partnership law. Those changes increase the priority of partnership creditors vis-à-vis personal creditors in the partners' personal assets and also increase the effective size of the claim that partnership creditors can assert against the personal assets of individual partners.

One likely reason for this evolution lies in improved mechanisms for controlling opportunism toward creditors on the part of corporate shareholders, hence making the full limited liability that characterizes the corporate form workable for a broader range of firms. These mechanisms include, for example, improved accounting standards, more extensive disclosure, more sophisticated credit rating services, and other institutional monitors. They also include more specialized forms of regulation, such as the mandatory deposit insurance, and accompanying federal financial supervision now imposed on most US banking institutions.

A second reason lies in the increasing availability of the corporate form, and other limited liability forms, to small-scale enterprise. Until well into the twentieth century, the corporate form was designed almost exclusively for large-scale enterprise and did not accommodate the types of specialized arrangements (such as shareholder voting agreements and restrictions on share transferability) needed for small firms. Small-scale enterprise was therefore effectively restricted to the partnership form even for those firms that would otherwise have chosen

---

[42] The company limited by guarantee is still in common use in some Commonwealth jurisdictions but is now used almost exclusively to form non-profit entities of the sort formed in the United States under a non-profit corporation statute, which is lacking in UK law. Davies (1997: 10–11).

limited liability. It therefore made sense to apply to partnerships an intermediate form of defensive asset partitioning (with priority in personal assets for personal creditors) as a compromise: it allowed owners of a firm to pledge their personal assets to firm creditors when, as was often the case, that was the efficient thing to do, but still provided at least some ability to insulate an individual's personal financial affairs from the vicissitudes of the firms he invested in.

In the course of the twentieth century, however, the corporate form became sufficiently flexible to accommodate the special needs of small firms. The result is that a firm of any size can choose freely between a rule of limited liability (by forming as a corporation, or, today, as a limited liability company or a statutory business trust) and a rule of unlimited liability (by forming as a partnership). The need for a compromise form of defensive asset partitioning has therefore disappeared, and it now makes sense to offer, to those firm owners who wish to pledge their personal assets to firm creditors, the greatest possible freedom to make such a pledge.[43]

2.7. Is Law Necessary for Defensive Asset Partitioning?

Given that strong defensive asset partitioning—limited liability—is evidently efficient for most firms, it remains to ask whether organizational law is necessary to establish this form of partitioning, as it is to establish affirmative asset partitioning.

2.7.1. Establishing Limited Liability by Contract

In the absence of organizational law, the default rule would presumably be unlimited joint and several liability for a firm's owners of roughly the type found

---

[43] Ribstein (1992: 430 n. 65) offers a different view. He argues, first, that the partnership form is moving closer to the corporate form because the 'exhaustion principle', under which partnership assets must be exhausted before partnership creditors can pursue individual assets, has been extended from contract creditors under the UPA, to contract and tort creditors under the RUPA; see Bromberg and Ribstein (1988: § 5.08(g)). We are unpersuaded, because tort liability is, in our view, irrelevant to the legitimate functions of organizational law. See Section 2.7.2, discussing the distinction between organizational and tort law. In addition, Ribstein (1997: 65–7) argues that the shift in priorities under the Bankruptcy Reform Act of 1978, under which the creditors of individual partners lost their priority in the assets of these partners, was an instance of inefficient federal intervention in an area of organizational law best left to the states. We disagree. The corporate form, once universally available, captures all of the creditor monitoring economies available under the old UPA priority rules for partners' creditors. Section 40(i) of the old UPA gave individual creditors priority in individual assets, which encouraged partnership creditors to ignore personal assets and individual creditors to monitor business interests only in so far as these were among the partners' personal assets. The corporate form, of course, puts business and individual creditors in virtually the same position. Given this, the partnership form retains value only as an unlimited liability alternative to the corporate form, which implies that the claim of partnership creditors should be strengthened—they should have the same claim on the assets of individual partners as do individual creditors.

in the contemporary (post-1978) general partnership. This is because, so long as the owners retain some minimal degree of control over the firm's managers (or are the managers themselves), the managers would be considered agents of the owners and the law of agency would therefore make each owner personally liable for all of the firm's debts.

Is organizational law necessary to reverse this default and permit the establishment of limited liability or other forms of defensive asset partitioning? To put the question more precisely, suppose there were a body of organizational law that permitted affirmative asset partitioning but did not provide for defensive asset partitioning. That is, suppose the only available legal entity were the modern general partnership. How difficult would it be to establish limited liability—or other forms of defensive asset partitioning—for a general partnership using only the tools of contract?

To accomplish this, it would be necessary for the partnership to insert, in its contracts with all of its creditors, provisions whereby the creditor waives any right to proceed against the partners' personal assets to obtain satisfaction of the creditor's claims against the firm. This might involve high transaction costs, at least if there were an effort to extend it to all of the firm's creditors, including the smallest trade creditors. While it might not be difficult to draft the necessary language for the waivers, it could be costly to induce all creditors—particularly small trade creditors who utilize standard-form contracts or invoices of their own that do not include such a waiver—to incorporate the waivers in their contracts with the firm.[44] On the other hand, even at their worst these transaction costs would be vastly smaller than the transaction costs, described earlier, that would be necessary to establish affirmative asset partitioning by contract. There would be no need to alter contracts between the individual owners and all of their individual creditors, and no need to confront the moral hazard associated with that contracting.

Indeed, there is historical experience with such a regime of limited liability by contract.[45] In England, prior to 1844, the corporate form was not generally available to manufacturing firms. Consequently, large manufacturing firms commonly formed as joint stock companies with transferable shares—a noncorporate form that had roughly the legal characteristics of a partnership, including joint and several personal liability for all of the firm's obligations. Between 1844 and 1855, manufacturing firms were permitted to incorporate, but still were denied limited liability. Only with the enactment of the English Limited Liability Act in 1855 was incorporation with limited liability made generally available. The pre-1855 unlimited liability regime did not, however, prevent the formation of large firms with multiple owners. By 1844, there were

[44] A further problem is the possible ambiguity as to precisely which assets belonged to the firm, and hence were available to satisfy its creditors. However, the analogous ambiguity in determining the extent of partnership assets has not proven to be insurmountable. In addition, this ambiguity can be reduced by acquiring assets in the name of the firm. See Ribstein (1991: 108).

[45] The English experience recounted here is discussed in detail in Blumberg (1995: § 1.03, at 9–23).

nearly one thousand joint stock companies in England, some with thousands of shareholders. These companies commonly sought to limit their members' liability for the firm's debts to third parties by such means as inserting the word 'Limited' after the company's name, putting an indication of limited liability in the company's stationery, and including limited liability clauses in the company's contracts.[46] The courts ultimately gave at least a partial blessing to these practices, holding that a standard 'limited liability' clause inserted into all of a joint stock company's contracts with creditors was effective,[47] although simply inserting such a clause into a joint stock company's deed of association would not bind creditors even if they had express notice of it.[48]

In sum, while organizational law plays a role in reducing the transaction costs of establishing defensive asset partitioning, that role is substantially less important than the role that organizational law plays in affirmative asset partitioning. The latter, unlike the former, would generally be quite impossible to establish without organizational law. This critical point has been missed by contemporary scholars who, recognizing that limited liability could be established by contract, have gone on to conclude that corporation law as a whole does no more than avoid unnecessary contracting costs by offering convenient default terms.[49]

2.7.2. Organizational Law Versus Tort Law

Although it is to some extent a question of interpretation whether organizational law is important for limiting the personal liability of owners toward a firm's contractual creditors, there is no doubt that organizational law is essential to shield owners of an organization from personal liability to tort victims. Almost by definition, basic contractual devices are insufficient to establish such protection.

---

[46] Ibid. § 1.03.2, at 15–16.
[47] *Hallett v. Dowdall* (1852) 21 L.J.Q.B. 98.
[48] *In re Sea, Fire & Life Assurance Co.* (1854) 3 De G. M. & G. 459, 475–77, 43 E.R. 180, 186–7.
[49] e.g. Posner (1976: 506) states that:

[Questions of tort liability] to one side, the primary utility of corporation law lies in providing a set of standard, implied contract terms, for example, governing credit, so that business firms do not have to stipulate these terms anew every time they transact, *although they could do so if necessary*. To the extent that the terms implied by corporation law accurately reflect the normal desires of transacting parties, they reduce the costs of transactions. . . . A corporation law that is out of step with [commercial] realities, and so induces contracting parties to draft waivers of the contract terms supplied by the law, is inefficient because it imposes unnecessary transaction costs (emphasis added).

Our argument here is that, when it comes to establishing affirmative asset partitioning, the parties could not 'do so if necessary' by contractual means absent organizational law, and that 'the primary utility of corporation law' thus lies in that partitioning. (To be sure, Posner's statement is arguably accurate if he is assuming that, absent corporation law, the parties could still resort to modern partnership law, and obtain affirmative asset partitioning by that means, building up the rest by contract.)

To say that organizational law is essential for the creation of limited liability in tort is not to say, however, that organizational law serves an important efficiency-enhancing purpose in doing so. Limited liability in tort is a doctrine of very dubious efficiency. Tort victims have no control over the type of legal entity that injures them. Consequently, to make the amount recovered by a tort victim depend upon the legal form of the organization responsible for the tort is to permit the externalization of accident costs, and indeed to invite the choice of legal entity to be governed in important part by the desire to seek such externalization.

Thus, while allowing the intentional use of the corporate form to limit liability in contract makes eminent sense, to permit the intentional use of the corporate form to limit liability in tort does not make sense. Of course, if unlimited shareholder liability for tort damages would interfere seriously with the tradeability of corporate shares, or if collection of excess liability judgments from numerous corporate shareholders would necessarily be a very costly process, then limited liability in tort might be justified, at least for publicly traded business corporations, as a regrettable necessity. But this does not appear to be the case. A much weaker form of defensive asset partitioning for corporate torts—namely, a rule of unlimited pro rata shareholder liability—would apparently protect the marketability of corporate shares without permitting shareholders to externalize the costs of corporate torts.[50]

In fact, corporate limited liability in tort appears to be a historical accident, perhaps encouraged in important part by the rarity, during the formative period of business corporation law in the nineteenth and early twentieth century, of tort liability sufficient to bankrupt a corporation. The increasing use of the corporate form for small businesses, together with the recent advent of potentially massive tort liability for environmental harms, workplace hazards, and injurious products, suggests that the issue should be revisited—as we have argued at length elsewhere.[51]

2.8. Does Organizational Law Serve Other Essential Functions?

We have argued here that provision for affirmative asset partitioning is an essential function of organizational law, in the sense that firms could not practicably be given this important attribute in the absence of organizational law. Defensive asset partitioning, though also a useful function of organizational law, is less important for the creation of large-scale enterprise. Moreover, whatever the utility of defensive asset partitioning, provision for defensive asset partitioning is not an essential function of organizational law, as we use the term 'essential'

---

[50] A rule of pro rata liability would need to be accompanied by subordination of tort claimants to contractual creditors in corporate bankruptcy, in order to keep the value of contractual claims independent of the personal wealth of individual shareholders. See Hansmann and Kraakman (1991: 1901–2).

[51] Ibid. at 1880–1.

here, since it would be feasible to establish defensive asset partitioning by contract even if the law did not make special provision for it.

It remains to ask whether organizational law serves other essential functions as well. That is, are there other important features of modern organizations that could not feasibly be established by contract in the absence of organizational law?

The question is posed squarely by the recent evolution of the statutory business trust, as exemplified by the Delaware Business Trust Act.[52] The statute provides for both affirmative asset partitioning and defensive asset partitioning, with the latter being in the form of full limited liability of the type found in business corporations. The statute leaves virtually all other aspects of organizational structure open, however, permitting the formation of limited liability legal entities with virtually any desired designation of owners, and with virtually any conceivable assignment of control and distribution rights among the owners. Given this highly protean form, why does Delaware need any other forms? Are Delaware's other statutory forms for legal entities—including business corporations, limited liability companies, non-profit corporations, cooperative corporations, general partnerships, and limited partnerships—now merely conveniences, serving the same function as privately provided standard-form contracts, or do they perform a more essential role, permitting the formation of types of firms that could not practicably be created in their absence using just the business trust statute with appropriate contractual additions and adjustments?[53]

In answering this question, there are three functions performed by organizational law that need to be considered, each of which involves relations among different groups of actors. The first is to govern relations between the firm—which is to say, the firm's owners and managers—and the firm's creditors. The second is to govern relationships among the firm's owners and between the firm's owners and managers. The third is to govern relations between the firm and its non-owner patrons. We deal with these three sets of functions in turn. We do not seek to explore the issues involved in detail, but simply to touch on the main issues.

2.8.1. Facilitating Contracting with Creditors

Organizational law often contains provisions other than asset partitioning that help a firm's owners bond themselves credibly to its creditors. These include, for example, limitations on the ability to pay dividends that would impair legal

[52] Delaware Business Trust Act, Del. Code Ann. tit. 12, §§ 3801–20 (1995).

[53] Ribstein (1999: 435–46) has argued in a similar vein for a 'contractual entity' statute that would provide investors with limited liability but none of the other provisions of a detailed standard form of legal entity. The Delaware Business Trust Act is in effect such a contractual entity statute, which provides for limited liability and—even more importantly—affirmative asset partitioning. Delaware Business Trust Act, Del. Code Ann., tit. 12, §§ 3803(a), 3805(b).

capital, and (at least in Europe) minimum capital requirements. In the absence of controlling provisions in organizational law, however, these matters could—like limited liability—evidently be governed feasibly by inserting appropriate terms in the firm's contracts with its creditors (Posner 1992: 396). Affirmative asset partitioning is unique in that it involves an assignment of property claims to creditors that could not effectively be made, on behalf of the firm's owners, by a contract just between those owners (or their collective agent, the firm's managers) and the firm's creditors. Once the law provides the means for affirmative asset partitioning, the owners of the firm can use simple contracts with the firm's creditors to make commitments as to such matters as the quantity and nature, e.g., riskiness, of the assets that the firm will hold, and hence will pledge to its creditors.

2.8.2. Facilitating Contracting among Owners and Managers

Much of organizational law—such as rules concerning governance of the firm and distribution of the firm's earnings—regulates relations among the owners of a firm and relations between the firm's owners and its managers. As others have observed, however, these matters could generally be handled relatively easily, in the absence of organizational law, just through privately supplied standard-form contracts (Easterbrook and Fischel 1991: 34–5).

  This is true, in particular, of fiduciary duties of care and loyalty, which are sometimes thought to be particularly dependent on the law. Consider, for example, the manager's duty of loyalty. This consists, in essence, of a promise on the part of the manager not to engage in self-interested transactions involving the firm's property and prospects. That promise—accompanied, if needed, by a definition in any appropriate level of detail of what types of transactions will be considered self-interested, and what forms of disclosure and approval are required—can simply be inserted into the firm's founding document and incorporated by reference in the employment contract with each of the firm's managers. The same is true of the duty of care. Indeed, even absent such explicit contracting, the law of agency would impose on managers, as a default rule, fiduciary duties of loyalty and care that are the rough equivalent of those that are imposed by most forms of organizational law.[54]

2.8.3. Transferability of Ownership

The law permits free transferability of ownership interests in some types of legal entities, such as the business corporation. Absent that legal doctrine, an owner might not be presumed to have the power to substitute another person for himself with respect to his rights and obligations toward his fellow owners and

---

[54] For a more extended discussion of contractual approaches to fiduciary duties, see Hansmann and Mattei (1998: 447–50).

toward third parties to whom the firm has contractual obligations. Yet both contractual rights and contractual duties can in general be made transferable, under the law of contracts, so long as all contracting parties expressly agree.[55] Thus, to establish free transferability of ownership interests absent specific organizational law doctrine to that effect, it should be sufficient to put terms to that effect in the owners' association agreement and into the firm's contracts with each of its creditors. This might be burdensome, but it would not be infeasible. The contracting costs involved would presumably be comparable to those of establishing limited liability by contract.

2.8.4. Withdrawal Rights

In some contemporary legal entities—such as the partnership-at-will—the firm's owners are free to withdraw their share of the firm's assets at any time. Other standard-form legal entities, however, permit limits on the withdrawal rights of individual owners. The business corporation is conspicuous among these; shareholders generally cannot withdraw their individual share of the firm's assets short of dissolution, and dissolution generally requires consent of the holders of at least 50 per cent of the firm's shares.

Could such limits on withdrawal rights be established in the absence of organizational law? There is room to doubt that they could be. Suppose, for example, that the co-owners of a business were to hold their joint property as tenants-in-common. Then, as we noted earlier,[56] they might not be able to agree to waive their individual rights to force partition of the property for more than a finite period of time. It is not a question of transaction costs; the law simply prohibits unlimited agreements not to partition. Thus, to mimic fully the attributes of all contemporary legal entities, arguably the law must not just make special provision for affirmative asset partitioning, but provide that co-owners can commit not to withdraw their share of jointly held partitioned assets unless there is agreement to that effect by the fraction of the co-owners that is stated in their contract of association.

We might think of this as a third element of asset partitioning. We have already noted two distinct elements of asset partitioning: priority of claims and liquidation protection from personal creditors of the firm's owners. The third element we are considering here is liquidation protection from the individual owners themselves. These two forms of liquidation generally go hand in hand. Strong-form legal entities, which are characterized by liquidation protection from the owners' personal creditors, also typically provide for substantial liquidation protection from the owners themselves. Or, put differently, the liquidation powers of an owner's personal creditors are generally the same as

---

[55] See Farnsworth (1990: § 11.11) (stating that contractual duties can be delegated, and the delegating party can be discharged from liability, if there is consent by the party to whom the duties are owed).

[56] See *supra* n 25.

those of the owner himself. For example, since personal creditors of a bankrupt corporate shareholder step into the bankrupt's role as shareholder, those creditors can force liquidation of the corporation's assets only if the shareholder held enough shares in the corporation—generally 50 per cent—to have been able to force liquidation himself.

2.8.5. Facilitating Contracting with Other Patrons: Non-distribution Constraints

Some legal entities embody a formal separation of control rights from distribution rights whereby those who control the firm are barred from appropriating the firm's net earnings, either currently or upon liquidation. That separation is a defining feature, in particular, of non-profit entities, including the non-profit corporation, the charitable trust, and the civil law foundation (Hansmann 1980).

Could organizations be given this attribute without the benefit of specially designed organizational law? While something close might be achieved using only contractual devices, it would fall short of a complete substitute.[57]

In this respect, then, the law of charitable trusts and non-profit corporations arguably adds something to the law, beyond asset partitioning, that is 'essential' in the sense we use here: it could not feasibly be replicated in the absence of organizational law.[58] Several qualifications are worth making, however. First, the non-distribution constraint is confined to several standard-form legal entities that are employed today for a relatively small subset of all organizations. Second, something close to the non-distribution constraint could evidently be

[57] An organization's founders could, presumably, put a non-distribution constraint in the contract of association that serves as the organization's founding document. To be fully effective, however, that provision would need to be unamendable, even by unanimous agreement of the organization's founders and controllers, since the purpose of the constraint is to protect third parties—donors and beneficiaries—against opportunism by controlling persons. That is, the constraint is a means by which those who control the organization bond themselves not to take a stake in the firm that will give them an incentive to exploit the firm's other patrons. The law, however, frowns on non-renegotiable contracts. See Jolls (1997: 208–9). Consequently, it is doubtful that founders could make the non-distribution constraint unamendable simply by entering into an agreement to that effect among themselves.

An alternative approach might be to have the firm make a contractual commitment to each donor, in return for the donor's contribution, to maintain and adhere to the non-distribution provisions in the charter. The result, however, would still not quite create the complete equivalent of the non-profit corporation. For, in most states of the United States, it is possible and indeed common to create non-profit corporations in which both donors and beneficiaries lack not just voting rights but also the right to sue the organization's managers either directly or derivatively, with the result that neither donors nor beneficiaries have any rights of control over the organization's managers. Arguably the tools of the common law are inadequate to achieve this result, in which perpetual obligations are imposed on self-appointing managers who cannot—because of the absence of control over them—be considered agents of any party in interest.

[58] The Delaware Business Trust Act, interestingly, specifically authorizes use of the business trust form for the formation of organizations of a non-profit character. Delaware Business Trust Act, Del. Code Ann., tit. 12, § 3801(a). The Act does not, however, make it clear how a non-distribution constraint is to be imposed under the Act.

achieved simply by contractual means. Third, the barriers to crafting a do-it-yourself non-distribution constraint arise not from transaction costs but from legal prohibitions of contestable utility. Fourth, the non-distribution constraint has a bonding character with substantial parallels to asset partitioning: it is a means by which those who control the firm pledge to its donors—who are effectively a subset of the firm's creditors—that the firm's assets and net earnings will not be diverted from the objects that the donors intended.

2.8.6. Essential Terms Versus Useful Terms

The preceding discussion has sought to show that, with the possible exception of some elements of the law of non-profit organizations, aspects of organizational law other than asset partitioning are not 'essential' in the sense that workable substitutes for them could not be found elsewhere in the law. This is not to say, however, that elements of organizational law other than asset partitioning are trivial and could be dispensed with costlessly.

There are a number of ways in which standard-form legal entities can reduce the costs of contracting for a firm's owners. Among these are (1) simplifying the drafting of the firm's charter; (2) helping to avoid mistakes in choosing the details of the organization's form; (3) putting all parties on notice of non-standard provisions (by effectively requiring that all non-standard provisions, and only those provisions, must be specifically set out in the organization's charter); (4) providing owners with a highly credible device for bonding their commitments to each other and to those with whom they and the firm deal; (5) facilitating the efficient evolution of standard-form provisions, which are in part a public good; and (6) permitting modification of existing relationships among the parties involved in a firm, without requiring the parties' explicit consent, when existing contractual arrangements prove inefficient.

These and other efficiencies offered by the various detailed rules governing standard-form legal entities are important. There is every reason to believe that those rules reduce significantly the costs of commercial activity. This is strongly suggested, for example, by the fact that most developed market economies provide for standard-form legal entities that are similar in their basic features. Our claim, however, is not that aspects of organizational law other than asset partitioning are not important. Rather, it is that the economies involved are not of the same order as those involved in asset partitioning. Or, put more strongly, the commercial order of a contemporary market economy could still be established without these features of organizational law, while it could not exist without legal provision for affirmative asset partitioning. The latter is the only important feature of modern firms for which substitutes could not be crafted, at any price that is even remotely conceivable, using just the basic tools of contract, property, and agency law.

2.8.7. Enabling Rules, Mandatory Rules, and Default Rules

The general view of organizational law today is that it is primarily enabling in character. That view is especially prominent in the literature on business corporations, which is, naturally, by far the largest body of contemporary organizational law scholarship. Within that body of scholarship, there has been an extensive debate on the extent to which corporate law is strictly enabling. That debate has focused largely on the extent to which corporate law imposes important rules that are mandatory in character rather than simply defaults. It generally deals with contractual terms that the parties could have adopted on their own, but which, instead of being left to the parties to choose, are either (a) prohibited, or (b) required.[59]

Our concern here, in contrast, is not with the limits that corporate law, or organizational law in general, imposes on parties' freedom to contract. Rather, we are concerned with the enabling aspects of the law. We are asking what organizational law permits parties to accomplish that they could not otherwise do. On this point, the existing literature is much thinner. On the rare occasions when the issue has been addressed with any directness in the contemporary literature, the answer suggested has typically been that the law plays no essential role in this respect, but rather just offers standard-form contractual provisions of the sort that might also be provided by law firms or other private actors.[60] Our answer, of course, is different.

2.8.8. Theories of Juridical Personality

There is a vast literature, with deep roots in nineteenth-century German scholarship, on the nature of juridical persons. The debate over competing conceptions of juridical persons that is the central preoccupation of that literature still shows some life today, in terms not much removed from those of a century ago (Bratton 1989; Hager 1989; Iwai 1999; Mark 1987; Phillips 1994; Schane 1986). One might think that there would be substantial overlap between the issues in that debate and those that we are dealing with here. Yet, while the literature on juridical persons sometimes points to a separate patrimony as a key characteristic of a juridical person,[61] that attribute is generally not the focus of analysis. Rather, the traditional literature is principally concerned with questions—such

---

[59] The issues and the literature in this debate, which reached its peak in the late 1980s, are well surveyed in Black (1990).

[60] e.g. Easterbrook and Fischel (1991), repeating the analysis offered earlier in Easterbrook and Fischel (1989: 1444–6); Posner (1992, 1976). This view also seems implicit in much of the literature debating the issue of mandatory rules, of which Easterbrook and Fischel's article forms a part. All of these analyses, we should note, are too brief and unfocused to offer a clear and well-argued-for position on the issue. Hence we refer here, in the text, to the views 'suggested' by these authors.

[61] For example, among the principal competing theories that emerged from the nineteenth-century debate, this is true both of the theory associated with Savigny and of that associated with Brinz. See Machen (1911: 255–7); Wolff (1938: 496–7).

as the power of the state versus the power of private organizations or the nature of group will—that are tangential to our concerns.

We have sought to offer here a definition of juridical persons that is simpler, clearer, and more functional than those that have characterized the traditional literature. Indeed, one reason we have used the term 'legal entity' rather than 'juridical person' is to avoid confusion between our analysis and the more traditional views.

2.9. HISTORICAL DEVELOPMENT

Given the critical role of law in permitting affirmative asset partitioning, it is natural to ask when and where, as a historical matter, affirmative asset partitioning evolved as a feature of organizational law. The answer to that question is difficult to determine from conventional sources. While there is extensive scholarship tracing the evolution of defensive asset partitioning (in particular, limited liability) (Blumberg 1987; Forbes 1986; Livermore 1935; Macey and Miller 1992; Orhnial 1982; Weinstein 2000), the evolution of affirmative asset partitioning appears to have been largely ignored in the literature on legal and economic history—a reflection, presumably, of the surprisingly low level of self-consciousness about affirmative asset partitioning in the literature generally. The exception is a recent paper by Paul Mahoney, which builds on an earlier version of this article to explore the history of corporate entities with particular emphasis on affirmative and defensive asset partitioning (for which Mahoney uses the terms 'forward' and 'reverse' asset partitioning, respectively) (Mahoney 2000).

Prior to the advent of the investor-owned business corporation, which is largely a creature of the past two centuries, partnership was the form commonly used for jointly-owned businesses. The interesting historical question, then, is when affirmative asset partitioning became a well-established aspect of partnership law.[62] It is possible to have a form of partnership that provides for collective agency without affirmative asset partitioning. We conjecture that this is the way that partnership law first developed, and that affirmative asset partitioning became a recognized feature of partnership law only much later.[63] We hope to explore these historical issues more thoroughly in subsequent work.

---

[62] While joint stock companies are a relatively recent development in Anglo-American law, corporations of a non-profit character—including universities, monasteries, and other eleemosynary institutions—have been common for nearly a millennium. See e.g. Davis (1905); Hansmann (1980: 843 n. 32). Whether or not it was self-consciously thought of as such, affirmative asset partitioning was apparently always a well-developed aspect of the latter corporations. Because the diffuse beneficiaries of those corporations were not considered owners of the corporation, however, it was presumably taken for granted that an individual beneficiary's creditors would have no recourse against a corporation's assets.

[63] Mahoney (2000) offers the view that the legal tools for both affirmative and defensive asset partitioning may have been available much earlier in the development of the partnership form. We address Mahoney's stimulating thesis in a forthcoming paper.

2.10. CONCLUSION

There is a strong tendency today to view organizational law as performing functions similar to those typically performed by contract law: providing a standard set of default rules that govern when contracting parties have not specifically decided otherwise, and perhaps providing as well some mandatory rules that protect the interests of parties who would otherwise be disadvantaged in the contracting process. These contractual functions of organizational law are undoubtedly useful. They do not, however, appear to be essential, in the sense that modern firms could not feasibly be constructed if organizational law did not perform them.

A far more important function of organizational law is to define the property rights over which participants in a firm can contract. At its essential core, organizational law is property law, not contract law. In particular, organizational law permits the formation of a floating lien on the pool of assets associated with a firm, and permits as well the assignment of that lien to the constantly changing group of creditors who transact with the firm, while shielding those assets from creditors of the firm's managers and owners. This type of affirmative asset partitioning, which plays a critical role in permitting the formation of the large nexuses of contracts that are employed to organize most modern business activity, could not otherwise be accomplished. By contrast, organizational law doctrine establishing defensive asset partitioning—including the rule of limited liability that is so often celebrated as a foundational achievement of organizational law—seems to be of distinctly secondary importance.

REFERENCES

Adler, B. E. (1997), 'A Theory of Corporate Insolvency', *New York University Law Review* 72: 343.

Alchian, A., and Demsetz, H. (1972), 'Production, Information Costs, and Economic Organization', *American Economic Review* 62: 777.

Baird, D. G., Jackson, T., and Adler, B. E. (2000), *Bankruptcy*, New York: Foundation Press.

Bebchuk, L. A., and Fried, J. M. (1996), 'The Uneasy Case for the Priority of Secured Claims in Bankruptcy', *Yale Law Journal* 105: 857.

Black, B. S. (1990), 'Is Corporate Law Trivial?: A Political and Economic Analysis', *Northwestern University Law Review* 84: 542.

Blumberg, P. I. (1987), *The Law of Corporate Groups: Tort, Contract, and Other Common Law Problems in the Substantive Law of Parent and Subsidiary Corporations under Statutory Law of General Application*, Boston: Little, Brown & Co.

Bratton, W. W. (1989), 'The New Economic Theory of the Firm: Critical Perspectives from History', *Stanford Law Review* 41: 1471.

Bromberg, A. R., and Ribstein, L. E. (1988), *Bromberg and Ribstein on Partnership*, New York: Aspen Publishers.

Buljevich, E. C., and Park, Y. S. (1999), *Project Financing and the International Financial Markets*, Boston: Kluwer Academic.

Cardozo Law Review (1986), 'Note: Partitions in Kind: A Preference without Favor', *Cardozo Law Review* 7: 855.

Committee on Bankruptcy and Corporate Reorganization of the Association of the Bar of the City of New York (1995), 'Structured Financing Techniques', *Business Lawyer* 50: 527.

Cribbet, J. E. (1975), *Principles of the Law of Property*, New York: Foundation Press.

Davies, P. L. (1997), *Gower's Principles of Modern Company Law*, London: Sweet & Maxwell.

Davis, J. P. (1905), *Corporation*, New York: G. P. Putnam's Sons.

Davison, K. A. (1994), 'Note: Cox v. Thee Evergreen Church: Liability Issues of the Unincorporated Association, Is It Time for the Legislature to Step in?', *Baylor Law Review* 46: 231.

Easterbrook, F. H., and Fischel, D. R. (1985), 'Limited Liability and the Corporation', *University of Chicago Law Review* 52: 89.

—— —— (1989), 'The Corporate Contract', *Columbia Law Review* 89: 1416.

—— —— (1991), *The Economic Structure of Corporate Law*, Cambridge: Harvard University Press.

Farnsworth, E. A. (1990), *Farnsworth on Contract*, Boston: Little Brown.

Forbes, K. (1986), 'Limited Liability and the Development of the Business Corporation', *Journal of Law, Economics and Organization* 2: 163.

Gahlon, J. M., and Stover, R. D. (1979), 'Diversification, Financial Leverage and Conglomerate Systematic Risk', *Journal of Financial and Quantitative Analysis* 14: 999.

Grossman, P. (1995), 'The Market for Shares of Companies with Unlimited Liability: The Case of American Express', *Journal of Legal Studies* 24: 63.

Hager, M. (1989), 'Bodies Politic: The Progressive History of Organizational "Real Entity" Theory', *University of Pittsburgh Law Review* 50: 575.

Halpern, P., et al. (1980), 'An Economic Analysis of Limited Liability in Corporation Law', *University of Toronto Law Journal* 30: 117.

Hansmann, H. (1980), 'The Role of Nonprofit Enterprise', *Yale Law Journal* 89: 835.

—— (1996), *The Ownership of Enterprise*, Cambridge, Mass.: The Belknap Press of Harvard University Press.

—— and Kraakman, R. (1991), 'Toward Unlimited Shareholder Liability for Corporate Torts', *Yale Law Journal* 100: 1879.

—— —— (2000a), 'Organizational Law as Asset Partitioning', *European Economic Review* 44: 807.

—— —— (2002), 'Property, Contract, and Verification: The Numerus Clausus Problem and the Divisibility of Rights', *Journal of Legal Studies* 31: 373.

—— and Mattei, U. (1998), 'The Functions of Trust Law: A Comparative Legal and Economic Analysis', *New York University Law Review* 73: 434.

Hart, O. (1995), *Firms, Contracts, and Financial Structure*, Oxford: Clarendon Press.

—— and Moore, J. (1990), 'Property Rights and the Nature of the Firm', *Journal of Political Economy* 98: 1119.

Hill, C. A. (1996), 'Securitization: A Low-Cost Sweetener for Lemons', *Washington University Law Quarterly* 74: 1061.

Iwai, K. (1999), 'Persons, Things and Corporations: The Corporate Personality Controversy and Comparative Corporate Governance', *American Journal of Comparative Law* 47: 583.

Jackson, T. H., and Kronman, A. T. (1979), 'Secured Financing and Priorities among Creditors', *Yale Law Journal* 88: 1143.

Jensen, M. C., and Meckling, W. J. (1976), 'Theory of the Firm: Managerial Behavior, Agency Costs and Ownership Structure', *Journal of Financial Economics* 3: 305.

Jolls, C. (1997), 'Contracts as Bilateral Commitments: A New Perspective on Contract Modification', *Journal of Legal Studies* 26: 203.

Kanda, H., and Levmore, S. (1991), 'Taxes, Agency Costs, and the Price of Incorporation', *Virginia Law Review* 77: 211.

Klein, B., et al. (1978), 'Vertical Integration, Appropriable Rents, and the Competitive Contracting Process', *Journal of Law and Economics* 21: 297.

Langbein, J. (1997), 'The Secret Life of the Trust: The Trust as an Instrument of Commerce', *Yale Law Journal* 107: 165.

Levmore, S. (1982), 'Monitors and Freeriders in Commercial and Corporate Settings', *Yale Law Journal* 92: 49.

Levy, H., and Sarnat, M. (1970), 'Diversification, Portfolio Analysis and the Uneasy Case for Conglomerate Mergers', *Journal of Finance* 25: 795.

Lewellen, W. G. (1971), 'A Pure Financial Rationale for the Conglomerate Merger', *Journal of Finance* 26: 521.

Livermore, S. (1935), 'Unlimited Liability in Early American Corporations', *Journal of Political Economy* 43: 674.

Lopucki, L. M., and Whitford, W. C. (1990), 'Bargaining over Equity's Share in the Bankruptcy Reorganization of Large, Publicly Held Companies', *University of Pennsylvania Law Review* 139: 125.

Macey, J., and Miller, G. (1992), 'Double Liability of Bank Shareholders: History and Implications', *Wake Forest Law Review* 27: 31.

Machen, Jr., A. (1911), 'Corporate Personality', *Harvard Law Review* 24: 253.

Mahoney, P. (2000), 'Contract or Concession? An Essay on the History of Corporate Law', *Georgia Law Review* 34: 873.

Mark, G. (1987), 'The Personification of the Business Corporation in American Law', *University of Chicago Law Review* 54: 1441.

Melicher, R. W., and Rush, D. F. (1974), 'Evidence on the Acquisition-Related Performance of Conglomerate Firms', *Journal of Finance* 29: 141.

Orhnial, T. (ed.) (1982), *Limited Liability and the Corporation*, London: Croom Helm.

Phillips, M. J. (1994), 'Reappraising the Real Entity Theory of the Corporation', *Florida State University Law Review* 21: 1061.

Posner, R. (1976), 'The Rights of Creditors of Affiliated Corporations', *University of Chicago Law Review* 43: 499.

—— (1992), *Economic Analysis of Law*, Boston: Little Brown.

Rajan, R., and Zingales, L. (1998), 'The Firm as a Dedicated Hierarchy: A Theory of the Origin and Growth of Firms' (National Bureau of Economic Research, Working Paper No. 7546, available at http://papers.ssrn.com/sol3/papers.cfm?abstract_id=139707).

Ribstein, L. E. (1991), 'Limited Liability and Theories of the Corporation', *Maryland Law Review* 50: 80.

—— (1992), 'The Deregulation of Limited Liability and the Death of Partnership', *Washington University Law Quarterly* 70: 417.

—— (1997), 'The Illogic and Limits of Partners' Liability in Bankruptcy', *Wake Forest Law Review* 32: 31.

—— (1999), 'Limited Liability Unlimited', *Delaware Journal of Corporate Law* 24: 407.

Schane, S. A. (1986), 'The Corporation Is a Person: The Language of a Legal Fiction', *Tulane Law Review* 61: 561.

Schwarcz, S. L. (1993), *Structured Finance: A Guide to the Principles of Asset Securitization*, New York: Practising Law Institute.

—— (1994), 'The Alchemy of Asset Securitization', *Stanford Journal of Law, Business, and Finance* 1: 133.

Scott, R. E. (1986), 'A Relational Theory of Secured Financing', *Columbia Law Review* 86: 901.

Smith, R., and Walter, I. (1997), *Global Banking*, Oxford: Oxford University Press.

Thomas, D. A. (ed.) (1994), *Thompson on Real Property*, Charlottesville: Michie Company.

Tracht, M. E. (1997), 'Contractual Bankruptcy Waivers: Reconciling Theory, Practice, and Law', *Cornell Law Review* 82: 301.

Weinstein, M. (2000), 'Limited Liability in California: 1928–1931' (University of Southern California, Marshall School of Business, University of Southern California Law School, Working Paper, available at http://marshallinside.usc.edu/mweinstein/research.html).

Weiss, L. A. (1990), 'Bankruptcy Resolution: Direct Costs and Violation of Priority of Claims', *Journal of Financial Economics* 27: 285.

Williamson, O. E. (1985), *The Economic Institutions of Capitalism*, New York: Free Press.

Wolff, M. (1938), 'On the Nature of Legal Persons', *Law Quarterly Review* 54: 494.

Woodward, S. E. (1985), 'Limited Liability in the Theory of the Firm', *Journal of Institutional and Theoretical Economics* 141: 601.

3

An Economic Analysis of Shared Property in Partnership and Close Corporations Law

JOHN ARMOUR and MICHAEL J. WHINCOP*

3.1. INTRODUCTION

The small firm has engaged the attention of law reformers in the United States of America for the last decade. Close corporation reform continues in many states, and the revisions to uniform partnership law, resulting in the Revised Uniform Partnership Act (RUPA),[1] have been well publicized (Weidner and Larson 1993). In addition to reform of 'traditional' business forms, recent years have seen the emergence of new business forms in US jurisdictions, such as the Limited Liability Company (LLC) and the Limited Liability Partnership (LLP) (Hamilton 1995; Ribstein 1995a; Bishop 1997). Similar reform efforts are now under way in Europe. In the United Kingdom, the recent Review of Company Law has made the needs of small companies one of its 'core concerns' (Company Law Review Steering Group 2001). Partnership law is currently under review in the United Kingdom for the first time in over a hundred years (Law Commission 2000), and reforms are also imminent in other European jurisdictions such as the Netherlands (Maeijer 1998). Furthermore, the proliferation of new statutory forms appears to be spreading to Europe with the introduction of the UK Limited Liability Partnerships Act.[2]

The task of the law reformer working in this area is a complex one. Small firms are very different from widely held, exchange traded firms, where wealth-maximizing governance institutions are obstructed by endemic collective action problems and high agency costs. The small firm differs radically in the capability of investors to be actively involved in the design of governance processes that lower agency costs (Easterbrook and Fischel 1991: 228–36; Miller 1992: 402–6).

* We thank Brian Cheffins, Joe McCahery, Riz Mokal, Larry Ribstein, Chris Riley, and Erik Vermeulen for helpful comments on earlier versions. We are also grateful for comments received following a workshop presentation at the University of Nottingham in March 2001, and a presentation in May 2001 at Tilburg University to the Conference on Close Corporation and Partnership Law Reform in Europe and the United States.

[1] See Revised Uniform Partnership Act (1997).
[2] Limited Liability Partnerships Act 2000 (UK). See Freedman (Chapter 10, this volume).

The lawmaker must focus on what role the law can uniquely serve in small firms without duplicating what parties can do for themselves.

Economic analysis of law has conventionally approached this question by explaining how the relations between investors, creditors, and managers are contractual and illustrating the governance problems arising from these incomplete contracts.[3] Its exponents often conclude that the functional role the law can serve in small firms is limited to the lower-order function of decreasing transaction costs by plugging gaps in contracts with suitable default rules (Easterbrook and Fischel 1991: 34–5). Yet this leaves a nagging question unanswered: Why does the state have a comparative advantage in the supply and enforcement of these terms over private interest groups and arbitrators, who respectively supply standard terms for, and adjudicate disputes arising under, other varieties of relational contract (Bernstein 1996: 1771–82; Hadfield 2001)? When 'rule competition'—both between jurisdictions and between public and private suppliers of terms—is included in the equation, the role of the statutory law reformer seems increasingly marginal (Ribstein 1995b: 376–7).[4]

Our answer to this problem rests in an appreciation of the law's role in giving proprietary effect to the entitlements that the participants share. With a few exceptions, law and economics scholarship has failed to consider the proprietary foundations of intra-firm governance. This neglect is surprising. These proprietary foundations are the most important instance where law performs a unique function, a function neither Coasean trade nor private provision can easily emulate.[5] A study of proprietary entitlements offers promise for uniting developments in the economics of the firm with legal scholarship. Finally, the principal organizational alternatives for small firms—close corporations and partnerships—are most meaningfully differentiated according to the proprietary effect those firms give to organizational entitlements.

At the outset, it should be made clear that this analysis is an internal critique that extends the existing theory. Consequently, it does not consider social objectives of the state other than facilitation of private parties' goals. This does not imply that other social goals are considered irrelevant. On the contrary, a

---

[3] There are too many works in this genre to cite. An authoritative exposition of the theory is found in Easterbrook and Fischel (1991). For its application to English law, see Cheffins (1997); Whincop (2001a).

[4] Ribstein suggests three possible sources of comparative advantage: (1) publication of statutes at state expense lowers the costs of learning about the law for citizens; (2) statutes may be able to create larger network benefits and thereby enjoy greater uptake; and (3) only statutes can introduce mandatory creditor-protection penalties, which may be prohibitively costly to contract for privately. We do not find the first two accounts compelling. On the one hand, there is no a priori reason why publication of private terms cannot be adequately funded through user fees, and, on the other hand, empirical research has demonstrated that private terms may have very significant network benefits (Whincop 2001b). The third account is in some respects similar to the one developed here.

[5] This point is made in Hansmann and Kraakman (Chapter 2, this volume), who claim that this analysis extends only to what they term 'affirmative asset partitioning'. This understates the range of rules relevant to business organizations—which differ between organizational form and which are similarly non-replicable by private contracting.

proprietary analysis provides more scope for considering, for example, issues of distribution than does a contractarian model (Whincop 1999: 33–5). A study of how the law can most efficiently facilitate parties' goals is nevertheless useful for two reasons. First, an understanding of how private parties use law to achieve their goals is crucial to the design of successful regulation intended to direct parties' efforts towards the attainment of particular social goals. Second, so long as the enhancement of efficiency is a goal for the law, it is important to understand how best to attain it.

Section 3.2 examines how and why activities are organized in firms. Recent economic theories of the firm have gone beyond a purely contractual model by emphasizing the role of property rights as a governance mechanism. In these theories, firms consist of a relational contract and a pool of assets that support its governance. The way in which *ex post* entitlements to assets are divided up might be seen as simply another set of terms in the relational contract. This dyadic conception of property rights neglects the significance of the distinction between rights *in rem* and *in personam*. Property rights, being of the former variety, bind the world. This difference has particular significance where entitlements to assets are shared.

Section 3.3 shows that factors such as wealth constraints, time and expertise constraints, and decision-making and risk-bearing costs mean that all the incidents of ownership of a firm's assets cannot be placed in one person's hands. Instead, they must be divided among participants. This gives rise to agency and hold-up problems, including some that arise where an insider contracts with an outsider in a way that would undermine the governance leverage accorded to other insiders under the sharing arrangement. Obvious examples include selling the assets, or new entitlements to them, and pocketing the proceeds.

The law has a choice here. It may protect insiders by automatically invalidating such transactions. This indicates that the insiders' entitlements are *in rem*; they bind third parties. The result of such a legal rule is equivalent to supplementing a dyadic governance arrangement with contracts binding all possible outsiders to defer to its terms. The cost of entering those contracts would be prohibitive. Alternatively, the law may allow the new contract to trump the insiders' entitlements as would happen if they were purely personal. This would make intra-firm governance solutions less credible, as they would remain vulnerable to such *ex post* side deals.

However, giving the arrangement proprietary effect imposes costs on uninformed outsiders. Accordingly, the law must trade-off the facilitation of *ex ante* optimal arrangements between insiders with the minimization of costs to outsiders. Because the outsiders' costs are endogenous to the range of terms offered, the law limits the flexibility insiders have to define their proprietary entitlements. This accounts for the partitioning of organizational terms into forms rather than maintaining a continuous spectrum of terms.

Section 3.4 applies this theory to examine differences between close corporations and partnerships. There are important differences between the forms that respond to the proprietary problems we have described: agency rules, asset partitioning, and entry and exit of firm participants.

Section 3.5 considers the implications of the analysis. The fact that parties are unable to replicate these solutions privately means that they are forced to select from a limited legal menu of forms. While it is possible to tell stories about why particular sets of rules may have efficiency-enhancing properties, the limits placed upon the set of possible organizational structures presents a very real possibility that the law may exhibit constrained inefficiencies.

3.2. THE THEORY OF THE FIRM AND ITS IMPACT ON ORGANIZATIONAL LAW SCHOLARSHIP

3.2.1. Principal Themes in the Theory of the Firm

The theory of the firm begins with Coase (1937). For Coase, the managers of firms did deliberately what a market did spontaneously—both allocated resources to different uses. The firm internalized transactions that would otherwise occur across a market interface. Coase explained that internalization economized on the transaction costs of using markets.

The rediscovery of Coase by economists in the 1970s provided the theoretical platform for most economic analysis of organizational law. First, Alchian and Demsetz (1972) and then Jensen and Meckling (1976) developed a neoclassical theory of the firm (NTF) (Bratton 1989). Under NTF, corporations and other organizations were nexuses for contractual relations. The contracting problem was the creation of incentives for agents to maximize value, in the light of risk aversion and imperfect information. These works focused research attention on how markets mitigated agency costs, and how solutions to residual contracting problems were endogenous to contracts (Easterbook and Fischel 1991: 8–22). Although the listed public corporation was the dominant paradigm for analysis, several scholars adapted the model to consider the governance properties of close corporations and partnerships (Easterbrook and Fischel 1991: 228–36; Johnston 1992).

Second, Williamson (1985) regarded the contracting problems associated with relations in firms as being qualitatively different from those transacted across a market interface. These contracting problems arose from the confluence of opportunism and specialized assets generating quasi-rents. Quasi-rents are characterized as supracompetitive profits generated by the match between assets in the exchange—the differential between the value the parties generate working within the exchange and what they can gain in the market (Klein, Crawford, and Alchian 1978). Firm hierarchies acted as the governance structures necessary to protect quasi-rents against opportunistic dissipation. This perspective represented a more institutional theory of the firm (ITF) (Bratton 1989). These works focused scholarship on examining specific governance processes, such as the functioning of the board of directors.

Like ITF, the property rights theory of the firm (PRTF) recognized the contracting problems created by the quasi-rents arising from asset-specific investments (Grossman and Hart 1986; Hart and Moore 1990; Hart 1995). However, ITF sought to examine the governance institutions needed for transactions organized within a firm, whereas PRTF examined the anterior question of how the allocation of the rights of control over tangible assets influences the division of quasi-rents (and thus the need for supplementary governance institutions).

This focus on control in the PRTF was linked to the concept of property rights. In a world of zero transaction costs, where there are no exogenous limits on the capacity to verify information to a court, control or power would be empty terms. Obligations and payoffs would be negotiated and agreed in a contract for all possible future states. But because those contracts cannot be written or reliably enforced by courts, much behaviour in the transaction will depend on what each party can do, rather than what they are required to do. A recurrent concept in the PRTF was residual control—the strategy space of a party, with respect to an asset, that has not been cut down by a formal contract. Ownership of the property rights in the asset confers residual control. The allocation of residual control between parties will therefore affect whether, and to what extent, parties seek to renegotiate *ex post* the *ex ante* agreement in relation to division of the quasi-rents. The party owning the property rights is capable of holding up the contract's performance (e.g. by refusing to let the other have access to the assets he controls) as a means of renegotiating the division of surplus. The other party's hold-up threats are less credible in the absence of residual control. The allocation of residual control will also determine the parties' incentives to make further investments in specific to the assets so controlled. The person with control has an increased incentive; the other person's incentive will normally decrease. In the case—as in a firm—where there are a number of related contracts, each involving distinct specialized assets, the firm becomes a bundle of assets subject to the same ownership interests (Grossman and Hart 1986). Likewise, organizational governance is the set of constraints (including the allocation of property rights) on the processes for dividing quasi-rents between contractors (Zingales 1998).

3.2.2. The Functions of Organizational Law

The theory of the firm has in turn influenced the theory of organizational law. To date, this has mainly been driven by the idea in NTF and, to a lesser extent, ITF, that the firm is a nexus of contracts. This gave rise to a 'contractarian' theory of organizational law. By characterizing organizations as contracts, which are costly to form and perform, economic analysis can justify legal rules to the extent that they reduce transaction costs. Law can reduce transaction costs by emulating those provisions that the parties might themselves contract for. The state can capture economies of scale in the design and supply of 'standard terms', but law may increase transaction costs to the extent that it imposes mandatory rules that limit the parties' freedom to achieve other, pre-ferred arrangements. This latter point underlies the common prescription for legal rules as defaults capable of displacement (Goetz and Scott 1985: 261–2).

Internal weaknesses have, however, become apparent in this contractarian account (Charny 1991: 1844–7; Schwartz 1998).[6] The first question is whether the state has any comparative advantage in supplying 'off the rack' terms (Easterbrook and Fischel 1989: 1444–6). Standard terms are also typically developed by professionals working in a particular field, e.g. in bond indenture documentation (Smith and Warner 1979b: 122–4). It is likely that most organiza-tional terms could be supplied in this fashion—the development of the joint stock partnership in England prior to the Joint Stock Companies Act of 1844 is illustrative (Davies 1997: 29–30). Furthermore, decentralized, private provision of terms may also foster desirable innovation (Hadfield 2001).

To be sure, there are some types of contract terms for which the state does have a comparative advantage. These include 'muddy', open-ended standards, such as fiduciary duties, which are costly to specify *ex ante* and are best left to *ex post* definition by an adjudicator (Ayres 1992: 1403–7). However, these terms only account for a small subset of organizational law.

The second problem is that modern contract economics has stressed the importance of limitations in courts' ability to verify whether a particular out-come, specified in a contract, has occurred. Even if contracts were costless to write, parties would still leave gaps because terms conditioned on unverifiable information are simply unenforceable (Schwartz 1992: 279–80). For a court to 'fill in the gaps' in circumstances where the parties would not include a term themselves is inefficient. Furthermore, even if parties would want a term to be supplied, determining its optimal specification is a highly contingent exercise, which depends on the scale of transaction costs, the distribution of information, and the incidence of market power (Ayres and Gertner 1992: 732–4, 740–2). The economies of scale that might be captured by the supply of default rules seem to be small (Schwartz 1992: 279–80, 287–90).

One might rightly infer from this that much of the intra-firm governance of substantive outcomes takes place at a sublegal level, through norms and stand-ards supported by the threat of second-party sanctions (Rock and Wachter 2001). The operation of such arrangements relies on outcomes being observable to the parties, without the need for costly verification by an adjudicator. In this light, an important function of organizational law is to exclude legal enforce-ment from the day-to-day governance of firms.

Such an account of governance nonetheless makes presuppositions about the nature of the property rights created in these governance arrangements. A substantial degree of state enforcement against non-parties is a precondition for the parties to self-enforce these incentive-compatible property rights. As one shall see, such state enforcement cannot be replicated by private suppliers of terms.

---

[6] Owing to space constraints, this chapter does not consider non-economic critiques.

3.3. SHARED OWNERSHIP AND PROPERTY LAW

3.3.1. The Residual Control Concept and the Sharing of Entitlements

PRTF makes extensive use of the residual control concept in modelling the governance of firm contracts. The use of the term 'residual' implies that the span of control covers all states of the world which are not specified by law or contract *ex ante* (Hart 1995: 30). This definition has much in common with Honoré's well-known account of legal ownership (1961: 108–9, 126–8). In summary, ownership confers upon an individual the maximum 'enjoyment space' that is legally attainable in respect of a given asset, after taking into consideration regulatory restrictions and subsisting contracts over the assets (Honoré 1961: 141–2; Hart 1995: 30). In practice, however, the property rights we observe in firms exhibit greater complexity than these definitions of control or ownership. The complexity inheres in the sharing of property rights and residual control. Sharing these rights is sometimes an optimal response to the governance problems (Hart and Moore 1990: 1135–6, 1140), and more frequently to the presence of wealth constraints and specialization of labour and risk bearing (Fama and Jensen 1983: 305–9). It is necessary to consider, first, what these sharing mechanisms are, and second, how sharing mechanisms affect the relationship between the parties sharing entitlements and outsiders to the firm.

3.3.2. Sharing Arrangements Used in Firms

Parties may wish to share ownership of assets for a variety of reasons and in a range of different modalities. As emphasized by PRTF, shared ownership will in some circumstances be an optimal governance mechanism for hold-up problems. An important example is outside financing. Money supplied by a financier is a paradigm firm-specific investment, and shared ownership can be used as a means to minimize the expected hold-up costs. The partitioning of property rights can be effected in more than one way. Where financiers have expertise about the firm's business, they may share ownership of the assets in parallel: their entitlements to residual control will be coterminous. This mode of sharing, in its unmodified form, requires both parties to make all ownership decisions by unanimity. In order to reduce the costs of decision-making, it is possible for them to agree to allow each other to act unilaterally, or if there are more than two co-owners, by majority (Hart 1995: 48).

Alternatively, ownership may be shared sequentially. This involves partitioning entitlements across states of the world. These states can be defined according to any description that a court can verify (e.g. the passing of time, default in payment, or service of a notice). Prior to the occurrence of the specified state of the world, residual control is exercised by or on behalf of one party; when the specified state of the world occurs, rights revert to the other party. Incomplete contracting theories of financial structure explain simple debt contracts as a form of sequential sharing of ownership (Hart 1995: 95–115; Hart and Moore 1998). Provided the debtor does not default, he is entitled to exercise residual control. Should default occur, the creditor has power to sell the debtor's assets and to retain the proceeds up to the value of the outstanding debt.[7]

Hold-up problems are by no means the only reason for shared ownership. Time and expertise constraints will often make it efficient for a party who would otherwise be a sole owner to employ an agent to manage certain parts of the firm's assets. Similarly, in situations of parallel sharing, the costs of decision-making will lead co-owners to specify that one of their number, or an additional agent, shall be responsible for certain types of ownership decisions. Each of these cases involve a third mode of sharing ownership: delegation (Hart 1995: 61–2).[8] The agent is entitled to exercise, for the purposes specified by the principal, some subset of the ownership rights relating to the asset. Such delegation may be exclusive, whereby the principal is unable to exercise the delegated rights during the continuance of the arrangement, or non-exclusive, whereby both principal and agent may exercise the delegated rights. In both cases, the delegation may be terminated at the will of the principal.[9]

3.3.3. Costs of Shared Ownership and the Role of Property Law

Sharing ownership rights creates a risk of opportunistic behaviour by one co-owner at the expense of others. For example, a parallel sharing arrangement that uses a unanimity rule for decision-making enables one co-owner to hold up the others by denying consent. In a delegation, the principal may hold up an agent (who has invested in human capital specific to the asset over which ownership rights have been delegated) by threatening to terminate the relationship. The contours of the sharing arrangement and the disposition of residual control can be designed in advance to minimize the expected risks of opportunism. Minority hold-up can be avoided by using majority rule in parallel sharing arrangements.[10] Hold-up of an agent can be avoided by using a parallel sharing structure instead of a delegation.

In each of the cases surveyed so far, the costs of opportunism are minimized by the parties' agreement *ex ante*. In legal terms, it is irrelevant whether the parties have contracted among themselves about how the assets will be used or

---

[7] Since the process of sale is costly, default ought to occur only where the value of the assets is less than the sum due: otherwise it is in the debtor's interest to pay (Leff 1970).

[8] There is a parallel here with the constitutional rules explored by Buchanan and Tullock (1962), who identified the cost of decision-making and the capacity for members to impose externalities on each other as the principle variables traded off by changing the degree of consent required for collective action.

[9] It will be seen that exclusive delegation involves sharing the subset of ownership rights sequentially, with the terminating event being the principal's consent. Non-exclusive delegation is akin to parallel sharing with a decision-making structure that allows each co-owner to act unilaterally.

[10] Of course, this brings with it a risk of cross-opportunism by the majority.

actually shared ownership rights between their number. Different considerations are raised where opportunistic behaviour involves a transaction with an outsider—one who is not, at the beginning of the transaction, a party to the sharing arrangement between the parties to the firm. Such transactions could occur under any of the sharing arrangements we have considered. All that is required is for one of the insiders to be able to benefit by granting some type of ownership claim over the assets to an outsider. This could be through selling the asset or using it to support a loan and employing the proceeds to fund a personal project. Alternatively, a self-serving insider could attempt to grant rights under the shared ownership arrangement to a friendly outsider, and thereby capture a majority to expropriate the other insiders.

If insiders were unable to prevent transactions of this sort from occurring, they would need to monitor each other extensively. Alternatively, they could try to secure the cooperation of outsiders by obtaining promises that the outsiders will respect the internal terms of the asset-sharing arrangement. The costs would, however, be prohibitive. Property law assists parties by making the terms of the sharing arrangements automatically enforceable against third parties. This is achieved where the parties' rights are proprietary (*in rem*), as opposed to merely personal (*in personam*). Wesley Hohfeld (1919: 72), who conceived of all legal relations in dyadic terms, classified proprietary rights as 'multital' relations, which he contrasted with the personal rights he classified as 'paucital' relations:

A paucital right, or claim (right in personam), is either a unique right residing in a person (or single group of persons) and availing against a single person (or group of persons); or else it is one of a few fundamentally similar, yet separate, rights availing respectively against a few definite persons. A multital right, or claim (right in rem), is always one of a large class of fundamentally similar yet separate rights, actual and potential, residing in a single person (or single group of persons) but availing respectively against persons constituting a very large and indefinite class of people.

By allowing parties to make their rights under asset-sharing arrangements proprietary (creating multital rather than paucital relations), property law allows them to make credible commitments not to engage in the sorts of opportunistic behaviour considered above. In other words, through private ordering parties may do more than simply transfer property rights predefined by law; they may, to an extent, define the scope of the property rights themselves. Such a 'contractible' property law is appealing—parties may select governance arrangements that maximize their wealth, even if they involve asset sharing. In a world of positive transaction costs, that result is otherwise difficult to achieve because of the costs incurred in binding an indefinitely large class of outsiders to observe such an arrangement.[11]

---

[11] It is important not to confuse a contractible property law with opting out of a default rule: the latter involves the exclusion of rights applicable between the contractors, whereas the former involves opting into an arrangement that binds outsiders.

The appeal of such arrangements must be weighed against their effect on third parties. Let A and B share the rights in asset X according to contract k_i, in which A is conferred residual control. Let the marginal gain to the parties of k_i over l_i, a governance arrangement that does not involve sharing, be called G_{k_i}. A will deal with outsiders from the set, O ($O = \{C, D, E, \ldots, N\}$). If k_i is enforced against O, each member of O takes the risk that A has power under k_i to transfer title under the trade proposed. One may describe that risk as λ, the product of the gains from trade multiplied by the risk that A lacks power under k_i. Alternatively, the outsider incurs transaction costs, t, to determine the effect of k_i. In some states of the world enforcing k_i decreases welfare:[12]

$$\sum_{n=C}^{N}\min(\lambda_n, t_n) > G_{k_i}$$

The law responds to this problem in three ways. First, the law may make available a very limited menu of sharing arrangements, K, from which k_i may be selected (Merrill and Smith 2000: 38–41). In these cases, outsiders are presumed to know the contours of the sharing arrangement involved (i.e., $t_n \to 0$). For example, outsiders are presumed to know that a partner has authority to bind the firm in the usual course of its business.

Second, the law may mandate that the parties give notice of a particular sharing arrangement (Baird 1983). In one sense, this decreases t_n. It may also be justified where the gains from trade are sufficiently high that a member of O confirms authority in the normal course of business, so that registration occurs simply to standardize transactional practice (i.e. $\lambda_n > G_{k_i} > t_n$). This is reflected in requirements for registration of statutory business forms, and in mandatory rules requiring suffixes such as 'Ltd.' or 'Inc.' to be appended to business names (Macey 1995: 439–40).

Third, the law may limit the multital effect given to k_i. Limitations are enforced *ex post facto*, depending on a comparison between t_n and the cost to B of preventing A from purporting to act inconsistently with k_i, called u_n. Thus, multital effect is denied where $t_n > u_n$, since B has lower costs of avoiding unauthorized transactions than N's cost to determine the status under k_i. The law will use this method where K's operation is heavily fact contingent (either because the contract is highly incomplete or because of idiosyncrasies in sharing arrangements), and also where the value of t_n is highly variable (e.g. where some transactions are obviously suspicious). These issues are most likely to arise in delegations, where residual control is predicated on acting in the principal's best interests.

---

[12] Even where that inequality does not hold, specialized sharing arrangements impose costs on outsiders. In a Coase-theoretic world, where $t = 0$, an efficiency problem never arises as authority is never in doubt, but then non-enforcement of K is not problematic either, because B may contract costlessly with O.

3.4. Business Organizations and Property Law: The Case of Partnerships and Close Corporations

3.4.1. Introduction

This section applies the theory developed in Section 3.3 to the case of differences between types of organizational form open to small firms, in particular, close corporations and partnerships.[13] The foregoing analysis suggests that the most significant differences between organizational forms will occur not at the level of terms that affect only insiders, but at the more foundational level of the terms which, through choice of form or customization within forms, allow insiders to affect multital relations.[14] Unlike insider terms, which affect relations only between participants who choose to contract with the firm, these are not privately replicable. The principal foundational rules are considered below.

3.4.2. Asset Partitioning

First, rules are necessary to delimit the pool of organizational assets, which bond the firm's operating contracts, from the personal assets of the participants. These 'asset partitioning' rules, as Hansmann and Kraakman (Chapter 2, this volume) call them, determine the extent to which: (1) a party with a claim against organizational assets may attach participants' personal assets (defensive asset partitioning (DAP)) and (2) a party with a claim against participants' personal assets may attach organizational assets (affirmative asset partitioning (AAP)). As Hansmann and Kraakman (ibid.) show, these rules differ across organizational forms. While in partnerships DAP is weak,[15] in close corporations statutorily prescribed limited liability limits creditors' recourse to insiders' personal assets to any amount unpaid on their shares.[16] Hansmann and Kraakman (ibid.) argue that DAP does not modify multital relations. Each contractual creditor could be asked to agree to limit recourse to organizational assets—indeed, these waivers were standard practice in dealings with UK joint stock partnerships prior to the Limited Liability Act of 1855.[17] However, the

---

[13] Due to space constraints, rules relating to LLPs (of both the US form and the UK form) and LLCs are not considered in detail. The analysis in the text would be readily applicable to the differences between these forms as well.

[14] It is worth emphasizing once again that the current analysis does not consider the justifications for, and the scope of, mandatory restrictions on the contractibility of insider terms. Obviously, the supply of such mandatory terms, if desirable, would be another area in which the state has comparative advantage over privately supplied terms.

[15] In the United Kingdom, partners share joint and several personal liability for partnership debts. Partnership Act 1890, 53 & 54 Vict., ch. 39, § 9 (UK). Where both the partner and the firm are insolvent, partnership creditors must first exhaust partnership assets, and then rank equally with the partner's personal creditors against his personal assets (Morse 2001: 237).

[16] Companies Act 1985, ch. 6, § 1(2)(a) (UK); Insolvency Act 1986, ch. 45, § 74(2)(d) (UK).

[17] *Hallett v. Dowdall* (1852) 18 L.J. Q.B. 2, 118 E.R. 1; *In re Merchant Traders' Ship, Land and Insurance Association* (1852) 5 De G. & Sm. 386, 393–4, 64 E.R. 1165, 1168; *In re European*

same is not true of limited liability for non-contractual claims (Ribstein, Chapter 6, this volume). The putative efficiency of limited liability for both types of claim has been extensively debated (Easterbrook and Fischel 1985; Ribstein 1991; Hansmann and Kraakman 1991; Bratton and McCahery 1997). We have nothing to add, save to reiterate that the benefits of limited liability are likely to be at their most modest in close corporations.

Conversely, AAP in close corporations is slightly stronger than for partnerships-at-will (Hansmann and Kraakman, Chapter 2, this volume). Corporate and partnership creditors have priority in liquidation over the personal creditors of equity investors (shareholders or partners respectively), with respect to organizational assets.[18] However, shareholders' personal creditors cannot initiate liquidation of the firm (unless the shareholder holds a formal majority), whereas the personal creditors of a partnership-at-will can force its dissolution. This guaranteed freedom from liquidation is useful for small firms that want to 'lock-in' assets during a developmental phase, and it ensures that value is not destroyed by unbundling complementary assets (Rock and Wachter, Chapter 4, this volume). However, partnership's AAP inferiority is mitigated by the entitlement of the partnership agreement to contract into liquidation protection by opting out of dissolution at will.[19]

3.4.3. Agency: Creating Claims against Organizational Assets

A second group of rules is necessary to delimit the circumstances under which claims by participants may be created against the organizational assets.[20] This encompasses the law of contractual agency and doctrines of vicarious liability and attribution, which perform a related function for non-contractual claims.

The law of apparent authority applies both to partnerships and close corporations, so that in circumstances under which outsiders would be reasonably entitled to expect that an agent occupying a particular position would have authority, the courts will infer a representation from her principal to that effect.[21] In effect, this applies a least-cost-avoider standard to determine the allocation of loss for unauthorized transactions as between the firm and an outsider (Rasmusen 2001; Whincop 1997: 303–6). However, the baseline for the

---

Assurance Society, 1 Ch. D. 307, 322–3 (Eng. C.A. 1875); cf. *In re Sea, Fire & Life Assurance Co.* (1854) 3 De G. M. & G. 459, 43 E.R. 180; *In re Norwich Equitable Fire Assurance Co.*, 27 Ch. D. 515 (Eng. C.A. 1887).

[18] Insolvency Act 1986, § 107 (UK) (providing that shareholders' claims rank behind those of corporate creditors); Morse (2001: 237) (noting that unpaid personal creditors rank behind unpaid partnership creditors in respect to partnership assets).

[19] Partnership Act 1890, 53 & 54 Vict., §§ 26, 32 (UK); *Moss v. Elphick* [1910] 1 K.B. 846 (Eng. C.A. 1910) (right to dissolve partnership by notice ousted by agreement that partnership may only be terminated by mutual agreement).

[20] Of course, no such specialized set of rules is necessary to delimit the circumstances under which participants may create claims over their own personal assets.

[21] *Freeman & Lockyer v. Buckhurst Park Properties (Mangal) Ltd.* [1964] 2 Q.B. 480 (Eng. C.A. 1964); cf. *Hely-Hutchinson v. Brayhead Ltd.* [1968] 1 Q.B. 549 (Eng. C.A. 1967).

authority differs from one organizational form to another (DeMott 1997: 597–9). In a partnership, each partner has authority, implied by law, to bind the firm to any contract entered into for the purpose of carrying on the firm's business in the ordinary course.[22] An equivalent entitlement is not conferred on a close corporation shareholder, which is typically reserved for the managing director or CEO (Pennington 2001: 147–8). This allows for efficient separation of risk-bearing and control, where not all of the investors are equally adept at the firm's business, or where levels of trust are limited. It is, of course, possible for close corporations to emulate the partnership rule by conferring greater actual authority on individual owner-managers. However, the reverse transformation is not so readily achievable. Restricting the authority of a partner is conceivable, but the restrictions, to be effective, must be communicated to the attention of all outsiders.[23] The costs of this would likely be prohibitive.[24]

3.4.4. Dynamic Asset Partitioning: Entry and Exit of Assets from the Pool

Third, rules are required to govern how assets enter and exit the organizational pool. The entry of assets is unlikely to involve significant opportunism by one insider against others. Consequently, the selection of assets invested at the outset is a matter to be negotiated between investors. After establishment, the law need only channel assets acquired on behalf of the organization into the organizational asset pool. Property acquired by a contract to which a corporation is a party automatically becomes part of its asset pool. For partnerships, assets bought with partnership property are presumed to become partnership property, although this is rebuttable by evidence of contrary intention.[25] This difference reflects the relative porosity of the partition between personal and organizational assets with respect to partnership creditors.

There is considerable scope for opportunism by insiders over the exit of assets. Fiduciary duty law governs these situations in both partnerships and close corporations. In general, transactions not entered bona fide in the firm's best interests are proscribed (Law Commission 2000: 181–3). A transaction with an outsider that involves a breach of fiduciary duty may leave the outsider liable to a proprietary claim by the organization for restitution of its property.[26] A

---

[22] Partnership Act 1890, 53 & 54 Vict., § 5 (UK).

[23] One fairly extreme solution is not to publicize the fact that the 'manager' is a partner, relying on the proviso to Partnership Act 1890, § 5 ('does not know or believe him to be a partner'). However, if more than one manager is desired, this becomes impossible (Morse 2001: 107–9).

[24] The desired outcome could, however, be achieved using a Limited Partnership form, under which a limited partner does not have authority to bind the firm. See Limited Partnerships Act 1907, 7 Edw., § 6(1) (UK). A list of limited partners is made publicly available through registration.

[25] Partnership Act 1890, 53 & 54 Vict., § 21 (UK).

[26] See e.g. *Rolled Steel Products (Holdings) Ltd. v. British Steel Corp.* [1986] Ch. 246, 295–8, 307 (Eng. C.A. 1984) (finding that third party with notice of directors' abuse of power held corporate assets as constructive trustee); cf. Companies Act 1985, § 35A (UK) (stating that where third party deals in good faith with board of directors, mere notice of excess of power will not invalidate a transaction). Clearly, transactions involving insiders dealing with assets owned by the firm, or in

bona fide purchaser takes free of any equitable claims the organization may have, whereas an outsider who has notice of the irregularity is deemed to hold the assets in constructive trust for the firm. Like apparent authority, this is another application of a least-cost-avoider standard in allocating a loss between the firm and an outsider (Fox 1998: 403–4; Schwartz and Scott 1991: 488–94).

In a close corporation, transfers of assets to shareholders are likely to be regulated by provisions restricting distributions—whether by way of dividend or repurchase of shares.[27] Like limited liability for contract creditors, these rules could be emulated if shareholders promised creditors not to make such distributions (Armour 2000: 375–7) Such contracts were in fact used in UK joint stock partnerships formed in the early nineteenth century.[28]

Finally, the law on fraudulent conveyances serves a multital function analogous to the proprietary operation of fiduciary doctrine, with exceptions for bona fide transactions for value.[29] These rules are impossible to emulate contractually, given the need to trade with an indefinitely large number of creditors. In England and the United States of America, the applicable law is the same for partnerships and close corporations, although there are substantial interjurisdictional differences. However, it is by no means axiomatic that the applicable law must be the same across organizational forms. Australian law provides an example where the law on voidable transactions involving close corporations undoes more transactions than the general bankruptcy provisions applicable to partnerships.[30]

3.4.5. Granting Ownership Interests

Fourth, rules are needed to limit participants' power to make outsiders part of the sharing arrangement.[31] There are two paradigmatic problems. One involves unilateral attempts to alter rights shared in parallel between equity investors, such as by bringing in new investors. In a partnership, the default rules require unanimous consent to the addition of new partners.[32] The close corporation default rule is that shares are freely transferable. This provision is commonly varied, and transfer restrictions typically require board approval. Furthermore, although directors may be entitled to issue new shares under the corporate contract, that power is subject to fiduciary duties. Therefore, the issue of shares for

which the firm is interested, are also proscribed. However, such restrictions could in principle be emulated by contract between insiders. It is only where the restrictions affect outsiders generally that such restrictions become multital in their scope.

[27] Companies Act 1985, pts. V, VIII (UK).

[28] See e.g. *Evans v. Coventry* (1857) 8 De. G. M. & G. 835.

[29] Insolvency Act 1986, §§ 238, 339, 423 (UK); Unif. Fraud. Transf. Act, § 8 (1984), 7A U.L.A. 351 (1999); 11 U.S.C. § 548 (1994).

[30] See Corporations Act 2001, §§ 588FA–588FJ (Aust.) (close corporations); Bankruptcy Act 1966, §§ 120–5 (Aust.).

[31] This group of rules could alternatively be considered a subset of the rules linking claims to assets. See *supra*, Section 3.4.3.

[32] Partnership Act 1890, 53 & 54 Vict., § 24(7) (UK).

a clearly improper purpose (e.g. to dilute a controlling shareholder) will invalidate the share issue.

The second problem involves equity investors transferring wealth to themselves from existing creditors by altering the risk profile (either by switching from low-risk to high-risk projects (Jensen and Meckling 1976: 333–43) or by devaluing the existing creditors by raising new debt of equal or higher priority). Neither partnerships nor close corporations can give direct multital effect to a promise not to engage in a particular form of business activity,[33] or to raise further capital (Bjerre 1999: 312–13, 337–8). However, by granting a security interest to the first creditor, others can do something similar. A security interest prevents the debtor from alienating collateral without the secured creditor's consent (Smith and Warner 1979a) and, through the creditor's priority in insolvency, ensures that subsequent borrowings will not dilute their claims (Schwartz 1989). Furthermore, it does so in a way that alters multital relations: a security interest is 'self-enforcing' in that it binds outsiders (Schwartz 1997: 1412–13).

The law of security interests forms part of the menu of property law structures that the law supplies to facilitate the governance of commerce. Registration is typically a prerequisite to their perfection.[34] Although security interests can be created by and used in any organizational form, it is possible in the United Kingdom for a company, but not a partnership, to grant a 'floating charge' (floating lien) (Law Commission 2000: 257–8). This form of wraparound security interest is thought to facilitate lender governance of small firms (Scott 1986: 926).

3.4.6. Anticommons and Insolvency Law

Equity investors and creditors share ownership rights sequentially. Should the firm default on its debts, then equity investors and their delegates must turn the assets over to creditors. In turn, the creditors share ownership claims among themselves in parallel. During the firm's solvency, it makes sense for creditors to be able to exercise their rights unilaterally, but once they become residual claimants this gives rise to severe hold-up or anticommons problems. Hence insolvency law steps in, imposing collectivity on the exercise of creditors' rights (Jackson 1986: 7–19). Insolvency law also provides means, such as voluntary administration in the United Kingdom,[35] or Chapter 11 reorganization in the United States,[36] by which hold-up problems can be reduced by allowing decisions to be made through majoritarian processes for the financial restructuring

---

[33] The doctrine of *ultra vires* at one stage performed a function along these lines. However, the dynamic inefficiencies it gave rise to—locking companies into particular businesses when these were no longer worthwhile investments—far outweighed the benefits it brought in terms of the ability to commit credibly not to divert assets into high-risk projects (Cheffins 1997: 529–31).

[34] See e.g. Companies Act 1985, pt. XII (UK); U.C.C. §§ 9–301, 9–302, 3A U.L.A 6, 14 (Supp. 2001).

[35] Insolvency Act 1986, Pt. II (UK).   [36] 11 U.S.C. §§ 1101–74 (1994).

of a potentially viable firm. This can create frictions where the fit between the insolvency procedure and the organizational form may not be ideal (Ribstein 1997: 52–6).

While the terms of the arrangement by which close corporation shareholders or partners exercise their collective rights are frequently agreed upon, this is not possible for the collective exercise of creditors' rights. In theory, firms might contract with their creditors over a procedure to govern the resolution of financial distress, but might be unable to commit not to borrow on different terms (Adler 1993: 336). What is needed is for the state to give multital effect to a set of 'insolvency' terms selected by the firm. English law indirectly allows this by enforcing a secured creditor's floating charge in insolvency, through the receivership process, even against the liquidator.[37] This procedure captures informational efficiencies by allowing a relational lender to run the insolvency proceeding (Armour and Frisby 2001: 79–91). Again, because of the restrictions on the grant of a floating charge, this is only possible in a close corporation, not in a UK partnership.

3.5. IMPLICATIONS AND CONCLUSION

This chapter began by demonstrating the importance now attached to property rights, rather than contracts, in the economic theory of the firm. The regnant theory of organizational law is nevertheless still rooted in the contractarian model. We have explained how the importance of property rights requires legal scholars to understand the significance of property law's functions in supporting governance arrangements—in particular the sharing of residual control and the enforcement against third parties of terms in the sharing arrangement. We examined the importance of the proprietary role of the law in the differentiation of the assets of the firm from the personal assets of the investors, the entry and exit of assets from the firm, the exercise of managerial power, the creation of new ownership interests, and the resolution of anticommons problems in insolvency.

In developing this argument, we have shown how these proprietary entitlements are differentiated across the discrete standard forms available for the organization of small firms. That argument itself reveals why the law is organized into a limited menu of standard forms rather than a continuum of term choices—the menu reduces the costs that contract choices can impose on outsiders by limiting the number of possible choices (Ribstein 1995a: 381–3).

Because of the unique role played by the state in defining proprietary entitlements, lawmakers should appreciate how changing these proprietary entitlements are the reforms most likely to impact economic efficiency. They are, at

---

[37] *In re David Lloyd & Co.*, 6 Ch. D. 339 (Eng. C.A. 1877); *In re Northern Garage Ltd.*, [1946] 1 Ch. 188; *Sowman v. David Samuel Trust Ltd.*, [1978] 1 All E.R. 616; *In re Potters Oils Ltd.*, [1986] 1 W.L.R. 201.

once, the areas of greatest promise and the areas of greatest problem. The efficiency of a number of these rules is, however, debatable. This suggests the need to examine apparently unnecessary frictions in some areas of the law with a view that there may be constrained inefficiencies: in other words, that law reform can genuinely improve outcomes.

We also cannot assume that the historical sequence of reforms to the law in this area necessarily demonstrates an efficient evolutionary trend, as some theorists allege (Ribstein, Chapter 6, this volume). Even if the laws maximized the welfare of the equity investors, they may impose higher externalities on third parties who must learn about the effect of new organizational forms whether they trade with them or not (Merrill and Smith 2000: 26–35). Those third parties may be less effective (because more diffusely organized) interest groups in the law reform process.

REFERENCES

Adler, B. E. (1993), 'Financial and Political Theories of American Corporate Bankruptcy', *Stanford Law Review* 45: 311.

Alchian, A. A., and Demsetz, H. (1972), 'Production, Information Costs and Economic Organization', *American Economic Review* 62: 777.

Armour, J. (2000), 'Share Capital and Creditor Protection: Efficient Rules for a Modern Company Law?', *Modern Law Review* 63: 355.

—— and Frisby, S. (2001), 'Rethinking Receivership', *Oxford Journal of Legal Studies* 21: 73.

Ayres, I. (1992), 'Making a Difference: The Contractual Contributions of Easterbrook and Fischel', *University of Chicago Law Review* 59: 1391.

—— and Gertner, R. (1992), 'Strategic Contractual Inefficiency and the Optimal Choice Of Legal Rules', *Yale Law Journal* 101: 729.

Baird, D. G. (1983), 'Notice Filing and the Problem of Ostensible Ownership', *Journal of Legal Studies* 12: 53.

Bernstein, L. (1996), 'Merchant Law in a Merchant Court: Rethinking the Code's Search for Immanent Business Norms', *University of Pennsylvania Law Review* 144: 1765.

Bishop, C. G. (1997), 'The Limited Liability Partnership Amendments to the Uniform Partnership Act (1994)', *Business Lawyer* 53: 101.

Bjerre, C. S. (1999), 'Secured Transactions Inside Out: Negative Pledge Covenants, Property and Perfection', *Cornell Law Review* 84: 305.

Bratton, W. W. (1989), 'The "Nexus of Contracts" Corporation: A Critical Appraisal', *Cornell Law Review* 74: 407.

—— and McCahery, J. A. (1997), 'An Inquiry into the Efficiency of the Limited Liability Company: Of Theory of the Firm and Regulatory Competition', *Washington and Lee Law Review* 54: 629.

Buchanan, J. M., and Tullock, G. (1962), *The Calculus of Consent*, Ann Arbor: University of Michigan Press.

Charny, D. (1991), 'Hypothetical Bargains: The Normative Structure of Contract Interpretation', *Michigan Law Review* 89: 1815.

Cheffins, B. R. (1997), *Company Law: Theory, Structure and Operation*, Oxford: Clarendon Press.

Coase, R. H. (1937), 'The Nature of the Firm', *Economica* 4: 386.

Company Law Review Steering Group (2001), Modern Company Law for a Competitive Economy: Final Report.

Davies, P. L. (1997), *Gower's Principles of Modern Company Law*, London: Sweet & Maxwell.

DeMott, D. A. (1997), 'Agency and the Unincorporated Firm: Reflections on Design on the Same Plane of Interest', *Washington and Lee Law Review* 54: 595.

Easterbrook, F. H., and Fischel, D. R. (1985), 'Limited Liability and the Corporation', *University of Chicago Law Review* 52: 89.

—— —— (1989), 'The Corporate Contract', *Columbia Law Review* 89: 1416.

—— —— (1991), *The Economic Structure of Corporate Law*, Cambridge, Mass.: Harvard University Press.

Fama, E. F., and Jensen, M. C. (1983), 'Separation of Ownership and Control', *Journal of Law & Economics* 26: 301.

Fox, D. (1998), 'Constructive Notice and Knowing Receipt: An Economic Analysis', *Cambridge Law Journal* 57: 391.

Goetz, C. J., and Scott, R. E. (1985), 'The Limits of Expanded Choice: An Analysis of the Interactions between Express and Implied Contract Terms', *California Law Review* 73: 261.

Grossman, S. J., and Hart, O. D. (1986), 'The Costs and Benefits of Ownership: A Theory of Vertical and Lateral Integration', *Journal of Political Economy* 94: 691.

Hadfield, G. K. (2001), 'Privatizing Commercial Law', *Regulation* 24: 40.

Hamilton, R. W. (1995), 'Registered Limited Liability Partnerships: Present at the Birth (Nearly)', *University of Colorado Law Review* 66: 1065.

Hansmann, H. B., and Kraakman, R. (1991), 'Towards Unlimited Shareholder Liability for Corporate Torts', *Yale Law Journal* 100: 1879.

—— —— (2000), 'The Essential Role of Organizational Law', *Yale Law Journal* 110: 387.

Hart, O. (1995), *Firms, Contracts, and Financial Structure*, Oxford: Clarendon Press.

—— and Moore, J. (1990), 'Property Rights and the Nature of the Firm', *Journal of Political Economy* 98: 1119.

—— —— (1998), 'Default and Renegotiation: A Dynamic Model of Debt', *Quarterly Journal of Economics* 113: 1.

Hohfeld, W. N. (1919), *Fundamental Legal Conceptions as Applied in Judicial Reasoning*, ed. W. W. Cook, New Haven: Yale University Press.

Honoré, A. M. (1961), 'Ownership', in A. G. Guest (ed.), *Oxford Essays in Jurisprudence*, Oxford: Oxford University Press.

Jackson, T. H. (1986), *The Logic and Limits of Bankruptcy*, Cambridge, Mass.: Harvard University Press.

Jensen, M. C., and Meckling, W. H. (1976), 'Theory of the Firm: Managerial Behavior, Agency Costs, and Ownership Structure', *Journal of Financial Economics* 3: 305.

Johnston, J. S. (1992), 'Opting In and Opting Out: Bargaining for Fiduciary Duties in Cooperative Ventures', *Washington University Law Quarterly* 70: 291.

Klein, B., Crawford, R. G., and Alchian, A. A. (1978), 'Vertical Integration, Appropriable Rents, and the Competitive Contracting Process', *Journal of Law & Economics* 21: 297.

Law Commission (Law Commission for England and Wales and the Scottish Law Commission) (2000), Partnership Law, A Joint Consultation Paper.

Leff, A. A. (1970), 'Injury, Ignorance and Spite—The Dynamics of Coercive Collection', *Yale Law Journal* 80: 1.

Macey, J. R. (1995), 'The Limited Liability Company: Lessons for Corporate Law', *Washington University Law Quarterly* 73: 433.

Maeijer, J. M. M. (1998), 'Memorandum to the Dutch Ministry of Justice with respect to the Bill regarding the (Personal) Partnership (Persoonlijke Vennootschap)' (unpublished manuscript).

Merrill, T. W., and Smith, H. E. (2000), 'Optimal Standardization in the Law of Property: The Numerus Clausus Principle', *Yale Law Journal* 110: 1.

Miller, G. P. (1992), 'The Economic Efficiency of Close Corporation Law: A Comment', *Washington University Law Quarterly* 70: 399.

Morse, G. K. (2001), *Partnership Law*, London: Blackstone Press.

Pennington, R. R. (2001), *Company Law*, London: Butterworths.

Rasmusen, E. (2001), 'Agency Law and Contract Formation' (Harvard Law and Economics, Discussion Paper, available at http://papers.ssrn.com/sol3/papers.cfm?abstract_id=6761).

Ribstein, L. E. (1991), 'Limited Liability and Theories of the Corporation', *Maryland Law Review* 50: 80.

—— (1995a), 'The Emergence of the Limited Liability Company', *Business Lawyer* 51: 1.

—— (1995b), 'Statutory Forms for Closely Held Firms: Theories and Evidence from LLCs', *Washington University Law Quarterly* 73: 369.

—— (1997), 'The Illogic and Limits of Partners' Liability in Bankruptcy', *Wake Forest Law Review* 32: 31.

Rock, E. B., and Wachter, M. I. (1999), 'Waiting for the Omelet to Set: Match-Specific Assets and Minority Oppression in Close Corporations', *Iowa Journal of Corporation Law* 24: 913.

—— —— (2001), 'Islands of Conscious Power: Law, Norms, and the Self-Governing Corporation', *University of Pennsylvania Law Review* 149: 1619.

Schwartz, A. (1989), 'A Theory of Loan Priorities', *Journal of Legal Studies* 18: 209.

—— (1992), 'Relational Contracts in the Courts: An Analysis of Incomplete Agreements and Judicial Strategies', *Journal of Legal Studies* 21: 271.

—— (1997), 'Priority Contracts and Priority in Bankruptcy', *Cornell Law Review* 82: 1396.

—— (1998), 'Incomplete Contracts', in P. Newman (ed.), *The New Palgrave Dictionary of Economics and the Law*, London: Macmillan Reference.

—— and Scott, R. E. (1991), *Commercial Transactions: Principles and Policies*, New York: Foundation Press.

Scott, R. E. (1986), 'A Relational Theory of Secured Financing', *Columbia Law Review* 86: 901.

Smith, C. W., and Warner, J. B. (1979a), 'Bankruptcy, Secured Debt and Optimal Capital Structure: A Comment', *Journal of Finance* 34: 247.

—— —— (1979b), 'On Financial Contracting: An Analysis of Bond Covenants', *Journal of Financial Economics* 7: 117.

Weidner, D. J., and Larson, J. W. (1993), 'The Revised Uniform Partnership Act: The Reporters' Overview', *Business Lawyer* 49: 1.

Whincop, M. J. (1997), 'Nexuses of Contracts, the Authority of Corporate Agents, and Doctrinal Indeterminacy: From Formalism to Law and Economics', *University of New South Wales Law Journal* 20: 274.

Whincop, M. J. (1999), 'Painting the Corporate Cathedral: The Protection of Entitlements in Corporate Law', *Oxford Journal of Legal Studies* 19: 19.

—— (2001a), *An Economic and Jurisprudential Genealogy of Corporate Law*, Aldershot: Ashgate Dartmouth.

—— (2001b), 'An Empirical Investigation of the Terms of Corporate Charters and Influences on Term Standardization in a Laissez-Faire Environment' (Griffith University, Working Paper, available at http://papers.ssrn.com/sol3/papers.cfm?abstract_id=231048).

Williamson, O. E. (1985), *The Economic Institutions of Capitalism*, New York: Free Press.

Zingales, L. (1998), 'Corporate Governance', in P. Newman (ed.), *The Palgrave Dictionary of Economics and the Law*, London: Macmillan Reference.

4

Waiting for the Omelet to Set: Match-Specific Assets and Minority Oppression in Close Corporations

EDWARD B. ROCK and MICHAEL L. WACHTER*

4.1. INTRODUCTION

Closely held corporations ('close corporations') form an important subset of corporations with concentrated ownership.[1] The category includes an interesting variety of enterprises, including the traditional 'mom and pop' businesses, high-tech start-ups, and mature publicly held corporations post leveraged buy-outs. More generally, close corporations are important because of their number and because even the largest publicly held corporations often start out as closely held corporations. As such, close corporations are incubators for tomorrow's publicly held corporations.

Two sets of problems have arisen repeatedly in closely held corporations, but only rarely in publicly held firms. The first, now resolved, revolved around the enforceability of attempts by participants to tailor the terms set by the general corporation law. Because states historically have provided one corporation law for all corporations, participants in closely held corporations have often tried to modify the statutory structure by contract to serve their needs. These variations have raised the question of the extent to which parties can contract out of the rules provided by the statute. The evolution towards greater flexibility was long, and at times, hard fought, but it no longer is a central issue. Today, participants in the close corporation can largely tailor its terms to their purposes.

The second set of problems, and the focus of this chapter, falls under the caption of 'protection of minority shareholders'. To what extent should the law

* This chapter was first published in the *Iowa Journal of Corporation Law* 24: 913 (1999). We are grateful for comments from Howard Chang, Zohar Goshen, Lawrence Hamermesh, Peter Huang, Michael Klausner, Dale Oesterle, Steven Rosenblum, David Skeel, and participants in presentations at the National Bureau of Economic Research (NBER) Conference on Concentrated Ownership, University of Colorado, University of Pennsylvania, Georgetown, and the American Bar Association. As part of the NBER conference, this chapter also appears as a chapter in (Morck 2000).

[1] Closely held corporations are typically defined as corporations for which there is no public market for shares and, sometimes, no market at all. An alternative and largely co-extensive definition is corporations with few (typically defined as less than twenty-five) shareholders. See e.g. American Law Institute (ALI) (1994: § 1.06).

provide protection to minority shareholders from 'oppression' by majority shareholders, beyond what the parties have contracted for? This set of questions, unlike the first set, remains alive and controversial. It has been the subject of an enormous amount of judicial and legislative effort, much of which has been devoted to expanding the rights of minority shareholders. The questions raised go to the very core of what corporations are about.

There are several repeated scenarios that raise the issue of 'minority oppression'. Consider the following:

Case A: There is a falling-out between the majority shareholder, Major, and the minority shareholder, Minor, both of whom work in the business. Major fires Minor, who then can either hold on to his shares, which pay no dividends (all distributions are through excessive salaries), or sell them back to the firm for whatever the majority shareholder is willing to offer. A variant arises when there are three equal shareholders, A, B, and C. After a falling-out, A and B gang up on C and fire him, at which point he is left with shares that pay no dividends and which only the firm is willing to buy.[2]

Case B: The majority shareholder or group of shareholders enter into a transaction with the firm, in which, for example, the firm buys back a portion of the majority shareholders' shares without making the opportunity available to the minority shareholders.[3] Easier variants of this scenario include the full range of transactions of controlling shareholders with the firm, including compensation, selling and buying property, and diversion of corporate opportunities.[4] More difficult variants include the situation in which the majority shareholder takes advantage of opportunities that are not clearly corporate opportunities, such as developing a more liquid market for shares in which the minority shareholders would like to participate, but are not offered the opportunity.[5]

Case C: The majority shareholder sells its majority (controlling) stake to a third party without giving the minority shareholder an opportunity to participate.

This chapter addresses the question of what, if anything, the courts should do for the minority shareholders in cases where the parties have not provided for the problem by contract.[6] Our basic answer is that courts should not do anything except enforce the participants' contracts and vigorously prevent non pro rata distributions to shareholders. This second principle provides a guide to the expansion of minority shareholder protection against 'oppression'.[7]

---

[2] See e.g. *Wilkes v. Springside Nursing Home, Inc.*, 353 N.E.2d 657 (Mass. 1976); *In re Topper*, 433 N.Y.S.2d 359 (N.Y. Sup. Ct. 1980).

[3] Classic examples are *Donahue v. Rodd Electrotype Co.*, 328 N.E.2d 505 (Mass. 1975) and *Nixon v. Blackwell*, 626 A.2d 1366 (Del. 1993).

[4] See e.g. *Crosby v. Beam*, 548 N.E.2d 217 (Ohio 1989); *Alaska Plastics, Inc. v. Coppock*, 621 P.2d 270 (Alaska 1980).

[5] See *Jones v. Ahmanson & Co.*, 460 P.2d 464 (Cal. 1969).

[6] For a very interesting and important game theoretic analysis that arrives at many of the same points as we do but from a different direction, see Johnston (1992). Other important treatments that overlap with ours are Easterbrook and Fischel (1991: 228–52) and O'Kelley (1992).

[7] There is a third problem which is not normally thought of as a 'close corporation problem' but which is, namely, 'piercing the corporate veil'. This is the issue of when a creditor can 'pierce the

We proceed as follows. First, we make a fundamental break with the traditional legal treatment of the problem of 'minority oppression' by rejecting the analogy between close corporations and partnerships, and the intuitions and implications that flow from it. We also show that the alternative argument, which emphasizes the low agency costs of close corporations, needs to be expanded upon to explain the Silicon Valley-type of start-up close corporation. Second, we illustrate that the close corporation form is best suited to companies that require extensive investments in match assets. In such cases, the close corporation acts as an incubator and the lock-in is a benefit, not a cost. Low agency costs are more likely a result of the choice of forms and not the reason the form is adopted in the first instance. Third, we argue that the problem of minority oppression combines two fundamentally separate problems: in the employment context, the issue raised by the 'employment-at-will' doctrine; and the quite separate problem of controlling shareholder attempts to make non pro rata distributions of firm assets. Building on an earlier analysis of employment-at-will, we then show that the same rule of judicial non-intervention that governs the employment relationship solves closely similar problems in the close corporation context. This rule, combined with vigorous judicial enforcement of the rule of no non pro rata distributions, including ancillary enforcement of minority shareholder informational rights, and limitations on the ability of control shareholders to sell shares to the firm, allows the close corporation to maximize the value of its match assets. We conclude by drawing the implications of the analysis for a larger theory of close corporations.

4.2. Defining the Issue

There are two types of structures that fall under the heading of close corporation. One is the traditional close corporation, often small-scale and family owned. The other is what we will call the 'Silicon Valley start-up'.[8] Several traits typically characterize the closely held firm: there are few shareholders; no public market for the shares; and a substantial overlap between suppliers of capital and suppliers of labour. Due to the overlap between managers and shareholders and the absence of public markets, the shareholder/managers of the close corporation are in continuous contact with each other. The lack of a public market causes the parties to be locked into their investments to a much greater extent than in either the partnership or the publicly traded corporation. Because

corporate veil' of limited liability in order to reach the assets of the shareholders. Although formally a question that arises in both publicly held and close corporations, the issue arises only in close corporations—in the United States, at least. This issue is, however, beyond the scope of the chapter.

[8] Today, substantial literature exists on the structure and governance of venture capital start-ups. See Barry et al. (1990: 456); Gompers (1995); Gorman and Sahlman (1989); Lerner (1994, 1995); Sahlman (1990: 493); Lerner and Merges (1998). For a more comprehensive description of the 'private equity' market, see Fenn et al. (1995).

the majority shareholders elect the directors and control the management of the corporation, minority shareholders are particularly vulnerable if there is a falling-out with the majority.

4.2.1. Existing Positions

In their famous and influential article, John Hetherington and Michael Dooley (1977: 2) expressed the intuition that lies at the heart of the evolution of minority shareholders' remedies for 'oppression': that, in all important respects, 'the close corporation is the functional equivalent of the partnership'.[9] In their view, participants choose the corporate form over the partnership form simply to take advantage of limited liability. The problem with close corporation law, they argue, is that despite this functional equivalence, shareholders cannot exit their investment as easily as partners who always have the power to trigger a buyout by dissolving the partnership 'by the express will of any partner at any time'.[10] To them, the difficulty of exit is a flaw in the legal structure. Their proposed solution is legislation that provides shareholders of close corporations with the same exit option that partners classically possess.

Indeed, it is their intuition that lies at the heart of the evolution of minority shareholders' remedies for 'oppression'. Although the law has not gone as far as they had proposed, it has moved in that direction—driven, at least in significant measure, by an acceptance of their core claim of equivalence. Courts have been more willing to order dissolution and buyouts when convinced that the majority has engaged in oppressive conduct and have also been more willing to find oppressive conduct when the minority's reasonable expectations have been violated.

The literature has also explored the conditions under which oppression—that is, opportunistic behaviour—is likely to occur. This literature also provides support for buyouts and other remedies for minority oppression (Thompson 1993; Mahoney 2000).

---

[9] For a classic judicial expression of the same intuition, see *Donahue v. Rodd*, 328 N.E.2d 505, 512 (Mass. 1975).

[10] Uniform Partnership Act (1914: § 31(2)). While the dissolution may be wrongful, it will nonetheless be effective and will immediately trigger a winding up of partnership affairs with the pro rata distribution of net proceeds. The Revised Uniform Partnership Act (RUPA), which is in effect in some states, has tried to limit the potential damage to going concerns caused by this power, but individual partners retain much of their power to dissociate from the partnership and, by doing so, to trigger a buyout regime without triggering dissolution of the partnership itself. Thus, under §§ 601 and 602 of the RUPA, a partner may dissociate from the partnership at will, at any time, rightly or wrongly. Revised Uniform Partnership Act (1997: §§ 601, 602). Under § 602(a), partners have the power to withdraw at any time, a power that is immutable under § 103(b)(6). See ibid. §§ 602(a), 103(b)(6), 601 cmt. 2. Under § 701, if a partner is dissociated from the partnership, and the partnership continues, the partnership must buy out the dissociated partner's interest for 'the amount that would have been distributable to the dissociating partner . . . if, on the date of dissociation, the assets of the partnership were sold at a price equal to the greater of the liquidation value or the value based on a sale of the entire business as a going concern', less any damages caused by wrongful dissolution.

Taking a different approach, Frank Easterbrook and Daniel Fischel (1991: 228–52) have provided an alternative agency cost argument. They argue that the small number of shareholders and the overlap of managers and shareholders naturally align the interests of the two. This occurs for a variety of reasons. First, because managers are typically the residual claimants, actions taken by them will directly affect the value of their investment. The alignment is strengthened when shareholders have a large percentage of their wealth tied up in the venture. Furthermore, because the shareholders cannot easily alienate their holdings, they will be focused on maximizing the return. Second, participants in close corporations often have familial or other personal relations. The bond between them constrains conflict of interests. The result of the close alignment and the familial bond is that close corporations can have very low agency costs.

In the Easterbrook and Fischel view, companies choose the close corporate form to maximize the return on their low agency costs. If they wanted to, the companies could have adopted the partnership model, contracted for shareholder agreements, or adopted specific protections for minority shareholders in the articles of incorporation. Consequently, those who choose the corporate form without modification should be assumed to prize stability of operations. The implications of their approach to the minority oppression debate are clear. Providing ease of dissolution or buyouts would only serve to weaken the bonds that align the parties' interests. Consequently, controlling shareholders in close corporations should be held to the same fiduciary standards as directors in publicly traded corporations, and no additional protections should be accorded to minority shareholders.[11]

But is the Hetherington and Dooley intuition correct? Are close corporations nothing more than 'incorporated partnerships'? Do close corporations better serve the interests of the participants when exit is easy? Are Easterbrook and Fischel correct that the primary virtue of the close corporation is that it reduces agency costs and that no additional protection should be accorded minority shareholders? In order to answer these questions, we must open the lens wider to place close corporations in a broader context. With a wider lens, we can see that any explanation for the close corporate form has to be able to explain the second type of close corporation: the Silicon Valley start-up.

4.2.2. Our Position and the Silicon Valley Start-Up

In Silicon Valley, close corporations are started when the entrepreneur has an idea for a new product or service, such as a network switch. In the initial stage, the venture attempts to develop the new product. Whether the product will be

---

[11] Easterbrook and Fischel, on one side, and Hetherington and Dooley, on the other, have provided for a grand debate that has engaged not only the academic literature, but also courts faced with allegations of minority oppression. For example, to Easterbrook and Fischel, minority oppression is no more likely in the close than in the public corporation and should not be a cause of action with distinctive standards and remedies. See Easterbrook and Fischel (1991: 231).

successful is unknowable because its precise form and potential revenue streams have not yet taken shape. At this stage, the company will have relatively few shareholder/managers who supply the ideas, the initial capital for the venture, or both.

In the early stages of developing this new switch, the venture is highly dependent on these individuals for either the critical ideas or the financial capital. In addition, it is these individuals who believe in the high potential value of the network switch. Their investments of human and financial capital are made with the expectation that the pay-off to the investment could be huge if the development stage idea can be implemented. But if the project were to falter, the value of these development stage investments would be nil. During this period, outsiders are unlikely to attach a similarly high value to the potential pay-off to the concept. In this sense, the investments in our hypothetical are match-investments and the assets being created are match assets: they have great value to insiders and little value to outsiders.[12] A defining characteristic of the Silicon Valley start-up is that its key assets are specific to the match.

The intensity of match assets creates a second important characteristic of close corporations. Between the time of the initial investments in research, development, and marketing, and the time at which the world can see if the switch will be a commercial success, it will be difficult to convince outsiders to invest in the project. Second stage venture capitalists may be interested in the venture, but given the still unproven value of the concept, will need to be brought in as insiders. To outside investors, the high cost of learning and staying informed about the switch's potential value makes them unwilling bidders at a price that values the match assets at the insiders' valuation. As a consequence, the company will be capital constrained with no easy access to outside financing at an appropriate valuation of the assets.

If any of the company insiders could trigger dissolution of the enterprise midstream, the forced sale of the match assets would result in substantial losses to the participants. Either the insider with the deepest pocket would buy the assets or the assets would be sold at a low price equal to the outsiders' bid price. If critical insiders could credibly threaten dissolution, they could use the threat to extract a greater share of the value of the enterprise. The resulting potential for opportunism would interfere with inducing optimal investment.[13] The problem

---

[12] Investments in match are defined as investments that are more valuable to the contracting parties than to a third party. We use the term 'match-specific' investment in this chapter in place of the more common 'firm-specific' training for several reasons. First, the term 'match-specific' investment captures the broader range of activities that create a good partnership, including training and learning-by-doing, but also including adaptations to each other's styles of interaction. In addition, the term is more general and does not restrain the investments to take place inside of a firm. Finally, the term match-specific leads one to identify the specific asset created or improved by the parties' investments.

[13] We define 'rent-seeking', or, more generally, 'opportunism', to be the expenditure of resources or efforts by one party in order to transfer resources from the other party to itself. This investment by the rent-payers wastes the joint profits of the parties because it creates no new wealth. Moreover, rent-seeking by one party typically causes the prospective rent-payer to expend resources in order to protect its share of the joint investment.

is akin to making an omelet: between the time the eggs are broken and the omelet sets, the cook knows his grand plan for the omelet, but to outsiders, the half-cooked omelet is unappetizing. Forced sales of half-developed switches and uncooked omelets go poorly.

In our approach, low agency costs are a natural result of the choice of form, but not the reason for adopting it. The close corporation will always have lower agency costs than an otherwise identical publicly owned company as a consequence of the small number of shareholders and the overlap of shareholders and managers. But agency costs do not explain why any given firm would adopt the close corporation form. The important exception, noted by Easterbrook and Fischel (1991: 229–30), is the family business. In a family business, low agency costs pre-exist in the familial relationship and the parties can thus capitalize on it by adopting the close corporation form (ibid.). However, the Silicon Valley start-up is different. These shareholder/managers are unlikely to have pre-existing familial ties and hence are unlikely to bring low agency costs to the formation of the close corporation. For at least the Silicon Valley start-up, the explanation for the choice of form is an operational factor: the need to lock-in parties while developing vulnerable match-specific assets. Reduced agency costs are the result rather than the cause.

The problem of match-specific investments in a context with substantial asymmetry of information characterizes many other centrally important economic relationships. The employment relationship in which an employee with match-specific training is more productive than an employee hired from the external labour market provides a classic example. That employment relationship provides a critical foundation for our analysis precisely because most or all of the shareholders of close corporations are also employees.

Focusing on match assets also shows the fundamental differences between classical partnerships and close corporations. The dissolution-at-will feature of classical partnerships means that the form will best fit enterprises in which there are few if any assets that are not easily sold to third parties. In such cases, the benefits of dissolution-at-will are clear: by providing an easy exit, it prevents opportunistic rent-seeking. And the costs are minimal: when there are no sunk costs, when the principal assets are easily divided or sold, dissolution-at-will causes little harm. Thus, for a small law firm in which partners have their own clients, but wish to share office space, staff, and occasionally to refer business to other lawyers in the office with greater expertise or receive referrals, the partnership form is optimal. If the firm breaks up one day, very little value is trapped. Indeed, as one would predict, small law partnerships dissolve and reorganize constantly.

If participants can trigger dissolution-at-will, they will be unwilling, *ex ante*, to make investments in match for fear that, *ex post*, they will be held up. Because of this problem, when there are high investments in match, such as the Silicon Valley start-up, the costs of a rule of easy dissolution are huge. The traditional close corporation manifests the same features, although in a less highly articulated form. As in the Silicon Valley start-up, at the early stage of a new venture, the product or service will have no revenue but high costs. Similarly, once the initial investments of human and physical capital are made, the participants are locked in. In one respect, the traditional family business close corporation poses an even more difficult problem of protecting match investments. Unlike the Silicon Valley start-up, the traditional close corporation often expects to remain privately held indefinitely: the nature of the products or services is often such that selling to a third party is never a live option. However, traditional close corporations come in many forms and, at least in their formative years, many often hope to develop a product or service that may eventually be successful enough to be saleable to a third party.

Easy dissolution would also make it even more difficult to raise equity or debt capital than it already is. If the firm were required to retire the capital of an existing owner who sought to cash out, the cash constrained close corporation would be forced to raise new capital in a potentially unfavourable climate. Indeed, the shareholder dissension that characterizes a 'minority oppression' case is likely to be highly correlated with negative events in the firm. A legal rule favouring easy exit threatens to shift the engine for raising new money into reverse, forcing capital to be retired under unfavourable conditions.

Similarly, the lock-in of the corporate form is important to creditors. In a setting of limited liability, creditors cannot be repaid from the individual wealth of the owners of a bankrupt company. In return, and in distinction to the rules of partnership, they are protected by the existence of an entity that is difficult to dissolve by the current owners. It is only with this protection that the squabbles among those who manage the company will be of limited interest to the creditors. Nowhere is this more important than in the close corporation, whose assets are difficult to value and whose current realizable market value—at forced sale—may be considerably below its future value. In such a setting, easy dissolution or buyout increases the risk of bankruptcy, thereby reducing the creditworthiness of the company. The traditional judicial reluctance to order dissolution or a buyout of minority shareholders lowers the credit risk of close corporations and allows them to borrow at more favourable terms.

Clearly, not all close corporations will be marked by heavy investments in match. Parties can, and do, choose alternative corporate and non-corporate forms based on very different motivations. In addition, parties sometimes make mistakes in their choice of form. In this regard, the analysis can be interpreted as defining the paradigm close corporation that is best served by the legal rules. Choose the close corporation form when heavy investments in match make restrictions on exit valuable. Choose the partnership form when exit is not costly and the parties can be given free rein to withdraw from the match.

4.3. LEGAL SETTING

In this section, we describe the legal and non-legal features of the close corporation. In so doing, we show how minority oppression arises and how it is constrained. This begins to set the stage for providing an answer to how the three cases noted at the outset should be resolved.

4.3.1. Core Solution: The Corporate Form

The standard, off-the-rack, corporate form provides a robust solution to the problem caused by threats of opportunistic exit. The standard form has several relevant terms. Directors are elected by a plurality of the shares.[14] Dissolution requires a board resolution and a vote of the majority of the shares.[15] Individual shareholders have no general right to sell their shares back to the firm.

The lock-in of the close corporation is created by the interaction of these terms with the absence of a public market for the shares. But the lock-in only affects the minority shareholder (Minor). The majority shareholder (Major) can dissolve the corporation through a board resolution and a vote of a majority of the shares. The individual minority shareholders have no power to trigger dissolution. Minor likewise has no right to be bought out because, under the standard corporation laws, no shareholder has a general right to be bought out. If Major dissolves the corporation, Minor will receive a pro rata share if and when the firm is dissolved.[16] In the mean time, Minor has a very limited right to be bought out by the firm—namely, the right to judicial appraisal upon a merger and, sometimes, a sale of all or substantially all of the assets.[17]

In addition to the lock-in provided by the statutory form, there are additional core properties of the form provided by a combination of statute and case law. The single most important combination is the prohibition on non pro rata distributions during the life of the firm combined with the close scrutiny of self-dealing transactions that attempt to evade this prohibition. The restrictions on non pro rata distributions are quite clear and derive from several sources. A majority shareholder may not pay itself dividends without also paying the same per share dividend to the minority shareholders.[18] It would be clearly illegal—and easily challenged—if the majority shareholder paid itself $10 per share in dividends, while only paying minority shareholders $1 per share.

Indirect means of distribution are also constrained. For example, if the majority shareholder attempts to divert assets by entering into a contract with

---

[14] See e.g. Del. Code Ann. tit. 8, § 216 (1974).   [15] See e.g. ibid. § 275.

[16] See e.g. ibid. § 281(a)(4).

[17] See e.g. ibid. § 262(a); Revised Model Business Corporation Act (RMBCA) § 13.02.

[18] Del. Code Ann. tit. 8, § 170 (1998); RMBCA § 6.40. The interpretation of these two sections is that, by definition, a dividend is a pro rata distribution. See Welch and Turezyn (1993: § 170.2, at 340–1).

the firm on preferential terms, the contract is subject to close judicial scrutiny. In addition, the majority shareholder bears the burden of establishing that the transaction is 'entirely fair' to the corporation, where 'entirely fair' is, when possible, defined by an arm's length market comparison. Compensation agreements are subject to a similar, but somewhat less exacting rule (ALI 1994: § 5.03). Generally, to avoid the 'entire fairness' scrutiny, compensation agreements must be authorized in advance by disinterested directors or disinterested shareholders, and even then, these are subject to scrutiny by the court under a 'waste' standard. Similarly, attempts by the majority shareholder to take opportunities that belong to the corporation, or to use corporate assets for its own benefit, are limited (again imperfectly) by the 'corporate opportunity' and related doctrines (ibid.: §§ 5.10–5.14).

While no one believes that these rules eliminate non pro rata benefits of control, most corporate law scholars agree that they significantly limit the magnitude of such diversions. As Cliff Holderness and Dennis Sheehan's (2000) empirical investigation suggests, legal restraints are surprisingly effective and probably the primary protection for minority shareholders. By limiting non pro rata distributions, these provisions go a long way to making the relationship incentive compatible. So long as the majority shareholders cannot prefer themselves in distributions, minority shareholders can depend on the majority to protect its interests.

The provisions addressing end-game scenarios are a second set of equally important standard protections that facilitate and protect the beneficial lock-in. When, for example, the majority shareholder triggers dissolution in order to take its capital out of the enterprise, the minority shareholders share pro rata in the net proceeds.[19] Similarly, if the firm merges with another firm, shareholders receive equal shares and minority shareholders have a right to be bought out at 'fair value', whether the firm survives or disappears.[20] Under section 13.02 of the Revised Model Business Corporation Act (RMBCA), minority shareholders are also entitled to appraisal if the firm sells all or substantially all of its assets.[21]

Attempts by Major to circumvent these rules are constrained. If, for example, Major engineers a 'squeeze-out merger' to rid itself of minority shareholders, Minor will be entitled to a judicial valuation of its shares, often with favourable procedural protections. Under Delaware law, Minor will be entitled to appraisal.[22] In addition, Minor may also be entitled to bring a breach of fiduciary duty action.[23] In evaluating such a squeeze-out merger, the Delaware court will place the burden on Major to prove the entire fairness of the price.[24]

---

[19] See e.g. Del. Code Ann. tit. 8, §§ 275, 281 (1998); RMBCA §§ 14.02–14.05.
[20] See Del. Code Ann. tit. 8, §§ 251, 262 (1998); RMBCA §§ 11.01–11.06, 13.01–13.02.
[21] RMBCA § 3.02.   [22] Del. Code Ann. tit. 8, § 262.
[23] See generally *Weinberger v. UOP, Inc.*, 457 A.2d 701 (Del. 1983).
[24] See *Kahn v. Tremont Corp.*, 694 A.2d 422, 433 (Del. 1997).

4.3.2. Majority Opportunism and the Remedy for 'Minority Oppression'

But the very provisions that protect against opportunistic exit create the problem of opportunistic lock-in. Consider Case A, above.[25] When Major has a falling-out with Minor, and Minor is left holding a minority interest in a firm controlled by Major, the standard corporation codes do not give Minor any right to be bought out, nor any right to dissolve the corporation. As a result, Minor may find itself locked into an investment that pays no dividends, in which Major makes all the decisions, and from which the only exit is to sell to Major at Major's bid price.

The core protection against majority oppression is the prohibition on non pro rata distributions and the related prohibitions on self-dealing, discussed above. The doctrine of 'minority oppression' can be understood as a supplemental judicial response to this problem. Over the last twenty-five years, in response to the perceived plight of the locked-in minority shareholder, courts and legislatures have modified the law to provide remedies to minority shareholders that are not available to shareholders of publicly held corporations.[26] This has been done in a variety of ways. First, legislatures in many states have broadened the circumstances in which minority shareholders may force the judicial dissolution of a corporation. In addition, legislatures have expanded the range of remedies beyond dissolution; namely, to include judicially mandated buybacks at a 'fair price' (Thompson 1993: 718–22). In most jurisdictions, shareholders can petition for dissolution on the grounds of illegality, fraud, misapplication of assets, or waste (ibid. 708). 'Oppressive conduct' by the majority shareholder is often listed as a basis for dissolution.[27] Similarly, frustration of a 'shareholder's reasonable expectations' is often a ground for dissolution (Thompson 1988: 199). In other jurisdictions, shareholders' 'reasonable expectations' are the measure of whether or not the majority shareholder has oppressed the minority. Second, judges have become more willing to order dissolution or a buyout, particularly if they are convinced that majority shareholders have engaged in 'oppressive conduct' or that shareholders' 'reasonable expectations' have been violated. Third, courts have made it easier, substantively and procedurally, for minority shareholders to bring suit against majority shareholders for breach of fiduciary duties.

[25] See Section 4.1.

[26] In the following extremely cursory summary, we follow the excellent treatment provided by Robert Thompson (1993). For further details, see Thompson (1988). For even more details, see O'Neal and Thompson (1986 and 1995 Supplement); O'Neal and Thompson (1991); O'Neal and Thompson (1985).

[27] See e.g. RMBCA § 14.30(2)(ii) ('The court may dissove [*sic*] a corporation . . . in a proceeding by a shareholder if it is established that . . . the directors or those in control of the corporation have acted, are acting, or will act in a manner that is illegal, oppressive, or fraudulent.'). Under RMBCA § 14.34(a), when shares are closely held, 'the corporation may elect, or, if it fails to elect, one or more shareholders may elect to purchase all shares owned by the petitioning shareholder at the fair value of the shares.'

Minority shareholders have benefited from several trends. First, courts have tended to make the fiduciary duty owed by majority shareholders stricter. Second, courts have shown an increased scepticism towards whether the majority has fulfilled its duties. Finally, courts have broadened the situations in which a minority shareholder can bring a (procedurally simple) direct suit in place of a (procedurally complex) derivative suit. Together, these developments have moved close corporation law towards partnership law, both with regard to the ease of dissolution as well as with regard to the duties owed by one shareholder towards the others.

These various doctrines have proved difficult to contract out of (Oesterle 1995: 888). Because the doctrines find their foundations in either a contractual 'covenant of good faith' or a fiduciary duty, and because contracts waiving such duties are typically void, a straightforward contractual opt-out will not be effective. Similarly, contractual attempts to divest courts of authority to dissolve the corporation are generally void. Ironically, while the overwhelming trend in close corporation law has been to permit tailoring of the standard terms by contract, the area of minority protection has stood out as an exception.

In summary, a cause of action has evolved for 'shareholder oppression' or, perhaps more accurately, as Robert Thompson (1993: 708) suggests, for 'shareholders' dissension'. This cause of action has increased the ability of shareholders of the close corporation to turn to a third party decision-maker for relief from what shareholders argue is oppression or unfair conduct by the controlling shareholders. Although the cause of action is still evolving and its boundaries remain obscure, these developments have increased the bargaining power of the minority, *ex post*, vis-à-vis the majority.

The critical question is whether such developments are likely to benefit the participants in close corporations. The close corporation is the ideal form for enterprises with a high density of match assets because of, and not despite, its lock-in feature. Accordingly, the development of shareholder oppression law may interfere with the efficiency of the close corporation form. To reduce this possibility, what principles should guide its evolution?

4.3.3. When a Legal Solution?

The possibility of opportunistic behaviour does not itself provide a sufficient basis for judicial or legal intervention. While the problem of opportunism is pervasive in relationships characterized by investments in match and asymmetry of information, such problems are only sometimes solved by legal intervention. To put it somewhat differently, the issue is when does a non-legally enforceable, norm-governed relationship serve the parties' interests better than a third party, law-governed relationship?

From this perspective, one cannot understand the role of legal intervention in the close corporation until one first understands the extent to which the relationship is already self-governed by non-legally enforceable norms enabled by the core legal form. We proceed in several steps. First, because many minority oppression cases are employment-related and the employment relationship is the best example of a relationship with match investments and asymmetrical information that is almost entirely norm-governed, we start with a brief summary of that analysis. Second, we apply that mode of analysis to the close corporation, examining the analogous non-legally enforceable structures that constrain opportunistic behaviour. Third, we examine the fundamental legal protections that make that self-government possible. With that groundwork laid, we turn to the appropriate judicial role in rooting out residual opportunism.

4.4. CONSTRAINTS ON OPPORTUNISM

4.4.1. The Employment Relationship and Investments in Match

The employment relationship, and particularly the relationship between managers and the firm, is often characterized by large investments in match (Rock and Wachter 1996; Wachter and Wright 1990). These include employee investments identifying the employer, in understanding and improving job performance, and in learning the organizational and operating structures of the company and its core competencies. The company in turn invests in identifying and training the employee in the above factors and in the monitoring of the employee's performance to determine the most profitable future path of joint match-investments. Many of these investments are match-specific and would be lost if the employee left the company.

Given the magnitude of the sunk investments in match, the threshold question is why the parties enter an ongoing relationship without adopting (legally enforceable) contract terms to protect their interests. The explanation is twofold. First, the costs of contracting over the multitude of interactions would be extremely high in a relationship that is continuous and evolving. Second, self-enforcing, but not legally enforceable, norms emerge to constrain opportunistic behaviour.

The widespread but puzzling features of the employment relationship can be best understood as a remarkably robust set of self-enforcing employee protections. Consider, for example, why firms choose to discharge an employee for inferior performance rather than adopting a less severe penalty, such as reduction in wages. While this may initially seem to be in conflict with the presumed interest of the parties in maintaining the employment relationship, asymmetric information requires termination rather than a wage reduction. Because of asymmetric information, employees know their work effort, but firms do not. Firms can learn by monitoring, but constant monitoring is very costly. To save on costs, workers are infrequently monitored. The harsh penalty is driven by the low detection rate. If most shirking goes undetected, workers must be penalized an amount greater than the expected loss of any specific incident.

However, this optimal deterrence explanation does not explain why the penalty for inferior performance cannot be a large salary reduction. The answer is that if the firm could simply declare that an employee was under-performing and cut his or her salary, the employer would have an incentive to overstate underperformance, thereby reducing costs and increasing profits. Channelling the employer's response into discharge is thus incentive-compatible. In declaring inferior performance, the company must accept the loss of the employee. The company is willing to do this if the employee's performance is indeed inferior, but not otherwise. The practice of laying off workers during a slowdown, rather than reducing wages, can be understood in a similar fashion.

From this perspective, the legal doctrine of employment-at-will—the doctrine according to which companies can discharge employees for good reasons, bad reasons, or no reasons at all—is best understood as a rule of judicial non-intervention, and not the incorporation of a substantive term of the employment relationship (Rock and Wachter 1996). Even the critics of the rule do not claim that companies often discharge workers for bad reasons or no reasons. When the substantive norm that governs the employment relationship seems to be 'no discharge without cause', why would the parties prefer a legal rule that says 'no intervention'? The answer follows from the preceding analysis.

An enforceable contract must be specified *ex ante* in terms that can be verified *ex post* by the third-party enforcer. In the employment context of continuous and evolving interactions, such a contract would invariably be incomplete. Consequently, the expectations of the parties would be difficult to establish at any given time. Since much of the information is asymmetrically available to one party, many of the outcomes cannot be verified by third parties.

In this context, legal enforcement of the norm of 'no discharge without cause' would undermine the norm-based system because of the difficulties of *ex post* third-party verification. As a starting point, proving just cause would require that the employer engage in additional detection costs, which reduces the value of the match. In addition, the third party would have to learn enough about the internal norms of the firm to determine whether a violation of the norm was meaningful enough to constitute 'cause'. Moreover, the presence of investments in match increases the likelihood of error when third parties enforce the norms because the valuations of those assets depend not on market prices but on the parties' own valuations. From the employer's perspective, just cause exists when the continuation of the match with the particular employee has negative net present value, including the reputational cost of taking too tough or too easy a stance in the face of the perceived violation.

Self-enforcing norms better serve the parties' interests. On the one hand, they allow the party with the detailed information to act on his or her knowledge at low cost. At the same time, they protect the uninformed party by forcing the informed party's actions into channels that make opportunistic behaviour unprofitable.

In cases where norms are insufficient to deter opportunistic behaviour, other non-legal remedies are available. The parties are involved in repetitive inter-actions, and the employer is also a repeat player in the competitive external labour markets. Both make it costly for an employer to act opportunistically. In the ongoing employment relationship, bad play by the employer generates retributive bad play by the employees, whether in concert or individually. This can take the form of hard-to-detect work slowdowns, bad-mouthing the employer in the public domain, or even covert vandalism and theft. Such actions cause direct losses to the employer and force an increase in monitoring, which is also costly. In the labour market for new employees, a reputation for bad play is similarly costly in the form of increased difficulty in attracting or retaining the best employees. Finally, in the case of non-supervisory employees, unionization is an effective alternative, forcing the relationship into the domain of explicit contracting with a collective bargaining agreement.

Given these advantages, the resilience of the employment-at-will doctrine in the employment relationship is unsurprising. Whenever courts encroach on the doctrine through a theory of contractual interpretation, one finds that the par-ties, to the extent permitted, contract around the interpretation by specifying, for example, that the terms of the employment handbook are not to be taken as legally binding. The best explanation for this resilience is that, in a relationship characterized by match investments and asymmetry of information, the parties are best served by self-enforcing rather than third-party enforced agreements. It is not that opportunistic behaviour is eliminated entirely, only that the benefits of the flexible norm-governed relationship outweigh the costs of residual oppor-tunism.

We now turn to the analogous problem in the closely held corporation.

4.4.2. Close Corporation: Non-legal Constraints on Opportunism

As in the employment context, many of the persistent features of the close corporation provide substantial, albeit non-legally enforceable, protection against opportunities for abuse that are opened up by the form itself. In this sub-section, we explore how these non-legal constraints operate, and show that the seemingly detrimental lock-in of the close corporation, supplemented by the prohibition on direct and indirect non pro rata distributions, renders the form largely incentive-compatible. By locking in Minor, and prohibiting non pro rata payments, Major, in seeking to maximize the value of his stake in the firm, like-wise will maximize Minor's stake.

This is particularly true in the case when the close corporation is like an unfin-ished omelet. Like the shareholders' individual inability to trigger dissolution, the lack of a market prevents exit or opportunistic threats of exit, except under narrowly defined circumstances. Locked in together, the parties can count on each other's dedication to cooking the omelet properly. This issue is also han-dled, at least in the Silicon Valley start-up, by legally enforceable contracts that protect early investors through particular financing structures.[28] In general then, the close corporation forces the investor into a high degree of illiquidity, an unfavourable state from a traditional investment perspective, but an illiquidity that serves the interests of the parties by locking up participants in the enterprise.

A variety of other features of the close corporation can be understood as supplementing and complementing this structure. The overlap between suppliers of capital and labour reduces information asymmetries and transaction costs. Whether in the traditional or Silicon Valley variety, the overlap puts all the relevant players into continuing contact, providing both the entrepreneur and the capital suppliers with continuing information on their own and on the company's performance.

The result is that the operations of the close corporation are akin to the stylized employment relationship discussed above. The same types of self-enforcing norms are operational. In both cases, the participants are engaged in repetitive interactions where the parties can sanction each other for bad play and can apply the appropriate sanctions more reliably than third parties who cannot observe and monitor the behaviour of the parties. In the close corporation, the ability of the participants to identify improper behaviour will be much greater than the ability of any third party. Moreover, the ability of the participants to punish bad behaviour will likewise be great. The disenchanted minority shareholder/manager armed with greater access to company performance information has more leverage to sanction bad play by the employer than does the individual manager in a public corporation.

Indeed, if anything, the results found in the employment relationship are stronger in the case of the close corporation because of Easterbrook and Fischel's (1991: 228–52) point on agency costs.[29] The most difficult problem in the employment relationship is aligning the interests of the employees with the company. Pay for performance, particularly stock options for senior executives, reduces the misalignment in the public company; however, the device is both imperfect and costly to the shareholders. In the close corporation, pay for performance is a natural result of the fact that employees are also shareholders. More generally, in the public corporation's employment relationship, senior executives and shareholders occupy mostly independent spheres. In the close corporation, the spheres overlap. The wide governance mandate of its board of directors results from the overlap of roles between capital and labour providers. The shareholder/employee is involved in the governance issues normally reserved for shareholders in the publicly held corporation and for employees in the employment relationship.

---

[28] See Sahlman (1990: 489–503) (outlining the contract and analysing the relationship between external investors and the venture capital firm); Gompers (1995: 1464) (discussing the contracting costs incurred by venture capitalists).

[29] See Section 4.2.1, para. 4, et seq.

The robustness of the norm protection is illustrated by the high-tech sector. The occasions for opportunistic renegotiation that arise from sequential performance are a particular problem in high-tech start-ups. Venture capitalists (VC) worry that the entrepreneurs, after accepting early financing from the VC, will find other financing once the idea proves its worth, or will quit and go to work elsewhere after the VC has invested millions of dollars. Entrepreneurs worry that the venture capitalists will find other managers once the idea has been committed to paper and has proven its worth. These concerns, which are simply a special and detailed case of the more general problems of the close corporation, are the subject of intense contracting and research. We will illustrate by considering a few details.

The VCs protect themselves in several ways (Barry 1990: 461–3; Gompers 1995; Gorman and Sahlman 1989; Lerner 1995; and Fenn et al. 1995: 32–3). First, a surprising stylized fact of the Silicon Valley start-up is that the VCs have the right to replace the entrepreneur with a professional manager (Hellmann 1998: 58). In addition, the terminated entrepreneur often can be forced to sell his stock back to the firm at cost—well below its actual value. Finally, entrepreneurs do not automatically receive generous severance packages.

Thomas Hellmann explains why the venture capitalists would demand such terms as a response to a hold-up problem (ibid. 60). Entrepreneurs gain private benefits of control, which lead them to stay on longer than they should. By contrast, the VCs' incentives are much better aligned with maximizing firm value, and, moreover, they are better situated to identify better professional managers. In Hellmann's model, unless the VC receives the right to displace the entrepreneur, it will not invest optimally in searching for replacement managers.

How the entrepreneurs protect themselves is equally interesting. After all, if the VC has the right to terminate the entrepreneur, which triggers a stock buyback at cost, there would seem to be an incentive to do so. The entrepreneur's protections here are entirely non-legal, but they are substantial. Most importantly, VCs are repeat players in the start-up business and are likely to be constrained on a number of fronts. First, they compete to provide financing for the most promising start-ups and are thus likely to be constrained by reputational effects in their aim to maintain their position in relation to other start-up companies. In addition, the VC has to replace the entrepreneur with another person. Wrongful discharge of the chief executive officer, even if protected from judicial second-guessing by the employment-at-will doctrine, is not a strong starting point in any recruitment process. Finally, the discharge will raise questions with other capital suppliers. It is a negative signal under the best of circumstances and is likely to raise the company's cost of capital. Of course, this is precisely the story we earlier told about employment-at-will more generally, and the fact that employment-at-will governs even in a domain of such intensive contracting as the Silicon Valley high-tech sector is further support for our analysis.

That still leaves open the question of why the entrepreneur's stock position can be bought out at cost. The likely answer here, as stressed throughout the chapter, is the difficulty of determining market value for a start-up company that does not trade in a public market. The contract term that sets the buyback price at cost, however, is a default setting. Again, the VC will have a strong reputational incentive to deal fairly with the discharged entrepreneur, including paying a higher price if one can be reliably determined.

Another feature that is particularly striking is the absence of any general right to trigger dissolution or to be bought out at a pro rata share of firm value. The choice made in the high-tech sector, where contracting is most explicit, is to leave the lock-in in place and to avoid judicial valuation of hard-to-value assets, even at the cost of some residual opportunism. This is consistent with the more general reactions to the special close corporation articles of corporation codes, promulgated by some jurisdictions in response to developments in the law and academic commentary. However, few firms avail themselves of the opportunity to organize under such statutes. On the contrary, close corporations seem to stubbornly adhere to organizing under the general corporation codes.

4.5. The Proper Judicial Role in the Three Cases

We have argued that the lock-in effect of the corporate form is what makes it so attractive for firms that benefit from extensive investments in match. We have argued further that there are a variety of structural features that limit the incentives and constrain the ability of the participants to act opportunistically—the principal threat to optimal match investment. In addition, the law limits significantly the non pro rata distribution of assets from the corporation and provides for pro rata treatment upon dissolution and merger. Moreover, the law provides for a judicial valuation of minority shares in a sharply limited number of situations. Finally, participants are free to contract for additional or different terms, an opportunity which participants liberally use.

The remaining question is what room, if any, is there for further judicial intervention on behalf of minority shareholders? The concern is that judicial attempts to protect minority shareholders against opportunistic behaviour will jeopardize the web of features and protections that make the close corporation form so attractive and popular for firms with substantial match-specific assets.[30] In guarding further against the potential for minority oppression, do we end up increasing the potential for opportunism in the relationship by providing Minor with more chances to act opportunistically against Major?

---

[30] A weaker proposal would be to make the minority protection a default setting, from which firms could opt out. The experience of states that have special optional close corporation provisions suggests that there would be boilerplate opt-out option provisions from default settings. The widespread contracting around departures from the employment-at-will doctrine through the interpretation of employee handbooks likewise suggests that any variation must be mandatory to be effective.

4.5.1. Case A: Employment-at-will as Minority Oppression?

Consider Case A,[31] in which Major fires Minor. Minor, the terminated minority shareholder, invested in match-specific assets related to a new network switch, with the expectation that he would share in the returns generated from the venture. We are concerned that Minor will not be able to share the fruit of his efforts now that he has had a falling-out with fellow shareholder Major. Moreover, having lost his job, we are also concerned that Minor will be forced by both economic necessity and the absence of a liquid market for shares to sell his shares at a fraction of the pro rata value of the firm. The Minors of the world, never certain whether they will end up on the wrong end of a disagreement, will not invest optimally in match-specific assets unless their employment and investment expectations are protected.

There are two variations of Case A that must be considered. First, assume that Major is the entrepreneur who supplies the ideas and has 60 per cent of the stock, while Minor supplies the money and owns 40 per cent. What possibilities for opportunism arise in the absence of any special protections for minority shareholders? Suppose that, after Minor has invested his money and the idea is developing well, Major says 'I want an additional 10% of the equity or else you will never see a dime of profit', or any number of variants that amount to the same idea. Is this a credible threat? Clearly the answer is 'no'. First, because of the restrictions on non pro rata distributions, if Minor does not get any dividends, neither will Major. Second, if Minor is providing more than money (management advice, industry contacts, etc.), then Major may still need him. Third, the market and the need for a stream of additional capital will constrain Major's ability to threaten Minor. In these circumstances, Minor will be unwilling to put more capital into the business. Moreover, other potential investors are also likely to refuse when they learn of the incident. As long as Minor remains a material owner of the company, or is known in the financial community, those in the financial community who are considering investments will undoubtedly learn of Major's opportunism. Empirical research on the high-tech sector confirms that the financial individuals are quite good at contracting for particular devices that protect against this sort of opportunism (Gompers 1995).

Now consider the reverse scenario. Major supplies the financial resources and holds 60 per cent, while Minor is the entrepreneur who supplies the ideas and possesses 40 per cent. Once Minor commits his idea to patentable paper, Major fires Minor. Minor has neither an employment agreement nor any shareholders' agreement that provides for a buyout right. Does Minor have a claim on our sympathies?

In this case, a threshold question is whether Minor's contribution is 'one off'. If it is, then Minor opens himself up to opportunistic renegotiation if Minor commits the contribution before Major finishes performing. However, when the

---

[31] See Section 4.1.

contribution really is 'one off', without the necessity for ongoing involvement (the scenario that gives rise to the threat of opportunism), there is an easy transactional solution: a licence or sale. The individual (or individuals) who discovers something important, but has nothing further to contribute, should license or sell the idea to Major, who will then develop it. Similarly, when the capital provider has only a single investment to make and has nothing else to contribute, he should buy limited partnership shares with a VC who can then control the opportunistic Major's because of their superior knowledge and network. Of course, the one-time, would-be financier may purchase the patent or license it, only to go broke due to his own lack of good follow-up ideas. The critical fact, however, is the following: when the contribution is indeed 'one-off', no business reason exists to use the corporate form.

Focus, then, on the difficult cases that will involve plaintiffs who believe they are still making contributions to the firm. If brought before a third party for resolution, Major will provide one of two explanations—either that Minor was fired because Minor has been shirking or that Minor is not suited to the current demands of his job or needs of the firm. In other words, Major will allege that Minor is no longer making valuable contributions. Minor will maintain that he was fired because Major wanted to take Minor's ideas for himself and capture all of the gains.

This is precisely the same problem that is addressed in employment law by the employment-at-will doctrine. In this case, sorting out the truth raises the precise difficulties of relying on a third party to resolve employment disputes. It is very difficult for the court to determine *ex post* what the parties' reasonable expectations were *ex ante*. Even if the court could determine the parties' expectations, performance is largely unobservable; therefore, the court will be unable to determine whether the expectations have been satisfied. As in the employment context, Major and Minor know much more about who is telling the truth than a judge could ever discover. In addition, valuing the relationship of specific assets to determine if opportunism has occurred and, if so, to set damages, is, in theory and in practice, necessarily speculative. Finally, permitting Minor to sue for 'oppression' or breach of 'reasonable expectations' will, as in the employment context, undermine the web of self-enforcing relationships that provides the principal protection for investments in match.

Against this background, consider the classic Case A case, *Wilkes v. Springside Nursing Home, Inc.*[32] Wilkes, along with three others, established a nursing home, with the work and profits apportioned more or less equally.[33] After a falling-out, the others forced Wilkes out of active participation in the management of the enterprise and cut off all corporate payments.[34] Wilkes alleged that his termination constituted a breach of the fiduciary duties owed to him by the majority shareholders.[35] According to the court, 'The severance of Wilkes from the payroll resulted not from misconduct or neglect of duties, but

---

[32] *Wilkes*, 353 N.E.2d 657 (Mass. 1976).   [33] Ibid. 659.   [34] Ibid. 661.   [35] Ibid.

because of the personal desire of [the other shareholders] to prevent him from continuing to receive money from the corporation'.[36] In holding for Wilkes, the court stated:

A guaranty of employment with the corporation may have been one of the 'basic reason[s] why a minority owner has invested capital in the firm'. The minority stockholder typically depends on his salary as the principal return on his investment, since the earnings of a close corporation . . . are distributed in major part in salaries, bonuses and retirement benefits. Other non-economic interests of the minority stockholder are likewise injuriously affected by barring him from corporate office. Such action severely restricts his participation in the management of the enterprise, and he is relegated to enjoying those benefits incident to his status as a stockholder. In sum, by terminating a minority shareholder's employment or by severing him from a position as an officer or director, the majority effectively frustrate the minority stockholder's purposes in entering on the corporate venture and also deny him an equal return on his investment.[37]

The court then recognized the extent to which the controlling group needed 'room to maneuver in establishing the business policy of the corporation'.[38] As a compromise, the court established a 'legitimate business purpose' test: 'When an asserted business purpose for their action is advanced by the majority, . . . we think it is open to minority stockholders to demonstrate that the same legitimate objective could have been achieved though an alternative course of action less harmful to the minority's interest.'[39] Because the majority had not shown a legitimate business purpose in terminating Wilkes's involvement in the firm, the court held for Wilkes.

In addition, there is a second argument suggested that raises some additional issues. The court notes that '[o]ther non-economic interests of the minority stockholder are likewise injuriously affected by barring him from corporate office. Such action severely restricts his participation in the management of the enterprise, and he is relegated to enjoying those benefits incident to his status as a stockholder.'[40] The exact thrust of the court's argument here is somewhat unclear. One reading of this claim is that there are valuable, non-economic benefits that come with participation in the firm. To the extent that this is the argument, it simply amplifies the no-just-cause claim.

However, there is a much more relevant alternative reading—namely, that terminating Wilkes's participation in the firm made it impossible for him to continue to monitor his co-shareholders, and because of the asymmetry of information that characterizes the close corporation form, this rendered his continued participation as a shareholder untenable. This is an argument that differs both from the faulty employment-at-will concerns as well as from the non pro rata distribution concerns that will be discussed below.[41]

---

[36] Ibid.

[37] *Wilkes* (*supra* n. 32) at 662–3 (quoting Northwestern University Law Review (1957: 392); O'Neal and Thompson (1991: § 1.07).

[38] *Wilkes* (*supra* n. 32) at 663.   [39] Ibid.   [40] Ibid. 662.

[41] See Section 4.5.3.

Could the other shareholders in Wilkes have been behaving opportunistically? Could they have terminated Wilkes's relationship with the firm in order to expropriate his investment, considering that he had already committed whatever special skills and knowledge he possessed? Absolutely. Opportunistic behaviour is clearly possible in such circumstances. Yet that alone is not sufficient to justify the court's response, namely, a case-by-case analysis of terminations to determine if the firm acted with a 'legitimate business purpose' and with no 'less harmful alternatives'.[42] That is the same as stating that because opportunistic behaviour is possible in the employment relationship, a court should scrutinize each termination to see if it was for just cause.[43]

Case A and *Wilkes* both present situations in which the majority shareholder(s) could have been behaving opportunistically. However, in both cases, there are numerous non-legal constraints on such behaviour. If Major treats Minor badly, Major will have greater difficulty convincing current shareholder/employees to continue investing time, money, and effort in the enterprise, as well as convincing prospective investors, or prospective employees to join the firm on the same terms that Minor did. These are the reputation and self-help stories described earlier.

Suppose that Minor's idea or plaintiff Wilkes's stake is so valuable that Major is willing to suffer whatever reputational cost will be incurred by acting badly? Minor and Wilkes are still not unprotected. If Major successfully markets, develops, or sells Minor's patent, or if Springside Nursing Homes sells the nursing home to a national chain, Minor and Wilkes are still protected by the rule of no non pro rata distributions. If Major ultimately decides to liquidate or sell the firm in order to take its profits on Minor's invention, Minor will likewise receive its share. In the mean time, Minor will be in a position to make Major's life difficult by making requests for information and threats of litigation. Finally, if these protections are insufficient and the problem is significant, future Minors always have the option of specifying additional protections by contract.

On the other side of the equation, permitting judicial scrutiny of Minor's or Wilkes's termination is in effect to undermine the very advantages of the informal, non-legally enforceable set of protections that constitute relational 'contracts'. As we have argued elsewhere (Rock and Wachter 1996) in connection with the employment-at-will doctrine, the attempt to root out residual opportunism—opportunism that slips through the network of legal and nonlegal constraints—threatens to undermine the self-enforcing character of the overall relationship. Moreover, as we will discuss in more detail below, the court's difficulty in determining whether a discharge was for a 'legitimate business purpose' is aggravated by the difficulty of valuing match assets in awarding Minor the 'fair value' of his shares in a judicially mandated buyout.

---

[42] *Wilkes* (*supra* n. 32) at 663.
[43] This, of course, is precisely the argument that opponents of the employment-at-will doctrine make.

The *Wilkes* case is a good example of the difficulties courts have with the employment issues that frequently overlay close corporation cases.[44] For example, was the court correct in saying that there was no legitimate business purpose in terminating Wilkes's employment? On the one hand, we are told that there was no misconduct and that Wilkes 'had always accomplished his assigned share of the duties competently'.[45] The court, however, made no attempt to determine whether Wilkes's services were still needed. Apparently he was not replaced, suggesting overstaffing. By not appreciating the norms of the employment relationship, the court stumbled badly, inferring a right to continued employment, subject only to proof of misconduct. Such a right is so far at variance with employment practice anywhere that its insertion in the case undermines the logical application of the legitimate business purpose standard.

4.5.2. Case B: Stock Buybacks as Minority Oppression?

Consider Case B: Major forces the firm to buy back a portion of Major's shares (while leaving Major in control) at an entirely fair price, without giving Minor a proportionally equal opportunity to cash out. The principal variant of Case B is one in which the Major Group, the controlling shareholder group, buys back the shares of a member of the control group without giving Minor a proportionally equal opportunity to cash out. In either case, does Minor have a claim on our sympathies? In this instance, we are concerned that Major, even if its transaction with the firm meets the 'entire fairness' valuation standard, receives a benefit that Minor does not—the ability to cash out a portion of his holdings, when doing so is profitable. We are also concerned that the ability of Major to 'have his cake and eat it too' will undermine Minor's incentive to invest optimally in the firm by breaking the beneficial lock-in feature of the corporate form.

This is the issue in *Donahue v. Rodd Electrotype*.[46] In *Donahue*, the controlling shareholder, Dad, distributed most of his shares to his children who worked in the business. Subsequently, his sons wished that Dad would retire, but he would only do so if he could sell some of his remaining shares back to the firm (with the remainder distributed later to his sons).[47] The firm bought back Dad's shares without offering an equal opportunity to the minority shareholders, who challenged the buyback as a breach of fiduciary duty.[48] After a lengthy discussion of the extent to which close corporations are really little more than incorporated partnerships, a discussion which is not only wrong but unnecessary to the decision of the case, the Supreme Judicial Court of Massachusetts held that 'if the stockholder whose shares were purchased was a member of the

---

[44] The importance of employment disputes and the employment-at-will doctrine in the close corporation setting is stressed generally in Johnston (1992).

[45] *Wilkes* (*supra* n. 32) at 664.   [46] *Donahue*, 328 N.E.2d 505 (Mass. 1975).

[47] Ibid. 510.   [48] Ibid. 511.

controlling group, the controlling stockholders must cause the corporation to offer each stockholder an equal opportunity to sell a ratable number of his shares to the corporation at an identical price'.[49]

Nixon v. Blackwell likewise involved a stock repurchase plan.[50] In *Nixon*, the firm established an Employment Stock Option Plan (ESOP) that held company stock and provided departing shareholder/employees the right to receive cash for their interest in the ESOP when they retired.[51] In addition, the company established key-man insurance policies that allowed proceeds from the plan to be used to purchase stock in executives' estates.[52] The non-employee minority shareholders objected on the grounds that they were not provided an equal opportunity to sell their shares.[53] The Delaware Chancery Court held that it was 'inherently unfair' for the controlling shareholders to provide liquidity for themselves without providing comparable liquidity for the non-employee share-holders.[54] The Delaware Supreme Court reversed, holding that the stock repur-chase plans served a legitimate corporate interest by maintaining an overlap between employment and ownership and that the defendants met the 'entire fairness' standard.[55]

Plaintiffs claimed that the preferential repurchase of shares was a breach of fiduciary duty. The claim raises the question of the extent to which preferential repurchase schemes are problematic, not solely because the price is too high (a version of pure self-dealing), but because they undermine the alignment of interests between the majority and minority shareholders that makes the firm work. There are two aspects to the claim here. First, as described in more detail below, to the extent that a high density of match assets characterizes close cor-porations, it becomes very difficult for the court to determine whether the repur-chase price was entirely fair, because there is no market benchmark.[56] Second, even if one could value the shares, the preferential repurchase can be objection-able because it undermines the incentive-compatible lock-in that is the great attraction of the legal form. These aspects of the problem lie at the heart of both *Nixon* and *Donahue*, and are not explicitly discussed in either decision. These are very different situations than those that occurred in Case A because they do not raise the intra-firm employment questions that made the prior case so difficult.

These cases also differ from the classic non pro rata distribution of firm assets. Here, the firm receives something of value in return for cash—shares of the firm. Normally, under the duty of loyalty, transactions between a fiduciary and the firm are not per se void or voidable. Rather, they are judged under the entire fairness standard and, if entirely fair, are valid.

The question is whether regulating such transactions is necessary to supple-ment the prohibition on non pro rata distributions, and, if so, how to do so. The

---

[49] *Donahue (supra* n. 32) 518. [50] *Nixon*, 626 A.2d 1366 (Del. 1993).
[51] Ibid. 1371. [52] Ibid. 1371–2. [53] Ibid. 1373.
[54] *Blackwell v. Nixon*, No. CIV.A.9041, 1991 WL 194725, at 5 (Del. Ch. 1991).
[55] *Nixon (supra* n. 32) at 1377. [56] See Section 4.5.3.

dimensions of the problems, and the trade-offs among different approaches, are complex. First, one needs to maintain the beneficial lock-in of participants that harnesses the self-interested efforts of the controlling shareholders in the interests of all participants. Second, one must prevent non pro rata distributions which can be made by the advantageous purchase or sale of shares. Third, one needs to maintain flexibility in the management of the firm's capital structure and compensation practices. Finally, one needs to provide for the orderly exit of participants.

Three types of cases must be accounted for. First, the control group may decide to buy out a minority shareholder. In such cases, there is little potential for opportunism. Second, the control group may decide to buy out a shareholder/employee who is exiting, or who has exited, the firm, as in both *Donahue* and *Nixon*. Here, the potential for opportunism is greater. The control shareholders may prefer one of their own over outside non-employee shareholders, and there may be disguised self-dealing. On the other hand, as continuing shareholders/employees, they will also bear a pro rata share of the cost. Finally, the controlling shareholder sells shares to the firm without relinquishing control. This is the most dangerous circumstance—the controlling shareholder has a clear incentive to receive an excessively high price, while not giving up any of the private benefits of control.[57]

How does the law handle this range of cases? One reading of the law is to generalize *Donahue* into a general prohibition on the selective buyback of shares in close corporations—that is, an equal opportunity rule. This rule largely eliminates the opportunistic use of buybacks, but at the cost of impairing the firm's flexibility in adjusting its capital structure, compensation policies, and providing exit to shareholders. A second possibility is to generalize *Nixon* into a general standard permitting selective stock repurchases whenever they are 'entirely fair'. This preserves the firm's flexibility in compensation and in providing exit, but at the cost of diluting the beneficial lock-in. A final plausible possibility is that both *Donahue* and *Nixon* were correctly decided within their individual domains. *Nixon* addressed one aspect of the more complicated middle cases. Note that the Delaware Supreme Court's ruling in *Nixon* emphasized that the buyback was pursuant to a long-standing corporate policy to which the minority apparently did not object when first instituted, and that the company adopted the policy to benefit the corporation. Indeed, the court viewed the policy as a form of deferred compensation that provided the firm with flexibility to adopt standard deferred compensation packages, which were used in other firms to encourage superior employee performance. Moreover, the court

---

[57] A related issue is presented by *Kahn v. Tremont Corp.*, 694 A.2d 422 (Del. 1997). In that case, Harold Simmons was the controlling shareholder of Valhi Corp., which owned NL Industries. Simmons was alleged to have used his control over a third corporation, Tremont, to cause Tremont to buy Valhi-owned shares of NL Industries at an excessively high price. Simmons was able to reduce his holdings in NL Industries without giving up control, at an allegedly excessive price, without other shareholders having an equal opportunity to cash out.

emphasized how the policy was applied in an entirely non-discriminatory fashion among retiring employees. In contrast, the Delaware Chancery Court viewed the policy not as a deferred compensation practice, but as a straight financial structure issue that granted members of the control group preference over non-employee shareholders in cashing out.

As in Case A, courts must be careful not to confuse employment relationship issues with straightforward capital structure questions. If courts prevent firms from adopting deferred compensation plans because of an equal opportunity rule on the exit end, close corporations will not be able to develop optimal incentive-based compensation mechanisms. In evaluating such cases, courts must look to both the compensation and the financial capital aspects of the situation, with particular attention to indicia of self-dealing.

Because of the potential for self-dealing when a control group buys out one of its own, the entire fairness rule applies. Under the entire fairness rule, the Delaware courts look at both 'fair dealing' and 'fair price'. According to the Delaware Supreme Court, fair dealing was established by the fact that the company adopted stock purchase plans for legitimate corporate purposes (maintaining the overlap between ownership and control) and provided plans to the shareholders/employees on a non-discriminatory basis. Interestingly, the issue of whether the price paid for the shares was excessive did not arise.

In the close corporation context, both fair price and fair dealing can be problematic. Whether a repurchase plan is discriminatory depends on how the relevant group is defined. In *Nixon*, the Chancery Court found the plan discriminatory because it did not treat employee and non-employee shareholders equally.[58] Although the Delaware Supreme Court could have found the situation non-discriminatory because it treated all employee shareholders equally, it ultimately held that the discrimination against non-employee shareholders was justifiable.[59] Similarly, relying on fair price is problematic when, as we discuss in more detail elsewhere, the valuation problem is often intractable.

How, then, can one understand *Donahue* and its relation to *Nixon*? The primary difference between the two cases is that the control group in *Donahue* was a family group. One may worry that the payment to Dad is disguised self-dealing, that the more Dad gets for his shares the less the children who work in the business will have to contribute to buy him an apartment in Miami. The very family relations that Easterbrook and Fischel (1991) emphasize as important in reducing agency costs within the close corporation significantly increase the potential for self-dealing when the family group is dealing with non-family shareholders.

If the existence of a family relationship significantly increases the risks of self-dealing, then one can understand *Donahue* as consistent with *Nixon*. Reading them together, the standard in both cases is entire fairness, a standard not met in *Donahue* because of a (conclusive) presumption that the repurchase was not entirely fair. One can also understand the role of equal opportunity here. If

---

[58] *Blackwell* (*supra* n. 54) at 6.   [59] *Nixon* (*supra* n. 50) at 1379.

adopted by the control group, it is powerful evidence that the transaction is entirely fair. In cases like *Donahue*, offering minority shareholders an equal opportunity to exit reverses the presumption that buying back Dad's shares redounds to the sons' individual benefit by relieving them of some other financial obligation.

Appreciate, for a moment, the subtlety of the structure. While the firm is developing or producing omelets, and therefore has a reputational stake in not breaching its agreements, there are a variety of structural features that align interests, and the principal legal restriction is no non pro rata distributions. In other words, the majority shareholder can refuse to pay dividends, but only at the cost of all of the shareholders' capital remaining trapped in the firm. This lock-in, plus the other features outlined above, provides a strong incentive for the majority shareholder to maximize firm value, thereby protecting the minority shareholders' investments as well.

But the lock-in is not absolute. As reconstructed above, the law has evolved to permit sufficient flexibility to allow the firm selectively to offer some shareholders the opportunity to cash out without offering the same opportunity to all shareholders, when doing so benefits the firm. In doing so, the law distinguishes according to the potential for opportunistic behaviour by controlling shareholders. Thus, when the firm buys shares from non-controlling shareholders, the business judgement rule applies. When it buys shares from members of the control group who are exiting, the entire fairness standard applies, with 'equal opportunity' being powerful evidence of entire fairness. Finally, when the firm buys back shares from a controlling shareholder or shareholding family who is remaining in the firm, the potential for self-dealing is so great that entire fairness is not satisfied absent equal opportunity.

Once, however, the company enters the last period—defined by the distribution of a firm's equity capital—the norm against non pro rata distributions again protects locked-in minority shareholders. The rule of no non pro rata distribution means that minority shareholders are able to cash out at the pro rata valuation. Major, as the majority owner, gets to define when the omelet is finished and signals that fact by voiding the lock-in, either by dissolution, merger, or an initial public offering of stock. But, now, Minor gets to exit, either through a pro rata share of the firm equity in dissolution, or through an appraisal proceeding if the firm is merged into another firm, or by selling out to the market after a public offering of shares.

The rule against non pro rata distributions is the linchpin—it is the rule that prevents the participants from jumping out of these channels. So long as non pro rata distributions are controlled, remaining problems that arise between shareholders can be handled by analogy to employment-at-will, where courts should not intervene in the absence of an explicit contract.

The analysis, then, largely parallels the employment-at-will account. In both cases, locking participants into a relationship in which there are substantial investments in match is valuable because it avoids the hold-up problem (i.e.

threatening to leave before the omelet is done). It also: forces the parties to resolve the problems themselves, avoiding defections; provides high-powered incentives to succeed; and prevents the parties from threatening to impose heavy costs (by threatening expensive litigation) as a way of renegotiating the division of the joint surplus.

In this sense, the principles applied in Cases A and B are the same. In Case A, Minor wants to be cashed out, at least if he cannot continue as an employee. In Case B, Major wants to be cashed out, at least if he can continue in control. On our analysis, the answer is the same in both cases: neither can cash out without the other shareholders cashing out to the same degree. And, in both cases, the reason is the same: the omelet may not be finished yet. Major gets to decide when the omelet is finished, but once Major declares the omelet finished, Minor shares pro rata. Meanwhile, neither gets to pull out equity.

4.5.3. The Courts' Comparative Advantage: Do Cases A and B Differ?

Our analysis sharply distinguishes between Cases A and B. But, say some, our distinction misses the point of what the courts are doing in these cases, and in particular, why it is important for courts to intervene in Case A situations.[60] The problem, they say, is that courts cannot distinguish between market rates of compensation and excessive compensation, and therefore should and do protect minority shareholders' employment in the firm as a second-best technique for protecting their investment expectations. On this view, unless you protect the expectation in employment, including the expected salary, the financial investment in the firm becomes worthless. That is, if pro rata distributions are to be defended, Case A must be treated like Case B in the sense of judicial intervention to protect the minority shareholder.

But this argument misses the fundamental reason that courts should not and generally do not intervene in employment cases. The argument incorrectly assumes that a court is better at distinguishing discharge for cause from 'minority oppression', and when the remedy is a buyout, calculating 'fair value', than it is in figuring out whether payments by the firm to the majority shareholder constitute a non pro rata distribution to a shareholder. In fact, because of the presence of significant investments in match, exactly the opposite is the case, and the court is likely to be far better at policing non pro rata distributions than employment issues.

Compare the two inquiries. In Case A, the court must first determine whether a termination was for cause or, more or less equivalently, for a legitimate business purpose. Having determined that a termination was unjustified, the court must then either order reinstatement or, more likely given the bad blood between participants, either order dissolution of the corporation or a buyout of the minority shareholder at fair value. In either case, the court will have to

---

[60] We owe the acute articulation of this point to the comments of Robert Thompson.

calculate the value of the firm because, given the presence of substantial investments in match, the highest valuing buyer in a dissolution will most likely be the majority shareholder.

The first inquiry faces all of the problems that have been discussed with regard to the employment-at-will doctrine. Not only is the for-cause/fair-value standard a much harder standard to apply, it does not even eliminate the need to police non pro rata distributions. Even if an employee shareholder has been discharged for cause, so long as he is a shareholder, his financial investment in the firm must still be protected against such distributions by the majority.

The second inquiry is even worse. If we are correct that the close corporation form is most appropriate for firms with substantial investments in match, the valuation problem will be intractable. A market valuation will be unavailable (because the assets are worth much less to third parties than to the participants in the enterprise), and a cash-flow analysis will face all of the informational problems that make it impossible to sell the assets to third parties.

Generally, a company's assets are valued by first estimating the future discounted stream of the free cash flow that they generate, and then attaching a multiple that reflects the discount rate and the risk associated with the cash flow. The estimate of free cash flow is based on several factors, including the past performance of the company in generating revenue, the performance of comparable assets in other companies, and the market outlook for the products produced by the assets. This standard valuation methodology, while adequate for established firms, does not work well in most close corporations because the required data is not available. The company may have very limited past performance, the management may be too untested to allow reliable future predictions, and the company's products or services may be too novel to allow easy comparisons with seasoned firms. It requires time to determine whether the product ideas will work out and produce free cash flow of any given size.

Indeed, the difficulties of valuing the assets of the close corporation are, at least in the Silicon Valley context, an important explanation for why the company continues to be privately held. By the time enough information is available on likely performance to value the match assets of the close corporation, it is time for the close corporation to go public. Similarly, for firms furthest from access to a public market, the valuation problems are the greatest. Take, for example, the classic mom and pop corporation. When mom and pop are the enterprise, it is difficult to distinguish any ongoing market value from the value provided by the principals. The enterprise's match assets may be so tied to mom and pop that no independent valuation can be attributed to the firm's other assets. Moreover, in this case, generating additional years of performance data will not bring the firm closer to a reliable market valuation. Valuing the firm by looking at the sale value of comparable firms would also be stymied by the distinctiveness of the enterprise and the difficulty in identifying comparables. Finally, when comparable companies can be found, one's confidence in the resulting valuations will be challenged by the thinness of the market.

By contrast, consider the judicial inquiry under the norm of no non pro rata distributions in Case B. First, in so far as the claim is one of a failure to pay dividends, the inquiry is straightforward: as long as no one is receiving dividends and the earnings are retained in the corporation, the court can defer to the discretion of the board, knowing that everyone's earnings are equally locked in. Second, consider the manifold varieties of basic self-dealing, ranging from excessive salaries to non pro rata dividends, to diversion of corporate opportunities to sales to or purchases from the corporation. This is the classic domain of the duty of loyalty. The basic principle here is that the majority shareholder will bear the burden of establishing entire fairness, where entire fairness is defined with reference to an unconflicted arm's length transaction.

Consider salaries as an example, although the analysis applies equally to other transactions with the corporation. The standard is a market standard: are the controlling shareholders receiving more than the market wage? When, as is often the case, the controlling shareholders set their own salary, standard corporate law analysis imposes the burden of establishing entire fairness on the controlling shareholders—that is, showing that the wage is at or below the comparable market level. While plaintiffs typically fail in challenges to dividend policy or employment policy, they apparently fare substantially better in challenges to excessive compensation.[61]

Moreover, courts have already had experience in determining, in the tax context, whether close corporation salaries are excessive.[62] When there were tax advantages to paying dividends as above market salary, the IRS scrutinized such payments on precisely this basis. As the tax preference for distributions in salary disappears, determining whether a salary meets the market test is likely to be easier because relevant benchmarks will be less distorted.[63]

In addition, the courts have at their disposal their traditional methods of shaping the decisional process by allocating burdens of proof. Thus, the courts will be more deferential to salaries that are set by independent outside directors than by the majority shareholders themselves. For example, the problem of diversion of profits to majority shareholders through excessive salaries seems non-existent in the Silicon Valley high-tech context, in part at least because managers' salaries are set by, or at least in consultation with, the venture capitalists.

[61] *Donahue v. Rodd Electrotype*, 328 N.E.2d 505, 514 n.15 (Mass. 1975) ('Attacks on allegedly excessive salaries voted for officers and directors fare better in the courts . . . What is "'reasonable compensation" is a question of fact . . . The proof which establishes an excess over such "reasonable compensation" appears easier than the proof which would establish bad faith or plain abuse of discretion.'); see also *Alaska Plastics v. Coppock*, 621 P.2d 270 (Alaska 1980); *Crosby v. Beam*, 548 N.E.2d 217 (Ohio 1989).

[62] See e.g. *Alaska Plastics* (*supra* n. 61) 270.

[63] In this context, it is worth observing that changes in the tax law undermine the received wisdom that close corporations pay out all their earnings as salary, benefits, or pension payments to avoid double taxation of earnings (once at the corporate level and once at the shareholder level). With the advent of corporate forms and tax rules that permit 'pass through' taxation, this avoidance strategy has lost much of its justification. Without double taxation, why pay out everything as salary?

While judicial intervention in Case A forces courts to value the firm with the associated problems created by the high density of match-specific assets, no such difficulties bedevil Case B. In the salary context, the question is whether a salary is excessive relative to market equivalents. In the context of other transactions with the firm, the issue is likewise whether the terms of the transaction between the majority shareholder and the firm meet the market test. In the case of dividends, the question is only whether all shareholders receive the same amount.

Indeed, the only times the court must enter the thicket of valuing the firm are when the firm is being sold (by a merger or a sale of assets, in some jurisdictions), when the minority shareholders request appraisal, and when there is a selective stock repurchase. In the case of an arm's length merger, the shareholders have the opportunity to receive the same consideration as the majority shareholder, but believe that their shares are worth more. But, in those circumstances, precisely because the firm is being sold, there is at least one measure of valuation available. Moreover, because all shareholders share equally in the proceeds of a sale or dissolution, the majority shareholder is likely to represent the interests of the minority shareholders. Major is unlikely to sell the firm unless it has reached the stage where its third party value is beginning to approach the value to the participants.[64] As discussed earlier, selective stock repurchases present genuinely difficult issues.

The focus on preventing non pro rata distributions points the way towards incremental modifications within the existing framework to increase the level of enforcement without entering the thickets of 'for cause', without disturbing the employment-at-will standard, and without judicial valuation. For example, once it is clear that the issue is preventing non pro rata distributions, the courts should make it easier to challenge contracts between the controlling shareholder and the firm. Consider *Crosby v. Beam*,[65] in which the majority shareholders entered into self-dealing contracts with the firm, including unreasonable salaries, use of corporate property, life insurance, low interest loans, and so forth.[66] The legal issue was whether the minority shareholders must challenge the agreements through a derivative suit, which is subject to the demand requirement and in which any recovery is paid into the corporate treasury, or whether the minority shareholders could bring a direct suit.[67] The court, after a long discussion of how, in a close corporation, the majority shareholders owe fiduciary duties to the minority shareholders, held that the suit could be brought as a direct suit, with recovery going directly to the plaintiffs:

Given the foregoing, if we require a minority shareholder in a close corporation, who alleges that the majority shareholders breached their fiduciary duty to him, to institute a

---

[64] A more difficult problem arises when it is the majority shareholder who is buying out the minority shares. Under these circumstances, the court has no choice but to enter the difficult problem of valuation, and, although it can and does seek to avoid the difficult valuation questions by encouraging the use of independent negotiating structures to mimic an arm's length sale, its success in doing so is only limited.

[65] *Crosby (supra* n. 61).   [66] Ibid. 218.   [67] Ibid. 219.

derivative action pursuant to Federal Rule of Civil Procedure 23.1, then any recovery would accrue to the corporation and remain under the control of the very parties who are defendants in the litigation. Thus, a derivative remedy is not an effective remedy because the wrongdoers would be the principal beneficiaries of the recovery.[68]

According to our analysis, the court got it half right. The fact that the majority is accused of engaging in a self-interested transaction with the firm is, of course, central and, in a derivative suit, would fully justify excusing demand as obviously futile and allowing the plaintiff to proceed directly to the merits of the action. But if the guiding principle is preserving the beneficial lock-in effect of corporate form against attempts at non pro rata distributions, then the correct result is that any excessive payments go back into the corporation where they remained locked up until the majority chooses to make some sort of pro rata distribution. This is an adjustment to the procedural requirement for derivative suits in the light of the special nature of close corporations (or, perhaps, simply an application), but is a quite different sort of adjustment than that adopted by the Ohio Supreme Court in Crosby.

Along the same lines, an appreciation of the central issue will lead courts to give less deference to the board of directors in setting its own compensation or in approving asset distributions of other sorts. Finally, it makes it clear that, in the absence of some independent decision-maker, the burden of proof falls on the majority shareholder to justify salaries and other payments as entirely fair.

4.5.4. Case C: Is the Sale of Control for a Premium a Non Pro Rata Distribution?

In the close corporation, we take the rule of no non pro rata distributions to have the status of a commandment. It is the principle that makes the whole thing work, which allows minority shareholders to rely on majority shareholders to manage the firm in the general shareholder interest. It is this principle that allows for optimal investment in match-specific assets. Finally, enforcing this principle frees the courts from having to enter into the impossible (and destructive) tasks of sorting out, on the one hand, whether a discharge of a minority shareholder/employee was for cause and, on the other hand, how much the firm is worth.

What then does one make of Case C, in which Major sells its majority block to a third party who is unwilling to buy the minority shares on equal terms? In the United States, the general common law rule is that the majority shareholder may sell its holdings and a buyer may buy its holdings without offering the minority shareholders an opportunity to participate.[69] The principal exception is when the majority or controlling shareholder has reason to believe that the buyer will loot the corporation (Clark 1986: 478–98). There are a few cases to

---

[68] *Crosby* (*supra* n. 61) (citing O'Neal and Thompson (1986: § 8.11).
[69] See e.g. *Zetlin v. Hanson Holdings, Inc.*, 397 N.E.2d 387 (N.Y. 1979).

the contrary, but this is the general rule (Elhauge 1992). Much has been written on the efficiency of competing rules governing sales of control. We cannot enter that thicket here, but must address the relationship between sales of control and non pro rata distributions and, more generally, the connection between sales of control and firms with heavy match investments.

Case C seems to be an interesting and difficult mix of Cases A and B. When the majority shareholder sells control, he thereby terminates his relationship with the firm, while taking a larger than pro rata share of firm value. On its face, the majority shareholder's sale might seem to violate the no non pro rata distribution norm, or, at the very least, the related norm governing end games. When a majority shareholder sells its block, it gets cash at a time when the other shareholders do not. Moreover, the minority cannot even check the impact of the sale on their share of the presale equity of the firm. Finally, unlike an arm's length merger or dissolution in which the shareholders share on an equal basis, often with a right of appraisal, here the minority shareholders not only do not share, but also have no right to appraisal. In short, we worry that the majority shareholders will sell out the minority shareholders in the process of selling control. As before, we worry about this prospect to the extent that it undermines the minority shareholders' willingness to invest in match-specific assets, thereby reducing the parties' joint surplus.

Yet the situations also seem quite different. For example, the sale of a majority block differs from the non pro rata payment of dividends in several important respects. First, the sale of the blocks results in a change of control, while the various non pro rata distributions leave the incumbent controller in place. Second, the new controller steps into the shoes of the old controller with all of the same restrictions on non pro rata distributions, restrictions which, suggests the work of Holderness and Sheehan (2000), may be surprisingly effective. Third, to sell a majority block, one needs to find a buyer. This imposes a barrier that is not present in non pro rata distributions.

At least in form, there is no difference between Major selling his shares to a new Major and any Minor selling its shares to a new Minor, except perhaps the amount received for the shares. There is, indeed, an active market for shares of closely held Silicon Valley start-ups, in which (sophisticated) minority shareholders sell their shares to other (sophisticated) investors pursuant to Rule 144A.[70]

Why might minority shareholders, *ex ante*, agree to permit the majority shareholder to sell its block without an equal opportunity rule, despite the extent to which the sale may be in tension with the beneficial lock-in and the principle of no non pro rata distributions? This old chestnut of corporate law looks somewhat different against the backdrop of our emphasis on match investments. Take again, as given, that the close corporation is characterized by a large percentage of match assets. Moreover, assume that the lock-in of the

---

[70] Private Resales of Securities to Institutions, 17 C.F.R § 230.144A (1997).

corporate form, with exit at the close of play, is part of what renders the form incentive compatible.

The principal concern with permitting sales of a majority block is that the buyer and seller may collude to impose additional costs on third parties—here, the minority shareholders. Absent third-party effects, one can trust the buyer and seller to figure out what is best for them.[71] So long as the constraints on private benefits of control are reasonably binding, the likelihood of third-party effects is small and one can leave it to the buyer and seller of control to negotiate terms.[72] In such cases, the seller will sell only if the buyer is better at managing the corporation than the seller, which will benefit the minority. Indeed, because of the difficulties in valuation, the buyer will likely have to be substantially better than the seller.

The key point in the close corporation context is that private benefits of control are restrained by a set of formal and informal sanctions. For example, suppose the trapped minority believes that the planned sale, through one mechanism or another, will itself diminish the value of its investment. One remedy is to sue for a breach of the duty of loyalty. Whether or not the minority wins, such suits raise a red flag for any diligent new person thinking of becoming a controller. The reaction of the potential buyer is now threefold. First, he doubles the due diligence concerning the information provided by the majority. Presumably the disgruntled, frozen-in person might even be helpful here in supplying information. Second, the potential entrant may think twice about buying into a close corporation where the minority is disgruntled. In some circumstances, this may lead the buyer to insist on buying 100 per cent of the corporation. Third, the buyer may react by a standard 'curse on both their houses' and choose to pull his bid entirely or to bargain hard to buy the controller's share at a cheap price. In brief, because of the fewness of numbers, the parties can hurl mud at each other with great effectiveness.

Another consideration figures in as well: the orderly exit of controllers. Sometimes the majority shareholder gets tired of being the majority shareholder, or knows that he has lost his effectiveness. Sometimes, also, the firm is not yet ready to be sold to a third party because the omelet is not yet cooked. How do you make sure that there is someone around to play the role of majority shareholder, with all its burdens and risks? The common law answer may be the legal equivalent to the informal rule in voluntary organizations that you cannot

---

[71] One might also worry that the exiting controller is selling a lemon and the entering controller does not know that. But even if this occurs, the minority is no worse off—instead, it is just as badly off as before. Moreover, this should not be a likely event. Those who buy into an existing close corporation are, in general, likely to be a highly diligent group. Indeed, they are likely to be more careful than the controller who entered at the outset.

[72] This is the core of Elhauge's (1992) channelling explanation for existing doctrine: the looting cases (highly liquid assets—big premium) identify those cases in which the likelihood of collusion between buyer and seller are highest; the free sale cases, by contrast, are situations in which it is difficult for buyer and seller to collude successfully, either because of the nature of the (illiquid) assets or for other reasons.

stop chairing a committee until you find a replacement. Because the omelet is not yet finished, it will be very difficult to convince a third party to take over the omelet business, and it is possible that the majority shareholder will have to take a substantial discount in order to induce a third party to take over. In such cases, the minority shareholders are beneficiaries, not because the buyer will have bribed the controller to leave, but because the controller has bribed the new controller to enter.[73]

If this is more or less right, then the incentive compatible rule in the close corporation context—so long as the prohibition on non pro rata distributions is reasonably well enforced—is the same as in the public corporation context; namely, that absent a shareholders' agreement to the contrary, any shareholder, majority or minority, is free to sell to whomever is willing to buy (except a looter). The buyer, majority or minority, steps into the shoes of the seller and is locked in to the same extent.

This means that in the articulation of the pro rata principle, one must emphasize that it applies to distributions. On this view, the control on diversions of the cash flow does most of the work. Indeed, this may support Elhauge's (1992) argument that the laissez-faire rule is most appropriate for those situations, or, more generally, those systems in which non pro rata distributions are sharply limited, while the equal opportunity rule may better fit those situations in which such distributions are badly controlled.

4.5.5. Minority Shareholders' Informational Rights

In the earlier discussion, we discourage judicial intervention in Cases A and C. In both cases, however, there are potential problems with respect to the minority's access to company information which, if addressed, would strengthen our case. Recall the argument suggested in *Wilkes*: once Minor is terminated, the underlying asymmetry of information will make it untenable to continue as a minority shareholder. This is an important argument, as we have argued that the asymmetry of information associated with a high density of match-specific investments is part of what makes the close corporation form appropriate, and that the overlap between shareholders and managers helps manage that asymmetry of information.

On the one hand, it may be that this untenability is optimal for the parties under the circumstances. Both the high-tech sector and the traditional close corporation sector show that mandatory provisions that provide for the buyback of employee

---

[73] The difficulty of valuation may enter in another way. Because the omelet is only partly cooked, it would be extremely difficult for a court to determine whether the selling majority shareholder got too much—i.e. whether he was paid a 'premium' for control. This may be the reason why courts focus on preventing non pro rata distributions, rather than on measuring the extent to which the majority shareholder was overpaid. But, of course, a rule preventing a majority shareholder from selling control for a premium need not involve judicial valuation: an equal opportunity rule would be as easily implemented here as it was in the *Wilkes* case.

shares upon termination of employment at either cost or book value (easily measured amounts that are often far below actual, pro rata value) are quite common.

But, as the Case B cases indicate, it is not always the case that it is untenable to be a minority non-employee shareholder. Whether, and the extent to which, such a position may be tenable depends, in part, on the extent to which the courts police the norm of non pro rata distributions. This, in turn, depends on the extent to which courts provide for and enforce minority rights to information. Like the enforcement of the norm against non pro rata distributions, enforcing minority informational rights protects the beneficial characteristics of the close corporation form, without dragging the courts into either adjudicating employment-at-will issues or firm valuation.

To operate effectively, however, Minor must know when Major is acting opportunistically. Minor, as either a shareholder/employee or as only a shareholder, has the ability to impose or threaten Major with informal sanctions. When Minor is employed, he has all of the normal methods of sanction that apply to an employee. In his role as a shareholder in a closely held company, Minor also holds considerable power to impose sanctions. But if Minor is either discharged from the company or left employed, but in a non-managerial capacity, he is unlikely to learn the requisite information necessary to know when and how to act.

Minority shareholder information rights come from two sources: state law and federal law. Under state law, shareholders are entitled to substantial information. Delaware corporate law provides:

Any stockholder, in person or by attorney or other agent, shall, upon written demand under oath stating the purpose thereof, have the right during the usual hours for business to inspect for any proper purpose the corporation's stock ledger, a list of its stockholders, and its other books and records, and to make copies or extracts therefrom. A proper purpose shall mean a purpose reasonably related to such person's interest as a stockholder.[74]

As interpreted, title 8, section 220 of the Delaware Code provides minority shareholders of the close corporation with substantial rights to information. First, 'in the case of a close corporation, inspection rights will be liberally construed in favor of a minority stockholder' (Welch and Turezyn 1993: § 220.6.2, at 466). Second, finding out the facts necessary to determine if Major is engaging in self-dealing, or mismanagement, are both clearly 'proper purposes' under Section 220 (ibid.).[75]

The US federal securities laws provide the second principal source of informational rights for minority shareholders. Although close corporations are not subject to the periodic disclosure obligations, section 10(b) of the Securities

---

[74] Del. Code Ann. tit. 8, § 220(b) (1998). Minority shareholders have similar informational rights under the RMBCA §§ 16.01–16.04 (1997).

[75] In addition, minority shareholders who are in litigation with the corporation have substantial rights to information under the civil discovery rules, whether in federal or state court.

Exchange Act and rule 10b-5 apply fully.[76] Rule 10b-5 has proved most important in end-game scenarios. Minor, who is terminating his relationship with the
firm, negotiates to sell his shares back to the firm or to the majority shareholder.
At the same time, unbeknownst to Minor, Major is engaged in serious discussions with a potential acquirer of the firm or with an investment banker who
wishes to take the firm public. Sometime after Minor sells his shares, the acquisition is announced, which places a value on the firm far in excess of what Minor
received. Minor sues, alleging that, had he known of the merger discussions, he
would not have sold his shares. In such circumstances the courts have held that,
when Major is buying out Minor, Major has a duty to disclose all material non-
public information, including negotiations to sell the firm or take it public.[77]

This structure fits well with our previous analysis. Like the vigorous enforcement of the norm against non pro rata distributions, so, too, the enforcement of
these informational rights protects the incentive compatibility of the close corporation form. The state law rights to information help to alleviate (although
clearly not eliminate) the underlying asymmetry of information while Minor is
a shareholder. Major's duty under 10b-5 to disclose material facts or abstain
from buying Minor's shares protects and reinforces the end-game norm: upon
liquidation or merger, shareholders share equally.[78]

---

[76] Under rule 10b-5:

It shall be unlawful for any person . . . (a) To employ any device, scheme, or artifice to defraud,
(b) To make any untrue statement of a material fact or to omit to state a material fact necessary
in order to make the statements made, in the light of the circumstances under which they were
made, not misleading, or (c) To engage in any act, practice, or course of business which operates
or would operate as a fraud or deceit upon any person, in connection with the purchase or sale of
any security. 17 C.F.R. § 240.10b-5 (1997).

On the applicability of 10b-5 to close corporations, even in the sale of the entire business, see
Landreth Timber Co. v. Landreth, 471 US 681 (1985).

[77] See e.g. *Michaels v. Michaels, Michaels and Hyman-Michaels*, 767 F.2d 1185, 1194–97 (7th
Cir. 1985); *Holmes v. Bateson*, 583 F.2d 542, 558 (1st Cir. 1978); *Rochez v. Rhoades*, 527 F.2d 880,
887–88 (3d Cir. 1975); *Thomas v. Duralite Co.*, 524 F.2d 577, 584 (3d Cir. 1975).

[78] There is an additional set of issues that arise when Minor is subject to a mandatory buyback
provision upon termination of his relationship with the corporation. The issue arises whether and
when Major has a duty to disclose news that may be of significance to Minor in deciding whether to
terminate his relationship with the firm. *Jordan v. Duff and Phelps*, 815 F.2d 429, 440–41 (7th Cir.
1987); *Smith v. Duff and Phelps*, 891 F.2d 1567, 1575 (11th Cir. 1990). A related issue is whether such
a mandatory buyback provision should be read to displace the employment-at-will presumption in
the employment relationship. The answer has been negative. See e.g. *Ingle v. Glamore Motor Sales,
Inc.*, 73 N.Y.2d 183, 189 (N.Y. Ct. App. 1989) (mandatory buyback provision does not get share-
holder/employee any protection against at-will discharge). Indeed, in some cases, the buyback provisions explicitly provide that 'nothing herein contained shall confer on the Employee any right to
be continued in the employment of the Corporation'. *Jordan*, 815 F.2d at 446. Finally, the question
also arises whether the firm can fire an employee simply in order to trigger the mandatory buyback
provision. *Gallagher v. Lambert*, 549 N.E.2d 136, 138 (N.Y. 1989) (no breach of fiduciary duty to
terminate minority shareholder triggering mandatory buyback, even if firing is motivated by desire
to take advantage of lower valuation); *Knudsen v. Northwest Airlines*, 450 N.W.2d 131, 132 (Minn.
1990) (stock option agreement that expires when employee ceases to work for employer does not
imply any covenant of good faith termination for cause). Compare the majority opinion of Justice
Easterbrook in *Jordan*, 815 F.2d at 439, with Justice Posner's dissent, 815 F.2d at 446. These issues,
while fascinating, are beyond the scope of this chapter.

4.6. Conclusion

The close corporation form is ideally suited to enterprises in which there is a high density of match-specific assets. The limitations on exit, combined with the rule against non pro rata distributions, largely prevent opportunistic behaviour by the majority shareholder towards the minority shareholder. By locking both into the enterprise, the majority shareholders, in maximizing their own wealth, will, to a large extent, also maximize the wealth of the minority. Indeed, many of the persistent features of close corporations can best be understood as self-enforcing mechanisms to protect the participants from misbehaviour by fellow participants.

This is not to say that all enterprises that use the close corporation form make use of these attributes. An important conclusion of this chapter is that by isolating the distinctive features of close corporations, we identify those enterprises that are best suited for the close corporation form. The enterprises that most value the lock-in are precisely those Silicon Valley start-ups with new products that need time to set. The close corporation, in its best use, thus serves as an incubator for tomorrow's publicly owned corporations.

After examining the extent to which the enterprise form itself constrains opportunistic behaviour by participants, we analysed the classic problem(s) of minority oppression in the close corporation. As we understand it, minority oppression can best be understood as a combination of two separate and separable problems. The first aspect, captured in Case A, is a version of precisely the same problem that, in employment law, arises under the heading of employment-at-will: the situation in which Major terminates Minor's employment. Here we demonstrated that the law, by adopting the same passive stance as it does in the employment context, avoids threatening and undermining the self-enforcing structure in place.

The second aspect of the problem, captured in Case B, is fundamentally different from employment-at-will and involves attempts by Major to make non pro rata distributions of company assets. Here, we showed that vigorous judicial enforcement of a prohibition on such distributions, including the vigorous protection of ancillary rights to information, is necessary to enforce norms of non-opportunism. We further showed that courts are much better at sorting out issues of this sort than employment-at-will issues because doing so does not require either relying on unverifiable factors or valuing assets that the courts are unable to value.

Out of our appreciation of the beauty of the close corporation come several conclusions. First, our analysis implies that the parties themselves, rather than the courts, are best able to resolve the nasty employment issues that animate many bitter close corporation cases. Second, the analysis indicates that vigorous judicial enforcement of the sacred norm against non pro rata distributions is necessary to block the attempts of majority shareholders to profit from self-dealing transactions with the corporation. Finally, with an expanded menu of enterprise forms, there is little cost in allowing the close corporation to maintain its distinctive qualities. Firms that are not waiting for the omelets to set can choose another form that allows easy exit of capital suppliers.

REFERENCES

American Law Institute (ALI) (1994), *Principles of Corporate Governance: Analysis and Recommendations*, St. Paul: American Law Institute Publishers.

Barry, C. B., et al. (1990), 'The Role of Venture Capital in the Creation of Public Companies: Evidence from the Going-Public Process', *Journal of Financial Economics* 27: 447.

Clark, R. (1986), *Corporate Law*, Boston: Little, Brown and Company.

Easterbrook, F. H., and Fischel, D. R. (1991), *The Economic Structure of Corporate Law*, Cambridge, Mass.: Harvard University Press.

Elhauge, E. R. (1992), 'The Triggering Function of Sale of Control Doctrine', *University of Chicago Law Review* 59: 1465.

Fenn, G. W., et al. (1995), 'The Economics of the Private Equity Market' (Board of Governors of the Federal Reserve Staff, Study No. 168, available at http://netec.wustl.edu/WoPEc/data/Papers/fipfedgss168.html).

Gompers, P. A. (1995), 'Optimal Investment, Monitoring, and the Staging of Venture Capital', *Journal of Finance* 50: 1461.

Gorman, M., and Sahlman, W. A. (1989), 'What Do Venture Capitalists Do?', *Journal of Business Venturing* 4: 231.

Hellmann, T. (1998), 'The Allocation of Control Rights in Venture Capital Contracts', *RAND Journal of Economics* 29: 57.

Hetherington, J. A. C., and Dooley, M. P. (1977), 'Illiquidity and Exploitation: A Proposed Statutory Solution to the Remaining Close Corporation Problem', *Virginia Law Review* 63: 1.

Holderness, C. G., and Sheehan, D. P. (2000), 'Constraints on Large Block Shareholders', in R. Morck (ed.), *Concentrated Corporate Ownership*, Chicago: University of Chicago Press.

Johnston, J. (1992), 'Opting In and Opting Out: Bargaining for Fiduciary Duties in Cooperative Ventures', *Washington University Law Quarterly* 70: 291.

Lerner, J. (1994), 'Venture Capitalists and the Decision to Go Public', *Journal of Financial Economics* 35: 293.

—— (1995), 'Venture Capitalists and the Oversight of Private Firms', *Journal of Finance* 50: 301.

—— and Merges, R. P. (1998), 'The Control of Technology Alliances: An Empirical Analysis of Biotechnology Collaborations', *Journal of Industrial Economics* 46: 125.

Mahoney, P. (2000), 'Trust and Opportunism in Close Corporations', in R. Morck (ed.), *Concentrated Corporate Ownership*, Chicago: University of Chicago Press.

Morck, R. (ed.) (2000), *Concentrated Corporate Ownership*, Chicago: University of Chicago Press.

Northwestern University Law Review (1957), 'Symposium: The Close Corporation', *Northwestern University Law Review* 52: 345.

Oesterle, D. A. (1995), 'Subcurrents in LLC Statutes: Limiting the Discretion of State Courts to Restructure the Internal Affairs of Small Business', *University of Colorado Law Review* 66: 881.

O'Kelley, C. R. (1992), 'Filling the Gaps in the Close Corporation Contract: A Transaction Cost Analysis', *Northwestern University Law Review* 87: 216.

O'Neal, F. H., and Thompson R. B. (1985), *O'Neal's Oppression of Minority Shareholders*, Wilmette: Clark Boardman Callaghan.

—— ——(1986, and 1995 Supplement), *Close Corporations: Law and Practice*, Wilmette: Clark Boardman Callaghan.

—— ——(1991), *O'Neal's Oppression of Minority Shareholders: Protecting Minority Rights in Squeeze-Outs and Other Intracorporate Conflicts*, Deerfield, Ill.: Clark Boardman Callaghan.

Rock, E. B., and Wachter, M. L. (1996), 'The Enforceability of Norms and the Employment Relationship', *University of Pennsylvania Law Review* 144: 1913.

Sahlman, W. A. (1990), 'The Structure and Governance of Venture-Capital Organizations', *Journal of Financial Economics* 27: 473.

Thompson, R. (1993), 'The Shareholder's Cause of Action for Oppression', *Business Lawyer* 48: 699.

Thompson, R. B. (1988), 'Corporate Dissolution and Shareholders' Reasonable Expectations', *Washington University Law Quarterly* 66: 193.

Wachter, M. L., and Wright R. (1990), 'The Economics of Internal Labor Markets', in D. J. B. Mitchell and M. A. Zaidi (eds.), *The Economics of Human Resource Management*, Oxford: Basil Blackwell.

Welch, E. P., and Turezyn, A. J. (1993), *Folk on the Delaware Corporation Law: Fundamentals*, New York: Aspen Publishers.

5

Bracketed Flexibility: Standards of Performance Level the Playing Field

CLAIRE MOORE DICKERSON*

5.1. INTRODUCTION

Standards of performance such as good faith and fiduciary duty make bargaining possible. Because standards of performance level the playing field, they enable the more vulnerable party to express its preferences and thus to bargain. The standards have this effect because they are both flexible and precise.

Unfortunately, the standards of performance are under siege in the United States of America and in Europe. While some of the strongest criticism of the standards concerns their vagueness, their flexibility allows parties to negotiate meaningfully and thus to express their preferences. Consequently, far from being sources of distortion, the standards give a voice to those who otherwise would not be heard. To use a political analogy, the standards enable, in the commercial realm, democratic voice. Amartya Sen (1999: 16, 43) champions respect for this voice because no 'functioning democracy' has experienced famine. This is an affirmative reason to have standards of performance.

Although there is general agreement that the standards are flexible, the claim that they are precise is counterintuitive. While there is general acceptance of a floor—that is, of a minimum standard—the common complaint about the standards' vagueness presupposes the lack of a clear ceiling. In fact, actual behaviour supported by law reveals that the standards of performance have an identifiable floor and a self-executing ceiling. By confirming the existence of a floor and a ceiling, I show that the standards are precise within a prescribed range; indeed, further specification would merely destroy the flexibility.

The flexibility of the standards provides the subtlety; their precision provides the predictability. Despite the current challenge to the standards, US law still supports them, and because the standards' flexibility and precision make bargaining possible, business law should continue that support.

* This chapter is based on an article of the same title published in the *Iowa Journal of Corporation Law* (2001) 26: 1001, and on a presentation delivered 18 May 2001 at the conference on the Close Corporation and Partnership Law Reform in Europe and the United States, organized by the Center for Company Law of Tilburg University. My thanks to the Center for Company Law, the faculty of law of Tilburg University, the conference participants, and to the conference sponsors, Linklaters & Alliance, and the Anton Philips Fund. Thanks, also, to research assistant Daniel A. Birnhak, Rutgers Law School, 2003.

5.2. STANDARDS OF PERFORMANCE ARE FLEXIBLE AND DESIGNED TO LEVEL THE PLAYING FIELD

Standards of performance are flexible and designed to level the playing field. They play a larger, more important role than merely to reduce agency costs, the role often used to justify good faith or fiduciary duty (Easterbrook and Fischel 1982: 702). Standards of performance often make the bargain possible.

5.2.1. Levelling the Playing Field

Starting with an analogy to pollution, assume a downstream landowner who values clean water more than the upstream polluter values the right to pollute. Assume further that the downstream owner does not have the money to pay the upstream polluter to clean its effluents. In this context, the downstream owner is powerless. Regulation can level the playing field so that the downstream owner—before regulation, the weaker party—has the power to negotiate meaningfully. The downstream owner then can obtain the clean water that this owner values more than the polluter values the permission to pollute (Markovits 1984: 1176–7, 1194). Standards of performance similarly operate to level the playing field in the context of contracts and of business organizations. They do so by correcting for unequal power and for conflicts of interest.

In order for the standards to level the field effectively, the greater the conflict and inequity of power, the higher must be the applicable standard. The four examples below, two from contract law and two from unincorporated business entity law, reflect this direct relationship between the standards of performance on the one hand, and power and conflict on the other (Dickerson 1995: 979–91). Before beginning our discussion of contract law, note that contract law is relevant to unincorporated businesses in part because contracts play a significant role in the formation of organizations, and in part because of decades of 'nexus of contract' analogies (Jensen and Meckling 1976: 311 n. 3). In an arm's length transaction governed by contract law—that is, on a level playing field—each party is assumed capable of self-defence. In that context, any behaviour to a standard higher than opportunism conforms to contract law's theory of good faith and is appropriate. This result makes sense because neither party can overpower the other, even though their interests can conflict. The relative power equilibrium keeps abuse to a minimum.

In effect, the level of good faith in an arm's length transaction is another way of describing conformity with the parties' expectations. At least in the United States of America, this means an objective perspective with a touch of the subjective: what would a reasonable person in the parties' position expect?

Higher on the graph, the standard of performance reflects the obligations of a contracting party with significant control, for example, a party whose performance is the sole basis for calculating another party's return. Consider the percentage lessee, whose rent obligation depends on the lessee's own sales. Not only does the lessee have commercial power over the lessor because the lessor's return depends on the lessee's performance, but the lessee's interest clearly is in conflict with that of the lessor: if the lessee can maintain profits while pushing sales down, the lessee pays less rent and further increases profits. In the United States of America, that person will be held to a 'best efforts' standard, both because the landlord is at the mercy of the tenant, and because the tenant has an inherent conflict.[1]

Moving up the graph yet farther, we find, for example, the non-managing partner in a general partnership. The other partners would expect some minimum level of honesty and concern for the firm's well-being, but we also know that each partner invests in a firm in order to make profits. Thus, while a partner traditionally has a fiduciary duty of loyalty to the fellow partners, the partner expects (that word again) profits. Although an expectation of profits is a prerequisite to partnership, some degree of self-interest is inherent in the ordinary partnership relation.

There is at the very least a potential conflict for a partner who does not have a role in management, but does have an acknowledged self-interest in acquiring profit. The risk could, for example, become manifest in a situation similar to theft of corporate opportunity: a partner, not involved in management, but still understood to be part of the firm, is informed of an opportunity because of that relationship. The partner, possessing the information, has the power to be a disloyal agent of the partnership and to steal the opportunity instead of taking only the aliquot share through the partnership. Such a disloyal agent breaches the fiduciary duty applicable to partners, a performance standard higher than best efforts (Dickerson 1995: 979–91).

Further up the graph we find the partnership's managing partner in whom the fellow partners are placing their faith. In the classic partnership, not only do the other partners depend on the managing partner's performance in order to maximize the value of their investment in the partnership, but they also rely on that managing partner to avoid activities that would create personal liability for all owners.

Thus, the managing partner clearly has power; specifically, the power to determine the future of the firm as a whole. The managing partner in this way has the power to choose for the firm a transaction in which the managing partner already has a personal interest. This is in addition to the conflict of interest inherent in the managing partner's desire to make a profit through the partnership. In the United States of America, the managing partner is held to a standard

---

[1] See e.g. *Dickey v. Philadelphia Minit-Man Corp.*, 105 A.2d 580, 583 (Pa. 1954) (heightened standard for percentage lessee, except when there is a substantial minimum payment of rent under the lease).

even higher than best efforts, but without denying the managing partner's legitimate desire for a share of partnership profits.[2]

The highest level on the graph for a business organization still is lower than the standard applied to a trustee because the trustee, not the beneficiary, has total control over the corpus, and the trustee's conflict is inherent in that power. The trustee can, as a factual matter, do anything with the corpus, often without the beneficiary being aware and, therefore, is expected to behave selflessly. Indeed, the trustee, contrary to even a managing partner, is expected to take actions detrimental to the trustee if the actions benefit the corpus for the beneficiary.

This schematic description is doctrinally accurate whether the standard technically is good faith, fiduciary duty, or something else entirely—as is the case in some jurisdictions other than the United States of America when, for example, they focus on avoiding duress (Whittaker and Zimmermann 2000: 19, 39, 45). Thus, efforts to reduce the duty in the United States of America by speaking about good faith instead of fiduciary duty may have no practical effect; all that matters is relative power and conflict (Dickerson 1995: 979–91). Titles are less important than reality. Thus, if there is a titular managing partner, but another partner has all the facts regarding a particular transaction, functionally the latter partner's duty rises. By taking into account the transactor's power and conflict, the person owing lower standards in most contexts can actually owe a higher standard in other contexts. This nuanced approach prevents the standards from providing so much protection to the usually vulnerable party that this party acquires excessive power in the particular circumstance. Thus, the standards level the playing field, but they do not overcorrect and tilt the field in favour of the formerly weak.

This flexible standard of performance serves to level the playing field. The standard puts the parties in a position that allows them to bargain meaningfully. It is as though the downstream landowner, by regulation, were awarded the right to be free from pollution. Because the landowner then has an asset (the right) to sell, there is a basis from which the landowner can bargain with the polluter. In this same way, because the flexible standard grants the non-managing partner the right to have the managing partner not abuse its power despite the latter's conflict, the managing partner must engage the other partners. For example, if the managing partner requests permission to compete with the partnership in a particular transaction, the other partners know that they have no obligation to accede to the request, and that the managing partner is under a duty to disclose all information relevant to the negotiation. In this way, the

---

[2] See *Hawthorne v. Guenther*, 917 S.W.2d 924, 934 (Tex. App. 1996) (stating that managing partner owes 'co-partners the highest fiduciary duty recognized by law'); *Heller v. Hartz Mountain Indus., Inc.*, 636 A.2d 599, 603 (N.J. Super. Ct. Law Div. 1993) (holding that managing partner is held to 'strictest possible obligation' to co-partners); *Saballus v. Timke*, 460 N.E.2d 755, 760 (Ill. App. Ct. 1983) (managing partners held to heightened duty).

flexible standard allows the parties to form, in accordance with their true preferences, a contract or even a business organization.

5.2.2. Limited Liability in the Mix

Limited liability, when combined with a reduction of standards of performance, substantially eliminates accountability. The practical consequences are significant because the expansion of limited liability is one of the major changes suggested for unincorporated businesses. Over the past ten years, partnerships in the United States of America have acquired the option of limited liability,[3] and various new limited liability forms have evolved.[4] Thus, limited liability is an inevitable backdrop against which to consider standards of performance; in turn, as seen above, standards of performance make bargaining possible. This expansion of limited liability has not only taken the United States of America by storm, but is also gaining credibility in the United Kingdom, as evidenced by the Limited Liability Partnership statute adopted in 2000.[5]

What is the impact of this burgeoning limited liability on standards of performance? The limited liability of all owners in unincorporated businesses should not perceptibly affect the level of the standards of performance applicable to those owners. This is counterintuitive: limited liability appears principally

---

[3] The original limited liability partnership statute was adopted in Texas in 1991. Tex. Gen. Laws, ch. 901, § 84. See Hamilton (1995: 1065). The limited liability partnership provisions are found in the regular partnership statute. Twenty-eight states, Puerto Rico, and the Virgin Islands, have adopted statutes based on the Revised Uniform Partnership Act (RUPA) (including its 1994 predecessor, substantially similar to the 1997 revision, except for lacking the limited liability partnerships provisions). The National Conference of Commissioners on Uniform State Laws (NCCUSL). Louisiana never adopted any version of the UPA. Twenty-one states still operate under statutes derived from 1914 text.

RUPA provides for limited liability by amending, *inter alia*, § 101(5) to add the definition of the limited liability partnership, § 306(c) to limit liability, and § 1001 to provide for election of limited liability partnership status. States that have not yet adopted the upgrade from UPA to RUPA, but nevertheless wish to authorize the limited liability partnership form, have most importantly amended the liability provisions, in particular UPA § 15. See e.g. NY Partnership Law § 26 (where § 26(a) is identical to § 15 of the UPA, and §§ 26(b)–(d) of the New York Partnership Law provide for the registered limited liability partnership and the extent of any remaining liability).

[4] Other forms different from the classic general or limited partnership, and different from the corporation, have evolved recently. For example, there is now the limited liability company (LLC). See e.g. Uniform Limited Liability Company Act; Del. Code Ann. tit. 6, § 18 (2000). The first LLC statute was adopted in 1977, and the form flourished after 1988 when the US Internal Revenue Service facilitated the form's classification as a partnership for federal tax purposes (Ribstein 1997: 20). Every state now has an LLC statute, and the American Bar Association (ABA) has approved the NCCUSL's Uniform Limited Liability Company Act (Vestal 1998: 450).

Since 1993, a few states have adopted the concept of the limited liability limited partnership (LLLP). Texas and Delaware had an LLLP statute version by 1993. Tex. Rev. Civ. Stat. Ann. Art. 6132a-2.14; Del. Code Ann. Tit. 6, § 17-214. In each case, the state's limited partnership statute was amended to allow a limited partnership to register as a limited liability limited partnership under the state's general partnership statute, thus sheltering even the general partner from personal liability. For a list of states that have adopted an LLLP statute, see Callison (1992: § 30A.05, at 30A-10).

[5] I am, however, dismayed that 2000 UK Limited Liability Partnership statute mentions standards of performance only very indirectly. See Limited Liability Partnerships Act (2000).

to reduce the risk of being a partner,[6] and thus to reduce the damage that a managing partner can inflict on fellow partners. To this extent, it apparently diminishes the managing partner's power, although not necessarily the conflict of interest. Since it appears to reduce power, limitation of liability seems consistent with reduction of the standard of performance owed by a managing partner to fellow partners.

Consider an analogy to corporations formed in the United States of America and, to a lesser degree, in the United Kingdom.[7] Although this chapter discusses only the responsibility of managers who are owners, consider specifically the director of a corporation. In very broad outline, whether or not the director is also a shareholder, the business judgement rule protects that director from liability, absent gross negligence or some form of disloyal behaviour. In other words, the US business form that for the past century has provided owners with limited liability also gives the managers wide latitude.

Nevertheless, the better result—at least for firms that are not publicly held— is to hold an owner-manager to the same high standard of performance whether or not the business limits the liability of owners.[8] We already recognize that a person who is both a manager and an owner should be held to a higher—not lower—standard than a non-manager owner because of the manager's extra power. Although the fact that all owners are protected by the limited liability provisions does appear to reduce the owner-manager's potential impact, consider the effect on that owner-manager directly. An owner that manages one of

[6] Two scholars do argue that, instead, the real purpose of limited liability is to protect the business from the owners' debts (Hansmann and Kraakman, Chapter 2, this volume at 23–31; reprinted from Hausmann and Kraakman 2000: 387–440).

[7] Directors in UK corporations are held to a different standard than are those of US corporations since, generally, disinterested directors of a US corporation can cleanse a transaction and shareholders do not typically have significant input. By contrast, normally shareholders of a UK corporation, rather than its disinterested directors, are privileged to cleanse a transaction, but disinterested directors of UK corporations must receive full, formal notification of a corporate opportunity, and must reject it, before the interested director can take it (DeMott 1999: 245–6, 267–8).

[8] Arguably, publicly held businesses are different, because they tend to reflect a clearer separation of ownership from management, which creates a different problem of agency cost. The separation is attenuated with respect to a shareholder (even a shareholder of a publicly held corporation) who also is a manager. Nevertheless, the corporation cannot as a practical matter be publicly held unless there is significant separation, meaning that the manager-shareholder will tend not to have as much control as the owner-manager of a closely held business. Further, the manager-shareholder of a corporation is more likely than the owner-manager of a closely held business to have diversified financial interests (Easterbrook and Fischel 1989: 1441). There are, of course, a few manager-shareholders of publicly held corporations who resemble owner-managers of private firms, for example, Viacom's Sumner M. Redstone. See *Paramount Communications Inc. v. QVC Network Inc.*, 637 A.2d 34, 38 (Del. 1994) (describing Mr Redstone as the controlling shareholder of publicly held Viacom).

There already is evidence that at least some courts are applying the business judgement rule to managers of limited liability companies, at least when the Operating Agreement incorporates by reference fiduciary duties under applicable corporate law. See *Froelich v. Erickson*, 96 F. Supp. 2d 507, 520 (D. Md. 2000). In any event, because of the defendant's conflict of interest, it would have been an inappropriate case to apply the business judgement rule even if the entity were a corporation. The business judgement rule is not applicable in corporate law when there is a conflict of interest, and thus should not protect an LLC's management in the event of such a conflict (Murdock 2001).

the new limited liability business forms still has the full management authority of a managing partner. Due to the limitation on liability, however, the owner-manager is far less accountable than is the traditional managing partner. First, the owner-manager becomes unaccountable to third parties, beyond any initial investment in the firm. Second, unless subject to a sufficiently high standard of performance, the owner-manager will be unaccountable to fellow-owners as well. With respect to this balance of power, the owner-manager's unaccountability offsets the manager's decreased impact on co-owners who benefit from limited liability.

On the other hand, the standard imposed on the owner-manager should be higher than that applicable to a director who is not a shareholder, because of the inherent conflict in being both an owner and a manager. It makes sense that the schema requires increased responsibility when the manager is also an owner, even in a limited liability entity. Frequently, more passive investors do demand that managers become owners in order to align the managers' interests with those of the non-manager owners. Nevertheless, a higher standard of performance remains appropriate because the combination of management power and ownership still creates a conflict. In any event, aligning the managers' interests with the investors' interests merely increases the probability that the managers act as the non-manager owners would have done. It does not eliminate all situations where the managers have access to an opportunity that, because of their power, they can appropriate. In such a case, these managers can do serious damage even if the other owners are not subject to personal liability.

Doctrinally, standards of performance are flexible, and their flexibility levels the playing field. The standards are effective because their flexibility depends on the transactor's power and conflict. That flexibility even takes into account the owners' limited liability in the modern forms of business organization. On the other hand, the principal threat to the standards' effectiveness is that the salutary flexibility eases into vagueness. As discussed in the following section, these flexible standards do remain effective because they are bracketed by boundaries that protect their precision.

5.3. The Standards of Performance Are Precise and Predictable

To ascertain how precise the standards are, consider both the floor and the ceiling.

5.3.1. The Floor

The principal criticism of standards of performance has focused on the distortions that result when parties are forbidden from entering into a transaction that they both agreed to freely. In other words, if at least one of the parties is prevented from behaving to a standard as low as that to which the parties agreed, this, according to the neoclassical economists, entails a waste of resources (Posner 1998: 104). As the previous discussion of the downstream landowner illustrates, however, the argument fails if the parties were in fact unable to bargain freely, because the resulting agreement does not reflect preferences. The weaker party would have lost the shelter of the standards through the appearance of agreement, but without having truly bargained. Indeed, the standards will not be able to level the playing field unless they can force the parties to conform to a higher standard than that to which they appear to have agreed.

On the other hand, the standards' commendable flexibility may trigger an unintended consequence. Instead of levelling the field, the standards may well tilt it if their contours are so vague as to be unknowable. In this case, prudent parties may be driven by the standards' imprecision to adopt a standard higher than whatever is mandated. This concern about excessively high performance touches on the rule-versus-standard debate articulated brilliantly by Duncan Kennedy twenty-eight years ago (Kennedy 1976). It also touches on the distinction between risk, which is measurable, and uncertainty, which is not (Bernstein 1996: 133, 219). In a way, we are again talking about a by-product of the standards' flexibility, but I will show that the by-product is risk and thus is calculable within a range.

Note that the concept of the floor itself is not in controversy; even the fiercest critics of standards of performance accept some type of floor. Bad faith and opportunism, for example, are universally condemned because they produce inefficient results (Posner 1998: 130–1; Williamson 1985: 64–7; DeMott 1994: 71). Further, this floor is supported by parties' behaviour even without legal intervention. At least where the reputational effects are sufficient, business people do act according to a standard even higher than required by law (Macaulay 1963: 63–4). The actual floor therefore is a behavioural norm (Turner 1991: 4–5), reinforced by the law's articulation of the flexible good faith and fiduciary standards.

Given that there is a floor defined by behaviour, it is sensible to use statutory and judicial pronouncements to support the floor. The potential abuse that falls through the floor is an abuse of power, and a powerful transactor who has a conflict of interest may be unrestrainable by purely extralegal means. The good faith and fiduciary standards discussed above provide a flexible support; the problem is what happens above the floor.

5.3.2. The Ceiling

To assert there is a ceiling above this floor is more controversial. Together with the floor, the ceiling allows the flexible standards of performance to escape vagueness. Not only are the standards defined and limited by power and conflict, and not only are they limited by a floor, but the ceiling, too, increases predictability. The flexibility of the minimum performance requirement may be frustrating, of course, but the frustration is attenuated if the transactor knows the maximum required performance. Those who reject standards of performance most strenuously, asserting that they create distortions, are in fact concerned about overprotection—about a lack of ceiling (Easterbrook and Fischel 1986: 294–5; Ribstein 1993: 54–5). What is the highest level of performance that the law demands in a particular circumstance? Put differently, where is the safe harbour?

If the opponents of standards believe that the sky is the limit, that there is no meaningful ceiling, they are reasonable when they fear an inefficient result. They are reasonable when they fear that, despite the standards' nuanced flexibility, the standards may ultimately tilt the field in favour of the formerly vulnerable party. However, classic doctrine confirms that there is a ceiling, and one that protects both parties while merely levelling the field. For example, while a partner traditionally has an obligation to the co-partners, the partner is nevertheless expected to seek profits and, unlike a trustee, does not have to sacrifice for other partners. This provides a safe harbour. The ceiling is further described by two games taken from a study by behavioural economists Gary Charness and Matthew Rabin (2000).

5.3.2.1. *Behaviour Describes an Observable Ceiling*

In general terms, each game consists of two parts. First, one player in a group has a choice to take a prize or to enter the game. For ease of discussion, I will call each of the first players 'Albert', although the study does not discuss gender. If an Albert chooses to enter the game, he does so by giving the other player, whom I will call 'Barbara', a preordained choice. In the first game (Game One), Albert can take the entire prize, at which point Barbara receives nothing. Astonishingly, 17 per cent of the Alberts act to all appearances hyper-generously and forgo the sure prize. The next surprise is that almost two-thirds of the Barbaras respond to their Albert's generosity in a self-regarding, Pareto suboptimal way.[9]

The Barbaras' grasping response to the Alberts' hyper-generosity is consistent with the traditional game theoretic perspective on the prisoners' dilemma where, in the absence of an infinite time horizon, initial cooperation may well

---

[9] In Game One, A chooses (800, 0) or lets B choose (400, 400) vs. (750, 375) (forty-two participants). Eighty-three per cent of the Alberts chose to keep the full 800 and leave Barbara with nothing, displaying the kind of self-interest that the neoclassical economists have taught us to expect. However, 17 per cent of the Alberts decided to enter the game and thus gave each Barbara the choice of sharing the 800 evenly between Albert and Barbara, or of having Barbara give Albert 750 and keep only 375 for herself. Sixty-two per cent of the Barbaras chose to share 800 evenly (400 to each of Albert and Barbara), instead of sharing a total of 1,125 (750 to Albert and 375 to Barbara) (Charness and Rabin 2000: 29). The Barbaras' decision is Pareto suboptimal because society gains 800 instead of 1,125; it is self-regarding because each Barbara's decision to preserve the last 25 (400 versus 375) would cost her Albert 350 (400 versus 750). The traditional ultimatum game starts from the opposite assumption: Albert acts selfishly, and Barbara punishes him by depriving herself in order to spite him (Jones 2001).

trigger defection.[10] Clearly, this game does not reflect reciprocity, since almost two-thirds of the Barbaras repaid their Albert's generosity by the meanest kind of greed.[11] However, the other game (Game Two) does suggest that the impetus behind the Barbaras' grasping behaviour in Game One is something more than a mere failure to cooperate. The result in Game Two cannot be explained by simply asserting that people in the second half of any game tend to be grasping because Game Two's outcome is very different.

In Game Two,[12] Albert's original choice is either to give Barbara the entire prize and keep nothing or to enter the game. The rational decision for Albert is to enter the game: if he does not enter, he is sure to receive nothing, but if he does enter, Barbara cannot put him in a worse position than receiving nothing, and she could decide to let him share in the prize. Thus, it is unsurprising that all the Alberts decide to enter the game (Kahneman and Varey 1991: 127, 150–1). What is surprising is the Barbaras' response in Game Two: when confronted with an Albert who acts rationally but not particularly generously, more than half the Barbaras respond in the most generous way by giving up the right to receive the entire prize in order to share it with this rational Albert (Charness and Rabin 2000: 29).

In summary, in Game One, when an Albert has acted hyper-generously and forgoes a sure prize, almost two-thirds of the Barbaras respond in a self-regarding, Pareto suboptimal way. In Game Two, when an Albert has acted rationally but not particularly generously, over half of the Barbaras respond very generously. Thus, the Barbaras' grasping response to the Alberts' hyper-generosity in Game One cannot be explained by arguing that people in the second half of any game will tend to be grasping; clearly that did not happen in Game Two.

The authors of the study express puzzlement at the result of Game Two (ibid. 30), but I offer the following explanation that reconciles the seeming inconsistencies between Games One and Two. In many cases, the irrational negotiator succeeds beyond normal expectations because the inherent unpredictability of irrational positions renders that negotiator a particularly formidable and

---

[10] The games do not disclose the time horizon: the Alberts and Barbaras may not have expected further iterations, in which case cooperation would not be expected (Axelrod 1984: 10–11).

[11] The time horizon may not be infinite. Difference aversion is another possible explanation for the Barbaras' greedy behaviour, since a Barbara arguably does not want her Albert to receive more than she does. However, that cannot be the full explanation because, in a dictator game that has Barbara decide only the second part, without Albert's first, generous move, only 38 per cent of the Barbaras, instead of the 62 per cent in Game Two, chose the greedy alternative (Charness and Rabin 2000: 28).

[12] In Game Two, A chooses (0, 800) or lets B choose (0, 800) vs. (400, 400) (thirty-two participants). All the Alberts chose to enter the game: they chose to give up the certainty of receiving nothing, as against the possibility that their Barbara would accept to share the 800. Once in the game, only 44 per cent of the Barbaras were selfish and took the whole 800; over half (56 per cent) of the Barbaras gave up 400 to which they had a right and passed those 400 to their Albert (Charness and Rabin 2000: 30). In Game Two, either choice of Barbara provides society with the same value, i.e. 800.

dangerous opponent (Schoonmaker 1989: 138; Adler and Silverstein 2000: 96). The Barbaras in Game One are confronted with an irrational (albeit hyper-generous) Albert whose irrational behaviour makes him dangerous. Why is he hyper-generous? What will he do next? A majority of the Barbaras respond in a self-protective way. In contrast, the Barbaras in Game Two are confronted with an Albert who is neither particularly generous nor ungenerous, but who is rational and, therefore, predictable. In that context, the Barbaras are less self-regarding.

These games help us think about predictability. They help us analyse the difference between uncertainty, which is unmeasurable, and risk, which is measurable and thus quantifiable. Irrational Albert of Game One represents uncertainty even though he is acting generously; a majority of the Barbaras punish him. Earlier, I noted that the Barbaras, faced with an irrational negotiator, would ask themselves why 17 per cent of the Alberts choose to be hyper-generous; precisely because of this uncertainty, there is no answer to that question. In contrast, Albert in Game Two represents risk, which is predictable and thus quantifiable, and a majority of the Barbaras reward him by sharing the prize.

In short, Albert's hyper-generous behaviour in Game One is higher than any applicable standard of performance, and he has pierced the ceiling. The Barbaras provide the extralegal constraint: if Albert behaves too well he will be punished rather than rewarded because parties seek certainty. Therefore, the standard of performance is self-limiting because, if Albert behaves too well, Barbara's reaction eliminates his incentive to over-perform again. This ceiling simultaneously provides other Alberts with a safe harbour because an Albert who behaves as selflessly as the hyper-generous 17 per cent who entered Game One can be confident that, far from violating a duty to Barbara, he has exceeded every obligation.

To summarize, a majority of Barbaras punish an Albert's irrationally generous behaviour; they reward an Albert's rational, predictable behaviour. Albert in Game One engages in behaviour that is too generous, and almost two-thirds of the Barbaras effect a Pareto suboptimal split that deprives society of value. Importantly, these Barbaras punish each Albert by leaving him with the least possible amount, and thus deprive Albert of far more than the Barbaras' individual gain.[13] The Barbaras' behaviour has defined the Alberts' ceiling.

5.3.2.2. *The Ceiling, Applied*

The challenge is to ascertain how, as a practical matter, the ceiling manifests itself and, together with the floor, describes a standard of performance sufficiently precise to satisfy practical expectations. In short: how do Game One and

---

[13] In Game One, the Barbaras leave each Albert with 400 instead of 750, although each Barbara would have forgone only 25 (from 400 to 375) to have provided her Albert with the extra 350 (Charness and Rabin 2000: 28).

Albert's hyper-generosity manifest themselves in the context of contracts and unincorporated businesses?[14]

In the context of arm's length contracts without special circumstances such as percentage leases, the floor is the familiar absence of opportunism and absence of bad faith, to use two formulations. Moving to the top of the standard of performance: the ceiling is behaviour so aberrant that, to use the objective perspective, a reasonable person in Barbara's position would wonder whether Albert is dangerous. Barbara has no legal basis on which to sue Albert for Albert's generosity, of course, since Albert's hyper-generous behaviour certainly is not illegal. Instead, it is the relationship itself that will control Albert, because his generosity is not reciprocated. Thus, there is a socially constructed, extra-legal constraint on excessively generous behaviour.

Essentially the same result occurs if, for example, Albert is a partner. If Albert as a partner behaves with unexpected selflessness, that behaviour will be contained because the other partners will view it as dangerous and will not reciprocate. We know that a partner traditionally has a duty to benefit the firm, subject to the partner's expectation of profits from the partnership. Imagine a partnership in which Albert has a valuable asset that he is considering contributing to the firm. He also believes that his partner, Barbara, tends to shirk. Thus, he believes that any increase in value of the partnership will in unprovable ways disproportionately benefit Barbara, even if his ownership share increases to reflect his contribution. Barbara's shirking, if proved, would be a violation of her duty to the partnership, and Albert is under no duty to contribute a new asset. What should Albert do?

The doctrine-based recommendation to Albert would in all likelihood be that he should retain the asset. Based on the analysis outlined in this chapter, the result would be the same. However, if he were in a group like the 17 per cent of hyper-generous Alberts in Game One, he would contribute the asset to the partnership in the hope that Barbara would work harder and that both partners could benefit proportionately through the firm. In response, most of the Barbaras would continue to shirk subtly and would derive a disproportionate benefit from the new asset. While Albert has not violated a duty by contributing the asset, his generosity will not be rewarded or otherwise supported, except in the unlikely event that his Barbara's shirking is proved. Thus, unexpectedly generous behaviour is self-limiting. This is how we know that there is a ceiling, and that the ceiling is defined and enforced by extralegal means.

The definition of the ceiling as well as the floor thus is socially constructed; the corollary is that it can be socially destroyed. That definition will be less vulnerable if law encourages it. Thus, it is important to know the extent to which law supports this extralegal ceiling created by behaviour. We already know that

---

[14] It is unnecessary to speak further of Game Two because (1) the game reflects generosity only by Barbara without describing the consequences of Barbara's actions, and (2) the contribution of this game to the analysis here is thus merely to underscore that a Barbara's grasping behaviour in Game One is not purely due to her appearance in the second tranche of the game.

there exists a minimum commercial behaviour and that the law supports the standard of performance's floor by focusing on potentially abusive behaviour. The law tells the party to the contract not to be opportunistic, and it tells the inevitably conflicted partner of the partnership not to abuse the position of power.

In contrast, the law does not directly address the ceiling: it does not tell the party to the contract or the partner (Albert in our examples) not to be too generous. However, it does tell Barbara, once she acquires the choice and thus the power and conflict, not to be abusive, as abuse is defined within the relevant context. She has to take into account how able Albert is to bargain freely, including how diversified Albert is, for example (Easterbrook and Fischel 1986: 274). If Barbara's response falls through the floor of the standard of performance, the law offers Albert protection against abuse. If Game One's Albert gives up the prize because, for example, Barbara fraudulently misrepresented facts, Barbara's behaviour is abusive. Not only is Albert's behaviour not censured, but he will be protected, at least indirectly, because Barbara's behaviour will be punished. On the other hand, if a *compos mentis* but hugely generous Albert turns over the full prize to Barbara, Albert has pushed through the ceiling of required behaviour and will not normally be protected.

Assume, for example, that Albert is a partner and the partnership agreement requires the first distributions of partnership assets to be those stipulated in Game One. Under these circumstances, Albert should be able to keep the full prize; that was the behaviour of 83 per cent of the Alberts.[15] However, when 17 per cent of Alberts hyper-generously enter the game, and Barbara has a choice, she becomes the person with power, acting pursuant to a contract that was entered into properly. Under these facts, when she seizes that choice, Barbara has some potential for liability, depending on the reason why those 17 per cent of Alberts behaved hyper-generously. She is especially at risk if there is a significant question about Albert's competence. Here, the flexibility of the standard applies to Barbara, because Barbara owes a duty to Albert. On the other hand, if Barbara has no liability, she keeps the prize because Albert was hyper-generous, and the law supports the extralegal ceiling on Albert's behaviour. If Barbara does have liability, Albert was in all probability more gullible than hyper-generous.

We can see what has happened: the players describe the maximum standard of performance that, like the floor, varies by context, including the transactor's power. The law, by contrast, does not directly determine what behaviour is the maximum demanded of a transactor. Instead, the law stipulates when the other party's response is abusive. If, for example, Albert's behaviour is generous beyond what is required by law, Game One reveals that this behaviour may

---

[15] Assume for these purposes that, in order to avoid unravelling the standard of performance, the agreement was negotiated and signed in accordance with the same standard of performance applied to operations. At a minimum, we have to know that the parties, including Barbara, intended to enter into this agreement.

encourage Barbara to grab the maximum benefit even at Albert's expense. The fact that Barbara reacts in a brutally selfish manner without liability is an indication within the context provided by law that Albert exceeded the maximum required standard.[16] Thus, the law does indirectly confirm that Albert exceeded the maximum standard of behaviour, and it thus does support extralegal constraints on hyper-generosity, such as those reflected in Game One. In this way, the law supports the extralegal efforts to rein in uncertainty.

5.4. STANDARDS OF PERFORMANCE MUST BE MANDATORY, OR THEY UNRAVEL

Understanding that the standards of performance are flexible and precise, should standards of performance be mandatory, or should these standards instead be waivable? In the United States of America there has been a significant push, partly by statute and partly by judicial decision, to conclude that even default standards are waivable.[17] This is an unfortunate development.

The problem with waivers is that it is precisely when a party is asked to waive protection that the party may be unable to bargain freely. It is deeply ironic that courts are invited to apply the lowest contract-law standard of performance when reviewing a waiver of the highest standard applied to operations. Instead, if the parties purport to agree that neither shall owe heightened duties to the other, that agreement at minimum should be subject to scrutiny on the same level as the duties to be waived. Otherwise, the standard unravels to the lowest applicable level. For example, assume that all partners execute a partnership agreement that allows each to compete freely with the partnership. Even though the agreement itself is a contract, remember that partnership formation, of which the contract is merely an element, is consensual rather than contractual.[18] The agreement thus should be scrutinized as of the time of formation, even though doctrine otherwise rarely admits that even good faith applies to contract formation. The relevant questions are: At the time when the agreement was

---

[16] If Barbara acts abusively, she may actually be liable, but that liability would be based on her own actions, not those of Albert.

[17] The default standards are probably not waivable on a blanket basis, however. Larry Ribstein, a long-time supporter of the contractarian perspective, doubts that full blanket waivers will be permissible even for Delaware LLCs (Ribstein 1999: 445).

[18] See Uniform Partnership Act (UPA) § 6(1) (making no reference to contract); see also UPA § 6(1), cmt., 6 (expressly stating that a voluntary association, but not a contract, is needed for partnership formation); RUPA § 202 (making no reference to contract); UPA § 202, cmt. (discussing intent and noting that what distinguishes a partnership from agency is co-ownership). If co-ownership is the distinguishing factor, then a partnership is not necessarily contractual, because an agency relationship is not necessarily contractual. See Restatement (Second) of Agency § 1 (1984) (referencing consent, not contract); see also UPA § 1, cmt. b (expressly stating that the agency relationship does not require a contract). As the drafters of the evolving Restatement (Third) of Agency confirm, common law still maintains that the agency relationship is not essentially contractual. See Restatement (Third) of Agency § 1.01 cmt. c (T.D. No. 2 2001) (the agency relationship depends on assent and consent; there is no reference to contract).

entered into, were all parties in a position to negotiate freely? And what were the parties' reasonable expectations concerning how a particular provision would be interpreted?

Furthermore, it is important to scrutinize the standards closely, taking into account the context, because the standards are bigger than any one aspect of contract or unincorporated business law. The underlying, interrelated concepts are that behavioural norms provide us with a practical definition of Albert's floor and ceiling, within which the standards' flexibility works its corrective effects. These concepts specify, for example, that the ceiling is located where Albert's action creates uncertainty, and that this extralegal ceiling on Albert's behaviour is supported by the standard of performance the law imposes on Barbara. Unless destroyed by statute, the concepts apply to all relationships within the business organization, not only to operations (already a huge arena). For instance, the concepts apply even to dissolution. Dissolution is a means of exit, and the question of whether a party should be able to exit under specific circumstances is essentially a question of who is behaving abusively—the person seeking the exit or the person seeking to retain control of the business?[19]

The standards have a broad impact on business relationships and permeate our commercial lives. As we learn how norms are formed and supported, we have to consider that we permit unbargained-for abuse when we start from the assumption that all parties are already on a level playing field and that the markets therefore are the proper arbiters of all disputes. Since norms are central to this analysis, we must remember that there is also a feedback effect on society at large. Thus, the norms we embrace in our commercial lives affect those of the greater society.

5.5. CONCLUSION

If the law speaks only in terms of bargains and markets, and assumes, contrafactually, a level playing field, it may well limit effective bargaining. The standards of performance are designed to rectify a pre-existing inequality and to correct the playing field's tilt. They do so by introducing the flexible standard that rises in direct proportion to the transactor's power and conflict of interest. These standards are predictable as well as nuanced. They are subject to both a floor and a ceiling: a floor defined by commercial realities which the law supports directly, and a ceiling (within a range defined by commercial behaviour), which the law supports indirectly.

---

[19] There is a relationship between fiduciary duty and anti-oppression remedies (Rock and Wachter, Chapter 4, this volume, at 103–4; reprinted from Rock and Wachter 1999: 923–4). Some states establish a statutory remedy for certain minority shareholders who have been, *inter alia*, oppressed. NY Bus. Corp. Law § 1104-a. Even a state that provides less protection for shareholders who also are employees on the premiss that the at-will employment doctrine trumps all rights of employees, it recognizes that the absence of fiduciary rights are attenuated by the anti-oppression statute. *Ingle v. Glamore Motor Sales. Inc.*, 535 N.E.2d 1311, 1313–14 (N.Y. 1989).

Our efforts in the United States of America to reduce or even eliminate heightened standards of performance are wrong-headed and should be rejected. Certainly, they should not be exported. Standards of performance that are flexible, but cabined, make efficient bargains possible.

REFERENCES

Adler, R., and Silverstein, E. (2000), 'When David Meets Goliath: Dealing with Power Differentials in Negotiating', *Harvard Negotiation Law Review* 5: 1.

Axelrod, R. (1984), *The Evolution of Cooperation*, New York: Basic Books.

Bernstein, P. (1996), *Against the Gods: The Remarkable Story of Risk*, New York: John Wiley and Sons.

Callison, J. W. (1992), *Partnership Law and Practice: General and Limited Partnerships*, St. Paul: West Group.

Charness, G., and Rabin, M. (2000), 'Social Preferences: Some Simple Tests and a New Model' (Berkeley University, Working Paper, available at http://iber.berkeley.edu/wps/econ/E00-283.pdf).

DeMott, D. (1994), 'Do You Have the Right to Remain Silent?: Duties of Disclosure in Business Transactions', *Delaware Journal of Corporate Law* 19: 65.

——(1999), 'The Figure in the Landscape: A Comparative Sketch of Directors' Self-Interested Transactions', *Law and Contemporary Problems* 62: 243.

Dickerson, C. M. (1995), 'From Behind the Looking Glass: Good Faith, Fiduciary Duty and Permitted Harm', *Florida State University Law Review* 22: 955.

Easterbrook, F. H., and Fischel, D. (1982), 'Corporate Control Transactions', *Yale Law Journal* 91: 698.

—— —— (1986), 'Close Corporations and Agency Costs', *Stanford Law Review* 38: 271.

—— —— (1989), 'The Corporate Contract', *Columbia Law Review* 89: 1416.

Hamilton, R. (1995), 'Registered Limited Liability Partnerships: Present at the Birth (Nearly)', *University of Colorado Law Review* 66: 1065.

Hausmann, H., and Kraakman, R. (2000), 'The Essential Role of Organizational Law', *Yale Law Journal* 110: 387.

Jensen, M., and Meckling, W. (1976), 'Theory of the Firm: Managerial Behavior, Agency Costs and Ownership Structure', *Journal of Financial Economics* 3: 305.

Jones, O. (2001), 'Time-Shifted Rationality and the Law of Law's Leverage: Behavioral Economics Meets Behavioral Biology', *Northwestern University Law Review* 95: 1141.

Kahneman, D., and Varey, C. (1991), 'Notes on the Psychology of Utility', in J. Elster and J. Roemer (eds.), *Interpersonal Comparisons of Well-Being*, Cambridge: Cambridge University Press.

Kennedy, D. (1976), 'Form and Substance in Private Law Adjudication', *Harvard Law Review* 89: 1685.

Macaulay, S. (1963), 'Non-Contractual Relations in Business: A Preliminary Study', *American Sociological Review* 28: 55.

Markovits, R. S. (1984), 'Duncan's Do Notos: Cost-Benefit Analysis and the Determination of Legal Entitlements', *Stanford Law Review* 36: 1169.

Murdock, C. (2001), 'Limited Liability Companies in the Decade of the 1990s: Legislative and Case Law Developments and Their Implications for the Future', *Business Lawyer* 56: 499.

Posner, R. (1998), *Economic Analysis of Law*, New York: Aspen Publisher.

Ribstein, L. (1993), 'The Revised Uniform Partnership Act: Not Ready for Prime Time', *Business Lawyer* 49: 45.

—— (1997), 'Changing Statutory Forms', *Journal of Small and Emerging Business Law* 1: 11.

—— (1999), 'Limited Liability Unlimited', *Delaware Journal of Corporate Law* 24: 407.

Rock, E., and Wachter, M. (1999), 'Waiting for the Omelet to Set: Match-Specific Assets and Minority Oppression in Close Corporations', *Iowa Journal of Corporation Law* 24: 913.

Sen, A. (1999), *Development as Freedom*, Oxford: Oxford University Press (first published by Alfred A. Knopf).

Schoonmaker, A. (1989), *Negotiate to Win: Gaining the Psychological Edge*, Upper Saddle River: Prentice-Hall.

Turner, J. (1991), *Social Influence*, Buckingham: Open University Press.

Vestal, A. (1998), 'Special Ethical and Fiduciary Challenges for Law Firms under the New and Revised Unincorporated Business Forms', *Texas Law Review* 39: 445.

Whittaker, S., and Zimmermann, R. (2000), 'Good Faith in European Contract Law: Surveying the Legal Landscape', in R. Zimmermann and S. Whittaker (eds.), *Good Faith in European Contract Law*, Cambridge: Cambridge University Press.

Williamson, O. (1985), *The Economic Institutions of Capitalism*, New York: Free Press.

PART II
EVOLUTION OF PARTNERSHIPS AND CLOSELY HELD BUSINESSES

6

The Evolving Partnership

LARRY E. RIBSTEIN*

6.1. INTRODUCTION

The recent *Centros* decision[1] raises important questions about the future of European law, particularly the law of business organizations. By characterizing a corporation as eligible for the privileges and immunities of a full-fledged citizen of its state of origin, including the right to establish a branch in a country outside its origin that is subject to home-state law,[2] this decision sets the stage for increased jurisdictional competition for European business law. Although *Centros* does not eliminate the rule that the law of the country in which a firm has its 'real seat' or main office governs its internal affairs,[3] it invites erosion to this doctrine by giving some firms a way to avoid its effect.

Centros might spur regulators either to more aggressive efforts to harmonize European business law or to embrace jurisdictional competition for business law (Ebke 2000). This chapter advocates the latter approach. Focusing on US partnership law, which has developed recently in a setting of open competition among the fifty-one US jurisdictions, this chapter demonstrates that jurisdictional competition is preferable to a regime in which firms must comply with the rules of all states in which they do business, or in which a single lawmaking body provides all the rules.

Until relatively recently, partnership law was uniform across US jurisdictions, all but one of which had adopted the 1914 Uniform Partnership Act almost verbatim. During this stable era of partnership law, the partnership form was characterized by decentralized management directly by the owners, personal liability of members, and dissolution upon dissociation of a member. These features kept partnerships closely held, predominantly family affairs.

But partnership always has contained within it powerful seeds for change. Partnerships have been governed mostly by contract rather than, like corporations, constrained by the concept of state 'creation'. These seeds have now germinated. The stable era of partnership ended in the United States around

* Presented at International Conference on Close Corporation and Partnership Law Reform in Europe and the United States, Tilburg University, 17–18 May 2001.
[1] European Court of Justice, 9 March 1999, C-212/97.   [2] Ibid.
[3] For discussions of the implications of *Centros*, see Ebke (2000); Wymeersch (2000); Gilson (2000).

1988 and was replaced by a period of rapid development and change. Partnership law itself is now non-uniform across US jurisdictions. More importantly, the partnership form itself has split into sub-forms, particularly including the limited liability company (LLC) and the limited liability partnership (LLP), that provide a continuous spectrum of forms.

This recent history in the United States has important lessons for Europe as it embarks on partnership law reform. A single set of business association rules issued by a central planner cannot meet the needs of various types of firms or respond to firms' changing business needs. Central planning is hostage both to inherent limits on human knowledge and foresight and to interest group politics. Rather, firms should be able to pick suitable rules by making both 'horizontal' choices among the various jurisdictions and 'vertical' choices of business forms within jurisdictions. Moreover, more efficient rules can emerge from jurisdictional competition for business formations, and from an evolutionary process in which more efficient forms become more prevalent and less efficient forms fall into disuse (Kobayashi and Ribstein 1999b; Ribstein and Kobayashi 1995). The primary engine of efficiency is parties' ability to contract for the applicable law, including choosing a firm's internal governance rules through choice of state of organization (O'Hara and Ribstein 2000; Ribstein 1993a). There is significant evidence that permitting horizontal and vertical choice of business forms produces efficient outcomes.[4] In particular, the recent rapid changes in partnership and related business forms in the United States discussed above provide a kind of laboratory in which to test the efficiency of various regulatory approaches. New and more efficient legal structures have evolved that regulators could not have envisioned only a few years ago.

Moreover, the 'lock-in' effects that some theoreticians imagined have not impeded the evolution of business forms. Instead of being locked in, inefficient old forms have been swept away. This is the world that *Centros* potentially opens to Europe.

The chapter proceeds as follows. Section 6.2 broadly describes partnerships, contrasting the traditional and new varieties, and partnership with corporation. Section 6.3 discusses the forces that have shaped partnership in the United States, primarily firms' ability to engage in horizontal choice among jurisdictions and vertical choice among business forms. Section 6.4 discusses the evolution in partnership terms wrought by these competitive forces. This process suggests that optimal partnership rules defy top-down theorizing and planning. Section 6.5 presents some implications of the analysis, particularly for present and future European law. Section 6.6 presents concluding remarks.

---

[4] See Section 6.3.3.5.

6.2. THE NATURE OF PARTNERSHIP

This part broadly describes the subject of this chapter. Section 6.2.1 shows that the partnership form, though mutable, is essentially defined by its contrast with the corporate form. Sections 6.2.2 and 6.2.3 broadly describe the beginning and ending points of the evolutionary process described below in Section 6.2, while Section 6.3 provides more detailed descriptions.

6.2.1. Partnership vs. Corporation

Partnership is fundamentally a contractual entity. Courts[5] and commentators (Bromberg and Ribstein 2001b: § 2.05(a)) often describe partnership as proceeding from contract, and as arising from the intent of the purported partners.[6] By contrast, the corporation is often described as a state-created legal 'person'.[7] The most famous expression of that view is in *Trustees of Dartmouth College v. Woodward*,[8] which characterized a British Crown charter granted to Dartmouth College as 'a contract, on the faith of which, real and personal estate has been conveyed to the corporation',[9] and thus entitled to protection under the 'contract clause' of the US Constitution.[10] Constitutional protection came as part of a Faustian deal by which the firm recognized the state (in this case, the Crown) as its creator. According to Chief Justice Marshall, the corporation was a 'mere creature of law',[11] suggesting that it had rights that private contract could not create. This characterization reflects entrepreneurs' early practice of obtaining special state charters that granted permission to incorporate. Special chartering, however, long ago was replaced by general incorporation, in which the state's only involvement in creating the corporation is accepting articles of incorporation for filing.[12]

Although the advent of general incorporation reinforced the view of the corporation as a contract among the parties to the firm, vestiges of the corporate person theory survive through shareholders' limited liability for torts and the special corporate choice of law rules. With respect to tort liability, it might seem that, because the firm's owners cannot insulate themselves from tort creditors solely by contracting among themselves, limited liability is a state privilege, and that the firm is to some extent a creation of the state rather than of private contract. This is inaccurate, since limited liability is simply a feature of a particular

[5] e.g. *Bradley v. Bradley*, 554 N.W.2d 761 (Minn. App. 1996); Bromberg and Ribstein (2001: § 2.05(d)).

[6] *H. T. Hackney Co. v. Robert E. Lee Hotel*, 156 Tenn. 243, 300 S.W. 1 (1927) ('A partnership can only arise by a voluntary contract of the parties').

[7] See Ribstein (1995a) (discussing various constitutional implications of entity view).

[8] 17 U.S. 518 (1819).   [9] Ibid.   [10] U.S. Const. Art I, § 10, cl 1.

[11] 17 U.S. 518 (1819).

[12] For a discussion of the evolution of American corporate law from special to general incorporation, see Butler (1985); Shughart and Tollison (1985).

type of contract.[13] More importantly for present purposes, limited liability provided an excuse for distinguishing corporations from other types of contracts
that did not exist for partnerships. Similarly, the corporate person theory
supports the 'internal affairs' choice of law rule that applies the law of the incorporating state to certain legal issues. Without this rule, corporations would be
subject to the vagaries of enforcement of contractual choice of law. By contrast,
a state-created corporate 'entity', like any other state citizen, is subject to the
protection of the creating state. Again, the apparent distinction between corporations and other contracts, though illusory,[14] shaped the different legal treatments of corporations and partnerships. In short, incorporated firms exchanged
their autonomy as contracts for favours accorded state-created entities. This
gave states some excuse for applying special restrictions on contracting that they
would not apply to ordinary contracts. Partnerships, by contrast, never made
this Faustian deal. Partners traditionally are vicariously liable for debts of the
firm. Moreover, while they can select the law of a particular state to govern their
contract, and in the United States courts normally enforce these clauses,
enforcement is not as invariable as the application of the incorporation state's
rule under the US 'internal affairs' rule (Bromberg and Ribstein 2001b: § 1.04).

Distinctions between partnerships and corporations seem to be diminishing.
Partnership-type businesses such as LLCs and LLPs have limited liability based
on state filings and are subject to corporate-type internal affairs rules (Bromberg
and Ribstein 2003: ch. 6; Ribstein and Keatinge 1992: ch. 13). There is an
increasing trend towards recognition of partnerships as 'entities'.[15] However,
the entity characterization is simply a way to summarize the effect of partnership law for various (although not necessarily all) purposes and does not change
the fundamental nature of partnership.[16] Partnerships remain contractual
despite these corporate trappings (Ribstein 1997b).

---

[13] See Ribstein (1995a: 101–3). By the same token, limited liability is a feature of a creditor's contract with the firm vis-à-vis other creditors. The fact that a state filing is a prerequisite to enforcing
limited liability does not make the term non-contractual, any more than does the filing requirement
for secured credit. Nor does the fact that limited tort liability may create an externality, which is true
of other types of contracts, or that it is infeasible to opt into or out of this rule by private contract,
which reflects Coase's insight that legal rules matter in the presence of transaction costs. See Coase
(1960). Whether or not limited liability involves a special type of contracting problem, see Armour
and Whincop (Chapter 3, this volume) justifies special regulation, the main point in the text is that
regulation cannot properly be justified simply by designating the relationship as 'non-contractual'.

[14] See Ribstein (1993a) (comparing enforcement of contractual choice of law for corporations
and for other types of contracts).

[15] See e.g. Revised Uniform Partnership Act (RUPA) (1994: § 201).

[16] For a discussion of the many cases applying both entity and aggregate characteristics of partnership, see Bromberg and Ribstein (2003: § 1.03). It is not clear the extent to which RUPA § 201 will
change the results in these cases. For a criticism of the RUPA provision on this basis, see Bromberg
and Ribstein (2001: § 8.201).

6.2.2. The Traditional Partnership

Although partnerships have remained true to their basically contractual nature, the specific rules of partnership have changed significantly. That change and its explanations are the focus of this chapter. The basic model of the partnership set forth in the Uniform Partnership Act (UPA) is for a very closely held and informal firm. Each partner has by default an equal power to control the business and to share in profits, irrespective of his capital investment.[17] Thus, each partner is both a co-principal and an agent in a principal–agent relationship. As an agent, a partner can bind the business to acts within the scope of the agency,[18] while, as a principal, a partner is personally liable for the acts of the firm's other partners and employees.[19] It follows from their role as co-principals that each partner can veto important acts, such as amending the partnership agreement and admitting new partners.[20] It follows, in turn, from these significant management powers and partner liability that partners cannot freely transfer all of their partnership rights,[21] and instead exit by cashing out of or liquidating the firm, in either case through at least a technical dissolution.[22]

6.2.3. The New Partnership

Many of these basic default rules have carried over into modern US law, including the Revised Uniform Partnership Act of 1994 (RUPA), but with some important modifications. Partners now can limit the agency power of non-managing members, at least in real estate transactions.[23] The partners' personal liability for the debts of the firm has been qualified by requiring creditors to first exhaust partnership assets, even in tort cases.[24] Exit provisions have been significantly revised to eliminate the absolute requirement of dissolution upon partner dissociation.[25]

Even more important than these changes in general partnership law, the partnership form has split into other forms. This, in effect, reserves general partnerships only for the most informal relationships. LLCs, while having many partnership characteristics, have the 'corporate' features of limited liability, an option for centralized management and, under many statutes, even restrictions on dissociation of members (Ribstein and Keatinge 1992). LLPs are essentially general partnerships with limited liability. This allows firms to eliminate vicarious liability, while retaining the general partnership form, which may be advantageous in complying with regulation and facilitating transition from general partnership.

---

[17] See Uniform Partnership Act (UPA) (1914: § 18(a), (e)).   [18] Ibid. §§ 9–14.
[19] Ibid. § 15.   [20] Ibid. § 18(g), (h).   [21] Ibid. § 27.   [22] Ibid. §§ 29–31, 38.
[23] See RUPA § 303.   [24] See ibid. § 307.
[25] See ibid. § 103 (permitting partnership agreement to waive provisions of act except for those listed); § 801 (providing for continuation of the firm in certain situations). See Section 6.4.5.

As discussed below, these changes resulted from jurisdictional competition in the US federal system, and have made the partnership form more adaptable to business needs.

6.3. COMPETITION AND CHANGE

This section discusses the principal force that produced the changes discussed above—jurisdictional competition within the US federal system. As I have discussed previously (1998d), other forces also play a role in change, particularly contractual avoidance and external shocks such as tax law changes. This chapter emphasizes jurisdictional competition in order to focus on the potential effects of the *Centros* case. Sections 6.3.1 and 6.3.2 distinguish two forces of jurisdictional competition—'horizontal' choice among jurisdictions, and 'vertical' choice among the various business forms available in each jurisdiction. Section 6.3.3 discusses the effects of competition, particularly including eroding formerly mandatory state and federal rules. Section 6.3.4 discusses the non-trivial regulation that survives competition. These limits on firms' ability to avoid mandatory rules indicate that jurisdictional competition is a dynamic process that confines regulation but does not eliminate government's power to regulate efficiently.

Before beginning this analysis, it is important to note the significant difference between the horizontal and vertical choice discussed here and an alternative 'menu' approach to business association statutes that offers firms choices with respect to each of several issues. Although jurisdictions might compete to provide different menus, menu options in themselves are not comparable to horizontal choice because a single rulemaker determines the options. Nor are menus comparable to vertical choice, since menu options arise in a single business form rather than offering choices among distinct business forms. This issue relates to the costs and benefits of 'linkage', discussed below.[26]

6.3.1. Horizontal Choice

Horizontal choice arises in the United States because firms at low cost can choose the rules that govern their internal structure by organizing under the rules of any 'incorporation' state while doing business or locating assets in one or more 'host' states. Thus, horizontal choice arises by contract alone, unconstrained by the firm's location. Firms' ability to contract for any state's internal rules prevents states from imposing strong and costly regulation on firms' internal structure. While this rule initially applied mainly to corporations, more recently it has spread to unincorporated firms such as the LLC and LLP, which permit corporate-type choice through filings in the state of organization.[27] Until

---

[26] See Section 6.4.8.
[27] See RUPA § 106, which is subject to contractual variation pursuant to ibid. § 103.

relatively recently, general partnerships had less flexibility because they were subject to general choice of law rules and the Uniform Partnership Act had been adopted in fifty of the fifty-one US jurisdictions. However, general partnership has moved closer to other business associations with the promulgation of the Revised Uniform Partnership Act in 1994 by the National Conference of Commissioners on Uniform State Laws, and the spread of LLP provisions. RUPA introduced to US partnership law both non-uniformity and explicit recognition of contractual choice of law.[28] LLP provisions, which have been adopted in every state and were added to RUPA in 1997, accelerated these changes by permitting general partnerships to select the governing state law through corporate-type filings.

Because this chapter seeks to offer lessons from the United States for Europe, it would be useful to describe briefly the conditions that create jurisdictional choice. To begin with, it has been thought that constitutional protection under the Commerce, and Privileges and Immunities clauses in the US Constitution enabled interstate competition for corporate governance (Butler 1985; Shughart and Tollison 1985). But the Constitution has played a smaller role in facilitating this competition than these commentators suppose. Because corporations are artificial persons they are not protected by the Privileges and Immunities Clause.[29] Thus, their ability to do business outside their states of incorporation under the formation state's rules, including rules regarding limited liability, depends solely on comity between host and incorporation states rather than on the Constitution.[30] Nor does the 'dormant Commerce Clause'[31] in the US Constitution support horizontal choice. Although the Clause theoretically might be interpreted to compel a state to enforce a firm's internal rules in order to permit it to do business in several states, in fact states can protect local creditors and shareholders and other internal interests as long as they do not discriminate against foreign corporations (Ribstein 1993a: 287–94). Finally, the Full Faith and Credit Clause of the US Constitution[32] does not in itself require states to give full effect to other states' laws, as distinguished from judicial decrees or other state acts.

More critical to horizontal competition in the United States are the constitutional rules, cultural, and institutional factors that provide an environment

---

[28] See RUPA § 103(b)(9), 106(b) (providing that any such filing supersedes any contradictory choice of law selected in the agreement).

[29] See *Paul v. Virginia*, 75 U.S. (8 Wall.) 168, 181 (1869) (corporations are 'mere creation of local law' and therefore have no constitutional right under the privileges and immunities clause to do business outside their states of incorporation).

[30] By contrast, the European constitution applied in *Centros* characterizes a corporation as eligible for the privileges and immunities of a full-fledged citizen of its state of origin.

[31] See U.S. Const. art I, § 8, cl 3 (providing that Congress has the power '[t]o regulate Commerce . . . among the several states . . .').

[32] See U.S. Const. art IV, § 1 (providing that '[f]ull Faith and Credit shall be given in each State to the public Acts, Records, and judicial Proceedings of every other State. And the Congress may by general Laws prescribe the Manner in which such Acts, Records and Proceedings shall be proved, and the Effect thereof').

conducive to interstate competition (Kobayashi and Ribstein 1999a). The Commerce Clause at least forbids states from imposing trade barriers against out of state firms by discriminating against them merely because they are not incorporated locally. More basically, firms are subject to constitutional protections such as due process wherever they do business in the United States. Apart from the Constitution, firms can do business in every state under the same basic legal institutions and language. Thus, firms' mobility is not inhibited by significant variations in the business environment among the states.

The ability to do interstate business, in turn, gives host states incentives to recognize incorporation state rules. Interest groups in each state stand to gain or lose in the resulting interstate competition. Accordingly, they push for rules that make their jurisdictions inviting to, or at least do not repel, interstate firms (Kobayashi and Ribstein 2001b). In particular, lawyers gain from promoting use of the state's courts and of their own expertise as business planners.[33] State legislators may therefore stand to gain more from welcoming interstate firms and offering them friendly terms than by appeasing groups that would gain from the application of local law.

A Europe governed by a strong application of the *Centros* decision is both more and less conducive to jurisdictional competition than the United States. It is more conducive in the sense that it offers constitutional protection for foreign incorporation. On the other hand, it is less conducive because the basic structures such as common language and institutions make it harder for multijurisdictional firms to operate in Europe than in the United States. This difference makes constitutional protection of foreign incorporation even more important in Europe than in the United States. Moreover, as discussed below in Section 6.4, this difference ultimately may prevent US-style jurisdictional competition from arising in Europe and necessitate changes in how the competition model should be applied in this context.

6.3.2. Vertical Choice: Choice of Form

Firms can choose rules not only from among states, but also within states from among a variety of business forms. A multiplicity of statutory forms provides different sets of default rules for different types of firms, which are valuable where the costs of customized contracting are high (Ribstein 1995d). Among other things, these rules serve to form the basis of interpretive networks of rules (Klausner 1995; Ribstein 1995d: 378). Although private organizations can generate forms, statutory promulgation is often helpful in generating networks and in providing enforcement mechanisms (Ribstein 1995d: 378–80).

Multiple business forms are beneficial because they offer alternative coherent bundles of rules for different types of firms (ibid. 380–3). The traditional part-

---

[33] See Ribstein (2001c, 1994); Macey and Miller (1987) (discussing lawyers' role in corporate context).

nership form discussed above offers one such bundle in the sense that strong co-management and dissolution-at-will naturally complement partners' personal liability.

Even more importantly for present purposes, multiple forms within each state provide an additional dimension of regulatory competition that can break down inefficient mandatory rules. Thus, multiple forms offer opportunities for regulatory arbitrage.[34] Consider, for example, the role of multiple business forms in facilitating moves from mandatory fiduciary duties to enforcement of fiduciary waivers, or from vicarious partnership liability to limited liability. Legislators may resist such moves either because of opposition from strong interest groups such as trial lawyers or because of genuine policy concerns about the costs of permitting free bargaining. But permitting the move in one of several standard forms may not trigger the same level of opposition because the rule will apply only to firms that are willing to incur the switching and other costs of adopting favourable business forms,[35] and therefore are most likely to be benefited by the rule. In this way, partnership-type business forms can be used as proving grounds to test increased flexibility in internal governance rules.[36]

6.3.3. Effects of Choice

This subpart discusses the effects of horizontal and vertical choice in eroding mandatory rules and contributing to the evolution of the partnership form. Sections 6.3.3.1 and 6.3.3.2 discuss erosion of state and federal rules. Section 6.3.3.3 discusses the advantages of offering different forms for different types of firms. Section 6.3.3.4 shows that choice does not have to lead to chaos, but instead may lead to convergence on uniform rules where this is efficient. Finally, Section 6.3.3.5 shows evidence of the effectiveness of choice of law and choice of form notwithstanding the 'lock-in' effect some commentators have feared.

6.3.3.1. Erosion of State Restrictions

There have been two eras in which horizontal competition among states and vertical competition among forms eroded traditional restrictions on the internal structure of business associations. Innovations spread from single states and business forms, leading to a gradual process of nationwide recognition. These developments demonstrated the power of horizontal and vertical competition in breaking down state-imposed barriers to contractual freedom.

In the first era, competition broke down the practice of special chartering involving state legislators' sale of charters to individual firms. Beginning with

---

[34] See Huang and Knoll (2000: 190) (discussing regulatory arbitrage as a respect in which capital structure adds value to the firm).

[35] See Section 6.3.3.5.

[36] See McCahery and Vermeulen (Chapter 7, this volume) (discussing the possibility of regulatory arbitrage in Europe through the introduction of a new LLC business form).

New Jersey and Delaware, states passed general incorporation statutes, and firms formed under these statutes gradually were recognized in other states.

The second era is the recent history of the partnership form. Even after the spread of general incorporation, closely held firms that wanted limited liability had to be satisfied with unaccommodating corporate default and mandatory rules. Centralized management through a board of directors, restricted transferability of ownership interests, voting according to ownership interests, and continuation of the firm following a member's exit all are unsuited to closely held firms. Corporations' contracts for partnership-type governance rules were sometimes strictly interpreted or simply not enforced (Ribstein and Letsou 1996: ch.5). While states adopted statutory and judicial rules for so-called 'incorporated partnerships', firms that adopted such forms remained exposed to the default rules of the chosen corporate form beyond the specific partnership-type provisions they agreed to.

The logical response to this situation was giving firms the option to adopt partnership-type business forms that included limited liability. But US tax law reduced the benefits of adopting limited liability partnership-type forms by essentially applying two-tier corporate taxation to such firms. The next section discusses the change in federal tax law that accommodated the development of partnerships with limited liability. That change unleashed state competition regarding partnership-type limited liability forms. The LLC spread rapidly from two states in 1988 to all fifty-one jurisdictions only six years later. As LLCs evolved, they became more flexible and better adapted to closely held firms' needs.[37]

These new forms not only brought new flexibility in themselves, but also helped loosen the rules of existing forms. States developed LLPs and changed the older limited partnership form. Moreover, the greater contractual freedom permitted in the partnership form appears to be spreading back to the traditionally more constrained corporate form. Some states, particularly Delaware, recognized the contractual nature of partnership by passing statutes that explicitly provided for enforcement of broad fiduciary duty waivers.[38] This provided a precedent for dropping restrictions on corporate waivers (Ribstein 1991b).[39]

6.3.3.2. Erosion of Federal Rules

A federal system subordinates state law, in some respects, to federal law. This would seem to significantly constrain state competition.[40] However, it is

---

[37] See Section 6.4.

[38] The first such statute was appended to Delaware's limited partnership statute. See 6 Del. Code. § 17-1101(c)–(d).

[39] Indeed, one possible result is Delaware's recent authorization of charter provisions permitting contracting with regard to corporate opportunities, similar to provisions in LLC and partnership statutes. See Delaware General Corporation Law, § 122(17).

[40] Viewed more positively, federal law can be viewed as providing a vertical dimension of jurisdictional competition that constrains inefficient state law. See Breton and Salmon (2001).

important to keep in mind that state law often defines the terms and the contexts in which federal law operates. Thus, changing state rules can reduce the impact of federal constraints.

A good example of this process concerns federal tax constraints on state business forms. Federal tax law once restricted the availability of limited liability by using this feature as an important part of the test for whether a firm was eligible for the corporate tax.[41] Although the Internal Revenue Service (IRS) nominally applied a four-factor test that required at least two corporate characteristics in addition to limited liability to hold that a firm was a tax 'corporation', it had signalled that limited liability alone could cause a firm to be considered a corporation by initially proposing that the first LLCs be taxed as corporations.[42]

While the IRS was pondering LLCs, state legislatures and businesses were changing the limited partnership form (Ribstein 1995d).[43] Businesses formed limited partnerships with corporate general partners, thereby giving them virtually complete limited liability. Also, state legislatures eroded the 'control rule' pursuant to which limited partners who participated in control took on the personal liability of general partners. This forced the IRS to make increasingly fine distinctions in order to maintain the tax distinction between corporations and partnerships. It had to choose between greatly broadening the corporate tax and making official what the changes in the limited partnership form now implied. In 1988 the IRS chose to classify a Wyoming LLC as a partnership for tax purposes.[44] This led to the rapid development and spread of LLC statutes,[45] and the development of the LLP (Ribstein 1995b, 1996).

[41] For a discussion of the policy arguments for basing tax classification on limited liability and a history of the erosion of this approach, see Maine (2000). For arguments against this approach to tax classification, see Ribstein (1992). Maine notes that the IRS ultimately accepted a broader-based entity approach to classification that led to reduction and eventual elimination of a limited liability test, but does not explain why this occurred.

[42] See 45 Fed. Reg. 75,709 (1980). Although the Service later withdrew the regulations (see I.R.S. News Release IR-82-145 (16 Dec. 1982); I.R.S. Announcement 83-4, 1983-2 I.R.B. 30 (14 Jan. 1983)), it issued a private letter ruling classifying an LLC as a corporation (Priv. Ltr. Rul. 83-04-138 (29 Oct. 1982)) and decided that it would not issue additional private rulings concerning LLC classification (see Rev. Proc. 83-15, 1983-1 C.B. 676).

[43] This activity was at least partly attributable to the Tax Reform Act of 1986, which, among other things, caused top corporate tax rates to exceed top individual rates and eliminated the lower tax on 'capital gains'.

[44] Rev. Rul. 88-76, 1988-2 C.B. 361.

[45] A court recently noted the effect of the change in tax classification rules on the development of LLC law. See *In re Garrison-Ashburn*, L.C., 253 B.R. 700, 706-7 (Bankr.E.D.Va. 2000): the Virginia statutory requirement that prevented the continuity of life corporate attribute from attaching to Virginia limited liability companies necessarily permitted events over which the company had no control to jeopardize its very existence, potentially in the prime of its economic life. With the change in the IRS regulations, it was no longer necessary to avoid this corporate attribute. Potentially serious problems could be avoided by eliminating dissolution upon enumerated unforeseen events. As of 1 July 1998, a Virginia limited liability company may have, effectively, perpetual existence. The same Act that gave Virginia limited liability companies perpetual existence also added § 13.1-1040.1, which addressed events causing a member's dissociation. The events that previously led to the dissolution of the company now result in the member's dissociation.

6.3.3.3. Variation and Adaptability

Increased choice of form not only eroded federal and state restrictions on form, but also allowed firms to customize their contracts to suit their individual needs. As discussed in more detail below, the currently available range of business forms suits firm-specific preferences in such respects as degree of formality and centralization of management. State laws offering several different sets of default rules allow a firm to adopt a set of rules that is coherent in the sense that the different rules work together, that invites efficient gap-filling by courts, and that helps ensure efficient application of regulatory provisions (Ribstein 1995d: 380–3). This permits more efficient matching of default rules with various types of firms.

Consider, for example, the choices offered by the three leading business forms. The general partnership form suits very closely held firms managed directly by their owners not only in terms of its default management rules,[46] but also its rules regarding owners' power to bind the firm.[47] In contrast, in limited partnerships management and control are sharply separated, as exemplified by the limited partnership 'control rule', which penalizes limited partners who participate in management.[48] The LLC falls between these extremes, offering a choice between centralized and decentralized management, multiple sets of fiduciary and agency rules to suit both options, and more ambiguous treatment under regulatory statutes (Ribstein and Keatinge 1992; Ribstein 1995b).

6.3.3.4. Evolution of Business Forms

The important question about the erosion of regulation and the variations in state statutes is whether these changes efficiently meet firms' needs. Some might argue that, on the 'supply side' of regulation, legislators are not adequately motivated to make efficient changes because this does not serve the objectives of powerful interest groups. Indeed, powerful groups might actively oppose changes that erode existing regulation these groups favour. Others might argue that there is a 'demand side' problem in the sense that firms will be impeded from making choices among laws and forms that optimally suit their needs because they are locked into existing forms. Still others might claim that state competition will produce a 'race-to-the-bottom', where firms perversely choose statutes that are socially inefficient, perhaps because they hurt creditors.

Several arguments support the proposition that business forms will evolve efficiently. First, with respect to the role of interest groups, there is strong reason to believe that lawyers can be the engines of efficiency. Transactional lawyers have much to gain from promoting efficient business laws in their states. Such laws give firms incentives to physically locate in the enacting state and to hire local lawyers who are proficient in local law. The potential free-rider problem is ameliorated by state lawyer licensing laws that exclude lawyers from

---

[46] See UPA § 18; RUPA § 401.   [47] See UPA § 9; RUPA § 301.
[48] See Revised Uniform Limited Partnership Act (RULPA) (1985: § 303).

some of the benefits of practising under a law of a state in which they are not licensed and by the fact that lawyers earn individual reputational benefits from participating in law reform efforts (Ribstein 2001c). These factors help solve the 'supply-side' of regulation by giving a particular interest group the incentive to drive efficient law reform.[49]

A second argument for efficient evolution is that, as Armen Alchian (1950) has observed, even if legislators lack knowledge, motivation, and foresight to supply efficient laws, such laws may nevertheless emerge through the 'adaptive mechanism' of the marketplace. Evolution through experimentation is consistent with Hayek's (1939) observation that 'if left free, men will often achieve more than individual human reason could design or foresee' (Alchian 1950; Vihanto 1992: 416). These insights are relevant to both common law (Rubin 1977) and statutory law (Kobayashi and Ribstein 1997). In other words, it is necessary to look beyond the actions of individual participants in the process to the outcome of the process itself. For example, although particular firms or interest groups caused enactment of the first LLC and LLP statutes,[50] these statutes are best viewed merely as mutations that spurred the evolutionary process. The ultimate form and success of LLCs and LLPs depended on the ensuing process of jurisdictional competition rather than on the circumstances in which these business forms were born.

Third, there are strong arguments against 'lock-in' or 'path dependence' as constraints on efficient evolution of statutory forms. These terms can be taken to refer to individuals' or firms' inability to adopt terms that, but for lock-in, would optimally suit their needs.[51] The most coherent explanation of lock-in is 'network externalities', which holds that, because individual economic actors do not internalize all 'network' benefits, the most efficient products are not necessarily the ones that succeed in the market (Farrell and Saloner 1985: 71–2; Katz and Shapiro 1996). This theory has been applied to business association standard forms, which depend on networks of users to create beneficial features such as case law and expertise (Klausner 1995). But there are several problems with this theory. Among other things, it is not clear what should be considered an 'externality', since market actors can internalize the benefits from creating networks, and it will rarely be clear whether a product or business form has failed because of its inherent defects or because of network externalities.[52]

---

[49] For writers who have noted the supply-side problem, see Cumming and MacIntosh (2000); Tjiong (2000) (noting the absence of an appropriate political 'feedback mechanism' to translate firm mobility into optimal regulation).

[50] In the case of LLC statutes, a single firm, Hamilton Brothers Oil Company, and its lawyers and accountants, caused the adoption of the initial Wyoming statute. For accounts of the history of the LLC, see Carney (1995); Goforth (1995); Hamill (1998). LLP statutes were instigated to protect Texas law firms against liability in connection with the collapse of savings and loan institutions. See Bromberg and Ribstein (2003: § 1.01); Fortney (1997); Hamilton (1995).

[51] For discussions of alternative meanings of lock-in, see Liebowitz and Margolis (1995); Ribstein (1998d); Roe (1996).

[52] For a summary of alternative explanations for apparent network externality phenomena, see Kobayashi and Ribstein (2001a).

Fourth, a race-to-the-bottom is unlikely to occur with respect to closely held firms. Unlike publicly held corporations, legislators would not be competing for franchise fees.[53] Indeed, it has been argued that, because of this, there would be inadequate supply-side competition to provide closely held business forms (Ayres 1992). But as noted above, transactional lawyers help drive this competition, and they do not have strong incentives to promote business forms that hurt creditors. Moreover, the strong trial lawyer bar has incentives to protect their tort creditor clients.

Apart from theory, the recent history of unincorporated business forms in the United States strongly supports efficient evolution through horizontal and vertical choice. First, and perhaps most strikingly, the LLC form has evolved rapidly since 1988 into a dynamic entity offering such features as flexible management and corporate-type continuity, rather than locking in the early Wyoming version of the LLC, which was based closely on the limited partnership (Kobayashi and Ribstein 2001a; Ribstein 1995d).

Second, LLC statutes have spontaneously evolved towards uniformity with respect to the types of provisions for which uniformity is most efficient.[54] This compares favourably with the effects of the 'official' Uniform Limited Liability Company Act promulgated by the National Conference of Commissioners on Uniform State Laws (Ribstein and Kobayashi 1995).

Third, there is evidence specifically refuting the role of network externalities in the development of unincorporated business forms. The LLP is very similar to the LLC except that it is designed to overcome network effects by permitting partnerships to access the existing network of general partnership case law and forms while opting into limited liability. If network externalities really did impede efficient evolution, partnership-type firms likely would opt for the LLP rather than the LLC form. In fact, the opposite has occurred, and firms' choices between forms depend on state-specific regulatory and tax considerations rather than network effects (Kobayashi and Ribstein 2001a).

This evidence suggests what might happen in a post-*Centros* Europe in which firms have greater ability to make horizontal and vertical choices. Indeed, there is direct evidence against a race-to-the-bottom in both Europe and the United States showing that firms tend to choose high-quality securities regimes even when they can choose lower-quality regimes.[55]

---

[53] For the leading franchise-fee-competition explanation of corporate law, see Cary (1974).

[54] See Kobayashi and Ribstein (1997). For example, uniformity would be most efficient in transactions involving third-party creditors who deal with many different firms and therefore face high potential information costs of sorting out the rules applicable to each firm.

[55] See Choi (2001) (showing that firms that had been sued under the securities laws and investigated by the Securities and Exchange Commission (SEC) tend to make US-regulated securities offerings rather than foreign offerings, indicating that they are using the US federal securities laws to allay investor mistrust); Jackson and Pan (2001: 691) (finding that the market demanded more securities disclosures than required by the minimum standards in EU directives and noting that 'market developments in European capital markets to date do not offer support to critics of regulatory competition who claim that the issuer choice proposals would prompt a race to the bottom in international securities regulation').

All of this is not to say that business forms that evolve from horizontal and vertical choice necessarily are optimal. Firms may encounter some friction, including the effect of local regulations that firms can avoid only by locating their physical business elsewhere, that may limit firms' mobility enough to prevent development of optimal forms. For example, law firms necessarily are subject to ethical rules of the profession that apply in each state in which the firm practises. This keeps firms from avoiding inefficient ethical rules, such as rules that restrict non-competition agreements and that therefore would help prevent opportunistic exit (Hillman 2001; Ribstein 2001a). The main point for present purposes is not that evolution operates perfectly, but that offering some jurisdictional choice is likely to yield more efficient results, at least in the context of business forms, than rules promulgated by a single rulemaker.

6.3.3.5. Competition and Regulation as a Dynamic Process

Critics of federalism might argue that many of the effects described in Section 6.3.3.4 are inefficient, particularly including the erosion of federal and state regulation. However, it is important to keep in mind that erosion and evolution do not sweep away all regulation. With respect to state regulation, for example, professional firms must comply with substantial local regulations even if they can operate under the 'internal affairs' rules of any state's business association statute.[56] Avoidance of regulation involves such difficulties as choosing contractual terms that would not be optimal but for the regulation, the need to vote and revise existing agreements when switching forms, and the extra costs of organizing under the law of a favourable jurisdiction and then doing business as a 'foreign' firm in the home state. Thus, regulation will continue to be effective even with jurisdictional choice except to the extent that firms derive strong net benefits from avoiding the regulation even taking into account market constraints. Moreover, it is important to keep in mind that firms have market-based incentives to serve customers' needs even if they legally could adopt the rules of a lax jurisdiction.

6.4. The Output of the Process: The Elements of Partnership

This section discusses the specific effects of the processes described in Section 6.3. It shows the extent to which partnerships have been engaged in a continuous process of change that has increased partnership-type business firms' adaptation to firms' needs. The following subparts review features of the general standard partnership form introduced in Section 6.2 and show both the theoretical uncertainty concerning what these features should look like and how experimentation in the 'laboratory' of state laws has responded to this uncertainty.

---

[56] This will also be true under *Centros*, which explicitly preserved a role for professional regulation.

6.4.1. Partner Liability

The default rule for US partnerships still is vicarious liability of partners for the firm's debts.[57] This reflects partners' incentives as profit-sharers and co-managers to monitor the firm and the potentially high moral hazard from limited liability when owner-managers deal with creditors.[58] Since creditors in these circumstances usually would demand personal guarantees from owners,[59] making vicarious liability the default rule for contracts would economize on transaction costs. Owners of very closely held firms would gain little from tort limited liability because the 'firm's' torts often can be attributed to the owners' acts (Thompson 1994).

Nevertheless, as discussed in the following subsections, it is not clear that vicarious liability should be the default rule for some, or even any, partnership-type firms, and this uncertainty is reflected in variations in partner liability between the extremes of limited and vicarious liability.

6.4.1.1. Limited Liability for Closely Held Firms

Even if vicarious liability is efficient for some firms, particularly including owner-managed partnerships, limited liability may be an efficient default rule for other firms. Although commentators have highlighted the advantages of limited liability in facilitating public trading of shares (Easterbrook and Fischel 1985; Woodward 1985), limited liability also may be valuable in some closely held firms, particularly where ownership and management are specialized, and even in some cases where owners manage the firm (Ribstein 1991b). If this is the case for many closely held firms, it follows that limited liability should be available as a default rule rather than forcing firms to enter into non-recourse contracts with casual trade creditors, and to their owners to bear vicarious liability in tort suits where non-recourse contracts are not feasible. Alternatively, it may be efficient to adopt modified forms of limited liability, such as focusing vicarious liability on managers or providing for limited liability only for certain types of debts. Indeed, as discussed below in this section, various forms of vicarious and limited liability have been tested in the 'laboratory' of state law.

It has been argued (Hansmann and Kraakman 1991) that shareholder limited liability for corporate torts is inefficient, and therefore is not part of the 'essential' role of business forms.[60] From the standpoint of the present chapter's

---

[57] See UPA § 15; RUPA § 306.

[58] For analyses of vicarious liability based on the principal's ability to monitor, motivate or select agents, see Kornhauser (1982); Sykes (1984).

[59] See Mann (1997: 26–37) (showing evidence that most small firm debt is backed by the owners' personal guarantees).

[60] See Hansmann and Kraakman (Chapter 2, this volume, reprinted from Hansmann and Kraakman 2000: 387–440) (distinguishing limited liability from 'affirmative asset partitioning', or shielding the entity's assets from claims by owners' creditors). See also Armour and Whincop (Chapter 3, this volume) (analysing the 'essential' role of affirmative asset partitioning in a broader framework of business organization rules).

analysis, the main question is whether this assertion about inefficiency can be refuted by every state's acceptance of tort limited liability, including in closely held firms. One commentator has suggested that states' adoption of limited liability business forms is not evidence of efficiency because this was done over a brief period, without significant public debate, primarily at the behest of lawyers.[61]

In order to establish the inefficiency of the spread of LLC statutes, critics must ask why business lawyers were able to steamroll over all other interest groups in all fifty-one US jurisdictions. States could have prevented the spread of limited liability within their borders had they chosen to do so simply by failing to recognize the LLC liability limitation.[62] Nor did LLC statutes move in under cover of night. The process took eight years from the time of the tax ruling that made LLCs viable until the last LLC statute was passed, during which time Westlaw reports that 350 law review articles were published with 'limited liability company' in the title. And trial lawyers, who long have vigorously pressed for extension of tort liability and opposed attempts to reform state tort and professional liability laws, lobbied hard against LLC statutes in several states, including Missouri, Ohio, Tennessee, Washington, and Oklahoma (Goforth 1995: 1271–5, 1279–81), as well as against the California LLP act (Ainsworth 1995: 2). Finally, between the 1977 passage of the Wyoming law and the 1988 tax ruling, LLC statutes faced the significant federal tax classification hurdle, during which time opponents of limited liability might have prevailed at the federal level.

A benign explanation of the spread of LLC statutes is that they reflected closely held firms' increasing need for limited liability because of the increase in tort and malpractice exposure. Thus, LLC statutes represented a reverse swing of the tort pendulum after the tort revolution in the United States had left firms exposed to excessive tort risk. The statutes spread so quickly because by the time of the 1988 tax classification rule the need for them was well recognized. In other words, the rapid spread of LLC statutes indicates the inefficiency not of the new rule, but rather of the pre-1988 tax rules that had constrained the passage of LLC statutes prior to that date (Ribstein 1991b). It also shows how a dynamic system is able to react to inefficiency by providing an opportunity for regulatory arbitrage.

6.4.1.2. *Exhaustion of Firm Assets*

Owner liability rules do not involve a choice simply between the extremes of vicarious and limited liability. One option is requiring creditors to sue the partnership and exhaust its assets before they can recover from partners. Under US partnership law, partners traditionally are directly liable only to tort-type creditors such as accident victims. However, several US jurisdictions, including

---

[61] See Callison (Chapter 8, this volume). See also Goforth (1995) (comprehensive state-by-state review of state adoption of LLC statutes showing the role of lawyers and business groups).

[62] For a discussion of the conflict of laws issue, see Ribstein and Keatinge (1992: § 13.04).

those adopting RUPA (Ribstein and Keatinge 1992: § 307) require both contract and tort creditors to exhaust partnership assets. The exhaustion rule is consistent with the so-called 'dual priorities' rule of the Uniform Partnership Act, which gives partnership creditors priority only in the assets of the partnership and not in those of individual partners.[63] This form of limited liability represents a compromise between full-fledged corporate-type limited liability and full-fledged vicarious liability. The US rule contrasts with partners' joint and several liability for all partnership debts in most other countries (Heenen 1975: 140–4).[64]

These alternative rules raise the issue of which is best for partnership. The exhaustion rule obviously raises collection costs for creditors, while reducing partners' burden of paying and then seeking indemnity from their firm. Creditors' costs arguably would exceed those of partners, who deal regularly with the firm. On the other hand, the exhaustion/dual priorities rule arguably is consistent with the growth and increased acceptance of limited liability even in closely held firms (Ribstein (1992).[65] It also may be a reasonable compromise for some firms between vicarious and full-fledged limited liability where personal liability addresses moral hazard problems but creditors' costs of suing the firm are not much higher than those of owners.

Since the efficiency of the exhaustion rule is unclear from the standpoint of pure theory, it should be tested in the laboratory of state laws. With NCCUSL's promulgation of across-the-board exhaustion in RUPA, coupled with increased availability of contractual choice of law in general partnerships, states can accept or reject the RUPA rule, and firms can choose from among the various state rules. If states tend to adopt, say, the RUPA across-the-board exhaustion rule, and if firms tend to choose these statutes, this would indicate that this rule is efficient for most partnership-type firms.

The problem with a competition solution to these issues, however, is that federal bankruptcy law in the United States stifles full-fledged competition regarding the nature of limited liability. Bankruptcy law, among other things, overrules the dual priorities rule by providing for direct access by partnership creditors through the bankruptcy trustee to assets of bankrupt individual partners, and bankruptcy courts have enjoined creditors' actions against

---

[63] See UPA § 40(i).

[64] As discussed in the Joint Consultation (Law Commission and Scottish Law Commission 2001), England adopts a joint and several liability approach, while Scotland adopts an entity/exhaustion approach. The discussion in the text concerning the merits of both approaches indicates that there may be less certainty about which rule partnership law reformers in the United Kingdom should choose than is apparent from the Joint Consultation report.

[65] Conversely, it has been argued that, since a universally available corporate form 'captures all of the creditor-monitoring economies available under the old UPA priority rules for partners' creditors . . . the partnership form retains value only as an unlimited liability alternative to the corporate form, which implies that the claim of partnership creditors should be strengthened—they should have the same claim on the assets of individual partners as do individual creditors' (Hansmann and Kraakman 2000: 428 n. 60).

non-bankrupt partners.[66] All firms are subject to these rules in federal bankruptcy proceedings regardless of the otherwise applicable state law.[67]

6.4.1.3. *Limited Liability for Torts Only*

Another possible approach to owner liability would be a rule of personal liability for contract but limited liability for torts. This approach would address the infeasibility of contracting out of vicarious liability as to tort creditors while providing by default for the liability that most contract creditors of closely held firms apparently want.[68] On the other hand, vicarious liability may not be the efficient default rule for contract claims, and distinguishing two sets of creditors imposes extra transaction costs on the firm (Bromberg and Ribstein 2003: § 3.02; Ribstein 1996: 329–31). Although the original Texas rule distinguished contract and tort claims (Bromberg and Ribstein 2001a: § 1.01(a)), less than a third of the LLP statutes now take this approach. (ibid.: table 3-1) Thus, the laboratory of state laws generally has rejected what appears to be an awkward liability rule.

6.4.1.4. *Limited Liability in Limited Partnerships and the Control Rule*

A third approach to owner liability is the mixed liability rule for limited partnerships, in which general partners have vicarious liability but limited partners have limited liability unless they participate in control.[69] This rule can be rationalized as a way to permit limited liability investments in an unincorporated firm, while minimizing the potential moral hazard problem with limited liability in closely held firms by giving managers an incentive to act in creditors' interests (Ribstein 1999b: 979). The control rule no longer unduly restricts limited liability, as it did when firms had few other limited liability options, now that firms can combine separation of ownership and control and limited liability by forming LLCs.

The main counterargument is that too few firms would opt for this approach to justify continuing to offer it. As with the other issues discussed in this chapter, the best way to answer this question is through the 'laboratory' of state competition. State law and contractual variations have made vicarious liability in limited partnerships vestigial. Limited partners' control liability under the existing version of the Revised Uniform Limited Partnership Act (RULPA) has been

---

[66] For discussions and criticisms of these and other effects of bankruptcy law on partnerships, see Ribstein (1998b, 1997c).

[67] It has been argued that the transaction costs of entering into contracts regarding creditors' access to separate pools of owner and firm assets make legal default rules on such matters particularly important and binding (Hansmann and Kraakman 1991). But this does not preclude variation in these rules. Indeed, as transaction costs make legal default rules more valuable, they should also increase the value of competition and evolution regarding such rules in order to help ensure the rules' efficiency. Uniformity may be efficient if the rules are complex, entailing learning costs by third-party creditors. See Kobayashi and Ribstein (1997) (showing evidence that LLC rules regarding matters of this sort are, indeed, more uniform). However, the efficiency of uniformity does not necessarily follow from high costs of contracting around the default rule.

[68] See Mann (1997).   [69] See RULPA § 303.

reduced through an extensive safe harbour for permissible control acts to a type of partnership by estoppel based on misrepresentation of general partner status.[70] At the same time, general partners can avoid liability by the simple expedient of incorporating.

The advent of the LLP continued this evolutionary process. Several states explicitly permit limited partnerships to organize as limited liability limited partnerships (LLLPs), and thereby eliminate the vicarious liability of general partners and, in some cases, also of limited partners who participate in management (Bromberg and Ribstein 2003: ch. 5). LLLPs raise still further questions. On the one hand, now that limited partnerships easily can opt into full-fledged limited liability, it might be argued that the limited partnership statute should tighten the control rule and general partner liability for the general partners that do not make the election, thereby preserving two distinct alternatives. On the other hand, it might be argued that, since most limited partnerships will elect LLLP status if it is available, the statute should eliminate vicarious liability for limited partnerships as simply a trap for the unwary, thereby making the LLLP in effect the 'default' limited partnership. This issue was debated in the context of NCCUSL's revision of the (Re-RULPA) (Ribstein 1999b: 971). The final version of Re-RULPA provides for default personal liability of general partners.[71] However, the Reporter reflected the confused history of the revision on this issue in the following note to the April 2001 draft:

Having consulted severally with a majority of the Commissioners on the Drafting Committee, the Reporter believes that the Committee will vote to 'flop' on the 'flip'—i.e., to provide that, as a default rule, the general partner of a limited partnership is liable for the debts of the entity. If the Reporter's prediction is wrong (not an unprecedented event), the changes indicated above (and elsewhere) will simply be removed.[72]

This suggests that the vicarious liability rule for limited partnerships is determined by how a particular committee feels at a particular time. But the laboratory of state legislatures considering whether to adopt Re-RULPA ultimately will, and should, determine this issue.

6.4.1.5. *Limited Liability as a Default Rule for All Partnerships*

Limited liability in limited partnerships raises an additional question about the future of vicarious liability in general partnerships. If the state laboratory ultimately should decide that vicarious liability is simply a trap for limited partnerships, why not for general partnerships as well? One might respond that general

---

[70] See RULPA § 303 (1985).

[71] The final version of Re-RULPA provides for default personal liability of general partners. See National Conference of Commissioners of Uniform State Laws, Revision of Uniform Limited Partnership Act (1976) with 1985 Amendments, Draft for Approval, § 404(a) (August 2001) (Re-RULPA), available at http://www.law.upenn.edu/bll/ulc/ulc_frame.htm.

[72] Re-RULPA § 404, Note 9 (April 2001), available at http://www.law.upenn.edu/bll/ulc/ulc_frame.htm.

partnerships are the default entity, unlike limited partnerships, which the parties must commemorate by a state filing. But limited liability, like vicarious liability, also can be seen as a prescribed legal consequence of a particular relationship. The decision by the vast majority of firms to opt for limited liability arguably suggests that this is the efficient rule and that the legal consequence of forming a partnership should change accordingly. Full-fledged vicarious liability may not be an efficient default rule for a significant number of firms, since the collection costs of actions against individual partners and the increased monitoring costs of both partners and creditors under a vicarious liability rule probably exceed any benefits to creditors from the availability of a direct action (Ribstein 1991b). Once again, this is a complex issue that is best decided in the laboratory of state law.

6.4.2. Partners' Financial Rights

There are several theoretically possible default rules for partners' shares in profits and losses, including equally, or 'per capita' pro rata according to partners' financial contributions; and per capita or pro rata by class of holder depending on their liability for the firm's debts and management responsibilities. As discussed below, these default rules reflect varying assumptions concerning firms' management and liability structures. As with the other issues discussed in this chapter, the appropriate rule or mix of rules is difficult to determine a priori. US partnership law provides that partners share equally in profits and losses after paying non-partnership creditors.[73] Indemnification by the partnership and contribution by individual partners reconciles partners' loss shares with their vicarious liability for all partnership debts. Partnership statutes also deny partners interest and rent in addition to their profit shares except where they specifically contract to loan or lease property to the firm.[74] These rules contrast with the pro rata sharing rule for corporations, and with the partnership rule in some non-US jurisdictions.[75]

The partnership equal sharing rule raises significant policy issues.[76] Fred C. Dobbs (Humphrey Bogart) observed in 'The Treasure of the Sierra Madre' that 'in any civilized place the biggest investor gets the biggest return'. The rule might be defended as based on the assumption that, in the absence of contrary agreement, the partners' profit share compensates them for all of their investments in the firm, including their credit contribution to a vicarious liability firm. This would explain why the default rule does not hold in limited liability firms

---

[73] UPA § 18(a); RUPA § 401(b).   [74] See UPA § 18(c) and (f); RUPA § 401(d) and (h).

[75] For example, German law provides for sharing on the basis of capital shares. See Heenen (1975: 108).

[76] This markedly contrasts with the peculiar view of Smith (2001), who sees the rule as playing an essential role in partnership and explains this through evolutionary biology. Smith's paper ignores considerations underlying default rules as distinguished from actual contracts in particular firms (illustrated by the Fred C. Dobbs pronouncement), variations across types of partnership-like firms, cross-country differences and, in general, the adaptability of business forms.

and is so often varied by contract in firms where the equal-contribution assumption does not hold.[77] The rule applies as a default rule even in firms where the parties' contributions are not in fact equal because it is difficult to design a default rule that will better suit a large number of firms. But to what extent should this result prevail even in the face of clear expectations to the contrary in particular firms? A rigid rule would encourage costly contrary agreements, seemingly inconsistent with the transaction cost reducing function of default rules. Thus, for example, should partnership law provide for a different default rule in LLPs where the assumption of credit contributions does not hold?[78] On the other hand, offering many different default rules imposes information costs on firms.[79]

Again, the laboratory of state laws should resolve these issues through horizontal and vertical competition. States can offer hybrid or variant partnership statutes that alter some of the default rules, including those regarding allocation of financial rights. For example, limited partnership statutes provide for pro rata financial rights,[80] and most LLC statutes so provide for all members.[81]

6.4.3. Management and Control

Management and control default rules theoretically vary on a continuum according to their flexibility or rigidity, from rules providing for equality among partners with fixed categories of authority, to those creating classes of owners and managers with particular levels of authority. The less definite the members' default authority, the greater the uncertainty costs associated with determining that authority and the need to allocate those costs between the firm and third parties. Default partnership rules treat all partners equally regarding management and control: partners participate directly in management;[82] each partner has one vote rather than apportioning votes by the value of money contributions as under corporate law;[83] and all partners vote on the firm's decision, with a majority vote required to approve all 'ordinary' decisions and unanimity for extraordinary decisions, including amendment of the agreement and admission of new partners.[84]

Equality rules for management, like those for financial rights discussed above, suit very closely held firms in which the partners' combinations of capital,

---

[77] Indeed, courts often assume a contrary agreement in this situation. See e.g. *Warren v. Warren*, 784 S.W.2d 247 (Mo. App. 1989) (holding that partners who provided substantial time and vital services deserved extra compensation).

[78] See generally Bromberg and Ribstein (2003: ch. 4) (discussing possible differences between applications of partnership law to LLP and non-LLP general partnerships).

[79] Moreover, the 'linkage' of general partnership default rules with LLPs is arguably an advantage of LLPs. See generally Kobayashi and Ribstein (2001a).

[80] See RULPA § 503 (1985).

[81] See Ribstein and Keatinge (1992: app. 5-1) (tabulating statutes).

[82] See UPA § 18(e); RUPA § 401(f).   [83] Ibid.

[84] See UPA § 18(h)–(i); RUPA § 401(i)–(j).

service, and credit contributions can be assumed to equalize. At the same time, majority-vote rules avoid the high coordination costs of requiring unanimity on ordinary decisions.[85] The rules regarding a partner's power to bind the firm in transactions with third parties reflect this equal allocation of power. Under US law any partner normally can bind the firm in ordinary business transactions with third parties.[86] Similarly, because the default rules assume that partners are full-time co-managers, their acts in the ordinary course of business trigger partnership tort liability, as do acts by full-time employees of other types of firms.

But even many closely held firms do not fit the model of active worker-management. For example, larger partnerships need to centralize authority to minimize decision-making costs. Because of the basic partner equality assumption, the firm bears the burden of notifying third parties of limitations on partners' authority to bind the firm.[87] RUPA makes only a slight concession to this problem by providing a mechanism for binding third parties in real estate transactions where third parties can easily check a central record.[88]

There is, therefore, a need for default rules that suit centralized management even in closely held firms. The limited partnership was once the only alternative set of default rules US law offered for closely held firms. The limited partnership form clearly delineates classes of managing general partners, who have vicarious liability for the debts of the firm and can bind the firm in transactions with third parties, and non-managing limited partners, who have limited liability unless they participate in control[89] and no power to bind the firm.[90]

The traditional limited partnership does not, however, suit the many closely held firms in which investor-employees want substantial say even if they do not exercise day-to-day control. State statutes initially accommodated this need by diluting the limited partnership control rule and permitting limited partners to participate more actively in management without losing their limited liability. These state statutory developments were reflected in 1976 and 1985 versions of the Uniform Limited Partnership Act, which offered increasing levels of management flexibility.[91] Re-RULPA completely eliminates the 'control rule'.[92] However, eliminating the clear demarcation between general and limited partners simultaneously raises general-partnership-type problems of third party uncertainty in determining member authority.

The LLC offers a compromise form of 'chameleon' management: the firm can choose either direct partnership-type control by the members or centralized control by managers that is closer to, but not as rigid as, the limited partnership

---

[85] See generally Buchanan and Tullock (1962) (describing optimal voting rules). Armour and Whincop (Chapter 3, this volume), argue that decisions should be made by at least a majority vote. But the parties might decide to reduce the costs of consensus through sub-majority voting and delegation.

[86] See UPA §§ 9–13; RUPA §§ 301–305.   [87] See UPA § 9; RUPA § 301.

[88] Ibid. § 303.   [89] See ULPA § 7; RULPA § 303.

[90] See RULPA § 403(a) (providing that general partner of a limited partnership has the same rights and powers as a general partner in a general partnership).

[91] Compare RULPA § 303 (1976) with RULPA § 303 (1985).   [92] See Re-RULPA § 303.

format.[93] With this greater flexibility comes greater uncertainty for third party creditors than in limited partnerships as to whether particular individuals have authority to bind the firm. For example, limited partnership statutes generally provide that the certificate is notice to third parties that those designated therein as general partners are such.[94] LLC statutes generally do not have comparable provisions (Ribstein and Keatinge 1992: app. 4-1). Thus, under most statutes courts would apply agency rules that would require the firm to notify third parties which non-managing members lack binding authority (ibid. § 8.05). However, some states, particularly Delaware, make the operating agreement binding as to members' and managers' authority, thereby effectively requiring third parties to check this agreement when dealing with the firm (ibid. App. 8-1).

The main point for present purposes is that the laboratory of state law, and not uniform law drafters, has produced governance structures that efficiently reflect the variety of firms' needs. Even where rules are embodied in NCCUSL's uniform partnership, limited partnership, and LLC acts, NCCUSL generally has followed rather than led the process (Ribstein and Kobayashi 1995). For example, the LLC chameleon management structure had evolved in many state statutes before being included in ULLCA (Ribstein 1995b).

6.4.4. Partners' Property Rights in the Firm

Partners have the right to sell or otherwise alienate their rights to distributions but, unlike corporate shareholders, cannot transfer their rights to participate in control without their co-partners' consent.[95] Like the other partnership default rules, this assumes that each partner is a co-manager and therefore not fungible with other investors as in a corporation.

These rights raise at least two important issues. First, to what extent should partners be able to protect their interests in the firm from their individual creditors? The rights of partners' creditors must be balanced against those of the non-debtor owners to continue to exercise their substantial management rights free from creditors' interference. These owner and creditor rights may collide in partnerships. Unlike in a publicly held firm, an individual partner may be able to exercise significant control over the partnership, and thereby restrict distributions that creditors otherwise would be able to reach by levying on the partner's interest. Moreover, unlike in a corporation, the creditor who levies on, or 'charges', a partnership interest cannot, by foreclosure, take over the voting power of the stock because the charging creditor is no more than a transferee of the partner's financial rights.[96] Instead, the creditor's rights are subject to those of the holders of the ownership rights, including the debtor himself.

---

[93] See Ribstein and Keatinge (1992: app. 8-1) (summarizing and tabulating state statutes).
[94] See RULPA § 208.   [95] See UPA § 27; RUPA § 503.   [96] See UPA § 28; RUPA § 504.

The laboratory of state law has dealt with this issue. State general partnership statutes vary as to whether a charging creditor can foreclose on the debtor's partnership interest.[97] This is a significant issue under general partnership law because foreclosure permits the creditor to obtain a judicial dissolution and liquidation of a partnership without an unexpired term.[98] Foreclosure and dissolution rights may or may not carry over from general to the limited partnership statutes under current law. Although these statutes do not explicitly provide for dissolution by members' creditors,[99] they incorporate general partnership terms to the extent that these are not inconsistent with the limited partnership statute,[100] thus raising the question whether the general partnership provision on the assignees right to compel dissolution is 'inconsistent',[101] as one leading case has held.[102] Re-RULPA will apparently clarify that issue through a special limited partnership provision that permits judicial dissolution actions only by or for a partner.[103] On the other hand, ULLCA provides for judicial dissolution on application by transferees of interests.[104] This sets the stage for evolution and competition among both states and business forms on this issue.

The second issue regarding partner property rights concerns free transferability of management rights. Since restricted transferability assumes that members are co-managers, it arguably follows that the default rule should differ in firms where that assumption does not hold. Partnership-type statutes including rules based on centralized management arguably should provide for free transferability of management rights for non-managing members. Yet restricted transferability of management rights is still the rule for all interests in partnership-type firms. This may be because such transferability is the tax and regulatory dividing line between corporate-type and partnership-type firms.[105] This may be an example of tax and regulation trumping efficient state law evolution of business forms. On the other hand, a transferability-based distinction among business forms may be more efficient than other bases because it is less likely to induce firms to make inefficient tax or regulation-induced adjustments in form (Ribstein 1991b: 471–3).

---

[97] See Bromberg and Ribstein (2001: § 3.05(d)(3)(v)).

[98] See UPA § 32; RUPA § 801(6). This means that a partnership's creditors, unlike those of a corporation, do not have the type of 'affirmative asset partitioning' that gives them 'liquidation protection' against owners' creditors. See Hansmann and Kraakman (2000: 394).

[99] See RULPA § 801 (1985).   [100] See RULPA § 1105.

[101] See Ribstein (1995b) (discussing general linkage issue).

[102] *Baybank v. Catamount Construction, Inc.*, 141 N.H. 780, 693 A.2d 1163 (1997) (holding that assignee of interest may not compel dissolution).

[103] See Re-RULPA § 802.   [104] See ULLCA § 801(a)(5).

[105] See IRC § 7704 (providing that partnerships with freely transferable shares are subject to double corporate taxation). Prior to check-the-box, transferability also was one of the attributes that distinguished corporations from partnerships under the classification rules. See Treas. Reg. § 301.7701-2(a)(2).

6.4.5. Fiduciary Duties

Fiduciary duties minimize agency costs associated with the separation of ownership from management rights (Jensen and Meckling 1976). Thus, they arguably should apply when partners act as agents. By contrast, imposing fiduciary duties when partners act as owners to protect their interests, as in voting on partnership transactions, selling their ownership interests, exiting the firm, or expelling other partners, actually could increase agency costs by inhibiting partners from monitoring managers. It follows that fiduciary duties should not apply, or at least not strictly require unselfish conduct, when partners act as owners rather than as managers or agents. Apart from optimal default rules, fiduciary duties are part of the contract among the partners and therefore should be subject to contrary agreement (Easterbrook and Fischel 1993; Ribstein 1997b). Finally, the statutes should provide some mechanism for enforcing fiduciary duties, again subject to contrary agreement. The following subsections raise issues concerning fiduciary duties that can be, and have been, addressed in the laboratory of state laws.

6.4.5.1. Managers vs. Owners

To what extent should default duties reflect degrees of centralization of management? This issue mirrors those regarding financial rights, agency, and transferability discussed above. Given the model of co-equal ownership in the general partnership, it would seem to follow that partners would not have default fiduciary duties—that is, would be able to act selfishly subject to general contract and good faith principles. However, the UPA is ambiguous. Section 21, titled 'partner accountable as a fiduciary', requires partners to 'account to the partnership for any benefit and hold as trustee for it any profits derived by him without the consent of the other partners' from partnership transactions, with no explicit qualification as to whether the partner was, in fact, acting as a fiduciary in the transaction. Indeed, the classic statement of fiduciary duties, by Justice Cardozo in *Meinhard v. Salmon*, was applied to a partner:

Not honesty alone, but the punctilio of an honor the most sensitive, is then the standard of behavior. As to this there has developed a tradition that is unbending and inveterate. Uncompromising rigidity has been the attitude of courts of equity when petitioned to undermine the rule of undivided loyalty by the 'disintegrating erosion' of particular exceptions. Only thus has the level of conduct for fiduciaries been kept at a level higher than that trodden by the crowd. It will not consciously be lowered by any judgment of this court.[106]

Close analysis of partnership cases, however, reveals that courts, in fact, attend to the nature of specific contracts in applying fiduciary duties (Ribstein 1997b). This is consistent with the language of UPA § 21, which imposes a trust only on profits derived without co-partner consent.

---

[106] *Meinhard v. Salmon*, 249 N.Y. 458, 164 N.E. 545, 546 (1928).

The Revised Uniform Partnership Act, however, confuses the law by taking the cases' fiduciary language more seriously than their actual holdings. RUPA § 404 defines 'general standards of partner's conduct', to include an explicit 'duty of loyalty' and a 'duty of care'. In order to deal with the many cases noted above in which partners were held not to be acting as fiduciaries, RUPA § 404 (e) and (f) qualifies these general duties as follows:

(e) A partner does not violate a duty or obligation under this [Act] or under the partnership agreement merely because the partner's conduct furthers the partner's own interest. (f) A partner may lend money to and transact other business with the partnership, and as to each loan or transaction, the rights and obligations of the partner are the same as those of a person who is not a partner, subject to other applicable law.

These provisions are unclear (Ribstein 1993b). At their broadest, they can be taken to negate the general 'standards' elsewhere in § 404. The most straightforward interpretation is that partners are not subject to a fiduciary duty when they are not acting as fiduciaries. This can be reconciled with the remainder of § 404, which does not impose a fiduciary duty on all partners, but literally only defines the 'only fiduciary duties a partner owes to the partnership'—that is, when one is owed.

Because of its ambiguity, RUPA § 404 eliminates whatever advantage might otherwise have been derived from statutory definition of partners' fiduciary duties. This problem is exacerbated by the limited waivability of fiduciary duties under RUPA discussed below. Unfortunately, many of the states that are adopting RUPA, which number exceeds a majority of US jurisdictions, are taking along with it these undesirable features of RUPA. This illustrates the potential harm that can be caused by promulgation of uniform law proposals (Kobayashi and Ribstein 1997).

Horizontal and vertical choice and statutory and common law evolution, however, mitigate the harm caused by RUPA. In particular, many LLC statutes clearly separate the fiduciary duties of managing members from the looser good faith duties of non-managing members.[107] A similar rule is emerging in limited partnership case law (Bromberg and Ribstein 2001b: § 16.07(a)), and in Re-RULPA.[108] Statutory provisions explicitly authorizing fiduciary duty contracts, discussed in the next subsection, further mitigate problems under standard-form provisions.

Questions concerning the consequences of centralization of management also arise regarding disclosure duties. It has been argued that, when ownership and management are separated, the non-managing owners should have relatively weak access to information to reflect their weak fiduciary duties regarding use

---

[107] See Ribstein and Keatinge (1992: 9-1) (describing and tabulating statutes).
[108] See Re-RULPA § 305 (describing limited duties of limited partners). The Reporter's Note to ibid. § 305(b) makes clear that '[t]he obligation of good faith and fair dealing is not a fiduciary duty, does not command altruism or self-abnegation, and does not prevent a partner from acting in the partner's own self-interest'.

of the information they obtain (Callison and Vestal 2001). But it also could be argued that isolation from control creates a greater need for information and therefore justifies stronger information rights. Indeed, courts follow this approach when determining the applicability of the US securities laws.[109]

These questions are best resolved through firm-specific contracts that reflect variations concerning the potential for member abuse of information and through evolution of statutory default provisions in different states and business forms. For example, perhaps the information rights of limited partners, who are completely locked out of control by the limited partnership 'control rule', should differ from those of non-managing LLC members who are not similarly impeded. Even within a given business form there is room for several different approaches. Reflecting these uncertainties concerning the optimal rule, US jurisdictions have shown remarkable variability regarding members' information rights in LLC statutes.[110]

6.4.5.2. Waiver of Fiduciary Duties

Whatever the statutory rules concerning fiduciary duties in partnership-type firms, they clearly should be, and essentially are, subject to contrary agreement (Ribstein 1997b). There are strong policy reasons for permitting contractual tailoring of duties to particular relationships. Among other things, there may be considerable costs associated with empowering partners to sue under broad and ambiguous fiduciary duty rules (Ribstein 2001b). The arguments against enforcement of fiduciary duty waivers are based mainly on the inability of contracting parties to protect themselves against oppressive contracts or to foresee potential harm—arguments that should have no more traction in business association contracts than in contracts generally (Butler and Ribstein 1990; Easterbrook and Fischel 1985).

In any event, since partnerships, like other business associations, clearly are voluntary relationships, contracts inevitably will hold sway. If a state forbids waivers in one or more forms, the parties can select a different business form or type of relationship, or they can contract for the law of another state. The issue, then, is not whether the law forbids fiduciary duty waivers, but how costly it makes them.

Delaware has taken the lead in enacting legislative provisions that explicitly permit contracting around partnership-type fiduciary duties. These provisions first entered Delaware's limited partnership act,[111] and now are also found in

---

[109] These laws apply to the offer or sale of a 'security', the existence of which has been held to depend significantly on whether the investor's participation in management was significant in producing the expected return. See generally Ribstein (1991a) (discussing the application of this case law to partnerships).

[110] For a summary of LLC statutory variations, see Callison and Vestal (2001: 287–91). These authors are particularly stubborn in resisting the data provided by the state law laboratory. While demonstrating significant jurisdictional variation despite the existence of a uniform law, and condemning that law's approach (ibid. 279–80), Callison and Vestal nevertheless advocate that this issue be dealt with in uniform laws (ibid. 291–2).

[111] See also Ribstein (1991b).

Delaware's LLC[112] and general partnership[113] acts. Delaware courts have interpreted these provisions expansively to give full range to freedom of contract, subject to reasonable interpretation of fiduciary duty provisions, including general contractual good faith duties (Bromberg and Ribstein 2003: § 16.07(h)(5); Ribstein and Keatinge 1992: § 9.04). A few other states also permit full waiver of fiduciary duties in partnership-type limited liability firms.[114]

Should statutes give parties the same freedom to waive fiduciary duties in all types of partnership-type firms? One might argue that there should be more stringent limits on contracting in general partnership, which is the default form for very informal firms, than in LLCs and limited partnerships that require a filing and are usually done with the advice of counsel. On the other hand, since fiduciary duties may be inappropriate for closely held owner-managed general partnerships,[115] restrictions on waiver may be most costly for such firms. Again, these issues arguably are appropriate for resolution in the state law laboratory. If, despite competition among forms, freedom of contracting does not spread to the partnership form, this provides some evidence that firms forming general partnerships prefer to be bound by restrictions on waiver.[116]

A corollary to the point that partnership fiduciary duties are essentially contractual and subject to testing and evolution through competition and variation in state laws is that any excessive or inadequate fiduciary duties are attributable to restrictions on competition and variation. For example, attorney ethical rules in the United States are not subject to competitive forces and therefore may constrain efficient evolution (Ribstein 2001a). In particular, ethical rules constrain law firms from restricting opportunistic exit and competition,[117] thereby leading to the sort of conduct Professor Hillman (2001) condemns.

6.4.5.3. Enforcement of Duties

Partners have rights against the partnership for their shares of profits or other compensation and indemnification, and against individual partners for contribution towards partnership losses or for damages for breach of fiduciary duty. US law traditionally held that partners could not enforce these rights except in an action called an 'accounting', generally brought on dissolution, that resolves all of the partner's rights and obligations in a single proceeding.[118] However, some cases recognized partners' rights to sue without an accounting,[119] and

---

[112] Del. Code, tit. 6, § 18-1101.   [113] Ibid. § 15-103(b)(8).

[114] See Bromberg and Ribstein (2001a: § 8-103) (discussing general partnership provisions); Ribstein and Keatinge (1992: app. 9-1) (tabulating LLC provisions).

[115] See Section 6.4.5.1.

[116] To the extent that the general partnership form applies by default when firms have not chosen some other form, vertical and horizontal choice may be illusory. By the same token, however, the ability to contractually waive statutory terms is, by hypothesis, irrelevant in this setting.

[117] See Ribstein (1998a) (discussing how these restrictions may injure clients).

[118] See Bromberg and Ribstein (2001: § 6.08(c)) (discussing accounting 'exclusivity' rule).

[119] The leading case is *Sertich v. Moorman*, 162 Ariz. 407, 783 P.2d 1199 (1989).

RUPA explicitly permits partners to use non-accounting actions to enforce partnership rights.[120]

Although the RUPA approach seems sensible, it is not free from doubt. Given the potential for litigation to disrupt the partnership relationship, the partnership default rule arguably should restrict such suits until global resolution on dissolution and winding up, when there is no more relationship to preserve (Levmore 1995). That seems particularly logical in the very closely held general partnership. However, in firms with centralized management, partner suits may be needed as a way to police agents. Once again, this issue is appropriate for resolution in the laboratory of state laws. There is, in fact, variation among the states, particularly regarding explicit recognition of derivative suits in LLCs.[121]

6.4.6. Dissociation and Dissolution

As with other partnership issues, there is a range of policy choices regarding partner exit from the firm. On the one hand, given the restricted transferability of and limited market for partnership interests, in order to have a viable ability to exit the firm, partners need to be able to either dissolve the firm or sell interests back to the firm or the other partners. Partner exit rights give partners control over their investments and thereby constrain co-partners' opportunism more effectively than the weaker powers to vote or to sue for co-partner misconduct (Levmore 1995). Moreover, the stronger are partners' ownership rights in the firm's assets, the stronger are their incentives to participate in developing these assets (Grossman and Hart 1986). On the other hand, partner exit rights invite opportunistic conduct in the form of withdrawing property that is the product of joint investment, or threatening to do so in order to extort a payoff from their co-partners. This risk of opportunism, in turn, dilutes the partners' incentives to invest in the firm.[122] In general, the problem is one of finding the right balance between these costs of exit and of continuity.

Partnership law in the United States began with the single UPA rule that each partner can dissolve the firm at will, even if contrary to the partnership agreement.[123] This sort of strong exit rule is appropriate for very closely held firms that consist of particular individuals making unique contributions and that change fundamentally when one individual leaves. However, the rule probably does not suit many partnerships that want rules that encourage the partners to stay (Ribstein 1987). Partners always have been able to contract around the UPA default rule by entering into a partnership agreement in which they agree to continue the firm notwithstanding a partner's exit (Bromberg and Ribstein 2001: § 7.13). The UPA also provides a kind of default continuation agreement for partners who agree to a partnership for a particular term or undertaking

---

[120] RUPA § 405.   [121] See Ribstein and Keatinge (1992: app. 10-1) (tabulating statutes).
[122] For discussions of the opportunism problem in closely held firms, see Ribstein (1987); Rock and Wachter (Chapter 4, this volume).
[123] See UPA (1914: §§ 31, 38).

pursuant to which the leaving partner must pay damages and is not entitled to share in the goodwill of the continuing firm.[124] Under either type of agreement, partner dissociation would cause only a technical dissolution after which the business of the firm would continue. But these agreements may not provide enough continuity for many firms because strong default exit rules may be traps lying in wait for partners who have neglected to provide for continuity in a particular situation. Moreover, even a technical dissolution may raise questions concerning the continuity of the partnership's rights and obligations in contracts with third parties.[125]

RUPA eliminates even technical dissolution in the event of certain types of partner dissociation, as where the partner dissociates wrongfully, or by death, or bankruptcy[126]—the sorts of sudden departures where forcing buyout or liquidation can wreak the most havoc. Thus, as the states consider and adopt RUPA, they now offer a choice between UPA and RUPA exit rules.[127]

Even more importantly, states have developed additional variations through LLC and limited partnership statutes. In particular, some statutes have eliminated not only default dissolution upon member dissociation, but also the right to dissociate itself, meaning that members can take their services elsewhere but may not be able to remove their investments from the firm.[128] This evolution was driven to some extent by the federal tax law changes that allowed much more flexibility in the types of firms that are entitled to elect partnership-type taxation.[129] It has also been affected by estate tax laws that impose higher taxes on interests in firms governed by state laws that provide by default for liquidation on partner dissociation (Ribstein and Keatinge 1992: ch. 18).

Has state competition produced an optimal mix of exit rules? Eliminating partners' default exit right swings the pendulum towards permitting oppression of locked-in partners. Indeed, close corporations long were plagued by such problems, which triggered complex and unpredictable judicial remedies to relieve minority oppression. (ibid. § 5.05(c)). The application of estate tax rules irrespective of the rights provided for in the agreement may have encouraged legislatures to provide for a higher level of default continuity than would have been the case apart from tax considerations. State competition and evolution arguably has produced an optimal mix of rules if tax considerations are taken into account.

---

[124] UPA §§ 31, 38.

[125] See Bromberg and Ribstein (2001: § 7.14(b)) (discussing effect of dissolution on partnership's executory contracts).

[126] RUPA § 801(2).

[127] See Bromberg and Ribstein (2003: ch. 8) (presenting chart on state adoptions of RUPA and summarizing state variations on RUPA provisions).

[128] See ibid. § 17.01(c), n. 19 (listing limited partnership provisions); Ribstein and Keatinge (1992: app. 11-1) (tabulating LLC statutes).

[129] See Section 6.3.3.2.

6.4.7. Switching and Changing Forms

The many new forms that have been developed and the changes within forms discussed above raise problems as well as benefits. The basic issue is how to balance the benefits of legal evolution against the need to protect the rights of parties who are caught up in the changes (Ribstein 1997a).

To begin with, the proliferation of statutory standard forms creates a need for procedures that simplify the task of moving from one form to another. The traditional way of doing so in a general partnership was to dissolve and liqui-date the firm, triggering tax, and other costs of discontinuity. But the states have reduced switching costs by providing merger and conversion procedures that allow partnerships to combine with or become other types of entities without dissolving (Ribstein and Keatinge 1992: § 11.16). This promotes legal evolution by encouraging existing firms to move to the new forms. On the other hand, the ability easily to switch into limited liability forms may hurt third party creditors of the original business, among others.

This raises the broader topic of the effect of changes within statutory forms. Again, while these changes are an inherent part of the beneficial evolution described above, they may frustrate the expectations of those who have relied on the existing rules. For example, members or partners may have relied on dis-solution and dissociation-at-will, and therefore may be hurt by changing the rules to restrict these rights.

Case law applying common law creditor-protection rules or the Contract Clause of the US Constitution may protect parties' expectations. The problem with these approaches, however, is that they are applied *ex post* by courts, and therefore may frustrate the expectations of some parties while attempting to protect those of others. Here, too, it is worth seeing what the laboratory of state laws might accomplish regarding, for example, rules specifying prospective application of changes in dissociation and dissolution provisions.

6.4.8. The Limits of Variation in Business Forms

How many different business forms should there be? Here, too, important pol-icy choices lie along a spectrum and are best addressed through state law com-petition and variation. On the one hand, this chapter has shown the advantages of alternative business forms in facilitating regulatory arbitrage and providing different business rules to suit different types of firms.[130] Thus, there is a cost to 'linking' business forms or, at the extreme, 'unified' business entity laws—the vertical equivalent to 'harmonization'.

On the other hand, linkage does have the important benefit of permitting firms to use case law, customs, and forms associated with both of the linked forms that aid in the application and interpretation of the statute and private

---

[130] See Section 6.2.2.

agreement, thereby encouraging the development and use of new business forms (Kobayashi and Ribstein 2001a). The greater the number of forms, the greater are owners' and third parties' information costs of selecting and dealing with firms, and the less the potential for standardization and development of private forms and case law interpretations. This suggests that standard forms should not provide every feasible combination of default rules.

Since the current menu of choices has emerged from substantial state competition and evolution of the past few years, there is reason to believe that it efficiently reflects firms' needs. However, from a theoretical standpoint there is an additional option the states might consider—an open-ended 'contractual entity' that enables firms to have the advantage of limited liability without having to confine themselves to an existing set of default rules (Ribstein 1999b). This open-ended form might 'incubate' new standard forms by encouraging parties to enter into new types of contracts.

6.5. IMPLICATIONS OF THE ANALYSIS

The above analysis holds lessons for law development, including those underway in Europe. Most importantly, this chapter demonstrates the benefits of 'horizontal' jurisdictional competition to facilitate market-testing, variety, and evolution of laws. The United States may have an inherent advantage in this respect over individual European countries where there are no significant subordinate political entities. It has been pointed out that '[f]or most of the last 300 years, the richest nation in the world has had a federal structure' (Weingast 1995: 3).[131] In other words, federal systems are likely to beat unitary jurisdictions in international competition.

The US model also might work for Europe as a whole. The disappearance of international trade barriers may reduce the significance of whether countries are allied in a US-style federal system. This suggests that the best path for Europe is to facilitate competition regarding business association laws rather than eliminating competition through 'harmonization'. To the extent that centralizing law-drafting functions is desirable, it can be best accomplished through promulgation of 'model' laws rather than by compelling uniformity through federal mandates (Ribstein and Kobayashi 1995).

There may be, however, significant differences between Europe and the United States that prevent the development of US-style competition in Europe. This difference is not constitutional, since there may be a firmer constitutional basis for jurisdictional competition in post-*Centros* Europe than in the United States.[132] Rather, inherent legal, cultural, language, historical, and other differences among European countries may play a greater role in constraining firms'

---

[131] For other historical and comparative discussions of different federal systems, see Riker (1964); Hayek (1939).
[132] See Section 6.3.1.

ability to choose from among different jurisdictions. Also, jurisdictional competition in Europe must overcome the 'real seat' choice of law rule, which *Centros* has not necessarily displaced. And lawyers may not be able to take the lead in law reform in Europe as they have in the United States because of differences between lawyers' role and the structure of the bar in the two contexts. All of this is not to say that jurisdictional competition cannot arise in Europe. For example, LLP legislation in England apparently was provoked by competition from Jersey (McCahery and Vermeulen, Chapter 7, this volume). Moreover, *Centros* might provoke erosion of the real seat rule as new firms establish in the United Kingdom to avoid the rule. However, jurisdictional competition in Europe may never take the full-fledged US form.

These differences suggest that it may be appropriate to design legal rules to compensate for the reduced feasibility of competition in the European context. These rules might mimic competition by providing for menus of business features within individual statutes.[133] Although a menu offered by a single lawmaker is not equivalent to jurisdictional choice, menus may be a viable second-best way to facilitate adaptation and variation given inherent constraints on jurisdictional competition.

Europe may differ from the United States not only in terms of the competitive dynamic, but also in terms of the optimal rules and therefore the likely outcome of an efficient competition. In particular, there may be less need for limited liability for small firms given the reduced threat of tort liability in Europe as compared to the United States. The growth of limited liability in the United States may be attributable to the revolution in tort liability.[134] In Europe, by contrast, limited liability in small firms arguably adds little protection since owners of small firms would be liable for their own acts in any case, and most of their remaining business and personal liability would be insurable or subject to limitation by contract.[135]

6.6. CONCLUDING REMARKS

As this chapter shows, enforcing jurisdictional choice can have profound benefits for the evolution of business law. Since humans cannot accurately foresee

---

[133] A menu approach has been recommended for the American system to deal with the supposed problems created by network externalities. See Klausner (1995). However, network externalities probably do not impede jurisdictional competition in the United States sufficiently to justify reliance on this method there.

[134] See Section 6.4.1.1.

[135] See *Williams v. Natural Life Foods Ltd.* [1998] 1 W.L.R. 830; [1998] 2 All E.R. 577; WL 1043679 (1998), in which the House of Lords held that an employee of a limited company was not personally liable for his own negligent misstatement because, under *Hedley Byrne and Co. Ltd. v. Heller and Partners Ltd.*, (1964) A.C. 465, there was an absence of reliance sufficient to create a special relationship between plaintiff and defendant that would justify liability for negligent misrepresentation. This is a contract-type privity argument that may not have held up against wide-open tort theories in the United States.

and provide for the future, a market-oriented evolutionary process is preferable to government-imposed rules. Markets, and not government, have the wisdom necessary to guide firms in an uncertain world. Thus, policymakers should be wary of top-down planning and the hegemony of theory untested in the markets. Policy reform should focus on the mechanisms of legal evolutions and markets for law rather than on the substantive provisions of business law. These lessons have important implications for Europe as it enters the post-*Centros* age.

REFERENCES

Ainsworth, W. (1995), 'Trial Lawyers Learn to Live with Limited Liability', *Recorder* 26 June.

Alchian, A. A. (1950), 'Uncertainty, Evolution, and Economic Theory', *Journal of Political Economy* 58: 211.

Ayres, I. (1992), 'Judging Close Corporations in the Age of Statutes', *Washington University Law Quarterly* 70: 365.

Breton, A., and Salmon, P. (2001), 'External Effects of Domestic Regulations: Comparing Internal and International Barriers to Trade', *International Review of Law and Economics* 21: 135.

Bromberg, A. R., and Ribstein L. E. (2001), *Bromberg and Ribstein on Partnership*, New York: Aspen Publishers.

——— ———(2003), *Bromberg and Ribstein on Limited Liability Partnerships and the Revised Uniform Partnership Act*, New York: Aspen Publishers.

Buchanan, J., and Tullock, G. (1962), *The Calculus of Consent: Logical Foundations of Constitutional Democracy*, Ann Arbor: University of Michigan Press.

Butler, H. N. (1985), 'Nineteenth Century Jurisdictional Competition in the Granting of Corporate Privileges', *Journal of Legal Studies* 14: 129.

——— and Ribstein, L. E. (1990), 'Opting Out of Fiduciary Duties: A Response to the Anti-Contractarians', *Washington Law Review* 65: 1.

Callison, J. W., and Vestal, A. W. (2001), '"They've Created a Lamb with Mandibles of Death": Secrecy, Disclosure, and Fiduciary Duties in Limited Liability Firms', *Indiana Law Journal* 76. 271.

Carney, W. J. (1995), 'Limited Liability Companies: Origins and Antecedents', *University of Colorado Law Review* 66: 855.

Cary, W. L. (1974), 'Federalism and Corporate Law: Reflections upon Delaware', *Yale Law Journal* 83: 663.

Choi, S. J. (2001), 'Assessing the Cost of Regulatory Protections: Evidence on the Decision to Sell Securities Outside the United States' (Yale Law and Economics Research Paper No. 253, UC Berkeley Public Law Research Paper No. 51, available at http://papers.ssrn.com/paper.taf?abstract_id=267506).

Coase, R. H. (1960), 'The Problem of Social Costs', *Journal of Law and Economics* 3: 1.

Cumming, D. J., and MacIntosh, J. G. (2000), 'The Role of Interjurisdictional Competition in Shaping Canadian Corporate Law', *International Review of Law and Economics* 20: 141.

Easterbrook, F. H., and Fischel, D. R. (1985), 'Limited Liability and the Corporation', *University of Chicago Law Review* 52: 89.

—— —— (1993), 'Contract and Fiduciary Duty', *Journal of Law and Economics* 36: 426.

Ebke, W. F. (2000), 'Centros—Some Realities and Some Mysteries', *American Journal of Comparative Law* 48: 623.

Farrell, J., and Saloner, G. (1985), 'Standardization, Compatibility, and Innovation', *RAND Journal of Economics* 16: 70.

Fortney, S. S. (1997), 'Seeking Shelter in the Minefield of Unintended Consequences— The Traps of Limited Liability Law Firms', *Washington and Lee Law Review* 54: 717.

Gilson, R. J. (2001), 'Globalizing Corporate Governance: Convergence of Form or Function', *American Journal of Comparative Law* 49: 329.

Goforth, C. R. (1995), 'The Rise of the Limited Liability Company: Evidence of a Race between the States, But Heading Where?', *Syracuse Law Review* 45: 1193.

Grossman, S., and Hart, O. (1986), 'The Costs and Benefits of Ownership: A Theory of Vertical and Lateral Integration', *Journal of Political Economics* 94: 691.

Hamill, S. P. (1998), 'The Origins behind the Limited Liability Company', *Ohio State Law Journal* 59: 1459.

Hamilton, R. W. (1995), 'Registered Limited Liability Partnerships: Present at the Birth (Nearly)', *Colorado Law Review* 66: 1065.

Hansmann, H., and Kraakman, R. (1991), 'Toward Unlimited Shareholder Liability for Corporate Torts', *Yale Law Journal* 100: 1879.

—— —— (2000), 'The Essential Role of Organizational Law', *Yale Law Journal* 110: 387.

Hayek, F. A. (1939), 'The Economic Conditions of Interstate Federalism', *New Commonwealth Quarterly* 5.

Heenen, J. (1975), 'Partnerships and Other Personal Associations for Profit', *International Encyclopedia of Comparative Law* 13: 97.

Hillman, R. W. (2001), 'Professional Partnerships, Competition, and the Evolution of Firm Culture: The Cases of Law Firms', *Iowa Journal of Corporation Law* 26: 1061.

Huang, P. H., and Knoll, M. S. (2000), 'Corporate Finance, Corporate Law and Finance Theory', *Southern California Law Review* 74: 175.

Jackson, H. E., and Pan, E. J. (2001), 'Regulatory Competition in International Securities Markets: Evidence from Europe in 1999', *Business Lawyer* 56: 653.

Jensen, M., and Meckling, W. (1976), 'Theory of the Firm: Managerial Behavior, Agency Costs, and Ownership Structure', *Journal of Financial Economics* 3: 305.

Katz, M. L., and Shapiro, C. (1996), 'Systems Competition and Network Effects', *Journal of Economic Perspectives* 8: 93.

Klausner, M. (1995), 'Corporations, Corporate Law, and Networks of Contracts', *Virginia Law Review* 81: 757.

Kobayashi, B. H., and Ribstein, L. E. (1996), 'Economic Analysis of Uniform State Laws', *Journal of Legal Studies* 25: 131.

—— —— (1997), 'Evolution and Uniformity', *Economic Inquiry* 34: 464.

—— —— (1999a), 'Contract and Jurisdictional Freedom', in F. H. Buckley (ed.), *The Fall and Rise of Freedom of Contract*, Durham, N.C.: Duke University Press.

—— —— (1999b), 'Uniformity, Choice of Law and Software Sales', *George Mason Law Review* 8: 261.

—— —— (2001a), 'Choice of Form and Network Externalities', *William and Mary Law Review* 43: 79.

—— —— (2001b), 'A Recipe for Cookies: State Regulation of Consumer Marketing Information', (George Mason Law and Economics Working Paper No. 01-04, available at http://papers.ssrn.com/paper.taf?abstract_id=261073).

Kornhauser, L. A. (1982), 'An Economic Analysis of the Choice between Enterprise and Personal Liability for Accidents', *California Law Review* 70: 1345.

Law Commission and Scottish Law Commission (2001), *Partnership Law: A Joint Consultation Paper* (Law Commission Consultation Paper No. 59 and Scottish Law Commission Discussion Paper No. 111).

Levmore, S. (1995), 'Love It or Leave It: Property Rules, Liability Rules, and Exclusivity of Remedies in Partnership and Marriage', *Law and Contemporary Problems* 58: 221.

Liebowitz, S. J., and Margolis, S. (1995), 'Path Dependence, Lock-in and History', *Journal of Law, Economics and Organization* 11: 205.

Macey, J. R., and Miller, G. (1987), 'Toward an Interest-Group Theory of Delaware Corporate Law', *Texas Law Review* 65: 469.

Maine, J. A. (2000), 'Linking Limited Liability and Entity Taxation: A Critique of the ALI Reporters' Study on the Taxation of Private Business Enterprises', *University of Pittsburgh Law Review* 62: 223.

Mann, R. J. (1997), 'The Role of Secured Credit in Small-Business Lending', *Georgetown Law Review* 86: 1.

O'Hara, E. A., and Ribstein, L. E. (2000), 'From Politics to Efficiency in Choice of Law', *University of Chicago Law Review* 67: 1151.

Ribstein, L. E. (1987), 'A Statutory Approach to Partner Dissociation', *Washington University Law Quarterly* 65: 357.

—— (1991a), 'Private Ordering and the Securities Laws: The Case of General Partnerships', *Case Western Reserve Law Review* 42: 1.

—— (1991b), 'Unlimited Contracting in the Delaware Limited Partnership and its Implications for Corporate Law', *Iowa Journal of Corporation Law* 17: 299.

—— (1992), 'The Deregulation of Limited Liability and the Death of Partnership', *Washington University Law Quarterly* 70: 417.

—— (1993a), 'Choosing Law by Contract', *Iowa Journal of Corporation Law* 18: 245.

—— (1993b), 'The Revised Uniform Partnership Act, Not Ready for Prime Time', *Business Lawyer* 49: 45.

—— (1994), 'Delaware, Lawyers and Choice of Law', *Delaware Journal of Corporate Law* 19: 999.

—— (1995a), 'The Constitutional Conception of the Corporation', *Supreme Court Economic Review* 4: 95.

—— (1995b), 'The Emergence of the Limited Liability Company', *Business Lawyer* 51: 1.

—— (1995c), 'Linking Statutory Forms', *Journal of Law and Contemporary Problems* 58: 187.

—— (1995d), 'Statutory Forms for Closely Held Firms: Theories and Evidence from LLCs', *Washington University Law Quarterly* 73: 369.

—— (1996), 'Possible Futures for Closely Held Firms', *University of Cincinnati Law Review* 64: 319.

—— (1997a), 'Changing Statutory Forms', *Journal of Small and Emerging Business* 1:11.

—— (1997b), 'Fiduciary Duty Contracts in Unincorporated Firms', *Washington and Lee Law Review* 54: 537.

—— (1997c), 'The Illogic and Limits of Partners' Liability in Bankruptcy', *Wake Forest Law Review* 32: 31.

Ribstein, L. E. (1998a), 'Ethical Rules, Agency Costs and Law Firm Structure', *Virginia Law Review* 84: 1707.

—— (1998b), 'Partner Bankruptcy and the Federalization of Partnership Law', *Wake Forest Law Review* 33: 795.

—— (1998c), 'Partnership', in *New Palgrave Dictionary of Economics and the Law*, London: Macmillan Reference Limited.

—— (1998d), 'Politics, Adaptation and Change', *Australian Journal of Corporate Law* 8: 246.

—— (1999a), 'Limited Liability Unlimited', *Delaware Journal of Corporate Law* 24: 407.

—— (1999b), 'Limited Partnerships Revisited', *University of Cincinnati Law Review* 67: 953.

—— (2001a), 'Ethical Rules, Law Firm Structure, and Choice of Law', *University of Cincinnati Law Review* 6: 1161.

—— (2001b), 'Law v. Trust', *Boston University Law Review* 81: 553.

—— (2001c), 'Lawyer Licensing and State Law Efficiency' (unpublished manuscript, available at http://hal-law.usc.edu/cleo/papers/alea/Ribstein.pdf).

—— and Keatinge, R. A. (1992), *Ribstein and Keatinge on Limited Liability Companies*, St. Paul: West Group.

—— and Kobayashi, B. H. (1995), 'Uniform Laws, Model Laws and ULLCA', *Colorado Law Review* 66: 947.

—— and Letsou, P. V. (1996), *Business Associations*, New York: Matthew Bender.

Riker, W. (1964), *Federalism: Origin, Operation, Significance*, Boston: Little, Brown and Company.

Roe, M. (1996), 'Chaos and Evolution in Law and Economics', *Harvard Law Review* 109: 641.

Rubin, P. H. (1977), 'Why is the Common Law Efficient?', *Journal of Legal Studies* 6: 51.

Shughart II, W. F., and Tollison, R. D. (1985), 'Corporate Chartering: An Exploration in the Economics of Legal Change', *Economic Inquiry* 23: 585.

Smith, T. A. (2001), 'Equality, Evolution and Partnership Law' (University of San Diego Law and Economics, Research Paper No. 11, available at http://papers.ssrn.com/paper.taf?abstract_id=262407).

Sykes, A. O. (1984), 'The Economics of Vicarious Liability', *Yale Law Journal* 93: 1231.

Thompson, R. B. (1994), 'Unpacking Limited Liability: Direct and Vicarious Liability of Corporate Participants for Torts of the Enterprise', *Vanderbilt Law Review* 47: 1.

Tjiong, H. I. T. (2000), 'Breaking the Spell of Regulatory Competition: Reframing the Problem of Regulatory Exit' (Max-Planck Project Group, Preprint No. 2000/13, available at http://papers.ssrn.com/paper.taf?abstract_id=267744).

Vihanto, M. (1992), 'Competition between Local Governments as a Discovery Procedure', *Journal of Institutional and Theoretical Economics* 148: 411.

Weingast, B. (1995), 'The Economic Role of Political Institutions: Market-Preserving Federalism and Economic Development', *Journal of Law Economics and Organization* 11: 1.

Woodward, S. (1985), 'Limited Liability in the Theory of the Firm', *Journal of Institutional and Theoretical Economics* 141: 601.

Wymeersch, E. (2000), 'Centros: A Landmark Decision in European Company Law', in T. Baums (ed.), *Festschrift for Richard M. Buxbaum*, London: Kluwer Law International.

7

The Evolution of Closely Held Business Forms in Europe

JOSEPH A. McCAHERY* and ERIK P. M. VERMEULEN

7.1. INTRODUCTION

This chapter grows out of the ongoing debate among European academics on the need for an expansion of the menu of business organization forms to meet the needs of firms at all levels. Advocates of such reforms claim that company law structures in Europe, which provide a highly developed legal framework and limited liability, are cumbersome and costly for closely held firms to apply. Proponents who favour reform suggest that lawmakers address the problems by devising new business organization statutes that are more varied, less complex, and can potentially enhance efficient outcomes. Traditionally the business organization law available for small businesses has been structured around the needs of larger, publicly owned companies. In most jurisdictions, closely held business forms are burdened by a number of regulatory requirements causing firms to incur substantial costs in carrying out their normal business activities. Moreover, the imposition of many of the European Community's (EC) harmonized company law provisions on small firms is viewed as disproportionate and over-regulatory, and tends to impede the development of an efficient supply of legal rules. The current debate on the regulation of closely held firms can be explained in terms of a trade-off between the need for creditor protection, in case of firm failure, and the commitment to supply legal rules, which give owners the ability to maximize wealth (DTI 1999: 57).

European scholars who express concern about the importance of mandatory requirements as a mechanism to protect creditors and other interests in the firm have justified harmonized rules as a means to avoid a race to the bottom (Deakin 2001). According to this view, the mandatory rules, such as minimum capital requirements, disclosure rules, and accounting rules play a fundamental role in the development of the regulation of companies in Europe. The law and economics perspective stands in contrast to the EC's uniform approach (Romano 1993). A large body of work has focused on the benefits and costs of uniformity. On the one hand, uniform rules have the advantage of simplicity

* An earlier and different version of this chapter was published in the proceedings of the Tilburg University Law School Conference on Close Corporation and Partnership Law Reform in Europe and the United States, and in the *Iowa Journal of Corporation Law*.

and lower administrative costs. Moreover, uniform rules are more appealing to the extent that the benefits of regulation are the same for all firms. On the other hand, uniform rules lead to higher costs for different types of firms. If firms are heterogeneous, efficient regulation calls for the provision of diverse menus of rules in order to reduce the risk of suboptimal uniformity. In the EC context, the common thread in this body of work has been the effort to demonstrate that harmonized rules are cumbersome and costly measures that are not sufficient to regulate externality problems. For instance, minimum capital requirements aimed at protecting the welfare of creditors are costly and haphazard restrictions, which interfere with private orderings while promoting inflexible financial structures (Enriques and Macey 2001: 1186–94; Freedman 2000: 335–8). Consequently, the ability of private parties to obtain superior protection in the market demonstrates, in certain circumstances, the EC mandatory law framework cannot be an efficient approach to limit externalities.

More recently, the relative merits of designing legal rules aimed at the needs of the closely held firm has been stimulated by product and capital market pressures to supply the most competitive business statute for small and medium businesses (SMEs) (DTI 1999: 58). While scholars have debated the advantages of private company statutes for more than a decade, the discussion of competition-based lawmaking for limited liability companies in Europe represents a new departure. Given the presence of market-driven pressures, national regulators are being forced to begin making changes in their corporate law regimes. However, in the absence of freedom of choice in corporate law, it cannot be assumed that lawmakers will generate optimal business law forms for different types of firms.

Indeed, to the extent that national lawmakers have few revenue-based incentives for researching and designing the optimal rules for all types of firms, they have attempted—for the most part—to apply governance structure and mandatory provisions designed for publicly held firms to their closely held counterparts. Thus, the persistence of the suboptimal statutory frameworks is explained by the failure of small firms to lobby lawmakers to create a new business organization form that benefits their special needs. Ultimately, the issue posed is whether, in the absence of regulatory competition, the 'integrated framework' that seems to prevail across Europe will dominate, or whether as a result of increased competition, the 'free standing approach', which involves creating a separate limited liability company statute for small firms, can emerge.[1] Under the circumstances, concentrated incumbents may have the political power necessary to constrain the struggle between the two approaches, and the current bundle of rules may persist despite the possibility of an alternative that promises to yield greater value.

---

[1] To be sure, many European jurisdictions have a separate limited liability vehicle for closely held firms, e.g. the German limited liability company (Volhard and Stengel 1997: 6–8).

The current debate addresses the relative merits of each model. Reform-minded scholars have pointed to the efficiency-enhancing characteristics of the US Limited Liability Company (LLC) and Limited Liability Partnership (LLP), which are tailored to meet the special needs of closely held businesses (Ribstein, Chapter 6, this volume). On the other hand, critics have questioned the effectiveness of these new forms for small businesses and whether they promote economic welfare (Freedman 2000: 327–34). An important reason why commentators are concerned about the new closely held firms is that, by virtue of the organizational structure, there is a natural fear of opportunism that may turn out to be harmful to participants in these firms (Vestal, Chapter 12, this volume). Nevertheless, the LLC is becoming very attractive because it provides for small companies a standard-form contract that combines the most attractive features of partnerships and corporations (Ribstein and Kobayashi 2001). From a European vantage point, the new business statutes are attractive if they are likely to enhance the productivity of small firms. However, the efficiency-enhancing characteristics of the new legal structures may be a weak factor in a politically constrained environment. The combination of organized interest group pressure and the significant switching costs could limit the allure of new business statutes. In such circumstances, policymakers may be strongly disposed to adapt the main features of the existing regime.

The aim of this chapter is to give consideration to the possibility of making available new business forms in the EU based on the LLC, which could lead to an increase in the number of start-up firms as well as satisfying the contracting needs of a range of SME firms. This chapter examines the theoretical arguments about the importance of new organizational forms, inspired by the LLC, for entrepreneurs and SMEs. An important question is whether the introduction of regulatory competition is necessary to overcome the difficulties encountered in promulgating a vehicle that has few mandatory rules. One goal of our chapter is to extend the debate over regulatory competition to closely held organization forms. In principle, one could imagine a European member state becoming the dominant producer of law as product by moving first to establish a legal infrastructure and a bundle of rules that fully benefit the firms incorporating in the jurisdiction. More specifically, the point of this chapter is to show how the development of an innovative business organization form like the LLC—which arguably has significant cost advantages for a broad class of closely held firms (particularly start-ups)—can be expected to strengthen the company law regime of the state choosing to create the statutory innovation, thereby potentially inducing rival member states to supply similar sets of rules.

The purpose of our chapter is not to show that the introduction of a new free-standing form will induce competitive lawmaking in Europe, but that its emergence may create additional pressure on legislatures to respond faster and more effectively to the changing needs of start-ups and other closely held firms. Solving the problems of European company law will take more than the introduction of competition between member states. As such, the approach taken in this chapter has the potential to shed light on the nature of institutional and legal problems that pervade the company lawmaking process and offer insights into how a new organizational approach could affect changes.

This chapter has five sections. Section 7.2 begins by setting out the recent history of European company law. A competitive environment for reincorporations has yet to develop due to the *siège réel* doctrine that governs in most member states. In recent years, however, the combination of a new decision by the European Court of Justice (ECJ) and the legislative blockage in the EC's company law harmonization program has stimulated considerable interest in the competition between jurisdictions. While the real seat doctrine continues to restrict firm mobility, the ECJ's recent judgment in *Centros*[2] and *Überseering*[3] may, in the near term, encourage the introduction of competitive lawmaking within the European Union (EU). This discussion extends the analysis by pointing out that member states may gain by competing to supply flexible business organization forms for closely held businesses. In fact, some of this sort of competition is stimulated by cross-border tax competition (Carney 1997: 327; Code of Conduct Group 1999). Consequently, there are adequate incentives for governments to create better business organization vehicles. However, the recent expansion of private business forms that have appeared over the last decade are disadvantaged by a legal framework that includes European company law requirements, particularly the imposition of a minimum capital requirement and other disclosure rules, and legal rules that derive from public company law. This chapter argues that there are a number of interest group barriers (e.g. notaries) that prevent member states from adopting legal business structures that would make closely held firms better off. The legal regimes that entrepreneurs use for their businesses are likely to give rise to high costs and do not meet the full range of contracting needs for, for instance, banks and suppliers of private equity and entrepreneurs.

However, this chapter suggests that the United Kingdom, which has important differences from Delaware, has recently taken the necessary steps to provide a wide menu of business forms. We maintain that the combination of interest group pressures and a suitable company law regime is confirming evidence that the conditions are favourable for regulatory competition. Further support for this view is evidenced by the interest of government regulators to supply new business statutes in response to the threat of competition posed by offshore jurisdictions for reincorporating entities. Even though there is significant pent-up demand across Europe for businesses to incorporate in low-regulation jurisdictions, it is nevertheless difficult to predict with certitude the circumstances that would lead to the development of regulatory competition in the LLC context.

---

[2] Case C-212/97, *Centros Ltd. v. Erhvervs- og Selskabsstyrelsen* [1999] E.C.R. I-1459; [1999] 2 C.M.L.R. 551.

[3] Case C-208/00, *Überseering BV v. NCC Nordic Construction Company Baumanagement GmbH* [2002] ECR I-9919.

Section 7.3 analyses the institutional and legal structures in the United States and Europe that give rise (albeit to differing degrees) to competitive lawmaking in the field of partnership-type business forms. In Section 7.4, we argue that the creation of a separate statute, based on the US LLC, is desirable because it would result in substantial benefits to entrepreneurs and investors leading to the erosion of barriers that limit the introduction of these statutes. We argue, despite the potential efficiency-enhancing effects of such a form, there may be considerable resistance to its adoption. We conjecture, however, that an entrepreneurial state could be well placed to begin changing their legal structures in response to the needs of the business community. Section 7.5 concludes.

7.2. Reflections on European Company Law

In this section, we briefly describe the current developments in European company law. Three central trends appear to emerge. First, the basic requisites for regulatory competition are missing in the EC. Second, in terms of the debate over competitive lawmaking, the emergence of new judgments from the European Court of Justice (ECJ), which apparently reflects changes within the EC about decentralized lawmaking, provides evidence that regulatory competition for newly formed corporations is an imminent possibility. Third, the development of new statutory organization forms for closely held firms could be stimulated by increased competitive pressures.

7.2.1. Developments in European Corporate Law

One of the most important debates in European company law is whether the market for corporate law will ultimately emerge within the European Union, and if so, whether it will be based on a Delaware-like model in which companies can freely select their country of incorporation (Ebke 2000: 625–8). The virtual absence of any lawmaking behaviour that arguably resembles American charter competition, in the face of mounting economic pressure to reduce existing levels of regulation, suggests that there are substantive legal and procedural barriers to the establishment of jurisdictional competition in the European Union. Indeed, European company law seems to be immune from the evolutionary pressures of competitive lawmaking due largely to the implementation of the European Directives that have given the substantive corporate law of the member states a mandatory quality. The framework of European corporate law can be viewed largely as a patchwork quilt of mandatory rules on accounting standards, capital maintenance, disclosure standards, domestic mergers, the formation of companies, and securities regulation. The gaps in the company law harmonization programme are significant (Hopt 2002: 189–93). They can be traced to fundamental disagreements among member states with regard to employee participation, the EC's subsidiarity principle and its presumption favouring decentralized regulation, and the reluctance of member states to implement the harmonized rules (Wouters 2000: 275). As well as having little legislative success with key aspects of the EC's harmonization agenda, the diversity in corporate law norms in the various member states is thought significant enough to create an additional structural barrier to the Community's economic integration efforts. For instance, at the national level, there are noticeably few incentives for lawmakers to modify regulatory design or reform inefficient rules because of legislative inertia and special interests. At a fairly high level of generality, the differences in the normative arrangements between the continental and common law systems partly explain the deeply rooted conflict among the member states over the direction and pace of the company law harmonization programme. These insights provide important clues as to why only a small number of EC-level policy initiatives have met with legislative success.

At present, the debates about the blockage of company law harmonization initiatives all attempt to deal with the substantive conflicts and practical administrative concerns among member state governments and their difficulties in arriving at a productive compromise. It is under such conditions that a number of scholars have argued that increased exposure to competitive market pressures could, in the absence of legislative change, alter the pattern of existing governance structures. For example, John Coffee (1999) has asserted that the impressive recent growth of continental European stock markets could have a beneficial influence on regulatory reform, reinforcing a shift towards increased levels of disclosure and investor protection. For a number of reasons, the EC has been successful in its efforts to harmonize securities law. It is reasoned that, given the close relationship between securities regulation and corporate law, it should be possible by extension to replicate the success with corporate law harmonization (Coffee 1999: 658–9). Still, despite the increase in capital markets pressures, a strong coalition of interest groups and other path-dependent forces have largely limited the ability of lawmakers to alter or substantially modify inefficient rules in the European Union.

Scholars who have expressed concern about the barriers to legal convergence have argued that the increased European cross-border acquisition of firms operating in weakly protective governance systems by companies with better access to external capital will have a positive effect for investors and may prompt corporate governance transformations. For some commentators, it will be the decline of the governance and funding role of main banks, and the corresponding influx of institutional shareholders from high-quality corporate governance systems, that will likely trigger a disruption in ownership patterns and the stability of control-oriented governance systems based on exclusionary relations between main banks and firms (Gordon 1998). The post-2000 decline in the high technology stock market and the diminishing pace of IPOs will, if anything, add additional pressures, which are already formidable, for governance reform. As a result, the changing market relations will give way to increased competition and formal convergence. The common thread of this diverse body of work has been the effort to identify changes in capital market activity and regulation with the convergence of corporate governance institutions.

The traditional European perspective on company law stands in contrast to the functional convergence model of legal change. Most European scholars are not optimistic about the prospects for market-induced reform of the institutional and legal infrastructure in the EC, notwithstanding the partial harmonization of securities regulation. Fundamentally, the forces, which encourage the development of higher disclosure standards and investor protection, have not had sufficient political support to induce changes to the EC's corporate law structure. The recent inability of the EC Council of Ministers to adopt the 13th Directive on Takeovers is an obvious example of the ability of large German-based corporations, and family-owned firms, which benefit from the current inefficient practices, to block transformational measures (McCahery et al. 2003). Viewed in this light, it would appear that the institutional environment of European decision-making, notwithstanding the advent of a more flexible approach to company law harmonization, is ill-suited for the introduction of agency-reducing corporate law.

It should also be stressed that, besides the existing institutional barriers at the EC level, the development of corporate law has been constrained by several other factors. First, reincorporation costs in Europe make firms immobile. Under the *siège réel* doctrine, which is followed by the majority of member states in the European Union, a corporation is regarded as fully formed and constituted in the jurisdiction where its headquarters are located. A reincorporation triggers taxes on hidden reserves—effectively restricting demand for firms to opt out into different national governance systems. Second, European patterns of corporate regulation and equity capitalization do not open up market opportunities for revenue-seeking jurisdictions. National governance systems do not allow for much shareholder litigation and some restrict shareholder voting rights. Third, Europe's normative landscape is complex. Crucially, labour codetermination in Germany and employee participation structures elsewhere create a barrier to a regulatory system directed to the preferences of managers and shareholders (Wymeersch 1998: 1045). This dampens the demand for responsive lawmaking in the European Union. It is not surprising, therefore, that national legislatures and non-shareholder groups are happy with the current institutional arrangement that impedes legal reforms aimed at improving the welfare of shareholders.

However, even though the dynamics of European company law have not changed fundamentally in more than thirty years, recent developments in EC case law could eventually undermine the *siège réel* doctrine and set the stage for strong competition among jurisdictions in furnishing corporations with optimal rules. This chapter takes the occasion of the European Court of Justice's recent decisions in *Centros* and *Überseering* to enter the debate about the desirability of competitive lawmaking in the EU. The *Centros* case, which appears to question the Court of Justice's *Daily Mail* judgment[4] that the *siège réel* doctrine is compatible with the freedom of establishment, has injected new interest in the need for more flexibility and contractual freedom in EC company law. Proponents of regulatory competition submit that *Centros* permits start-up companies to select the least costly legal system. For example, Ronald Gilson (2001), in trying to explain the implications of the ECJ's judgment for the introduction of regulatory competition, argues that the *Centros* case creates a hybrid mechanism of formal and functional convergence. He contends that the mechanism is form, in the sense that what is at issue is the selection of binding rules of business organization law, but functional, in the sense that as a result of the ECJ's decision, European law is sufficiently flexible to allow at least newly formed firms to adapt their governance structures in response to changing economic conditions.

Even though regulatory competition may not be the aim of the ECJ's intervention, *Centros* could very well usher in a new era of competitive lawmaking with regard to business forms in Europe. Of course, commentators may take refuge behind a phalanx of obscure and convoluted statements in the ECJ's decision in order to defend the *siège réel* doctrine (Halbhuber 2001: 1409). That said, the conclusion that *Centros* stimulates regulatory competition is in line with the policy laid down by the European Commission in the 1985 White Paper on Completing the Internal Market. This new approach to lawmaking aims to limit harmonization efforts to the essential minimum and provides for mutual recognition of national regulations (Woolcock 1996: 289–90). It is only to be expected that the ECJ will continue along the path it set about developing in *Centros*. The *Centros* decision constitutes the necessary causal conditions for further evolution of the regulatory competition framework. The ECJ's judgment also affects litigation decisions and the lawmaking process in general. In this respect, it is worth pointing to the *Überseering* case, referred to the ECJ by the Seventh Chamber of the German Supreme Court, which involved a Dutch close corporation (Besloten Vennootschap (BV)) that had moved its actual central administration to Germany. In its judgment of 5 November 2002, the ECJ found that where a firm incorporated in accordance with the law of a member state (A) in which it has its registered office is deemed, under the law of another member state (B), to have moved its actual centre of administration to member state B, Articles 43 EC and 48 EC preclude member state B from denying the legal capacity and, consequently, the capacity to bring legal proceedings before its national courts for the purpose of enforcing rights under a contract with a firm established in member state B. But even if one takes the view that the *siège réel* doctrine is not wholly contrary to European Union law and decides that the matter must be dealt with by future legislation or conventions, European lawmakers will be on the brink of embracing competitive lawmaking in the context of business forms.

---

[4] *R v HM Treasury & Commissioners of Inland Revenue, ex parte Daily Mail & General Trust PLC* [1988] ECR 5483.

As a consequence of *Centros* and *Überseering*, start-up firms can choose from among the number of member states that offer less restrictive regulations and more favourable conditions to long-term relational contracting. As noted above, the absence of minimum share capital requirements is also an attraction for many small undercapitalized firms. In this context, the United Kingdom, which has signalled its commitment to regulatory responsiveness by offering a varied and high-quality corporate law, could be well-placed to establish itself, like Delaware in the United States, as the leading state for incorporations in Europe (Cheffins 1997: 435–40). To be sure, charter fees and franchise taxes, which provide a high-powered incentive to Delaware to enter the competition for business forms, do not encourage the United Kingdom. However, the United Kingdom could dominate firms' domicile choice as a side-effect of its aspiration to attract large volumes of business and risk capital. The United Kingdom has a substantial body of case law and a highly respected judiciary that could be an important advantage in this respect. The United Kingdom also has a responsive legislature that may be motivated to develop amendments to its company law regime in response to demands in the marketplace. Another attractive feature that could have a significant effect on attracting firms is that UK company law is significantly more flexible vis-à-vis other European jurisdictions. Furthermore, the popularity of the United Kingdom for larger companies and financial intermediaries suggests that it will be willing to offer legal rules that may be attractive for these firms. To the extent that the United Kingdom attracts a large number of new companies and is seen as the jurisdiction where a company might keep its corporate headquarters, lawmakers have incentives to provide legislation that can attract firms incorporated in other states.

Paradoxically, further harmonization could be the last resort for member states to protect their present system against the competitive pressures of the United Kingdom (Ebke 2000: 658; Ribstein, Chapter 6, this volume). Viewed in the context of deregulation, simplification of laws and subsidiarity, there is not much prospect of the EU issuing new directives and extending their scope to closely held business forms. Indeed, recent evidence shows that a number of member states that are highly vulnerable to the pressures of market competition, such as Germany, may be driven to institute reforms to their closely held business forms so as to stem the flow of out-migrating firms to the United Kingdom (Bachmann 2001: 365). The foregoing developments suggest that the UK company law regime poses a competitive threat to EC member states and could be well positioned to compete successfully for out-of-state incorporations as this market fully develops. Moreover, even if UK lawmakers lack a charter revenue motive to attract foreign corporations, they will seek to provide legal rules that are attractive to firms' managers because British business lawyers and accountants will benefit from increased fee revenue (Cheffins 1997: 435). Unlike their counterparts in the United States, the British bar associations have yet to step in to solve collective action problems regarding the drafting and enactment of beneficial legislation. Of course, UK lawyers and accountants will be even more willing to undertake the commitment to develop new corporate law when they face competition from other states to retain in-state companies. As will be shown, British accountants have, to the extent they are sufficiently incentivized to externalize costs, mobilized to lobby lawmakers to enact legislation in order to meet their demands and preferences.

7.2.2. Recent Developments in Closely Held Company Structures: The European Union

The previous section argued that the recent ECJ's decisions in *Centros* and *Überseering* should encourage the development of competitive lawmaking for entrepreneurs, SMEs, and other newly incorporating firms. According to the analysis presented above, the United Kingdom may stand to benefit from meeting the needs of businesses by supplying them with a full range of limited liability forms that can create value. In this section we focus on the factors that led the United Kingdom to enact a separate LLP statute into English law. This section will finish by discussing other initiatives to reform business organization laws in continental Europe and at the level of the European Union.

7.2.2.1. United Kingdom

For many years, European policymakers have been concerned with introducing new organizational forms intended to provide cost advantages for entrepreneurs and small firms. The existing body of empirical evidence, however, reveals that few jurisdictions have rushed to supply flexible business organization statutes that offer cost-saving advantages for closely held businesses. In this context, we have witnessed recently a new UK initiative from the Department of Trade and Industry that involves the establishment of new partnership arrangements that may entail economic benefits for individual firms. Prompted by competition from offshore LLPs, particularly that of Jersey, UK lawmakers recently promulgated a Limited Liability Partnership Act.[5] The legislation introduces a vehicle that has legal personality, a partnership governance structure, limited liability, and partnership tax treatment.[6] In drafting this legislation, the Department of Trade and Industry responded to the pent-up demand from existing partnerships, which wished to transfer to limited liability partnership (LLP) status. Although the LLP Act was initially drafted to address the profes-

---

[5] Limited Liability (Jersey) Law 1997. Motivated by liability and tax considerations, British accountants provided a wholly crafted statute to Jersey lawmakers, a largely passive and accessible body, that decided to adopt the statute. In speedily adopting the statute, Jersey signalled its commitment to a comprehensive set of business forms for foreign organizations. However, high switching costs and doubts about the prospective benefits of incorporating as a Jersey LLP may explain Jersey's failure to capture a share of the UK partnership market, see Freedman and Fitch (1997: 414–15) (enumerating potentially serious problems for firms intending to move to Jersey); (Payne 2000: 134).

[6] The Limited Liability Partnerships Act 2000 and the Finance Act 2001 provide that LLPs be classified as tax partnerships.

sional negligence concerns of large accounting and other service providers in England, the statutory provisions, as enacted, cover all types of businesses.

Yet even if it represents a new policy direction in partnership law, it cannot be viewed as creating a successful, low-cost solution for SMEs—notwithstanding the flexibility and access to lower cost rules afforded by the introduction of the Act. Among other considerations, firms that opt into the LLP form are required to comply with many of the provisions of Part VII of the Companies Act 1985, concerning the preparation of audits and publication of accounts, some provisions of the Companies Act in relation to the registration of charges, the delivery of accounts; the investigation of companies and their affairs, and the Insolvency Act in relation to voluntary agreements, administrative orders, and the winding up of the business. As a consequence, with respect to some operating formalities, the LLP resembles a corporation. In some other respects, and chiefly its decision-making rules, the LLP resembles a partnership. However, the new LLP makes it very costly for entrepreneurs and small firms to structure their relationships through this particular type of business organization form. Even though the LLP supplies its internal members limited liability, the disadvantages of the flimsy statute, which requires firms to comply with corporate default rules, outweigh the practical benefits of the legal form. Hence, unlike its US namesake, the UK LLP is not a general partnership with limited liability. On the contrary, like the US LLC, the UK LLP is a hybrid between a partnership and a corporation. Both business forms are intended to allow firms to obtain the benefits of limited liability while retaining the tax treatment of a partnership. However, they are superficially more similar to a corporation, in that many provisions of the statutes draw directly from the corporate model.[7]

In short, the United Kingdom has responded to the demands of a particular class of firms (i.e. multinational professional service firms) that possess the resources and capacity to draft a comprehensive operational agreement to meet their special requirements. The outcome is that, while the LLP extends limited liability to all types of firms, the effect of high transaction costs will arguably limit its suitability for most SMEs. While there are significant, unanticipated drawbacks during the pioneering stage of the LLP statute, the statutory framework may eventually evolve into a more efficient regime. Assuming that a large number of firms convert to the LLP form, the increasing use of the law should lead to the creation of more beneficial statutory terms. If the LLP proves to be insufficiently flexible and ill-suited to meet all of the needs of small and medium

---

[7] The ULLCA draws many provisions from RUPA. However, many state statutes adopt a more corporate law approach, see Hamilton (2000: 25). As for the UK LLP, it is likely that where there is no agreement and the Regulations do not help, the default position is corporate law. This is reflected in s 1(5) of the LLPs Act 2000, which states that, except for as otherwise provided by this Act or any other enactment, the law relating to partnerships does not apply to a limited partnership. See Comment Company Lawyer (2000: 96) (noting that the international tax treatment of an LLP by non-UK countries may not be transparent because an LLP is not actually a partnership but rather a corporate body); Freedman, Chapter 10, this volume (arguing that 'LLP' is a misnomer for the UK legal form, which is closer to a corporation).

firms, lawmakers might—in the light of the government's policy to provide the most competitive legal firms possible for commercial businesses seeking limited liability and transferability of shares—eventually take steps to adopt new legislation targeted to the needs of the class of firms effectively barred from switching to the LLP form.[8] However, while the prospects for new legislation depend on the success of the lobbying efforts of organized interest groups in combination with the threat of external competition, in the absence of a revenue-based incentive, it is far from clear whether lawmakers will undertake a new company law initiative for the benefit of unorganized small firms.

7.2.2.2. France

A second example of responsive lawmaking in Europe is the 1994 introduction of the société par actions simplifiée (SAS) and its subsequent modification in 1999.[9] In recent years, the competition between states for real inflows of capital has caused member states to adopt a variety of new business forms designed to stem the outflow of taxable resources. The pressure of competition from the Dutch private company (Besloten Vennootschap, or BV), which is viewed as a more suitable closely held business form, stimulated French lawmakers to adopt a new organizational structure that has significant cost benefits for firms (Wouters 2000: 286 n. 120; Wymeersch 2004). As conceived, the SAS creates the opportunity for partners in a joint venture—and for other purposes—to adopt a legal structure that is truly flexible in the organization and control of the firm. This vehicle allows for parties to choose the firm's decision-making structure and the contents of its by-laws. Arguably, the SAS holds out the potential to provide cost-saving benefits that may attract new incorporations, allowing France to compete effectively with Germany, the Netherlands, and the United Kingdom. By making the corporate structure more adaptable to the business needs of SMEs and allowing its shareholders to be both individuals and legal entities, the French government would probably have increased the number of new domestic businesses, and perhaps a small subsection of SMEs. Regardless of whether business activity increases as a result of the adoption of the SAS, cri-

---

[8] See Freedman (Chapter 10, this volume). Despite its complex and cumbersome quality, the earliest empirical evidence on registrations of LLPs compiled by Jordans shows that, in fact, SMEs are most attracted to this new limited liability vehicle. Astonishingly, more than 75% of the 600 or so of the LLPs registered since 6 April 2001 have been drawn from the wider business community. See News Digest (2001: 317). Allegedly, SMEs are attracted to the LLP, as this form has important advantages over other business forms, such as the private company and the general partnership. For instance, by forming an LLP a firm avoids paraphernalia associated with companies, while obtaining credibility. Moreover, the LLP might be viewed as a focal point around which a new network will arise. That professional firms are lagging behind other business firms could partly be explained by the reluctance of professionals to disclose their financial details (Freedman, Chapter 10, this volume; Peel and Eaglesham 2002). Nevertheless, the publication of the Statement of Recommended Practice for Accounting for LLPs is expected to increase interest in the LLP even more. As at 8 July 2002, 2,580 LLPs had been registered in England and Wales.

[9] Law No. 94-1 of Jan. 3, 1994 J.O., Jan. 4, 1994, p. 129; Law No. 99-587 of July 12, 1999, J.O., July 13, 1999, p. 10396. See (Guyon 1999).

tics argue that the complexity of the SAS may lead to incomplete contracting, since the statute fails to supply a comprehensive statutory template that the parties can fall back on when establishing the distribution and allocation of powers and responsibilities. There are a substantial number of issues that parties cannot contract for themselves *ex ante* due to the absence of sufficient legal precedent necessary to write joint venture agreements.

Moreover, provisions in the French civil code relating to the companies (as well as all the SA provisions) apply to the SAS (Lazarski and Lagarrigue 2000: 108 and n. 10). It is clear that incorporation under the SAS framework may be costly and problematic. Not only are the general corporate law provisions complex and onerous, but management must take steps to draft by-laws in order to ensure that general corporate law provisions are not applicable. It is clear, moreover, that the judicial application of the corporate law provisions to the SAS might also lead to some uncertainty. Even if contract parties are willing to accept the challenge of drafting an agreement for the SAS, transaction costs, information asymmetries, and strategic behaviour could prevent them from bargaining their way to an optimal agreement. Consequently, even if the SAS can provide more flexibility for closely held firms, the costs involved in complex legal drafting to adapt the public corporation framework to the needs of a close corporation will discourage most firms from incorporating under the SAS. If this is the case, the difficulties in modifying the SAS to benefit small and medium firms could prove problematic. Indeed, French lawmakers have been slow to revise the inefficient statutory provisions that have a costly impact on smaller firms (ibid. 106). By allowing SMEs to employ the SAS framework, without the value of corresponding benefits for these enterprises, French lawmakers were apparently more motivated by calculations of self-interest to offer window-dressing than introduce reforms that have redistributive effects. As with the UK LLP, government lawmakers will likely achieve much more by developing a variety of legal rules that are directly beneficial to closely held firms.

7.2.2.3. Germany

Whilst bereft of competitive pressures, the German legislature has made several amendments to its traditional partnership forms through the revision of the Commercial Law in 1998.[10] For instance, the German legislature followed the recommendation of the European Commission that member states should introduce the continuity of partnerships into their national laws. In this view, the unsophisticated entrepreneurs should not be victimized by inefficient fallback provisions that oblige them to dissolve their businesses (e.g., in the event of the unforeseen death of any partner) (see § 131(3) of the German Commercial Code (Handelsgesetzbuch—HGB)). In all likelihood, the continuity of business is the appropriate default rule. It may well reduce transaction costs because most partners will be spared the need to reach a private agreement on this issue.

---

[10] The German legislation has reformed several provisions of partnership law as part of the Handelsrechtsreformgesetzes in 1998 (Schmidt 1998).

The revision of the Commercial Code does not benefit partnerships generally, however (see § 131(3) of the German Commercial Code (Handelsgesetzbuch—HGB)). It only applies to the commercial partnerships formed and registered for commercial purposes, such as general partnerships and the limited partnership.[11] The law concerning the civil partnership,[12] which does not have commercial objects (e.g. agriculture, forestry, educational and professional activities), does not recognize the continuity of the partnership as a legal principle. The death or bankruptcy of any partner causes the dissolution of a German civil partnership when nothing to the contrary has been agreed.

While there is no distinction between civil and commercial law in Commonwealth countries, the principle has been deeply rooted in continental European jurisdictions. In partnership law, it entails that professional service firms are prohibited in principle from using a commercial partnership. While the distinction may be explained by history rather than compelling logic, there are nevertheless several important consequences attached to the commercial qualification of a partnership (Kessler and Schiffers 1999). Most importantly, commercial partnerships are generally characterized as legal entities by code or by judicial usage. Typically, entity status can be acquired by official registration. But even when legal personality is not explicitly conferred to commercial partnerships, which is the case in Germany, there is a preponderance of entity-based features: the partnership has its own rights and obligations; the partnership may sue and be sued in its own name; and the partnership can hold title to property (see § 124 of the German Commercial Code (Handelsgesetzbuch—HGB)).

Yet the difference between civil and commercial partnerships is gradually diminishing over time. Commercial law reform in Germany has broadened the scope of general and limited partnerships not explicitly regulated by the commercial code (see § 105(2) of the German Commercial Code (Handelsgesetzbuch—HGB); Schmidt 1998: 62). The only prerequisite is that the partnership must be entered in the commercial register. Moreover, case law and commentary increasingly attribute entity features to 'external' civil partnerships, which enter into legal relationships with third parties (Gummert 1995). In fact, it might be argued that the German legislature has more or less confined the entity status of the civil partnership (see § 190 of the German Business Transformation Act (Unwandlungsgesetz—UmwG)).

Despite the improvement, the question of whether the civil partnership may sue and be sued in its own name is still open to dispute (Gummert 1995; Schmidt 1997: 1805–18). Furthermore, despite the efforts to attribute entity features to

---

[11] Business participants who want to form a partnership for the purpose of conducting a trade or business regulated by the commercial code must register as either a general partnership (offene Handelsgesellschaft (oHG)) or a limited partnership (Kommanditgesellschaft (KG)), which are governed by the second book of the German Commercial Code.

[12] The German civil partnership (Gesellschaft des bürglichen Rechts (GbR)) is governed by § 705 and further of the German Civil Code (Bürgliches Gesetzbuch (BGB)). The rules laid down in the civil code also apply to commercial partnerships to the extent that the Commercial Code is silent.

partnerships, creditors generally maintain their right to enforce their claims against partners individually. Partly because of the acceleration of malpractice claims, professionals organized as civil partnerships had to find another way to structure their business with some kind of limited liability protection. In order to meet their special needs, the German legislature promulgated a professional limited liability partnership (Partnerschaftgesellschaft) in 1995 and 1998.[12] The German limited liability partnership offers the benefits of the ability of partnerships to sue and be sued in its own name and adopts techniques for limitations of liabilities arising from contractual and tort claims against the partnership.

In response to British legislative initiatives, German academics do recommend that domestic lawmakers become more involved in responsive lawmaking. Corresponding pressures have not sufficiently emerged in practice to warrant German legislative attention to the competitive pressures highlighted in the academic debate. Nevertheless, Germany's popular commercial partnership-type business form, the GmbH & Co KG (Meyer 2002: 182), which has already created considerable learning and network effects in Germany, has the potential to increase Germany's share of the European venture capital industry. Furthermore, the limited partnerships with shares (Kommanditgesellschaft auf Aktien— KGaA), in which the general partners have exclusive management control and the limited partners may transfer their shares freely, appears to respond to the pent-up demand for more easily tradeable equity investments.[14] As interests in venture capital funds already change hands increasingly in the secondary market, the conversion to a combination of limited partnership and public corporation, which offers ready access to liquidity and market price, could be a viable alternative. In order to be competitive, legal and fiscal complications regarding these hybrid business forms should be minimized. Although Germany has recently created law and regulations clarifying the positions of these vehicles,[14] more needs to be done

[13] Initially the Partnerschaftgesellschaft, which is regulated by the Gesetz über Partnerschaftsgesellschaften Anghöriger Freier Berufe (Part GG), was not very popular. Indeed, at the time of enactment, case law also paved the way for professionals to incorporate. See BGH NJW 1994, 786 and BaytObLG NJW 1995, 1999, and Sommer (1995). Recently, the German legislature acknowledged professional corporations such as the Anwalts-GmbH (Römermann 1999). Professionals have the choice of either selecting the Partnerschaftgesellschaft or incorporating. Since both procedures appear to be costly and cumbersome to individuals (for instance, the Partnerschaftgesellschaft statute is linked awkwardly to both the civil and commercial partnership rules), they had often attempted to limit their liability by publicly limiting the authority to act for the partnership and adding 'limited liability' (mit beschränkter Haftung, mbH), to the civil partnership's name. This attempt to introduce limited liability into the partnership form was rejected by the German Supreme Court (BGH v. 27.9.1999—11 ZR 371/98). The Court stated that a partnership's liability could not be limited by either a name extension or other indication.

[14] This hybrid form was used frequently in the period when corporations existed by virtue of a concession by the government. Currently, the KgaA is viewed as an intermediate business form between the close corporation and the public corporation (Meyer 2002: 186–7).

[15] For example, the enactment of the conversion code (Umwandlungsgesetz) in 1994 simplified the procedure of converting a GmbH or GmbH & CoKG to a GmbH & Co KGaA. See Halasz et al. (2002). The popularity of the KgaA may increase with the recognition of the German Supreme Court in 1997 (BGH v. 24.2.1997—II ZB 11/96, BGHZ 134, 302) that a corporation could be the sole partner in a limited partnership with shares.

to make them the standard structure for European venture capital funds. For instance, consideration should be given to codifying 'safe harbour' provisions that state to what extent a limited partner may participate in the control of the firm so as to improve certainty and accessibility to foreign investors. The law should also be more generous in liability protection for a limited partner, if the formation of the limited partnership or the admission of the limited partner have not been filed in the commercial register.[16]

7.2.3. Developments at the EU Level: The European Private Company

The foregoing discussion of the difficulties in changing national corporate law regimes to create a framework that meets the needs of closely held firms leads to a general observation: the linkage of public corporation law to closely held firms is likely to be inefficient. States seldom supply default rules that are optimal for the operation of closely held firms. This raises the question whether it is necessary from a cost-benefit standpoint to propose the adoption of a common set of European rules for closely held firms.

While EC regulators have pursued harmonization of public corporations and the protection of shareholders in order to achieve further Community integration, there has been no real attempt to adopt a series of similar measures for the benefit of closely held companies (Boucourechliev 2001). Over the last decade, Brussels lawmakers have adopted a series of approaches to the development of common rules, notably the 12th Directive and the European Economic Interest Grouping. Beginning in 1995, a group of European business leaders and legal experts of different nationalities, brought together on the initiative of CREDA, the research centre of the Paris Chamber of Commerce and Industry, have been attempting to develop an appropriate organizational structure for SMEs.[17] The group has proposed the introduction of a draft European Private Company

---

[16] § 176(1) of the German Commercial Code (Handelsgesetzbuch—HGB)) states that a limited partner who agreed with the commencement of the business is unlimitedly liable for the limited partnerships' debts and obligations incurred before the registration of the partnership in the commercial register § 176(2) provides that a new limited partner is unlimitedly liable for debts and obligations incurred after his admission and before the amendment to the registration. For an example of § 176, see Schmidt (2002). This article gives an intended limited partner explicit protection from general partner liability if he erroneously believed he was a limited partner and did not give a third party any reason to believe—in good faith—that he was actually a general partner at the time of the transaction. Re-RULPA § 303 provides that a limited partner is not personally liable, even if the limited partner participates in the management and control of the limited partnership.

[17] In general, Brussels lawmakers have focused on publicly held corporations and their equivalents. Over the last decade, they have adopted a series of approaches to the development of close corporations, notably the Twelfth Directive on single member companies and the EEIG (Lutter 2000: 7–8). However, the High Level Group of Company Law Experts released, on 4 November 2002, the final Report on a Modern Regulatory Framework for Company Law in Europe which stated that the EPC is not considered a priority for the European Commission in the light of the concern to pass a Tenth and Fourteenth Directive on cross-border mergers and the transfer of registered or head office. Recently, the EC accepted the recommendation of the High Level Group that a feasibility study be conducted to assess the implications of a legal statute for SMEs (Commission of the European Communities 2003: 21–2).

(EPC), which is designed to be flexible enough to accommodate all types of firms in different business situations (Helms 1998: 1–3). In contrast to the European Company, which is grounded on the German Aktiengesellschaft and therefore mainly aimed at publicly held firms, the EPC has been designed so as to offer closely held firms, which are particular SMEs wishing to develop on the European market, a Europe-wide, simple and effective form that meets their specific requirements. The draft EPC regulation is very concise, comprising only thirty-eight articles (CCIP/CNPF 2001). The EPC draft articles of association require that parties specify the rights of the shareholders, the organization and operation of the company, and the powers of its governing bodies. These steps appear to make the EPC a less complicated and a more flexible form of business entity. For example, the draft EPC regulation offers substantial flexibility to vary the firm's decision-making structure by providing, like the US LLC, the opportunity to vary from a shareholder-managed governance structure to a manager-managed structure. Usually most European close corporations are viewed as owner-controlled firms; consequently, the new form may offer parties more flexibility than other business forms.

The drafters have incorporated few mandatory rules into the EPC regulation, which should suit the needs of different types of firms. At first blush, the flexibility of the EPC structure, combined with limited liability, would be sufficient to outweigh the absence of some defaults and the utilization of certain EC Directives. However, few believe that the new draft EPC regulation can resolve the practical difficulties that prevent its immediate adoption and implementation by the member states. Besides the resistance from national groups, there is concern that the draft regulation holds out few cost-saving benefits for small firms. The first problem is that, despite the significant differences between close and public corporations, the draft EPC regulation, which is designed to offer enterprises in the European Union a genuine European corporate form, incorporates the Second EC Directive, which presents an insuperable barrier (Schutte-Veenstra 2001: 322). Second, the draft EPC regulation supplies few default rules that the parties can adopt off-the-rack.[18] From a small firm vantage

---

[18] The European Private Company aspires to become an all-purpose vehicle with respect to closely held business forms. The draft regulation (see Appendix, this volume) allows business parties much leeway in organizing their firm and the relationship between them. In order to help parties save substantially on transaction costs, the drafters of the EPC regulation have created a model standard form 'Articles of Association' (art 13). Model A is a standard form for small 'member-managed' quasi-partnership firms. Model B is intended to meet the needs of larger businesses with one or more 'passive' investors. Statutory ambiguity and linking problems are likely to ensue from the 'unified business form' approach, which expects all types of closely held business firms to organize under one statute. With respect to the EPC, the vexed question is one of which fiduciary duties courts will apply to shareholders of an EPC. The Regulation and the Model Articles of Association are silent on this issue. The Explanatory memorandum, however, states that the EPC should be viewed as a company 'not issuing shares to the public, and the shareholders of which are bound by a strong bond of partnership, a true company of associates'. Unless these complex issues are resolved by the drafters, we can expect few firms to be willing to opt into this European business form, given the uncertainties. It might be argued that the omission will lead to incomplete contracting, since

point, the costs involved in creating their own contract-based rights are substantial, and parties will obviously have few incentives to reorganize under the
current draft EPC regulation. It should, however, be possible for the drafters to
create default terms that enhance the private ordering by making the law clear
and predictable to parties governed by such terms. Presumably, the number of
firms that would be forced to incur the costs of contracting around the untai-
lored default rules is very small. The foregoing point about the evolution of the
draft EPC regulation suggests that the persistence of inefficient terms may be
due to the inability of the drafters to overcome the EC company law inertia that
prevents the promulgation of off-the-rack standard-form contracts tailored to
meet the needs of small firms.

7.2.4. Path Dependency

The previous section asserted that the needs of close corporations are not easily
met through the adaptation of public corporation statutes or EC Directives,
emphasizing the theoretical importance of making available a coherent set of
standard forms that provide limited liability and direct management in a separate statute. Not surprisingly, a free-standing legal business form may be necessary to modify the current corporate law framework, which is inefficient and
burdensome for closely held and public firms. Much as in the US context, a
separate framework may be necessary for closely held firms because of the
uncertainty created by the judicial interpretation of EC Directives (which were
intended to regulate public corporations) by the ECJ (Wouters 2000: 265–6;
Ayres 1992: 387–8).

In the light of these and other factors, what explains the persistence of inefficient rules for closely held firms in Europe? There are a number of explanations.
First, even if a particular business organization form would make closely held
firms more efficient, it may not be in the interests of most lobby groups (i.e.
professional advisers and creditors) to modify the law to allow more efficient
forms to emerge. Predictably, governments respond by failing to adopt value-
increasing legislation from which they could derive valuable tax revenues and
other economic benefits. Consequently, lawmakers present a good case for
adapting the existing, suboptimal regime to meet the needs of small firms (DTI
1999: 64–5).

Second, there are few incentives to introduce legal innovations. The standardization of provisions in corporate codes may account for the lock-in to the existing mandatory provisions. Many law-and-economics scholars take for granted

the Regulation and model Articles of Association fail to supply a comprehensive statutory framework. The fact that art 12 of the Regulation provides that the 'matters governed by this Regulation
shall not be subject to application of the law of Member States, even with respect to those points
which it does not settle expressly' only complicates the practical use of this form. In addition, the
reference to the general principles of the Regulation, Community company law, and the general
principles common to national laws (see art 12 of the Regulation) does not exactly clarify the
gap-filling discretion of courts.

that when network externalities or learning effects are present, the value of a contractual term increases (Kahan and Klausner 1996). Statutory terms under the public corporation codes confer large network benefits to users of those statutes. In most EC member states, the majority of firms are organized under the provisions of a general corporate code. Such codes not only create large network benefits, but firms also expect to obtain further benefits as new companies incorporate. The learning benefits which come from the use of the corporate code also explain why most parties that originally opted into the general corporation code have an incentive to continue to use the regime (Bratton and McCahery 1995: 1900). If these benefits are taken into account, newly formed companies will likely migrate to the business corporation statutes that confer larger network benefits to the user. This will mean that demand will be higher than it otherwise might be, which in turn will lead to the supply of standardized terms rather than customized terms that benefit small firms. Because standardized terms offer certainty, business lawyers, when advising clients about incorporation decisions, will recommend a standardized term— even if suboptimal—rather than draft a customized term that could lead to a higher expected value for a client (Bernstein 1995: 248). The result, in turn, is that continuous use of the dominant business form, even if not ideally suited for some firms, will serve to reduce the incentives for lawmakers (and lawyers) to innovate. Like other areas of law reform in continental Europe, the reluctance to diverge from the existing company law framework means that, even if new business forms were adopted, parties might be unwilling to substitute the standard form for non-standard terms (DTI 1999: 64). In short, the benefits that accrue to a standardized general corporation regime may be sufficient to outweigh the benefits that small firms could realize by shifting to a separate statute designed for small companies.

7.3. The Prospect of Regulatory Competition in Europe

The potential introduction of new business forms holds out the prospects of overcoming the negative effects of lock-in. We now turn to regulatory competition theory and ask whether competitive lawmaking provides sufficient incentives to create adequate demand for the introduction and diffusion of new LLC and partnership-like forms in Europe. The recent development of closely held business forms appears to be consistent with the assertion that even imperfect regulatory competition is an effective means to bring about more efficient laws.

7.3.1. The US Experience: Competition among States

In the context of corporate law, regulatory competition (a legislative process in which governments endeavour to provide a more favourable regulatory environment to promote the competitiveness of domestic businesses or to attract more business activity from abroad) (Woolcock 1996; Bratton and McCahery 1997b: 220–43) has been well publicized in the United States (Romano 1993). The US legal system traditionally views business organization law in general as a local matter reserved to the states' governments (Bebchuk 1992: 1438). Consequently, the corporation statutes of some states may differ appreciably from those of most other states on many critical matters. Once US business owners decide to incorporate, they must select an attractive state of incorporation. Under traditional conflict-of-laws rules, courts will respect this choice even if the corporation in question has no other contact with the chosen state. The corporate laws of the incorporating state govern the basic rights and duties of a corporation and its participants. As a result, the revenue generated by the charter fees and franchise taxes, which can be collected directly from incorporating firms, gives smaller states a high-powered incentive to provide attractive rules (Romano 1993: 38). The ability of firms to incorporate in those states with the most attractive legal regimes, and the eagerness of states to 'steal' corporations from each other, have led to the emergence of a potentially robust market for incorporations in the United States.

At the end of the nineteenth century, New Jersey and Delaware, concerned about incorporation decisions, adopted modernized general incorporation statutes. Eventually, Delaware's statute made it the leading incorporation state in the United States since the 1920s, presently serving as the state of incorporation for nearly half of the corporations listed on the New York Stock Exchange and more than half of all Fortune 500 firms (Romano 1993: 6–17; Fisch 2000: 1061). In addition, Delaware is also the leading destination for firms that opt to reincorporate. Clearly, Delaware's value to incorporating firms is more than an up-to-date statute. The possibility of other states rapidly free-riding on the efforts and resources of the Delaware legislature by copying its statute would entail Delaware's lead being exhausted in a very short period of time. Free-riding by other states acts as a severe disincentive to invest any resources in legal innovation. If the possibility existed of other states rapidly free-riding on its legislative efforts and resources, Delaware would not consider legal change so as to keep its rules attractive for a variety of firms in the future (Ayres 1995: 545–50). Nevertheless, the attractiveness of Delaware as the incorporating state lies in significant 'first-mover' advantages in the production of corporate charters. For instance, the less easily replicated judicial expertise and other enduring advantages, such as a well-developed corporate case law, learning and network benefits, herd behaviour, and the superiority of Delaware's specialized chancery court, arguably preserve Delaware's leading position over time (Easterbrook and Fischel 1991: 212–13; Fisch 2000: 1063; Kahan and Kamar 2001: 1212–14; Romano 1985).

Delaware's corporate law plays a key role in the evolution of corporations in the United States, not only because regulatory competition has caused a widespread diffusion of its law (Carney 1997), but also because Delaware law provides an alternative set of rules that serve firms and their legal advisers across the country. Consequently, many commentators have dealt with the vexed question of whether the choice of Delaware's corporate law eventually leads to value maximization. In other words, is regulatory competition better described as a 'race-to-the-bottom' or as a 'race-to-the-top'? This question has been debated extensively in the US literature. Since this discussion is likely to become increasingly relevant to Europe it is worth providing a brief summary of the literature here (Bebchuk et al. 2002: 1800–1812; Daines 2001: 528).

7.3.2. Regulatory Competition: 'Race-to-the-bottom' or 'Race-to-the-top'?

As management decides where to incorporate, it is generally agreed that Delaware has produced corporate statutes that are attractive to incumbent management. Cary (1974), who started the debate on regulatory competition, argued that in order to attract corporations, Delaware had systematically tilted its corporate law to favour management at the expense of shareholders, creating a race-to-the-bottom. Against this background, Cary viewed regulatory competition as a means to achieve a suboptimal level of regulations and proposed a federal corporate statute that set minimum standards in selected areas of corporation law. Shortly after Cary's article was published, Winter (1977) criticized the race-to-the-bottom thesis. He argued that regulatory competition is an effective means to discipline self-interested government authorities, to promote innovation, and to supply optimal rules and regulations. In this view, management chooses the state of incorporation to maximize shareholder welfare. If this were not the case, corporations would raise less money from investors, and the value of a firm's stock would decline relative to stock in a similar firm incorporated in a state with value-maximizing laws, thereby increasing the probability of the incumbent management being displaced by a hostile takeover. In this view, regulatory competition induces states to enact corporate rules that are beneficial to shareholders. The race-to-the-bottom thesis offers no theoretical or empirical explanation of why shareholder investors, who are generally risk-averse, voluntarily entrust their money to managers who have no incentive to maximize their welfare or invest in firms incorporated in Delaware. Conversely, empirical work by Romano (1985: 265–83) and Daines (2001) supports Winter's assessment by demonstrating that Delaware law actually maximizes value, thereby undermining Cary's position that shareholders are victimized by regulatory competition (Easterbrook and Fischel 1991: 214–15; but cf. Bebchuk et al. 2002: 1886–90).

Yet some commentators continue to point to possible shortcomings of the competitive process that ensue from the divergence between the interests of managers and public shareholders (Bebchuk 1992; Bebchuk et al. 2002). In their view, the development of state anti-takeover legislation perfectly exemplifies the shortcomings of regulatory competition. Because of the ability of firms' management to capture state legislation, states (including Delaware) have developed anti-takeover statutes and judicial decisions permitting the use of defensive tactics that are overly protective of incumbent managers at the expense of shareholders (Bratton and McCahery 1995: 1887–9). If the possibility of shareholder exit by tender to a hostile offeror is severely threatened, market mechanisms cannot adequately align the interests of managers and shareholders. By providing a constant and credible risk of hostile acquisitions, the takeover market creates a powerful incentive for managers to restrain from managerial self-dealing. Assuming that the 'market-for-corporate-control' is economically efficient in that it increases firm value, regulatory competition has serious implications for the race-to-the-top thesis. Consequently, according to this argument, mandatory federal rules should at least ensure that the market for corporate control remains active, robust, and competitive (Bebchuk 1992; Bebchuk and Ferrell 1999).

It is doubtful, however, that US business organization laws will be placed under federal jurisdiction in the near future. Although it is conventional wisdom among US scholars that regulatory competition produces a race-to-the-top with respect to some areas of corporate law (Bebchuk and Ferrell 1999: 1171), it certainly has its flaws. First, states do not pursue regulatory competition solely by offering rules that meet their clients' needs. High-powered interest groups within a particular state induce the competitive process because of considerable tangible benefits. It has been argued that Delaware's corporation law is devised to maximize the amount of work performed by lawyers who are members of the Delaware Bar (Macey and Miller 1987: 491–8). By providing standards and ambiguous default rules rather than rules that are clear in application, Delaware law enhances the amount of litigation in the state (Bratton and McCahery 1995: 1887–8; Kahan and Kamar 2001: 1217). Delaware lawmakers thereby respond to the lobbying efforts of in-state lawyers who are able to capture a considerable share of the incorporating revenues, due to litigation-increasing standards.

Furthermore, since Delaware can rely on its dominant position in the market for incorporations, it could allow itself to prevent the emergence of optimal legal rules that would prevail in a perfectly competitive market (Kahan and Kamar 2001: 1252). Finally, recent empirical research indicates that regulatory competition in the context of corporate law is imperfect as not only the product quality, but also the location of the 'seller' plays a pivotal role. It appears that since firms display a marked home preference with respect to business forms, states are more successful in retaining in-state firms than attracting out-of-state business formations (Bebchuk and Cohen 2001). Thus, Delaware closely resembles a monopolistic 'seller' possessing market power and competitive advantages that other jurisdictions cannot replicate. The increasing return mechanisms act as substantial barriers to other states wishing to enter the market for out-of-state business formations.

Nevertheless, the shortcomings of regulatory competition are hardly a ringing endorsement of centralized lawmaking. Regulatory competition may not automatically yield an efficient outcome, but its legal product is arguably superior to what a centralized regime would produce. Even though it might be argued that the absence of competitive conditions gives domestic special interest groups less power to influence national lawmaking (O'Hara 2000: 1579–88), a centralized legislature in a federal regime is likely to be the object of the same or more intensive lobbying (Romano 2001: 573). In addition, that path-dependence factors will miraculously dissipate under a centralized regime is simply not plausible. Then again, the presence of conditions conducive to regulatory competition gives a state legislature at least some incentive to be responsive to changing needs and conditions of the business environment. Not doing so could arguably detract from the state's leading position.

To illustrate the point, let us suppose that regulatory competition induces state legislatures to benefit special interest groups, and local Bar members in particular. As we have seen, the Bar has an incentive to lobby for arbitrary amendments that give rise to judicial clarification. The leading state is likely to respond to the lobbying efforts as statutory modification and updates make it more difficult for other states to develop copycat legislation (Ayres 1995: 558–9). Yet interest groups appear to play a seemingly innocuous role when competitive forces from outside the legal system are present. It is therefore reasonable to infer that regulatory competition results in laws that are more public-regarding (Carney 1997). Even in the case of the enactment of anti-takeover legislation in Delaware, which suggests a stronger negative participation of the organized Bar in a competitive lawmaking process (Bratton and McCahery 1995: 1887), it is vital to note that Delaware's takeover statute has not been an innovative step, but rather a reluctant reaction to contemporary developments (Ayres 1995: 555–6). Interest groups' gain from inefficient legal procedures and increasing litigation is arguably constrained by jurisdictional competition, which appears to provide a safety valve against harmful laws (Romano 1993: 862). The recent history of state takeover laws demonstrates the merits of state competition. That some jurisdictions have no or only mild anti-takeover regulation restricts how far other jurisdictions can go, as well as the influence of interest groups, especially when the milder laws are in leading states. That said, the moderation in lobbying efforts varies from one type of law to another. Because firm particip-ants adopt business organization laws *ex ante*, the presence of competitive forces may well predict that lawyers' involvement in this field will produce a more efficient outcome.

7.3.3. Regulatory Competition and Closely Held Business Forms: The US Experience

The recent development of closely held business forms in the United States appears to be consistent with the assertion that even imperfect regulatory competition is an effective means to bring about more efficient laws. To be sure, closely held firms usually employ local business forms. They are mostly organized according to the business organization laws of the state in which they have their principal place of business (Johnson 1997: 255). For many closely held firms, the relatively high costs of operating outside the formation state may exceed the benefits of organizing under a more efficient foreign business form (Ribstein 1992: 266). They must usually pay charter fees and franchise taxes to the formation state—not only for organizing within that state, but also for maintaining the entity status. In addition, they must pay (sometimes overlapping) taxes to the local state for the privilege of doing business there. More importantly, local business lawyers may be loath to give legal advice on the laws of other states. Generally, closely held firms, which are naturally hesitant to obtain legal services, have no alternative but to employ a domestic business form. This seems especially true of small and informal partnerships, as the participants may have no real expectations concerning the applicable law. In addition, the business organization laws for partnerships used to be remarkably uniform, making choice-of-law decisions largely irrelevant. For instance, the Uniform Partnership Act has been adopted in fifty of the fifty-one US jurisdictions, although there were variations in the wording of the Act.

The weak financial incentives for states to compete for closely held firms suggest that competitive lawmaking has no influence on the evolution of partnership-type business forms (Ayres 1992: 376–8; Bratton and McCahery 1997a: 675). Until fairly recently, state legislatures did not exert themselves in researching and drafting closely held business organization laws. However, recent empirical research seems to indicate that jurisdictional competition has gained a foothold in this area of the law as well.[19] The limited liability company (LLC) bandwagon that rolled across the United States in the early 1990s indicates that most states are responsive to competitive forces in the drafting and enactment of these business organization laws (Goforth 1995: 1271–2; Macey 1995: 447). Increasingly, states have supply-side incentives to take a proactive attitude towards legislative innovations in the field of organization laws, so as to capture and retain closely held firms. For instance, new entrepreneurial ventures are more mobile than large publicly held corporations in terms of the low decision-making costs of changing their state of organization in response to inefficient legal rules. Hence, smaller states that have acknowledged Delaware's

---

[19] It appears firms participants in partnership-type business forms had no expectations concerning the applicable law, as there has long been a high degree of uniformity in state partnership law. Yet uniformity has broken down with regard to traditional partnership forms, and has never existed with respect to limited liability partnership and limited liability company forms, thereby increasing the importance of choice-of-law issues. In fact, state legislatures increasingly provide explicitly for statutory enforcement of formation state law for new entities, such as LLPs and LLCs. The Revised Uniform Partnership Act (RUPA) § 106(a) replaces the complex Restatement (Second) of Conflicts § 294, stating that subject to contrary agreement the law of the place of the chief executive office is applicable to relations among the partners and between the partners and the partnership (O'Hara and Ribstein 2000: 1204–5) (arguing that for the sake of predictability and certainty, the internal affairs of partnership-type business entities should be governed by the law of the jurisdiction in which they are formed; unregistered general partnerships should be governed by the law of the state of their principal place of business instead of the chief executive office). But see Vestal (1994: 256)(arguing that the Restatement (Second) rule meets the goals underlying the choice-of-law rules better than RUPA, which allegedly sacrifices the last vestiges of fiduciary-based partnership law).

supremacy with regard to corporate law may want to shift to another playing field not dominated by Delaware (Ribstein 2002: 39). By focusing on closely held business forms, these states may be able to 'skim a little cream' from Delaware (Kahan and Kamar 2002).

Still, Delaware does seem to have non-financial supply-side incentives to keep up with legislative innovations in the field of business organization laws in general. First and foremost, Delaware has to live up to its reputation of having a good business climate. Not doing so could have a bad spillover effect on its public corporation business (Romano 1992: 415). Conversely, publicly held firms could infer from its general pre-eminence in business organization laws that Delaware should also be responsive to their particular concerns. Second, even though the formation of partnership-type business forms would only constitute a small percentage of the franchise tax draw, Delaware's lawmakers have every reason to increase the share in the market for closely held firms, including joint ventures and investment funds (Bratton and McCahery 1997a: 677). As in corporate law, Delaware periodically amends its partnership-type business forms to keep them current and to maintain its national pre-eminence. Delaware has increasingly become a major forum of choice for the organization of limited liability companies and limited partnerships, for instance.

Because states do not have a high-powered incentive to compete for franchise fees, some US commentators conclude that the evolution of new closely held business forms must be efficient. They point to a body of evidence supporting the rationale that regulatory competition produces welfare-enhancing outcomes (Ribstein, Chapter 6, this volume). It might be argued that Delaware's Limited Partnership Act, like its corporate law statute, primarily accommodates the needs of the managers—the general partners—who choose the place of organization and, correspondingly, that it tends to be less protective of the investors, the limited partners (Bromberg and Ribstein 1999: § 12.25(c)). However, since there is generally less or no separation between ownership and control in closely held firms, an inefficient trend in closely held business form legislation, like the anti-takeover statutes and judicial decisions, is unlikely to occur (Miller 1992: 407). The LLC, for instance, tends to evolve towards efficiency. First, by supplying the best features of corporations and partnerships, it offers an innovative solution for closely held firms locked into the less efficient corporation framework. The combination of flexible management, corporate-type continuity, and limited liability presents clear advantages over both the traditional corporate and the partnership forms for a wide range of closely held firms. The inherent benefits of the LLC could help overcome disadvantageous increasing return and herd behaviour effects. Second, even though regulatory competition promotes diversity and experimentation, it appears that in the event of uniformity being efficient, LLC statutes have evolved towards uniformity (Ribstein and Kobayashi 2001: 118–19). The evidence, thus, suggests that the linking of the evolution of closely held business forms to regulatory competition generally should constitute a race-to-the-top.

Yet critics have questioned the efficiency of this 'product of regulatory competition' (Callison, Chapter 8, this volume; Freedman 2000). They contend that, by virtue of their organizational structure, the new business forms create the conditions for opportunism, which may harm minority participants (Callison and Vestal 2001: 275). More importantly, critics are concerned about third parties. On this view, limited liability is not wholly efficient in the context of closely held firms. The proliferation of LLC statutes is only an indication of the legislatures' responsiveness to the business lawyers, who supported the LLC so as to increase fee revenues, and other special interest groups (Bratton and McCahery 1997a: 682–4; Callison, Chapter 8, this volume; Goforth 1995: 1272–4). In the light of the rapid enactment of new statutes by rivals, numerous state legislatures promulgated LLC legislation almost without hesitation, thereby failing to consider public welfare aspects. When other interest groups (e.g., trial lawyers) opposed the expansion of limited liability beyond the realm of corporations, because of the possibility of creditors being detrimentally affected, they were generally no match for their opponents. The upshot is that even if a variety of legal restraints, such as mandatory insurance and minimum capital requirements, are necessary to avoid the adverse consequences of expanding limited liability, legislatures are politically blocked by a suboptimal trend in a competitive federal system (Bratton and McCahery 1997a: 667). Furthermore, to the extent that the extension of limited liability to partnership-type business forms is a piece of interest group legislation, courts are unlikely to respond with a coherent set of principles to guide judicial veil-piercing, which could limit the effects of excessive risk-taking in certain cases by allowing creditors to reach the personal assets of internal firm participants.

Clearly, this has important implications for the efficiency of the lawmaking process in the US federal system. If the costs of limited liability are felt outside of the state providing the limited liability vehicle, a race-to-the-bottom could occur. Yet it does not necessarily lead to the conclusion that the effects of regulatory competition on closely held business forms are undesirable and inefficient. For instance, law and economics scholars are divided about the merits of the efficiency of limited liability (Easterbrook and Fischel 1991: 41–4; Leebron 1991; Hansmann and Kraakman 1991; Grundfest 1992; Alexander 1992). On the one hand, proponents argue that limited liability fosters entrepreneurship (Klein and Zolt 1995: 1029–30), facilitates capital formation, and protects firms against the troublesome developments in liability law (Oesterle 1995: 881). The debate on the efficacy of limited liability for partnership-type business forms traced the outlines of the debate in corporate law on the subject of the extent to which limited liability should be restricted or curtailed (Ribstein 1991: 101–6). On the other hand, opponents have questioned the efficiency presumption of limited liability for closely held firms. In this view, the efficiency presumption of limited liability for closely held firms is under threat due to a series of interventions about its suitability in this context. The basic argument here is that limited liability is thought to have little impact on monitoring costs, liquidity, and risk diversification in firms that often do not separate ownership from control, have no intention of raising outside capital, and in which parties are often required to place all their eggs in a single basket. In fact, limited liability introduces the prospect of opportunistic behaviour, i.e. attempts by the participants to shift the risk of business failure to outsiders (Easterbrook and Fischel 1991: 49–61; Freedman 2000: 331–2). More recently, building on earlier analyses, some have argued that limited liability should not be considered as part of the essential role of business organization law, unlike conferring legal entity status (Hansmann and Kraakman, Chapter 2, this volume).

Because there is little empirical evidence to support either the efficiency or inefficiency of limited liability for closely held firms, this is a very complex question to which there is no straightforward answer (Bratton and McCahery 1997a: 635). Despite the absence of evidence, many scholars argue that the benefits of extending limited liability to closely held forms outweigh the costs. It has been argued, for example, that the rapid diffusion of limited liability within the United States contravenes the argument that LLC statutes are inefficient. In reality, the ready acceptance of tort limited liability by all fifty-one states shows that the pent-up demand for limited liability was significant, and the absence of notable opposition by the malpractice and tort law lobbies indicates that the perception of risks was not so excessive as to justify expenditure to block adoption of this new form (Ribstein, Chapter 6, this volume). Alternatively, the rapid adoption of LLC statutes merely reflected the delayed, but necessary, response by businesses and legislatures to tort law litigation movement, which had increased costs for parties overall.[20] Ultimately, neither of these claims provides theory or evidence that suggests that limited liability for small firms is likely to be efficient.

Of course, the uncertainty surrounding the efficiency of limited liability does not lend support to the introduction of federal regulations, such as minimum capital requirements, to protect voluntary and involuntary creditors to the firm. The reliance by some US states on these signalling devices to balance the levels of risk-taking is deceptive.[21] By their very nature, these devices—which are

---

[20] For instance, in an era of excessive liability claims, professionals may refuse to provide their services in overly risky situations. The fear of legal liability also results in professionals taking more precautionary steps that have minimal expected benefits. Professionals hope that the use of limited liability vehicles lightens the liability burden.

[21] In almost all states, regulatory competition has broken down the anachronistic mandatory capital requirements for corporations and LLCs. Most states in which minimum capital requirements for limited liability vehicles were practically universal three decades ago have sent these requirements into oblivion, since their protective effect was insufficient and only discouraged entrepreneurship. Ironically, the first LLP statutes were reluctant to provide partners with fully fledged limited liability protection. The first versions of the first LLP statute in Texas, for example, only shielded partners from liability claims created by errors, omissions, negligence, incompetence, or malpractice committed by other partners or by employees supervised by other partners. In addition, it required an LLP to carry at least $100,000 of liability insurance or provide $100,000 of funds specifically designated and segregated for the satisfaction of judgments against the partnership. Slowly but surely, though, the idea of a corporate-type limited liability for partnerships—liability

often poorly designed and outdated—tend to impede innovation, entry, and investment, and consequently create unnecessary barriers to trade and social welfare.[22] In any event, direct creditors, which are not the main beneficiaries of such legislation, are able to bargain efficiently so as to avoid any risk that may arise in connection with any contracts involving such firms.[23] More perversely perhaps, involuntary creditors are often unable to adequately protect themselves under these devices, given their lack of information and bargaining power. For some type of firms, reputational barriers may well prove a more effective constraint when embarking upon risky projects. We must also bear in mind that firms will be much better off when they use limited liability vehicles that are acceptable to customers, banks, employees, and regulatory bodies in the state in which they are geographically located. The conclusion is that the market for limited liability forms is unlikely to increase the risks for most parties, and in the light of the degree of openness and competition in the market, may produce business organization laws that parties will prefer.

7.3.4. The Evolution of Business Organization Law in Europe

The evolution of European business organization law may well turn on the prospect of national lawmakers finding a compelling reason to abandon the defence of well-entrenched legal forms and the mandatory rules that reinforce their position and consequently block the diffusion of new innovative legal rules. However, given the way in which lawmakers have responded up to now, the emergence of new separate legal statutes responsive to the needs of closely held firms would appear unlikely, particularly in the absence of the conditions necessary for competitive lawmaking. In most European jurisdictions, the SME business community is not likely to play a featured role in the development of corporate law legislation. Aside from the United Kingdom, where accountants already have played a central role in the adoption of an LLP statute, the national lawmaking process is led by civil servants who give priority to the preferences of large firm managers. Thus, unless SMEs and affiliated interest groups have the ability to influence the pattern of lawmaking, any statutory changes made

---

protection for both tort and contract claims without minimum capital requirements—seems to be accepted. See Bromberg and Ribstein (1999); Hamilton (1995); Ribstein (2002). The reasoned acceptance of LLPs is yet another indication of the efficiency of easily accessible limited liability vehicles.

[22] In Europe, the current debate on the regulation of closely held firms can be explained in terms of a trade-off between the need for creditor protection in the case of firm failure and the commitment to supply legal rules that enable owners to maximize wealth.

[23] Closely held firms, although they are organized as limited liability vehicles, frequently extend liability to firm participants in the form of personal guarantees. Furthermore, since participants in a closely held firm have a substantial portion of their wealth tied up in the firm, they are unlikely to take excessive risks. See Meyer (2002: 250) (noting that empirical research in Germany shows that most participants in closely held firms cannot shield their personal liability in the case of bankruptcy). Thus seen, protection is perhaps illusory, but this illusiveness is no reason to prevent entrepreneurs from flocking to limited liability forms (Booth 1995: 562–3).

will not be particularly beneficial to closely held firms. Nevertheless, we argue that where national lawmakers may decide to enter the regulatory competition arena by bringing to the fore legal rules that are acceptable to different interest groups, new statutes could promote the emergence of an efficient set of legal provisions and undoubtedly foster the conditions for competitive lawmaking.

It is important for responsive lawmakers to concentrate on the needs of closely held firms, not so much to attract these firms to their jurisdiction, but to create positive spillover effects. Highly developed legislation for business firms at all levels signals that a jurisdiction is responsive to the demands of the business society. Furthermore, by having a legal framework in place for the smallest and simplest firms, jurisdictions mitigate the cost of statutory ambiguity and, hence, negative spillover effects for business forms that focus on meeting the needs of more sophisticated firms. From this perspective, introducing an LLP form designed with the 'think small first' approach in mind is arguably necessary to prevent distortion of choice-of-business-form decisions and the resulting legal problems that arise when economic actors choose suboptimal structures.[24] This would allow choice of business forms to send a clearer signal about the parties' organizational needs, which is attractive to more sophisticated parties who do not want courts meddling in the internal affairs of the firm. It is submitted that there may be less need for liability protection for these very small firms. However, it simply cannot be denied that many small firms, whether encouraged by 'legal' advisers or not, choose a business form because it furnishes them with the limited liability feature.

An LLP form should be formally linked to the default provisions of standard general partnerships.[25] This could be achieved simply by making the LLP provisions part of the general partnership statutes (RUPA 1997: § 306(c) and § 1001). Even though limited liability diminishes the harm that partners can

---

[24] Here, LLPs are viewed as a legal form for business associations consisting of two or more partners. However, US commentators point to the discriminating effect of having an easily accessible and flexible limited liability vehicle in place for businesses with two or more owners. In this view, a 'one-person LLP' should be recognized that not only allows individual entrepreneurs easy access to liability protection, but also gives them the advantage of the affirmative asset portioning that they lack when they conduct their own business as a sole proprietor, because there is no separation between the proprietors and the business they own (Hansmann and Kraakman, Chapter 2, this volume). Easily accessible limited liability vehicles for the smallest firms obviously raise the question of why limited liability is not simply a default rule for business forms at all organizational levels. Limited liability would then become an opt-out rather than an opt-in provision. In view of path-dependence factors, however, it might be argued that lawmakers are generally not willing to prescribe to a limited liability default rule (Klein and Zolt 1995; Weidner, Chapter 13, this volume).

[25] For an overview of the different forms of linkage between statutory business forms, see Ribstein (1995a). Besides the situation in which business form statutes are linked in the sense that rules from one statute are applied to a business form created under another statute, Ribstein distinguishes three other variations on linkage: (1) explicit linkage (one statute governs two business forms); (2) implicit linkage (a business form statute imports language from other business form statutes); (3) implicit de-linkage (firms may waive certain provisions of a particular business form statute and so create a different business form).

inflict on each other, firms that opt for an LLP form, i.e. the small 'mom and pop' businesses, arguably expect the same default rules as if they were organized as a standard partnership (Dickerson, Chapter 5, this volume). In fact, the LLP form should be the realization of the 'incorporated partnership' with easy exit provisions and broad fiduciary duties. Linkage also has the advantage that general partnerships can easily convert to an LLP without having to deal with the cumbersome formalities of changing to a completely new form. Finally, by organizing as an LLP the firm has access to the same network and learning benefits as the general partnership form.[26]

Yet outside the realm of small closely held business forms, linking involves significant costs (e.g., increased information costs and uncertainty, distortions in the signalling function of business forms, decreased coherence of terms, erroneous gap-filling by courts, and negative spillover effects) that outweigh possible linking benefits (Ribstein 1995a: 203–6). It is therefore suggested that a menu of separate business statutes would be more efficient in providing firms at different levels with different sets of default rules. In this respect, alternative business forms imply varying levels of control and commitment and help firms to tailor the organization of the business to their idiosyncratic needs. These distinct sets not only help to define the firm participants' expectations *ex ante*, but also assist judiciaries and arbitrators in filling gaps in the statute or the parties' contracts *ex post*.[27] Another advantage is that it is easier for lawmakers to create coherent and clear benefits for 'de-linked' business forms, which are consequently better able to attract firms to their network (Ribstein, Chapter 6, this volume).

The diversity of business firms could be a problem in designing appropriate sets of default rules. Most firms do not fit into a single mould. There are simply too many different types of firms, resulting in statutes that are either too constraining or too flexible and vacuous. An array of business forms could easily lead to inconvenience and confusion, thereby raising the partners' costs of choice and third parties' information costs of dealing with these different forms (Goetz and Scott 1985; Freedman 1999). It is surely inefficient to provide a business form for every possible type of firm. A greater number of business forms

---

[26] See Ribstein, Chapter 6, this volume. In the United States, the LLP is formally linked to the general partnership form and is therefore linked to the existing network of partnership law. In order to benefit from this network, firms could be expected to prefer the LLP to the LLC, which is not explicitly linked to the general partnership. However, empirical research shows that firms prefer the LLC business form (Ribstein and Kobayashi 2001). This evidence does not prove that network and learning benefits do not influence the choice-of-business-form decision. It suggests rather that other factors have played a more important role. For instance, LLCs used to give a broader protection against claims against the firm than LLPs. Moreover, if lawyers and other business advisers promote the formation of an LLC, the LLC may act as a focal point around which economic actors expect a new network to arise.

[27] It might be argued that the business form is becoming detached from the substance of how the firm is run. Admittedly, concerned outsiders of the firm, such as investors and creditors, are interested mainly in the substance of how the firm is run. However, standard forms can reduce the outsiders' cost of learning the terms of each of the firms with which they contract (Ribstein 1995b: 375).

would not only overshoot the target of economizing on formation and information costs, but would also hamper the potential of conferring large network and learning benefits, which play a role in choice-of-business-form decisions.

The question is therefore of how many business form statutes there should be. The evolution of business forms in the United States provides some tentative answers. It is argued that the current menu of choices in the United States (consisting of the general partnership, LLP, LLLP, LLC, and a flexible corporate form, among others) efficiently reflects firms' needs (Ribstein, Chapter 6, this volume). The impact of regulatory competition on the emergence and development of these business forms indicates that lawmakers contemplating reform must have taken the wishes and requirements of business firms into account. However, as most business forms are still evolving in the United States, it may be too simple merely to emulate the US approach, particularly given distinct legal and economic cultures within Europe. For instance, the US menu does not supply straightforward answers to the question of the extent to which business forms should be linked to each other. On the one hand, the development of the LLLP and the Re-RULPA suggests that the linkage between general and limited partnership law resulted in confusion in interpreting and applying limited partnership statutes (Vestal 1995). On the other hand, the evolution of the LLC reflects a tendency towards a process of ultimate linking—i.e. combining separate business forms into a single unified form. First, the LLC statutes are largely linked to general and limited partnerships and corporations. To the extent that LLC statutes do not contain explicit linking provisions, the 'pick and mix' of provisions of other business forms could entail implicit linking problems. If the statutes are silent on a particular issue, the import of general partnership provisions could imply that gaps should be filled with other partnership law rules. In the absence of statutory authority, courts could decide to extend general partnership principles to the LLC and to treat different business forms alike. For instance, since the Uniform Limited Liability Company Act (ULLCA) uses identical language to RUPA for its fiduciary duties, it is obvious that there will be some undesired spillovers from one business form to the other (ULLCA 1995: § 409). Second, even though most LLC statutes provide for decentralized management by default (Ribstein and Keatinge 1999: § 8.02), it is also possible to opt for centralized management (ULLCA 1995: § 203). This raises the issue of whether other default rules should also differ according to the parties' choice. In this respect, ULLCA provides for different fiduciary duty provisions, but similar dissociation and dissolution provisions. Courts could view this as a legislative omission and decide to apply corporate law rules to centralized management LLCs when the underlying relational contract remains silent. The incorporation of corporate governance principles could transform the LLC into an all-purpose vehicle, in which uncertainty and linking problems abound. However, in the light of the jurisdictional competition, the emergence of a corporate-type LLC could also indicate that the menu of business forms in the

United States is evolving towards a more efficient set of forms that reflects the preferences of a variety of firms (Ribstein, Chapter 6, this volume).

In Europe, as we have seen, the pressures of competitive lawmaking have also induced domestic lawmakers to take action and initiate law reform projects with respect to business organization law. To the extent that these lawmakers had few revenue-based incentives for researching and designing the optimal rules for all types of firms, they have attempted—for the most part—to apply the legal provisions designed for typical small partnerships or large publicly held enterprises to a wide range of closely held firms. The issue here is whether, in the context of regulatory competition, the 'integrated framework' that seems to prevail across Europe will dominate, or whether, as a result of increased competition, the 'free-standing' approach, which involves creating separate business forms, can emerge. Because most national legislatures in Europe voluntarily apply the EU Directives on publicly held corporations to the closely held corporate form (implicit linkage), it might be argued that the integrated approach prevails. This suggests that a major source of lock-in for most jurisdictions appears to be the implicit linkage of close and public corporation structures. We proposed, in contrast, that in a competitive legal environment, where the signalling function of business forms becomes more important, business forms for firm organization provided for by law should be adapted to prevailing forms of ownership and incentive structures. Given the significant role of a specialized judiciary and related case law in conferring large benefits to firms, a 'de-linked' legal form that has distinctive statutory qualities for a certain group of business firms is arguably better equipped to commit courts and arbitrators to future responsiveness.

It seems clear that as Europe enters the competitive lawmaking environment, lawmakers will mainly focus on the needs of business firms that are most likely to engage in forum shopping. Since the Directives regarding publicly held corporations have reduced the feasibility of competition in the context of large corporations, European lawmakers will begin to turn their attention to 'closely held firms', such as large professional firms, venture capital funds, joint ventures, and start-ups generally. Although jurisdictional competition in Europe is still in a developmental stage, the empirical evidence lends support to this view. We can already foresee a pattern of regulatory competition in the context of business organization law that prompts competitive lawmakers to innovate by initiating law reforms and introducing new legal entities that are better equipped than the traditional partnership and corporate forms to meet the (changed) needs of these firms. In the next sections, we briefly review the evidence bearing on our claim that there is an urgent need for European jurisdictions to develop modern business organization statutes for professional service firms, venture capital funds, and joint ventures and start-ups.

7.3.4.1. *Professional Service Firms*

Due to its many advantages, the general or civil partnership form has long dominated the professional service industries (Levin and Tadelis 2002; Milgrom and Roberts 1992: 522–3). First, because the professional partnerships are very human capital-intensive and the need for physical and financial capital is small, the partnership governance structure, in which mutual self-monitoring is the default, was more efficient than having an outsider attempt to monitor the partners. The free-rider problem, which seems to loom in large professional service firms, was partly mitigated by informal incentive mechanisms. The professionals teaming up with partners that were doing similar sorts of work and shared common educational backgrounds arguably stimulated incentive mechanisms. Not only did the partners' similar type and ability solve monitoring problems, but it also reduced decision-making costs in partnership (Kandel and Lazear 1992). While malpractice claims were uncommon, the partners' being unlimitedly liable for the firms' debts helped to overcome the monitoring problems and, more importantly, to send a signal of quality commitment to a market in which clients cannot perfectly observe and monitor the professional's performance. It is submitted that, since market monitoring failed, the partnership's principle of redistributing profits among the partners also played a pivotal role in guaranteeing a high quality of service. The redistribution of profits provided a disincentive for partners to bring in new employees, resulting in an incentive to hire only people that could meet the high quality standard (Levin and Tadelis 2002: 2).

Recent trends in professional service industries have put serious pressure on the ethos of efficiency of traditional partnership law. The acceleration of liability claims resulted in a stampede away from the unlimited liability feature. But even without the liability problems, there are other pressures working against the traditional partnership form. It is obvious that the many partners (sometimes over 1,000) of a large, international law or accounting firm cannot all be involved in the day-to-day decision-making process. Large professional firms often appoint a committee or use a corporate management structure to deal with daily affairs (Peel and Eaglesham 2002). However, unlike shareholders in a typical publicly held corporation, the non-managing partners are not passive investors but specialists in different areas who, by forming alliances, capture potential gains and diminish the variance of income. Ironically, the specializations that emerge in large professional service firms are the main reasons why partnerships unravel, and its monitoring and incentive systems fail (Carr and Mathewson 1998: 499).

Another emerging problem is the destabilization of professional service firms. If one takes a closer look at large law firms, one sees that a recent change in the culture of law practice also imposes a burden on the traditional partnership form (Hillman 2001). There is considerable evidence that the instability of law firms can be attributed to the decisions of lawyers to move their practices (and sometimes departments within firms) elsewhere. Enhanced monitoring by corporate counsel has made the market knowledgeable about the quality of a law firm's legal services. As a result, the large corporate clients will be more likely to leave a particular law firm if the quality level is not sufficient. This reduces the importance of the firm's brand name as a sunk commitment to assuring the delivery of quality, and shifts the goodwill balance from the firm to the lawyers themselves. This has stimulated the level of competition among law firms who have focused on hiring lawyers with a large clientele whose reputation may attract even more clients. Certain corporate clients are likely to follow their favourite lawyers from firm to firm. Consequently, the value of goodwill and undermined loyalty of lawyers to their firms has eroded significantly. Law firms have become confederations of individual lawyers, in which partners have their own clientele but wish to share office space, equipment, and staff. In this respect, limited liability vehicles seem to fit into the changed business climate.

This increase in the mobility of lawyers took place in the presence of strong and mandatory fiduciary duties. In practice, the standards are much lower, largely due to the high litigation costs and difficulties of pursuing damages under an indeterminate standard. For the most part, partners' fiduciary duties are matters of process and disclosure. At the same time, attorney ethics rules, such as the norm of client choice, are generally consistent with the substantive laws of partnership. It is recognized that the recent decline in lawyers' loyalty to firms has been matched equally (or even exceeded) by the demise of the firms' loyalty to lawyers, a development evident in the activities of firms that systematically review their membership to eliminate less productive partners (Vestal 1997, 1998). The experience of law firms under this new regime shows that most have quickly adjusted by changing their hiring, promotion, and retention practices.

These trends may be working against traditional partnerships in favour of the corporate form, but the latter is not free of difficulties. For instance, the demand for high levels of public revelation of the firm's financial details (and the partners' profit shares) is viewed as particularly cumbersome. Moreover, corporate law statutes contain unwanted default rules and often do not offer the freedom to tailor the statutory provisions to meet the needs of professional services firms. It appears that large professional services firms prefer a highly flexible business form that allows partners to adopt a more corporate-style decision-making and monitoring structure, has highly flexible and waivable fiduciary duties, and provides for limited liability without losing partnership-type flexibility and privacy (Ribstein 1999a: 418–20).

7.3.4.2. Venture Capital Funds

The previous subsection has found evidence that suggests that professional service firms would benefit from the introduction of a de-linked LLP statute. In this subsection, we again suggest that most of the evidence favours the enactment of a business organization form that makes it possible to emulate the most efficient US venture capital contracts.

It seems clear from the recent history of the reform of the private equity limited partnership, the standard organization form used by venture capitalists in the United States, the United Kingdom, and continental Europe to supply finance to start-up firms (Gompers and Lerner 1999; Lerner and Schaor 2002), that governments have strong incentives to create efficient legal rules designed to meet the needs of these funds. To be sure, the success of the venture-capital funds experienced a climax during the bubble years of the late 1990s when they succeeded in turning innovative ideas rapidly into gold. However, the fact that the venture capital industry has undergone a profound change over the past few years, in that venture capital funds have lost most of the millions of dollars invested in high-technology firms, does not mean that these funds went out of fashion. In reality, with bank credit becoming harder to come by, venture capital funds are still the only hope for start-ups (Saunders and Schmeits 2002: 139–52). The adaptability of these funds is a necessary quality in an ever-changing business environment.

In the United Kingdom, the limited partnership organizational form owes its popularity mainly to the venture capital industry. In particular, the tax benefits, the flexibility surrounding its structure and terms, and its fixed life make the limited partnership the dominant venture capital fund vehicle. Individuals and institutions invest in a limited partnership and delegate all investment and monitoring decisions to the venture capitalist, who acts as the general partner. These limited partnerships share publicly held and closely held aspects: passive owner-investors entrust their money to powerful and entrenched owner-managers who have substantial discretion over the funds. The flexibility of this business form allows the internal and external firm participants to enter into covenants and schemes that align the incentives of venture capitalists with those of the outside investors and reduce agency costs (Gompers and Lerner 1999: 29–55; Sahlman 1990: 489–94). Despite several drawbacks, such as limited partnership shares not being publicly tradeable and the archaic law governing this form, the UK limited partnerships have become the standard structure used by European venture capitalists in general (Myners 2001: 155). That said, the UK's prominent position is under threat from other jurisdictions that have introduced or plan to design modern legislation on limited partnerships. It is not surprising, therefore, that policymakers are planning to revise the Limited Partnership Act 1907 by proposing to abolish the rule on the maximum number of partners (presently limited to twenty) and introduce 'safe harbour' provisions similar to those found in the Delaware Revised Uniform Limited Partnership Act and Jersey's limited partnership form. These provisions clearly establish that limited partners may participate in the control of the firm so as to improve certainty and accessibility to foreign investors. The threat of competition, combined with the lobbying efforts of venture capitalists and sophisticated investors will arguably make UK limited partnership law more sophisticated and suitable for venture capital investment. Consequently, the limited partnership law reform fits the UK government's objectives of creating modern business organization forms that support the needs of a competitive economy.

7.3.4.3. *Joint Ventures and High-tech Start-ups*

In this subsection, we show that many of the contractual provisions for dealing with joint ventures and venture-sponsored firms are particularly ineffective and tend to increase transaction costs for entrepreneurs and investors. We show that parties, in the presence of such costs, would favour the introduction of business organization statutes that could serve their needs while yielding substantial governance benefits.

Joint ventures blur the line between a closely held firm and a long-term relational contract through the market. A joint venture is often described as a 'quasi-firm', as the joint venture, owned and actively co-managed by usually pre-existing, independent firms that pool resources for a specific objective, resembles long-term relational contracts in many important respects. First, the independent joint venture partners are often simultaneously competitors out-side the scope of the venture (Pèrez-Castrillo and Sandonís 1996). Second, since joint ventures usually involve the development of a particular product, their average life span is not usually very long. Third, joint venture partners may rely more on renegotiation and reputational incentives than on the firm's organiza-tional structure. In fact, joint ventures may be merely contractual arrangements that do not involve any joint ownership of assets. However, they usually employ some kind of firm-like organizational structure. This is especially true of joint ventures that explicitly employ a legal business form.

Joint venture partners may prefer to specify their rights and duties in an agreement when those prescribed by law are deemed inappropriate (Chemla et al. 2002: 1). For instance, they may rely on explicit buyout options rather than vague and open-ended fiduciary duties to overcome the consequences of incom-plete contracts (Holmström 1999: 81). These vague concepts may increase the transaction costs of negotiating the terms of the agreement and even foreclose potentially productive ventures. This is especially true of joint ventures between rival enterprises that want to deal at arm's length outside the scope of the jointly held firm. These venturers normally do not want to be hampered by broad con-cepts of trust while renegotiating their deals. Yet contractual provisions are obviously not the only sufficient means of overcoming the consequences of incomplete contracts. It appears that the equity structure also plays a significant role in the financial and organizational design of joint ventures (Hauswald and Hege 2002). Theoretical and empirical research indicates that a corporate-type equity structure is very useful to create optimal incentive mechanisms and to allocate control and ownership rights that help to alleviate or resolve oppor-tunistic behaviour in joint ventures (Belleflamme and Bloch 2000). Moreover, corporate-type share capital facilitates easy transfer and listings opportunities. In this view, a joint venture business form statute should therefore, in addition to the contractual freedom to specify the rights and duties of the joint venture parties, provide for a corporate-type management and equity structure and limited liability protection.

Such a business form could also be attractive to firms backed by venture capital, which, like joint ventures, have to deal with a 'double-sided moral hazard' problem. Both the entrepreneurs and the venture capitalists must be actively involved in the venture for several reasons. The setback of the 'new economy' has shown that the passive investors who merely provide capital are not sufficient to fertilize a promising and innovative idea. Consequently, the venture capitalists closely monitor their investments, actively participate in the venture's strategic decisions and furnish the venture with value-added services. These services (e.g. identifying business opportunities and management assistance) are often more important than their financial resources. In this respect, start-up firms are typical closely held firms. However, these firms also resemble publicly held corporations. For instance, in order to help make the venture a success and to professionalize the internal organization, outside directors are brought inside the firm, thereby separating effective control and management from risk-bearing (Hellmann 1998: 58).

The next section will discuss in more detail which organizational and legal structures are favourable for the formation and development of innovative start-ups and joint ventures. It is suggested that the introduction of a legal framework, in which equity, contractual, and non-legal incentives interrelate, is crucial to further stimulate the development of a successful venture capital market in Europe.

7.4. PROVIDING A FREE-STANDING LIMITED LIABILITY COMPANY

At first glance, it appears that an LLC statute that affords a workable menu of beneficial provisions and is attractive enough to be widely used could provide a focal point around which new networks might arise. The fundamental problem, however, is to develop an LLC form that is desirable for many SMEs and is likely to be adopted in most member states. In such circumstances, the question is to what extent the drafters of the proposed LLC statute should endeavour to build on earlier attempts to coordinate private company law in the European Community. While there is great appeal to the utilization of existing frameworks, it is important—given Europe's excessive reliance on mandatory law—to produce a statute that functions as a coherent whole and is sufficiently attractive from a cost-benefit perspective to persuade firms to opt-in to the new form. In order to achieve this objective, the design of a new business statute should be tailored so as to supply firms with limited liability, flexible legal rules, and preferential tax treatment. Such a proposal would enable business ventures to better structure their legal identity in respect of their organizational requirements and could attract (semi-) strong interest groups. In making this projection, US scholars have argued that new business forms tend to be efficient because they offer small firms comprehensive sets of terms that limit the drafting and information cost burdens while providing limited liability and sometimes even free transferability of shares (Oesterle 1995: 919–20; Ribstein 1995b; Talley 1999: 1002). Hence, the creation of an off-the-rack standard-form contract designed to meet the needs of SMEs is the legal equivalent of a simple, low-cost incorporation. To the extent that the new business statute offers firms and legal decision-makers a set of simple and coherent terms, the legislation will provide an acceptably low-cost vehicle for business planning and operation and the resolution of conflicts. We suspect that the supply of clear and simple default rules will be regarded as value-enhancing. The adoption of the default terms will also provide firms with opportunities that otherwise might not be available which, in turn, could improve the competitive position of a state's corporate law regime.

Thus, if the new statute were to offer the appropriate protections and incentives that draw start-up firms into its framework, we should expect support from a number of organized businesses and professional groups. In this respect reference can be made to the emergence of the LLP in the United Kingdom. As a prerequisite to success, the inherent benefits of the new form must exceed the benefits lost by leaving the current private corporate law. It might be suggested that these considerations alone do not support a convincing counter-story to the foregoing analysis. But if we look to the governance benefits that emerge from the introduction of new business statutes, we expect that an innovative model form, if adopted and suitably tailored, will attract those new-style, entrepreneurial firms that cannot benefit from the older, existing legal forms (Rock and Wachter, Chapter 4, this volume; Ribstein, Chapter 6, this volume). Furthermore, evidence from the United States shows that the introduction of a new form could provide the necessary impetus to help erode the mandatory nature of EC corporate law rules.

The introduction of a new, separate statute modelled on the US LLC holds out the prospect of overcoming the negative lock-in effects that inhibit the adoption of new statutes. The attractiveness of the US LLC statutes can be contrasted with other similar-styled business forms. The American form provides virtually a complete shield against personal liability (this is important given the risk inherent to a highly innovative start-up) without cumbersome formation and capital maintenance rules. As for the consideration for the payment of 'shares', most LLC statutes provide that contributions may be made to the firm in many different forms, such as 'tangible or intangible property or other benefits to the company, including money, promissory notes, services performed, or other agreements to contribute cash or property, or contracts for services to be performed' (Uniform Limited Liability Act 1995: § 401; U.L.A. 1995: 455). These LLC statutes provide extreme flexibility with respect to internal organization. Although a legal entity, an LLC is best viewed as a contract among the members of the firm. The operating agreement even overrides the articles of organization in the case of a conflict. A great majority of LLC statutes provide for decentralized management directly by the members unless otherwise provided.

However, the default rule for the governance structure of the LLC is not optimal for those entrepreneurial firms that wish to attract external capital and attempt to limit their exposure to risk and opportunism through a combination of contractual measures and the active monitoring of management (Callison 2000: 114; DeMott 1997: 614). The principal–agent literature shows that the failure to separate ownership from control will limit the benefits of specialization in the firm's decision-making. For example, if members are prepared to undertake the financial risk and supply services for the firm's ventures, it does not necessarily follow that these members will be equally suited and talented to make the appropriate management decisions about the allocation of firm resources. Second, the integration of ownership and control means undifferentiated management decision-making, which entails a more cumbersome, costly, and restricted process. Finally, a member-dominated firm will suffer higher costs due to the absence of monitoring and intervention devices to intervene on behalf of investors.

To be sure, the difficulty of the failure to separate ownership from control could be overcome by careful drafting of the firm's LLC agreement. In fact, some LLC statutes provide that a firm may be centrally managed if the statute provides for decentralized management but allows the parties to contract around the statute (Ribstein and Keatinge 1999: § 8.02). However, devising the optimal LLC structure is difficult to achieve. On the one hand, the flexibility afforded by LLC statutes takes into account the diverse organizational needs of a variety of firms. In this regard, the LLC statute can play a significant role in business planning and design. On the other hand, there is an important trade-off between a high degree of flexibility and the cost of specificity. Indeed, as US evidence shows, extensive tailoring of default rules of an LLC statute to satisfy the needs of venture-capital-backed firms may be problematic due to the effort and transaction costs involved in contracting around the statutory defaults. It appears that investors are reluctant to choose and modify an LLC statute despite its beneficial tax treatment and flexible structure.

An optimal free-standing business form should also allow investors to exit their investments via an IPO. Even though the US LLC allows for publicly traded 'units' (which are nothing more than depository receipts for the owners' property interests), the efficiency of selling units is called into question because underwriters are probably unwilling to employ 'units' on a large scale. If European lawmakers wish to create a favourable business environment for new firms, they should design an LLC statute that permits owners to have a share capital that is similar to corporate forms. We suspect also that the incentive and protection mechanisms, which are necessary to prevent opportunistic behaviour, may be best achieved by the employment of corporate-type stock.

7.4.1. The Prospects for the Emergence of an LLC-type Form in Europe

In terms of assessing the likelihood of the enactment of a new LLC-type statute into national law, there are several classes of firms that might be attracted by its cost-saving benefits. The first class is made of prospective start-up firms that will only come into existence in the new limited liability form if the form is available. It is expected that low formation costs will appeal to potential entrepreneurs who cannot afford a typical European corporate form. If the new form also provides an extensive set of protective default provisions for both investors and entrepreneurs, the number of start-ups may very well increase. The second class consists of future start-ups, which, but for the new form, would employ the more costly corporate form. The third class contains prospective portfolio companies that, at the insistence of investors, will convert into the proposed LLC-like form. A fourth class contains the existing portfolio firms for which cost savings will accrue in the event of reorganization to this form, with the savings exceeding the cost of reorganization. Presumably, the number of firms in this last class will be very small, as dramatic contractual changes are not likely during the firm's development phase.

The appearance of more successful start-ups will undoubtedly foster prosperity and economic welfare. However, the powerful forces of efficiency and public welfare alone are not always sufficient to prompt lawmakers to undertake reforms along these lines. Granted that special interest groups can sometimes help to persuade the legislature that this is a propitious moment for reform, the question remains which powerful groups will support the proposal and what are the chances of its eventual enactment. In this case, the alliance of market sector interest groups may emerge as a strong interest group. In most jurisdictions, the domestic equity exchanges conceivably could join in the lobbying process. In a period of fierce competition among European stock markets, good listing opportunities for an attractive business vehicle could result in the desired spurt of listings. Finally, entrepreneurial firms will have high-powered incentives to lobby for this innovative business form, which disposes of the cumbersome, time-consuming formation requirements and bolsters entrepreneurship.

In terms of assessing the prospects of success, we expect that on the positive side some business lawyers may have sufficient incentives to support reform proposals. They can expect increased fees as a consequence of many classes of firms being attracted to a new, low-cost business vehicle. Conversely, the notaries—lawyers who specialize in incorporations and have qualified to issue a notarial deed—could organize themselves as a significant interest group, blocking innovative measures and frustrating attempts at effective implementation. In continental Europe, a notary deed is usually required for all incorporations. Given the notaries' well-entrenched position and proximity to the lawmaking process, establishment of new forms would preferably not require issuance of such a deed. If an LLC statute were to gain adherence amongst investors and popularity with business lawyers, the notaries' fee revenues might therefore drop substantially. Since their losses are probably more acute than the possible gains of the business lawyers generated by the pent-up demand, the notaries will have a particularly high-powered incentive to block this new form. Since both types of lawyers often practise together in law firms, these professionals will strongly disfavour reform. However, well-organized professional firms, if they lack sufficient choice to shield their liability, may have sufficient incentives to exercise political influence over legislatures to supply an LLC-type form that they prefer. We expect further that Treasury and Revenue officials employed by national governments will be opposed to legislative action to the extent that the new business form's tax treatment implies revenue losses and could well organize interest group opposition to the introduction of new forms. However, the rapid diffusion of LLC statutes in the United States suggests that these considerations are secondary to most lawmakers.

7.4.2. Predicted Result

If we compare and weigh the competing interests on the demand side of legislation, we cannot predict with certainty the likelihood of enactment of a statute by national governments across Europe. The outcome will depend largely on the political power of the alliance of market sector interest groups. However, an adequate prediction cannot be made without taking into account the supply side of the legislation process. Legislative procedures reduce the stakes interest groups have in regulation, and, as a consequence, the supply side (i.e. the political and regulatory institutions) plays a decisive role with respect to a new legal form. As far as governmental institutions are maximizers of public welfare, an innovative business form might be enacted if the policymakers are convinced that it is beneficial to an increase of government revenue, job-creation, and technology developments. Conversely, some governments, which have sufficient resources and a well-organized interest group, may choose to act entrepreneurially themselves. They may be motivated to lift the curse that rests on Europe's small and medium-size business environment by actively attempting to 'attract investment or business activity or to promote the competitiveness of indigenous industries' by adopting a more favourable business form. If the future brings a significant increase in the number of start-up firms to the most favourable jurisdictions, as envisaged by the ECJ's recent case law, increases in interest group pressure can be expected. As noted earlier, the United Kingdom would be a likely candidate to enter the competitive lawmaking environment for the supply of legal product. As such, a leading state could reap the benefits by coming to the fore with a set of rules that are ideally suited to SMEs in need of outside capital. If such a state were among the early group of movers to adopt a corporate-type LLC form, it could very well create a focal point leading to the selection of a new generation of business forms by a significant number of domestic and foreign firms (Bratton and McCahery 1997b). This could, in turn, give such a state the lead in start-up formations and, due to favourable IPO opportunities, a more vibrant and competitive financial market.

7.5. CONCLUSION

The needs of closely held firms are not easily met through the adaptation of a European business form, emphasizing the theoretical importance of making available a coherent set of standard forms. Despite the increased pressures from SME organizations and professionals, law reforms tend to be piecemeal and reactionary, leading to the creation of inefficient legal codes and a paucity of limited liability vehicles. This chapter has shown that new business forms may be necessary to modify the current framework, which seems to be inefficient and burdensome for closely held firms of all kinds.

We offered a number of explanations with respect to the persistence of inefficient rules for closely held firms. First, even if a given business form would make closely held firms more efficient, it may not be in the interest of most lobby groups to modify the law to allow more efficient business forms to emerge. Predictably, legislatures respond by failing to adopt value-increasing legislation from which they could derive tax revenue and other economic benefits. Second, European firms have considerably less freedom to adopt particular provisions that match their own needs. The existing structure of corporation law imposes significant costs on closely held firms that are required to comply with highly formalistic and technical requirements. Third, the standardization of provisions in corporate codes may account for the lock-in to the existing mandatory framework. When increasing returns are present, the value of the existing provisions increases. In most European member states, the majority of closely held firms are organized under the provisions of close corporation codes. These codes not only create considerable learning benefits, but firms also expect to obtain further benefits as new firms incorporate under the same code. Moreover, because the standardized corporate form offers certainty, business lawyers, when advising clients about choice of business form decisions, tend to recommend the close corporation—even if it is suboptimal. The conclusion is that continuous use of the close corporation—even if not ideally suited to a wide range of closely held firms, will serve to reduce the incentives of lawmakers to innovate. In most European jurisdictions, the SME business community is not likely to play a featured role in the evolution of business forms.

One strategy for law reform, explored in this chapter, would attempt to meet the needs of close corporations through deregulation and modification of the general provisions of corporation law. Proponents of this approach would reconceptualize corporation law by allowing greater contractual flexibility. Typically, this means providing a separate statute that offers a bundle of legal rules regarding transferability of rights, dissolution, and internal governance rules. The promulgation of the LLP in the United Kingdom and the SAS in

France clearly demonstrates the movement towards the establishment of new arrangements that could involve economic benefits for individual firms. A second factor, coinciding with these changes, is the renewed debate within the European Union about the merits of regulatory competition, which could eventually give rise to a market for business formations. Our view is that if Europe succeeds in creating conditions more conducive to competitive lawmaking, one could expect more states to be involved, as in the United States, creating a variety of legal rules that are beneficial to different types of closely held firms.

Finally, we considered the merits of the competitive lawmaking process in the United States. Commentators have rightly noted that some provisions created by state competition have led to outcomes that would not be considered desirable. For instance, state lawmakers seem to conduct their business experiments without an underlying theory, thereby creating complexity and undesirable results. In this view, the benefits of a well-designed and theoretically appropriate model of business organization laws outweigh the benefits of competitive lawmaking. Yet one must weigh up all the benefits and costs of jurisdictional competition. New partnership law, which resulted in an increased choice of form in the United States, provided a kind of laboratory for business organization law reform in which to test new regulatory approaches. By doing so, new partnership law helped erode restrictions on the formation and operation of business firms in general. In this view, the ultimate outcome of regulatory competition rather than the initial experiments must be taken into account.

From a European perspective, it does not matter which side one takes. Obviously, there are substantial legal and cultural barriers to the near-term development of a US-type market for business forms. Consequently, despite the pent-up demand for low-cost business forms across Europe, we find it difficult to predict the circumstances that would lead to the development of regulatory competition within the European context. In any event, our analysis questions whether the introduction of regulatory competition is necessary to overcome the difficulties in promulgating a new business vehicle with few mandatory rules. In particular, this chapter has attempted to extend the debate about competitive lawmaking to the closely held business forms. We have shown that one could imagine a European member state becoming the dominant producer of business organization laws as products by being the first to establish a legal infrastructure and a bundle of rules that fully benefit firms organizing under its laws. Indeed, we argue that the development of an innovative business organization form can be expected to strengthen the business organization law regime of the state choosing to create the statutory innovation, thereby potentially inducing rival member states to supply similar sets of rules.

On a final note, the relatively unimportant role that state competition has played, thus far, in the development of business forms within the European Union means that more attention must be paid to creating adjustments in the lawmaking context that would play a role in stimulating regulatory competition and experimentation in legislative products. To some extent a private legislature or association of lawyers could facilitate the introduction of legal rules that meet the needs of distinct firms while introducing standards that reflect the ever-changing dynamics of the environment in which the firm operates. Our analysis suggests that the standardization of law, in conjunction with regulatory competition, could serve as the much-needed stimulus for legal innovation and change within the European Union.

REFERENCES

Alexander, J. C. (1992), 'Unlimited Shareholder Liability through a Procedural Lens', *Harvard Law Review* 106: 387.

Ayres, I. (1992), 'Judging Close Corporations in the Age of Statutes', *Washington University Law Quarterly* 70: 365.

—— (1995), 'Supply-side Inefficiencies in Corporate Charter Competition: Lessons from Patents, Yachting and Bluebooks', *Kansas Law Review* 43: 541.

Bachmann, G. (2001), 'Grundtendenzen der Reform geschlossener Gesellschaften in Europa Dargestellt am Beispiel des britischen Reformprozesses und der Europaischen Privatgesellschaft', *Zeitschrift für Gesellschafts Recht* [ZGR] 351.

Bebchuk, L. A. (1992), 'Federalism and the Corporation: The Desirable Limits on State Competition in Corporate Law', *Harvard Law Review* 105: 1435.

—— and Cohen, A. (2001), 'Imperfect Competition and Agency Problems in the Market for Corporate Law', Harvard University Law School and John M. Olin Working Paper, Oct. 2001.

—— and Ferrell, A. (1999), 'Federalism and Corporate Law: The Race to Protect Managers from Takeovers', *Columbia Law Review* 99: 1168.

—— Cohen, A., and Ferrell, A. (2002), 'Does the Evidence Favor State Competition in Corporate Law', *California Law Review* 90: 1775.

Belleflamme, P., and Bloch, F. (2000), 'Optimal Ownership Structures in Asymmetric Joint Ventures', Working Paper, Queen Mary, University of London.

Bernstein, L. (1995), 'The Silicon Valley Lawyer as Transaction Cost Engineer?', *Oregon Law Review* 74: 239.

Booth, R. A. (1995), 'Profit-Seeking, Individual Liability, and the Idea of the Firm', *Washington University Law Quarterly* 73: 539.

Boucourechliev, J. (2001), 'The Ideas behind the European Private Company and Its Interest for Economic Actors', *Ondernemingsrecht* 11: 318.

Bratton, W. W., and McCahery, J. A. (1995), 'Regulatory Competition, Regulatory Capture, and Corporate Self-Regulation', *North Carolina Law Review* 73: 1861.

—— —— (1997a), 'An Inquiry into the Efficiency of the Limited Liability Company: Of Theory of the Firm and Regulatory Competition', *Washington and Lee Law Review* 54: 629.

—— —— (1997b), 'The New Economics of Jurisdictional Competition: Devolutionary Federalism in a Second-Best World', *Georgetown Law Journal* 86: 201.

Bromberg, A. R., and Ribstein, L. E. (1999), *Bromberg and Ribstein on Limited Liability Partnerships and the Revised Uniform Partnership Act*, New York: Aspen Law and Business.

Callison, J. W. (2000), 'Venture Capital and Corporate Governance: Evolving the Limited Liability Company to Finance the Entrepreneurial Business', *Journal of Corporate Law* 26: 97.

——and Vestal, A. W. (2001), ' "They've Created a Lamb with Mandibles of Death": Secrecy, Disclosure, and Fiduciary Duties in Limited Liability Firms', *Indiana Law Journal* 76: 271.

Carney, W. J. (1997), 'The Political Economy of Competition for Corporate Charters', *Journal of Legal Studies* 26: 303.

Carr, J., and Mathewson, F. (1998), 'Law Firms', in P. Newman (ed.), *The New Palgrave Dictionary of Economics and the Law*, vol. 2, London: Macmillan Reference Limited.

Cary, W. L. (1974), 'Federalism and Corporate Law: Reflections upon Delaware', *Yale Law Journal* 83: 663.

CCIP/CNPF (2001), 'Draft for a Regulation Relating to the Rules Governing the European Private Company: A Close Company', *Ondernemingsrecht* 11: 331.

Charny, D. (1991), 'Competition among Jurisdictions in Formulating Corporate Law Rules: An American Perspective on the "Race to the Bottom" in the European Communities', *Harvard International Law Journal* 32: 423.

Cheffins, B. (1997), *Company Law: Theory, Structure and Operation*, Oxford: Oxford University Press.

Chemla, G., Habib, M., and Ljungquist, A. (2002), 'An Analysis of Shareholder Agreements', Working Paper, University of British Columbia.

Code of Conduct Group (1999), Report from Code of Conduct Group to ECOFIN Council on 29 Nov. 1999, SN 4901/99.

Coffee, J. C. (1999), 'The Future as History: The Prospects for Global Convergence in Corporate Governance and Its Implications', *Northwestern University Law Review* 93: 641.

Comment Company Lawyer (2000), 'Limited Liability Partnership: Available at Last', *Company Lawyer* 22: 65 and 96.

Commission of the European Communities (2003), 'Communication from the Commission to the Council and the European Parliament, Modernizing Company Law and Enhancing Corporate Governance in the European Union—A Plan to Move Forward', COM (2003) 284 final, 21.5.03.

Company Law Review Steering Group Department of Trade and Industry (DTI) (1999), *Modern Company Law for a Competitive Economy: The Strategic Framework*, London: DTI.

Daines, R. (2001), 'Does Delaware Law Improve Firm Value', *Journal of Financial Economics* 40: 525.

Deakin, S. (2001), 'Regulatory Competition Versus Harmonization in European Company Law', in D. Esty and D. Geradin (eds.), *Regulatory Competition and Economic Integration*, Oxford: Oxford University Press.

DeMott, D. A. (1997), 'Agency and the Unincorporated Firm: Reflections on the Design on the Same Plane of Interest', *Washington and Lee Law Review* 54: 595.

DTI (Department of Trade and Industry) (1999), *Company Law in Europe: Recent Developments in Core Principles of Companies Regulation in Selected National Systems*, London: DTI.

Easterbrook, F. H., and Fischel, D. R. (1991), *The Economic Structure of Corporate Law*, Cambridge, Mass.: Harvard University Press.

Ebke, W. F. (2000), 'Centros—Some Realities and Some Mysteries', *American Journal of Comparative Law* 48: 623.

Enriques, L., and Macey, J. R. (2001), 'Creditors versus Capital Formation: The Case against the European Legal Capital Rules', *Cornell Law Review* 86: 1165.

Fisch, J. E. (2000), 'The Peculiar Role of the Delaware Courts in the Competition of Corporate Charters', *University of Cincinnati Law Review* 68: 1061.

Freedman, J. (1999), 'The Quest for an Ideal Form for Small Businesses—A Misconceived Enterprise?', in B. A. K. Rider and M. Andenas (eds.), *Developments in European Company Law*, Volume 2/1997: *The Quest for an Ideal Legal Form for Small Businesses*, London: Kluwer Law International.

—— (2000), 'Limited Liability: Large Company Theory and Small Firms', *Modern Law Review* 63: 317.

—— and Fitch, V. (1997), 'Limited Liability Partnerships: Have Accountants Sewn up the "Deep Pockets" Debate?', *Journal of Business Law* 1997: 387.

Gilson, R. J. (2001), 'Globalizing Corporate Governance: Convergence of Form or Function', *American Journal of Comparative Law* 49: 329.

Goetz, Ch. J., and Scott, R. E. (1985), 'The Limits of Expanded Choice: An Analysis of the Interactions between Express and Implied Terms', *California Law Review* 73: 261.

Goforth, C. R. (1995), 'The Rise of the Limited Liability Company: Evidence of a Race between the States, But Heading Where?', *Syracuse Law Review* 45: 1193.

Gompers, P. A., and Lerner, J. (1999), *The Venture Capital Cycle*, Cambridge, Mass.: MIT Press.

Gordon, J. N. (1998), 'Deutsche Telekom, German Corporate Governance, and the Transition Costs of Capitalism', *Columbia Business Law Review* 1998: 185.

Grundfest, J. A. (1992), 'The Limited Future for Unlimited Liability: A Capital Markets Perspective', *Yale Law Journal* 102: 387.

Gummert, H. (1995), 'Die Haftung für gemeinschaftliche Schulden', in B. Riegger and L. Weipert (eds.), *Münchener Handbuch des Gesellschaftsrecht*, Band 1, München: Ch. H. Beck'sche Verlagsbuchhandlung.

Guyon, Y. (1999), 'L'Élargissement du domaine des sociétés par actions simplifiées (loi du 12 juillet 1999, art. 3)', *Rev. Soc'y* 3: 505.

Halasz, Ch., Kloster, L., and Kloster, A. (2002), 'Umwandlungen von GmbH und Gmbh&Co. KG in eine GmbH&Co. KgaA (I) und (II)', *GmbHRundschau* 93: 310 and 359.

Halbhuber, H. (2001), 'National Doctrinal Structures and European Company Law', *Common Market Law Review* 38: 1385.

Hamilton, R. W. (1995), 'Registered Limited Liability Partnerships: Present at the Birth (Nearly)', *University of Colorado Law Review* 66: 1065.

—— (2000), *The Law of Corporations*, St. Paul: West Group.

Hansmann, H., and Kraakman, R. (1991), 'Toward Unlimited Shareholder Liability for Corporate Torts', *Yale Law Journal* 100: 1879.

Hauswald, R., and Hege, U. (2002), 'Ownership and Control in Joint Ventures: Theory and Evidence', Working Paper, CentER, Tilburg University.

Hellmann, Th. (1998), 'The Allocation of Control Rights in Venture Capital Contracts', *Rand Journal of Economics* 29: 57.

Helms, D. (1998), *Die Europäische Privatgesellschaft*, Köln: Verlag Otto Schmidt.

Hillman, R. W. (2001), 'Professional Partnerships, Competition, and the Evolution of Firm Culture', *Journal of Corporation Law* 26: 1061.

Holmström, B. (1999), 'The Firm as a Subeconomy', *Journal of Law, Economics & Organization* 15: 74.

Hopt, K. J. (2002), 'Common Principles of Corporate Governance in Europe, in Convergence and Diversity', in J. A. McCahery, P. Moerland, T. Raaijmakers, and L. Renneboog (eds.), *Corporate Governance Regimes and Capital Markets*, Oxford: Oxford University Press.

Johnson, J. J. (1997), 'Risky Business: Choice-of-Law and the Unincorporated Entity', *Journal of Small and Emerging Business Law* 1: 249.

Kahan, M., and Kamar, E. (2001), 'Price Discrimination in the Market for Corporate Law', *Cornell Law Review* 86: 1205.

—— —— (2002), 'The Myth of State Competition in Corporate Law', *Stanford Law Review* 55: 679.

—— and Klausner, M. (1996), 'Path Dependence in Corporate Contracting: Increasing Returns, Behavior and Cognitive Biases', *Washington University Law Quarterly* 74: 347.

Kandel, E., and Lazear, E. (1992), 'Peer Pressure and Partnerships', *Journal of Political Economy* 100: 801.

Kessler, W., and Schiffers, J. (1999), 'Rechtsformwahl', in W. Müller and W.-D. Hoffmann (eds.), *Bech'sches Handbuch der personengesellschaften*, München: C. H. Bechk'sche Verlagsbuchhandlung.

Klein, W. A., and Zolt, E. M. (1995), 'Business Form, Limited Liability and Tax Regimes: Lurching toward a Coherent Outcome?', *University of Colorado Law Review* 66: 1001.

Lazarski, H., and Lagarrigue, A. (2000), 'The "New" SAS, Legal and Tax Considerations', *European Taxation* 40: 106.

Leebron, D. W. (1991), 'Limited Liability, Tort Victims, and Creditors', *Columbia Law Review* 91: 1565.

Lerner, J., and Schaor, A. (2002), 'The Illiquidity Puzzle: Theory and Evidence from Private Equity', National Bureau of Economic Research (NBER) Working Paper 9146.

Levin, J. D., and Tadelis, S. (2002), 'A Theory of Partnerships', Working Paper, Stanford University.

Lutter, M. (1998), 'Limited Liability Companies and Private Companies', in D. Vagts (ed.), *International Encyclopedia of Comparative Law*, vol. 13, ch. 2, Tübingen: Mohr Siebeck.

—— (2000), 'Das Europäische Unternehmensrecht im 21. Jahrhundert', *Zeitschrift für Unternehmens- und Gesellschaftsrecht (ZGR)* 29: 1.

Macey, J. R. (1995), 'The Limited Liability Company: Lessons for Corporate Law', *Washington University Law Quarterly* 73: 433.

Macey, J. R. and Miller, G. P. (1987), 'Toward an Interest-Group Theory of Delaware Corporate Law', *Texas Law Review* 65: 469.

McCahery, J. A., Renneboog, L., Ritter, P. and Haller, S. (2003), *The Economics of the European Takeover Directive*, Brussels: Centre for European Policy Studies.

Meyer, J. (2002), 'Die GmbH und andere Handelsgesellschaften im Spiegel empirischer Forschung (I) und (II)', *GmbHRundschau* 93: 177 and 242.

Milgrom, P. R., and Roberts, J. (1992), *Economics, Organization and Management*, Upper Saddle River: Prentice-Hall.

Miller, G. P. (1992), 'The Economic Efficiency of Close Corporation Law: A Comment', *Washington University Law Quarterly* 70: 399.

Myners, P. (2001), 'Institutional Investment in the UK: A Review', 6 March 2001, www.hm-treasury.gov.uk/media/OF7AO/157.pdf.

News Digest (2001), 'Limited Liability Partnership: Available at Last', *Company Law* 22: 65.

Oesterle, D. A. (1995), 'Subcurrents in LLC Statutes: Limiting the Discretion of State Courts to Restructure the Internal Affairs of Small Business', *University of Colorado Law Review* 66: 881.

O'Hara, E. A. (2000), 'Opting Out of Regulation: A Public Choice Analysis of Contractual Choice of Law', *Vanderbilt Law Review* 53: 1551.

—— and Ribstein, L. E. (2000), 'From Politics to Efficiency in Choice of Law', *University of Chicago Law Review* 67: 1151.

Payne, J. (2000), 'The Limited Liability Partnership Bill: A New Legal Entity Poised to Enter onto the Commercial Stage', *Company Law* 21: 133.

Peel, M., and Eaglesham, J. (2002), 'Personal Protection versus Financial Privacy', *Financial Times*, 9 January 2002.

Pèrez-Castrillo, J. D., and Sandonís, J. (1996), 'Disclosure of Know-how in Research Joint Ventures', *International Journal of Industrial Organization* 15: 51.

Ribstein, L. E. (1991), 'Limited Liability and Theories of the Corporation', *Maryland Law Review* 50: 80.

—— (1992), 'Efficiency, Regulation and Competition: A Comment on Easterbrook and Fischel's Economic Structure of Corporate Law', *Northwestern University Law Review* 87: 254.

—— (1995a), 'Linking Statutory Forms', *Law and Contempory Problems* 58: 187.

—— (1995b), 'Statutory Forms for Closely Held Firms: Theories and Evidence from LLCs', *Washington University Law Quarterly* 73: 369.

—— (1999), 'Limited Liability Unlimited', *Delaware Journal of Corporate Law* 24: 407.

—— (2002), 'Aftermath of Enron May Test Limits on Professionals' Liability', 12 Legal Opinion Letter (Washington Legal Foundation), 22 March 2002.

—— and Keatinge, R. R. (1999), *Ribstein and Keating on Limited Liability Companies*, New York: Aspen Law Publishing.

—— and Kobayashi, B. H. (2001), 'Choice of Form and Network Externalities', *William and Mary Law Review* 43: 79.

Romano, R. (1985), 'The State Competition Debate in Corporate Law', *Journal of Law, Economics and Organization* 1: 225.

—— (1992), 'State Competition for Close Corporation Charters: A Commentary', *Washington University Law Quarterly* 70: 409.

—— (1993), *The Genius of American Corporate Law*, Washington, D.C.: AEI Press.

—— (2001), 'The Need for Competition in International Securities Regulation', *Theoretical Inquiries in Law* 2: 364.

Römermann, V. (1999), 'Erste Praxisproblem mit der Neuregelung des Anwalts-GmbH', *GmbHRundschau* 88: 526.

Sahlman, W. A. (1990), 'The Structure and Governance of Venture-Capital Organizations', *Journal of Financial Economics* 27: 473.

Saunders, A., and Schmeits, A. (2002), *Topics in Corporate Finance, The Role of Bank Funding for the Corporate Sector: The Netherlands in an International Perspective*, Amsterdam: Amsterdam Center for Corporate Finance.

Schmidt, K. (1997), *Gesellschaftsrecht*, Köln: Carl Heymanns Verlag.

—— (1998), 'HGB-Reform und gesellschaftsrechtliche Gestaltungspraxis', *Der Betrieb* 1998: 61.

—— (2002), 'Was wird aus der unbeschränkten Kommanditistenhaftung nach § 176 HGB? Auslegung, Vetagsgestaltung und Gesetzgebung Gesetzgebung vor einer haftungsrechtlichen Neubesinnung', *GmbHRundschau* 93: 341.

Schutte-Veenstra, J. N. (2001), 'The EPC from the Perspective of the EC Directives on Company Law', *Ondernemingsrecht* 11: 319.

Sommer, M. (1995), 'Anwalts-GmbH oder Anwalts-Partnerschaft? Zivil- und steuer-rechtliche Vor- und Nachteile', *GmbHRundschau* [*GmbHR*] 86: 249.

Talley, E. (1999), 'Taking the "I" out of "Team": Intra-Firm Monitoring and the Content of Fiduciary Duties', *Journal of Corporate Law* 24: 1001.

Vestal, A. W. (1994), 'Choice of Law and the Fiduciary Duties of Partners under the Revised Uniform Partnership Act', *Iowa Law Review* 79: 219.

—— (1995), 'A Comprehensive Uniform Limited Partnership Act? The Time Has Come', *University of California, Davis Law Review* 28: 1195.

—— (1997), ' "Assume a Rather Large Boat . . .": The Mess We Have Made of Partnership Law', *Washington and Lee Law Review* 54: 487.

—— (1998), 'Law Partner Expulsions', *Washington and Lee Law Review* 55: 1083.

Volhard, R., and Stengel, A. (1997), *German Limited Liability Company*, West Sussex: John Wiley & Sons.

Winter, R. (1977), 'State Law, Shareholder Protection and the Theory of the Corporation', *Journal of Legal Studies* 6: 251.

Woolcock, S. (1996), 'Competition among Rules in the Single European Market', in W. W. Bratton et al. (eds.), *International Regulatory Competition and Coordination: Perspectives on Economic Regulation in Europe and the United States*, Oxford: Clarendon Press.

Wouters, J. (2000), 'European Company Law: Quo Vadis?', *Common Market Law Review* 37: 257.

Wymeersch, E. (1998), 'A Status Report on Corporate Governance Rules and Practices in Some Continental European States', in K. J. Hopt et al. (eds.), *Comparative Corporate Governance: The State of the Art and Emerging Research*, Oxford: Oxford University Press.

—— (2004), 'About Techniques of Company Law in the European Union', in G. Ferrarini, K. J. Hopt, J. Winter, and E. Wymeersch (eds.), *Modern Company and Takeover Law in Europe*, Oxford: Oxford University Press.

Young, S. (2000), 'Limited Liability Partnerships—A Chance for Peace of Mind', *Business Law Review* 21: 257.

8

Federalism, Regulatory Competition, and the Limited Liability Movement: The Coyote Howled and the Herd Stampeded

J. WILLIAM CALLISON*

8.1. INTRODUCTION

Choice of business entity decisions historically have involved considering and balancing three factors: (1) the extent to which owners and managers are personally liable to business creditors and tort victims under the applicable commercial law; (2) the tax and regulatory treatment of the business entity, including whether the entity and its owners will be subject to a single or double taxation; and (3) the owners' current investment preferences and the need to attract additional capital to the entity.[1] Focusing on these factors, US business organization law has undergone fundamental change since 1988. The Limited Liability Company (LLC) emerged into a significant new organizational form (Callison and Sullivan 1994, and 2000 Supplement), and the traditional general partnership and limited partnership forms mutated to permit limited liability protection for owners that historically had unlimited personal liability.[2] As a result, business owners are not forced to suffer the tax disadvantages resulting from state law incorporation in order to obtain corporation-like limited liability protection.

These changes resulted from an elaborate interplay between the two separate spheres that influence the selection of US business entities—federal income taxation and state business organization law—and the momentum for these changes rapidly accelerated when the Internal Revenue Service (IRS) pronounced that Wyoming LLCs, which provide limited liability protection to all

* I would like to thank Maureen Sullivan for her helpful comments. This chapter was originally presented at the International Conference on Close Corporation and Partnership Law Reform in Europe and the United States, Tilburg University, 17–18 May 2001.

[1] See Callison (2000) (discussing the difficulty of obtaining outside capital with contemporary LLC governance structures and encouraging consideration of alternative board-directed structure).

[2] See Uniform Partnership Act (UPA) § 15 ('All partners are liable (a) jointly and severally for everything chargeable to the partnership under sections 13 and 14 (b) jointly for all other debts and obligations of the partnership . . .'); Revised Uniform Limited Partnership Act (RULPA) § 403(b) ('Except as provided in this [Act], a general partner of a limited partnership has the liabilities of a partner in a partnership without limited partners to persons other than the partnership and the other partners.').

owners and managers, receive favourable partnership taxation.[3] By 1996, all fifty states and the District of Columbia had enacted LLC statutes. Following on the heels of the LLC revolution, Texas created the limited liability partnership (LLP) in 1991, and thereby permitted general partners in professional partnerships to avoid joint and several malpractice liability by filing a registration statement and using the 'LLP' appellation in the partnership name.[4] The remaining forty-nine states and the District of Columbia quickly enacted LLP legislation, and several states extended the LLP concept to limited partnerships (LLLPs), in which general (but not limited) partners historically have joint and several liability for entity debts and obligations.[5]

Although, the decoupling of partnership tax classification from personal liability finally occurred in 1988, it had its antecedents in the IRS's relaxation of tax classification rules with respect to limited partnerships. After a steady crescendo in the early 1990s, it climaxed in 1996 when the IRS issued regulations providing that most multiple member unincorporated business organizations are taxed as partnerships, unless the organization makes an affirmative election to be taxed as a corporation.[6] Upon the regulations' issuance, any requirement that unincorporated business organizations retain partnership-like business characteristics to obtain partnership federal income tax treatment disappeared.

The recent history of this US business organization law revolution started with Wyoming's entrepreneurial creation of the LLC alternative[7] and the

---

[3] Rev. Rul. 88-76 (1988).

[4] UPA (1997) (generally referred to as the Revised Uniform Partnership Act (RUPA)) contains typical LLP language:

SECTION 306. PARTNER'S LIABILITY.

(a) Except as otherwise provided in subsections (b) and (c), all partners are liable jointly and severally for all obligations of the partnership unless otherwise agreed by the claimant or provided by law.
(c) An obligation of a partnership incurred while the partnership is a limited liability partnership, whether arising in contract, tort, or otherwise, is solely the obligation of the partnership. A partner is not personally liable, directly or indirectly, by way of contribution or otherwise, for such an obligation solely by reason of being or so acting as a partner. This subsection applies notwithstanding anything inconsistent in the partnership agreement that existed immediately before the vote required to become a limited liability partnership under Section 1001(b).

See Hamilton (1995). See generally Callison (1992: Ch. 30A) (discussing limited liability partnerships and limited liability limited partnerships, including different protections offered by different statutes).

[5] States with limited liability limited partnership ('LLLP') provisions include: Arizona, Arkansas, Colorado, Delaware, Florida, Georgia, Iowa, Maryland, Minnesota, Missouri, North Dakota, Pennsylvania, Tennessee, Texas, and Virginia. The current draft of the Proposed Revisions to the Uniform Limited Partnership Act (1976) with Amendments (Re-RULPA) incorporates LLLP status as a default rule, although not without some controversy.

[6] Treas. Reg. § 301.7701-1-3. The regulations became effective 1 Jan. 1997. See Callison (1997).

[7] The fact that Wyoming was the first state to adopt LLC legislation is not insignificant. Wyoming is the least populated state in the United States, and has a small, informal, and accessible legislature. The Wyoming LLC Act passed, without committee hearings, one day after it was introduced. In addition, oppositional forces did not rally in Wyoming, as they might have in more populous states. In part, this may have been due to the speed with which the Wyoming LLC Act was adopted. Thus, Wyoming was the perfect state for a well-organized interest group, in this case a single oil and gas company and its professional advisers, to push special purpose legislation.

resulting pressure on traditional federal entity tax classification rules. The federal tax regulators eventually responded by changing the classification rules and permitting limited liability firms to be taxed as partnerships. This change was undertaken with a focus on federal tax law and an indifference to the state law sphere. These tax changes enabled massive and rapid state legislative reaction to eliminate personal liability for organizational debts and obligations in order to enhance the states' pro-business environment.[8] As the state legislatures rushed to create LLCs, LLPs, and LLLPs, little attention was paid to theoretical or normative aspects of the extension of limited liability protection to these firms.[9] Although some commentators adopt a triumphal state-law-first attitude when discussing the LLC's emergence,[10] the states' uncritical adoption of limited liability in reaction to tax regulatory changes can be viewed as a 'race-to-the-bottom' (Cary 1974; Fischel 1982) in which historic liability rules were jettisoned in order to create a more favourable business environment and to protect those individuals who form and operate businesses without regard to the moral hazard resulting from the change. The rise of US limited liability firms demonstrates the risk occurring when two separate, important, and uncoordinated spheres combine to fashion business organization law.

This chapter describes the different tax treatment of US tax corporations and US tax partnerships, as well as the IRS's and the courts' original position that unincorporated business organizations cannot possess a majority of corporate business characteristics and be taxed as partnerships. It then considers the genesis of the LLC form and the process whereby the IRS abandoned its historic approach and divorced income tax classification from business characteristics. It concludes by addressing the normative and theoretical questions that went unasked, and therefore unanswered, during the ensuing period of rapid statutory change and by posing questions concerning the interplay of independent federal and state regimes in business organization law.

---

[8] When limited liability protection is available, the owners of most firms prefer to separate their personal assets from their business assets. When such separation is legally recognized (i.e. when the courts respect the separate legal personality of the entity and refuse to use equitable principles to 'pierce the veil'), firm creditors can recover only from firm assets and personal creditors can recover only from personal assets. See Hansmann and Kraakman, Chapter 2, this volume (describing the essential role as 'asset partitioning' and distinguishing between 'affirmative' and 'defensive' partitioning).

[9] The lack of a unifying theory between disclosure rights and fiduciary responsibilities has been noted in Callison and Vestal (2001).

[10] See e.g. Hamill (1998: 1461) ('The invention of the LLC exemplifies the states responding to the inequities and distortions of the current federal business tax system.'). See also Hamill (1996).

8.2. The Aggregate-Entity Distinction in US Federal Tax Law

8.2.1. Aggregate Treatment of Partnerships/Entity Treatment of 'Associations Taxable as Corporations'

US tax law reflects an aggregate-entity dichotomy, with entities that are classified as partnerships generally being subject to aggregate tax treatment and entities that are classified as 'associations taxable as corporations' generally being subject to entity tax treatment. The LLC's creation and its acceptance as the entity-of-choice in numerous situations result from these divergent tax regimes and the fact that partnership taxation is favourable for many businesses. For many years until 1997, the aggregate-entity tax status of unincorporated business organizations derived from the presence of aggregate or entity characteristics under state law, and 'state law aggregate/state law' entity generally matched 'tax law aggregate/tax law' entity. Thus general partnerships, which imposed joint and several general partner liability,[11] in which interests were not freely transferable,[12] in which management authority and ownership were not separated,[13] and which dissolved upon partner dissociation,[14] were viewed as aggregates under state law and treated as partnerships under federal tax law. Conversely, corporations, which do not impose shareholder liability, in which shares are freely transferable, in which management authority and share ownership are separated, and which do not dissolve upon shareholder dissociation, were taxed as entities. Limited partnerships were taxed as aggregates or as entities depending on the presence or absence of corporate characteristics.

8.2.1.1. Partnership 'Aggregate' Taxation

The partnership tax provisions, contained in Subchapter K of the Internal Revenue Code (IRC), begin with a concise statement that partnerships are subject to a single level of taxation at the partner level, 'A partnership as such shall not be subject to the income tax imposed by this chapter. Persons carrying on business as partners shall be liable for income tax only in their separate or individual capacities.'[15] Partnership tax items, including income and loss, are allocated to the partners, who include them on their own tax returns.[16] Further, IRC § 704(b) provides partnerships with wide latitude to allocate income and losses among the partners.[17]

IRC § 705 provides that each partner separately determines the adjusted basis of his or her partnership interest.[18] This adjusted basis is important in determining, among other things, the partner's gain or loss from partnership distributions,[19] the adjusted basis of property (other than money) distributed to

---

[11] UPA § 15.　　　　[12] UPA §§ 18(g) and 27.　　　　[13] UPA § 18(e).　　　　[14] UPA § 29.
[15] IRC § 701. For discussions of partnership tax rules, see McKee (1997, and 2002 Supplement); Willis (1997, and 2002 Supplement).
[16] IRC § 702(a).　　　　[17] IRC § 704(b).　　　　[18] IRC § 705.　　　　[19] IRC § 731(a).

the partner,[20] the amount of gain or loss recognized on the sale or exchange of the partner's partnership interest,[21] and the limitation on the partner's ability to deduct his or her share of partnership losses on the partner's individual tax return.[22] Because partnerships are treated as tax aggregates, partners generally are treated as sharing partnership level liabilities[23] and an increase in a partner's share of partnership liabilities increases the basis of the partner's partnership interest.[24] This increased basis can permit the partner to deduct greater partnership losses on the partner's individual tax return.[25]

In addition, a partnership is treated as an aggregate of its partners in connection with the property contributions to the partnership, and neither the partnership nor any partner recognizes gain or loss on the contribution of property to a partnership in exchange for a partnership interest.[26] The aggregate nature of partnerships generally permits partners to receive distributions of money and property from the partnership without realizing taxable income.[27]

Partnerships are treated as entities in some regards, including: (a) a partnership has its own taxable year;[28] (b) a partnership does not terminate unless certain events occur;[29] (c) partners may engage in transactions with a partnership in a capacity other than as a partner, and the transaction generally will be treated as one between the partnership and a person who is not a partner;[30] and (d) most tax elections are made by the partnership rather than the partners.[31] These entity characteristics, while significant, are not as important as the aggregate characteristics that create tax efficiency and encourage partnership use.

8.2.1.2. Corporate 'Entity' Taxation

In contrast with tax partnerships, the income of a regular, or 'C' corporation, is subject to double taxation.[32] Corporate income is taxed at the corporate level as it is earned,[33] and it is taxed again at the shareholder level when shareholders receive dividend distributions.[34] In the event the corporation does not pay dividends, the shareholders have a second-level tax when they realize gain through the sale, redemption, or liquidation of their stock.[35] S corporations, which are not detailed in this chapter, generally permit corporate tax items to pass through to the shareholders, resulting in a single tax level, but S corporations are subject to qualification limitations not imposed on partnerships[36] and do not provide numerous tax advantages available to partnerships (Eustice 1984).

---

[20] IRC § 732.　　[21] IRC § 741.　　[22] IRC § 704(d).　　[23] IRC § 752(a).
[24] IRC §§ 752(a), 722.
[25] IRC § 704(d). The partner's ability to deduct losses may be further limited by the IRC § 465 'at risk' rules and the IRC § 469 'passive loss activity' rules. These rules are not applicable to all partners.
[26] IRC § 721.　　[27] IRC § 731.　　[28] IRC § 706.　　[29] IRC § 708(b).
[30] IRC § 707.　　[31] IRC § 703(b).
[32] For an authoritative discussion of corporate tax rules, see Bittker and Eustice (2000).
[33] IRC § 11 (corporations subject to tax on their taxable income).
[34] IRC § 61(a)(7) (gross income includes dividends).　　[35] IRC §§ 61(a)(3), 1(h).
[36] IRC § 1361(b).

Similarly, if a regular corporation incurs tax losses, such losses remain trapped at the corporate level and can be used only to offset corporate income. Unlike partnerships, corporate losses do not pass through to offset other shareholder income items. If a loss corporation never has taxable income, the tax benefit of the losses is obtained only indirectly to the extent the shareholders have a loss on the disposition or worthlessness of their stock.[37]

Entity characterization also affects the shareholder's contribution of property to the corporation in exchange for stock, which is taxed to the shareholder unless the contributing shareholders own 80 per cent or more of the stock immediately after the corporation.[38] The corporation's distribution of property to the shareholders also is subject to double taxation as though the corporation sold the property to a third party for fair market value and distributed cash equal to such fair market value to the shareholder.[39]

8.2.2. Historical Partnership-Corporation Classification Criteria

8.2.2.1. *The* Morrissey *Case and the Kintner Regulations*

Historically, classification of an unincorporated business organization as a partnership or a corporation posed difficult issues, in part because the defining IRC provisions were vague.[40] Entity tax classification was further complicated by the fact that state law categorization of unincorporated business organizations did not control their tax classification. Thus, it was possible for state law limited partnership with sufficient corporate characteristics to be taxed as a corporation.

In 1935, the US Supreme Court held, in *Morrissey v. Commissioner*, that a trust so 'resembled' a corporation that it would be taxed as a corporation despite the fact that it was not incorporated under state law.[41] The Court identified several fundamental corporate characteristics, including limited liability, continuity of life, free transferability of interests, and centralized management, and held that the business attributes of the trust made it 'sufficiently analogous to corporate organization to justify the conclusion that Congress intended that the income of the enterprise should be taxed in the same manner as that of corporations'.[42] The Court did not establish objective standards for determining whether a specific business relationship resembled a corporation and, although the *Morrissey* analysis was extended to other forms of unincorporated organizations, the tax classification waters remained murky.

The IRS adopted the *Morrissey* approach in its so-called Kintner regulations.[43] These regulations, until they were revoked in 1997 as part of the IRS's simplification efforts, described six characteristics relating to an organization's

---

[37] IRC § 1211(b).   [38] IRC § 351(a).   [39] See IRC § 336.   [40] IRC § 7701.
[41] *Morrissey v. Commissioner*, 296 U.S. 344, 357–60 (1935) ('The inclusion of associations with corporations implies resemblance; but it is resemblance and not identity.').
[42] Ibid. 360.   [43] Treas. Reg. § 301.7701-2 and -3 (repealed effective 1 Jan. 1997).

classification as a corporation or a partnership: (1) associates; (2) an objective to carry on business for a joint profit; (3) continuity of life; (4) centralized management; (5) limited liability; and (6) free transferability of interests. Because partnerships and corporations each have associates and a joint profit objective, the Kintner regulations provided that tax classification depended on the presence or absence of the remaining corporate characteristics—limited liability, continuity of life, centralized management, and free transferability. Unincorporated business organizations were classified as tax corporations only if they possessed at least three of the four pertinent characteristics.[44] Although the Tax Court indicated that the four corporate characteristics were equally weighted,[45] until the advent of the LLC form, neither the courts nor the IRS were pressured to address the question whether an organization providing limited liability protection to all owners could be taxed as a partnership.[46]

[44] The Kintner regulations established a bias towards partnership tax classification. This was due to the fact that, when the regulations were issued, organizations that provided professional services generally could not organize as corporations under state law due to legislative suspicion of limited liability protection in the professional services context. However, such organizations frequently preferred corporate taxation in order to obtain pension plan advantages and to subject business income to then-lower tax rates. The Kintner regulations were then anti-taxpayer and pushed such professional service firms into partnership tax status. At the same time, state legislatures responded to lobbying activities and began giving professionals the right to form professional corporations and professional associations, typically with malpractice insurance requirements, which enabled such firms to obtain corporate tax treatment. Subsequently, limited partnerships began to be used for real estate, oil and gas, research and development, and other syndications in which partnership status was desirable. The pro-partnership bias of the Kintner regulations facilitated such tax-motivated transactions.

In 1977 the IRS issued its so-called '48-hour regulations', which if adopted would have eliminated the 'preponderance of corporate characteristics' test of the Kintner regulations in favour of a 'resemblance' test thought to more closely mirror *Morrissey*. A business organization that possessed an equal number of corporate and non-corporate characteristics would not automatically have been classified as a tax partnership; instead, the IRS indicated that it would look further to determine whether the organization more resembled a corporation or a partnership. Prop. Reg. §§ 301.7701-1 to -3, 42 Fed. Reg. 1038 (5 Jan. 1977). These proposed regulations were withdrawn on 6 Jan., 1977. 42 Fed. Reg. 1489 (7 Jan. 1977).

[45] See *Larson v. Commissioner*, 66 T.C. 159, 172 (1976), acq., 1979-1 C.B. 1 (entity that lacked corporate characteristics of limited liability and continuity of life classified as tax partnership). The Tax Court noted that it gave equal weight to each characteristic and stated: 'This apparently mechanical approach may perhaps be explained as an attempt to impart a degree of certainty to a subject otherwise fraught with imponderables.'

[46] This was principally due to the fact that general partners in general and limited partnerships had personal liability under state law. The regulations provided that the limited liability corporate characteristic could be present in a limited partnership where the general partner had no substantial assets other than its partnership interest and was a mere 'dummy' acting as an agent of the limited partners. Treas. Reg. § 301.7701-2(d)(2) (repealed). The author is not aware of instances where the IRS ruled that such a limited partnership would be subject to partnership taxation due to the absence of two other corporate characteristics. Instead, limited partnerships were structured to avoid general partner 'dummy' characterization.

8.2.2.2. The Stress Begins—Initial Regulatory Reactions to the Limited Liability Company

In 1977 the Wyoming legislature responded to one oil and gas company's lobbying initiative and enacted the first limited liability company statute.[47] The Wyoming LLC Act provided that LLC members are not personally liable for LLC debts, obligations, and liabilities.[48] In addition, the Wyoming Act provided that LLCs can be member-managed or manager-managed,[49] that LLCs dissolve upon any member's dissociation unless all the remaining members agree to continue the LLC's business under a right to do so stated in the articles of organization,[50] and that assignees of LLC membership interests do not have any management participatory rights or become members without the other members' unanimous consent.[51] Thus, although Wyoming LLCs possessed the limited liability corporate characteristic,[52] they lacked the continuity of life,[53] and free transferability[54] characteristics and, if the four factors set forth in the Kintner regulations were equally weighted, Wyoming LLCs would be classified as tax partnerships.

The IRS's initial reaction to Wyoming LLCs was mixed. On 17 November 1980, it issued proposed regulations which, if adopted, would have provided that LLCs could never be taxed as partnerships.[55] The IRS's accompanying Notice of Proposed Rulemaking states:

The proposed regulations provide that an organization with associates and a joint profit motive shall be classified as an association [taxable as a corporation] if no member is personally liable for debts of the organization under local law. The Internal Revenue Service believes that the term 'partnership' can apply only to an organization some member of which is personally liable under applicable local law for the debts of the organization. Since a limited liability company does not satisfy this condition, it cannot be classified as a partnership. Consequently, the limited liability company must be classified as an association . . . without regard to the presence or absence of other corporate characteristics.[56]

The next day, on 18 November 1980, the IRS privately ruled that a Wyoming limited liability company lacked continuity of life, and free transferability of interests, and was therefore classified as a tax partnership despite the fact that it

---

[47] For a history of the LLC form, see Hamill (1998).   [48] Wyo. Stat. § 17-15-113.

[49] Wyo. Stat. § 17-15-116.   [50] Wyo. Stat. § 17-15-123.   [51] Wyo. Stat. § 17-15-122.

[52] The Kintner regulations provided that an organization possesses the limited liability corporate characteristic 'if under local law there is no member who is personally liable for the debts of or claims against the organization'. Treas. Reg. § 301.7701-2(d)(1) (repealed).

[53] The continuity of life corporate characteristic existed under the Kintner regulations when the organization does not dissolve upon a member's dissociation. Continuity did not exist if member dissociation caused dissolution unless all remaining members agreed to continue the organization's business. Treas. Reg. § 301.7701-2(b)(1) (repealed). The unanimity consent requirement was subsequently changed to a 'majority in interest' requirement.

[54] An organization had the free transferability characteristic under the Kintner regulations if members have the power to substitute for themselves, with all rights of ownership, a person who is not a member. Treas. Reg. § 301.7701-2(e)(1) (repealed).

[55] Prop. Reg. § 301.7701-2(a)(2)–(4).   [56] 45 Fed. Reg. 75709 (11 Nov. 1980).

afforded limited liability protection to all members.[57] The ruling was not a reversal of the proposed regulations, since it noted that the proposed regulations had been published. However, the ruling also stated that the proposed regulations were not effective until 1 January 1983 for organizations formed on or before 17 November 1980. In tandem, the proposed regulations and the private letter ruling demonstrate that the IRS believed that the then-effective Kintner regulations mandated equal weighting of the four corporate characteristics and that it also believed that the regulations should be amended so that the presence of limited liability protection would trump the other three Kintner factors.

Two years later, on 10 January 1983, the IRS withdrew the 1980 proposed regulations and announced that it was undertaking 'a study of the rules for classification of entities for federal tax purposes with a special focus on the significance of the characteristic of limited liability'.[58] On 14 March 1983, the IRS announced that it would not issue rulings concerning LLC tax classification.[59] Despite the withdrawal of the proposed regulations, the IRS was at best ambivalent towards the possibility of combining favourable partnership tax treatment and limited liability protection, and additional states did not enact LLC legislation.[60]

8.2.3. The Tax Significance of Owner Liability Crumbles: Revenue Ruling 88-76 and Its Aftermath

In 1988 the IRS withdrew its no-ruling position[61] and issued a precedential public ruling classifying Wyoming LLCs as partnerships for federal income tax purposes.[62] The LLC stampede was on! In 1990, two states enacted LLC legislation; in 1991, four states; in 1992, ten states; in 1993, eighteen states; and by 1996 all fifty states and the District of Columbia recognized LLCs. All LLC statutes provide that members and managers are not personally liable for entity debts, obligations, and liabilities,[63] and most provide that members are not

---

[57] Priv. Ltr. Rul. 8106082 (18 Nov. 1980).

[58] Announcement 83-4 (10 Jan. 1983). The proposed regulations drew heavy criticism, principally from representatives of equipment leasing trusts and US persons participating in foreign business enterprises that had received partnership classification despite having limited liability protection. See Hamill (1998: 1468).

[59] Rev. Proc. 83-15, 1983-1 C.B. 676, superseded to same effect by Rev. Proc. 83-22, 1988-1 C.B. 680.

[60] Florida, which enacted LLC legislation in 1982 in an attempt to attract foreign investment but which conceived of LLCs as tax corporations, was the sole exception.

[61] Rev. Proc. 88-44, 1988-2 C.B. 634.

[62] Rev. Rul. 88-76, 1988-2 C.B. 360 (relying on the Tax Court's holding in *Larson v. Commissioner*, 66 T.C. 159 (1976), that each corporate characteristic must be given equal weight, and ruling that Wyoming LLCs are taxed as partnerships because they lack the characteristics of free interest transferability and continuity of life).

[63] See e.g. Uniform Limited Liability Company Act (ULLCA) § 303(a) ('[T]he debts, obligations, and liabilities of a limited liability company, whether arising in contract, tort, or otherwise, are solely the debts, obligations and liabilities of the company. A member or manager is not personally liable for a debt, obligation, or liability of the company solely by reason of being or acting as a member or manager.'). Several states permit members and managers to elect personal liability. See e.g. Texas Civ. Stat., art 1528n, § 4.03.A (Texas).

proper parties to lawsuits establishing or enforcing such obligations. The IRS issued additional public and private rulings that LLCs formed in states other than Wyoming can be classified as partnerships.[64] In addition, the IRS reacted to practitioner pressures and took regulatory positions that made it relatively easy for LLCs to avoid corporation classification while adopting operating agreement provisions permitting them to closely parallel corporate business advantages.[65] Finally, in 1996 the IRS abandoned the classification business and issued regulations permitting most multiple member unincorporated business organizations to be classified as partnerships, without regard to the absence of corporate characteristics.[66] Within a relatively short time period, the IRS moved from rules connecting aggregate partnership tax treatment to aggregate organizational characteristics (with unlimited liability potentially recognized as the lynchpin characteristic) to rules disconnecting partnership tax treatment from business characteristics. At the heart of the matter, the IRS 'de-linked' limited liability from tax classification, and the states reacted by permitting new limited liability business forms. The coyote howled and the herd stampeded.

8.3. WHY THE RAPID ADOPTION OF LIMITED LIABILITY IN NON-CORPORATE BUSINESS ORGANIZATIONS?

The rapid expansion of limited liability principles into unincorporated business organization law resulted from a confluence of evolutionary forces and political power. First, strict separation of unlimited liability and partnership taxation already had eroded in the 1960s and early 1970s. Second, other methods for avoiding personal liability had developed over preceding years, arguably resulting in the 'death of liability' and a relative indifference to the existence of personal liability for firm obligations. Third, business lawyers advocated for LLC legislation without organized resistance from the plaintiffs' tort bar or other interested parties. Thus, the legislatures failed to consider the public policy aspects of expansive limited liability protection before they acted, and the expansion of limited liability protections occurred for pragmatic rather than theoretical or normative reasons. In a sense, the limited liability movement was unchallenged and its success came too easily.

9.3.1. Path Dependence and the Limited Liability Company

Current scholarship on corporate governance, notably recent writing by Lucian Bebchuk and Mark Roe, supports a conclusion that the corporate structures and rules that an economy has at any given time are functions of the rules and

---

[64] See Callison and Sullivan (1994: § 12.2) (listing classification rulings).
[65] See e.g. Rev. Proc. 95-10, 1995-1 C.B. 501 (setting forth conditions for classification rulings).
[66] Treas. Reg. §§ 301.7701-1 to -3.

structures present at an earlier time (Bebchuk and Roe 1999: 130).[67] In this view, initial ownership structures have direct effect on subsequent ownership structures, and initial ownership structures also have indirect effect on subsequent ownership structures through their effect on the legal rules governing ownership structures (ibid. 129).[68] Unless structures are static, changes are evolutionary and historically derived. Although Bebchuk and Roe use path-dependence theory as a comparative law tool to explain persistent differences in corporate ownership and governance among advanced economies, this theory also helps explain the evolution of US business organization structures. The enactment of the Wyoming LLC Act and the IRS's regulatory response to Wyoming LLCs introduced dynamic forces into business organization law, and law responded by referring back to, and evolving from, existing structures and rules.

The strict dichotomy between corporations, with limited liability protection and double taxation, and partnerships, with unlimited liability and single taxation, eroded prior to the advent of LLCs. First, beginning with the IRS's 1960 issuance of the Kintner regulations, businesses seeking partnership taxation while providing limited liability protection for at least some participants began using the limited partnership form. It was not a large step to provide further liability isolation by using a corporate general partner, and the IRS cooperated by accepting that limited partnerships with a corporate general partner could be taxed as partnerships (assuming the corporation had either some modicum of independence from the limited partners or that it met net worth requirements).[69] Second, in 1958 Congress provided that certain small business corporations, now referred to as S corporations, would be taxed on a pass-through basis.[70] Although neither innovation completely solved the liability–tax dilemma,[71] these alternative entity forms set the stage for further evolution and the creation of limited liability entities.

---

[67] Bebchuk and Roe state their claim formally as follows: 'Let us denote by S subl and R Subl the corporate structures and rules that an economy has at time T subl, and let us denote by S sub0 the structures that the economy had at an earlier time T sub0. Our claim is that S subl will be a function not only of R subl, the legal rules prevailing in the economy, but also of S sub0, the corporate structures that the [economy] had initially. . . . Our claim is that R subl, the legal rules that an economy has at a given time T subl, are a function of S sub0, the corporate structures that the economy had initially at T sub0'. See also Kahan and Klausner (1996); Roe (1991, 1996: 645).

[68] The first, direct, effect is referred to as structure-driven path dependence and the second, indirect, effect is referred to as rule-driven path dependence.

[69] See e.g. Rev. Proc. 89-12, 1989-1 C.B. 798; Rev. Proc. 92-33, 1992-1 C.B. 782; Rev. Rul. 93-91, 1993-2 C.B. 316. See also Hamilton (1997) (noting that a limited partnership with a nominally financed corporation as its sole general partner departs radically from the rule of general liability for partnership debts and becomes a limited liability entity not unlike a corporation). Hamilton dates such entities to the late 1960s and attributes them to tax shelter activities, notably in the real estate and oil and gas businesses, in which partnership loss pass-through was critical and due to the risk of which promoters sought liability protection.

[70] IRC § 1365(a) (S corporation generally not subject to taxation), § 1366 (pass through of tax items to shareholders).

[71] For example, limited partnerships did not work when the limited partner investors sought management participation. S corporation status imparted various restrictions on the number and type of shareholders and on capital structure, and S corporations are not as tax efficient as partnerships.

First, promoters incurred sunk costs in adapting to limited liability entity forms.[72] Second, the judiciary and third parties, such as banks and voluntary creditors, began to adapt their practices to the closely held limited liability entity.[73] Third, network externalities emerged as originally creative entity structures became familiar (Bebchuk and Roe 1999: 141). Fourth, the expansion of limited liability caused parties to become vested in limited liability protections and thereby to increase their valuation of such protections.[74] Finally, a limited liability status quo was created, and any subsequent departure from this status quo would create transaction costs.[75] Thus, the LLC grew on an already tilled field, and LLC adoption appears as a natural evolutionary step from the prior legal regime.

8.3.2. Liability Was Dead or Dying

In 'The Death of Liability', Professor Lynn LoPucki noted (1996: 4) that '[t]he liability system currently is mired in controversy over who should be liable, for what conduct, and for how much money. Yet this grand debate may be over the arrangement of the deck chairs on the Titanic. To hold a defendant liable is to enter a money judgment against the defendant. Unless that judgment can be enforced, liability is merely symbolic.' LoPucki notes that the systems for enforcing money judgments are failing due to the deployment of legal structures that render potential defendants judgment-proof. These systems include the use of secured credit (ibid. 14–19), shareholder limited liability (ibid. 20–3), national sovereignty (ibid. 32–8), property ownership structures (ibid. 30–2), and the lack of incentives to cause purchase of liability insurance (ibid. 76–80). LoPucki also notes that the introduction of computer technology makes it easier to maintain judgment-proof status by reducing the costs of recordkeeping (ibid. 3) and that the social norms that once prevented reputable businesses from deploying judgment-proofing strategies have eroded (ibid. 5). He concludes that this process may be irreversible (ibid.). Taking LoPucki's perspective one step further, the extension of statutory limited liability protection to unincorporated business organizations may not have been perceived as a meaningful step, and the state legislatures may merely have fallen in line with current trends eliminating the practical significance of unlimited liability.

---

[72] Bebchuk and Roe refer to these as 'sunk adaptive costs' (1999: 139–40).
[73] Bebchuk and Roe refer to these as 'complimentarities' (ibid. 140–1). For example, Hamilton (1997) discusses the adaptation of fiduciary duty principles to limited partnerships with corporate general partners.
[74] Bebchuk and Roe (1999: 140–1) refer to these as 'endorsement effects'.
[75] Bebchuk and Roe refer to these as 'multiple optima' (ibid. 142).

8.3.3. Lawyers Present at the Birth

Business lawyers were present at the birth of LLCs, and it can be argued that the rapid adoption of the form resulted from their persuasion and power. LLC legislation was the product of the public choice model of legislation, in which all substantive values and ends are regarded as private and subjective, and the legislature is conceived of as a marketplace where votes are the medium of exchange (Michelman 1977: 147–53).[76] Based on the lack of legislative debate and conversation concerning the expansion of limited liability, LLCs were not the product of the public interest model of legislation, in which the legislature is considered a forum for identifying public values and acting towards those ends (ibid.).[77]

8.4. THEORIES OF LIMITED LIABILITY REVISITED IN THE CONTEXT OF ALTERNATIVE BUSINESS ENTITIES

Although there has been considerable academic discussion of limited liability principles, there was little legislative discussion concerning whether, and the extent to which it is desirable, to extend limited liability protection to unincorporated business organizations. Thus, in a few short years, the state legislatures eliminated a bedrock legal principle for non-corporate entities and did so without considering the costs of change.[78]

[76] For discussions of the interest group theory of regulation, see Stigler (1971); Peltzman (1976); Macey and Miller (1987). For applications of interest group theory to LLC formation, see Bratton and McCahery (1997: 664–6) (arguing that business lawyers were a force in LLC enactments and noting that potential negative voices, specifically state treasurers, bankers, and the tort plaintiffs' bar, were not vocal); Macey (1995: 452–3) (noting that organized lobbying caused states to adopt LLC legislation and concluding that the 'decisional calculus' is much different in the courts). Hamill (1998) takes cognizance of the role of business and tax lawyers in pushing LLC legislation.

[77] Michelman argues that the coexistence of these two opposed models of legislative legitimacy is connected with a philosophical controversy between opposed notions of human freedom and thought. The public interest model derives from a philosophical tradition, associated with Aristotle, Kant, and Rousseau, that conceives of individual freedom in such a manner that its attainment depends on the possibility of communal and objective values that are jointly recognized by members of a group and determinable through reasoned interchange among them. On the other hand, Michelman notes that there is an individualist and subjectivist conception of the human experience, in which values are nothing but individual preferences that have no significance apart from what individuals are actually found choosing to do under situations that confront them. In this conception there is no objective good apart from allowing the maximum feasible satisfaction of private preference as revealed through actual choice. Michelman argues that the public choice conception is the foundation for modern economic efficiency analysis and the resulting allocation of resources to their highest paying employments.

[78] See Hamilton and Ribstein (1997: 691) (Hamilton claims that 'what bothers me is that the states that have broadened the LLP have in effect reversed the default rule without in any way considering or justifying that action'). See also Gabaldon (1992: 1394–5) (claiming that unlimited liability is the popularly perceived natural state for equity owners); Hillman (1997) (observing that persons associated with business activity have long sought to limit their liability and noting that there was at prior times 'a level of inquiry, a quality of debate, and an awareness of history that is largely absent from contemporary discussions of limited liability').

8.4.1. Economic Efficiency and Limited Liability

It has been widely noted that corporate law limited liability provisions create incentives for excessive risk-taking by permitting corporations and their owners to avoid the full costs of their activities. On the other hand, using a cost-benefit approach these incentives frequently are assumed to be the cost of securing efficient capital financing for corporations. The existing legal economics literature leaves open the question of limited liability 'efficiency', that is whether benefits outweigh costs or costs outweigh benefits, and there is a paucity of empirical data supporting either claim. Further, a focus on economic efficiency fails to take into account other values that might impact the limited liability debate.

8.4.1.1. Efficiency Theory of Limited Liability

Leading proponents of the efficiency theory of corporate limited liability, such as Frank Easterbrook and Daniel Fischel, focus on the monitoring, liquidity, and diversification problems that equity investors in publicly held firms likely would confront with joint and several liability and conclude that limited liability reduces transaction costs and enhances efficient operation of the securities markets, thereby lowering the costs of capital and increasing economic output and public welfare (Easterbrook and Fischel 1985, 1991). Easterbrook and Fischel identify (1985: 94) six critical differences between limited liability and unlimited liability regimes. First, they argue that limited liability reduces shareholder need to monitor managers (ibid. 94)[79] and that the monitoring costs associated with unlimited liability would discourage or prevent equity investment (ibid. 94–5). Second, because joint and several liability renders each shareholder liable for the firm's entire debt and permits shareholders who pay more than their share of firm liabilities to recover from other shareholders through contribution, they argue that unlimited liability forces shareholders to incur intershareholder wealth monitoring costs (ibid. 95–6).

Third, Easterbrook and Fischel argue that limited liability facilitates free transferability, market creation and liquidity, thereby providing managers with incentives to maintain high stock prices (ibid. 96). Fourth, they argue that shares in an unlimited liability regime would be hard to value due to potential liability, and that share prices would not be homogeneous because they would depend in part on the wealth of individual investors and their willingness to bear loss risk.[80] Thus, limited liability enhances market efficiency.

---

[79] This argument interacts with the argument that limited liability enhances liquidity and permits market creation, which market facilitates marketplace supervision through the corporate takeover market.

[80] Because a variance in personal wealth would result in a variance in the risk associated with a particular investment, in an unlimited liability regime investors with different amounts of wealth would place different values on the same equity shares, and high-risk shares would become more attractive to those with less wealth. See Halpern et al. (1980).

Fifth, Easterbrook and Fischel argue that by reducing the monitoring and risk costs of unlimited liability, limited liability permits portfolio diversification. Because diversification lowers shareholder risk, it lowers the firm's cost of capital and makes it more efficient (Easterbrook and Fischel 1985: 97; Manne 1967). Sixth, they argue that limited liability reduces shareholder risk aversion, and thereby frees the firm's managers to make riskier investments permitting greater returns (Easterbrook and Fischel 1985: 97). Thus, in their view limited liability permits a more productive firm investment policy, since high-risk investment strategies may produce innovations.

Easterbrook and Fischel acknowledge (ibid. 103–4) the moral hazard that results when investors can realize all the benefits of their investments but are protected from liability for losses and costs incurred by third-party tort claimants.[81] However, they claim that the magnitude of unsatisfied tort liability is minimal because managers, who have undiversified, firm-specific human investments in the firm, will not risk loss of their investment through uninsured tort liability (ibid. 108–9). After considering the benefits and costs of a limited liability regime, Easterbrook and Fischel (ibid.) conclude that the benefits outweigh the costs.

8.4.1.2. Application of the Efficiency Theory to Limited Liability Companies

Although Easterbrook and Fischel specifically excluded closely held firms from their analysis (ibid. 110), other legal-economics scholars have endeavoured to encompass LLCs within the Easterbrook–Fischel efficiency theory, thereby providing a cost-benefit foundation for limited liability alternative entity forms. For example, Jonathan Macey notes (1995: 450–1) several social benefits from limited liability protection in LLCs, including that (a) creditors are in some contexts superior risk bearers to shareholders; (b) limited liability permits LLC investors to diversify their holdings; and (c) limited liability obviates the need for LLC members to monitor their co-members. He argues (ibid. 451) that these economic foundations for limited liability are valid even in closely held, private LLCs. Although Macey recognizes that there are reasonable arguments for and against granting firms the ability to obtain limited liability with respect to tort victims, he summarily concludes that the arguments in favour of limited liability are 'far stronger' than the arguments against it. However, he notes that 'public policy issues regarding the relative merits of limited liability never entered the debates about whether to permit limited liability companies' (ibid. 451–2). Macey looks to the courts, particularly in their application of corporate veil-piercing doctrine, as the final arbiter of limited liability in cases of excessive risk-taking (ibid.: 452).

Following the Easterbrook–Fischel approach, Larry Ribstein argues (1995: 106) that limited liability is efficient in closely held firms because it permits

---

[81] Easterbrook and Fischel argue that there are no negative externalities with respect to contract creditors in a limited liability regime, since such creditors can bargain *ex ante* for additional compensation to offset their increased risk.

investor diversification, permits ownership without requiring excessive agency monitoring costs, and minimizes the need for creditors and shareholders to incur costs to monitor shareholder wealth. In addition to arguing that 'there is no a priori basis for believing that limited liability in close corporations externalizes costs' (ibid. 109), Ribstein states that there may be efficiency reasons for extending limited liability to involuntary tort creditors. These include higher credit costs or undertaking monitoring of activities, or both, as a result of the firm's dealings with voluntary investors (ibid. 127–8). Ribstein states that '[t]his shows that tort risk will be sufficiently internalized that the benefits of limited liability outweigh its costs to voluntary creditors' (ibid.).

8.4.1.3. Economics-Based Criticisms of Efficiency Theory

8.4.1.3.1. Pro Rata Theory

Henry Hansmann and Reinier Kraakman (1991) examine and discount the conventional efficiency-based claims for limited liability and conclude that there is no reason to assume that unlimited liability would discourage shareholder investment except in firms that impose net costs on society.[82] They state that limited liability protection in closely held firms provides an incentive for shareholders to cause the corporation to spend too little on accident-avoiding precautions, encourages overinvestment in hazardous industries, and may induce shareholders to choose too large or too small a scale for the firm (ibid. 1882–3). They note that these incentives are exacerbated if the firm relies heavily on borrowed capital or if the shareholders can withdraw capital from the firm prior to the time when tort liability attached (ibid. 1884). Assuming that shareholders are risk-averse, Hansmann and Kraakman note that tort damages serve dual efficiency functions of avoiding harms and distributing risk among the injurer and victim so that the less risk-averse person bears most of the risk (ibid. 1886).

When liability insurance is unavailable, Hansmann and Kraakman argue that both efficiency functions often will be served best when individual shareholders bear less than the full loss (ibid. 1886–7); and conclude that policymakers should consider combining unlimited liability with more flexible pro rata damage rules in order to achieve an efficient result (ibid. 1887). They claim that in a pro rata regime investors would not need to monitor other investors' wealth levels and would retain incentives to diversify their portfolios (Leebron 1991: 1578–9). However, when liability insurance is available, as it is for most firms, they argue that the case for unlimited shareholder liability is strengthened because shareholders with assets sufficient to cover a tort judgment will have an incentive to purchase full insurance, which, in turn, will give the shareholder efficient incentives to internalize costs with respect to level of care and magnitude of investment

---

[82] It is ironic that Hansmann and Kraakman created legal-economics-based fissures in the limited liability mantle just as states began wholesale enactment of LLC and LLP statutes.

(Hansmann and Kraakman 1991: 1888–9). Thus, Hansmann and Kraakman conclude that most of the benefits of limited liability identified by efficiency theory would be solved by adoption of a pro rata liability rule. At the same time, they maintain that adoption of such a rule would reduce or eliminate the limited liability system's perverse incentives creating excessive moral hazard, and Hansmann and Kraakman conclude that '[a]t a minimum, . . . the burden is now on the proponents of limited liability to justify the prevailing rule' (ibid. 1880).

The pro rata liability theorists have coherently argued that limited liability is economically inefficient, even for public corporations. It is notable that critics of pro rata theory primarily have attacked it on the basis of its feasibility, and not on the basis of its cost-benefit analysis.[83] These criticisms of pro rata liability address problems with respect to large, publicly traded firms and do not support continuance of a limited liability regime for closely held corporations and alternative business entities such as LLCs.

8.4.1.3.2. Other Economics-Based Criticisms

It should not be surprising that other legal-economics scholars have questioned the extension of the Easterbrook–Fischel efficiency theory, originally stated in the context of publicly held firms, to closely held entities in general and to LLCs in particular. For example, Stephen Presser (1992: 159–60) concludes that the economic efficiency arguments are 'little more than a roundabout way of stating the obvious and traditional justification for the rule of limited liability . . . that limited liability reduces the potential costs of purchasing shares, and thus encourages investment'.

William Bratton and Joseph McCahery (1997) inquired into the efficiency implications of LLC statutes, hoping that the economic literature would yield a new theoretical spin on limited liability. Such a theoretical spin would provide guidance on whether the law should presume limited liability *vel non*. Instead, they found that the economic literature supports no such presumption (ibid. 631). First, Bratton and McCahery note that the Hansmann–Kraakman pro rata theory strongly challenges all standing economic justifications for limited liability in small firms, and that proponents of limited liability in closely held firms fail to confront the pro rata theory (ibid. 631). They then focus on two assertions central to applying efficiency theory to LLCs—that limited liability enables diversified shareholding and that limited liability leads to an efficient firm investment policy—and conclude that the connection between ownership structure and firm performance is theoretically and empirically inconclusive and highly contestable (ibid. 640–52).[84] They note that some economic models show

---

[83] See Grundfest (1992) (arguing that offshore investments are attachment-proof and that investors can arbitrage the risks of limited liability, such that share prices would be unaffected); Alexander (1992) (arguing that jurisdictional requirements for enforcement of shareholder liability would impose large administrative costs). Hansmann and Kraakman respond to these criticisms in (1992).

[84] They note that there are no conclusive empirical studies on point (ibid. 651).

that incentive devices such as collateral provide a sufficient alignment of management incentives and limit the effects of risky decisions (ibid. 643–6), and that other economic models show that under some conditions concentrated (rather than diversified) shareholding may increase productivity (ibid. 648–52). Bratton and McCahery argue that, taken together, these models controvert the assumption that limited liability enhances productivity by encouraging portfolio diversification (ibid. 632).

Richard Booth (1994) also attempts to refute the economic arguments offered in defence of limited liability and justifies limited liability based on the idea that contract creditors may refuse to negotiate with shareholders without it. He restates the Easterbrook–Fischel efficiency arguments favouring limited liability and argues that these positions are unpersuasive, since there is no reason to conclude that investors would refuse to invest in firms unless they are relieved of personal liability or offered benefits in addition to market return on investment (ibid. 147–53). Booth concludes that the real reason for a limited liability regime in closely held entities is to shift the burden to negotiate for personal liability to contract creditors, and thereby to eliminate a barrier to contracting between the entity and its creditors (ibid. 157–61).

8.4.1.4. Observations

Cost-benefit analysis is a utilitarian theory.[85] Utilitarianism, like other liberal political theories, adopts the principle that government should be neutral towards the moral, religious, and other views espoused by its citizens.[86] Legal-economics scholars frequently transplant liberal tenets from the religious and moral spheres to the economic sphere. Some such scholars align themselves on liberalism's freedom axis and argue that government should not impose itself on people's business through regulation, unless market failures dictate such regulation.[87]

---

[85] In 'Utilitarianism', John Stuart Mill (1861: 210) defined utilitarianism as:

The creed which accepts as the foundation of morals, Utility, or the Greatest Happiness Principle, holds that actions are right in proportion as they tend to promote happiness, wrong as they tend to produce the reverse of happiness. By happiness is intended pleasure, and the absence of pain; by unhappiness, pain, and the privation of pleasure.

See Sidgwick (1907) (summarizing the development of utilitarian moral theory).

[86] Fundamentally, liberal political theory concerns itself with the question of autonomy, of what it means for the individual to be free to define and pursue his or her own ends. Autonomy can be viewed to include an ideal of freedom and an ideal of equality. Freedom can be obtained by limiting the use of the state's power, and equality requires a more active state intervention to distribute the goods used to measure equality, including money, power, genetic resources, and education. Thus, in the liberal view 'justice' involves the balance between freedom and equality, and different theories strike different balance.

See Rawls (1999); Dworkin (1977); Nozick (1977); Ackerman (1980).

[87] This approach has a long history. For example, in 'On Liberty', John Stuart Mill (1859: 226) writes: 'The only freedom which deserves the name, is that of pursuing our own good in our own way, so long as we do not attempt to deprive others of theirs, or impede their efforts to obtain it.'

By partaking of utilitarianism's blend of welfarism, sum-ranking, and consequentialism, the cost-benefit approach to policymaking suffers from utilitarianism's defects.[88] First, cost-benefit analysis limits its scope to certain measurements of well-being, such as pleasure,[89] or wealth maximization,[90] and judges the effect of variables against such defined values. Other values, which are deemed less significant or are not capable of measurement, tend to be ignored. Second, as discussed above, cost-benefit analysis requires measurement and empirical analysis; and both can be flawed.[91] What Easterbrook and Fischel view as a net positive, Hansmann and Kraakman view as a net negative, and Bratton and McCahery view as unresolved. Third, cost-benefit analysis sacrifices individual interests to whatever social good is being measured, and thereby neglects personal autonomy and integrity.[92]

Although economic approaches to policymaking can permit valuable insights, a strong argument can be made that these approaches are only tools and should not dictate the ultimate contours of social and economic relationships.[93] The legislatures did not engage in an efficiency analysis before expanding limited liability protection, and therefore did not weigh alternative approaches or, even assuming that such weighing could be accomplished, decide the appropriate role to be placed on efficiency.

8.4.2. Theories of the Firm and Limited Liability

People are generally held liable for their own actions and the actions of their agents, and not for the actions of other persons who are outside of their control

---

[88] See Sen and Williams (1982: 4–5) (describing utilitarianism as a combination of (a) welfarism, through which a state of affairs is judged exclusively on the basis of utility information related to that state, (b) sum-ranking, which merges individual utility bits into one total lump, losing in the process the identity and separateness of individuals, and (c) consequentialism, in which this information is carried to the judgement of all variables such as actions, rules, and institutions). Sen and Williams specifically note that utilitarianism neglects personal autonomy and lacks interest in personal integrity.

[89] In *Animal Liberation*, Peter Singer (1991) uses utilitarian principles to argue that animals should be brought into the field of concern, since they are capable of pain. Singer argues that the world should be organized to consider whether animal suffering outweighs the human happiness created through such suffering. See also Singer (1979) (using utilitarian principles to argue that people in affluent countries have a moral duty to transfer wealth to those in poorer countries until economic equity is reached). It should be noted that early utilitarians held broad views on the content of 'pleasure'.

[90] See Posner (1979). Responses to the wealth maximization principle include Dworkin (1980); Kronman (1980). See also Posner (1980).

[91] See Robbins (1952: ch. 4) (arguing that it is impossible to make intersubjective utility comparisons); Sidgwick (1907: ch. 3) (arguing that it is difficult for any person to make intrasubjective utility comparisons due to the time line of experience and the constant relativization of memories).

[92] See Section 8.4.2.3.

[93] See Hamilton and Ribstein (1997) (authors have a dialogue concerning the role of legal economics in the expansion of limited liability protection to alternative entities and take very different perspectives).

or who are not acting on their behalf.[94] Agency principles support legal rules limiting liability to those persons who can assert control over business activities and who can therefore be held culpable for business wrongs.[95] In the context of widely held corporations, constraints on shareholder control of firm management support limited shareholder liability.[96] However, shareholders in closely held corporations frequently have the ability to control the firm's activity, but the law generally does not hold them personally responsible for corporate obligations and liabilities. This indicates that corporations are considered neither as extensions of their individual shareholders nor as agents acting on behalf of shareholder principals. Instead, the modern corporation is viewed as an entity existing separately from its owners and acting on its own behalf with responsibility to the owners.

This entity status traditionally distinguished corporations from other business forms, such as partnerships, which were considered aggregates through which owners carried on their own business. The recent extension of entity principles to partnerships and LLCs moved these alternative entities from a regime of vicarious agency liability to one of limited liability. However, this extension of entity theory is not a given, and consideration should be given to whether corporation-like separation of the organization and its participants is desirable. Contemporary corporate theory parallels contemporary liberal political theory, and criticisms of modern corporate theory parallel criticisms of liberal political theory. Even assuming that limited liability protection is a given in corporations, these criticisms raise questions concerning the basis for entity-owner separation and the desirability of extending limited liability protection to noncorporate firms.

8.4.2.1. Theories of Corporate Personhood

Beginning in the nineteenth century, corporations were considered artificial entities existing separately from shareholders and other participants and owing their existence to the states' positive law rather than the incorporators' private initiative.[97] Under this concession theory, public policy objectives could be pursued by state regulation of corporate activities and the relationship between

---

[94] See Blackburn (1999: ch. 3) (providing an introduction to the philosophical connection among freedom, control, and personal responsibility).

[95] Under agency law, a principal can have personal liability for his or her agent's acts. Restatement (Second) of Agency § 144 (1958). An agency relationship arises when one person, the principal, manifests consent that another person, the agent, shall act on his or her behalf and subject to his or her control, and consent by the other so to act. The requisite is a right to control rather than exercise of control.

[96] Similar restraints exist with respect to limited partners and support limited liability for limited partners.

[97] In *Trustees of Dartmouth College v. Woodward*, 17 U.S. (4 Wheat.) 518, 636 (1819), Justice Marshall referred to the corporation as 'an artificial being, invisible [and] intangible'. See Millon (1990: 205–6; 2001).

the corporation and its owners.[98] Limited shareholder liability, to the extent that it existed, could be viewed as a concession emerging from the political process and could be withdrawn at the state legislature's will.[99]

By the late nineteenth century, state regulation of corporations was thought to limit desirable expansion of the scale of business activity, and new theories emerged to reduce the substantive influence of state law on corporations. First, some opponents of governmental regulation argued that corporations were not artificial entities, but were instead mere aggregations of their owners that were not subject to regulation separately from their owners.[100] The anti-regulatory impulse of the aggregate theory had several downsides that limited corporate expansion. For example, treatment of corporations as though they were aggregates (i.e. as partnerships) suggested the possibility of unlimited shareholder liability.

Second, the artificial entity theory was supplanted in the early twentieth century by a 'natural entity' theory. Under this theory, the corporation's characterization as an 'entity' separate from its shareholders was retained, but the entity was considered the creation of private shareholder initiative, in which the state incorporation process was facilitative, rather than as a state concession (Millon 1990: 211). Incorporation was not viewed as a basis for significant state regulation. Since the corporation was treated as a separate entity, claims for limited liability protection could be justified without relying on state concession. However, as corporations became larger and more complex, and shareholders increasingly relied on professional managers, managerial accountability issues began to dominate and corporate law scholars focused their attention on internal corporate affairs. Defenders of shareholder economic interests used natural entity theory to argue for an 'aggregate' approach to internal corporate affairs, with the managers being responsible to the owners whose private initiative created the firm (ibid. 214). Thus, corporate theory gave the corporation an inherent entity/aggregate conflict, in which the corporation was treated as an entity for external and regulatory purposes but an aggregate for internal responsibility purposes. This anti-regulatory, shareholder-focused approach continued throughout the twentieth century, in restated form as a 'shareholder primacy' theory, despite scholarly attempts to use natural entity theory as

[98] Millon (2001: 207) (noting that incorporation to pursue private entrepreneurial objectives generated suspicion of monopolistic privilege and that such suspicion led to democratization of incorporation).

[99] See Cohen (1998: 445–7). In fact, throughout the nineteenth century, corporate shareholders did not enjoy complete limited liability protection, since state statutes made them liable to creditors of insolvent corporations for up to twice the value of their stock and 'trust fund' doctrines made them liable to creditors to the extent they paid in less than the par value of their stock.

[100] These arguments found support in the US Supreme Court's decision that attempts to tax corporations implicated individual constitutional rights because no distinction should be drawn between corporate property and shareholder property. *Santa Clara v. Southern Pacific Railway*, 118 U.S. 394 (1886).

a means to require that corporations recognize their social responsibilities as citizens (ibid. 220–5).[101]

The more recent conception of the corporation as a 'nexus-of-contracts' derives from shareholder primacy theory and is fundamentally aggregate in nature. Under the nexus-of-contracts approach, the importance of corporate personhood (including the concept of corporate citizenship) is reduced and the corporation becomes a bundle of market-driven contracts among shareholders, managers, and other firm participants (ibid. 230).[102] Managers are hired to act for the firm's shareholders, and the focus of corporate law remains internally directed at minimizing (now through contract rather than property rights principles) the 'agency costs' associated with the separation of ownership and control (ibid.).

Nexus-of-contract theory conceives of the corporation as nothing more than the product of individual actors freely contracting based on their own utility assessments and defines the role of corporate law as setting forth 'default rules', duplicating the terms that individual shareholders, management, and other contracting parties would have agreed to in the event of actual bargaining.[103] Neither corporations nor their shareholders are thought of as having external social or moral obligations independent of contract—the corporation since it is not a person, and the shareholders since they do not contract for broader social responsibilities.[104] The state continues to have a minimal regulatory role because the corporation is viewed as an outgrowth of multipolar private initiative rather than state concession. The anti-regulatory conception of corporate law, which arose with the natural entity theory, remains legitimate and supports limited shareholder liability. This revised aggregate approach, coupled with freedom of contract principles, does the opposite of the traditional partnership aggregate approach, in which the partnership is viewed as acting on the partners' behalf of and under their control and in which partners have unlimited liability (Callison 2001).

---

[101] Noting that the aggregate-based shareholder primacy conception reduced the corporation to the purely private financial interests of its shareholders. See Dodd (1932) (arguing that corporations are entities and therefore that corporations could act other than in shareholder interests). Berle and Means (1932) responded to Dodd's corporate responsibility position with the argument that shareholders had a property-based claim on the corporation that was superior to that of other potential constituencies. Corporate responsibility arguments re-emerged during the takeover period of the late twentieth century. See Nader et al. (1976).

[102] See Allen (1993: 1400) ('The corporation is seen as a market writ small, a web of ongoing contracts (explicit or implicit) between various real persons. The notion that corporations are 'persons' is seen as a weak and unimportant fiction.').

[103] Thus, corporate law has moved towards the public choice theory of legislation. The bargaining is hypothetical, rather than actual, and is based on an assumption of rationality in which the hypothetical bargaining parties obtain benefit to offset their risk. Thus, the purchaser of a corporation's products is assumed to rationally bargain for a reduced price in exchange for the greater risk imposed by shareholder limited liability.

[104] Fundamental issues of responsibility remain respecting persons who cannot be considered to have entered into contractual relationships. These issues are minimized by broadly defining the contracting persons to include not only traditional voluntary creditors, but also suppliers, customers, and employees. See e.g. Easterbrook and Fischel (1985: 104) (stating that 'employees, consumers, trade creditors, and lenders are voluntary creditors').

8.4.2.2. *Extension of Corporate Theory to Unincorporated Organizations*

The extension of limited liability protection to unincorporated business organizations can be viewed as part of the extension of theories of the corporation to such organizations. Recent changes in partnership law illustrate this point. At common law, a partnership was considered an aggregate of the individual partners, rather than a distinct legal entity separate from the partners. Taking this aggregate theory to its extreme, a partnership is nothing more than a relationship between persons acting for a common business purpose and such persons would jointly own assets, jointly incur obligations, and conduct a pro rata share of the partnership business in their own behalf. A pure aggregate theory of partnerships, which places emphasis on the individual rights and responsibilities of the partners rather than the collective rights and responsibilities of the partnership, was ill-suited for the commercial environment in which modern commercial partnerships operated. In response, the courts often adopted and applied an entity view of the nature of partnerships or reached decisions which, while not expressly based on an entity theory, are more easily reconciled with it than with an aggregate theory. In any case, the fact that the 1914 Uniform Partnership Act did not state either that a partnership is an aggregate or that it is an entity (although it generally adopts an aggregate approach, with entity twists) left room for evolution and case-by-case decision-making.[105]

In 1994 the National Conference of Commissioners on Uniform State Laws (NCCUSL) declared that the Revised Uniform Partnership Act (RUPA) was ready for adoption by the states.[106] RUPA § 201(a) states, 'A partnership is an entity distinct from its partners.' The Comment to RUPA § 201 provides 'RUPA embraces the entity theory of partnership. In light of the [Uniform Partnership Act's] ambivalence on the nature of partnerships, the explicit statement provided by subsection (a) is deemed appropriate as an expression of the increased emphasis on the entity theory as the dominant model.' Numerous 'since/then' results follow. For example, since RUPA partnerships are entities separate from their partners, then under RUPA such partnerships need not dissolve whenever a person is admitted to the partnership or dissociates from the partnership.

Although RUPA § 307(d) adheres to the new 'partnership-as-entity' model by providing that partnership judgment creditors generally may not execute against individual partner assets without first attempting to satisfy their claims from partnership assets,[107] RUPA § 306(a) backs away from fully embracing the entity form and leaves partners jointly and severally liable for partnership obligations. The Prefatory Note to RUPA states that 'the aggregate approach is retained for some purposes, such as partners' joint and several liability'. What

---

[105] For a full discussion of the aggregate–entity approach to partnership law, see Callison (1992: 3-1-11).

[106] At this time, a majority of the states have adopted RUPA in its 1992, 1994, or 1996 forms.

[107] This is contrary to the case law in some jurisdictions. See Callison (1992: 14–16).

one hand attempts to clarify, the other hand obfuscates—thus, under RUPA a partnership is an entity unless RUPA provides that it is an aggregate.

Yet, the RUPA drafters were quickly compelled to recognize the current thrust of modern law concerning participant liability. In the 1996 version of RUPA, NCCUSL adopted the limited liability partnership form and provides RUPA § 306(c) provides that 'an obligation of a partnership incurred while the partnership is a limited liability partnership, whether arising in contract, tort, or otherwise is solely the obligation of the partnership. A partner is not personally liable, directly or indirectly, by way of contribution or otherwise, for such an obligation solely by reason of being or so acting as a partner.' Following the aggregate–entity dichotomy, an LLP can be viewed as a partnership that declares that it does not follow the aggregate characterization of RUPA § 306(a) and instead is a separate entity for liability purposes.

Limited liability companies have a different history. They can be seen as firms that were not present for an initial aggregate characterization and that went straight to the natural entity stage. Thus, LLC statutes adopt a conception in which the firm and its owners are separate persons.

8.4.2.3. *Philosophical Approaches to Individual Autonomy*

Although legal-economics scholars use utilitarian cost-benefit approaches to consider the efficiency of corporate rules, both the natural entity and the nexus-of-contracts theories of the firm can be linked to a liberal philosophy that emphasizes the importance of individual autonomy rather than utilitarian social maximization principles.[108] The individualist case against utilitarianism derives from Kant's view that teleological principles involving the supremacy of utility as a good and developing conceptions of the right as that which maximizes the good, is not an acceptable basis for morality. Kant (1785, 1788) argued that an instrumental defence of individual rights, in which such rights are subjugated to good maximization, fails to respect individuals as ends in themselves who are worthy of respect.[109]

Some contemporary liberals extend the Kantian critique and argue that 'utilitarianism does not take seriously the distinction between persons'.[110] Thus, unlike teleological utilitarianism, contemporary Kantian liberals distinguish

---

[108] In this parlance, liberalism is not a political approach favouring a measure of social or economic equality, including through a more generous welfare state, but is instead a political philosophy embracing neutrality on the question of the good life. Indeed, liberal political philosophers differ greatly concerning whether equal possession of material goods should be a goal of the liberal state. Compare e.g. Nozick (1977), with Ackerman (1980), and Ackerman and Alstott (1999).

[109] This is the 'categorical imperative' which, in one version, requires that each individual be treated as an end in himself, not merely as a means for achieving other ends.

[110] Rawls (1999: 24). Rawls writes:

In working out the conception of justice as fairness one main task clearly is to determine which principles of justice would be chosen in the original position. . . . [I]t is an open question whether the principle of utility would be acknowledged. Offhand, it hardly seems likely that persons who view themselves as equals, entitled to press their claims upon one another, would agree to a principle which may require lesser life prospects for some simply for the sake of a greater sum of

between the 'right' and the 'good', and argue that it is appropriate for the state to affirm a fair framework of individual rights without supporting or affirming any particular ends.[111] Individual rights cannot be sacrificed for the common good, and individual rights cannot be founded on any particular view of a good life.

Contemporary liberalism is based on the separateness of persons, each of whom has his or her own interests, and each of whom has the right to pursue his or her own interests as a free moral agent. It begins with the presumption that people should be free to make their own choices about how to live their lives. Legal rules that mandate behaviour or prevent people from making bargains and entering arrangements they would otherwise enter are presumptively invalid because they interfere with individual autonomy. Conversely, liberalism values rules that permit people to live their own lives based on their own preferences, and to structure their relationships with others and to define their duties to them by means of consent. Contract is a critical focus of liberal philosophy, as it is through contract that autonomous individuals define their relationships with others. This emphasis on separation and autonomy, and on the ability of persons to define their rights and obligations through contract, readily supports the natural entity and nexus-of contracts theories of the firm and their approaches to limited liability protection.

advantages enjoyed by others. Since each desires to protect his interests, his capacity to advance his conception of the good, no one has a reason to acquiesce in an enduring loss for himself in order to bring about a greater net balance of satisfaction. In the absence of strong and lasting benevolent impulses, a rational man would not accept a basic structure merely because it maximized the algebraic sum of advantages irrespective of its permanent effects on his own basic rights and interests.

Bruce Ackerman takes a different approach and argues that liberalism requires application of the neutrality principle under which '[n]o reason [for a particular outcome] is a good reason if it requires the power holder to assert: (a) that his conception of the good is better than that asserted by any of his fellow citizens, or (b) that, regardless of his conception of the good, he is intrinsically superior to one or more of his fellow citizens' (1980: 11). Ackerman thus notes that 'the problem with utilitarianism is its teleological character, its effort to evaluate distribution rules by how much "good" they produce. Any such effort requires a specification of the good that will be contested by some citizens who insist on measuring their good by a different yardstick.'

Robert Nozick (1977: 30–3), despite his practical differences from Rawls, adopts the Kantian premiss that each person should be treated as an end rather than a means and denies the existence of any social entity above the individuals comprising it:

Side constraints upon action reflect the underlying Kantian principle that individuals are ends and not merely means. . . . Side constraints express the inviolability may not one violate persons. But why may not one violate persons for the greater social good? Individually, we each sometimes choose to undergo some pain or sacrifice for a greater benefit or to avoid a greater harm. . . . But there is no social entity with a good that undergoes some sacrifice for its own good. There are only individual people, different individual people, with their own individual lives. Using one of these people for the benefit of others, uses him and benefits the others. Nothing more. . . . To use a person in this way does not sufficiently respect and take account of the fact that he is a separate person, that his is the only life he has.

[111] For example, John Rawls (1999: 3–4) writes that '[t]he rights secured by justice are not subject to political bargaining or to the calculus of social interests'.

It is no surprise that a dominant political theory has strong critics—and contemporary liberalism is no exception. Some critics, including communitarian scholars (Sandel 1982, 1996; Walzer 1983),[112] critical legal studies scholars (Kennedy 1976),[113] and feminist legal scholars (West 1988; Young 1990), adopt a perspective on the relationship of individuals and society that contrasts with the liberal view of individual autonomy. In this view, individuals owe obligations to one another that exist independently of contract because they are born into a society, a shared community. As members of a community, individuals need to recognize interdependence and responsibility for the quality of all community members' lives. In this view, the state acts appropriately when it recognizes and enforces such duties and legal rules can be used to structure relationships among community members.

These theories, which can be loosely termed 'communitarian', support a radically different approach to business firms than the liberal, contractarian approach (Millon 1995). Rather than being a separate entity derived from the private initiative of autonomous individuals, the firm can be viewed as an association, a collective business community, which is not separate from its owners, and which does not separate the owners from responsibility to broader constituencies affected by the firm's activities.[114] Instead of conceiving of the corporation as an aggregation of natural persons associating only through market-driven contracts, the communitarians reject the argument that the market answers all questions concerning the assignment of legal rights and obligations and focus instead on non-market-driven responsibilities of persons to other members of the community. To the extent that the firm's activities create third-party liabilities, in this view it is possible to discuss allocating responsibility to firm members.

8.4.2.4. Observations

Different theories of the corporation have held sway at different times based on different social and economic needs. There is no one 'natural' and ever-dominant theory that tells us what kind of person the corporate entity is, or even

---

[112] See Sandel (1996: 13–14). He writes:

Kantian liberals thus avoid affirming conception of the good by affirming instead the priority of the right, which depends in turn on a picture of the self given prior to its ends. But how plausible is this self-conception? Despite its powerful appeal, the image of the unencumbered self is flawed. It cannot make sense of our moral experience, because it cannot account for certain moral and political obligations that we commonly recognize, even prize. These include obligations of solidarity, religious duties, and other moral ties that may claim us for reasons unrelated to a choice. Such obligations are difficult to account for if we understand ourselves as free and independent selves, unbounded by moral ties we have not chosen. Unless we think of ourselves as encumbered selves, already claimed by certain projects and commitments, we cannot make sense of these indispensable aspects of our moral and political experience.

[113] Kennedy (1976) (contrasting individualism with altruism and proposing that altruism is the appropriate morality for contractual relationships).

[114] See Callison and Vestal (2001: 292–306) (discussing the tension between autonomy and community in unincorporated business associations).

that the corporation is a separate entity at all, or what the characteristics of the corporation are assuming that it is an aggregation of individuals rather than an entity. Second, the 'natural entity' theory of the corporation was extended only recently to partnerships and other unincorporated business organizations. Third, the currently dominant view of the corporation connects to currently dominant views of individual autonomy. All of these suggest that firms are malleable rather than fixed, and that it is appropriate to consider what it is that legislators and other policymakers want the firm to accomplish when they are establishing legal rules and structures.[115]

8.4.3. Democratic Theory and Limited Liability

8.4.3.1. Democratic Arguments for Corporate Limited Liability and Its Expansion to Small Business Organizations

Stephen Presser (1992: 156) adopts a historian's attitude and argues that

to the nineteenth-century legislators in states such as New York, who mandated limited liability for corporations' shareholders, the imposition of limited liability was perceived as a means of encouraging the small-scale entrepreneur, and of keeping entry into business markets competitive and democratic. Without limitations on individual shareholder liability, it was believed, only the very wealthiest men . . . could possess the privilege of investing in corporations. Without the contributions of investors of moderate means, it was felt, the kind of economic progress states . . . needed would not be achieved.

In Presser's view, limited liability occurred because of a desire to maximize state wealth by encouraging investment and to encourage individual investment in smaller firms (ibid. 163). Thus, limited liability 'reflects democracy as much as economics' (ibid.) and, before limiting or eliminating corporate limited liability, there should be a robust public debate weighing and comparing the advantages of limited liability's incentive goals, including basic principles of democracy and economic expansion, and other policy goals (ibid. 178).

Professors William Klein and Eric Zolt (1995) expand on Presser's historical observations and argue that democracy and economic growth principles do not mean 'that the butcher, the baker, or the partners operating the general store should be entitled to limited liability', and that a more substantial scale was contemplated by legislators who created corporate limited liability (ibid. 1029–30). Although they note that the Easterbrook–Fischel efficiency theory

---

[115] Millon (2001: 56–7). Millon notes that a standard argumentative move is to follow a descriptive assertion, such as 'a corporation is an entity', with a normative claim, such as 'therefore shareholders have limited liability'. He concludes that 'just as it is possible to argue over whether the corporation is really an entity or, instead, is just an aggregation, acceptance of one position or the other settles nothing because there is no agreement over what kind of person the entity is, any more than there is consensus over how to think of the relationships among the natural persons who have associated with each other in the name of a corporation'. Millon suggests that it might be better to concentrate on the problem of personal obligation rather than the question of corporate personhood.

might support a firm-size-based distinction, Klein and Zolt conclude that an owner liability distinction based on firm size would be considered unsound, since it is inconsistent with a commitment to competition and democratic values (ibid. 1031–3). In their view, if economic efficiency reasons justify giving large firms limited liability, other considerations of efficiency and democracy require treating small firms, whether organized as corporations or as LLCs, in the same manner.[116]

8.4.3.2. *Observations*

Although the democracy argument for extending limited liability to alternative business entities has a compelling simplicity, several arguments can be made against it. First, democratic theory implies that persons who are situated the same should be treated the same. Klein and Zolt tease liability away from firm size and claim that size should not matter. They fail to note other distinctions that situate partnerships and LLCs differently from corporations, most notably beneficial partnership tax treatment. The fact that the IRS classifies limited liability firms as partnerships does not compel the states to follow suit and grant limited liability protection to all organizations that are taxed as partnerships. Instead, the states could maintain that partnership tax benefits should be offset by unlimited liability. Second, Presser notes that the legislature, which is the more democratic branch of government, extended limited liability protections to small-scale entrepreneurs. However, until recently legislatures did not extend limited liability to small-scale entrepreneurs that did not incorporate. This indicates that the democratic branch recognized differences between the corporate form and alternative forms that, irrespective of the entrepreneurial nature of businesses being undertaken, mandated different liability treatment.

8.5. Conclusion

In the United States, the move towards limited liability companies and limited liability partnerships was triggered by the federal tax regulators' elimination of any linkage between unlimited liability and favourable partnership taxation. It was not motivated by a theoretical or normative commitment to limited liability, and this chapter demonstrates that theoretical bases for extending limited liability protection to unincorporated business organizations are uncertain and indeterminate. Arguments can be made for efficiency and for inefficiency, for autonomy and for community, for democracy and for limits on equal treatment. In addition, this chapter illustrates that state legislative discussion about extending limited liability was not animated by public interest considerations.

---

[116] Klein and Zolt (1995: 1036) ('[O]ne thing should be clear: limited liability should not turn on choice of business form—not now, not ever').

The limited liability movement of the last twelve years demonstrates that the seemingly separate spheres of federal income tax law and state business organization law influence one another. It raises questions concerning a federal system in which the federal government is considered to dominate one realm, in this case tax collection; and, state governments are considered to dominate another, in this case enhancement of business enterprise and protection of citizen interests through business organization law. If one assumes that the states, acting alone, would not have chosen to extend limited liability protection or would have imposed conditions on such protection, the US experience demonstrates an inherent risk in a federal system. Federal change forced state changes.

Continued critical analysis of limited liability can lead to further change. First, state legislatures might require risk mitigation by imposing insurance or capitalization requirements or by charging franchise or other taxes. Second, state legislatures might provide statutory guidance concerning situations when the liability shield should be set aside. Third, analysis might guide the courts in developing coherent, theoretically grounded veil-piercing rules. The corporate veil-piercing concept has been described as a 'tempting but pointless discussion' (Wormser 1912), but a critical understanding of limited liability's purposes can provide logic and direction to judicial veil-piercing analysis.

Finally, a fuller understanding of federal–state interplay can be helpful both in the United States and with respect to the European Union. At a minimum, the lesson to be taken from the US experience is that significant changes at a federal level, combined with a right of freedom of establishment,[117] likely will force law changes at a state level. This leads to the question of whether, and to what extent, state sovereignty, state legislative decisions balancing private and public interests, and state traditions concerning individual autonomy and community should be swept aside in the name of federal community, and how appropriate deference can be given to individual state values in an era of federalism.

REFERENCES

Ackerman, B. (1980), *Social Justice in the Liberal State*, New Haven: Yale University Press.
—— and Alstott, A. (1999), *The Stakeholder Society*, New Haven: Yale University Press.
Alexander, J. C. (1992), 'Unlimited Shareholder Liability through a Procedural Lens', *Harvard Law Review* 106: 387.
Allen, W. T. (1993), 'Contracts and Communities in Corporation Law', *Washington and Lee Law Review* 50: 1395.
Bebchuk, L. A., and Roe, M. J. (1999), 'A Theory of Path Dependence in Corporate Ownership and Governance', *Stanford Law Review* 52: 127.
Berle, A., and Means, G. (1932), *The Modern Corporation and Private Property*, New York: Macmillan.

---

[117] See *Centros Ltd. v. Ehrvervs- og Selskabsstyrelsen* (European Court of Justice, 9 Mar. 1999).

Bittker, B. I., and Eustice, J. S. (2000), *Federal Income Taxation of Corporations and Shareholders*, Valhalla, N.Y.: Warren, Gorham & Lamont.

Blackburn, S. (1999), *Think: A Compelling Introduction to Philosophy*, Oxford: Oxford University Press.

Booth, R. A. (1994), 'Limited Liability and the Efficient Allocation of Resources', *Northwestern University Law Review* 89: 140.

Bratton, W. W., and McCahery, J. A. (1997), 'An Inquiry into the Efficiency of the Limited Liability Company: Of Theory of the Firm and Regulatory Competition', *Washington and Lee Law Review* 54: 629.

Callison, J. W. (1992), *Partnership Law and Practice: General and Limited Partnerships*, St. Paul: West Group.

—— (1997), 'New Entity Classification Regulations', *University of Colorado Law Review* 26: 3.

—— (2000), 'Venture Capital and Corporate Governance: Evolving the Limited Liability Company to Finance the Entrepreneurial Business', *Iowa Journal of Corporation Law* 26: 97.

—— (2001), 'Indeterminacy, Irony and Partnership Law', *Stanford Agora* 2: 73.

—— and Sullivan, M. A. (1994), *Limited Liability Companies: A State-by-State Guide to Law and Practice*, St. Paul: West Group.

—— and Vestal, A. W. (2001), ' "They've Created a Lamb with Mandibles of Death": Secrecy, Disclosure and Fiduciary Duties in Limited Liability Firms', *Indiana Law Review* 76: 271.

Cary, W. L. (1974), 'Federalism and Corporate Law Reflections upon Delaware', *Yale Law Journal* 83: 663.

Cohen, D. L. (1998), 'Theories of the Corporation and Limited Liability: How Should Courts and Legislatures Articulate Rules for Piercing the Veil, Fiduciary Responsibility and Securities Regulation for the Limited Liability Company?', *Oklahoma Law Review* 51: 445.

Dodd, F. M. (1932), 'For Whom Are Corporate Managers Trustees?', *Harvard Law Review* 45: 1145.

Dworkin, R. (1977), *Taking Rights Seriously*, Cambridge, Mass.: Harvard University Press.

—— (1980), 'Is Wealth a Value?', *Journal of Legal Studies* 9: 191.

Easterbrook, F. H. and Fischel, D. R. (1985), 'Limited Liability and the Corporation', *University of Chicago Law Review* 52: 89.

—— —— (1991), *The Economic Structure of Corporate Law*, Cambridge, Mass.: Harvard University Press.

Eustice, J. S. (1984), 'Subchapter S Corporations and Partnerships: A Search for the Pass through Paradigm (Some Preliminary Proposals)', *Tax Law Review* 39: 345.

Fischel, D. R. (1982), 'The "Race to the Bottom" Revisited: Reflections on Recent Developments in Delaware's Corporation Law', *Northwestern University Law Review* 76: 913.

Gabaldon, T. A. (1992), 'The Lemonade Stand: Feminist and Other Reflections on the Limited Liability of Corporate Shareholders', *Vanderbilt Law Review* 45: 1387.

Grundfest, J. A. (1992), 'The Limited Future of Unlimited Liability: A Capital Markets Perspective', *Yale Law Journal* 102: 387.

Halpern, P., et al. (1980), 'An Economic Analysis of Limited Liability in Corporation Law', *University of Toronto Law Journal* 30: 117.

Hamill, S. P. (1996), 'The Limited Liability Company: A Catalyst Exposing the Corporate Integration Question', *Michigan Law Review* 95: 393.

—— (1998), 'The Origins Behind the Limited Liability Company', *Ohio State Law Journal* 59: 1459.

Hamilton, R. W. (1995), 'Registered Limited Liability Partnerships: Present at the Birth (Nearly)', *University of Colorado Law Review* 66: 1065.

—— (1997), 'Corporate General Partners of Limited Partnerships', *Journal of Small and Emerging Business Law* 1: 73.

—— and Ribstein, L. E. (1997), 'Limited Liability and the Real World', *Washington and Lee Law Review* 54: 687.

Hansmann, H., and Kraakman, R. (1991), 'Toward Unlimited Shareholder Liability for Corporate Tort', *Yale Law Journal* 100: 1879.

—— —— (1992), 'A Procedural Focus on Unlimited Shareholder Liability', *Harvard Law Review* 106: 446.

Hillman, R. W. (1997), 'Limited Liability in Historical Perspective', *Washington and Lee Law Review* 54: 615.

Kahan, M., and Klausner, M. (1996), 'Path Dependence in Corporate Contracting: Increasing Returns, Herd Behavior and Cognitive Bias', *Washington University Law Quarterly* 74: 347.

Kant, I. (1785), *Groundwork of the Metaphysics of Morals*, New York: Harper & Row, 1964.

—— (1788), *Critique of Practical Reason*, New York: Liberal Arts Press, 1956.

Kennedy, D. (1976), 'Form and Substance in Private Law Adjudication', *Harvard Law Review* 89: 1685.

Klein, W. A., and Zolt, E. M. (1995), 'Business Form, Limited Liability, and Tax Regimes: Lurching Toward a Coherent Outcome', *University of Colorado Law Review* 66: 1001.

Kronman, A. T. (1980), 'Wealth Maximization as a Normative Principle', *Journal of Legal Studies* 9: 227.

Leebron, D. W. (1991), 'Limited Liability, Tort Victims, and Creditors', *Columbia Law Review* 91: 1565.

LoPucki, L. M. (1996), 'The Death of Liability', *Yale Law Journal* 106: 1.

Macey, J. R. (1995), 'The Limited Liability Company: Lessons for Corporate Law', *Washington University Law Quarterly* 73: 433.

—— and Miller, G. P. (1987), 'Toward an Interest Group Theory of Delaware Corporate Law', *Texas Law Review* 65: 469.

Manne, H. (1967), 'Our Two Corporate Systems: Law and Economics', *University of Virginia Law Review* 53: 259.

McKee, W. S., et al. (1997 and 2000 Supplement), *Federal Taxation of Partnerships and Partners*, Boston: Warren, Gorham & Lamont.

Michelman, F. I. (1977), 'Political Markets and Community Self-Determination: Competing Models of Local Government Legitimacy', *Indiana Law Journal* 53: 145.

Mill, J. S. (1859), 'On Liberty', reprinted in J. M. Robson et al. (eds.) (1969), *Collected Works of John Stuart Mill*, Toronto: University of Toronto Press

—— (1861), 'Utilitarianism', reprinted in J. M. Robson et al. (eds.) (1969), *Collected Works of John Stuart Mill*, Toronto: University of Toronto Press.

Millon, D. (1990), 'Theories of the Corporation', *Duke Law Journal* 1990: 201.

Millon, D. (1995), ' "Communitarianism" in Corporate Law: Foundations and Law Reform Strategies', in L. E. Mitchell (ed.), *Progressive Corporate Law*, Boulder, Col.: Westview Press..

—— (2001), 'The Ambiguous Significance of Corporate Personhood', *Stanford Agora* 2: 39.

Nader, R., et al. (1976), *Taming the Giant Corporation*, New York: Norton.

Nozick, R. (1977), *Anarchy, State and Utopia*, New York: Basic Books.

Peltzman, S. (1976), 'Towards a More General Theory of Economic Regulation', *Journal of Law and Economics* 19: 211.

Posner, R. A. (1979), 'Utilitarianism, Economics and Legal Theory', *Journal of Legal Studies* 8: 103.

—— (1980), 'The Value of Wealth: A Comment on Dworkin and Kronman', *Journal of Legal Studies* 9: 243.

Presser, S. B. (1992), 'Thwarting the Killing of the Corporation: Limited Liability, Democracy, and Economics', *Northwestern University Law Review* 87: 148.

Rawls, J. (1999), *A Theory of Justice*, Cambridge, Mass.: Harvard University Press.

Ribstein, L. E. (1995), 'Limited Liability and Theories of the Corporation', *Maryland Law Review* 50: 80.

Robbins, L. (1952), *An Essay on the Nature and Significance of Economic Science*, London: Macmillan Reference.

Roe, M. J. (1991), 'A Political Theory of American Corporate Finance', *Columbia Law Review* 91: 10.

—— (1996), 'Chaos and Evolution in Law and Economics', *Harvard Law Review* 109: 641.

Sandel, M. J. (1982), *Liberalism and the Limits of Justice*, Cambridge: Cambridge University Press.

—— (1996), *Democracy's Discontent: America in Search of a Public Philosophy*, Cambridge, Mass.: Belknap Press of Harvard University Press.

Sen, A., and Williams, B. (1982), *Utilitarianism and Beyond*, Cambridge: Cambridge University Press.

Sidgwick, H. (1907), *Methods of Ethics*, London: Macmillan Reference.

Singer, P. (1979), 'Famine, Affluence and Morality', in J. Rachels (ed.), *Moral Problems*, New York: Harper & Row.

—— (1991), *Animal Liberation*, London: Thorsons.

Stigler, G. L. (1971), 'The Theory of Economic Regulation', *Bell Journal of Economics and Management Science* 2: 3.

Walzer, M. (1983), *Spheres of Justice: A Defense of Pluralism and Equality*, Oxford: Robertson.

West, R. (1988), 'Jurisprudence and Gender', *University of Chicago Law Review* 55: 1.

Willis, A. B., et al. (1997, and 2001 Supplement), *Partnership Taxation*, New York: Warren, Gorham & Lamont, Incorporated.

Wormser, I. M. (1912), 'Piercing the Veil of the Corporate Entity', *Columbia Law Review* 12: 496.

Young, I. M. (1990), *Justice and the Politics of Difference*, Princeton: Princeton University Press.

PART III

LEGISLATIVE REFORM INITIATIVES IN THE UNITED KINGDOM AND THE UNITED STATES

9

Transatlantic Perspectives on Partnership Law: Risk and Instability

DEBORAH A. DeMOTT*

9.1. INTRODUCTION

General partnership law in the United States, although comparable to English law in many respects, has long differed from it on a fundamental question: If a partner wishes to terminate membership in a partnership, is the partner bound by a prior agreement to remain a member of the partnership? Different answers to this basic question carry corollary consequences for other provisions within partnership legislation. These differences have persisted through the twentieth century and remain evident in contemporary partnership legislation in the United States as contrasted with the reform alternatives for English partnership law[1] presented recently by the Law Commissions in their Consultation Paper on Partnership (Law Commission 2000: 8–9). My thesis is that partnership legislation in each country strikes a different balance in the inevitable trade-offs as between stability for the partnership association and risk as perceived by each individual partner. These trade-offs make the general partnership in the United States less stable as a form of business association but also reduce certain risks otherwise borne by individual partners.

The law applicable to general partnerships is a rich source of legal puzzles because the underlying concepts draw on doctrine from contract, agency, and property, doing so in ways that reveal tensions among them. In particular, elements of partnership law drawn from contract law may be at odds with partnership's inclusion of elements drawn from the common law of agency. Different elements dominate partnership law in England compared with the United States. This chapter begins by discussing the basic similarities in partnership law in the two countries, followed by the major difference. The chapter

* This chapter is based on a public lecture given at the Institute for Advanced Legal Studies, London, March 2001. I am grateful to the audience, and to Professors Evelyn Brody, Paul Davies, and Judith Freedman, for comments and suggestions.

[1] Throughout, references are to English partnership law. My intention is to exclude any reference to the Scottish law of partnership, which differs materially from partnership law in England and Wales.

then examines the consequences that follow from this difference and identifies points on which further empirical research would be illuminating.

Before examining the legal specifics, consider as an initial matter an analogy or visual metaphor. The points of partnership law examined in this chapter involve what may be termed architectural features or choices—basic decisions concerning the structure of the relationship among parties and their rights and powers as defined in large measure by the statute applicable to a particular type of business association. Architectural features in the law of business associations have consequences that pervade the particular body of law and explain many of its specific provisions. By analogy, an architect designing a vaulted building, at least one capable of standing for any appreciable time, develops a design that counteracts the forces of compression and tension that push downward and pull outward on the vault. Unsuccessful vaulted buildings fail to successfully play compression and tension off against each other and channel these forces safely to the ground. Designs for successful vaults—like the Pantheon and the domed cathedral in Florence—can span vast spaces, but the design's solution to the basic problem tends to implicate many other visual and functional elements in the building (King 2001: 28–31). For example, the coffers in the ceiling of the Pantheon's dome, a memorable visual feature, also lighten the load that the dome imposes. Likewise, the law applicable to any particular form of business association reflects a series of choices—whether made explicitly or implicitly—about basic structural questions; consequences of these basic choices are diffused throughout applicable law.

9.2. STATUTORY SIMILARITIES

To place the differences in context, it is important to begin by identifying common features of general partnership law in the two countries. In both countries, general partnership legislation covers the same subject-matter. Partnership is defined in § 1(1) of the Partnership Act 1890 as 'the relation which subsists between persons carrying on a business in common with a view to profit'. The counterpart definition in US legislation characterizes a partnership as an 'association' and partners as 'co-owners' who carry on a business for profit. These definitions do not differ materially in the subject-matter covered by partnership law.[2] Similarly, both countries' legislation contains provisions comparable in

---

[2] Uniform Partnership Act 1914 (UPA) defines a partnership in § 6(1) as 'an association of two or more persons to carry on as co-owners a business for profit'. Under § 202(a) of the Revised Uniform Partnership Act 1997 (RUPA), 'the association of two or more persons to carry on as co-owners a business for profit forms a partnership, whether or not the persons intend to form a partnership'. One consequence of characterizing partnership as a 'relation' as opposed to an 'association' is the need for additional terminology. Section 4(1) in the Partnership Act 1890 provides that '[p]ersons who have entered into partnership with each other are for purposes of this Act called collectively a firm, and the name under which their business is carried on is called the firm-name'. In contrast, UPA does not use the 'firm' terminology.

substance that exclude, from the scope of the general definition of partnership, certain relationships in which a person receives a share in the profits of a business but is not to be treated as a partner, such as repayment of a loan in amounts that vary with the profitability of a business.[3] Moreover, in both countries partners in a general partnership are its agents and as such hold power to bind the firm, in the words of the Partnership Act 1890 as to 'any act for carrying on in the usual way business of the kind carried on by the firm . . . unless the partner so acting has in fact no authority and the person with whom he is dealing either knows that he has no authority, or does not know or believe him to be a partner'.[4] Finally, in both countries, general partners have individual liability as a consequence of obligations incurred by the partnership.[5] This is commonly treated as a fundamental and defining element of general partnership. Indeed, the drafter of the 1914 uniform partnership legislation in the United States, William Draper Lewis (1915), wrote that the element of individual liability is 'the idea of every business man who deals with a partnership, that he is dealing

---

[3] See Partnership Act 1890, § 2; UPA § 7; RUPA § 202(c).

[4] Under the Partnership Act 1890, a partner is an agent of fellow partners as well as an agent of the firm. See Partnership Act 1890, § 5. In contrast, the UPA and RUPA characterize a partner as an agent only of 'the partnership'. See UPA § 9; RUPA § 301(1). Thus, partners in partnerships subject to US law are not each other's 'mutual agents', although they may be individually liable for obligations of the partnership that fellow partners have incurred. Moreover, in both jurisdictions, a partner who wishes to 'revoke' the authority of his or her fellow partners may do so only by dissolving the partnership or disassociating from it, a step which carries many complex consequences and which English law limits to partnerships-at-will. In contrast with the common law of agency, a partner's manifestation of intention to revoke a fellow partner's authority is ineffective. See Restatement (Third) Agency § 3.10(a) (Tentative Draft No. 2, 14 Mar. 2001).

The US legislation makes a partner's apparent authority dependent on the scope of the partnership business and does not additionally condition it on whether the third party knew or believed the actor to be a partner. See UPA § 9(1) ('Every partner is an agent of the partnership for the purpose of its business, and the act of every partner . . . for apparently carrying on in the usual way the business of the partnership of which he is a member binds the partnership, unless the partner so acting has in fact no authority to act for the partnership in the particular matter, and the person with whom he is dealing has knowledge of the fact that he has no such authority'); and (2) ('An act of a partner which is not apparently for the carrying on of the business of the partnership in the usual way does not bind the partnership unless authorized by the other partners'). Section 303(1) and (2) are comparable, except in two respects. Section 303(1) makes it explicit that a partner's apparent authority includes acts for carrying on in the ordinary course 'business of the kind carried on by the partnership', not just a partnership's particular business. Section 303(2) permits a partnership to limit the risk created by unauthorized acts by providing a notification to a third party that states the restrictions imposed on a partner's authority. Section 102(d) provides that a notification is effective upon its delivery to a person's place of business or other place that the person designates to receive communications. The point is to make the effectiveness of restrictions on authority not dependent on a showing of actual knowledge.

In contrast, the last part of § 5 in the Partnership Act 1890 carries the implication that if a third party who does not know that the person with whom dealing occurred is a member of a partnership, fellow partners are not liable on the obligation resulting from the partner's dealings with the third party. If so, § 5 rejects the common law doctrine of the undisclosed principal, as stated and applied in *Watteau v. Fenwick*, (1893) 1 Q.B. 346. For discussion of alternative interpretations of § 5, along with cases and commentary supportive of applying undisclosed principal doctrine in this context, see Morse (1995: 86–9).

[5] See Partnership Act 1890, § 9; UPA § 15; RUPA § 306(a).

with a group of persons who are directly and unlimitedly liable for partnership obligations'.[6]

A brief historical note may help here. The 1914 statute was highly successful; almost every state enacted legislation closely patterned on it, making partnership law less susceptible to state-by-state variation than other bodies of law, such as corporate law.[7] The effect of the 1914 statute was long-lived as well. The early 1990s saw the completion of a revised uniform statute for general partnership (generally known by its acronym, 'RUPA'), now the basis for legislation in many states, some embodying significant departures from the proposed uniform provisions.[8]

The original project that culminated in the 1914 uniform legislation did not have an entirely auspicious beginning. The first drafter, James Barr Ames, died mid-way into the project. Sad enough in itself, but his underlying theory as well as his draft diverged markedly from what appear to have been Lewis's views. As the language just quoted may imply, Lewis was committed to the view that a general partnership is necessarily an aggregate of discrete persons as opposed to an entity having a distinct juridical personality. Ames, in contrast, was a proponent of treating general partnerships as legal entities distinct from their members. Following Ames's death, and Lewis's appointment as his successor, Lewis gave advisers to the project two alternative drafts from which to choose, one drawn on the entity premise and the other on the aggregate premise. The advisers sided with Lewis, perhaps persuaded by his argument that it would be, at the least cumbersome, to explain how partners can have individual liability (a proposition to which Ames was also committed) when a third party has acquired rights and liabilities that in the first instance bind the partnership as an entity (Lewis 1915: 640–1).[9] Almost a century later, RUPA overcame this particular problem by distinguishing between primary and secondary liability. RUPA provides that a partnership creditor may not levy execution against the individual assets of a partner, otherwise liable on a claim, unless the creditor has

---

[6] Cf. Vestal (Chapter 12, this volume) (noting that decade of changes in law produced 'a widening gap between the popular conception of the partnership relationship and the legal restatement of the concept. It is my sense that the popular conception of the partnership relationship is much closer to the tort-based, relationship-driven model under the UPA and the common law than it is to the contract-based, immediate self-interest model under RUPA').

[7] The sole exception is the state of Louisiana. The Civil Code defines a partnership as 'a juridical person, distinct from its partners, created by a contract between two or more persons to combine their efforts or resources in determined proportions and to collaborate at mutual risk for their common profit or commercial benefit'. La. Civ. Code Art. 2801 (2001).

[8] For instances of non-uniform provisions in states that have otherwise adopted RUPA, see Vestal (Chapter 12, this volume).

[9] Lewis wrote that the entity theory, 'while it enables us to solve the rights of the separate judgment creditor of a partner in the partnership property, it makes it impossible to work out in a satisfactory way the rights of a firm creditor against the separate property of a partner' (Lewis 1915: 640). Lewis argued additionally that treating partnerships as entities would entail the creation of a system of registration (ibid. 641). However, RUPA, which treats partnerships as entities, does not require registration. See RUPA § 201(a) (stating that a partnership is an entity distinct from its members).

first recovered a judgment against the partnership itself and that judgment has been returned unsatisfied in whole or in part.[10]

It is clear that Lewis and Ames were aware of the formulations in the Partnership Act 1890, to the extent of using the statute as an interim drafting model in some respects. The 1890 statute originated with the work of Sir Frederick Pollock, who in 1879 drafted the initial bill to consolidate the law of partnership (Lindley and Banks 1995: 4).[11] Lewis recounts, though, that although in early drafts the wording in the English statute was followed verbatim when its substantive approach was adopted, by the end of the project all was redrafted to 'reduce the language to as simple a form as possible' (Lewis 1915: 621). Lewis takes particular authorial pride in having reduced, to twelve lines, the Partnership Act's one-page treatment of when a recipient of a share in profits is not a partner.[12]

9.3. THE MAJOR DISPARITY

Against this background, it is significant that the US legislation departed from the 1890 Act in one basic respect, a divergence that continues in RUPA. Under the Partnership Act 1890, as under the US legislation, a general partnership is a relatively fragile form of business association because many kinds of circumstances will cause a partnership to dissolve. These circumstances include the death of an individual partner and an agreement among partners to dissolve.[13] Dissolution is a complex doctrine. Its basic effect is to terminate the association among partners, which creates a right in individual partners to their share (net of claims owing to third parties and to other partners) of partnership property. Partners who wish to carry on post-dissolution may do so by forming a new partnership, but the claims incident to settling-up may erect practical obstacles on this course.

The intriguing difference among statutes is the effect each gives to a partner's stated intention or will to dissolve, when no other ground for dissolution is

---

[10] RUPA § 307(d). Comparable legislation in some states preceded RUPA. See e.g. *State Security Bank v. McCoy*, 361 N.W.2d 514 (Neb. 1985), applying Neb. Rev. Stat. § 25-316 (1985). See also Law Commission (2000: 137–40) (proposing alternative reform in which partnership's liability is primary and that of individual partners is secondary). Under RUPA § 307(c), a creditor may not satisfy a judgment against a partnership from the individual assets of a partner unless the creditor has also obtained a judgment against that partner. In contrast, one of the Law Commission's proposals is that a creditor be permitted to enforce a judgment against a partnership directly against a partner's assets without obtaining a judgment against that partner (ibid. 140).

[11] In 1865, legislation, known as 'Bovill's Act', clarified distinctions between partnership and various forms of debtor–creditor relationships. Sections 2 and 3 of the Partnership Act 1890 contain the gist of Bovill's Act (Morse 1995: 36).

[12] See Lewis (1915) (comparing Partnership Act 1890 § 2 with UPA § 7).

[13] Partnership Act 1890, §§ 32–5 (stating circumstances under which dissolution will occur); UPA § 29 (defining dissolution as 'the change in the relation of the partners caused by any partner ceasing to be associated in the carrying on as distinguished from the winding up of the business'), and §§ 31-3 (stating causes of dissolution and when dissolution may be ordered by a court).

present. Section 32 of the Partnership Act 1890 provides that such notice is effective to dissolve a partnership when it has been entered into for an undefined term.[14] In contrast, a partner's notice of intention to dissolve is ineffective when a partnership has been formed for a fixed term and that term has not yet expired, or when the partnership has been formed for a specific undertaking that has not yet been completed. In a partnership that is not a partnership-at-will, in other words, agreement among partners is a requisite for dissolution unless some other circumstance causes dissolution. Nor is a partner's notice to third parties that the partner shall no longer be bound by co-partners' acts operative when the notice is ineffective to dissolve the partnership.[15] In contrast, under § 31(2) of the Uniform Partnership Act, an individual partner's express will to dissolve effects dissolution when no other circumstance permits dissolution. This is so even when the dissolution contravenes a provision in the partnership agreement, as in a partnership for a fixed term or the completion of a specific project.[16]

Moreover, this basic difference persists in RUPA. The drafters of RUPA were concerned to develop terminology that distinguishes between a partner's departure from the firm and the 'various aspects of the process of disengagement from the relationship' (Weidner and Larson 1993: 7). A partner who departs from the firm 'disassociates' under RUPA.[17] 'Dissolution' follows only when the partnership's business is wound up. Although RUPA's consequences are not identical to those created by the Uniform Partnership Act in all respects, a partner has power to disassociate at any time by giving express notice that the partner so intends, even when the dissolution is wrongful because it breaches a provision of the partnership agreement.[18]

These basic differences illustrate the intellectual linkages between, on the one hand, partnership and, on the other hand, concepts and doctrines drawn from the common law and the tensions among these concepts and doctrines. The choice made by the Partnership Act 1890 reflects the dominance of contract.[19] Partners lack the power to dissolve in contravention of their agreement because that is the consequence of their prior agreement. As a consequence, relationships among partners, third parties, and partnership property should be more stable. Third parties who deal with the partnership are assured that the group who comprise the partnership will remain members consistent with the terms of the agreement, barring an occurrence like a partner's death, and are also assured

---

[14] Cases have defined a partnership with no fixed term to include a partnership in which partners have agreed that no dissolution may occur except by mutual agreement. See *Moss v. Elphick*, [1910] 1 K.B. 846. In effect, any agreement that limits a partner's right to dissolve by giving notice creates a partnership for a fixed term (Morse 1995: 32–3). It can be open to question whether such an agreement exists (ibid. 33).

[15] See Lindley and Banks (1995: 393–4) (noting that the Partnership Act itself is silent on the point whether a partner may unilaterally revoke the authority of a co-partner). Giving notice of a purported revocation may constitute a repudiatory breach of the partnership agreement, which would entitle the innocent partners to choose whether to affirm the agreement or treat the partnership as ended (ibid. 697).

[16] See UPA § 31(2).   [17] See RUPA § 601.   [18] RUPA § 601(1) and 602(a).

[19] Commentators on English partnership law emphasize its contractual nature. See Morse (1995: 4).

that, although many circumstances may diminish the value of partnership assets, a partner's wrongful dissociation will not be such a circumstance.

This stability should be of benefit to partners as well. Fellow partners are assured that a colleague may not leave the partnership simply by expressing the intention that it dissolve, which provides an assurance of ongoing association. Moreover, fellow partners should benefit from stability even though a court would not grant an order of specific performance that compels an unwilling partner to continue to provide services to a partnership.[20] If partners are unable to dissolve a partnership in contravention of their agreement, individual partners lose the ability to safeguard their individual resources against obligations that the partnership may incur following their departure from the firm. This is a relevant consideration given the joint and several nature of partners' individual liability.[21] That is, it is in all partners' interests to know that the individual assets of their fellow partners will remain available throughout the duration of the partnership and the liabilities that may ensue. Nonetheless, this assurance is not complete under the Partnership Act 1890 because a partnership may dissolve, for example, as a consequence of a partner's death or bankruptcy. In any event, the Law Commission's reform proposals are consistent with this point and, as discussed below, take the underlying point further than does the 1890 statute.[22]

A further implication of the dominance accorded contract is that a partner's repudiation of the partnership contract should not terminate the contract and convert the partnership into one of partnership-at-will. If the innocent partners wish to dissolve following the repudiation, some other route towards dissolution should be identified, such as agreement among the partners or an application to the court for an order dissolving the partnership (Law Commission 2000: 70).[23] Otherwise, if a partner repudiates the partnership contract, partners who

---

[20] See *C. H. Giles and Co. v. Morris* [1972] 1 W.L.R. 307, at 317–19 (discussion of bases for judicial reluctance to grant specific enforcement of contract involving more than a minor element of personal services or continuous personal services); Restatement (Second) of Contracts § 367(a) (1981) (stating that promise to render personal services will not be specifically enforced) and ibid. Comment b (discussion definition of personal service); see also Lindley and Banks (1995: 17–18 nn. 39–42) (stating that court would not decree specific performance of agreement for partnership-at-will, nor would court decree specific performance of agreement to perform personal services); Hillman (1985: 733) (noting that although court will not compel an individual to perform services on behalf of another, limitations on the availability of specific performance do not require the free dissolvability of partnerships because a partner's involvement in partnership may take a form other than provision of services).

[21] See Partnership Act 1890, §§ 9 and 12.

[22] The Law Commission (2000: 66) specifically considers whether a partner in a partnership of defined duration should have 'a right to withdraw' when the partnership agreement itself does not confer such a right. It provisionally rejects this possibility because '[t]he partners will have contracted to be in the partnership for a defined term; the law should respect that contract'.

[23] This argument is contra to the dictum stated in *Hurst v. Bryk* (2000) 2 W.L.R. 740, 746–50 (H.L.) that a repudiatory breach terminates the partnership contract. The dictum continues, though, with the reservation that the termination of the partnership contract does not automatically dissolve the partnership because the equitable jurisdiction of the court whether to decree dissolution should not be circumvented.

wish to continue the partnership are denied the financial stability for which they contracted originally if other less bold partners may exit freely in the wake of the partner who initially repudiated the contract.[24]

To be sure, one might wonder how comprehensively a partnership statute should be understood to control the resolution of partnership-related disputes and whether the statute ousts the applicability of common law doctrines completely or only partially. A full answer to this difficult question is beyond the modest scope of this chapter. As points of departure, though, one might consider the nature of partnership legislation and how the legislation itself addresses the possible applicability of other bodies of law. The Partnership Act 1890 has been characterized as substantially 'declaratory' in nature because its intention was largely to restate principles already developed in common law and equity cases (Morse 1995: 3–4). In some respects, although the UPA largely restates preceding law, it also reflects more choice among competing rules because its drafters considered and resolved points of doctrinal divergence among states (Lewis 1915: 623).[25] Both statutes expressly contemplate that other bodies of law may be applicable to partnerships. The Partnership Act 1890 preserves in § 46 'the rules of equity and common law applicable to partnership . . . except so far as they are inconsistent with the express provisions of this Act'. The UPA provides that '[i]n any case not provided for in this act, the rules of law and equity, including the law merchant, shall govern'.[26] RUPA provides that '[u]nless displaced by particular provisions of this [Act], the principles of law and equity supplement' the Act.[27] These formulations are not identical; the standard in the Partnership Act 1890 is inconsistency, compared with whether a case is 'provided for' in the UPA, and whether legal principle is 'displaced' by RUPA. Of the three formulations, the inconsistency standard in the Partnership Act 1890 is arguably the friendliest to applying extra-statutory law. In contrast, the UPA may contain provisions that can be interpreted to 'provide for' a case by generating a rule for decision by analogy or by extension.

In any event, one might accord controlling effect to the statute on matters that it addresses explicitly or by ready implication. These include the causes of dissolution, which partnership legislation itself specifies. It is inconsistent with statutory specification of the circumstances that cause dissolution to import an additional cause by applying common law contract doctrines, such as anticipatory repudiation.

In contrast with its English counterpart, partnership legislation in the United States assigns dominance to the agency elements in partnership. As noted above, all partners are the firm's agents, and when a partner's act binds the partnership, it creates individual liability for all partners. A defining element in the common

---

[24] If a partner wrongfully repudiates a partnership agreement, fellow partners no longer owe fiduciary duties to the partner who repudiated.

[25] However, the dearth of precedent in many states and 'confusion in legal theory' were more important causes of confusion in the common law of partnership in the United States.

[26] UPA § 5.   [27] RUPA § 104(a).

law of agency, in England as well as the United States, is the power held by both principal and agent to terminate an agent's actual authority: the principal by revoking authority and the agent by renouncing it.[28] From the standpoint of a principal, the power to revoke authority is a basic measure for controlling the agent and self-protecting against the risks present in a relationship in which another person's actions carry direct legal consequences for oneself. From the standpoint of an agent, the power to renounce authority enables the agent to move on to other activities and associations. The common law of agency recognizes the effect of revocation and renunciation even when they contravene a contract between principal and agent. The effect is to empower principal and agent to act on assessments of risk and self-interest that occur subsequent to an initial agreement between them.

In commenting on the 1914 uniform legislation as its drafter, Lewis wrote, simply and declaratively that, '[t]he relation of partner is one of agency. The agency is such a personal one that equity cannot enforce it even where the agreement provides that a partnership shall continue for a definite time' (Lewis 1915: 627).[29] Lewis also noted that uncertainty on the point had preceded the statute's resolution and that '[t]he English law is opposed to this view'.[30] The practical insights in the partnership context are that the ability to exit from the partnership is relevant to downside scenarios as well as upside scenarios. On the downside, the ability to exit at any time enables a partner to cut off the risk stemming from post-dissolution liabilities, at least once third parties have notice that the partner has left the firm. On the upside, having left the partnership, the now-former partner no longer owes fiduciary duties to former colleagues (excepting duties that follow the possession of confidential information) and, subject to contractual restraints, is free to compete and pursue opportunities that would otherwise fall within the partnership's ambit. In contrast, a contract-dominated view binds parties more tightly to their initial assessments of risk and self-interest.

9.4. Mitigating Elements

9.4.1. United States

I characterized this difference between general partnership law in the United States and England as involving an 'architectural' feature of partnership law, a basic design choice that carries many corollary consequences. This is because either choice has the potential to create harsh consequences, which various provisions in each statute may mitigate. Consider first the consequences of the agency-dominated design of the US legislation. If a partner has power to

---

[28] See Restatement (Third) Agency § 3.10 (1) (2001) (Tentative Draft No. 2); Reynolds (1997).
[29] This passage continues: 'The power of any partner to terminate the relation, even though [in] doing so he breaches a contract, should, it is submitted, be recognized.'
[30] Lewis notes this in footnote 8 on page 627 of his article.

dissolve at any time in contravention of the partnership agreement, the partner might use the power, or threaten to use it, when fellow partners will be unable to carry on the partnership's business. Upon dissolution, a partner has the right to receive that partner's share of partnership assets, minus the partner's share of liabilities. Partners who wish to carry on the business may be unable to raise the cash requisite to buy out the share of the partner who has dissolved. This prospect may create leverage in bargaining for opportunistic partners who threaten to dissolve unless fellow partners agree to sweeten the terms of the partnership agreement to the benefit of the partner who threatens dissolution. This consequence follows because the structure of partnership law also draws on property concepts by specifying circumstances under which a partner may compel the sale or division of partnership assets to complete a winding up.[31] A partner's premature withdrawal may also damage the partnership by reducing the willingness of third parties to deal with the shrunken firm or by leading third parties to demand better terms to induce them to deal.

Accordingly, both the 1914 legislation and RUPA contain provisions that reduce the risks that wrongful dissolution and dissociation otherwise would impose on fellow partners. Under both statutes, partners who have not wrongfully dissolved or dissociated have a claim against their now-former partner for damages caused by the dissolution or dissociation, which is to be subtracted from the now-former partner's account.[32] Additionally, some courts developed doctrines of bad-faith dissolution or dissolution in contravention of a partner's fiduciary duty. The leading case, *Page v. Page*, holds that a partner's power to dissolve a partnership 'like any power held by a fiduciary, must be exercised in good faith'.[33] RUPA does not explicitly address whether a partner's power to dissociate is subject to a good-faith or fiduciary-duty limit.[34] Both RUPA and the UPA enable partners who have not wrongfully dissolved or dissociated to continue to use partnership property to operate the business and both permit the

---

[31] In this respect general partnership shares some of the instabilities of tenancies-in-common. In US law, a tenancy-in-common carries the risk that a co-owner will seek a partition by sale, which will oust the other co-owners unless they purchase the property. For an extended treatment of this problem and its more general implications, see Dagan and Heller (2001).

[32] See UPA § 38(2)(a)(II) and (c)(II); RUPA § 602(c). RUPA is a bit kinder to partners who wrongfully dissociate because it does not exclude partnership goodwill in calculating the value of the wrongfully dissociated partner's partnership interest. Under RUPA, if the partnership's goodwill is damaged by the wrongful dissociation, the amount of damage is offset against the buyout price received by the wrongfully dissociated partner. Compare UPA § 38(2)(c)(II) with RUPA § 602(c) and Comment 3 and RUPA § 701, Comment 3.

[33] *Page v. Page*, 359 P.2d 41 (Cal. 1961).

[34] RUPA § 404(d) imposes a duty of good faith and fair dealing on partners in exercising rights and discharging duties to the partnership and to fellow partners. The facts of *Page* itself are unlikely to trigger the good-faith duty imposed by § 404(d). In *Page*, the partner who sought dissolution was also a creditor, and the attempted dissolution occurred when the partnership's business took a turn for the better but the amount of debt owing to that partner made it unlikely that a third party would buy the partnership's assets. RUPA § 404(f) provides that a partner may 'lend money to and transact business with the partnership, and as to each loan or transaction the rights and obligations of the partner are the same as those of a person who is not a partner, subject to other applicable law'.

deferral, until the partnership's term has expired, of payment to the partner who wrongfully dissolved or dissociated.[35] This right is conditioned on securing payment to the former partner of the partner's eventual share.[36] RUPA is friendlier to continuation because it provides that, following a partner's wrongful dissociation, winding up of partnership business will occur only if that is the express will of at least half of the remaining partners, determined within ninety days following the dissociation.[37] As a result, if a majority of the remaining partners so wish, they may continue the partnership's business. However, the partnership agreement may eliminate this possibility. As the statute is structured, continuation by the majority of remaining partners is the default rule, subject to ouster by contrary provision in the partnership agreement.[38] In contrast, the partnership agreement may not oust the statutory provisions that govern dissolution by court order or on the basis that carrying on the partnership has become illegal.[39]

Even with these mitigating elements, US partnership legislation has been criticized for its unwillingness to bind partners to the terms of their agreement. However, the critics disagree about the preferable alternative. Professors Bromberg and Ribstein (2001: § 7:03(d), § 7:60 n. 23) would make specifically enforceable a partnership agreement that explicitly limits a partner's power to dissociate. In contrast, Professor Hillman (1985: 735) would treat a partnership as indissoluble when the partnership agreement specifies a particular term or undertaking, which is consistent with the Partnership Act 1890. All agree on an underlying premise that in negotiating the terms of their prospective association as partners, parties should be permitted to strike a binding agreement that reflects each party's relative assessment of the risks that partnership will create and the benefits of assuring greater stability in the association (Hillman 1985: 731; Bromberg and Ribstein 2001: § 7.03(c), §§ 7:59–60).

This underlying premise is, however, open to question if the risks created by the agency that partnership creates are more difficult than other business risks to assess at the point of an initial agreement or if these risks are especially problematic in some other way. The demographics of partnership are also relevant. In particular, reflecting its status as the default form of organizational choice, general partnership law is applicable to business associations in which parties may lack the sophistication to strike a closely tailored bargain reflecting a balance among risks and opportunities as perceived by each participant, following

---

[35] See UPA § 38(2)(b) and (c)(II); RUPA § 701(h) and 801(2)(ii). Under § 38(2)(b), whether a partnership's business continues in the wake of a wrongful dissolution depends on whether all the remaining partners 'desire to continue the business in the same name, either by themselves or jointly with others'. Under RUPA § 801(2)(i), the business may continue unless at least half of the remaining partners expressly wish to wind-up.

[36] See UPA § 38(2)(c)(II); RUPA § 701(h).

[37] RUPA § 801(2)(i). A partner who dissociates within ninety days after another partner's wrongful dissociation does so rightfully. See ibid. § 602(b)(2)(i). The rightful dissociation is treated as an expression of will to wind up partnership business. See ibid. § 801(2)(i).

[38] See RUPA § 103.   [39] See RUPA § 103(b)(8).

careful analysis and professional counsel. For example, English authorities report that, at present, at least half of all partnerships have no comprehensive partnership agreement (Deards 2001: 362). This constituency may include members not readily able to assess the risks created by operating a business as a general partnership and unlikely to obtain sophisticated professional assistance to evaluate these risks so that they may be assessed in relation to benefits anticipated in a structure that binds partners to membership on stated terms.

Another way to characterize US partnership law is that it limits the extent to which partners may use pre-commitment strategies to reduce the risk of subsequent defections. A pre-commitment strategy consists of a person's voluntary actions that restrict future options when the person realizes that her preferences may differ in the future from her preferences at the time of committing. Precommitment may be rational when one anticipates greater benefit from credibly committing to stay a particular course, despite subsequent changes in preferences. For example, Ulysses pre-committed to staying his navigational course and to sailing past the Sirens when he directed his crew to bind him to the mast and to stop their ears against the Sirens' song (Elster 1979: 37–47).[40] The statutory power to dissolve is, of course, antithetical to pre-commitment.

As it happens, an additional limit on pre-commitment comes from general contract law. Suppose a partnership agreement provides that a partner who wrongfully dissolves the partnership or dissociates from it will lose any right to subsequent payment from the partnership, including the return of the partner's capital account and any share of profits to which the partner would otherwise be entitled. Such a provision is enforceable only if it can be characterized as a reasonable estimate of the damage the partnership will incur, as opposed to a penalty.[41] Thus, contract law itself limits the extent to which a partnership agreement may be structured to deter defections. Additionally, many cases testing the limits of such provisions involve contests between a partnership's remaining members and former partners engaged in competitive activities (Bromberg and Ribstein 2001: § 7:178–9). Contract law does not enforce promises that restrain competition if they are 'unreasonable', a determination that considers whether the restraint is necessary to protect the promisee's legitimate interests, whether it will result in hardship to the promiser, and whether

---

[40] Sometimes a pre-commitment strategy is not the wisest course. Ulysses would regret his crew's compliance with his instructions if, once past the Sirens, he sighted a sea monster but was unable—the crew's ears still being stopped—to warn them of the impending peril of being swallowed by the monster if the ship does not change course. Likewise, if Ulysses misunderstands the risk that the Sirens pose, his pre-commitment strategy may not be wise. See DiFonzo (2000: 944).

[41] See *Howard v. Babcock*, 863 P.2d 150, 151 (Cal. 1994) (provision in partnership agreement providing that partner would forfeit some or all rights to benefits upon withdrawal if partner entered into competition with partnership is enforceable; provision took only a 'reasonable toll' on departing partners who competed, and represented a reasonable attempt by partnership to estimate damages from loss as opposed to an unenforceable penalty). See also *Meehan v. Shaughnessy*, 535 N.E.2d 1255, 1266 (Mass. 1989) (partnership could not retain former partners' capital accounts and profit shares; capital contributions 'are not a form of liquidated damages to which partners can resort in the event of a breach' of the partnership agreement).

it is likely to injure the public.[42] These factors range well beyond partners' determinations of the advantage they mutually anticipate at the time of structuring their partnership agreement.

9.4.2. England

Similarly, the English legislation contains provisions that reduce the risks created by a contract-dominated design choice. There are several grounds on which a partner may petition the court for a decree of dissolution, including another partner's conduct that prejudicially affects partnership business and, more generally, circumstances that make it 'just and equitable' that the partnership be dissolved.[43] To be sure, US legislation states similar bases on which a court may order dissolution or dissociation.[44] Additionally, in both England and the United States, dissolution occurs automatically upon the occurrence of a partner's death or bankruptcy, unless the partnership agreement otherwise provides.[45] If the other partners wish, a partnership may be dissolved if a partner's share becomes subject to a creditor's charging order.[46] An unhappy partner in an English partnership may thus benefit if dissolution occurs fortuitously, for example as a consequence of a fellow partner's death or bankruptcy, because the partnership association then ends but the unhappy partner has not repudiated the partnership agreement.

Moreover, this perspective provides a framework for explaining why, in English law, with the exception of certain professional firms, partnerships are illegal if they have more than twenty partners.[47] Exceeding this number automatically dissolves the partnership on the basis of illegality.[48] This limitation is difficult to justify, especially in a framework largely dominated by contract, making it unsurprising that the Law Commission's consultation paper (2000: 56–9) identifies the size limit as an obvious target for abolition. The limitation may be explained, but not justified, by the risks created by a binding contractual undertaking that makes one individually liable on the basis of others' actions. One might sensibly proceed with caution before making such a commitment and might in particular wish to have ample information about prospective fellow partners. The statutory limit may represent a rough proxy for circumstances under which the cautious would decide to proceed. But this does not suffice as a justification for a mandatory size limit: individuals' preferences

---

[42] Restatement (Second) of Contracts § 188(1) (1981).   [43] See Partnership Act 1890, § 35.
[44] See UPA § 32; RUPA § 601(5).   [45] See Partnership Act 1890, § 33(1).
[46] See Partnership Act 1890, § 33(2); RUPA § 601(4)(ii) (partner may be dissociated following unanimous vote to expel if partner's transferable interest in partnership has become subject to charging order that has not been foreclosed).
[47] See Companies Act 1985, §§ 716 and 717 (excepting firms of solicitors, accountants, and stockbrokers). Other law has eliminated the restriction for other professions. See Law Commission (2000: 56 n. 55). The same numerical limit applies to limited partnerships formed under the Limited Partnership Act 1907. See § 4(2).
[48] See Partnership Act 1890, § 34.

for undertaking risk vary, as do partnerships' businesses, the risks a particular business typically entails, and the information available with which to assess risk.

9.5. FURTHER IMPLICATIONS

These underlying basic differences in general partnership law have implications outside the realm of partnership. In the United States, business associates who wish to avoid the instability of general partnership have many choices, including the long-standing choices of incorporating the business or organizing as a limited partnership. An innovation of the last couple of decades, limited liability companies (LLCs) are organized under statutes that permit, as with partnership, great organizational flexibility without the risk of individual liability for LLC members. Although the statutes governing these forms differ, none creates a power of dissolution or dissociation with the consequences that affect the stability of a general partnership.[49] In this context, it is possible to understand the general partnership as a penalty default.[50] That is, many if not most organizers of business firms may prefer characteristics that cannot be achieved through a general partnership; the structure of general partnership law creates incentives to choose other organizational forms. In contrast, in England, where the statute permits the formation of general partnerships with greater stability, the incentive to look elsewhere for alternate organizational choices may be weaker, as may be legislative incentives to produce them. English authorities report that almost 40 per cent of businesses with more than one owner choose to be partnerships, which may reflect either a good fit between partnership law and the needs of its users or the lack of better fitting alternatives (Deards 2001: 375).[51]

These basic differences may have further implications for other comparisons that could be examined. For example, are partners' fiduciary duties defined

[49] See e.g. Del. Code Ann., tit. 8, § 275 (stating procedure for dissolution of business corporation, initiated by resolution adopted by corporation's directors and approved by vote of majority of shares having right to vote); Unif. Limited Partnership Act § 801 (limited partnership is dissolved as specified in its certificate or in limited partnership agreement; upon written consent of all partners; or upon withdrawal of a general partner unless partnership has another general partner and partnership agreement permits partnership business to be carried on by remaining general partner, or unless within ninety days of withdrawal all partners agree in writing to continue and to appointment of one or more general partners if necessary or desired); Del. Code Ann., tit. 6, § 18-801 (LLC is dissolved as specified in LLC agreement; unless agreement provides otherwise, affirmative vote of two-thirds of members effective to dissolve LLC).

[50] This term was formally defined in the landmark article, Ayres and Gertner (1989).

[51] Aggregate data on the number of partnerships in the United States does not always distinguish among all firms that file a partnership tax return—some of which are LLCs—and firms that are organized as partnerships. For example, according to the 2000 edition of the *Statistical Abstract of the United States*, in 1997 in all industries active 'partnerships' numbered 1,759,000 with $1,296 billion in business receipts (U.S. Bureau of the Census 2000: table 858). However, inclusion in the 'partnership' category is based on tax-filing status, and thus may include firms organized as LLCs. In the same period, 4,710,000 corporate tax returns were filed, including 2,452,000 filed by subchapter S corporations (ibid. table 862). Total corporate receipts amounted to $16,610 billion. Data derived

more broadly and enforced more stringently in fixed-duration English partnerships than in partnerships governed by US law? Partners who are more firmly bound to each other by their prior agreement may be more vulnerable to various forms of opportunistic and self-serving conduct by fellow partners. It is noteworthy that the Law Commission's (2000: 179–85) comprehensive review of English partnership law does not propose any material change in partners' fiduciary duties, including any articulation of the extent to which those duties may be reduced by provisions in a partnership agreement, while proposing the addition of a statutory statement of a duty of good faith and fair dealing. In contrast, RUPA § 404(b) limits fiduciary duties to those explicitly stated. While § 103(a) explicitly provides that the partnership agreement shall govern partners' relations with each other, § 103(b) provides that an agreement may not eliminate partners' fiduciary duty of loyalty. Additionally, the Law Commission's review (ibid. 179) does not propose any material revisions to the mandatory duty imposed on each partner by Partnership Act 1890 § 28 to 'render true accounts and full information of all things affecting the partnership to any partner or his legal representatives'. RUPA, in contrast, permits a partnership agreement to restrict a partner's right of access to partnership books and records so long as the restriction is not unreasonable,[52] and appears to permit a partnership agreement to eliminate the duty imposed on each partner and the partnership by § 403(c)(1) to furnish 'without demand, any information concerning the partnership's business and affairs reasonably required for the proper exercise of the partner's rights and duties under the partnership agreement'.[53] In this respect RUPA is consistent with a pre-RUPA case that enforces provisions in a partnership agreement that specified partners' rights to receive information when the information was material to evaluating an offer received from the managing partner to purchase their interests.[54] English authority, in contrast, stresses the mandatory nature of the rights and duties created by § 28 of the Partnership Act 1890, even when the transactional context is the purchase by one partner of another's interest (Morse 1995: 112–13).

This basic difference may also carry implications for the relative extent to which particular remedies are sought. For example, in fixed-duration English

---

from partnership tax returns themselves—which ask whether the filer is organized as an LLC or a partnership—illustrate that the number of LLCs has increased rapidly. In 1998, 470,657 LLCs filed a partnership tax return, up from 349,054 in 1997 and 221,498 in 1996. See Zempel (1998: 69), in Internal Revenue Service, *Statistics of Income Bulletin*, Fall 2000. In 1998 the number of LLCs exceeded the number of limited partnerships. Like most partnerships, most LLCs operate in the finance, insurance, real estate, rental and leasing, and services sectors. The significance of partnerships in these sectors is a long-established trend (ibid. 62). In 1998 LLCs reported $1.2 trillion in total assets, which represents 23.2 per cent of total assets reported by all partnerships (ibid. 69). In all industries in 1998, LLCs reported 1,879,382 members (ibid. figure I).

[52] RUPA § 103(b)(2).

[53] Section 403(c)(1) is not explicitly insulated by § 103(b) from the effects of contrary provisions in the partnership agreement.

[54] See *Exxon Corp. v. Burglin*, 4 F.3d 1294, 1300 (5th Cir. 1993).

partnerships, is more use made of judicial dissolution as a mechanism to allow exit from the firm? And should the standards for judicial dissolution of a corporation on the 'just and equitable' ground be the same as those applicable to dissolution of a partnership? The differences between partnership and corporate structures cut in opposing directions. A general partnership's relative fragility means that more bases for exit may be available, in contrast with the relative durability of a corporation. But membership in a general partnership, unlike shareholding, creates an ongoing risk of individual liability for business obligations.[55]

It is open to question what to make of these differences in the light of the recent availability, in both countries, of limited liability options for general partnerships. The Limited Liability Partnerships Act 2000, like LLP legislation in the United States, makes it possible for two or more persons associated as partners to register as a limited liability partnership. Eligibility for English LLP status is not limited to professional services partnerships, although their concern about the risk of increasing liability on claims of negligence led to the legislation (Whittaker and Machell 2001). Eliminating individual partners' risk of liability to third parties for partnership obligations should significantly reduce the unattractiveness of enforcing partnership agreements that bind partners to each other for a fixed term. However, that risk remains present for partners who do not register their partnership as an LLP, including in particular the less sophisticated cohort within the realm of partnership. Partnerships that operate without a comprehensive written partnership agreement—as at least half of English partnerships reportedly do[56]—may be unlikely to register as an LLP, unless the newly available prospect of limited liability spurs an increase in the requisite attention to organizational formality.

Interestingly, the Law Commission's thoughtful Consultation Paper on partnership articulates throughout a reform philosophy of enhancing the duration of partnerships. For example, under the 1890 statute, a partner's death or bankruptcy automatically dissolves the partnership unless the partnership agreement provides otherwise. The Consultation Paper (Law Commission 2000: 67–9) questions whether the default should be shifted, such that a partner's death or bankruptcy would dissolve only the relationship between that partner and the others, unless the partnership agreement provides that it shall also dissolve the partnership. It is likely, as the Consultation Paper (ibid. 68) observes, that this change would accord with 'the presumed wishes of partners who have not provided for death or bankruptcy one way or the other in the partnership agreement', especially given that any of the partners could withdraw from the partnership if the agreement does not fix a term.

However, the preceding contrast with the US material suggests another perspective from which to assess the value of fortuitously occurring events that

---

[55] For the point that simple analogies between partnership and corporate law can be misleading, see Easterbrook and Fischel (1991: 249–50).

[56] See Section 9.4.1.

cause dissolution. Under the Partnership Act 1890, a fellow partner's death or bankruptcy may serve fortuitously as an escape hatch from a partnership when the agreement binds the partners for a fixed term and the causes of unhappiness or nervousness for a would-be escapee partner do not rise to the level that would furnish grounds on which to achieve escape through court-ordered dissolution. Shifting the default permits the agreement to bind even more tightly, which serves the interests of stability. Like the contract-dominated perspective more generally, permitting an initial agreement to bind more tightly may disserve the interests of partners who have reason to regret the commitment they previously made in the partnership agreement. For good reason, contract law is generally unsympathetic to the regret that may follow a commitment.[57] The general partnership, however, combines a risk of direct individual liability with a flat organizational structure that confers actual and apparent authority on all partners. It is not surprising that mature legal systems, like England and the United States, vary in how these interests and risks are resolved.

REFERENCES

Ayres, I., and Gertner, R. (1989), 'Filling the Gaps in Incomplete Contracts: An Economic Theory of Default Rules', *Yale Law Journal* 99: 87.

Banks, R. C. I. (Lindley and Banks) (1995), *Lindley & Banks on Partnership*, London: Sweet and Maxwell.

Bromberg, A. R., and Ribstein, L. E. (2001), *Bromberg and Ribstein on Partnership*, New York: Aspen Law & Business.

Dagan, H., and Heller, M. (2001), 'The Liberal Commons', *Yale Law Journal* 110: 549.

Deards, E. (2001), 'Partnership Law in the Twenty-First Century', *Journal of Business Law* 2001: 357.

DiFonzo, J. H. (2000), 'Customized Marriage', *Indiana Law Journal* 75: 875.

Easterbrook, F. H., and Fischel, D. R. (1991), *The Economic Structure of Corporate Law*, Cambridge. Mass.: Harvard University Press.

Elster, J. (1979), *Ulysses and the Sirens: Studies in Rationality and Irrationality*, Cambridge: Cambridge University Press.

Farnsworth, E. A. (1998), *Changing Your Mind: The Law of Regretted Decisions*, New Haven: Yale University Press.

Hillman, R. W. (1985), 'Indissoluble Partnerships', *University of Florida Law Review* 37: 691.

King, R. (2001), *Brunelleschi's Dome: The Story of the Great Cathedral in Florence*, London: Pimlico.

---

[57] For an extended discussion, see Farnsworth (1998). See also Bromberg and Ribstein (2001: § 1.02(b)) (observing that statutory dissolution provisions are useful because 'at the time of formation the parties may underestimate the possibility of problems concerning breakup; negotiations over dissolution may result in disagreement that causes the relationship to founder; and working out detailed provisions takes time and requires the expensive services of an attorney'). But see Ribstein (1990: 147) (criticizing non-waivable power to dissolve as a 'wholly-unjustified restriction on private ordering').

Law Commission (Law Commission for England and Wales and the Scottish Law Commission) (2000), Partnership Law: A Joint Consultation Paper, London: The Stationery Office.

Lewis, W. D. (1915), 'The Uniform Partnership Act', *Yale Law Journal* 24: 617.

Lindley and Banks, see Banks, R. C. I.

Morse, G. (1995), *Partnership Law*, London: Blackstone Press.

Reynolds, F. (1997), 'When Is an Agent's Authority Irrevocable?', in R. Cranston (ed.), *Making Commercial Law: Essays in Honour of Roy Goode*, Oxford: Clarendon Press.

Ribstein, L. E. (1990), 'A Mid-Term Assessment of the Project to Revise the Uniform Partnership Act', *Business Lawyer* 46: 111.

U.S. Bureau of the Census (2000), *Statistical Abstract of the United States*, Washington, D.C.: US Government Printing Office.

Weidner D. J., and Larson, J. W. (1993), 'The Revised Uniform Partnership Act: The Reporters' Overview', *Business Lawyer* 49: 1.

Whittaker, J., and Machell, J. (2001), *Limited Liability Partnerships: The New Law*, Bristol: Jordans.

Zempel, A. (1998), '1996 Partnership Tax Returns', Statement of Income Bulletin, Washington D.C.: Internal Revenue Service.

10

Limited Liability Partnerships in the United Kingdom: Do They Have a Role for Small Firms?

JUDITH FREEDMAN*

10.1. INTRODUCTION

The emergence of a new legal form, the limited liability partnership (LLP), in the United Kingdom in 2001 may be depicted by some as part of a general, evolutionary movement towards new limited liability vehicles, influenced by such moves in the United States.[1] Some are also suggesting that this new legal form, the first such innovation in the United Kingdom for over a century, will provide a more suitable vehicle for small, owner-managed firms than the ordinary limited company (Birds 2000: 39; Ward 2001).

This view of the LLP's development and potential will be questioned here. It will be shown that the UK LLP resulted entirely from political pressure from professional firms for limited liability in respect to their activities and from their unwillingness to incorporate. Although this new legal form has now been made available to all firms, not just the professions, it has not been designed with small trading businesses in mind, nor in response to small business concerns. The LLP legislation is complex and leaves much uncertainty, for example on the question of liability. It offers possibilities for tax reduction for some types of firm, but may distort commercial decisions due to this lack of tax neutrality between different legal forms.

It will be argued that the LLP is an unsuitable vehicle for most small, owner-managed, non-professional firms, at least in its present form and state of development. It will be some time, if ever, before it is of value to this type of small firm. Its importance should not be exaggerated.

* The author would like to thank the participants at the unincorporated business symposium at Tilburg University for their comments on the version of the chapter delivered there and also her colleague, Vanessa Finch, with whom she has worked on this area. A joint paper delivered with Vanessa Finch at the Institute of Advanced Legal Studies in July 2001 drew on an earlier version of this chapter, and the author thanks participants in the seminar for their comments. All responsibility for this chapter lies with the author.
    [1] That is, a 'race-to-the-top' argument. See Romano (1985); Winter (1977, 1989). Others are cautious about the validity of the race-to-the-top analysis. See Bratton and McCahery (1997); Macey (1995); Levmore (1992).

Prior to work on the LLP commencing, the Law Commission and Department of Trade and Industry (DTI) had both concluded, after consultation, that no new small business vehicle with limited liability was needed.[2] The UK limited company (the usual form of incorporation in the United Kingdom, used by small and large, private and public firms alike) is already flexible. The tax pressures that resulted in the growth of the LLP and the LLC in the United States, for example, do not apply in the United Kingdom.

The Law Commission was reviewing general partnership law during the time the LLP was under consideration. In addition, a major review of company law was under way (the Company Law Review), which included amongst its tasks a review of the appropriateness and need for simplification of company law for small, private firms. Regrettably, the LLP proposals, consultation, and implementation were conducted by the Department of Trade and Industry on a 'fast track' outside either of these other law reform exercises. This fragmented approach to business law reform is not ideal.

In order to provide a framework and reference point for the discussion that follows, Section 10.2 of this chapter briefly examines the needs of small businesses in relation to legal structure and outlines the arguments against the notion that the LLP will be an important new vehicle for ordinary small businesses. Section 10.3 then examines the pressures that led to the introduction of the LLP in the United Kingdom, and Section 10.4 evaluates the characteristics of the resulting legal vehicle. It is argued in conclusion, in Section 10.5, that this new legal creature is not the result of an evolutionary and competitive process that has produced an efficient result, but rather is the outcome of a political reaction to pressures, which has brought forth a strange legal vehicle of restricted value for small firms.

10.2. Limited Liability, Small Firms and LLPs: An Overview

10.2.1. LLPs: A New Corporate Form Open to All

The UK LLP was proposed initially to meet the perceived needs of professional firms, primarily auditors, who were complaining of unrealistic expectations and 'deep pockets' syndrome due to their inability to limit their liability (Department of Trade and Industry 1997). As the legislation was consulted upon and debated, it became clear that it was very difficult to sustain an argument that this new legal form should be limited to certain regulated groups of professionals (Freedman and Finch 1997; Trade and Industry Committee 1999: paras 30–9). The definition of professional was unclear; there were complaints of non-level playing fields between potential competitors for business, some of whom were classified as 'professional' and some not. Eventually, it was decided

---

[2] See Department of Trade and Industry (1997); Company Law Review (1994), discussed further in Freedman (1999).

to extend the legislation so that any two people could set up an LLP. Thus, there is no restriction of this legal form to professions in the United Kingdom.[3] Although in its origins the UK LLP is similar to those of LLPs in the United States, the resulting legal creation is very different. In fact, the LLP is a misnomer for the UK legal form, which is closer to a company than to a partnership as will be explained in Section 10.4 of this chapter.

10.2.2. The Needs of Small Businesses

Like the US LLP, the UK LLP combines tax transparency with limited liability without requiring the usual structures designed to protect shareholders from managers found in corporation law. For this reason, it has been seen as an ideal new form for small businesses, which combines the benefits of limited liability with the organizational flexibility of the partnership. It might be an alternative to trading either as a sole trader or general partnership, or, on the other hand, as an alternative to incorporation. It has even been suggested that the LLP 'is quite likely to take over as the main legal structure for small businesses' (Lowe 2000; Birds 2000; Ward 2001).

This reaction comes as no surprise. There has been a lengthy debate about the need for a simplified legal form for owner-managed small businesses in the United Kingdom (Department of Trade 1981; Chesterman 1982; Freedman 1994, 1999). Every proposal and consultation on the topic has resulted in a response showing no demand for a new legal form.[4] Nevertheless, intuitively, a combination of internal flexibility and limited liability seems ideal for small firms and each generation returns to examine it. There has been pressure to relax the provisions surrounding the limited company since 1855, when limited liability was first permitted through incorporation. Small businesses used the limited company in large numbers, though it was not designed for them. They then complained that it was not user-friendly and demanded simplification, resulting in the gradual introduction of exemptions and relaxations (Ireland 1983; Freedman 1994: 568). This pressure on the limited company form continues. This story seems likely to repeat itself with the LLP. Like the limited company, it does not seem to have been designed for small firms, yet it is now assumed that small firms will use it. This may well lead to pressure for modifications.

Why should such pressure to create a new legal form for small firms emerge? In brief, the problems claimed for the ordinary limited liability company appear to be primarily that complexity is introduced in the form of a layer of meetings and controls designed for separate ownership and control. Such meetings need

---

[3] In the United States, this varies from state to state, e.g. Iowa permits all general partnerships to register as LLPs and New York limits LLPs to professional partnerships. Commerce Clearing House (1997: § 804).

[4] For the most recent conclusion to this effect, see Company Law Review Steering Group (CLRSG) (2001).

to be provided for, within a corporate format, for the protection of shareholders who are not engaged in management. Arguably, they can be dispensed with where firms are owner-managed. Essentially, the LLP is thought to achieve this removal of the extra layer of formalities, since it does not set out detailed rules for internal governance.

One problem with this apparent advantage is that small firms that start out being owner-managed often cease to be so. The small firm is dynamic. Even if it does not grow, and many do not, it is highly likely to change as a result of death, marriage, divorce, and other family changes. A legal form that assumes that all owners are also engaged in management may be inflexible and may actually set up a barrier to growth. In theory, those concerned can change the legal arrangements if they become unsuitable, but this may be less than easy if the need to make the change arises at a crisis point, when it is not easy to get agreement from all. There may be a dispute, or a member of the family may be incapable due to sickness or age. These are familiar scenarios for those who read business law cases involving small firms. Change also incurs costs: again, a problem at a crisis point. It may be preferable for the legal vehicle adopted by the small firm to have provisions that allow the formalities to be invoked by a minority owner or to arise automatically when they are needed, rather than requiring major change at this stage.

In practice, the UK private company is already flexible and allows considerable scope for alteration of constitutional arrangements and waiver of meetings where this is agreed by the shareholders (Farrar and Hannigan 1988: 308–28). The Company Law Review Steering Group (CLRSG), after lengthy consultation, has recommended that decision-making procedures be simplified (CLRSG 2001). Currently, private companies have to elect into a regime in which meetings are not required and other relaxations apply (the elective regime) and written resolutions have to be unanimous. Under the proposals, the elective regime would become the default position, which would apply to all new companies upon formation unless they opted out of it. This is based on the 'think small first' principle that legislation should be drafted for the smallest companies, with add-ons for those with more complex requirements, rather than being designed for larger organizations and requiring the smaller firms to make decisions about opting out. Written resolutions would require only the same majority to be passed as resolutions passed at a meeting, and a new model constitution would be provided, written in plain language. This would not be mandatory but would be available as a standard form for those who wished to use it (ibid. ch 17, para 2.21.). There may be some argument that these changes relax the private company regime too far. Minority shareholders in a company covered by the default regime will need an ordinary resolution (51 per cent) to opt *into* the requirement for meetings. There may be some discussion to be had of the precise details of these proposals, but it is clear from the consultations of the CLRSG that there is strong support for a move in this direction, which seems likely to occur in due course.

A frequent complaint about the corporate form for small firms is that of the cost of formalities such as filing and other disclosures, and the cost of audit. Empirical research makes it clear that the cost of filing and of the statutory audit is a greater burden to small firms than are internal organizational requirements (Freedman 1994; Freedman and Godwin 1993; Hicks, Drury, and Smallcombe 1995; Manchester Business School 1991). It should be noted, however, that small companies already have various relaxations and exemptions in this area and, in response to continuing concerns, the CLRSG has proposed further relaxations as well as an increase in the thresholds applicable, so that a very high proportion of small companies will be covered by these exemptions (CLRSG 2001: paras 2.32–3). UK private companies have no minimum capital requirement.[5]

Despite these relaxations for small companies, and its general policy of ensuring that legislation meets the needs of small private companies, the CLRSG seems to have felt some continuing pressure to consider a completely new corporate structure for very small firms. Though it declined to do this, the pressure seems to have led to the statement, in the CLRSG's Final Report, that the LLP weakens the case for creating a new corporate vehicle designed for small companies, since the LLP may be 'particularly beneficial for businesses that seek limited liability while preserving the less formal internal governance and decision-taking arrangements familiar to many owner-managed businesses' (CLRSG 2001: para 2.7).

It must be recalled, however, that the CLRSG had not investigated the LLP itself, or studied its characteristics, since this was outside its terms of reference. The statement quoted may be seen, therefore, as something of a throwaway remark to distract critics of the CLRSG who had been pressing it to be more radical and consider new structures. By contrast, the Law Commission, examining partnership law and also excluded from looking at LLPs, took the view that the LLP is a legal form that most small and medium-sized businesses will not opt to use. In taking this view, they could largely ignore its introduction as irrelevant to the need to modernize and reform the general law of partnership (Law Commission 2000: para 1.15).

Whatever its origins, the CLRSG's remark is sufficiently important and prominent to suggest that the view that the LLP will assist small firms requires further investigation.[6]

10.2.3. Is the LLP Suitable for Small Firms?

In the author's view, the suggestion that the LLP legal form, as introduced in the Limited Liability Partnerships Act 2000, will prove suitable for ordinary

---

[5] See the discussion in Freedman (2000).

[6] The author was a member of a working party advising the CLRSG on matters relating to small private companies, but the role of the working party was advisory only. The author's views do not necessarily reflect the views of that working party or the CLRSG, nor are her views necessarily reflected in the Final Report.

owner-managed small trading firms is deeply flawed. The reasons for this view will be outlined here. Section 10.4 will examine the characteristics of the LLP in more detail in the light of these issues.

First, though now open to all, the LLP is not designed for small businesses. The LLP is being presented as offering flexibility and freedom as a result of its lack of rules on internal governance, but this also means that it offers no standard-form constitution. This will result in an LLP being more expensive to set up than an ordinary company, which has a standard-form constitution that is well tried and tested (set out in Table A, which can be found in a statutory instrument).[7] Under the CLRSG proposals, this standard form for limited companies is to be made more user-friendly than it is now; and, as explained above, the limited company in the United Kingdom is very flexible and there are proposals to make it more so.

Why should it be thought that providing a default framework for internal governance is a negative feature, when saving transaction costs by providing such standard forms is one of the rationales of business organizations provided by the state (Easterbrook and Fischel 1991)? The limited company model constitution provides a set of terms 'off the rack', which can save transaction costs. No doubt commercial providers will create their own standard forms for LLPs, but this is still likely to prove more expensive than using statutory standard forms, even if these later have to be modified. This was realized by those seeking to make the LLP more suitable for small firms as the LLP Bill passed through Parliament. They had initially thought that partnership law would apply to LLPs as a default, but a blanket application of partnership law was considered by the Department of Trade and Industry to be inappropriate as a result of the largely corporate characteristics of the LLP (Department of Trade and Industry 2000). The compromise reached was that default provisions were added to the LLP Regulations, reflecting some fundamental aspects of partnership law, although not imposing a general duty of good faith and subject to the general law and the terms of the LLP agreement (if any) reached by the parties.[8] Given that the general law governing LLPs is largely borrowed from company law, this partial adoption of partnership law could cause problems. We might expect some areas of confusion when the interaction of the Act, the Regulations, and LLP agreements come to be examined in litigation some years down the line. Certainly those relying upon the default provisions cannot assume that the courts will treat them in exactly the same way as an ordinary partnership, since the default provisions have to be read as subject to the general LLP legislation.

The second, and related problem with LLPs is that the method used—of adopting company law by reference with modifications in Regulations—has resulted in great complexity and a set of provisions that are very difficult to use, even for seasoned professionals. The primary legislation is short, but there are

---

[7] The Companies (Tables A to F) Regulations (1985), SI 1985/805.
[8] Limited Liability Partnerships Regulations (2001), SI 2001/1090, para 7.

sixty pages of secondary legislation.[9] These provisions will be even more difficult to use than the Companies Acts for small businesses, since the reader needs
to have open before him the Companies Acts, the LLP Act, and the Regulations,
and to cross refer continually. Consolidation of all these provisions has not been
attempted by the legislature but has been left to commercial providers (Morse
2001; Armour 2001). Not only does the reader have to juggle with the books, he
also needs a knowledge of both company and partnership law. Even with all this
information before him, there will be more unknowns and uncertainties about
the way in which the courts will interpret the legislation than in the case of a
company or partnership, given that this is an entirely new creation with features
of both companies and partnerships. There is no simplification here.

The third reason why LLPs are not more suited than incorporation to small
firms relates to accounts and the audit. The UK LLP has extensive disclosure and
filing requirements, including filing and statutory audit of accounts. This stems
from the link between limited liability and disclosure in UK doctrine (Sealy
1981). It is also the result of the pressure at an early stage (when the LLP was first
being mooted and was to be for professional firms only) for large professional
firms to be required to disclose this information. There is a contrast here with
US LLPs, which are not required to file accounts (Linsell 2000). The professional
partnerships dislike the disclosure required, especially the requirement to
disclose the remuneration of the highest-paid member. These requirements may
well be deterring some professional firms from using the LLP (ibid.). In the case
of very large firms, the disclosure requirements may be justified as the price they
are being asked to pay for limited liability.[10] Small LLPs are entitled to the same
exemptions and relaxations as are small companies. We can assume that further
relaxations to the small company audit and accounting regime will be extended
to small LLPs, so use of the LLP form would not make them worse off than those
using the corporate form, but lack of formalities cannot be presented as an
advantage for LLPs. General partnerships have none of these filing or audit
requirements.

Fourth, while it is clear in the United States that the LLP and LLC have major
tax advantages for small firms over incorporation, the UK tax position is quite
different. The double taxation of corporate profits experienced under the pure
classical system of corporate tax in the United States means that tax transparent
business forms bring serious tax savings. In the United Kingdom, corporate
distributions are not subject to such extensive double taxation as in the United
States, due to the availability of tax credits for shareholders on dividends in
many cases.[11] It follows that the tax pressures to move away from incorporation
are not so great for UK as for US small businesses. Indeed, due to the introduction of small corporation tax reliefs, such as a 10 per cent corporation
tax starting rate if relevant profits do not exceed £10,000,[12] incorporation may

9 Ibid.   10 The arguments on large firms are outside the scope of this chapter.
11 For a detailed review of UK corporation taxation, see Tiley (2000: 757–812).
12 Income and Corporation Taxes Act 1988, § 13AA(1).

be a beneficial way for small businesses to shelter profits in some circumstances.

This is a subtle area. Whether incorporation has tax advantages or not depends on the level of profits, pension issues, capital gains tax questions, and National Insurance payments (social security). The LLP is attractive to large professional partnerships because they have large numbers of highly paid individuals who must receive regular payments of salary. National Insurance contributions are much higher for employees of a company than for partners in these circumstances. There are also capital gains tax issues for large firms with frequent changes of ownership that may make a partnership tax regime beneficial (Mabey 2001). Small trading firms may well not find these features so advantageous. An owner-manager in a small firm may more easily take profits from a corporation by way of dividend, which carries a tax credit and is free of National Insurance contributions. The capital gains tax issues for a small owner-managed firm are quite different from those of a large professional partnership. Anti-avoidance provisions prevent the tax-effective use of LLPs for certain property investment and other purposes.[13] The LLP may actually be disadvantageous from a tax point of view, in some circumstances, as compared with operating as a general partner or sole trader, as losses available for relief against general income cannot exceed the capital contributed by the member.[14]

Finally, and perhaps most important, the main objective of the LLP is to bestow limited liability, at least on non-negligent members.[15] Small firms often gain little benefit from the apparent limited liability created by a limited liability legal form, since creditors will contract around this limitation by insisting on personal guarantees (Halpern, Trebilcock, and Turnbull 1980; Freedman 1994).[16] In this case, purporting to bestow limited liability could be nothing but a dangerous illusion. If firms do wish to expand and raise outside funding, so that the market rationale for limited liability is truly satisfied, incorporation is likely to be a better answer, since it clearly provides a structure for split ownership and management, as well as a structure that can be floated at some later stage.

For small firms for which limited liability is either unimportant or likely to be unobtainable, whatever legal form is used, the revision of general partnership law currently being undertaken by the Law Commission seems more important and potentially more helpful than the introduction of the LLP (Law Commission 2000). Generally, implementation of the proposals of the Law Commission on partnerships and the CLRSG on private companies would remove any arguments still remaining that the small business sector was in need of the LLP, at least the LLP as introduced in the United Kingdom.

---

[13] Finance Act 2001, Sch 25.
[14] Income and Corporation Taxes Act 1988, §§ 118ZA–118ZD (originally inserted by Limited Liability Partnerships Act 2000 and amended by Finance Act 2001).
[15] On the uncertainty surrounding the extent of the limitation on liability, see Section 10.4.3.
[16] Generally on the lack of advantage limited liability brings to small firms, see Freedman (2000).

We now turn to consider in greater detail the reasons for the introduction of the LLP and its characteristics, both of which underline the view that the UK LLP is unsuitable for small firms.

10.3. The Development of the UK LLP

The professions, particularly the audit profession, in the United Kingdom have been campaigning for a change to the rules on their liability for some time. In particular, they argue for a change to the law of joint and several liability, which they claim makes them vulnerable as the party with 'deep pockets' to full liability for losses in cases where the responsibility should be shared with others. In 1996, the Law Commission rejected the suggestion that the law on joint and several liability should be changed.[17] LLPs were seen as a kind of consolation prize for the audit firms. The Big Six, as they then were, had seen that LLPs helped them in the United States. Therefore, they pressed for LLPs in the United Kingdom, notwithstanding that the UK law on liability was probably more favourable to the audit firms than that in the United States.[18]

Two firms, Ernst & Young and Price Waterhouse, were at this time drafting a law for Jersey in the Channel Islands to introduce LLPs. They were threatening the UK government that they would go offshore if LLPs were not made available in the United Kingdom. Audit firms were, by this time, permitted to incorporate with limited liability in the United Kingdom,[19] so it is hard to avoid the conclusion that this pressure was motivated by tax considerations. Incorporation would have been costly in tax terms, for reasons referred to above, although the professional firms also argued that they did not wish to lose the partnership ethos. Whether the Jersey route would have worked for tax purposes is unclear. The Inland Revenue refused to give any assurances on this and the courts refused to give what amounted to an advance ruling on a hypothetical basis.[20] This was, however, in the run-up to the 1997 General Election and both main political parties, seeking to demonstrate that they were business-friendly and subjected to some extensive lobbying by professional bodies, promised that a UK LLP would be introduced.

As a result, an LLP Act was passed in July 2000 and came into force in April 2001. There was little opposition, although there was considerable discussion about the form of the legislation between the profession and government. A new procedure for evaluating proposed legislation was used which brought out some important and useful points,[21] although not all of these were followed through

---

[17] Common Law Team of The Law Commission (1996).

[18] This is discussed in more detail in Freedman and Finch (1997).

[19] The previous prohibition on incorporation was lifted from auditors by the Companies Act 1989, § 25.

[20] *R v. Commissioners of Inland Revenue, ex p Bishopp* [1999] STC 531; 72 TC 322.

[21] The draft legislation was subjected to pre-legislative scrutiny by the Trade and Industry Committee (1999). Oral evidence was taken mainly from the government and from the professions'

as thoroughly as might have been hoped, due to the political pressure to bring the legislation to fruition. In particular, the House of Commons Committee considering this legislation criticized the fact that consultation papers from the Department of Trade and Industry tended to give the impression that the proposal was a technical measure. The Committee felt that the consultation paper should have explained the demand for the new entity, analyzed the position in other jurisdictions, and discussed alternative means of producing the desired results. As the consultation paper did not do so, the Committee sought to fill in some of these gaps itself, because it felt there was a good case to be made (Trade and Industry Committee 1999: paras 5–6). The Committee was, however, critical of the approach that had been taken and also of the fact that the LLP proposals did not form part of the Law Commission or CLRSG's reviews. This was despite the fact that the Law Commission's original terms of reference for its partnership law review had included consideration of how the limited liability partnership structure might be made available to a wider range of businesses.[22] The Committee noted that this was not an ideal way to proceed and that the LLP regime should be designed as far as possible to be able to reflect the sort of changes to company and partnership law that emerged from the reviews (Trade and Industry Committee 1999: para 10). The Committee also considered that there was no justification for restricting eligibility to the LLP to professional partnerships (ibid. para 38).

The argument put to the House of Commons Committee by government was that the legislation was urgent due to the competition from Jersey and elsewhere. These other jurisdictions were prepared to provide LLPs. The Committee seemed convinced by this and for this reason was persuaded, for example, that the Regulations containing most of the detailed provisions could not go into the Bill but should be contained in secondary legislation. They did note, however, that they would have preferred to see the legislation all contained in one Bill (ibid. paras 81–2).

Despite the reservations of the House of Commons Committee, the legislation was dealt with by the Department of Trade and Industry and not put onto the wider business law reform agenda, which would have delayed implementation beyond what would have been acceptable to the professions. The detail remained in the Regulations, although some important changes were made to the Bill examined by the Committee, including the opening up of the LLP to all and not just the regulated professions. Nevertheless, the origins of the Act shaped it significantly, which is why many of its features and its basic disclosure regime are more suitable for large than small businesses. This is one major reason why it is mainly the Companies Acts, not the Partnership Act, that is applied in adapted form for use in regulating this new entity. Another reason may be

representative bodies. The dissenting voice was that of one academic: Professor Prem Sikka of the University of Essex. Other academic papers and written responses were also examined by the Committee.

[22] Company and Commercial Law Team of the Law Commission (1997).

that the officials in the Department of Trade and Industry were more familiar and comfortable with company law than with partnership law. They also seem to have considered that corporate personality would help to ensure limited liability overseas, but the other side of this coin is that overseas jurisdictions might not treat UK LLPs as transparent for tax purposes.

It is not at all clear that this story fits with an evolutionary analysis. The LLP was introduced as a result of concern about overseas jurisdictions but the process was not particularly well informed by an understanding of the position in those other jurisdictions and the new legal form created was different in important respects from those created elsewhere. Little benefit seems to have been derived from the existence of LLPs elsewhere for some years and the notion that jurisdictional competition has produced efficiency can be questioned in this case. This will be further examined in Section 10.4 of this chapter.

Before moving on to this examination, it is worth noting that the LLP is not necessarily a great success even for those for whom it was originally designed. The auditors continue to make representations for proportionate as opposed to joint and several liability. These have again been rejected by the CLRSG, although it is proposed to permit some exclusion of liability for audits contractually with the company and in tort with third parties subject to rules to be made by the Secretary of State.[23] The point here is that the introduction of LLPs has not reduced the glamour from auditors in particular for change in the law on liability, as it does not solve most of their problems. Since the assets of the LLP are all at stake, the firm could still be wiped out by a negligence claim. High levels of insurance are still needed. The partners' personal assets are protected to some extent, but that extent is not entirely clear.

In a survey for the magazine *Accountancy*, thirty-two of the top fifty audit firms replied to a questionnaire.[24] Six said they would be setting up as LLPs; twenty-two said they would not. Four were undecided. This is not a resounding vote of confidence in what was long awaited legislation designed to respond to a need expressed by these very firms. Some uncertainties remain about accounting treatment for LLPs and it may be that there will be more enthusiasm once these are resolved. Interestingly, though, only 20 per cent of registrations of LLPs by August 2001 had been for solicitors and accountants.[25]

Jordans, the business formation agents, report a greater than expected interest in LLPs with 600 LLPs registered by the end of August 2001, ahead of official predictions. More than three-quarters of these firms are not professionals, and Jordans claims that their professional customers are advising small and medium-sized enterprises to use the LLP. The benefits, they claim, are avoiding the Annual General Meeting and other paraphernalia associated with

---

[23] Section 310 of the Companies Act of 1985 currently prohibits any exclusion of liability. For the proposals of the CLRSG, see CLRSG (2001: paras 8.143–4).

[24] *Accountancy* (2001: 7).

[25] Businesses may now choose the new LLP status at Jordans. See their website at http://www.jordans.co.uk and follow the links to LLPs.

companies, obtaining credibility due to their corporate status, and borrowing more easily than ordinary partnerships.[26] Of course, the last of these is not an advantage over the corporate form, whilst the first of these advantages can be exaggerated, as discussed above. Further monitoring and research will be needed on the reasons why advisers are suggesting their clients should set up LLPs, and the level of customer satisfaction with this legal form.[27]

10.4. CHARACTERISTICS OF LLPS

Some characteristics of the LLP have been discussed already, but it is convenient here to gather together the main characteristics, which will help to determine the applicability of the legal form to small businesses.

10.4.1. Legal Nature

The UK LLP is a body corporate that exists as a legal person separate from its members.[28] As discussed above, this corporate personality route was adopted for various reasons including perceived concerns about international recognition of limited liability.[29] The Explanatory Notes to the Limited Liability Partnerships Act (LLPA) suggest that those drafting it saw a link between limited liability, having a separate legal personality and corporate characteristics, although, of course, these characteristics may be distinguished.[30] UK LLPS have continuing legal personality, so may hold property and continue in existence despite changes in membership. They have unlimited capacity. Partners are called members.

10.4.2. Formalities and Accounts

The UK LLP comes into existence only upon incorporation. An incorporation document containing specified information must be delivered to the Registrar of

---

[26] Ibid. The floating charge is available to LLPs and companies but not to general partnerships or sole traders.

[27] The cost of setting up a limited liability company through Jordans is £185 for a package that includes completed statutory registers and minutes of the first board meeting. The cost of a Jordans LLP is £488.75. This includes a standard-form partnership agreement prepared by a leading solicitor. Advisers clearly have some financial interest in promoting new legal forums, but presumably would be responsible enough, and certainly far-sighted enough, to do so only if the form would prove to be appropriate for the client. How well-informed advisers of small businesses are about the pros and cons of the LLP is another issue. Demand may have been stimulated by publicity and articles in professional journals.

[28] Limited Liability Partnerships Act 2000, § 1.

[29] Anecdotal evidence. For other reasons, see Section 10.3 above.

[30] Thus, Scottish general partnerships have separate legal personality but partners are individually liable in actions directed against the firm, Partnership Act 1890, § 4(2). US LLCs give limited liability without bestowing corporate characteristics.

Companies.[31] For an LLP to exist, two or more people must be associated for the carrying on of a lawful business with a view to profit. By contrast, a private company can be incorporated with only one member. This membership requirement is another drawback to the LLP as a legal form for small firms. The Companies Act was amended to conform with European Community policy so that a limited liability company could be formed and do business with one member.[32] An LLP, on the other hand, must have two members. If an LLP carries on business with a single member, that single member will become personally liable if he trades on for six months or more knowing he is the only member. This liability is a potential trap for the unwary, since it does not appear on the face of the Act but only by way of an application of an amended version of § 24 of the Companies Act 1985 by Schedule 2 of the LLP Regulations 2001. For one-person firms, the simplest approach will be to incorporate.

Designated members (there must be at least two) have certain administrative and filing duties.[33] The registrar must be notified of changes in membership and designated membership within fourteen days and of changes in addresses within twenty-eight days.[34] This requirement does not seem to be truly light touch regulation. In addition, accounts must be filed and audited to show a true and fair view under generally accepted accounting practice (GAAP) (though there are exemptions from audit for LLPs with turnover up to one million pounds).[35] Professional firms have reservations about disclosing this information, but small trading firms may be less concerned about this, especially as they have reduced disclosure requirements that permit them to keep certain information private. Nevertheless, there are quite extensive filing requirements which make the regulatory position of LLPs more onerous than that of ordinary partnerships.

Applying GAAP to LLPs is not a simple matter. GAAP applicable to companies may be inappropriate for LLPs because of the different legal rights to profits, for example. The Consultative Committee of Accountancy Bodies has issued a draft statement of recommended practice (SORP) to provide guidance on this, but its contents are controversial and the final SORP may not be agreed upon until 2002 (see now the postscript to this chapter) (CCAB 2001). Many of the concerns relate mainly to the large professional partnerships.[36] The draft does, however, require the valuation of long-term contracts to take into account a profit element in accordance with the relevant accounting standard for companies (Accounting Standards Board 1988). This could lead to a significant increase in the work in progress/stock level in the accounts of any general partnership converting to an LLP, although there is a debate about the extent to which

---

[31] Limited Liability Partnerships Act 2000, § 2.

[32] Companies (Single Member Private Limited Companies) Regulations (1992) SI 1992/1699 (implementing the Twelfth EU Company Law Directive 89/667 (1989)).

[33] Limited Liability Partnerships Act 2000, § 8.   [34] Ibid. § 9.

[35] Exemption threshold increased to £1 million on 26 May 2000. Companies Act 1985 (Audit Exemption) (Amendment) Regulations (2000) SI 2000/1430. The CLRSG has recommended a further substantial increase in this threshold.

[36] For example, problems with annuities and costing partners' time.

members' time and overhead should be included. The uncertainty over accounting for LLPs and the effect this might have on their tax treatment is a deterrent to using the LLP form, at least until the SORP is decided upon.[37]

10.4.3. External Relations

External relations are governed by § 6 of the LLPA. Contracts are with the partnership, entered into with members as agents, so that individual members will be bound only if there is also a contract with them personally. The usual rules of agency apply to determine who may bind the partnership. Generally, it will be the partnership that will be liable to third parties in tort, also. The objective of creating a limited liability partnership is to protect members who are not personally negligent or wrongdoing. It has been left to somewhat uncertain and evolving case law, however, to determine whether there is a separate cause of action against an individual member in tort.[38]

In the United States it seems clear, and is sometimes spelled out in the statute, that a partner in an LLP remains liable for his own omission, negligence, or misfeasance while being protected from liability where he was not involved in any way.[39] In the United Kingdom, it was initially assumed that this would be the case. If there was a duty of care owed by the individual wrongdoer he would be personally liable, as would the LLP, but not the other members.[40] This may be reasonably straightforward in the case of a physical tort where liability is based on a simple duty of care.

Greater problems arise in the case of negligent advice. The problem here is that an element of the duty being owed is to show that there was an assumption of personal responsibility for the negligent advice, and that the claimant relied upon that assumption of responsibility.[41] In the case of a professional partnership, in particular, the third party is actually likely to be relying not on the individual so much as on the partnership. He will be dealing with the partnership and relying on its name. The question then arises whether any individual partner ever assumed personal responsibility. It may be that the courts, in considering all the circumstances of whether there is an assumption of personal liability, will take into account the fact that an LLP exists. For this reason, it would have been helpful to have a clear statement in the legislation about whether or not the existence of the LLP was to impact upon personal liability.

---

[37] Jordans, although encouraging the use of LLPs, are concerned enough about this problem to point it out in a special note on their website at http://www.jordans.co.uk/. Follow the link to LLPs on the site, and then continue to the Thumbnail Guide to the Taxation of Limited Liability Partnerships (at the foot of the LLP homepage).

[38] Limited Liability Partnership Act 2000, Explanatory Notes, paras 15–16.

[39] The Texas legislation, for example, spells this out. See Hamilton (1995); cf. Alberta Law Reform Institute (1998: 62). Article 5 of the Limited Liability Partnerships (Jersey) Law 1997 also makes clear that a partner remains personally liable for any loss he caused.

[40] Limited Liability Partnerships Act 2000, § 6(4).

[41] *Hedley Byrne & Co. Ltd. v. Heller & Partners Ltd.* (1963) 2 All E.R. 575.

The UK legislature has chosen, however, to leave this entirely to the case law with consequent uncertainty.

The initial drafters of the LLPA thought that the individual member of an LLP would be liable for his own negligent advice. In this they seem to have been relying on some litigation going through the courts at the time they were preparing the Bill. In December 1996, the Court of Appeal had decided in *Williams v. Natural Life Foods Ltd.*[42] that a company director was personally liable for negligent advice on the basis that he had assumed personal liability. It seems to have been assumed by those drafting the Bill that this would apply to make individual negligent members of an LLP liable (though it would always have been a question of fact, so this is a somewhat surprising assumption). Paragraph 10 of the Explanatory Notes to the Bill said that a negligent member's personal assets will still be at risk. By way of example, under the general law, a professional person owes a duty of care to his client. Negligent advice given in breach of that duty by a member of an LLP will, in general, give rise to a potential liability on the part of that member as well as the LLP.[43]

The fact that individually negligent members would remain liable was seen as an important corollary to extending limited liability to non-negligent members and was repeated in the literature of the government, commentators, and the professional bodies.[44] During the passage of the legislation, however, the House of Lords overturned the Court of Appeal decision in *Williams* on the basis that in that case there was no assumption of personal liability.[45] This was a decision very much on the facts of its own case, but the policy aspect was significant. Lord Steyn stated that if it was accepted that the director was personally liable simply because he played a prominent role in negotiations, 'it would expose directors, officers and employees of companies carrying on a business as providers of service to a plethora of new tort claims'.[46]

The same reasoning could be applied to LLPs. For this reason, a clarifying amendment was proposed in the House of Lords, but this was rejected by government in favour of leaving the matter to the courts.[47] The rationale for this seems to have been that the government wanted the law of tort to develop naturally and in the same way for LLPs as for companies. This argument is understandable, but making clear the policy behind the LLP on liability of individual members would not have prevented the natural development of the law. A statement that the existence of the LLP was not intended to remove liability from a negligent or wrongdoing partner simply would have provided guidance on one factor for the courts to take into account when considering the

---

[42] [1997] 1 B.C.L.C. 131 (C.A.).

[43] House of Lords Explanatory Notes referring to the Limited Liability Partnerships Bill introduced to the House of Lords, 23 November 1999.

[44] See e.g. evidence given by the Department of Trade to the Trade and Industry Committee (1999: para 11); see also 608 Parliamentary Debate H.L. (5th set.), (2000) 1383 (comments of Lord Sharman).

[45] [1998] 2 All E.R. 577 (H.L.).   [46] Ibid. at 585. See now postscript.

[47] 608 Parliamentary Debate H.L. (*supra* n. 44).

circumstances and issues of a particular case and whether there had been an assumption of personal responsibility.

The *Williams* decision has been much debated.[48] It was distinguished by the Court of Appeal in *Merrett v. Babb*, where an employee surveyor was held liable for negligence even though he had been employed by a sole principal who had since become bankrupt.[49] The distinction was based on the fact that 'normally the director of a company is not personally liable for the actions of the company'—a policy distinction. Where LLPs lie has been left to the courts and to further litigation. This seems a strange decision, given that LLPs were designed to clarify partners' liability. Clearly partners will not be worse off in an LLP than in a general partnership, but incorporation might offer more complete protection. The facts of *Williams* themselves arose in relation to a small business and any advice to a small business choosing between incorporation and an LLP would need to take this personal liability uncertainty factor into account.

In addition to this possible liability for personal negligence or wrongdoing, all members may be required to contribute to the assets of an LLP in certain circumstances. That is, they must contribute on a winding-up if they withdrew property from the LLP over the two years preceding winding up at a time when they knew or had reasonable grounds for believing that the LLP was or would thereby become unable to pay its debts.[50] This clawback provision was held out as an important plank of protection, but has been watered down after pressure from the professions to become subjective. It is now in much the same terms as the wrongful trading test for company directors in § 214 of the Insolvency Act 1986. The member has to have known or should have concluded that the LLP had no reasonable prospect of avoiding insolvent liquidation. Whether he knew or should have known will be judged on the basis of his actual skill and knowledge as well as the knowledge and skill that could be expected from someone carrying on his function in relation to the LLP. This is partially objective, partially subjective, and replaces the more objective test in the original draft. The professions now seem much happier than they were with this clawback, which really only puts them in the same position as company directors are now. It does seem rational that the protection required for creditors should be no greater in the case of LLPs than that for companies, but there are many question marks over whether § 214 is stringent enough for companies: 'Sadly the experience with § 214 is that its bark has proved more powerful than its bite' (Milman 2000: 331).

In addition, there are some variations in the wording as between the provisions for LLPs and those for companies. Given this, and that courts may regard members of LLPs and company directors differently, there is some uncertainty about the operation of this clawback.[51]

---

[48] For a criticism of *Williams*, arguing that the case would have been decided differently in the United States, and Israel, see Cohen (2001). The House of Lords decision is supported in Grantham and Rickett (1999) and criticized by J. Armour (1999).

[49] [2001] EWCA Civ 214; [2001] 3 W.L.R. 1.   [50] Insolvency Act 1986, § 214A.

[51] For a more detailed discussion of this point, see Finch and Freedman (2002).

One reason for setting up an LLP rather than a general partnership is that floating charges are available to the former and not the latter. This may assist with borrowing, although in the case of very small businesses, lenders are apt to insist on personal guarantees in any event (Freedman 1994).[52] The LLP might be helpful for certain types of business, which could support a floating charge, but these are likely to be the minority in the case of very small firms.

10.4.4. Internal Relations

As noted above, internal relations are left to the members and no written constitution is required. If there is one, it need not be published.[53] This scheme is entirely suitable for the large professional firms for whom this legislation was first drafted. As the LLP was opened up to all, however, it was decided to introduce, in the regulations, default provisions, based on partnership law, for any firm not providing its own agreement.[54]

These default provisions include equal sharing of capital and profits and that every member may take part in management. Any aspect of partnership law not expressly referred to in these default provisions is not applicable, since the LLP is closer to a company than a partnership in certain important respects, such as property ownership, so that some partnership law would be inappropriate. There is no general duty of good faith, but there are specific duties in the regulations (subject to contrary agreement) to account for competing activities and use of partnership property. This 'half-way house' is the result of late pressure on the government. It is intended to give complete flexibility but then plug the gaps in cases where there is no agreement. The result is a very limited standard form that may not satisfy anyone. Just as there is pressure for a standard-form constitution for small companies, a pressure which the CLRSG has responded to, so we are likely to see pressure for a more comprehensive standard form for LLPs. Commercial providers are filling the gap, but this creates extra cost for business owners at start-up. More important, there must be doubts as to the way in which the courts will apply the default provisions. Will they follow partnership law or will they consider that they are starting with a blank sheet, given that the LLP is a completely different legal form? The use of provisions borrowed from partnership law does not guarantee the certainty of partnership law treatment in these circumstances.

Similarly, the application of company law provisions may not be straightforward. When it comes to disputes between members, § 459 of the Companies Act 1985 is applied. This permits a member to apply to the court on grounds of unfair prejudice and usually results in an order that that member (if unfair prejudice is proved) should be bought out by the other members. Inclusion of

---

[52] The empirical evidence suggests that the unavailability of floating charges is not a major concern for most partnerships.
[53] Limited Liability Partnerships Act 2000, § 5.
[54] Limited Liability Partnerships Regulations (2001) SI 2001/1090, Part VI.

this provision was contentious[55] and the section has been amended in relation to LLPs to permit the members of an LLP to exclude the right to make such an application for such period as shall be agreed by unanimous agreement in writing.[56] How the courts will apply § 459 to LLPs remains to be seen. It is curious that the ideas behind § 459 can be traced back to partnership law: here they are reapplied via a corporate route.

The internal relations of an LLP are therefore left very flexible but concerns about absence of provision have resulted in an uneasy mix of partnership and company law being put in place to plug any gaps. Just how this will develop will be a matter for the courts, but it may be hard to give definite advice to LLP users for some years.

10.4.5. Taxation

Without special tax provisions, the LLP would be taxed as a company. We have seen above, however, that a major advantage of the LLP for the large professional firms was to be taxed as partnerships. The major tax considerations relating to legal form have been outlined above.

The LLPA and the Finance Act 2001 provide for the LLP to be taxed as a partnership. This is not, however, done in an entirely straightforward way. Section 118ZA of the Income and Corporation Taxes Act 1988 (inserted by the subsequent legislation) provides that where a limited liability partnership carries on a trade, profession, or other business with a view to profit, then it is treated for tax purposes as a partnership. So, for example, company taxation will apply to clubs and societies using the LLP form. There are anti-avoidance provisions relating to the use of LLPs for investment activities. It is not clear how the fact that LLPs are essentially corporate will affect their tax treatment overseas, and this is also causing a level of uncertainty, although small businesses are unlikely to encounter this difficulty.[57]

The government is concerned about avoidance and adamant that LLPs should not provide opportunities for tax avoidance over the current entities used by business. It is perhaps rather naive to suppose that a new legal form designed to provide for a tax treatment not dictated by its characteristics would not be used to create tax advantages. For some small firms with special needs there may be tax advantages in having an LLP, especially capital gains tax advantages—and no doubt advisers are seeking these out, although there are

---

[55] The section is much criticized even in its company law context as it can result in complex and expensive litigation. The Law Commission has made proposals for reform of this section, which have now been tied in with the work of the CLRSG. Law Commission (1997).

[56] Limited Liability Partnerships Act Regulations (2001) SI 2001/1090, Sch 2.

[57] This difficult issue of entity classification is outside the scope of this chapter, which focuses on small businesses. The issue will be dependent on double taxation treaties to some extent. See Lang (2000). The issue was raised in the seventh sitting of the House of Commons (Standing Committee A) debates on the Finance Bill of 2001 (8 May 2001), at http://www.publications.parliament.uk/pa/cm200001/cmstand/a/st010508/pm/10508s01.htm.

many traps for the unwary, not least because tax treatment reverts to corporate tax treatment if the partnership ceases to carry on a trade or business with a view to profit. The considerations are complex and various, but tax transparency will not be as important to small firms in the United Kingdom as they are to those in the United States as a result of the different approach to corporate taxation in the United Kingdom. Rather than providing a new legal form with special tax treatment, the ideal would be for government to aim for similar tax treatment for all businesses so that choice of legal form would not be distorted by tax considerations. The differences between legal forms makes this difficult, if not impossible, to achieve (Freedman and Ward 2000).

10.5. CONCLUSION: EVOLUTION, DESIGN, OR MUDDLE?

The UK LLP was created as a result of political pressure arising in part from competition from overseas jurisdictions prepared to provide LLPs. The legal form created in the United Kingdom, however, is not the result of an evolutionary process directly related to those overseas legal forms. It is an artificial creation, a fusion of partnership and company law, created in this way as a direct result of its origins, the expertise made available for its creation, and the time limits due to political promises, which meant that it could not be considered as part of the very extensive programme of business organizations reform currently under way in the United Kingdom. The result is a legal form that combines corporate and partnership attributes. This may eventually create an interesting fusion but much uncertainty seems to lie in the way before the courts have delineated their approach to LLPs.

The LLP came about because of the needs of large professional firms. It remains to be seen whether it has met their needs. The availability of this legal form for all firms is welcome, in so far as there is no justification for confining it to professionals, but it occurred more by accident than design, as the result of practical considerations and arguments about parity. It was not designed to meet a perceived need. The case for the LLP as an ideal package for small trading businesses is not made out. Its rules governing external relations offer no simplification and little reduction of red tape as compared with companies. The extent to which limited liability is available for the wrongdoing or negligent member is unclear. There is certainly a greater regulatory burden than for general partners and sole traders. Internal relations are very flexible, as for general partnerships, but considerable freedom can also be achieved by UK private companies even now, and the proposals for the CLRSG would increase this freedom from regulation. The corollary of this freedom is the absence of a reasonably comprehensive standard-form constitution, meaning that LLPs will be well advised to have agreements either tailored for them, or standard forms purchased from commercial advisers. Many small firms do not seek limited liability and will find it difficult to obtain anyway, since creditors will require

personal guarantees and security. For these firms, the general partnership—
especially with some of the improvements proposed by the Law Commission—
already offers a stable vehicle for businesses.[58] The tax advantages of an LLP
over incorporation are not likely to be dramatic or straightforward for ordinary
small businesses and there may be tax disadvantages.

New legal forms create costs: the costs of transition to a new form, costs of
learning and taking advice about new forms, and the costs of litigation. More
legal forms mean more choices, but is that necessarily a good thing? All most
small businesses want to do is get on with their business. Intuitively, the LLP
may sound better tailored to the needs of a small firm than either the limited
company or the general partnership, but intuition is not necessarily reliable.
Those now arguing that LLPs are suitable for small businesses may bring pressure to bear for modifications and improvements of the LLP so that they become
the vehicle of choice for small firms in the future, but they are not the obvious
choice for most small firms at present.

POSTSCRIPT

Since this chapter was first written there have been various developments. In the
author's view, none of these has changed the fundamental argument that the
LLP is unsuited for small businesses as it stands.

Some of the uncertainty surrounding the LLP is settling down. For example,
on the accounting front the final agreed statement of recommended practice or
SORP was issued in May 2002 (King 2002). This attempts to meet a number of
the concerns previously expressed. It retains, however, a distinction between
members' profits (not deductible from profits and not included as costs in valuing work in progress) and salaries, which are treated as deductible; a distinction
criticized by the Institute of Chartered Accountants. This is a perfectly rational
distinction in the context of the proper analysis of a partnership but sits uneasily
with the application of accounting standards designed for companies, where
director's remuneration is all treated as deductible (though payments to shareholders are not). On some points answers could not be reached without seeking
Counsels' opinion. Preparers and auditors of accounts will be able to follow
most of the rules with which they are familiar in working with companies but
will also have to learn to deal with the modifications designed to deal with the
unique accounting conundrums raised by this special structure.[59]

The collapse of Enron and the subsequent impact on the audit firm Arthur
Andersen has been seen by some as strengthening the need for a limited liability

[58] Deborah DeMott (Chapter 9, this volume) argues that partnership law is already more stable
in the United Kingdom than in the United States and that this should make the incentive to create
alternative organizational choices weaker.

[59] The Consultative Committee of Accountancy Bodies Statement of Recommended Practice
'Accounting by Limited Liability Partnerships' (2002).

vehicle to protect non-negligent partners. Clearly the existence of an LLP cannot save a firm in serious difficulty—Arthur Andersen was an LLP—but it may assist those partners not immediately concerned with an issue. This is, however, of more relevance to professional firms than small trading firms who can in any event achieve the same, or maybe a better, measure of limited liability by incorporating if that is their main objective. It continues to be a question of fact whether an individual member of an LLP in the United Kingdom is liable for his own tortious act, since this has not been spelt out by the legislation. Where the act in question is a negligent misstatement, the key factor is whether the member actually assumed personal liability or whether the liability was intended to be confined to the partnership. It will be remembered that in the *Williams* case the fact that another legal person was in existence (there a company) was not seen as decisive but was nevertheless a relevant part of the fact situation. This left it unclear what the impact of the involvement of an LLP would be. In a subsequent case, Lord Hoffmann[60] has suggested that there is no special rule for the case where a company is involved (and by implication an LLP), but this was in a case involving fraud. It is submitted that where one of the elements of the tort concerned is assumption of personal liability as in negligent misstatement, the existence of a legal entity expressly designed to limit personal responsibility is a fact of some relevance, but how much relevance, it seems, depends on the particular facts of the case. Whether the existence of a limited company and an LLP both carry the same weight remains to be elaborated in the future. It remains possible that an LLP provides less protection for the individual business owner than would incorporation as a limited liability company.

It is still too soon to comment authoritatively on the take-up of the LLP form. By March 2002 there were still only two thousand LLPs registered in Great Britain in total,[61] which must be seen in the context of a monthly rate of limited liability company incorporations of around five to six thousand.[62] Current advice to small firms setting up is even less likely to be to use the LLP than when this chapter was first written, since small companies can obtain the benefit of a nil tax rate in some circumstances following the Finance Act 2002; a privilege not available to unincorporated firms. LLPs are being used for tax purposes for joint ventures and other arrangements, and do save large partnerships significant sums in National Insurance contributions, but a straightforward small business will usually obtain better tax breaks at present by using a limited liability company. It appears that the UK Treasury's attempts to encourage entrepreneurs through the tax system are not focusing on the LLP as a major vehicle for small businesses.

We continue to await legislation following the recommendations of the Company Law Review Steering Group, but it is expected that simplified

---

[60] *Standard Chartered Bank v. Pakistan National Shipping Corp. (No 2)*, [2002] UKHL 43; [2002] 2 All E.R. (Comm) 931.

[61] Companies in 2001–2002 (2002: table E4).

[62] Companies House Monthly Statistical Analysis (www.companieshouse.gov.uk).

provisions for small companies, including an improved standard-form constitution, will be produced by government over the next few years, making the limited company even less burdensome than it is now for use by small businesses
and further reducing any constitutional advantages the LLP might give.[63]

In sum, then, though the accounting position is now more settled for LLPs
than previously, the tax position currently frequently favours the use of a company for many small businesses and, in the end, this will often be what drives
the choice of a start-up vehicle for a business owner. It will be interesting to
watch the statistics over the next few years but, unless there are major changes
to the tax position, it seems unlikely that the LLP offers sufficient advantages to
become a widely used vehicle for small businesses.

REFERENCES

Accountancy (2001), 'Big Firms Say "Yes" to LLP Status', 30 April.
Accounting Standards Board (1988), Statement of Standard Accounting Practice No. 9,
    London.
Alberta Law Reform Institute (1998), 'Limited Liability Partnerships and other Hybrid
    Business Entities' (Issues Paper No. 4).
Armour, D. (2001), *Tolley's Limited Liability Partnerships: The New Legislation*,
    Croydon: Tolley.
Armour, J. (1999), 'Corporate Personality and Assumption of Responsibility', *Lloyd's
    Maritime and Commercial Law Quarterly* 1999: 246.
Birds, J. (2000), 'A New Form of Business Association for the Twenty-First Century',
    Company Lawyer 21: 39.
Bratton, W. W., and McCahery, J. A. (1997), 'An Inquiry into the Efficiency of the
    Limited Liability Company: Of Theory of the Firm and Regulatory Competition',
    Washington and Lee Law Review 54: 629.
CCAB, see Consultative Committee of Accountancy Bodies.
Chesterman, M. (1982), *Small Businesses*, London: Sweet & Maxwell.
CLRSG, see Company Law Review Steering Group.
Cohen, Z. (2001), 'Directors' Negligence Liability to Creditor: A Comparative and
    Critical View', *Journal of Corporation Law* 26: 351.
Commerce Clearing House (1997), 'Guide to Limited Liability Companies' 4th edn,
    Chicago: CCH.
Common Law Team of the Law Commission (1996), 'Feasibility Investigation of Joint
    and Several Liability', London: HMSO.
Company and Commercial Law Team of the Law Commission (1997), 'Partnership Law'
    (Initial Consultation Document), London: The Law Commission.
Company Law Review (1994), 'The Law Applicable to Private Companies',
    DTI/URN/94/529, London: DTI.
Company Law Review Steering Group (CLRSG) (2001), 'Modern Company Law for a
    Competitive Economy: Final Report' (also available at http://www.dti.gov.uk/cld/
    final_report/. Last accessed on 28 November 2002).

---

[63] For a discussion of these recommendations and the government's approach to implementation, see Freedman (2003).

Consultative Committee of Accountancy Bodies (CCAB) (2001), 'Accounting by Limited Liability Partnerships', *Accountancy* Sept.: 144.

—— (CCAB) (2002), Statement of Recommended Practice 'Accounting by Limited Liability Partnerships'.

Department of Trade (1981), 'A New Form of Incorporation for Small Firms', Cmnd 1871.

Department of Trade and Industry (1997), 'Limited Liability Partnership' (Consultation Paper), London: DTI.

—— (2000), 'Limited Liability Partnerships Regulatory Default Provisions Governing Relationship between Members' (Consultation Paper, available at http://www.dti.gov.uk/cld/llpbill/consdoc.htm. Last accessed 13 March 2003), London: DTI.

Easterbrook, F. E., and Fischel, D. R. (1991), *The Economic Structure of Corporate Law*, Cambridge, Mass.: Harvard University Press.

Farrar, J. H., and Hannigan, B. M. (1988), *Farrar's Company Law* (4th edn), London: Butterworths.

Finch, V., and Freedman, J. (2002), 'The Limited Liability Partnership: Pick and Mix or Mix Up?', *Journal of Business Law* 2002: 475.

Freedman, J. (1994), 'Small Business and the Corporate Form: Burden or Privilege?', *Modern Law Review* 57: 555.

—— (1999), 'The Quest for an Ideal Form for Small Businesses: A Misconceived Enterprise?', in B. A. K. Rider and M. Andenas (eds.), *Developments in European Company Law*, The Hague: Kluwer Law International.

—— (2000), 'Limited Liability: Large Company Theory and Small Firms', *Modern Law Review* 63: 317.

—— (2003), ' "One Size Fits All"—Small Business and Competitive Legal Forms', *Journal of Corporate Law Studies* 3: 123.

—— and Finch, V. (1997), 'Limited Liability Partnerships: Have Accountants Sewn Up the "Deep Pockets" Debate?', *Journal of Business Law* 1997: 387.

—— and Godwin, M. (1993), 'The Statutory Audit and the Micro Company: An Empirical Investigation', *Journal of Business Law* 1993: 105.

—— and Ward, J. (2000), 'Taxation of Small and Medium-Sized Enterprises', *European Taxation* 40: 158.

Grantham, R., and Rickett, C. (1999), 'Directors' "Tortious" Liability: Contract, Tort or Company Law?', *Modern Law Review* 62: 133.

Halpern, P., Trebilcock, M., and Turnbull, S. (1980), 'An Economic Analysis of Limited Liability in Corporation Law', *University of Toronto Law Journal* 30: 117.

Hamilton, R. W. (1995), 'Registered Limited Liability Partnerships: Present at the Birth (Nearly)', *University of Colorado Law Review* 66: 1065.

Hicks, A., Drury, R., and Smallcombe, J. (1995), *Alternative Company Structures for the Small Business*, London: Certified Accountants Educational Trust.

Ireland, P. (1983), 'The Triumph of the Company Legal Form', in J. Adams (ed.), *Essays for Clive Schmitthoff*, Abingdon: Professional Books.

King, H. (2002), 'SORP Points', *Accountancy* July: 102.

Lang, M. (2000), 'The Application of the OECD Model Convention to Partnerships: A Critical Analysis of the Report Prepared by the OECD Committee on Fiscal Affairs', The Hague: Kluwer Law International.

Law Commission (1997), Report No. 246 Shareholder Remedies, London: Stationery Office.

Law Commission (2000) (Law Commission for England and Wales and the Scottish Law Commission), 'Partnership Law: A Joint Consultation Paper' (Law Commission Consultation Paper No. 159 and Scottish Law Commission Discussion Paper No. 111).

Levmore, S. (1992), 'Partnership, Limited Liability Companies and Taxes: A Comment on the Survival of Organizational Forms', *Washington University Law Quarterly* 70: 489.

Linsell, R. (2000), 'Limited Liability Partnerships: Yes or No?', *Solicitors Journal* 144: 994.

Lowe, J. (2000), 'Limited Liability Partnerships Act 2000', *Company Law Club Newsletter*, 15 Sept.

Mabey, S. (2001), 'Tax and Transparency', *Accountancy* 122.

Macey, J. R. (1995), 'The Limited Liability Company: Lessons for Corporate Law', *Washington University Law Quarterly* 73: 433.

Manchester Business School (1991), 'Your Business Legal Structure', Manchester: The Forum of Private Business.

Milman, D. (2000), 'Limited Liability Partnerships: The Waiting Goes On', *International Company and Commercial Law Review* 2000: 329.

Morse, G. (ed.) (2001), *Palmer's Limited Liability Partnership Law*, London: Sweet & Maxwell.

Romano, R. (1985), 'Law as a Product: Some Pieces of the Incorporation Puzzle', *Journal of Law, Economics and Organization* 1: 225.

Sealy, L. (1981), 'The "Disclosure Philosophy"', *Company Lawyer* 2: 51.

Tiley, J. (2000), *Revenue Law* (4th edn), Oxford: Hart.

Trade and Industry Committee (1999), Fourth Report, H.C. 59, paras 30–9 (10 February 1999).

TSO (2002), 'Companies in 2001–2002', London: TSO.

Ward, G. (2001), 'New Accounting Rules for Limited Liability Partnerships' (Press Release, Institute of Chartered Accountants, available at https://www.icaew.co.uk/pressoffice/index.cfm? AUB=TB2I_25994. Last accessed 28 November 2002).

Winter, R. K. (1977), 'State Law, Shareholder Protection, and the Theory of the Corporation', *Journal of Legal Studies* 6: 251.

—— (1989), 'The "Race to the Top" Revisited', *Columbia Law Review* 89: 1526.

11

Limited Liability Partnerships and Partnership Law Reform in the United Kingdom

GEOFFREY MORSE

11.1. THE TWENTIETH CENTURY: INCREMENTAL CHANGE

For almost a century the United Kingdom has pursued a policy of legislative inactivity in the area of partnership law. The 1890 Act, itself substantially a codifying Act (Banks 2002: 4; Morse 2001: 7–10),[1] has only been amended in two minor respects since that date.[2] This policy of masterful inactivity has also been applied to the creation, or rather lack of creation, of any new business forms. The early years of the twentieth century were different. In 1907, some eighty years after it was first considered,[3] the Limited Partnerships Act introduced the limited partnership form with its distinction between general and limited partners;[4] the latter having limited liability but only at the expense of the loss of any management functions and so confining the form to a niche market today of venture capital and property investment vehicles and for agricultural tenancies in Scotland.[5] Similarly, the first decade of the century saw the decisive introduction of the private company in the Companies Act of 1907.[6] The private company has developed incrementally since then,[7] culminating in the single

---

[1] The effects of the Act as a partial codification can also be seen in § 46. See also *Geisel v. Geisel*, (1990) 72 D.L.R. (4th) 245.

[2] In 1959 § 35(a) as to dissolution of a partnership by the court on mental health grounds was repealed and replaced by the Mental Health Act 1959. See now §§ 95 and 96 of the Mental Health Act 1983. Section 22, applying the equitable doctrine of conversion to a partner's share of partnership property, was repealed by § 3(1) of the Trusts of Land and Appointment of Trustees Act 1996. Both these amendments therefore reflect changes in other areas of the law rather than partnership law per se.

[3] Companies, 1843, Parl. Papers 1844 Vol VII: commissioned report in 1837 by Mr Bellenden Kerr Q.C.

[4] See generally Banks (2002: Part Six); Morse (2001: 64–8).

[5] Law Commission Consultation 2001: 1–4.

[6] The basic definition was consolidated by the Companies (Consolidation) Act 1908. Initially private companies (which had to have between two and fifty members) were allowed to commence business immediately after registration and had certain exemptions from publicity. On the history of the private company, see e.g. Davies (1997: 12–13).

[7] The 1948 Act sub-classification into exempt and non-exempt private companies was repealed in 1967, which also removed most of the advantages of a private company. By way of contrast, more recent Companies Acts have sought to make the private company less restricted, see Davies (1997: 91–7).

member company introduced in 1992,[8] but which is in essence still the same concept as it was then—a public company freed from some of the controls applicable to such companies.

For the remainder of the twentieth century both these areas, of partnership law and the creation of new business forms, remained substantially free from parliamentary activity.[9] In essence therefore, during the whole of that period, the United Kingdom offered businesses two generic forms—the limited liability company, with its legal personality and limited liability, but subject to compliance costs including various formalities and controls, not least the disclosure of information; and the partnership, which has neither limited liability nor legal personality (except to some extent in Scotland) but requires no disclosure and has no formalities. Indeed it is a feature of UK partnership law that a partnership can exist without any of the partners being aware of the fact.[10] Although there are private and public companies they differ only in the application of the controls imposed, and sometimes that variation is predicated on economic criteria rather than form.[11] These two generic forms, the company and the partnership, are both available to and used by virtually the whole spectrum of economic and constituent enterprises. Partnerships range from the very large accounting and legal firms to the very small owner-managed business. Companies range from the one-man business, through the family business and the expanding business with external venture capital, to the substantial listed enterprise and the multinational giants.

In terms of the company the success of the single generic form as a vehicle for such a wide range of enterprises has been in some part due to the ability of the legislature to modify the control and compliance elements, albeit only undertaken in more recent times as part of the process of implementing EC directives, which gave the DTI access to valuable parliamentary time.[12] The result has been

[8] Introduced by the Companies (Single Member Companies) Regulations 1992, SI 1992 No 1699, implementing Dir. 89/667 EC (OJ L395).

[9] The exceptions to this being first the European Economic Interest Groupings (EEIG) introduced by the EEIG Regulations 1989 No 638 as implementing EC Council Reg. 2137/85 (see *Palmer's Company Law*, 23rd edn., para 16.201). There were 157 of these registered in the United Kingdom in 2000/1. The second is the Open-ended Investment Company introduced by Regulations in 1996 (SI 1996 No 2827) and now governed by their successor Regulations (SI 2001 No 1228). See *Palmer's Company Law*, part 5A. Other business forms have of course been created for specialized businesses, see *Palmer's Company Law*, paras 1.226 et seq.

[10] The factual nexus of carrying on a business in common with a view of profit is all that is required. See generally Morse (2001: 48–58). One of the possibilities canvassed by the Law Commissions of England and Wales and of Scotland in their 2000 Joint Consultative Paper on Partnership Law (Law Com. 159, London: HMSO) is for a registered partnership that would clearly require some formalities on formation, but that would still only be one form of partnership.

[11] These are concerned with the presentation and publication of accounts and involve a classification of companies into 'small', 'medium', and 'large' based on turnover, balance sheet total, and number of employees (CA 1985, § 247). See Davies (1997: 527–33).

[12] Thus, the 1980 Act implemented the second EC company law directive, Dir. 77/91 [1977] OJ L26/1; the 1981 Act, the fourth, Dir. 78/660 [1978] OJ L222/11; and the 1989 Act, the seventh and eighth, Dirs. 83/349 and 84/253 [1983] OJ L193/1 and [1984] OJ L126/20. Each of these Acts soon outgrew their original impetus. The recent slowdown in EC company law directives (and implementation by means of delegated legislation) is at least partly responsible for the fact that there has been no really significant companies legislation since 1989.

at least some response to the needs of small(er) businesses (e.g. the ability to elect out of certain formalities such as the need for an AGM[13]); to the need to maintain investor confidence in the larger ones (e.g. the revised rules on loans to directors in 1980[14]) and, very occasionally, to implement the complete abolition of outdated restrictions. Whilst recent events suggest that the second may be of some pressing concern it is not the subject of this chapter. Nor is the third, of which the abolition of the *ultra vires* rule is a simple example.[15] Over the years there have been abortive calls for the introduction of a separate small corporate form. In 1981 the DTI published a consultative document on the subject by Professor Gower[16] and in 1994 the Law Commission also considered the matter,[17] but neither led to the creation of a new form—albeit the 1981 report was influential in South Africa.[18] The recent Company Law Review Committee, instituted by the DTI and reporting to it in June 2001 (Modern Company Law for a Competitive Economy—Final Report[19]) also suggested the retention of the existing private company form rather than the creation of a new corporate vehicle, but with yet further modifications from the public company regime.[20] This recommendation has been accepted by the government in its 2002 White Paper, Modernising Company Law,[21] in the following terms:

I.6 The Government agrees with the review that a more appropriate way forward is to tailor the core of company law to fit the smallest companies, which are mostly private companies. Additional safeguards can be added as necessary, for example for public companies which offer their shares to the public. In general therefore the Bill[22] will, like the present Act, distinguish between public and private companies. But it will put private companies first.

Apart from the continuation of the rough and not always appropriate approximation between private and small companies inherent in this

---

[13] See CA 1985, § 379A, added by the 1989 Act.   [14] See now CA 1985, §§ 330–42.

[15] It is clear that the recast (in 1989) § 35 of the 1985 Act is intended to achieve this. There have been arguments to the effect that its wording is defective, but the impact of EC law on this implementation of part of the first directive would preclude any such argument, see Morse (1999: 54). The government has recently indicated that it proposes to abolish any last remnants of the *ultra vires* rule by giving companies unlimited capacity, see the White Paper: Modernising Company Law, Cm 5553, July 2002, para 2(2) and draft clause 1(5).

[16] A New Form of Incorporation for Small Firms, 1981, Cmnd 8171.

[17] Company Law Review, November 1994: The Law Applicable to Private Companies.

[18] By the South African Close Corporations Act 1984. See Henning, Cilliers, Benade, and Du Plessis: 'Close Corporations', in *The Law of South Africa*, First Reissue, Vol 4 Part 3 (1996), Butterworths SA.

[19] URN 01/942 and 943, DTI 2001. Available on http://www/dti.gov.uk.

[20] Ibid. at para 2.7. This was so even though the Group consistently adopted a policy of 'Think small first' and recommended legislation on the basis of that policy so that: (i) the law should be clear and accessible; (ii) accuracy and certainty should not be sacrificed unduly in an attempt to make the law merely superficially more accessible; and (iii) the legislation should be structured in such a way that the provisions that apply to small companies are easily identifiable (para. 2.34).

[21] Cm 5553, July 2002, HMSO.

[22] The White Paper in volume II contains a number of draft clauses for a future Companies Bill, although these are merely the first instalment of that Bill.

statement,[23] there is an apparent change of emphasis in that the core is to be designed for private companies with additions for public companies rather than it being for public companies with derogations for private companies. An examination of the draft clauses, however, suggests that just as before some will apply to all companies,[24] some only to private companies,[25] and some only to public ones.[26] The 'spin' might therefore prove to be more impressive than the reality.

But, by far the major factor in the success of the single corporate form is the ability of corporate lawyers to adapt the form to suit the needs of their clients. Two examples, one from each end of the spectrum, may be used to illustrate this. In terms of small companies the use of shareholder agreements to regulate the relationship between the members allows great flexibility, provided care is taken not to actually fetter the company's exercise of its statutory powers.[27] The courts have been willing to back these agreements even where they are intended to avoid the effects of a statutory provision (e.g. to prevent alteration of the company's constitution[28] or to entrench a member's right to veto any resolution by simply not turning up to the relevant meeting[29]). In terms of the largest multinational companies, company draftsmen have been able to develop forms to allow their growth, which raises the question as to whether the new (and much belated) European Company will be irrelevant except as political window dressing.[30]

The success of the partnership form as lending itself to all sizes of enterprise is of course its inherent flexibility. Being based on the concept of an agreement (express or implied) with only default terms imposed by the Act in the main, it can be used to effect group partnerships, sub-partnerships, and a myriad of other structures (Banks 2002: paras 5.79–81, 11.21–131); Morse 2001: 31–8). The larger firms, for example, are quite familiar with the terms: managing partner, equity partner, and salaried partner (Morse 2001: 70–5). Partnerships,

---

[23] See e.g. White Paper (*supra* n. 21), draft clauses 164–8, which purport to introduce a new right to a scrutiny report on the conduct of a poll. The question is posed in the White Paper as to whether this right should apply to private companies on the basis that in most cases they will be small, with few members who will each know how the others voted. It follows that the right to demand such a report in such companies may merely give rise to a mischief.

[24] Albeit sometimes applied with variations as between the two forms, see e.g. draft clause 149(4).

[25] See e.g. draft clauses 170–7.   [26] See e.g. draft clauses 13–16.

[27] *Greenwell v. Porter* [1902] 1 Ch. 530; *Puddephatt v. Leith* [1916] 1 Ch. 200; *Russell v. Northern Bank Development Corp. Ltd* [1992] 1 W.L.R. 588; [1992] B.C.L.C. 1016 (H.L.). See Gower (1997: 727–32).

[28] The *Russell* case (*supra* n. 27).

[29] *Harman v. BML Group Ltd* [1994] 1 W.L.R. 893 (C.A.); [1994] 2 B.C.L.C. 502. Other possibilities include the use of weighted voting on specific resolutions on the principles developed in *Bushell v. Faith* [1970] A.C. 1099 (H.L.).

[30] The Regulation to establish the European Company Statute, 2001/2157/EC [2001] OJ L294/1 will come into force on 8/10/2004, accompanied by a related Directive on employee involvement, 2001/86/EC. This idea was first put forward in 1959 and a draft statute first appeared in 1967. A later 1975 proposal was suspended in 1982 and not revived until 1992. There has been little enthusiasm in the United Kingdom for this proposal, although there are suggestions that the concept of a supranational corporate form could be extended to private companies. See *Palmer's Company Law*, paras 16.306–16.306.3.

however, do not confer either limited liability or legal personality on the partners—yet statistics indicate that there are nearly as many partnerships as there are companies (Law Commission 2000: 1.4). There are, of course, many reasons for this: for the regulated professions, the partnership form may be the only one allowed; for others, the benefits of the lack of compliance controls, which thereby allows for privacy and flexibility may far outweigh the advantages of limited liability (which may in any event be more illusory than real, except for trade creditors[31]) and the tax position may be preferable—partnerships being tax transparent whereas companies are not.[32] In some cases, of course, the choice of medium may simply depend upon the adviser consulted, who may or may not be well informed.

11.2. TURN OF THE CENTURY: CREATION AND REVIEW

But the end of the twentieth century, in addition to setting off the most fundamental review of company law for half a century, which the government has only recently started to digest,[33] also gave rise to the two topics for consideration in this chapter—the creation of a new (albeit mainly derivative) business form, the Limited Liability Partnership (or LLP), and the first general consideration of partnership law, by the Law Commissions of England and Wales and Scotland, for over a century. Indications from the DTI that the LLP was on the way first occurred in late 1996,[34] culminating in its availability as from 6 April 2001. The remit to the Law Commissions came from the DTI in November 1997 and the joint consultation paper was published in July 2000. The Commissions hope to have a final report and a draft bill sometime in the near future.[35]

What caused this burst of activity? It may well be the case that the ending, not only of the century but also the millennium, at least subconsciously and in part, inspired the DTI to set in motion the review of both company law and partnership law. It is also undoubtedly true that the company law review gained momentum from the dynamic presence of a particular individual at the DTI who chaired the steering group and who has progressed to a similar role in the

---

[31] Charges on personal assets on those running small businesses to secure business debts is, of course, the major reason for this.

[32] A company being a body corporate is subject to corporation tax (Income and Corporation Taxes Act § 832), which means that money taken out from a company is taxable either as emoluments or dividends. Partners are taxed as individuals and this has particular advantages for capital gains tax, whereby double taxation is avoided when an individual partner disposes of his or her share of the assets, see Inland Revenue Statement of Practice D 12. For VAT, however, both are taxed as separate entities.

[33] The Final Report of the Company Law Review Steering Group, Modern Company Law for a Competitive Economy (URN 01/942 and 943) was presented to the DTI in 2001. The DTI has now responded to part of that report in a White Paper, Modernising Company Law, Cm 5553, July 2002 (available on the DTI Company Law and Investigations website: www.dti.gov.uk/cld).

[34] Written answer to a parliamentary question, November 1996.

[35] Law Commission website: www.lawcom.gov.uk.

EU,[36] but it is impossible to know whether he also inspired its inception. On the other hand, the original idea for an LLP was solely the result of a political reaction to the concerns of large firms faced with substantial damages awards against them for negligence which the law of joint and several liability laid equally at the door of each partner, however remote from the action and on a scale that made insurance prohibitive. That reaction survived not only a change of minister but also of government. It may not be entirely a coincidence that the consultation paper on LLPs appeared in February 1997 and the reference on partnership law to the Law Commissions was formally made in November of that year. Partnerships were so to speak already in the frame.

11.3. Development and Nature of the LLP

Many countries have a business form called an LLP (Freedman 2000). Not one of those corresponds to the UK version, principally because the UK LLP, despite its name, is not a modified form of partnership but a modified form of company—it was suggested by one MP during the debates that it even fell foul of the Trade Descriptions Act.[37] The DTI in fact somewhat cavalierly dismissed any attempt to utilize the experience of other countries' LLPs on the basis that they were designed for different purposes than the UK form and in any event bore little comparison to each other.[38] The initial consultation paper of February 1997 stated that the LLP was designed to provide an up-to-date legal framework for certain professions and referred to 'recent developments' in other jurisdictions such as the United States and Jersey.[39] In effect this was a response to pressure for limited liability within a partnership relationship from professional firms and a threat to move offshore if it was not forthcoming.[40] This plea for limited liability was not new. In 1854 the House of Commons unanimously passed a resolution:

---

[36] High Level Group of Company Law Experts established by the European Commission, 1 September 2001 (see IP/01/1237). They have already published a consultation paper, A Modern Regulatory Framework for Company Law in Europe (April 2002), which bears a strong relationship to the recent UK company law reform process.

[37] Austin Mitchell MP, Hansard, HC 23 May 2000.

[38] DTI Response to the HC Select Committee on Trade and Industry, Fourth Report, HC 59 annex, 16 June 1999, para 26.

[39] Limited Liability Partnership: A New Form of Business Association for Professions, DTI, February 1997.

[40] HC Select Committee Report, HC 59, para. 26. But see Freedman and Finch (1997). The apparent threat from overseas LLPs came not only from those in the United States but also one specifically designed for the accountancy firms in Jersey. See Morris and Stevenson (1997) for an account of the Jersey LLP, which requires, *inter alia*, a £5m bond to be deposited by the members. Whether a move offshore would have been feasible for tax reasons was never finally settled, but the Revenue took the view that a Jersey LLP would be taxed as a company in the United Kingdom. See *R v. IRC, ex p Bishopp* [1999] S.T.C. 531.

that the law of Partnership, which renders every Person, who, though not being an ostensible Partner, shares the profits of a Trading Concern, liable to the whole of the Debts, is unsatisfactory, and should be so far modified as to permit Persons to contribute to the Capital of such Concerns on Terms of sharing their Profits, without incurring Liability beyond a limited amount.[41]

The DTI published the responses to the consultation paper and, despite a change in government, the matter was then remitted to the House of Commons Select Committee on Trade and Industry in 1999 for what proved to be the only general pre-legislative consideration of the proposals.[42] Originally the Law Commissions were invited to look at the width of availability of the LLP but never its introduction as such.[43] In fact they never examined the LLP at all, simply noting, without explaining why, that the vast majority of partnerships would be unaffected by its introduction (Law Commission 2000: para 1.15). The Select Committee were somewhat ambivalent as to the need for an LLP, stating that there was a failure by the DTI to set out a convincing case for its introduction[44] but also noting the 'very real possibility' of firms registering offshore.[45]

The Select Committee made one very significant change, however, to the proposals in that they successfully recommended that the LLP be made available to all and not just the regulated professions.[46] The drawback to this, however, is that the LLP was originally conceived as a vehicle for those professions and many of its provisions still bear the imprint of that original purpose.[47] The DTI continued onwards, publishing a draft bill and regulations in September 1998[48] and again in July 1999.[49] At that stage they considered the Bill to be final, although consultation on the regulations went on until May 2000.[50] The end result was the Limited Partnerships Act 2000 and the Limited Liability Partnerships Regulations 2000.[51] The former is a short framework Act, the latter sets out the details, the majority of which simply incorporate by reference substantial parts of the Companies Act 1985, the Insolvency Act 1986, and the Company Directors Disqualification Act 1986, as modified by the regulations. There are some new additions but very few in number. The Partnership Act 1890 is conspicuous by its absence from this list.

---

[41] Hansard 1854, 764, 800.

[42] HC Select Committee Report (*supra* n. 4).

[43] Partnership Law Initial Consultation Document, Law Commission, February 1997.

[44] HC, para 6.   [45] Ibid. para 26.

[46] Limited to businesses on formation but seems to allow for a subsequent change to a non-business form: the LLP Act 2000 § 2(1)(a) requires a business at the time of incorporation, but not thereafter. The tax authorities have certainly proceeded on the basis that an investment LLP is a real possibility, see Inland Revenue Tax Bulletin, December 2000; *Palmer's Limited Liability Partnership Law* (hereinafter *Palmer's LLP Law*), paras A1.85–A1.104.

[47] e.g. the lack of any formal requirement for an internal regulatory agreement and the fact that the LLP is to be treated as a partnership for direct tax purposes.

[48] URN 98/874. The LLP (Scotland) Regulations (2000) were not part of this process.

[49] URN 99/1025.   [50] A summary of responses was published then: URN 00/866.

[51] SI 2001 No 1090. For Scotland part of those Regulations are replaced by (and, due to the vagaries of devolution, other parts duplicated by) the LLP (Scotland) Regulations (2001) SI 2001 No 128.

There is therefore no easily accessible corpus of legislation available to potential users of the LLP, although some of us have attempted to produce an unauthorized version.[52] The DTI considered that this would be the best solution when this rather obvious defect was raised both by the Select Committee[53] and also by some of us during the consultation period—the result being outsourcing of legislation taken to its extreme.[54] There are many criticisms that can be made as to the legislative format adopted, not least its opaqueness—for example the modifications in the regulations provide that the word 'company' in the host section is to include and so is not necessarily replaced by, the words LLP[55]—thus making the sections relating to schemes of arrangement involving say both companies and LLPs interesting reading and an intellectual puzzle[56]—but business legislation should not be available only as a result of such an exercise. The end result is also cumbersome and requires subsequent changes by additional regulations whenever the 'host' section is altered.[57]

What then is an LLP? In essence it is a body corporate with limited liability in the sense that its members are not personally liable for its debts beyond their financial interests in the LLP itself, but with unlimited capacity.[58] It is incorporated by registration with an incorporation document fulfilling the role of the memorandum of association[59] and subject to many of the accounting and disclosure requirements and other controls applicable to companies.[60] But it has no shareholders or share capital, no directors, and no specific requirements as to meetings or resolutions. For insolvency purposes it is also treated as a company and is not only subject to all the controls and liabilities imposed on insolvent companies but also to its own additional clawback provision.[61] Externally, therefore, the LLP is a company but internally it may be run as the members wish—there is no formal legal requirement in the legislation for any written agreement. It was originally assumed that the professional firms for whom the form was initially intended would draft their own; at a late stage it was realized that this might not be the case with smaller enterprises and so there are a number of, rather hastily thought through, default terms in the regulations based on

---

[52] *Palmer's LLP Law*, Part C.   [53] HC 59, para 82.

[54] The previous attempt at such legislative techniques by the DTI in the Insolvent Partnerships Order 1992 was such a disaster that it had to be replaced within two years.

[55] See the LLP Regs 3(2)(a), 4(1)(a), 5(2)(a), and 6(2)(a).

[56] See *Palmer's LLP Law*, ch 10 and para C1-120.

[57] See e.g. the Limited Liability Partnerships (Particulars of Usual Residential Address) (Confidentiality Orders) Regulations (2002) SI 2002 No 915; the Limited Liability Partnerships (Competent Authority) (Fees) Regulations (2002) SI 2002 No 503; and the Limited Liability Partnerships (No 2) Regulations (2002) SI 2002 No 913. All these were required to mirror changes to the Companies Act to protect directors of companies in sensitive businesses, such as animal research, from attacks on their private addresses.

[58] LLP Act, §§ 1(3) and (4).   [59] Ibid. § 2.

[60] Including most of Part VII of the 1985 Act on accounting and audit, a modified annual return provision, the auditor controls and registration requirements of that Act are all applied by the LLP Regs.

[61] New § 214A of the Insolvency Act 1986 as applied to LLPs. See *infra* n. 103.

some of those in the Partnership Act[62]—the only obvious direct application of partnership law to LLPs, apart from direct taxation where an LLP is also to be treated as a partnership (another relic of its origins—as is the fact that changing from a partnership to an LLP is tax neutral whereas changing from a company to an LLP is not[63]).

The LLP is therefore a hybrid creature but based substantially on the corporate model—one possible reason for that is that there are problems of integrating legal personality into the partnership model (although it has also been suggested that the DTI were more familiar with company law and that it was a better vehicle for the large firms that were its original constituency—it is presumably for that reason that it is not possible to have a single-member LLP). The questions are: first, will it be used and, second, will it work? At first sight it looks an attractive vehicle both for large firms, preserving internal flexibility with the advantages of limited liability (albeit at the price of disclosure) and for small start-up businesses given its lack of internal regulations when compared with the private company—there can, for example, be no question of worrying about the esoteric rules concerning financial assistance for the acquisition of shares or the registration of special resolutions. For tax reasons it is not, however, an attractive vehicle for existing companies.

Some commentators have suggested that it will be widely used whereas others have a very different opinion. In their recent article, Vanessa Finch and Judith Freedman (2002) have no doubts:

> The desires of large partnerships have not been met, since they continue to seek the revision of joint and several liability laws. The requirements of small businesses are now, in any event, being met by steps currently being designed to improve laws relating to partnerships and limited liability companies. The financiers of business may see the LLP as a higher cost, higher risk entity than the limited liability company and this may discourage use of the LLP. The LLP is not so much a potentially popular vehicle of sophisticated design as one produced under pressure to a flawed plan.

In particular Finch and Freedman argue that there are simply too many uncertainties in the areas of law, accounting and taxation for the LLP for it to work. It is true that take-up so far has been modest (some 30 accountancy firms and very few law firms—by October 2002 only 1,373 LLPs had been registered and not all of these may be active (Finch and Freedman 2002: 478)), but it is very early days. It is necessary, therefore, to examine some questions to see if they are real and/or solvable so as to peer a little more closely into the crystal ball to see whether in time the LLP will blossom or whether it will be a mere footnote in the history of UK business law.

---

[62] LLP Regs 7 and 8. For the consultation process involved, see URN 00/617 and 00/865. The internal agreement is the subject of § 5(1) of the LLP Act.

[63] See *Palmer's LLP Law*, para A1.90 and the Inland Revenue Tax Bulletin, December 2000.

11.4. Will the LLP Provide Effective Limited Liability for the Professions?

Section 1(4) of the LLP Act provides that: 'The members of a limited liability partnership have such liability to contribute to its assets in the event of its being wound up as is provided by this Act.' It has nothing else to say about the personal liability of individual members in connection with the activities of the LLP.[64] When the LLP was first mooted as being a form of protection for partners against their joint and several liability for the negligence of one partner with whom they had little practical connection, it was suggested that this would not affect the personal liability of the negligent partner concerned—those actually responsible for say a negligent audit would remain personally liable, as would the LLP itself, but not the other members as such. This would preserve the professional ethos of personal responsibility.[65] That balance between limited liability and personal responsibility appears to have been achieved by the Jersey LLP, where the statute makes it clear that personal liability for a partner's own negligence is unaffected by the existence of an LLP.[66] Further, in many US LLPs personal liability applies both to the individual concerned and others supervising him or her (Finch and Freedman 2002). But there is no such provision under the UK statute and in fact the Government expressly rejected the idea of including one.[67]

The question of personal liability, unless it is resolved by the professional bodies themselves, is therefore a matter for the courts.[68] In effect the issue resolves itself into whether the courts will regard the personal liability of a member of an LLP as being in any way different from that of a director of a company. Both after all are bodies corporate and the LLP is directly based on the corporate rather than the partnership model. In the case of most torts there will be no problem, since normal principles of liability may well make both the member involved and the LLP liable, either vicariously or as joint tortfeasors,[69] but the position is more complex in connection with the tort of negligent misstatement, which is the one most likely to concern professional firms. This is because, unlike, say, the tort of deceit, liability depends upon there being a special

---

[64] Since § 6 of the LLP Act provides that all the members of an LLP are agents of it, contractual liability will usually rest with the LLP. Section 6 is in fact based on the partnership concept of agency rather than the corporate model but modified to take account of the LLP's legal personality. This may have some relevance to the reform of partnership law generally.

[65] See e.g. the Explanatory Notes to the LLP Bill as originally introduced into the House of Lords on 23 November 1999, [HL Bill 6] para 10.

[66] See the Limited Liability Partnerships (Jersey) Law 1997, art 5.

[67] The government refused to accept an amendment to this effect during the debate in the House of Lords—amendment No 28, HL debates, 24 January 2000, col 1381.

[68] The government has openly accepted that this is the position, see the Explanatory Notes to the LLP Act, paras 15 and 16.

[69] See e.g. *Daido Asia Japan Co Ltd v. Ines Charlotte Rothen*, 24/7/01 (Ch.), distinguishing *Standard Chartered Bank v. Pakistan National Shipping Corporation* [2000] 1 Lloyd's Rep. 218.

relationship between the parties based on an assumption of responsibility by the tortfeasor.[70] So whereas a director will be personally liable in deceit if he or she makes a deliberate or dishonest deception,[71] there will be no liability for negligent misstatements unless the director has assumed a position of special responsibility to the client. In *Williams v. Natural Life Foods Ltd*,[72] the House of Lords, overturning the Court of Appeal, held that on the facts the director had not assumed any such responsibility. But from that decision the principle has emerged that merely acting as a director of the company is not enough to give rise to such an assumption of responsibility and this has been applied in other cases since then.[73]

This is, however, what has been referred to as a developing area of company law.[74] But for present purposes the question is not where that law is going but whether the courts would take a different attitude to the personal liability of a member of an LLP for say a negligent report prepared for a client of the LLP than it does if the report had been prepared by a director for a client of the company. A negligent partner would of course always be liable under the principle of joint and several liability.

I cannot see why the courts should distinguish between an LLP and a company on this point. Finch and Freedman regard that proposition as being unacceptable on the basis that the LLP must be intended to diverge from company law in some respects if it is to be justified, as it was, on the basis of preserving the partnership ethos (Finch and Freedman 2002: 486). But that may be to confuse what the LLP started out as and what it became. It is a business form which, like a company, is open to all and is based squarely for external purposes on the corporate model. If there is to be a distinction in this developing area, which is possible, between those acting for an incorporated and those for an unincorporated business[75] (which is a different question), then that distinction must apply as between members of an LLP and partners in a partnership. After all § 1(5) of the LLP Act expressly provides that: 'Except as far as otherwise provided by this Act or any other enactment, the law relating to partnerships does not apply to a limited liability partnership.'

---

[70] This has been the position ever since the landmark decision creating the tort of negligent misstatement in *Hedley Byrne & Co Ltd v. Heller and Partners Ltd* [1964] A.C. 465. The purpose of the statement and the nature of the transaction are important in this context, see *Caparo plc v. Dickman* [1990] 2 A.C. 605.

[71] See e.g. *Credit Suisse First Boston Corporation v. Faris Al Rawi* [2002] E.W.H.C. 222 (Comm), 21/2/02.

[72] [1998] 1 W.L.R. 830, overruling [1997] 1 B.C.L.C. 131.

[73] *Noel v. Poland*, [2001] 2 B.C.L.C. 645. See also Armour, 'Corporate Personality and the Assumption of Responsibility' (1999) *Lloyd's Maritime and Commercial Law Quarterly* 246; Grantham and Rickett, 'Directors' Tortious Liability: Contract, Tort or Company Law?' (1999) 62 MLR 133.

[74] See e.g. *Partco Group Ltd v. Wragg*, unreported, 1 May 2002, giving leave to proceed to a full hearing on the question as to whether two directors of a target company owed a duty of care to the bidder on the basis of personal assurances etc.

[75] See *Merrett v. Babb* [2001] E.W.C.A. Civ. 214; [2001] 3 W.L.R. 1. In that case an employee of a sole trader was held liable for negligent misstatement but the circumstances were very different.

The problem therefore is not one which derives from the LLP form itself—it is in the possible distinction between incorporated and unincorporated businesses. Interestingly, if I am correct, then the LLP form gives members more immunity from liability for negligent misstatements than they originally sought from Jersey. Barring special circumstances, not only is there no joint and several liability on the members, there is also no individual liability on any member for a negligent misstatement. Yet the professions it seems are still seeking reform of the joint and several liability principle in partnership law.[76] It may well be that they are simply wary of the alleged uncertainty of the position of LLPs in this respect, but if they are rejecting the LLP it seems to be unlikely that this is because of the limited liability point—it must, on any interpretation, give far more protection than a partnership.

11.5. How Will the LLP Work Internally?

As we have seen, one of the main characteristics of the LLP is that, although it is subject to most of the company law rules relating to its external relations, virtually none of the rules relating to the internal relationships apply (there is one apparently anomalous exception which is considered below). Originally this distinction was made because the LLP was promulgated as leaving the professional firms free to regulate their own internal affairs by agreement just as they had done as partners.[77] Internal regulation was not required as part of the price of limited liability. When the LLP metamorphosed into a business form available to all, it was realized that not all such businesses would have such express agreements, so a number of default clauses were added at the eleventh hour.[78] These, as set out in regulations 7 and 8 of the LLP Regulations, are closely modelled on the relevant parts of §§ 24, 25, 28, and 29 of the Partnership Act.[79] Thus, the default provisions are taken from the partnership model (and § 5(1)(b) of the LLP Act expressly provides that they are derived from that source) so the question is as to how far that model will be applied generally to the internal relationships between the members. That in turn divides into two linked issues: first, will the courts apply partnership law concepts in the construction of all LLP agreements, express or implied, even if the larger LLPs adopt corporate-type constitutions; and, second, will they apply either a general

---

[76] This was made clear in responses to the Company Law Review, see the response of the ICAEW, July 2000. The Review also considered various ways of limiting the liability of auditors, see e.g. the Final Report, paras 5.34–5.36, 8.140–8.142. The climate may well have changed since then, however, and the government in its White Paper, Modernising Company Law, Cm 5553, July 2002, says at para 4.47 that it is considering the whole question of audit and auditors, post-Enron, and will come forward with its proposals in due course.

[77] The 1997 consultation paper from the DTI, URN 97/597, made this clear at para 2.2.

[78] DTI Consultation Paper: LLPs: Regulatory Default Provisions, URN 00/617.

[79] Not be transposed for LLPs, since the LLP may well be the owner of the LLP property, whereas partners individually own partnership property.

or limited fiduciary relationship as between the members *inter se* as distinct from the one that exists between each member and the LLP?

With regard to the first issue, Finch and Freedman are concerned that the courts may operate a two-tier approach and that the burden of litigation in this area will fall primarily on the smaller LLPs who rely on the default clauses, which are by no means fully comprehensive (e.g. they say nothing about financial matters) (Finch and Freedman 2002: 490). There is a very real issue here because the overarching supremacy of the corporate model is breached by the fact that internal affairs are entirely a matter for agreement, and that if there is no agreement on certain matters, then partnership solutions are provided. It is therefore possible, they argue, that the courts will construe some LLP agreements as if they were articles/shareholder agreements and some as if they were partnership deeds.

The LLP legislation is itself somewhat schizophrenic on this point. There is a default clause to the effect that there is no implied power of expulsion in an LLP,[80] but of course that, on the partnership model, can be overridden by express agreement.[81] At the same time the unfairly prejudicial remedy in § 459 of the Companies Act 1985 has been applied to all LLPs by the regulations subject to it being ousted by express agreement.[82] Thus, the courts may have to relate the partnership concept of expulsion exercised in good faith, with the corporate concept of unfairly prejudicial conduct.[83] Although its presence is somewhat anomalous, in the sense of incorporating a company law concept into an internal partnership model, § 459 may well provide at least one form of exit procedure for the smaller and less formal LLPs.

There are, of course, no answers to this question of interpretation just yet. But it seems to me that the more immediate perceived practical problem is rather that there is no model LLP agreement for small businesses to use.[84] The government refused to provide one but then there is no official partnership deed either

---

[80] See Reg. 8 of the LLP Regs.

[81] This is often the situation in practice. There is some doubt as to the exact procedure and standards expected of partners exercising such a power, but the need for basic good faith is not in doubt, see Banks (2002: paras. 10.110 and 10.120–10.129); Morse (2001: 165–9). The Law Commissions in their Joint Consultation Paper on Partnership Law (Law Com 159) have suggested that there should continue to be no default power of expulsion (Law Commission 2000: para 13.7).

[82] Subs (1A) to this effect was added to § 459 in its application to LLPs by Part I of Sch 2 to the LLP Regs.

[83] The meaning of that phrase was defined by Lord Hoffman in *O'Neill v. Phillips* [1999] 1 W.L.R. 1092, so that it requires some breach of the terms of the articles or other agreement which the complainant expressly or impliedly agreed that the affairs of the company should be conducted. In certain cases this could include equitable considerations. The test is whether the exercise of the power or other act in question be contrary to what the parties by words or conduct have agreed. As so put, there seems no inherent problem in applying that to LLPs.

[84] The Company Law Review proposed such a model constitution for small companies in Chapter 17 of its Final Report. This recommendation has been accepted by the government and even been applied by them to public companies in such a way that companies will have to expressly opt out of the relevant model and/or each individual provision (Modernising Company Law (Cm 5553, July 2002), para 2.5 and draft clause 11).

and that has not inhibited the use of partnerships.[85] The legal and business formation professions could clearly devise a number of different model LLP agreements just as they have model articles and partnership deeds. It will just take time. As to the question of interpretation of internal agreements it seems to me conceivable and perfectly rational for the courts to adopt a variable approach, sometimes adopting the articles/shareholder agreement model and sometimes the partnership deed model, depending upon whether the relationship between the members is in reality one of partnership or not. Company law after all has made that distinction, based on the existence or otherwise of so-called partnership qualities of mutual trust and management participation, ever since the landmark decision of the House of Lords in *Ebrahimi v. Westbourne Galleries Ltd*[86] and this has been carried forward into the current formulation of unfairly prejudicial conduct. To argue that such an approach to LLPs would be flawed on the basis of uncertainty is merely to argue that the LLP is new and will evolve its own jurisprudence, which in any event may not be all that new. Further such criticism sits ill with the criticism that an LLP is not sufficiently separate from existing forms of business entity.

An *Ebrahimi* form of distinction may also provide the answer to the second question as to whether, and in what circumstances, there is a fiduciary relationship between the members *inter se*. It is assumed that, given the corporate bias, there will be an obvious one as between the members and the LLP.[87] Consistent with its pro-corporate approach, the government rejected any idea of providing for an express duty of good faith as between the members.[88] But one of the default clauses applies § 28 of the Partnership Act thus requiring any member to render true accounts and full information of all things affecting the LLP to any member or his legal representative.[89] Thus, there can be a limited fiduciary relationship by default between the members (although the duties of good faith and non-competition, when implied as default clauses, are stated as being owed to the LLP). In my view the courts are more than capable of solving this issue—they are well versed in exploring the limits of fiduciary relationships—even the potential conflict between the duty of full disclosure to a member and the duty to the LLP to act in the best interests of the LLP as a whole, which might well provoke a conflict if the member seeking the information intends to damage the LLP as a result of obtaining it (it has been held in Canada that a partner can have access to a confidential document prepared

---

[85] The Law Commissions have provisionally suggested that there should be no such model agreement for partnerships, see Law Commission (2000: para 16.8).

[86] [1970] AC 360. See Davies (1997: 749–51).

[87] This can be predicated simply on the basis of the agency relationship between a member and the LLP.

[88] The DTI expressly stated that it had no wish to go much beyond the relationship that exists between a director and a company (DTI, Summary of responses: LLPs, URN 00/865, p 8).

[89] Reg. 7, LLP Regs. On the operation of § 28 in the partnership context, see Banks (2002: paras 16.02–16.09); Morse (2001: 143–4).

by a lawyer as to how to remove him, since it was prepared whilst he was still a partner[90]).

The courts have after all had to decide the circumstances in which, in the corporate context, directors can owe fiduciary duties to individual shareholders as well as to the company and those could easily be applied by analogy to members of an LLP.[91] The most recent explanation in the corporate context was given by Mummery LJ in *Peskin v. Anderson*.[92] If one substitutes LLP for company and members for directors/shareholders the solution to the fiduciary issue may well be as follows:

The fiduciary duties owed to the [LLP] arise from the legal relationship between the [members] and the [LLP] directed and controlled by them. The fiduciary duties owed to the [other members] do not arise from the legal relationship. They are dependent on establishing a special factual relationship between [the members] in the particular case. Events may take place which bring [some members] of the [LLP] into direct and close contact with [other members] in a manner capable of generating fiduciary obligations, such as a duty of disclosure of material facts to the [other members], or an obligation to use confidential information and valuable commercial and financial opportunities, which have been acquired by the [members concerned] for the benefit of the [other members] and not to prefer and promote their own interests at the expense of the [other members]
. . .

Those [fiduciary] duties are, in general, attracted by and attached to a person who undertakes, or who, depending on all the circumstances, is treated as having assumed, responsibility to act on behalf of, or for the benefit of another person. That other person may have entrusted or, depending on all the circumstances, may be treated as having entrusted, the care of his property, affairs, transactions or interests to him.

There will be LLPs where such duties attach and those where they do not. That does not seem to me to be any more of a problem than it is for companies or partnerships. It certainly should not put anyone off an LLP.

11.6. Is the Creditor/Member Balance Precise Enough to Encourage the Use of LLPs as against Companies?

Another of Finch and Freedman's arguments is that the creditor protection provisions in LLP law may create sufficient uncertainty in the minds of the banks and other lenders for them to advise their business customers against the use of the LLP as against the company. This argument is mainly predicated on the fact that, in addition to the application to LLPs of the wrongful trading, fraudulent preference, and transactions at an undervalue provisions applicable to companies, the additional creditor protection section (new 214A of the Insolvency Act

---

[90] *Dockrill v. Coopers & Lybrand Chartered Accountants* (1994) 111 D.L.R. (4th) 62.
[91] See e.g. *Percival v. Wright*, [1902] 2 Ch. 421; *Re Chez Nico Restaurants Ltd* [1991] B.C.C. 736; *Munro v. Bogie* [1994] 1 B.C.L.C. 415; *Platt v. Platt*, [1999] 2 B.C.L.C. 745.
[92] [2001] 1 B.C.L.C. 372 at 379.

1986 applicable only to LLPs) coupled with a rewording of § 74 of that Act as it applies to LLPs may have the reverse effect from that intended by making the LLP less creditor-friendly (Finch and Freedman 2002: 502).

Section 214A provides for the court, on the application of the liquidator, to order any member to repay any withdrawals made by him or her from the LLP within two years prior to the commencement of its winding up, if the member either knew or had reasonable grounds for believing that the LLP was unable to pay its debts at that time or would be so unable as a result of that and other contemporaneous withdrawals, and that the member either knew or ought to have known (based on his skill, knowledge, and experience and those of a person carrying out the same functions as the member) at that time that there was no reasonable prospect that the LLP would avoid going into insolvent liquidation.[93] Some of these phrases are clearly derived from wrongful trading[94] but others (such as the two-year limit) reflect rather more the preference and under-value provisions.[95]

Finch and Freedman, having conducted a detailed analysis of the wording of § 214A argue that it is possible that the courts may take either a lenient or a severe approach to members' liability under that section. In favour of the lenient approach, they argue, is the fact that there may be evidential difficulties for liquidators seeking to recover monies under § 214A and that subjective criteria may creep in (Finch and Freedman 2002: 505).[96] In addition liquidators may face funding difficulties in bringing actions under § 214A.[97] If that is the case, then § 214A will not assist creditors to any marked degree. On the other hand, if the courts take a hard-line approach,[98] then members may be tempted to take their money out before the two-year period,[99] which will have an adverse effect on creditors. On any interpretation, from the point of view of the members they

---

[93] The exact wording of § 214A is set out in Sch 3 to the LLP Regs. See also *Palmer's LLP Law*, para A9.40; Morse (2001: 247–9).

[94] Thus, the requirement 'of no reasonable prospect that the LLP would avoid going into insolvent liquidation' in § 214A(5) and the subjective/objective criteria to decide a member's awareness in § 214A(6) are derived directly from §§ 214(2)(b) and (4). The time factors are, however, different as between the two and there is no equivalent in § 214A to the defence in § 214(3) of the director taking every step to minimize loss.

[95] See § 240 of the IA 1986 applying the relevant time for both transactions at an undervalue and preferences. These provisions also apply to LLPs by virtue of Reg. 5 of the LLP Regs.

[96] In particular, it is argued that the omission of the words 'ought to have concluded' from § 214A in relation to awareness of the LLP's insolvency and the similarity in scope between § 214A and the preference sections may have a bearing on this.

[97] See *Palmer's Company Law*, para 15.461.1; *Re Oasis Merchandising Services Ltd*, [1997] B.C.C. 282 (C.A.).

[98] Actually withdrawing money from an LLP may be regarded by the courts as more heinous than simply carrying on business in a misguided attempt to save the company/LLP. Similarly whilst careful monitoring of the financial position may well be regarded as negating wrongful trading it may, conversely, be regarded as an aggravating factor if a member, knowing of the situation, withdraws money from the LLP. See e.g. *Re Produce Marketing Consortium (No 2)*, [1989] B.C.L.C. 520; *Re Purpoint Ltd*, [1991] B.C.L.C. 491; *Re Sherborne Associates Ltd*, [1995] B.C.C. 40; and *Re Brian D Pierson (Contractors) Ltd*, [1999] B.C.C. 26.

[99] Even taking a salary is potentially included in § 214A by § 214A(2)(a).

have nothing to gain from § 214A and much to lose—it simply does not apply to companies. Finally Finch and Freedman (2002: 509) argue that since § 74, as modified in its application to LLPs, allows members' claims to rank alongside those of creditors in a winding up (as opposed to being subordinated to them as in a corporate insolvency[100]) and for members' agreements to settle contributions to the LLP in such circumstances, that again may prejudice the creditors, although it hardly seems to prejudice the members in their choice between an LLP and a company.

In reality, however, the wrongful trading provisions have been little used in the corporate sphere (due at least in part to funding problems for liquidators but also due to the courts' attitude against using hindsight as foresight[101]) and for similar reasons,[102] it may be that § 214A will not play much of a role in the LLP sphere. The major creditors will protect themselves by a floating charge in either case.[103] From the point of view of the banks, therefore, the only question is whether unsecured overdrafts will be more expensive for an LLP than for a company and the only reason why that may be is if § 214A precipitates headlong rushes for the exit by members prior to the two-year deadline—everything else is the same. If that seems unlikely (since it requires a number of assumptions to be made such as a draconian approach by the courts and a sudden absence of funding problems), it may seem even more so if one considers the application of the Company Directors Disqualification Act to members of an LLP.[104] Disqualifications under § 6 of that Act have proved far more effective than wrongful trading in establishing behavioural norms for directors of sinking ships of all sizes.[105] There is no reason why it should not do the same for members of an LLP. Deliberate attempts to avoid § 214A may well constitute grounds for unfitness within § 6. There seems therefore to be no overwhelming reason why the creditor/member balance should influence a choice as between a company and an LLP.

Before we leave creditor protection it is worth noting that as opposed to the traditional partnership the LLP is friendlier to members in providing some limited liability whilst at the same time not altogether unfriendly to the major creditors who may take a much better security in the form of a floating charge—not available in partnership law.[106]

---

[100] As to what amounts to a members' claim, see *Soden v. British & Commonwealth Holdings plc*, [1998] A.C. 298.

[101] See e.g. *Re Sherborne Associates Ltd (supra* n. 98).

[102] Although the courts may take a harsher view of § 214A. But there are other problems, e.g. of evidence, which may make § 214A more of a threat than a reality.

[103] This will also protect them against the vagaries of the modified § 74 of the IA 1986.

[104] The 1986 CDDA is applied, as modified to LLPs, by Reg. 4 of the LLP Regs. Disqualification may work either way so that a director can be disqualified from being a member of an LLP and a member of an LLP from being a director. See *Palmer's LLP Law*, para A1.72 and ch 11.

[105] See e.g. *Re Continental Assurance Co of London plc*, [1996] B.C.C. 888; *Re Kaytech International plc*, [1999] 2 B.C.L.C. 351 (CA); *Official Receiver v. Vass*, [1999] B.C.C. 516; *Re Barings plc (No 5)*, [1999] 1 B.C.L.C. 433.

[106] The Law Commissions' provisional recommendation is that this should continue to be the case, unless a category of registered partnerships is to be introduced (Law Commission 2002: ch 22).

11.7. Other Residual Checks on Forming an LLP

In addition to the problems of accessibility of the legislation, the liability of individual members, the uncertainty regarding internal relationships and the creditor/member balance, there are of course other teething problems with the LLP. Two of these, raised by Finch and Freedman (2002: 478), relate to taxation and accountancy (ibid. 491 and 493). Being specialist issues, this is not the place to go into either of these problems in any detail. Nevertheless one or two observations may be made. Tax considerations are important but, as Finch and Freedman point out, they clearly vary from business to business (ibid. 491). It is true that the Revenue still regards the LLP as an alternative device to a partnership (having either deliberately or inadvertently missed its sea change to a modified company) and needs to consider the LLP in the corporation tax context—particularly in allowing for conversion from a company to an LLP and vice versa to be tax neutral.[107] So, for example, allowing an LLP formed as a start-up vehicle and which has evolved from an owner-managed enterprise to convert into a company without incurring any tax consequences from the actual process of change. Is it beyond the realms of reason to suggest that since, as we have seen, an LLP may be internally in effect either a modified company with no partnership ethos or a body corporate run very much on partnership lines, there could be some mechanism for allocating either the corporate or partnership tax regime as appropriate? Perhaps with a presumption for one mode with some form of election for the other. If there is a will for LLPs to succeed, then that could happen.

With regard to accounting controls, seen as a quid pro quo for limited liability, there are obvious tensions in applying corporate accounting rules to an entity that may be run internally on a partnership basis and is taxed as such. That is a matter for the accountancy profession and the DTI to sort out and the former has, over a year after the introduction of LLPs, finally produced a Statement of Recommended Practice on accounting by LLPs[108] and surely this is not going to be allowed to frustrate the LLP's development.

11.8. Reforming the Law of Partnership Generally

Whatever the future of the LLP may be, it is clear that partnerships as such are very much here to stay (Law Commission 2000: ch 1)—there will be no additional small business form in the foreseeable future[109] and limited liability

---

[107] See *Palmer's LLP Law*, paras A1.85–A1.104 and sources cited there.

[108] Accounting by limited liability partnerships, published by the Consultative Committee of Accountancy Bodies on 29 May 2002, available on www.ccab.org.uk. See also generally *Palmer's LLP Law*, ch 4.

[109] See the Final Report from the Company Law Review Steering Group, URN01/942, para 7, and the subsequent White Paper, Modernising Company Law, Cm 5553, July 2002, para 1.6.

is not necessarily seen as crucial by those who engage in such business (Law Commission 2000: para 1.11). The Law Commissions have as yet only produced their joint consultation paper on partnership law reform and not their final recommendations. The following therefore are comments on that consultation paper only. The LLP does have some relevance to this process, however, since, as we have seen, there are some aspects of partnership law attached to it, principally in the area of internal relationships[110] but also the application of agency law to LLPs.[111]

The adaptation of these partnership concepts to LLPs is significant for partnership law reform generally in two ways: first the LLP has legal personality on formation and so the adaptation of traditional partnership fiduciary duties and agency relationship as between the partners (devised in English law for a situation where there is no actual firm as a legal person) to the member/LLP scenario is of relevance to the similar problems that will arise if the traditional partnership is also to become a legal person, as is put forward as a possibility by the Law Commissions (Law Commission 2000: para 4.17). Second, in adapting the partnership agency model to LLPs, at least one significant change has been made to the borrowed statutory provision and which could be applied to all partnerships (Morse 2001: 257).

11.9. Acceptance of General Themes

It seems to me that there are three general themes in the proposals that are to be welcomed. The first is the introduction of legal personality for all partnerships, which will accord with public perception of a firm as an entity (Law Commission 2000: para 4.17). There might be thought to be problems with the concept of an informally created legal person (i.e. no one might realize that it does actually exist or when it came into effect, since it can arise simply by an association of persons carrying on a business with a view of profit[112]), but in practice since such matters as insurance and ownership of assets could be dealt with by the law of trusts and problems of theft etc. by a partner from the unknown firm covered by the need to show dishonesty, any such problems are outweighed by the advantages, not least the assimilation of partnerships into modern regulatory law (Morse 2001: 88–91). (The schizophrenic attitude of the tax regime whereby partnerships (and LLPs) are regarded as transparent for direct taxes but as an entity for indirect taxes will, however, continue.)[113]

---

[110] LLP Act, § 5. See *Palmer's LLP Law*, ch 5; Morse (2001: 259–64).

[111] LLP Act, § 6. See *Palmer's LLP Law*, ch 7; Morse (2001: 256–8).

[112] This causes some problems with 'contemplated partnerships' discussed below. The introduction of legal personality would not, unless the registered partnership is to be introduced, which seems unlikely, require any formalities for the formation of a partnership, which would still occur whenever the factual situation required by § 1 of the PA 1890 is fulfilled. The Law Commissions suggest minor amendments to § 1 but not to that basic principle (Law Commission 2000: para. 5.26).

[113] This is also the position with regard to LLPs.

The proposal that all partnerships should have legal personality[114] with the added provision that such personality should survive a change in the partners unless they provide otherwise (i.e. an opt-out model rather than an opt-in model as is suggested in the document) seems the most workable (Law Commission 2000: para 4.32). An alternative possibility of only giving such personality to a new form of registered partnerships (ibid. para 4.21 and ch 20) would defeat the object of the exercise and would I think have a very limited effect, since those firms that might register would probably either be those that would draft a constitution so as to take full benefit from automatic legal personality or incorporate as LLPs anyway. To introduce another costly and bureaucratic process is unnecessary.

One of the advantages of continuing legal personality is in fact the second theme of the proposals (ibid. para 4.32). This is that the association is to survive so far as possible after a change in the membership of the firm. Thus, where one partner leaves the firm for whatever reason the existing relationship between the remaining partners is presumed to continue. Thus, there would only be a dissolution as between the exiting partner and the other partners and not as between all the partners (which is technically the current position) (Morse 2001: 192).[115] So, for example, a partner will only be able to withdraw from a partnership-at-will by notice rather than dissolve it (Law Commission 2000: para 6.19) (thus avoiding the potential doomsday scenario nearly brought about by the activities of Mr Bingham chronicled in *Walters v. Bingham*) (Banks 2002: paras 24.21 et seq.; Morse 2001: 47).[116]

The third theme, which is to be welcomed, is the new approach to dissolution and winding up. In line with the second theme, dissolution per se would be limited to situations where the whole firm was to be dissolved (either voluntarily or compulsorily) (Law Commission 2000: paras 6.4, 6.7, 6.15, 6.25).[117] There are also the proposals for the winding up of a solvent partnership under court supervision with an independent officer having powers to act vigorously (ibid. para 8.60).[118] The current problems of partnership disputes consequent on a winding up are well documented in the report (ibid. paras 8.29 et seq.).

---

[114] Partnerships do have legal personality in Scotland under § 4(2) of the PA 1890. This is not necessarily the same concept as that being proposed by the Law Commissions, however, and has exercised the Commissions in their consultation document. See e.g. para 4.33 and *Major v. Brodie*, [1998] S.T.C. 491, where the English court struggled with the parameters of the legal personality of a Scottish partnership—not least because it had contradictory expert evidence on the point.

[115] For the potential consequences, see e.g. *Hadlee v. Commissioner of Inland Revenue*, [1993] A.C. 524 (P.C.).

[116] [1988] F.T.L.R. 260.

[117] In para 6.15 the Commissions suggest that there should be a general policy 'to give the maximum duration to partnerships which is consistent with the wishes or presumed wishes of the partners'.

[118] Summarized in Morse (2001: 205).

11.10. Proposals to be Welcomed as They Stand

The document makes a substantial number of detailed proposals and options for reform of specific provisions of partnership law. It is impossible in the space allocated to go through each of them but I would first like to mention a few of those that seem to me to be both sensible and timely before commenting on some areas that might require further thoughts and on others that appear to have been ignored in the consultation document.

Thus I welcome the proposed changes to the definition of a partnership in § 1 of the 1890 Act (e.g. it should be an association based on agreement to carry on a business through the firm with a view of profit but without necessarily having an agreed division of profits (Law Commission 2000: para 5.26))[119] and the proposed abolition of §§ 2 and 3 of the 1890 Act (ibid. paras 5.43 and 5.50). These sections today only cause problems rather than provide solutions as to the existence of a partnership and have served their purpose. To some extent modern case law suggests that the courts have already come to this conclusion and use § 1 as the key section.[120] I also (with almost everyone else) welcome both the Commissions' and the DTI's proposals to abolish the numerical limit of twenty on partnerships, which have now been implemented (Law Commission 2000: para 5.51).[121] The former system was both outdated and cumbersome and a strange way of regulating certain professions by means of exemptions from a numerical limit.[122]

I also welcome the proposals to rectify the anomaly in § 9 of the Act as to joint and several liability and to provide for primary and subsidiary liability where the firm has legal personality (Law Commission 2000: para 10.12; Morse 2001: 125; Banks 2002: paras 13.05 et seq.); the proposals to modernize the references to payments of interest in the Act (Law Commission 2000: para 7.26(b)); and the technical amendments to take into account legal personality (ibid. para 5.26).

---

[119] The question as to whether there is a need for a division of profits under the existing wording of § 1 is discussed in Banks (2002: para 2.10) and Morse (2001: 21).

[120] See e.g. *Vekaria v. Dabasia*, 1 December 1998.

[121] Having produced a consultation paper on the issue and having received very favourable responses, the DTI promulgated a statutory instrument to remove the limit by repealing §§ 716 and 717 of the Companies Act 1985 and amending § 4(2) of the Limited Partnerships Act 1907. That instrument, the Regulatory Reform (Removal of Twenty Member Limit in Partnerships etc.) Order 2002, SI 2002/3203, came into force on 21 Dec. 2002. The original reason for the limit, difficulty in bringing claims, has long since disappeared.

[122] This is because the exceptions to the limit are often couched in terms of membership of a professional or regulatory body, e.g. the Chartered Institute of Loss Adjusters. See Banks (2002: para 4.29 et seq.).

11.11. Areas Requiring Further Thought

There are a number of proposals in the report that do require perhaps some second or further thoughts.

11.11.1. Contemplated Partnerships

It is sometimes difficult to establish exactly when a partnership association has actually begun—there is, as yet, no registration procedure.[123] Thus, it is necessary to decide when the partnership obligations arise and, if legal personality is to be introduced, exactly when the firm itself comes into existence. In particular when does an agreement to set up a partnership actually evolve into the creation of a partnership? Following the decision of the Court of Appeal in *Khan v. Miah*[124] that arranging premises for a proposed restaurant, advertising the new venture etc. did not amount to a partnership, since the actual business of running the restaurant never got off the ground, the Law Commissions recommend that it should be sufficient for a partnership to exist if the actual carrying on of the business was an object rather than a reality (Law Commission 2000: para 5.22). But the House of Lords in that case[125] subsequently decided that there was no need for actual trading to begin for a partnership to exist. What is needed is a business activity carried on in common and the fact that assets had been so acquired and liabilities so incurred jointly was sufficient for that. It seems to me that that is a better criterion for establishing a partnership than merely having the object of actually carrying on a business where nothing may actually have been and might never be done (Morse 2001: 12–13). On the other hand the editor of the latest edition of *Lindley and Banks on Partnership Law* regards the decision in *Khan v. Miah* as giving rise to great uncertainty (Banks 2002: para 2.03). But his argument seems to be predicated simply on the basis that the facts will be different in each case.

11.11.2. Acceptance of Repudiatory Breach by One Partner

The House of Lords in *Hurst v. Bryk*[126] suggested that acceptance by the other partners of a repudiatory breach of the partnership agreement by one partner, which would end the agreement, should not amount to an automatic dissolution of the partnership relationship (since the partners had subjected themselves to equitable considerations that could override the common law doctrine of repudiation). This view could apply equally to the cases of frustration and rescission of the agreement (Morse 2001: 202–5; Banks 2002: paras 24.05 et seq.). As the

---

[123] It is unlikely that the system of registered partnerships canvassed by the Law Commission (2000: ch 22) will receive much support.
[124] [1998] 1 W.L.R. 477.   [125] [2000] 1 W.L.R. 2123.   [126] [2000] 2 B.C.L.C. 117.

Law Commissions pointed out, this would mean that the relationship would survive, but only as a partnership-at-will, which could be ended at any time by notice, or even by the acceptance of the repudiatory breach itself. Their suggested reform is to provide that acceptance of a repudiatory breach would end neither the contract nor the association. To effect that, an application would have to be made to the court for a dissolution—although they asked for views as to whether there should be an exception where a partner is locked out of the management of the firm for some time as a result (Law Commission 2000: paras 6.32, 6.33).

With respect I do not see how, consistently with the idea that a partnership is dependent upon an agreement, that association can remain intact on acceptance of a repudiatory breach of that agreement. There is also the considerable practical difficulty, as Lindley and Banks points out, of tying all the by now disenchanted partners into the firm pending a court dissolution, and thus exposing a partner who has, say been wrongly excluded from participation, to full joint and several liability during that period for which a subsequent indemnity might, at best, be cumbersome (Banks 2002: para 24.07). A better course would be to provide that such acceptance provides for an immediate withdrawal from the association by the person concerned, with continuity for the other partners, rather than a possible future dissolution, albeit partial (since other proposals would give the court that option), eventually coming from the courts. This would avoid problems of tying in all the partners, and logically fit with the general theme of providing for withdrawals rather than dissolutions (Law Commission 2000: para 6.15) and also with the law of contract.

11.11.3. Rights of Outgoing Partner to Share in the Profits Pending Final Settlement of Accounts

Section 42 of the Partnership Act 1890, currently provides that an outgoing partner (including a deceased partner) has a choice when the other partners continue the business pending the settlement of a final account. This is a choice as between a share of the profits attributable to the outgoing partner's share in the partnership assets or to interest on that share of the assets (currently 5 per cent but to be altered to cover fluctuating rates).[127] The Commissions have suggested that the profits share option should be removed on the basis of practicalities of ascertaining how much of those subsequent profits is due to the outgoing partner's share and how much to the personal efforts of the remaining partners (Law Commission 2000: para. 7.26). But in the light of the decision and comments of the Court of Appeal of Victoria in *Fry v. Oddy*[128] perhaps this should be reconsidered. In that case the question arose as to ascertaining the share of the profits attributable to the share of the assets of an outgoing partner in a firm of

---

[127] On § 42 generally, see Banks (2002: paras 25.25–25.37); Morse (2001: 222–8).
[128] [1999] 1 VR 542.

solicitors. The Court considered that in a modern legal practice profits were more and more attributable to the assets of the firm as opposed to the personal skills of each member of the firm. If that is correct and in times of low interest rates, it would seem harsh to remove the profits share option from § 42. In any event there is an argument that the continuing partners might be construed as holding that amount as constructive trustees for the outgoing partner.[129]

11.11.4. Competing or Complimentary Fiduciary Duties

The Law Commissions raise the issue as to the application of the current fiduciary duties owed by each partner to the other partners to a situation where the firm has its own separate legal personality and it carries on the business. This poses the question as to what duties should be owed by each partner to the firm and whether there should be any such duties still owed as between the members *inter se*. The Commissions have put forward three options: (i) that all duties should be owed only to the firm; (ii) that some duties should be specified as being owed to the firm (duty to account for profits, duty not to compete, duty to act bona fide for the benefit of the firm) and others as between the members (duty to give full information and accounts and duty of good faith in partnership relations); and (iii) that the duties of care and skill, account, and non-competition should be owed both to the firm and the other partners (Law Commission 2000: para 15.21).

The Commissions are concerned that if the duties are only owed to the firm, then there will be a problem for a minority partner having any redress against the majority for breach. One, rather cumbersome, answer to that is that it would be possible for a procedure to be devised to allow one partner to bring an action for a breach of duty owed to the firm subject to the majority being able to disclaim it if they are acting in good faith (as is suggested by the Commissions).[130] More realistically consideration should be given to adopting some form of default exit or resolution dispute procedure, though not necessarily based on § 459 of the Companies Act as has been applied to LLPs. This could take the form of a modified no-fault exit procedure if the partnership ethos of mutual trust etc. is broken. If such a default procedure is excluded by agreement, then the parties will surely have addressed their minds to exit procedures and provided accordingly. There is always the just and equitable winding-up provision in § 35 of the Act as a final back-up, which, if amended as the Commissions suggest, will allow the courts to allow for a withdrawal and not a full dissolution (Law Commission 2000: para 6.24).

---

[129] In so far as they are derived from assets, which could include goodwill, still partially owned by the outgoing partner. The Law Commissions' proposals should also be considered in the light of art 1 to the First Protocol to the European Convention on Human Rights.

[130] *Quaere* as to whether there is any concept of the derivative action in partnership law as it stands, see the Canadian case of *Watson v. Imperial Financial Services Ltd*, (1994) 111 D.L.R. (4th) 643; Morse (2001: 90).

It follows that I cannot see any reason why the duties should not be stated as being owed to the firm and exceptions where they may be owed between the partners could be left to the courts. It is clear that as controllers and agents for the firm the partners will owe fiduciary duties to it. To provide for additional express categorized fiduciary duties as between the members runs the risk of having competing duties; i.e. where a partner's duties to the firm and to another partner might actually conflict, as is a possibility with LLPs. If the answer to that is that it could be sorted out by the courts, then why not leave the question of duties as between the partners to the courts in the first place?

There is, as we have seen, a similar problem with regard to the internal relationships of members of LLPs. I can see no reason why the same basic solution as I have suggested for LLPs should not equally apply to partnerships; i.e. that the duties should be owed to the firm and only, additionally, to each other where there is a special factual relationship on the analysis of Mummery LJ in *Peskin v. Anderson*.[131]

Members of an LLP are not partners, however, and it could be argued that the partnership ethos requires an automatic fiduciary relationship as between the partners,[132] but I would suggest that to provide that all fiduciary duties are owed to the firm as arising from the legal relationship of direction and control between them and leaving the courts to apply fiduciary duties as between the partners on the factual relationship basis, i.e. where one partner has undertaken or is treated as having assumed responsibility to act for the other's benefit, allied to an exit procedure, will prove just as effective a protection for individual partners.

11.12. Areas Not Addressed by the Law Commissions

There are two areas of difficulty in partnership law which, if they were considered, have not been addressed in the Law Commissions' document. The accusation that these are only academic difficulties could only be addressed to the first of these and even there it has led to recent litigation in Australia and given that we only review partnership law every hundred years it might have been thought worthy of mention. The other area is very much before the courts in the United Kingdom.

11.12.1. Section 5 and the Doctrine of the Undisclosed Principal

The Law Commissions are of the opinion that § 5 of the 1890 Act, which sets out the circumstances where one partner may bind the others to a contract, is

---

[131] [2000] 1 B.C.L.C. 173.

[132] As has always been the case. See e.g. *Const v. Harris*, (1824) Turn & R 496, per Lord Eldon: 'In all partnerships, whether it be expressed in the deed or not, the partners are bound to be true and faithful to each other.'

'generally satisfactory' (Law Commission 2000: para 9.5). But that section has a proviso whereby the other partners will not be bound, even if the partner concerned is acting in the ordinary course of business of the firm, if either the person dealing with him knows that he has no authority (unexceptional) or does not know or believe him to be a partner. The latter appears to negative the doctrine of the undisclosed principal (i.e. where an agent is acting for an undisclosed principal, the third party may enforce the contract against the principal), despite some suggestions in case law to the contrary[133] and has led to academic debate as to when exactly the third party is unaware that the person he is dealing with is a partner (e.g. with whom).[134] Some consideration should be given as to whether the proviso should be maintained in its present form, including the trustee solution adopted in Australia (i.e. that the apparently unconnected partner is contracting as a trustee for the benefit of the firm rather than as an agent).[135] At the very least the amendment to the wording of the proviso in § 6 of the LLP Act, which imports § 5 of the PA into LLP law might be considered. There the restriction only applies if the person dealing with the member does not know that he/she is a member of the LLP rather than an LLP. Given that partnerships may have legal personality, such a limited restriction, i.e. that the third party did not know that the partner was a member of the firm involved, would at least reduce the potential for confusion.

11.12.2. Liability for Breaches of Express and Constructive Trusts by One Partner

The Partnership Act has three sections which apply to non-contractual partnership liability. Section 10 provides joint and several liability for all wrongs committed by a partner in the ordinary course of business of the firm;[136] § 11 for the misapplication of property either received by a partner within his authority as such and misapplied by him or brought into the firm and misapplied whilst in the firm's custody;[137] and § 13, which provides that no partner without notice is

---

[133] *Watteau v. Fenwick*, [1893] 1 Q.B. 346, cf. *Construction Engineering (Aus) Pty Ltd v. Hexyl Pty Ltd*, (1985) 155 C.L.R. 541.

[134] See Montrose, 'Liability of Principal for Acts Exceeding Actual and Apparent Authority' (1939) 17 Can Bar Rev 693; J. C. Thomas, 'Playing Word Games with Professor Montrose' (1977) 6 VUWLR 1. See Morse (2001: 105–9).

[135] *Construction Engineering (Aus) Pty Ltd (supra* n. 133).

[136] Section 10 reads: 'Where, by any wrongful act or omission of any partner acting in the ordinary course of the business of the firm, or with the authority of his co-partners, loss or injury is caused to any person not being a partner in the firm, or any penalty is incurred, the firm is liable therefore to the same extent as the partner so acting or omitting to act.' See Banks (2002: paras 12.83–12.110); Morse (2001: 110–16).

[137] Section 11 reads: 'In the following cases: namely—(a) where one partner acting within the scope of his apparent authority receives the money or property of a third person and misapplies it; and (b) where the firm in the course of its business receives money or property of a third person, and the money or property so received is misapplied by one or more the partners whilst it is in the custody of he firm; the firm is liable to make good the loss.' See Banks (2002: paras 12.111–12.140); Morse (2001: 116–19).

liable if a partner, being a trustee, improperly employs trust property in the business or on behalf of the firm in breach of trust (Banks 2002: paras 12.141–52; Morse 2001: 119–25). The Commissions have not recommended any changes of substance to these three sections (Law Commission 2000: paras 10.26 and 10.30), but this does seem to ignore recent problems that have arisen with regard to their application to the vicarious liability of partners for breaches of an express trust by one partner and, more importantly, their vicarious liability for what is known as accessory liability by one partner under constructive trusts.

Such accessory liability is based on a person either knowingly assisting in a breach of trust (knowing assistance—based on dishonesty)[138] or knowingly receiving trust property taken in breach of trust by another (knowing receipt—based on conscience).[139] If one partner is so liable, in what circumstances will the other innocent partners be vicariously liable if there is a partnership connection so as to bring §§ 10 or 11 into play?—they will, of course, each be individually liable if they have the requisite knowledge, etc.

Both the Court of Appeal and the House of Lords in *Dubai Aluminium Company Ltd v. Salaam*,[140] held that § 10 imposes a potential vicarious liability on the innocent members of a firm for the knowing assistance of one partner—liability for wrongs can include that. Thus, if the knowing assistance is done within the ordinary business of the partnership (i.e. it is an improper way of carrying out an ordinary activity of the firm),[141] the other partners will be liable vicariously just as they are for a tort committed by one partner. This decision reversed previous cases to the contrary which limited § 10 to vicarious liability for torts and crimes and has thus opened up § 10 to cover all forms of wrongs.[142] It seems clear therefore that their Lordships contemplated that § 10 would also apply to vicarious liability for the knowing receipt by a partner if that receipt is also within the ordinary business of the firm—it is also a wrong. They also concluded that there was no reason in law why a partner could not constitute himself as a constructive trustee in the ordinary course of the business.[143] But because knowing receipt, unlike knowing assistance, involves the property being received by a partner or the firm, it also requires consideration of §§ 11 and 13.

[138] The most recent formulation of this liability is by the House of Lords in *Twinsectra Ltd v. Yardley*, [2002] 2 All E.R. 377 (Lord Millett dissenting).

[139] The exact parameters of this liability are not yet certain, see e.g. *Bank of Credit and Commerce International (Overseas) Ltd v. Akindele*, [2000] 4 All E.R. 221.

[140] [2001] Q.B. 113 (C.A.); [2003] 1 B.C.L.C. 32 (H.L.).

[141] As for example in *Hamlyn v. John Houston & Co*, [1903] 1 K.B. 81 (C.A.). The C.A. and H.L. in the *Dubai Aluminium* case disagreed on the application of this concept to the facts of the case.

[142] The application of § 10 to knowing assistance cases seems also to have been tacitly assumed in *Agip (Africa) Ltd v. Jackson*, [1991] Ch. 547. Lindley and Banks appears underwhelmed by these decisions (Banks 2002: para 12.110).

[143] Lord Millett considered that the case of *Mara v. Browne* [1896] 1 Ch 199, was authority only for the proposition that it was outside the business of the firm for a solicitor to constitute himself a trustee de son tort and therefore that that case was wrongly applied to constructive trusts in *Re Bell's Indenture*, [1980] 1 W.L.R. 1217.

The difference between §§ 11 and 13 was explained by Millett LJ, as he then was, in *Bass Brewers Ltd v. Appleby*:[144]

Section 11 deals with money which is properly received by the firm (or by one of the partners acting within the scope of his authority) for and on behalf of the third party but which is subsequently misapplied. The firm is liable to make good the loss [i.e. vicarious liability]. Section 13 is concerned with money held by a partner in some other capacity, such as a trustee, which is misapplied by him and then improperly and in breach of trust employed by him in the partnership business. His partners can be made liable only in accordance with the ordinary principles of knowing receipt [i.e. personal liability].

Lord Millett further explained in the *Dubai Aluminium* case[145] that whilst § 10 is concerned with vicarious liability for the loss caused by a partner's wrongdoing, §§ 11 and 13 are concerned purely with the firm's liability to account for receipts. Under § 11 the firm is not vicariously liable for the misappropriation; it is liable to account for the money it received and cannot plead the partner's wrongdoing as an excuse for its failure. Section 13, on the other hand, limits the partners' liability for breaches of trust that will have taken place outside the firm's business—they would only be liable if they were guilty personally of knowing receipt.

With respect, once it has been established that § 10 can apply to all wrongs, the initial distinction between the vicarious liability of the firm for misapplications by knowing receipt under § 10 and its primary liability to account for misapplications under § 11 now seems more apparent than real. The question in relation to knowing receipt seems to be whether a partner's receipt can also be construed as a proper or business receipt by the firm for § 11 purposes or within the ordinary course of the firm's business for § 10—is there really any difference in practice? It is true that vicarious liability for knowing receipt under § 10 depends upon the wrongdoer having the requisite knowledge whereas there is no such express requirement in § 11, but that section does presuppose a misapplication by a partner which must now, by definition, also be a wrong for the purposes of § 10 liability.

The position is different with regard to breaches of an express trust by a partner. The Court of Appeal in *Walker v. Stones*[146] decided that partners could not be liable at all for a breach of an express trust by one partner under § 10, since otherwise it would contradict § 13. This was because if § 10 applied it would presuppose that individual trusteeships that a partner may undertake are in the ordinary course of business of a firm and would cover the exact situation described in § 13. This also seems to have been accepted by the House of Lords in *Dubai Aluminium*.[147] In so far as either case says that all express breaches of trust by a partner are outside § 10, however, it is submitted that that would seem

---

[144] [1997] 2 B.C.L.C. 700 at 711.   [145] *Supra* n. 14 at 61.
[146] [2000] 4 All E.R. 412.   [147] *Supra* n. 14.

to be too wide. Section 13 only applies to one specific fact situation—i.e. money taken in breach of trust and subsequently introduced into the firm by one partner. It could not apply where money is held by the firm, one partner becomes a trustee of it and then breaches his trust. That should be dealt with under §§ 10 or 11. There are also problems with the parameters of § 13 as to the meaning of notice.

The result of all this litigation is that there is some unnecessary complexity as to the interface between the three sections and this surely merits some discussion in a reform document. The reality is that those sections pre-date modern developments in accessory liability and restitutionary concepts. There are several possibilities: one would be to separate vicarious liability for torts and crimes, on the one hand, and for trusts and accessory liability, on the other; another would be to consider whether vicarious liability is appropriate at all for accessory liability, or alternatively whether restitutionary principles should be applied without any requirement of fault; or more radically and preferably to repeal §§ 11 and 13—leaving § 10 to deal with all questions of vicarious liability (i.e. was the wrong, of whatever type, done in the ordinary course of the business—thus excluding liability for the factual situation in § 13, but leaving tracing available as now (Banks 2002: para 12.152)—because the breach of trust takes place outside the firm, but including those currently in § 11—misapplication within the authority of a partner or whilst in the firm's custody, since it does not seem that that section's direct liability in practice adds anything to § 10 as it is now understood) and general principles to establish any personal liability.

REFERENCES

Banks, R. C. I. (Lindley and Banks) (2002), *Lindley & Banks on Partnership* (18th edn.), London: Sweet & Maxwell.

Davies, P. L. (1997), *Gower's Principles of Modern Company Law* (6th edn.), London: Sweet & Maxwell.

Finch, V., and Freedman, J. (2002), 'The Limited Liability Partnership: Pick and Mix or Mix-Up?', *Journal of Business Law* 2002: 475.

Freedman, J. (2000), 'Limited Liability: Large Company Theory and Small Firms', *Modern Law Review* 63: 317.

——and Finch, V. (1997), 'Limited Liability Partnerships: Have Accountants Sewn Up the "Deep Pockets" Debate?', *Journal of Business Law* 1997: 387.

Gower, L. C. B. (1997), *Gower's Principles of Modern Company Law*, by P. L. Davies with a contribution from D. D. Prentice, London: Sweet & Maxwell.

Law Commission (Law Commission for England and Wales and the Scottish Law Commission) (2000), *Partnership Law: A Joint Consultation Paper*, London: The Stationery Office.

——(2001), *Limited Partnership Act 1907: A Joint Consultation Paper*, London: The Stationery Office.

Law Commission (2002), *Partnership Law*, London: The Stationery Office.

Morris, Ph., and Stevenson, J. (1997), 'The Jersey Limited Liability Partnership: A New Legal Vehicle for Professional Practice', *Modern Law Review* 60: 538.

Morse, G. (ed.) (1992), *Palmer's Company Law*, 23rd edn., London: Sweet & Maxwell.

—— (1999), *Charlesworth and Morse: Company Law*, London: Thompson Professional Publishing Co.

—— (2001), *Partnership Law*, London: Blackstone Press.

—— (ed.) (2001), *Palmer's Limited Liability Partnership Law*, London: Sweet & Maxwell.

12

'Drawing Near the Fastness?': The Failed US Experiment in Unincorporated Business Entity Reform

ALLAN WALKER VESTAL

> These creatures you have seen are animals carven and wrought into new shapes.
>
> Dr Moreau (Wells 1896)

12.1. INTRODUCTION

The 1990s was an interesting decade in business organization law in the United States. At the start of the decade, firms could be organized as partnerships, limited partnerships, or corporations. At the end of the decade, we have reworked one traditional form, the general partnership, and added several new forms of firm life: limited liability partnerships, limited liability limited partnerships, and limited liability companies. The fundamental revision of another existing form, the limited partnership, is underway. More new forms of life are on the horizon: limited liability sole proprietorships, and single-member limited liability companies are being developed. And discussions are proceeding about wiping out all the different forms of firm life and creating a single form in their place.

It seems appropriate to now take a step back and question whether the decade was one of real accomplishment and reform or simply one of great change. So considered, the decade seems one of great change and little accomplishment.

The reform experience in the United States suggests three essential failures. First, our reformers proceeded without an underlying theory to guide their experimentation; they have acted because it was in their power to do so and not because of any consensus-based theoretical justification. Second, the want of an underlying theory led our reformers to engage in non-purposeful grafting and reshaping in their experiments. Third, there has been no justifiable social exchange in the process; social costs have been generated without any demonstrable and compensating social benefit.

The record suggests some useful observations about law reform in the United States and, perhaps, some cautionary words for our colleagues in the European Community as they consider parallel changes in their laws of unincorporated business ventures.

When I consider the experimentation in which we have engaged and the outcomes we have produced, I am reminded, perhaps a bit unfairly,[1] of the H. G. Wells story *The Island of Doctor Moreau.*

12.2. ANALYSIS

12.2.1. The Extreme Limit of Plasticity: The Want of an Underlying Theory

> You see, I went on with research just the way it led me. That is the only way I ever heard of true research going. I asked a question, devised some method of obtaining an answer, and got a fresh question. Was this possible or that possible? You cannot imagine what this means to an investigator, what an intellectual passion grows upon him! You cannot imagine the strange, colourless delight of these intellectual desires! . . . I wanted—it was the one thing I wanted—to find out the extreme limit of plasticity in a living shape.
>
> (Wells 1896: 136–7)

To say that the entire reform effort lacked an agreed upon underlying theory is an overstatement in two ways. First, parts of the reform effort had a generally accepted underlying theory.[2] Second, some analysts operated from essentially coherent underlying theories, although these were highly contested and were not the subject of general acceptance.[3]

An example of the first situation, where parts of the reform effort enjoyed an underlying theory with broad support, would be the move from the aggregate theory of partnerships to the entity theory. The Revised Uniform Partnership

---

[1] I would like to note that a great many of the changes worked in partnership law by the RUPA drafters made positive contributions to that body of law. Hillman, Vestal, and Weidner (2000). These modifications, which logically flowed from the initial limited vision of UPA revisions, were by and large well conceived and executed. The drafters, and especially the Reporter, Dean Don Weidner, deserve great appreciation for their labours. My criticisms are directed not at them, but at those who pushed to abandon fundamental principles of the prior regime.

[2] With respect to general partnerships, for example, Revised Uniform Partnership Act (RUPA) overall adopts a much more contractarian orientation than does the UPA, although the transition is imperfect. See Vestal (1995a: 55, 57–70) (comparing UPA and RUPA fiduciary regimes). The failure to make the fiduciary regime fully contractarian has been lamented by commentators of that persuasion. See Ribstein (1993: 45, 57–61); Hynes (1995, 1997).

[3] There is, for example, no convincing underlying theory to justify having either LLPs or LLCs, much less having them both. One commentator (Oesterle 1995: 881) noted the conclusory nature of the underlying theory: 'The ongoing revolution in small business structure is driven by the belief that limited liability should be available to businesses without a tax penalty. Some reformers are motivated by a perception that tort liability is out of control; others are motivated by a perception that a corporate level income tax is irrational.' These beliefs are not universally accepted and hardly justify the multiplication of forms we have seen over the last decade.

Act (RUPA) declares that '[a] partnership is an entity'.[4] This generally agreed upon evolution from the Uniform Partnership Act (UPA) model involves completely restructured provisions on the rights of partners, the forms of ownership, the presumptions under which property is assigned to either partners or the partnership, and the procedures under which creditors can satisfy their claims (Hillman, Vestal, and Weidner 2000: 4–5).

Examples of the second situation, where individual commentators had an underlying theory, if not one of general acceptance, would be the works of commentators on the right and left such as Bill Callison, Larry Ribstein, and Dennis Hynes. Others who, because of personal orientation or positions of leadership, had to adopt a more pragmatic and less ideological role, would include Don Weidner and Bob Hillman.

But having acknowledged the exceptions at the margins, it should be emphasized that taken as a whole the reform effort lacked a generally accepted, generally applied theoretical underpinning. This was true from the very start, with the American Bar Association (ABA) report (1987) on partnership revisions that started the entire reform effort. The ABA report was more in the nature of a list of technical corrections than it was a manifesto to reform unincorporated business organizations law along the dictates of a new theory.

The want of an underlying theory would not have been a problem if the 'reforms' had been simply a set of technical corrections. They were, of course, anything but mere technical modifications. The creation of the entirely new LLC form, one might reasonably conclude, should have been preceded by some generally agreed upon theoretical justification. But the phenomenal rise of the LLC form was driven by the result 'the elimination of personal liability for non-passive participants in a flow-through tax entity' not by any underlying theory (Hamilton 1995: 1065–7).

The failure to proceed from a widely accepted theoretical foundation led to some curiosities. One curiosity is the treatment of fiduciary duties and information disclosure rights under the Uniform Limited Liability Company Act (ULLCA) (Callison and Vestal 2000). In brief, ULLCA provides non-managing members the comprehensive information rights of partners, with the narrow fiduciary obligations of non-controlling shareholders.

Another curiosity is the treatment of partner agreements under RUPA. As a matter of general policy, RUPA adopts an agreement-primacy rule, under which the agreements of the partners are given primacy over the statutory provisions.[5] This general policy is consistent with the freedom of contract arguments advanced by several notable commentators. But the general rule is significantly undermined—in form at least—by the integration of a listing of points upon

---

[4] RUPA § 201.

[5] RUPA § 103(a): '. . . relations among the partners and between the partners and the partnership are governed by the partnership agreement. To the extent the partnership agreement does not otherwise provide, this [Act] governs relations among the partners and between the partners and the partnership.'

which the partnership agreement may not override the statute or may do so only within specified limits.[6] I have argued that these restrictions are not as significant as they might at first appear, but nevertheless the fact of the limitations is at odds with the freedom of contract analysis (Hillman, Vestal, and Weidner 2000: 38–53).

Also curious is the retroactive application of the new regime. RUPA provides[7] that it shall, after a rather brief transition period, apply to pre-existing partnerships (ibid. 385–9). RUPA has a clear preference for giving effect to the contractual agreements of the participants.[8] The retroactive application of RUPA clearly disregards the bargained for agreements of the participants in pre-existing partnerships. The retroactive application of RUPA is a curious break with the general policy (Vestal 1994; Ribstein 1993: 77–8).

One of my favourite curiosities is the RUPA approval of partner self-interest: '[a] partner does not violate a duty or obligation under this [Act] or under the partnership agreement merely because the partner's conduct furthers the partner's own self interest'.[9] There are two very different interpretations of the approval of self-interest; the language can be seen as either meaning nothing or meaning everything (Hillman, Vestal, and Weidner 2000: 204–5). Under the narrow interpretation, the language is merely an evidentiary rule that says very little.[10] Under the broader interpretation, the cited language is a broad-form insulation from liability based on the good faith and fair dealing standard.[11] The commentary and history from the section offer support to both interpretations, with perhaps a slight edge to the broader reading.[12] Professor Larry Mitchell (1996: 473–6) suggests yet a third reading of the self-interest language: that it establishes a benefit–detriment test for partners' self-interested transactions. Beyond the ambiguous endorsement of partners' pursuit of self-interest, the section contains a truly odd reordering of priorities as between the statute and the partnership agreement. Under RUPA § 103(a) the drafters clearly intended (with the limited exceptions provided in § 103(b)) for the partnership agreement to control over conflicting statutory provisions. But the self-interest provision reverses that rule by providing that 'A partner does not violate a duty or obligation . . . under the partnership agreement merely because the partner's conduct furthers the partner's own interest'.

---

   [6] RUPA § 103(b).   [7] RUPA § 1206.   [8] RUPA § 103(a).   [9] RUPA § 404(e).

   [10] Under this interpretation, the language could be paraphrased as: '[T]he fact that a partner directly personally benefits from the partner's conduct in the partnership context does not, without more, establish a violation of the partner's duties or obligations under RUPA or the partnership agreement.' Hillman, Vestal, and Weidner (2000: 204) (emphasis omitted).

   [11] I have suggested that: 'Under the broad interpretation, § 404(e) means that partners are free to pursue their short-term, individual self-interest without notice to or the consent of the partnership, subject only to the specific restrictions contained in the § 404(b) duty of loyalty in effect that the pursuit of self-interest cannot be a violation of the non-fiduciary obligation of good faith and fair dealing.' Hillman, Vestal and Weidner (2000: 204–5).

   [12] See ibid. The approval of self-interest language appears to have been an attempt to implement Professor Hillman's 'rebargaining' analysis (1987: 425, 442–6). Professor Weidner adopts the broader reading (2001: 1031, 8).

The curiosities—and others like them—are legacies of the failure to proceed from a widely accepted theoretical basis for such fundamental reforms.

12.2.2. Unexpected Gaps and Reversions: Non-Purposeful Grafting and Reshaping

> . . . there is still something in everything I do that defeats me, makes me dissatisfied, challenges me to further effort. Sometimes I rise above my level, sometimes I fall below it; but always I fall short of the things I dream. The human shape I can get now, almost with ease, so that it is lithe and grace-ful, or thick and strong; but often there is trouble with the hands and the claws,—painful things, that I dare not shape to freely. But it is in the subtle grafting and reshaping one must needs do to the brain that my trouble lies. The intelligence is often oddly low, with unaccountable blank ends, unex-pected gaps. And least satisfactory of all is something that I cannot touch, somewhere—I cannot determine where—in the seat of the emotions.
>
> (Wells 1896: 143)

The want of an underlying theory led our reformers to engage in non-purposeful grafting and reshaping in their experiments. Because there was not overall direc-tion to the effort, we ended up duplicating efforts in a confusing menagerie of forms. Why else would we have ended up with LLPs, LLCs, and a reworked form of the LP?

It also meant that in a rush to create the new forms we combined aspects of pre-existing forms in ways not well thought out or executed. I have already men-tioned the ULLCA dissonance between the information rights and fiduciary duties of non-managing members (Callison and Vestal 2000: 275–92). The problems were much broader. In the push to create the new business forms, the drafters freely borrowed from existing forms. At the lowest level, drafters have borrowed discrete terms and concepts from existing statutes. The Revised Uniform Partnership Act drafters, for example, borrowed various elements from the Uniform Commercial Code,[13] the Revised Model Business Corporation Act,[14] the Revised Uniform Limited Partnership Act,[15] the

---

[13] RUPA § 102 cmt. (§ 102 concepts and definitions of 'knowledge', 'notice', and 'notification' draw heavily upon UCC § 1-201(25)–(27)); RUPA § 103 cmt. 7 (§ 103(b)(5) is based on UCC § 1-102(3)); RUPA § 104 cmt. (§ 104 parallel to UCC § 1-103); RUPA § 106 cmt. (§ 106 'chief execu-tive office' concept is drawn from UCC § 9-103(3)(d)); RUPA § 403 cmt. 1 (§ 403(a) 'chief executive office' concept comes from UCC § 9-103(3)(d)).

[14] RUPA § 107 cmt. (§ 107 is adapted from RMBCA § 1.02); RUPA § 404 cmt. 1 (§ 404 title is drawn from RMBCA § 8.30); RUPA § 701 cmts. 6, 8, 10 (§ 701 procedure for purchase of dissociated partner's share is similar to dissenter buyout under RMBCA §§ 13.20–13.28, 13.31(b)); RUPA § 807 cmt. 2 (§ 807(a) revised priority rule initially in accord with RMBCA §§ 6.40(f), 14.05(a)).

[15] RUPA § 101 cmt. (§ 101(5) partnership agreement definition is adapted from RULPA § 101(9)); RUPA § 106 cmt. (rather disingenuously indicating that RULPA § 901 supports a proposition differ-ent from the main proposition but sufficiently analogous to lend support to RUPA § 106); RUPA § 107 cmt. (§ 107 is adapted from RULPA § 1106); RUPA § 402 cmt. (§ 402 language is suggested by RULPA § 605); RUPA § 403 cmt. 2 (§ 403(b) charge for document copies is in accord with RULPA § 105(b)); RUPA § 404 cmt. 6 (§ 404(f) language is drawn from RULPA § 107); RUPA § 502 cmt. (§ 502

Uniform Land Security Interest Act,[16] the Uniform Fraudulent Transfer Act,[17] the Restatement (Second) of Agency,[18] the Restatement (Second) of Contracts,[19] the Alabama Partnership Act,[20] the California Partnership Act,[21] the Delaware Code,[22] the Florida Partnership Act,[23] the Georgia Partnership Act,[24] and the Texas Partnership Act.[25]

At a somewhat higher level, drafters have modelled extensively revised forms on their precursors. The RUPA drafters, for example, quite appropriately started their drafting process with the existing Uniform Partnership Act.

At the highest level, drafters created entirely new forms of firm life by combining elements from different existing forms. Thus, the limited liability partnership can be seen as a form combining the risk attributes of a limited partnership or corporation with the control attributes of a general partnership. A limited liability sole proprietorship can be viewed as a form combining the risk attributes of a limited partnership with the control attributes of a sole proprietorship. Not surprisingly, the drafters of LLP statutes started with a partnership statute and engrafted limited liability protections. Both the American Bar Association and the National Conference of Commissioners on Uniform State Laws appointed committees to draft limited liability partnership acts; both groups based their work product on RUPA and simply added limited liability

---

limitation on partner's transferable interest compares to RULPA § 101(1) 'partnership interest' definition); RUPA § 601 cmt. 1 (§ 601 approach to dissociation is similar in approach to RULPA § 402); RUPA § 601 cmt. 5 (§ 601(4)(iii) is derived from RULPA § 402(9), § 601(4)(iv) is suggested by RULPA § 402(8)); RUPA § 601 cmt. 7 (§ 601(6)(iii) and (iv) are based substantially on RULPA § 601(4) and (5)); RUPA § 601 cmt. 9 (§ 601(8) is inspired by RULPA § 402(7)); RUPA § 601 cmt. 10 (§ 601(9) is based on RULPA § 402(10)); RUPA § 801 cmt. 8 (§ 801(5) language comes in part from RULPA § 802); RUPA § 807 cmt. 2 (§ 807(a) revised priority rule initially in accord with RULPA § 804).

[16] RUPA § 202 cmt. 3 (§ 202(c)(3)(v) language is taken from Unif. Land Security Interest Act § 211).

[17] RUPA § 302 cmt. 5 (§ 302(c) listed with cf. reference to Unif. Fraudulent Transfer Act §§ 8(a), 8(b)(2)).

[18] RUPA § 404 cmt. 1 ('Indeed, the law of partnership reflects the broader law of principal and agent, under which every agent is a fiduciary, see Restatement (Second) of Agency § 13 (1957)'); RUPA § 404 cmt. 2. (§ 404(b)(2) is derived from Restatement (Second) of Agency § 389, 391 (1957); § 404(b)(3) is derived from Restatement (Second) of Agency § 393 (1957)).

[19] RUPA § 404 cmt. 4 (citing Restatement (Second) of Contracts § 205 (1981) for proposition that '[t]he obligation of good faith and fair dealing is a contract concept, imposed on the partners because of the consensual nature of a partnership').

[20] RUPA § 204 cmt. 1 (§ 204 is influenced by Alabama partnership statute).

[21] RUPA § 303 cmt. 1 ('RUPA follows the lead of California . . . in authorizing the optional filing of statements of authority').

[22] RUPA § 803 cmt. (§ 803(c) is based on Delaware Laws, tit. 6, § 17-803).

[23] RUPA § 302 cmt. 7 (UPA § 10(2) omitted from RUPA following Florida model).

[24] RUPA § 101 cmt. (§ 101(2) debtor in bankruptcy definition is adapted from Ga. Code Ann. § 14-8-2(1)); RUPA § 104 cmt. (§ 104(b) is based on Ga. Code Ann. § 14-8-2(5)); RUPA § 204 cmt. 1 (§ 204 is influenced by Georgia partnership statute); RUPA § 302 cmt. 1 (§ 302 is adapted in part from Ga. Code Ann. § 14-8-10); RUPA § 302 cmt. 7 (UPA § 10(2) omitted from RUPA following Georgia model); RUPA § 303 cmt. 1 ('RUPA follows the lead of . . . Georgia in authorizing the optional filing of statements of authority').

[25] RUPA § 1006 cmt. (§ 1006 is similar to Tex. Rev. Civ. Stat. Ann. art 6132b-10.03 (Vernon Supp. 1994)).

provisions. In the various states, the pattern was to take the existing, UPA-based statute and engraft limited liability provisions.

Not all of these experiments have proved successful. At the first level, where the drafters have borrowed discrete terms or concepts, several of the resulting statutory provisions have been criticized as inappropriate. In one example, RUPA incorporates from the Uniform Commercial Code (UCC) the concept of a firm's 'chief executive office'[26] when determining what law governs the relations among the partners and between the partners and the partnership in a non-limited liability partnership.[27] This has been criticized as an inappropriate departure from the reasonable, widely accepted choice of law rules of the Restatement (Vestal 1995b; Hillman, Vestal, and Weidner 2000: 66–70). In a second case, RUPA diverges from the UPA on the treatment of knowledge and notice, and incorporates UCC-based concepts of 'knowledge', 'notice', and 'notification'.[28] But RUPA does not consistently use the concepts borrowed from the UCC and in substantive sections introduces additional concepts not found in the UCC.[29] The result is confusing and occasionally unclear. In a final example, RUPA uses a definition of 'partnership agreement'[30] adapted from the Revised Uniform Limited Partnership Act.[31] The UPA does not define the term.[32] The RUPA use of the RULPA-based definition of 'partnership agreement' has been criticized (Hillman, Vestal, and Weidner 2000: 22–5).

In the intermediate level, where the drafters have based revised forms on their statutory precursors, the process has caused some criticism. For example, by modelling RUPA on the UPA, the drafters worked from the combined statutory and common law regime of fiduciary duties governing the relations of the partners *inter se* (Vestal 1993; Hillman, Vestal, and Weidner 2000: 200). The drafters, however, made fundamental changes in the UPA regime, making the RUPA regime statutory and exclusive (Hillman, Vestal and Weidner 2000: 200–1), narrow (ibid. 201–7), temporally limited (ibid. 207–10), and broadly modifiable by the participants (ibid. 211–12).[33] To call the resulting regime

---

[26] RUPA § 106 cmt. ('the concept of a partnership's "chief executive office" is drawn from UCC Section 9-103(3)(d) ').

[27] RUPA § 106(a) ('Except as otherwise provided in subsection (b), the law of the jurisdiction in which a partnership has its chief executive office governs relations among the partners and between the partners and the partnership').

[28] Compare UPA § 3 with RUPA § 102 (Hillman, Vestal, and Weidner 2000: 31–3).   [29] Ibid.

[30] RUPA § 101(5) ('"Partnership agreement" means the agreement, whether written, oral, or implied, among the partners concerning the partnership, including amendments to the partnership agreement').

[31] RUPA § 101 cmt.

[32] The UPA does not define the term 'partnership agreement'. The term 'partnership agreement' is used only twice in the UPA. UPA §§ 32(1)(d), 38(2). More often, variations of the term are used. Several provisions refer to 'any agreement between the partners' or similar words. UPA §§ 18, 18(h), 19, 22(b), 38(1), 42, 43. In one section the UPA speaks of 'the agreement between the partners'. UPA §§ 31(1), 31(1)(d), 31(2).

[33] The character and extent of this difference is the subject of an ongoing academic debate. See Hynes (1995, 1997); Ribstein (1997); Vestal (1995b, 1997); Weidner (1995).

'fiduciary' has been called seriously misleading, but such is the legacy of the UPA and common law regime.

At the highest level, the combination of forms is suspect because the new forms extend limited liability for active participants and give participants flexibility in ordering their affairs *inter se* without articulating or justifying the costs, a problem discussed in the following section.

The want of an underlying theory also meant that we have a large amount of divergence at the state level, little of it purposefully directed. It will suffice to discuss two illustrations, among the most significant but not exhaustive of the list, the restrictions on partner modification of the statutory duty of loyalty and the question of whether the statutory listing of fiduciary duties is exclusive.

One of the RUPA restrictions on the partners' ability to override by their agreement statutory provisions relates to the duty of loyalty. The statute provides that the

> partnership agreement may not . . . eliminate the duty of loyalty under Section 404(b) or 603(b)(3), but:
>
> (i) the partnership agreement may identify specific types or categories of activities that do not violate the duty of loyalty, if not manifestly unreasonable; or
>
> (ii) all of the partners or a number or percentage specified in the partnership agreement may authorize or ratify, after full disclosure of all material facts, a specific act or transaction that otherwise would violate the duty of loyalty.[34]

This provision has been much criticized as being unclear and theoretically unsound (Hillman, Vestal, and Weidner 2000: 40–4). Neither has it been uniformly adopted without amendment by the various states. Two states, Delaware and Virginia, simply delete the duty of loyalty from the listing of sections as to which the partner's ability to override the statute is limited.[35] Alabama, Arizona, and Montana delete the 'manifestly unreasonable' qualifier.[36] Maryland takes a slightly different approach, eliminating the manifestly 'unreasonable qualifier' but adding: 'however, the partnership agreement may not be amended to expand or add any specific types or categories of activities that do not violate the duty of loyalty without the consent of all partners after full disclosure of all material facts.'[37] California, Idaho, and Washington move in the other direction by making the 'manifestly unreasonable' qualifier apply to both categorical exclusions and authorizations or ratifications of violations.[38] Oregon substitutes a different test, in this case an unconscionability test, for the 'manifestly unreasonable' test under RUPA.[39]

---

[34] RUPA § 103(b)(3).

[35] Va. Code Ann. § 50-73.81 (Supp. 1999); Del. Code Ann. tit. 6, § 15-103 (1999).

[36] Ala. Code § 10-8A-103 (Supp. 1999); Ariz. Rev. Stat. Ann. § 29-1003 (West 1997); Mont. Code Ann. § 35-10-106(2)(c).

[37] Md. Code Ann. § 9A-103(b)(3)(i) (West Supp. 1999).

[38] West's Ann. Cal. Corp. Code § 16103(b)(3); Idaho St. 53-3-103(b)(3); Wash. Rev. Code § 25.05.015(c)(ii) (Supp. 2000).

[39] Ore. R.S. § 67.015(2)(d). This is in line with the suggestion of Professor Hynes. Hynes (1995, 1997).

The second illustration of non-purposeful state variations is the question of whether the fiduciary duties listed in RUPA are exclusive. The RUPA intention is fairly clear: 'The only fiduciary duties a partner owes to the partnership and the other partners are the duty of loyalty and the duty of care set forth in subsections (b) and (c).'[40] Some adopting states have modified the RUPA language in ways which make, or arguably make, the fiduciary duty formulation non-exclusive. California, for example, deletes the word 'only' from the RUPA formulation, leaving open the interpretation that the California listing is not intended to be exclusive.[41] The legislative history gives some support to this interpretation.[42] Other states permit the non-exclusivity language with different degrees of confidence.[43]

Still other states change the statutory language in ways that allow the non-exclusive interpretation for a component of the statutory fiduciary duties. For example, RUPA defines the duty of loyalty in exclusive terms: 'A partner's duty of loyalty to the partnership and the other partners is limited to the following . . .'.[44] The Florida formulation is clearly non-exclusive: 'A partner's duty of loyalty to the partnership and the other partners includes, without limitation, the following . . .'.[45] Idaho and Oregon have a non-standard formulation only marginally weaker.[46]

12.2.3. The Persuasion Fades: An Uncertain Social Exchange

> These creatures of mine seemed strange and uncanny to you so soon as you began to observe them; but to me, just after I make them, they seem to be indisputably human beings. It's afterwards, as I observe them, that the persuasion fades.
>
> (Wells 1896: 143)

---

[40] RUPA § 404(a).　　　　[41] West's Ann. Cal. Corp. Code § 16404(a).

[42] The available California legislative history states that: '[CRUPA § 16404] establishes a comprehensive, but not exhaustive, definition of partnership fiduciary duties. A partner owes at least two duties to other partners and the partnership: a duty of loyalty and a duty of care. In addition, an obligation of good faith and fair dealing is imposed on partners.' Senate Rules Committee committee report from 27 Aug. 1996 hearing on AB 583 (emphasis supplied). This reading is also supported by the drafters' conclusion in the legislative history that 'the new fiduciary duty section makes no substantive change from prior law'. Senate Rules Committee committee report from 27 Aug. 1996 hearing on AB 583. Prior law, based on the UPA, would have included both statutory and common law components. Hillman, Vestal, and Weidner (2000: 212).

[43] Idaho, for example, adopted the formulation: '[t]he fiduciary duties a partner owes to the partnership and the other partners are the duty of loyalty and the duty of care set forth in subsections (b) and (c) of this section'; a non-standard provision that could be argued to be non-exclusive but which is more easily explained by Idaho's premature adoption of the penultimate draft of RUPA. Idaho St. § 53-3-404(a). Texas adopted a different formulation: 'A partner owes . . . (1) a duty of loyalty; and (2) a duty of care'. Tex. Rev. Civ. Stat. Ann. art 6132b-4.04(a) (West 1995). Like Wyoming, Texas abandoned the RUPA evolutionary path at an earlier draft.

[44] RUPA § 404(b).　　　　[45] Fla. Stat. Ann. § 620.8404(1).

[46] Idaho St. § 53-3-404(b) ('A partner's duty of loyalty to the partnership and the other partners includes the following . . . '.); Ore. Rev. St. § 67.155(2) ('A partner's duty of loyalty to the partnership and the other partners includes the following . . . '.).

As a matter of policy, perhaps the most disappointing result of the decade of reform is that there has been no social exchange in the process; social costs have been generated without any demonstrable and compensating social benefit.

Because we proceeded with reform without an underlying theory, there was, of course, no meaningful debate over that theory. Because there was no debate over the underlying theory, there was no public resolution of the allocation of social costs and benefits. The result is a series of substantial, non-consensual transfers of value. One such transfer was to partners, in the first instance lawyers and accountants, in the form of limited liability.[47] The reforms essentially gave such parties the benefits of limited liability, for those migrating from general partnerships, favourable tax treatment, for those migrating from corporations, and control, for those migrating from limited partnerships. Such transfers were from potential plaintiffs, especially tort plaintiffs, and from society in the form of a reallocation of the tax burden.

There is no clear compensating benefit to society from these transfers, except the perennial promise to create a better climate for business. Indeed, the very fact that LLPs and LLCs are so popular suggests to some commentators that the forms fail to strike an appropriate balance between private gain and social benefit. As Professors Bratton and McCahery (1997) have made clear, at the very least we have inadequate information upon which to base an extension of limited liability.[48]

Another social cost came in the loss of uniformity in business association laws. What is the compensating social benefit? Other than Professor Ribstein, who suggests that the atomization will lead to a type of spontaneous efficient uniformity, none is suggested.[49] While the path of atomization may be an eloquent argument for the federalization of business organization laws, it is a clear social cost for which no compensating benefit is even hinted at.

A final social cost came in the form of a widening gap between the popular conception of the partnership relationship and the legal restatement of the concept. It is my sense that the popular conception of the partnership relationship is much closer to the tort-based, relationship-driven model under the UPA and the common law than it is to the contract-based, immediate self-interest model under RUPA. When the reforms abandoned the old regime they both gave up a model of great value and created a fundamental dissonance between popular understanding and legal form. Both are regrettable changes, not reform.

---

[47] Professor Hamilton (1995: 1090–1) has characterized the move from a narrow to a broad shield against liability as 'gross overreaching by members of the legal profession'. Seemingly, nothing was expected. The debates of the various state legislatures evidence a pattern of shockingly little debate on these substantial changes in the law: 'The argument that this broadening of limited liability is necessary to make the shield of limited liability against malpractice claims more perfect seems to me a pretext for quietly obtaining limited liability for all partners in general partnerships without telling the world about it.'

[48] Professors Bratton and McCahery's (1997) analysis calls into serious question the economic efficiency justifications for the expansion of limited liability.

[49] I have offered a somewhat critical critique (1995a) of the Kobayashi and Ribstein spontaneous efficient uniformity analysis.

12.3. CONCLUSION: DRAWING NEAR THE FASTNESS

Cravings, instincts, desires that harm humanity, a strange hidden reservoir to burst forth suddenly and inundate the whole being of the creature with anger, hate, or fear. . . . First one animal trait, then another, creeps to the surface and stares out at me. But I will conquer yet! Each time I dip a living creature into the bath of burning pain, I say 'This time I will burn out all the animal; this time I will make a rational creature of my own. After all, what is ten years? Man has been a hundred thousand in the making.' He thought darkly. 'But I am drawing near the fastness.'

(Wells 1896: 143–4)

As with Dr Moreau's work in vivisection, our work in reform was hardly an experiment. We proceeded without an underlying theory of where we were headed, without a series of agreed upon goals or expectations. We made changes because they were possible, because the end result was new and different; because it could be done.

But now the persuasion fades. We are left, at the end of a tumultuous decade, with a system less uniform, less clear, less predictable, and less justifiable, than that which it replaced. We have given away significant social value with little or no compensation. And, having had no clear goals we are left, like Dr Moreau, with no clear end point—perhaps it will be the completion of the Revised Revised Uniform Limited Partnership Act, perhaps we will jump into a round of single form business entity experiments.

The decade was one of great change and little accomplishment. But 'after all', as Dr Moreau asked, 'what is ten years?'.

REFERENCES

American Bar Association (1987), 'Uniform Partnership Act Revision Subcommittee of the Committee on Partnerships and Unincorporated Business Organizations: Section of Business Law, American Bar Association, Should the Uniform Partnership Act be Revised', *Business Lawyer* 43: 121.

Bratton, W. W., and McCahery, J. A. (1997), 'An Inquiry into the Efficiency of the Limited Liability Company: Of Theory of the Firm and Regulatory Competition', *Washington and Lee Law Review* 54: 629.

Callison, J. W., and Vestal, A. W. (2000), '"They've Created a Lamb with Mandibles of Death": Secrecy, Disclosure and Fiduciary Duties in Limited Liability Firms', *Indiana Law Journal* 76: 271.

Hamilton, R. W. (1995), 'Registered Limited Liability Partnerships: Present at the Birth (Nearly)', *University of Colorado Law Review* 66: 1065.

Hillman, R. W. (1987), 'Private Ordering within Partnerships', *University of Miami Law Review* 41: 425.

——Vestal, A. W., and Weidner, D. J. (2000), *The Revised Uniform Partnership Act*, St. Paul: West Group

Hynes, J. D. (1995), 'Fiduciary Duties and RUPA: An Inquiry into Freedom of Contract', *Law and Contemporary Problems* 58: 29.

—— (1997), 'Freedom of Contract, Fiduciary Duties, and Partnerships: The Bargain Principle and the Law of Agency', *Washington and Lee Law Review* 54: 439.

Mitchell, L. E. (1996), 'The Naked Emperor: Arguing about RUPA's Fiduciary Provisions', *Washington and Lee Law Review* 54: 465.

Oesterle, D. A. (1995), 'Subcurrents in LLC Statutes: Limiting the Discretion of State Courts to Restructure the Internal Affairs of a Small Business', *University of Colorado Law Review* 66: 881.

Ribstein, L. E. (1993), 'The Revised Uniform Partnership Act: Not Ready for Prime Time', *Business Lawyer* 49: 45.

—— (1997), 'Fiduciary Duty Contracts in Unincorporated Firms', *Washington and Lee Law Review* 54: 537.

Vestal, A. W. (1993), 'Fundamental Contractarian Error in the Revised Uniform Partnership Act of 1992', *Boston University Law Review* 73: 523.

—— (1994), 'Should the Revised Uniform Partnership Act of 1994 Really be Retroactive?', *Business Lawyer* 50: 267.

—— (1995a), 'Advancing the Search for Compromise: A Response to Professor Hynes', *Law and Contemporary Problems* 58: 55.

—— (1995b), 'Choice of Law and the Fiduciary Duties of Partners under the Revised Uniform Partnership Act', *Iowa Law Review* 79: 219.

—— (1997), ' "Assume a Rather Large Boat . . .": The Mess We Have Made of Partnership Law', *Washington and Lee Law Review* 53: 487.

Weidner, D. J. (1995), 'RUPA and Fiduciary Duty: The Texture of Relationship', *Law and Contemporary Problems* 58: 81.

—— (2001), 'Partnership and LLP Law Reform Benefits and Risks: The U.S. Experience', *Iowa Journal of Corporation Law* 27: 1031.

Wells, H. G. (1896), *The Island of Doctor Moreau*, London: William Heinemann.

13

Pitfalls in Partnership Law Reform: Some US Experience

DONALD J. WEIDNER*

13.1. Introduction

I have been asked to address major pitfalls in partnership law reform, based on the Revised Uniform Partnership Act[1] experience. I think the two major pitfalls are a failure to learn from history and a failure to state clear, concise, and coherent principles. The best way to avoid these pitfalls is by properly harnessing available expertise and political support.

13.2. Failure to Learn From History

There are numerous examples of a failure to learn from history. I begin with 'the D word', RUPA's most notable failure to abandon a problematic approach.

13.2.1. Dissociation and Dissolution

Prior to the Uniform Partnership Act,[2] the term 'dissolution' was considered extremely confusing. The UPA, which borrowed shamelessly from the English Partnership Act of 1890, tried to resolve the confusion in two ways. First, it defined what 'dissolution' was. Second, it stated what dissolution was not. Dissolution was defined as 'the change in the relation of the partners caused by any partner ceasing to be associated in the carrying on as distinguished from the winding up of the business'.[3] Dissolution was not the same as termination, said the statute, which does not take place until the winding up of the partnership is complete.[4]

Seventy-five years later, by the time the RUPA project was getting under way, it was clear that the term 'dissolution' was still causing great confusion. For years, I submitted Drafts to the Committee without the word 'dissolution'. I had two basic reasons. First, however beautiful the initiated may have regarded the

---

* Dean Weidner served as the Reporter for the Revised Uniform Partnership Act from 1987 to 1994. The author wishes to express his appreciation to Robert W. Hillman for his helpful comments.
[1] RUPA, 6 ULA 1 (Supp. 2001)(hereinafter 'RUPA').
[2] UPA, 6 ULA 125 (1995)(hereinafter 'UPA').   [3] UPA § 29.   [4] UPA § 30.

'dissolution' construct, it simply caused too much confusion. Second, and I think this is part of what causes the confusion, the word itself is inapt, whether you view partnerships as aggregates or as entities. According to my *Oxford English Dictionary*, dissolution is 'separation into parts or constituent elements; reduction of any body or mass to elements or atoms; destruction of the existing condition; disintegration, decomposition.'

When a partner is being bought out, there is no 'atomization' or 'disintegration' of the partnership. The partnership continues, but without the departing partner. Even if a departure causes the commencement of a winding up of the business, there is no immediate atomization or disintegration. The partnership continues, but towards a new purpose, the winding up of the business. The departure simply causes a contraction in scope. The old statutory definition had the basic concept right, but the wrong word was chosen to carry the message of a contraction in scope. An inadequate statutory structure then was built upon the inapt word. The structure was inadequate because it failed to clarify the distinction between buyouts and wind-ups.

For years, the Committee worked from drafts of new breakup provisions that did not contain 'the D word'. The Committee drafts also contained a new structure that had separate articles for buyouts and wind-ups. The buyout in particular was defined with some specificity. Near the end of the project, certain members of an American Bar Association subcommittee stated that a partnership act without the word 'dissolution' would be so radical that it might not be adopted by the states. They did not want to change the new statutory structure or its substantive rules; they simply wanted the word 'dissolution' back in the statute. I was asked to add the word 'dissolution' to the subsequent draft so the Committee could 'see what it looks like'. I added the word in such a way as to make clear that it was unnecessary. Thus, wherever the previous drafts had stated that an event caused a winding up, the next draft said that the event caused a 'dissolution and winding up'. I added the word 'dissolution' as an obvious redundancy, so that it could easily be edited out, I thought, as soon as the scales fell from the eyes of the members of the Drafting Committee.

Not a single scale could be heard to fall. The Drafting Committee loved the new language, even though, as my fifteen-year-old daughter might say, it came from The Department of Redundancy and Needless Repetition Department. The Drafting Committee thought the final product was a wonderful compromise. I got the statute as I had structured it, and as the Committee had worked with it for years, with a switchboard article on departures and separate articles on buyouts and wind-ups, and the ABA subcommittee members got the word 'dissolution' reinstated. Most importantly, RUPA sounded less radical.

I take some small comfort in the fact that the State of Texas borrowed from our early efforts and adopted a revised partnership act that does not use the term 'dissolution'.[5] Despite the fact that this new act has been in force for a number

---

[5] See Tex. Rev. Civ. Stat. Ann. art 6132b-6.01.

of years, Professor Hamilton reports that the skies over Texas have not yet fallen. Nor, I hasten to concede, have the skies fallen over the now more than thirty jurisdictions that have adopted RUPA. On the other hand, thêre is needless confusion created by retaining a word that has always caused confusion and, without definition, changing its meaning. As we are about to see, the first revision of RUPA fell prey to this confusion.

13.2.2. Limited Liability

The RUPA Drafting Committee, and subsequent related law reform efforts in the United States, have been remarkably squeamish about the issue of limited liability. Like Nietzsche's news of the death of God, the reality of free access to limited liability has taken quite a while to sink in. By the time the RUPA project was commissioned, limited liability was widely available through the corporate form. It was also widely available through the limited partnership form, as evidenced by the fact that billions of dollars had been raised in limited partnerships that had sole corporate general partners. Our tax law had even come to conclude that these limited partnerships should be taxed as any other partnership.

Nevertheless, at the beginning of the RUPA project in 1987, the idea of making limited liability available to general partnerships was summarily rejected. In a memorandum I prepared for the Drafting Committee and published as an article in 1988, I noted that 'the state policy in favor of imposing personal liability on a profit sharer who takes part in the control of an unincorporated business has all but vanished' (Weidner 1988: 32). I suggested to the Committee that a system of registration could be created that would provide limited liability for general partners (ibid.). The suggestion was considered too radical, far more radical than the elimination of the word 'dissolution'. The Committee and the National Conference of Commissioners on Uniform State Laws (NCCUSL) kept to that opinion. Accordingly, when RUPA was 'finalized' in 1994, it contained no provisions for the limited liability of partners.

The RUPA project failed to keep pace with external developments on limited liability. The first limited liability partnership act, offering a limited liability shield to general partners, was adopted by Texas in 1991. Large law and accounting firms that were organized as partnerships wanted to eliminate the possibility of huge personal liability for professional malpractice claims arising out of a nationwide savings and loan association crisis. Within short order, LLP statutes were sweeping the nation. At the same time, limited liability company statutes were sweeping the nation. These statutes, in which the entity is a 'company' and the individuals are 'members', created entities that look very much like limited partnerships without general partners. It became clear that the general partnership form might be relegated to a very minor role, along with the aggregate theory, at least for all but inadvertent partnerships, if it did not offer a limited liability shield. Accordingly, in 1996, a mere two years after RUPA was 'finalized', limited liability partnership provisions were added.

The joinder of the limited liability partnership provisions to the rest of RUPA is not always pretty. Much is left to the Official Comments (Hillman, Vestal, and Weidner 2001). Furthermore, the Official Comments are inconsistent in the way they discuss partnership continuity. The Comments to § 1001 appear to disregard RUPA's new concept of dissociation and new role for the term 'dissolution' and reflect more of a UPA conception that a partnership dissolves every time a member leaves. In addition, the Comments are inconsistent with the concept, both under the UPA and under RUPA, that a partnership continues until, and only until, its winding up is complete.

Inconsistency with RUPA's concepts of dissociation and dissolution is reflected in the statement that 'a partnership that dissolves but whose business is continued under a business continuation agreement retains its status as a limited liability partnership without the need to refile a new statement'.[6] Under RUPA, if the partnership continues its business pursuant to a continuation agreement, there is no dissolution. Dissolution is the commencement of a winding up.[7] If the partners have contracted away the commencement of winding up when a partner departs, as they are permitted to do,[8] they have contracted away dissolution.

Inconsistency with the concept that a partnership continues only until its winding up is complete is reflected in the statement that 'limited liability partnership status remains even though a partnership may be dissolved, wound up, and terminated'.[9] A partnership is terminated when 'the winding up of its business is completed'.[10] Part of the winding up is the extinguishment of the partnership's obligations. It is technically inconsistent to suggest that partnership status continues after all the partnership's business has been concluded. Perhaps the inconsistency is an understandable effort to address the difficult issue of partnership termination.[11]

My strong recommendation for English and continental efforts is that the limited liability provisions be made a part of the core statutory undertaking. Stare the reality of limited liability in the eye and address it at the outset. Otherwise, a special limited liability SWAT team may crash into the statute at a later date and leave things a bit untidy, as SWAT teams tend to do. Much more importantly, if the partnership form cannot compete with other forms that offer limited liability, it will die on the vine. Limited liability companies have surpassed partnerships in their frequency of adoption, in part because that form delivered freedom from personal liability sooner than the partnership form. In

---

[6] RUPA § 1001, Official Comments (sixth paragraph).　　　　[7] RUPA § 801.

[8] RUPA § 103.　　　　[9] RUPA § 1001, Official Comments (sixth paragraph).

[10] RUPA § 802(a).

[11] It was difficult to determine when a partnership terminated under the UPA, and it continues to be a problem under RUPA. Even after all parties believe that a partnership's business has been completed, a liability may be asserted or an asset may be discovered. One way of responding is to say that the initial appearance of termination was deceptive. With respect to the liability shield, another response is to state—as the Official Comments appear to conclude—that each partner has a shield that continues even if the partnership no longer exists.

just a few years, people adopted the limited liability company, got used to it, and are sticking with it. The limited liability partnership now offers just as much, but the offer came too late.

13.2.3. Default Rule on Limited Liability

Default rules set on unlimited personal liability reflect how the law is tied to history. There are two separate questions with regard to limited liability. One is whether limited liability is available. Another is what is the default rule concerning limited liability. If limited liability is available by a perfunctory filing, why not reduce transaction costs and make it available without the filing? Stated differently, how formalistic will we continue to be?

A current 'hot' issue in the United States is the default rule for general partners in limited partnerships.[12] It is clear that general partners in limited partnerships can incorporate to avoid liability. It is also clear that limited partnerships can register as limited liability partnerships, thus eliminating the personal liability of the general partner. And, it is clear that the limited partnership form can be avoided entirely by using a limited liability company to obtain limited liability. Indeed, it also is now clear that the limited partnership form can be avoided by the use of a general partnership that registers as a limited liability partnership. Nevertheless, current law reform efforts are not yet at the point of saying that the default rule is limited liability for the general partner in a limited partnership. It simply sounds too radical. The emperor may have shed most of his clothes, we are willing to say, but surely he is wearing a thong.

13.2.4. At-Will Partnerships

A fundamental purpose of RUPA was to provide stability for partnerships that have contracted for stability. Because RUPA continued traditional terminology concerning 'at-will' partnerships, RUPA's definition of partnerships that have contracted for stability is unnecessarily narrow.

Under RUPA, a dissociation from an at-will partnership results in the winding up of the partnership, or, if you prefer, results in a 'dissolution and winding up'.[13] 'Partnership at-will' is defined as 'a partnership in which the partners have not agreed to remain partners until the expiration of a definite term or the completion of a particular undertaking'.[14] This definition does not embrace the full spectrum of partnerships that have contracted for stability. For example, consider a partnership agreement that provides that the partnership will continue until a majority of partners decides to the contrary. Has a 'definite

---

[12] See Meislik (2001: 8): 'No proposed revision to the Revised Uniform Limited Partnership Act (RULPA) has engendered more debate than whether, by default, general partners should have limited liability for the debts and obligations of the partnership.'

[13] RUPA § 801(1).   [14] RUPA § 101(8).

term' or 'particular undertaking' been provided for? For further example, consider a partnership formed to continue in perpetuity. Is there a 'definite term' or 'particular undertaking'? If not, the partnership is 'at-will' and can be wound up or 'dissolved and wound up', by any partner at any time. Yet there seems to be no reason to decline enforcement to a partnership agreement that states that it shall continue until a majority decides otherwise. Nor does there seem to be a compelling reason to preclude an agreement for a perpetual partnership (Hillman 1995:10–12).

13.2.5. Not-For-Profit Associations

RUPA should have been more accommodating to unincorporated associates seeking to opt in to the partnership form. RUPA provides that a partnership is an 'association of two or more persons to carry on a business for profit'.[15] The Official Comments hammer the point home to non-profits by stating that '[a]n unincorporated nonprofit organization is not a partnership under RUPA, even if it qualifies as a business, because it is not a "for profit" organization.'[16]

There does not seem to be any policy reason why other associations, falling just outside the traditional definition of partnership, or falling in a grey area, should not be allowed to opt in to the partnership form. The State of Delaware so concluded. When it adopted RUPA in 1999, it added supplementary language to the definition of partnership that provided that 'the association of two or more persons . . . to carry on any purpose or activity not for profit, forms a partnership when the persons intend to form a partnership'.[17] If a non-profit association can opt in to the partnership form, filing as a limited liability partnership should eliminate personal liability of the associates, at least in the absence of countervailing policy external to partnership law. Make the partnership form as useful as other forms or contribute to it becoming an endangered species.

13.2.6. Unintended Consequence of Entity Theory

When the UPA was being drafted at the turn of the last century, an entity approach was avoided in part because it was feared that it would be accompanied by or result in a diminution of fiduciary duties. Time has proved these concerns prophetic. RUPA's move to an entity theory has been accompanied by a significant reduction in the fiduciary duties of partners.

The reduction in fiduciary duties is consonant with the new rules on suits against partnerships and partners. In short, partners have assumed a lesser status with regard to partnership obligations to third parties (Hillman, Vestal, and Weidner 2001: 154–7).[18] The obligations are primarily those of the partnership.

---

[15] RUPA § 202(a).   [16] RUPA § 202(a), Official Comment 2.
[17] Del. Code tit. 6, § 15-202(a).   [18] RUPA § 307(d).

The assets are its. It and its assets should be pursued first. The partners are more like guarantors. In the case of a limited liability partnership, the partners are not even guarantors. In addition, partners are now third parties who can bring suit against the partnership and the other partners.[19]

Consider the impact these changes have on obligations within the partnership. What of the duties owed to partners to protect their interests in the partnership? Are those duties not now primarily those of the partnership? Are the partners themselves not now more supporting players? At the very least, it is now clearer that they can contract to be merely supporting players, guarantors whose obligations are limited to the letter of their guaranty.

13.3. FAILURE TO STATE CLEAR, CONCISE, AND COHERENT PRINCIPLES

The second major pitfall is the failure to state clear, concise, and coherent principles. Statutes can be too long. Statutory provisions can be too complex. Throughout the RUPA drafting process, there were participants who believed that we should attempt to answer, in the statute, every question that was raised in our discussions. Although a majority were not of this view, they did appear to believe that there was little or no downside to a very lengthy statute. I disagree. Statutes, or regulations, can be too long and too complex.

The state law of partnerships should have learned from the unfortunate experience of the tax law of partnerships. Some of the basic regulations on the taxation of partnerships and limited liability companies are hideously complex.[20] Lawyers, accountants, and business people who should be able to read the regulations on partnership allocations with relative ease now do not read them at all because of their complexity. Standard-form partnership, limited partnership, and limited liability company agreements contain complex boilerplate tax language that responds to this complexity. Most lawyers dealing with these agreements will never understand their complex allocation provisions, even though those provisions direct the economic consequences of the partnership. That, I believe, is unhealthy for lawyers and for the clients they serve. It also is unhealthy for the business form when an agreement among the parties becomes more like a government registration than a clear statement of the relationship.

13.3.1. Fiduciary Duty and Related Rules

The appropriateness of RUPA's policy restricting the fiduciary duties of partners has been discussed at length elsewhere.[21] I focus here on the length, complexity, and coherence of RUPA's provisions implementing this policy rather than on the policy itself.

---

[19] RUPA § 405(b). [20] See the Treasury Regulations under Int. Rev. Code of 1986, § 704(b).
[21] For extensive citations to authority including statutory variations, see generally Hillman et al. (2001: 200–15).

RUPA's new rules on fiduciary duties and related obligations are much longer than similar provisions under the UPA and are dispersed throughout RUPA.[22] The duty of loyalty and the obligation of good faith and fair dealing are set out in § 404. Partnership rights and duties with respect to information are contained in § 403. Separate mandatory minima on these rights and duties are explained in § 103(b). How they are contracted or terminated on dissociation is discussed in § 603.

These rules are more complex than they should be. To answer a question about a partner's duty on a breakup, and the extent to which it can be contracted away, all four sections may need to be consulted. Reading RUPA on this point is a little like reading the Internal Revenue Code when it is necessary to flip from provision to provision to get a complete statement of the applicable rule.

These rules also lack a clear statement of principle. It is not clear why certain rules are considered fiduciary and others are not. For example, it is not clear why the duty to provide information is not a fiduciary duty,[23] whereas the duty to share a partnership opportunity is.[24] What is the qualitative difference between a duty to share information about an opportunity and the duty to share that opportunity? This raises a broader point. The duties are stated as if they are separate, yet there is no 'bright line' separating them.

Interestingly, with all the complexity, the provision that I think is the clearest statement of principle has been lost in the shuffle. Early in the RUPA project, proponents of reining in fiduciary duties claimed that the biggest problem with calling a partner a fiduciary was that courts were likely to require a partner to be a selfless trustee. Case law, on the other hand, had recognized that there is a legitimate sphere for partners to pursue self-interest.

This basic problem was addressed in § 404(e), which provides: 'A partner does not violate a duty or obligation under this [Act] or under the partnership agreement merely because the partner's conduct furthers the partner's own interest.' This is a clear statement of principle that a partner need not be a disinterested trustee. Furthermore, it applies across the life of a partnership, from formation, through operation, to buyout or liquidation. It also avoids an unnecessary distinction between fiduciary duties and other obligations. Finally, it avoids drawing bright lines among fiduciary duties where none exists.[25] It is, in

---

[22] For an integrated discussion of these provisions, see Weidner (1997: 899–914).

[23] RUPA § 403.   [24] RUPA § 404.

[25] See also Del. Code Tit. 6, § 17-1101(d), which has been used as a model for other statutes, including limited liability company statutes:

> To the extent that, at law or in equity, a partner or other person has duties (including fiduciary duties) and liabilities relating thereto to a limited partnership or to another partner, (1) any such partner or other person acting under a partnership agreement shall not be liable to the limited partnership or to any such other partner for the partner's or other person's good faith reliance on the provisions of such partnership agreement, and (2) the partner's or other person's duties and liabilities may be expanded or restricted by provisions in a partnership agreement.

A related provision is Del. Code Tit. 6, § 17-1101(c): 'It is the policy of this chapter to give maximum effect to the principle of freedom of contract and to the enforceability of partnership agreements.'

short, a thoroughly appealing proposition that responds to a basic concern about fiduciary duty.[26]

Unfortunately, this rule acknowledging the legitimate pursuit of self-interest is lost in the shuffle of other provisions. The larger point is that the structure of the statute matters. Physical elevation within a statute can help, in the same way that placing a statute in a particular book can be influential in The Netherlands. The longer the statute, the easier it is to get overlooked.

Another RUPA provision that limits the notion of partner as trustee has also been relatively overlooked. Under the UPA, it had been said that a partnership is like a trust, and, like a trust, it continues until there is an accounting resolving that the trust purpose has been satisfied. This notion had been applied to require a formal accounting, in which all claims could be asserted, no matter how much time had passed.[27] This is changed under RUPA.

Stated somewhat differently, there is a downside to a partner's new freedom under RUPA to sue the other partners and the partnership. Once a partner's claim accrues, limitation periods start running. The partner must use it or lose it. This downside is in § 405(c), which provides that the accrual of any actions, and time limitations thereon, are governed by other law. RUPA also makes clear that a 'right to an accounting upon a dissolution and winding up does not revive a claim barred by law'.[28] The trust no longer continues until the trust purpose is satisfied. The partner is no longer a trustee.

13.3.2. Joint and Several Liability

RUPA at best overstates the situation when it declares that 'all partners are liable jointly and severally for all the obligations of the partnership unless otherwise agreed by the claimant or provided by law'.[29] This declaration of joint and several liability is inconsistent with other provisions reflecting RUPA's move to an entity theory.

Classically, a liability is 'joint and several' only if the obligee has the option of suing either all the obligors or any individual obligor or group of obligors. The classic idea is that each obligor is individually liable for the entire obligation and can be pursued independently of any of the other obligors (double recovery by the obligee, of course, not being permitted). Under pure joint and several liability, a plaintiff may select any one of the possible defendants, or any group of defendants, for suit. Thus, if a partnership obligation were a classic

---

[26] Not everyone is enamoured with this provision. Even though the direction of its thrust is clear, there are those who believe that the magnitude of the thrust is not clear enough. See Vestal, Chapter 12, this volume. It seems appropriate to emphasize that statutes cannot be drafted to answer all questions. Moreover, fiduciary decisions under RUPA will be informed by fiduciary decisions in other substantive areas.

[27] Another helpful analogy is to a mortgagor's equity of redemption, which does not generally disappear, affirmative action must be taken to foreclose it.

[28] RUPA § 405(c)(second sentence). See *Fike v. Ruger*, 754 A.2d 254 (Del. Ch. 1999).

[29] RUPA § 306(a).

joint and several liability, a plaintiff could proceed directly against any partner, recover a judgment against that partner, and levy execution against that partner. There would be no requirement to join or to proceed against the partnership or any of the other partners or to seek satisfaction first out of partnership assets.

The declaration of joint and several liability collides with the provisions on post-judgment relief stating that creditors must pursue partnership assets before pursuing the separate assets of partners.[30] Under RUPA, a partner's separate assets can be pursued first, but only by special contract. The partner must have agreed 'that the creditor need not exhaust partnership assets'.[31] The Official Comments explain that the post-judgment relief rule 'respects the concept of the partnership as an entity and makes partners more in the nature of guarantors than principal debtors on every partnership debt'.[32] Note the incoherence. Partners are not even principal debtors much less principal debtors who are jointly and severally liable.

As the introductory clause to the declaration of joint and several liability recognizes,[33] if a partnership is a limited liability partnership, all semblance of joint and several liability vanishes. Indeed, all liability for partnership obligations vanishes. RUPA declares that an 'obligation of a partnership incurred while the partnership is a limited liability partnership . . . is solely the obligation of the partnership. A partner is not personally liable, directly or indirectly, by way of contribution or otherwise, for such a partnership obligation solely by reason of being or so acting as a partner.'[34]

13.3.3. Failure with the Resulting Mixed Grill of Statutory Offerings

Today in the United States, there is a myriad of business forms, many of which accomplish, or can be made to accomplish, the same thing. There is no coherent rationale for the current cafeteria plan.

Relatively few of the specifics of business law reform of the past few decades seem to have registered on judges. To the extent this is because relatively few disputes wind up in court, this is not necessarily bad. One goal of statutes that contain a more complete set of rules is to save people the expense of litigating. On the other hand, something more may be going on, something much less positive. When matters do get to court, I am not confident that all the relevant statutes will be consulted. There are too many of them, they are too different, and no one wants to spend much time on them. Only experienced practitioners who specialize in business matters are very familiar with them. Many judges have little or no business experience. They may have been elected or they may have been appointed because of their positions on social, not business issues.

---

[30] RUPA § 307(d).
[31] RUPA § 307(d)(3). A creditor also may proceed directly against a partner's assets if liability is imposed on the partner by law or contract independent of the existence of the partnership.
[32] RUPA § 307, Official Comment 4.   [33] RUPA § 306(a).   [34] RUPA § 306(c).

Judges cannot be expected to spend a great deal of time learning the minutiae of business organization statutes. As many of them see it, there are simply too few cases to justify much attention, even in continuing judicial education programmes.

Complexity and incoherence may cause judges to apply a meta-theory all their own, perhaps by returning to the law of agency. Interestingly, as the ALI's Restatement of Agency project is unfolding, it has taken a very different approach to fiduciary issues than the approach taken in recent business law statutes designed to rein in fiduciary duties. The black-letter fiduciary duty provisions of the new Restatement of Agency are drafted almost as if the law-and-economics and freedom-of-contract movements of the past several decades had not taken place. It would be ironic if the individual or collective complexity or incoherence of business statutes designed to limit fiduciary duties and facilitate contracting out caused them to lose influence to the 'old time religion' of the Restatement of Agency. On the other hand, it would not be surprising for courts and practitioners alike to be attracted to the Restatement's clear and coherent statement of familiar doctrine.

The incoherence of law also affects how business law is practised. As transactions are entered into, most practitioners do not want to spend much time choosing a form. Business law experts are likely to be familiar with each form, and within a particular jurisdiction, are likely to be familiar with that state's variant, and how it differs from Delaware. But what of the general practitioner, who is often the person consulted by a start-up business? The general practitioner does not want to parse three or four statutes simply to select a business entity. The longer the statutes get, the more difficult they are to read, the less people will read them. Practitioners will pick one form and ignore the others.

Complexity and incoherence also affect the process of law reform. I had a recent experience on a law reform project in Florida that was disconcerting. A group of lawyers participating in a continuing legal education programme decided that we ought to dramatically overhaul our limited liability company law. Florida had adopted the second LLC law in the nation, and it was a rough early attempt in need of major overhaul. For example, it contained default rules among members that were most inappropriate—most of them were based on members' capital accounts. I was pleased to be asked to serve on the Drafting Committee, which I did, along with a number of distinguished and sophisticated attorneys. The Committee completely rewrote the statute in just a few months, over and among a relative handful of conference calls, and it was promptly enacted. The new statute made some important improvements but is flawed in important ways.

The two principal business forms, the partnership and the corporation, each had its own constituency on the LLC project. Each constituency wanted familiar doctrine inserted into the LLC statute. Consider the ever-controversial provisions on fiduciary duties and related obligations. Real estate and estate planning specialists were most familiar and most comfortable with the law of partnerships and limited partnerships. And so, when it came to state the rules on the fiduciary duties of members in limited liability companies, they wanted RUPA's rules put in the LLC statute. On the other hand, corporate specialists were most familiar and most comfortable with the law of corporations, and wanted corporate rules put in the LLC statute. The result was a compromise. Both were added. The provisions do not cohere. In short, RUPA protects partners from liability for breach of fiduciary duties by defining the duties narrowly and by providing that they can be contracted away. Corporate law protects managers from liability for breach of fiduciary duties by limiting shareholder remedies against managers. The new Florida LLC statute took a belt-and-braces approach by including both the partnership rules limiting duty and the corporate rules limiting remedies for breach of duty. The joinder is not at all pretty. Each set of rules is inserted as if the other does not exist. The point is that even business law experts active and dedicated enough to be influential in law reform are exhibiting dysfunctional behaviour because of the complexity and incoherence of business laws. The problem is compounded by the fact that, at the state level, there may be no effective structure for harnessing expertise in statutory drafting.

13.4. HARNESSING DIVERSE AND BALANCED EXPERTISE

The process of statutory revision is an intellectual, a legal, and a political one. There are two major, national law reform groups in the United States: The American Law Institute (ALI) and the NCCUSL. Many of the ALI's products are Restatements of doctrine announced by courts. These Restatements are not drafted as statutes. They are influential to the extent they are approved by the courts or expected to be followed by courts. NCCUSL's work is to draft statutes that will become adopted, ideally, by legislatures in every state. Approval of these two different kinds of products comes from two different branches of government, the courts in the case of the Restatements and the legislatures in the case of NCCUSL. Especially in the case of a legislative project, there is greater chance of success if it passes muster with the American Bar Association, or at least does not incur its wrath. The American Bar Association, and state bar associations, can mount extremely effective lobbying efforts.

The two groups, and I hope I am not overstating the point to make it, take different approaches to the composition of Drafting Committees. ALI has a Reporter (sometimes with a Co-Reporter or an Associate Reporter) who works closely with a group of 'Advisers'. The ALI Advisers tend to have deep expertise in the law under review. The Project also has a larger 'Members Consultative Group' to offer further advice before the projects are brought to the floor. Many of these members also have deep substantive expertise in the subject of the project. NCCUSL has a Reporter (also sometimes with a Co-Reporter or an Associate Reporter), who works closely with a Drafting Committee to bring projects to the floor. NCCUSL sometimes has Drafting Committees with much less substantive expertise in the subject of the project than the Advisers in an ALI project. Part of the reason may be that NCCUSL's Drafting Committees are made up of Commissioners who are political appointees from the various states rather than individuals selected for their deep substantive expertise in a particular area. This is not to say that Commissioners lack expertise, far from it. An additional part of the reason may be that NCCUSL does not always make a conscious effort to concentrate the greatest substantive expertise among its members on a Drafting Committee. An important part of being a Commissioner is to help NCCUSL products get enacted back home. The ultimate task of the Drafting Committee is to produce a statute that will be enacted by legislators throughout the country, many of whom are not even lawyers, much less specialists in the topic. A concept articulated to me is that a non-specialist Committee should be pleased with the product and prepared to sing its praises. The distinctive expertise of the Drafting Committee, and of the NCCUSL oversight process, is in what most states are not able to bring to bear on the drafting process: deep expertise in statutory drafting.

I believe it is important for the Reporter and the Drafting Committee to have deep and varied substantive expertise in the subject of the project. First, it makes the task much more efficient. Less time will be taken getting up to speed. Second, it leaves the project less susceptible to outside influences. Outside interest groups typically bring great expertise to bear on a project. Because of the political nature of the process of law reform and the need for legislative approval in the case of statutory law reform, a project must address the concerns of outside interests. But it should do so from a position of strength. Furthermore, if the project drags on too long, the outside representatives may change, and so may the focus of their attention. Indeed, new representatives may feel compelled to raise new matters simply to justify their participation. The focus of the project may be needlessly diverted to revisit old issues or to other less important issues.

The admixture of expertise is also important. It is important that the judiciary have very significant representation, even in a statutory project. Judges are often more resistant to the siren songs of the ideologue and of the special interest. Law reform, like other human activities, often suffers from a lack of broader context, including historical perspective. In this regard, I think that both judges and academics have a particular contribution to make. They often have more of a sense of history, of core concepts, and of analogous areas of the law, than the practitioner embroiled in transactions or litigation. They also have an ability to place proponents of particular points on a spectrum of opinion, to more quickly identify ideologues or other partisans. On the other hand, a weakness of many academics is that they are often ideologues themselves, inexperienced in practice or not used to compromise.

At the dawn of multidisciplinary practice, it is interesting that neither the accounting profession, nor the world of business or finance outside of law, tends to be represented on business law reform projects. Insights from lay business or finance people and from the business professoriate could be particularly useful on a wide range of provisions. Finally, law reform efforts could be aided by empirical research. From soup to nuts, the RUPA project was attempting to draft default rules of a sort that tend to be included in negotiated agreements. There was no empirical research to guide us, in part because empirical research on such matters is not fashionable, either in the academy or in the organized bar.

Without empirical research to guide statutory law reform projects, the insights of members of the practising bar are critical. It also is important to include those who labour in different segments of the economy. It is they who know how the law works in action, both in the conference room and in the court room. My greatest pleasure and honour has been working with the men and women of the practising bar who rise above ideology and special interest and give of their time to help make the law better for everyone. The best of this special breed should be identified and made an important part of every project.

REFERENCES

Hillman, R. W. (1995), 'RUPA and Former Partners: Cutting the Gordian Knot with Continuing Partnership Entities', *Law and Contemporary Problems* 58: 7.
——Vestal, A. W. and Weidner, D. J. (2001), *The Revised Uniform Partnership Act*, St. Paul: West Group.
Meislik, I. (2001), 'General Partner Liability: A Side-by-Side Debate' , Pubogram No. 2.
Weidner, D. J. (1988), 'A Perspective to Reconsider Partnership Law', *Florida State University Law Review* 16: 1.
——(1997), 'Cadwalader, RUPA and Fiduciary Duty', *Washington and Lee Law Review* 54: 877.

PART IV

THE EUROPEAN PRIVATE COMPANY AND PARTNERSHIP LAW REFORM IN THE EUROPEAN UNION

14

Private Companies in Europe and the European Private Company

ROBERT R. DRURY

14.1. INTRODUCTION

All of the major countries in Europe,[1] including all of the member states of the European Union, have got a private company form in their portfolio of business organizations.[2] The only major current exception to this pattern is the European Union itself, which can claim to have a public company vehicle in prospect in the shape of the European Company Statute and an existing European Economic Interest Grouping (EEIG) that in many ways is a rather hybrid structure lying halfway between a company and a partnership. A proposal for a European Close or Private Company has been put forward and has been the subject of an EU consultation exercise by the High Level Group of Company Law Experts.[3] This chapter will briefly outline the dissemination and development of the private company form throughout the member states of the European Union before considering the need for the introduction of a full range of vehicles at a supranational European level. It will then give further details of the proposal for the European Private Company.

14.2. POINT OF DEPARTURE

A somewhat cursory look at the private company forms in Europe tends to indicate that they relate to three moderately distinct models. There is the German GmbH type, the French SARL type, and the British private company type. This analysis is complicated by the fact that the French type was initially copied from the German GmbH, but has subsequently developed along a

---

[1] Austria, Belgium, Cyprus, Czech Republic, Denmark, France, Germany, Gibraltar, Greece, Guernsey, Hungary, Ireland, Isle of Man, Jersey, Finland, Liechtenstein, Luxembourg, The Netherlands, Norway, Poland, Portugal, Russia, Slovak Republic, Spain, Sweden, Switzerland, and the United Kingdom.

[2] In Sweden and Finland there is only one form of company, the aktiebolag (osakeyhtiö in Finnish), which can be either public or private.

[3] Access to this consultation exercise is available at: http://europa.eu.int/comm/internal_market/en/company/company/modern/index.htm.

different, if parallel, pathway. We should therefore begin with the GmbH, which was introduced into Germany in 1892.

At that time the joint stock company as well as general and limited partnerships had already existed for a long time. The joint stock company, having its origins in the trading companies of the 17th century, came into fashion in the years of economic boom following the Franco-Prussian war of 1870/71. . . . What the German business community needed in the late 19th century was a form of business organization which limited the liability of the entrepreneur, was simple, and typically designed for the smaller business. (Peltzer, Brooks, and Hopcroft 1996: 1)

The joint stock company did not fit that mould and so a new kind of company was developed that took the corporate personality and limited liability concepts from the joint stock corporation and the relationships between shareholders from the partnership (ibid.). The form has been an outstanding success. This original German form inspired Portugal to adopt the Sociedade por quotas by the Lei of 11 April 1901, Austria to adopt the GmbH by the law of 6 March 1906, Hungary to do the same in 1925 and Romania in 1933 (Ripert and Roblot 1989: 684).

Chronologically, the next significant point of departure might well be the evolution of the private company in Great Britain by 1907. Incorporation by registration under a general Act rather than by or under a special Act of Parliament was introduced in England in 1844 and limited liability for such registered companies was given in 1855. These Acts were consolidated into the Joint Stock Companies Act 1856, which for the first time also extended to Scotland.

It became clear in the portentous House of Lords decision of *Salomon v. Salomon Ltd*,[4] which acknowledged the separate legal personality of such companies, that the registered company could be used by de facto one-man companies and hence also by other small enterprises. This state of affairs was given formal recognition in the Companies Act of 1907, which exempted 'private companies'[5] from the requirement of issuing a prospectus or statement in lieu when offering shares to the public because this was applied only to 'public companies' (Schmitthoff 1972). This form extended also to Ireland, which until the passing of its Companies Act in 1963 was governed by English pre-1922 law, and that in effect meant the Companies Act 1907. The benefits flowing from this form have been appreciated by several European countries (e.g. France in the 1920s, the Netherlands, and Denmark more recently), but the fact that it was grafted on to a common law root meant that it was never copied exactly, in the same way as the GmbH and later the SARL were.

---

[4] [1897] A.C. 22.
[5] These were defined in the Act as those whose constitution restricted the right to transfer its shares, limited the number of its members to fifty, and prohibited any invitation to the public to subscribe for its shares or debentures.

The SARL arrived in France after the territorial changes brought about by the First World War. The inhabitants of Alsace and Lorraine had enjoyed the benefits of the GmbH when they were under German rule and wanted the same advantages once they were subject to French law. A law of 1924 had brought this about for the departements of Haut-Rhin, Bas-Rhin, and Moselle, and by the law of 7 March 1925 this was extended to the whole of the country. French businessmen had, for a long time, wanted the benefits of limited liability but without the complex rules that governed the société anonyme. They had pointed to the advantages obtainable in England under its private company regime. The new SARL proved to be a successful legal transplant, and by 1937 there were 52,549 such companies registered (Ripert and Roblot 1989: 682). However, it also had its drawbacks because it attracted some less scrupulous entrepreneurs, and there were many bankruptcies.

From 1935 onwards there were numerous reforms implemented that applied to the SARL rules designed to tighten up the regime governing the liabilities of the directors of the société anonyme. The SARL began to develop a distinctly French character that took it a little apart from its GmbH forebears. Its success did not go unnoticed, and it was adopted in Luxembourg in 1933 (Société à responsabilité limitée), in Belgium in 1935 (now called the Société privée à responsabilité limitée / Besloten vennootschap met beperkte aansprakelijkheid), Italy in 1942 (Societá a responsabilitá limitata), Spain in 1953 (Sociedad de responsabilidad limitada), Greece in 1955 (Etairia Periorismenis Efthinis), and, some would argue, by the Netherlands in 1971 (Besloten vennootschap met beperkte aansprakelijkheid) (ibid. 684).[6] Each country has adapted the form to its own system, but there are still basic similarities.

These adoption routes of the private company form are illustrated on the map in Figure 14.1.

What we seem to have experienced in the spread of the private company across the Europe of the twentieth century is a sort of cascade effect. From a point of origin in Germany in 1892 we have seen the GmbH private company form spread to Portugal and Austria in the early years of the century and later to Hungary and Romania. An important jump occurred in 1924/5 when the French adopted this form as the SARL, and from this source it had spread by the 1950s to Luxembourg, Belgium, Italy, Spain, and Greece. There was a separate development of the private company in England by 1907, which also applied to Ireland. A later impetus, brought about by the harmonization programme of the European Union and the need to confine the application of some of the directives to larger public companies, saw the introduction of the private company form into the Netherlands (1971) and Denmark (1973).

---

[6] However, another explanation is given by De Kluiver who asserts that given the pressures on the legislative process caused by work on other EEC Directives, the legislature merely adopted the rules for the (potentially) public company, i.e. the N.V., which was not offering its shares to the public, with certain modifications. See De Kluiver (1995: 109). Whether these modifications were inspired by French law or by the wording of the Directive is hard to say.

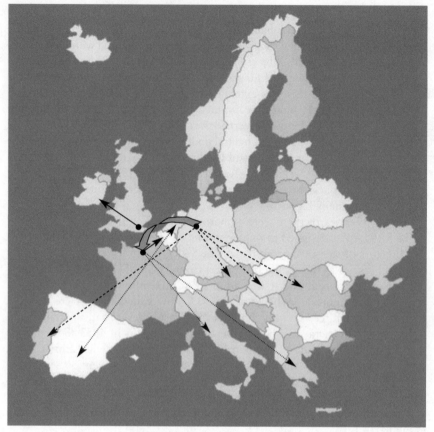

Figure 14.1. Adoption routes of the private company form

Sweden, following its later accession introduced the private company form, as a sub-type of the aktiebolag, in 1995.

It is difficult to determine the exact reasons for this pattern of spread of the private company. Earlier chapters of this volume have given details of the spread of the Limited Liability Company and other forms across the United States, within a vastly more compressed timescale. Ribstein's view (Chapter 6, this volume) is that this was due in no small measure to jurisdictional competition in a legal and constitutional environment that was at least not hostile to such a development. The ability to do business in every state in the Union, subject to the provisions of the now largely toothless qualification statutes, is based upon the almost universal application of the place of incorporation theory (Kozyris 1985) founded on recognition through comity. Thus, if one state does not have an appropriate legal vehicle for an enterprise such as an LLC statute, that enterprise, in theory, can use such a form from another state and trade under it in the original state. This brings pressure on the original state to introduce such a form in order to retain local businesses within the state's system, and as Ribstein (Chapter 6, this volume) suggests, pressure from local interest groups to make their jurisdiction inviting to interstate firms. In fact in the ordinary corporation field the pattern for small businesses is to use the local state corporation law rather than use the largely similar Delaware law or that of another jurisdiction to gain what are today fairly peripheral advantages. It is ordinarily not cost-effective for a small business to bother to seek an out-of-state incorporation. However, if the home state does not provide a form that has the fiscal attractions of the LLC, the dynamics of that equation may change.

Callison (Chapter 8, this volume) traces the rapid development of the LLC from the decision of the US Internal Revenue Service to accord Wyoming LLCs favourable partnership taxation status in 1988 to the adoption of the LLC in all fifty states and the District of Columbia some six years later. He likens this to the 'race to the bottom' mechanism. This race occurred in the United States particularly in the first third of the last century and saw a diminution in corporation law standards in an effort by some states, particularly New Jersey and then Delaware, to increase their revenue from initial and continuing incorporations.

The impact of one major player, in this case an oil and gas company lobbying the Wyoming legislature, has had a huge impact across this enormous country. In a pre-*Centros/Überseering* environment one would have said that the same process would not really have occurred in the European Union. The existence of the real seat theory in many of the member states effectively prevented trading through a pseudo-foreign corporate vehicle in order to gain from the advantages of incorporating in a more accommodating jurisdiction. European legal and cultural environments were not as amenable to the concept of jurisdictional competition as were those in the United States.

There are many reasons, including the harmonization programme of the EU itself, why such a competition would not have created the pressure on individual legislatures to adopt a particular corporate form in their country or to alter the rules governing the existing forms. We should therefore look elsewhere for an explanation of the spread of the private company in Europe.[7]

It is likely that internal demands for the availability of a small business vehicle bringing the benefits of limited liability without the rigours of public company style regulation proved a strong motivation in many countries. It certainly did in France in the 1920s. When this is coupled with an urgent need not to reinvent the wheel (which applies as strongly in the United States as elsewhere) the stage is set for the creation of a welcoming environment for legal transplants. In most countries, excluding Greece and initially Spain, these transplants have been an outstanding success.

---

[7] For the future, we will have to wait and see what difference the post-*Centros* availability of compulsory recognition of a branch in circumstances that look very like the migration of a primary establishment will make, and also take into account the demise of the real seat doctrine arising from the ECJ's decision in *Überseering*.

More recently the need to protect local small businesses from the sweeping application of EC company law harmonization directives has been a major factor. In this context we have seen, especially in the Netherlands and Sweden, an adaptation of the public company form with appropriate modifications, rather than the wholesale adoption of an 'exotic' form. The same mechanism also lies behind the development of the private company in Britain and Ireland.

While separate public company and private company types are known in all of the member states of the EU, the use that is made of them does differ considerably because of a whole range of factors. The extent of that diversity can be seen in Figure 14.2.[8] One extreme position is that of Greece where the private company, the Etairia Periorismenis Efthinis (EPE) is known, but little used compared to the public company, which constitutes the vast majority of the corporate population. The other extreme is represented by the UK, Germany, Netherlands, Austria, Spain, Sweden, and Ireland where the private company makes up almost the entirety of the number of companies, and the public company, although very important in economic terms, has relatively few adherents. In some states such as Belgium, Denmark, and Luxembourg the balance is different with the public company population being half that of the private company class. France is also different with the largest population of public companies, at around 160,000, which is particularly striking when compared, for example, to the 12,800 in the UK and the 7,800 or so in Germany, both of which represent broadly similar economies. This indicates that there is a different approach to the concept of the public company form. This form is traditionally used in France by the small and medium-sized firm as well as the large listed company. One major reason for this is the fact that an owner-manager of a private company (SARL), i.e. a majority shareholder appointed as manager, cannot take full advantage of all aspects of the social security provision in France. One can only do this if one is truly in the position of an employee, and having a majority shareholding in a private company does not, to French eyes, give the necessary degree of subordination of the employed manager to the employing company (Merle 1994: 182–3, 401). Hence majority shareholders who wish to both manage their company and enjoy the complete benefits of social security provision have to form public companies (sociétés anonymes) with themselves as the president in order to do so. As can be seen, in all countries except Greece, the introduction of the private company form has been an outstandingly popular innovation, obviously fulfilling the demands of the business community.

---

[8] Figure 14.2 is for illustrative purposes only because the data on which it is based comes from different sources and was compiled at different times (between 1995 and 2001). While it is not an absolute comparison, it does suffice to show broad general trends. It represents the proportion of the entire company population taking the private company and the public company forms, respectively.

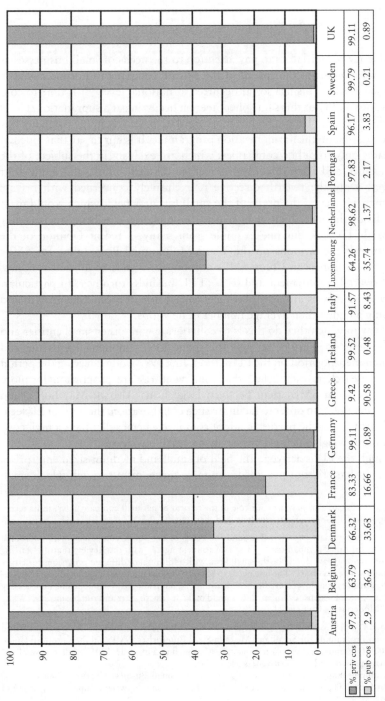

Figure 14.2. Proportions of private and public companies in member states

14.3. THE EUROPEAN UNION DIMENSION

The tendency of legislators to pay attention to the needs of small businesses as a motivating factor in the spread of the private company in Europe has been mentioned above. This has so far occurred at national level.[9] It is time to consider the possibility of this same phenomenon occurring at a supranational level inside the European Union. So far, most legislative activity in the company law field has centred on the harmonization programme. It is fair to say that much of this relates only to public companies, which are exclusively the subject of the second, third, and sixth directives as well as the fifth, ninth, and tenth draft directives. Only the twelfth directive is exclusively concerned with private companies. However, the needs of the small business field, which would most benefit from the introduction of a private company, are being increasingly recognized. To pick but one example from many, a recent Opinion of the Committee of the Regions on the Third Multiannual Programme for SMEs stated, 'In the European Union SMEs account for 99.8% of all undertakings, 66% of overall employment and 65% of EU business turnover. In particular, very small businesses are now playing a crucial role in promoting growth and generating a higher than average number of new jobs.'[10]

One way in which they do this is to collaborate with other small entities and by this synergy they are better able to expand their commercial activities and strengthen their position on the EU market. In a 1997 study covering the period 1989–95 researchers established that joint ventures are proportionally more common between SMEs than between large firms (Urban, Mayrhofer, and Nanopoulus 1997). In order to facilitate such collaboration, the present EU legal environment forces the parties to adopt complex schemes that have a high cost. Such burdens weigh particularly heavily on small businesses.

Although the EU is active in the field of small and medium-sized enterprises (SMEs),[11] it has still not provided a suitable mechanism through which small

---

[9] These needs can also play a major role in the reform of national company laws. In its recent White paper the UK Government acknowledged that

[c]urrent company law is designed around the needs of big public companies, with additional provisions for other companies. . . . The Government agrees with the Review that the starting point for company law should be the small firm, with additional or different provisions for larger companies where necessary. The law needs to balance various interests, including those of shareholders, directors, employees, creditors and customers, but it should avoid imposing unnecessary or inappropriate burdens. Company law should make it easy to start and run businesses. (White Paper, 'Modernising Company Law')

[10] Opinion of the Committee of the Regions on the 'Proposal for a Council Decision on a Third Multiannual Programme for Small and Medium-Sized Enterprises (SMEs) in the European Union (1997–2000) (presented by the Commission)—Maximizing European SMEs' full potential for employment, growth and competitiveness' (1997: 34).

[11] See, among many other initiatives, the 'European Small Business Charter' adopted by the Council in June 2000, which made the promotion of partnership between companies a priority of the Union.

businesses can collaborate and operate cost-effective transnational joint ventures. To be sure, there has been a regulation establishing the European Economic Interest Grouping,[12] but while this may provide a mechanism for cooperation between businesses of various sizes, its role is rather strictly circumscribed by the Regulation. Article 3 states that:

1. The purpose of a grouping shall be to facilitate or develop the economic activities of its members and to improve or increase the results of those activities; its purpose is not to make profits for itself. Its activity shall be related to the economic activities of its members and must not be more than ancillary to those activities.
2. Consequently, a grouping may not: (a) exercise, directly or indirectly, a power of management or supervision over its members' own activities or over the activities of another undertaking.

Hence a grouping cannot be used to set up a new business or to manage the businesses of its members more effectively. It was never intended by those who drafted the legislation to be a substitute for an operating company.

The entity that could fulfil these roles is the European Company (SE), which was introduced by a Regulation of 8 October 2001[13] and its partner Directive[14] covering the worker participation aspects. However, would this fulfil the needs and expectations of the SME sector? An Opinion of the European Economic and Social Committee on a European Company Statute for SMEs[15] stated that the SE 'is strongly influenced by the rules on public limited companies and was designed for big companies. Although it is undoubtedly a step forward the SE, which goes back more than thirty years, is based on an old concept, and its foundations clearly show the symptoms of this: it is cumbersome and complex, unsuited to SMEs' needs, and has difficulty in incorporating social advances.'

In its report on the last Draft Council Regulation on the SE, the European Parliament stresses that the draft 'does not take enough account of SMEs, when the European SME is the engine of a major part of the European economy' (H. P. Mayer report). This damning indictment is undoubtedly justified from a small business perspective. The original agenda for the SE was to provide a vehicle through which cross-frontier mergers and consolidations of large enterprises could take place that would produce entities of a size suitable to take on competitors from around the world, notably the United States and later Japan. Although the minimum capital has been reduced over the period of its gestation, the present requirement of €120,000 is still a hefty commitment for small businesses to make for a possibly risky international venture. It is essentially unsuited to the needs of the small business.

What would appear to be needed is a European private company form to complement that of the SE and thereby provide a range of supranational entities

---

[12] Council Regulation (EEC) No 2137/85 of 25 July 1985, OJ L199, 31/07/1985 pp. 1–9.
[13] Council Regulation (EC) No 2157/2001 of 8 Oct. 2001, OJ L294 of 10/11/2001 at p. 1.
[14] Council Directive 2001/86/EC of 8 Oct. 2001, OJ L294 of 10/11/2001 at p. 22.
[15] CES 363/2002 of 21 Mar. 2002.

Robert R. Drury

to cater for the full panoply of commercial demand inside the European Union. If such an entity were made available we would see a response to the needs of small businesses that parallels that which occurred in the individual member states.

Thoughts like this led CREDA, the research arm of the Paris Chamber of Commerce, to put together an international research project to investigate the prospects for a European close or private company. A team of researchers, of which the author formed a part, was drawn together from Germany, Netherlands, and the United Kingdom as well as from France. It was led by Mme Jeanne Boucourechliev whose book (Boucourechliev 1973) on a European SARL inaugurated the whole discussion of the subject. This team spent a couple of years discussing various ideas and working on the project before publishing its favourable conclusions in a book sponsored by the European Commission (Boucourechliev 1997). But one book clearly was not going to achieve the goals that CREDA had set itself.

A new sponsor was found in the shape of the Mouvement des Entreprises de France (MEDEF). They assisted in convening a smaller working party again with an international membership—France, Germany, and myself from the United Kingdom—which, in what seemed a very short space of time, produced a working draft of a regulation for a European Private Company. This has been refined, polished, published, and presented to the Commission. CREDA and MEDEF have held a series of seminars in several European cities (Paris, Brussels, London, Heidelberg, and Rotterdam) to rally support for the project.

A conference was held in Brussels in November 2000 to which leading civil servants from all of the member states were invited. The intention was to persuade these decision-makers that the project is a practical possibility that they can support with confidence in its viability. In addition to these seminars further work continued on the project as my colleague Andrew Hicks and I collaborated with Professor Hommelhoff and his team at the University of Heidelberg to produce the text of model articles of association, which are intended to be annexed to the completed draft Regulation.

Following the publication of the draft Regulation,[16] the European Economic and Social Committee held a public hearing on 22 October 2001, in which more than twenty European organizations concerned with the subject, as well as experts and lawyers took part. After the hearing the Committee published its own initiative Opinion.[17] This Opinion provided a strong endorsement for the thinking behind and the approach taken in the draft Regulation. It concluded as follows:

---

[16] The text of the draft Regulation on 'The European Private Company: A Close Company' is included as an appendix to this volume. The text is also available at the following URL: http://www.ccip.fr/etudes/dossiers/spe/index.html (inspected August 2003).
[17] CES 363/2002 of 21 Mar. 2002. This is downloadable from the following URL: http://www.esc.eu.int/pages/avis/03_02/op_March_en.htm (inspected September 2002).

7.1 An analysis of needs confirms the necessity for a European company project for SMEs, above all so that they can be treated on an equal footing with bigger companies—which are more concerned by the European Company statute—and to offer them a European label to facilitate their activities in the internal market.

7.2 To make it attractive, the new statute will have to remove the risk of multiple taxation and provide considerable legal flexibility, as well as facilities regarding setting-up formalities, advice and support for enterprise partnerships.

7.3 The EESC would set this project in the context of the conclusions of the European Council in Lisbon, i.e. improving European competitiveness and entrepreneurship and creating new activities and jobs. It must also promote employee participation at European level, a factor on which the success of integration depends.

7.4 The EESC therefore calls for the rapid setting-up of a simplified European statute for SMEs, as a complement to the European Company Statute.[18]

At the same time, in September 2001, the Commission set up a Group of High Level Company Law Experts with the objective of initiating a discussion on the need for the modernization of company law in Europe. Part of its remit was to consider the 'possible need for new legal forms (for instance, a European Private Company, which would be of particular relevance for SMEs)'.[19] The consultation document admits that '[T]he SE has been designed for large enterprises and may not meet all the expectations of the business community and in particular small and medium sized enterprises (SMEs), both independent and group's subsidiaries, which are the most important constituents of the European economy.'[20] It refers to the text of the draft Regulation and conducts a consultation exercise on the need for the European Private Company and on various technical issues related to the proposal. This consultation is now closed, and we await the results with considerable interest.

Having discussed the background and the history of this draft Regulation, it is now appropriate to consider the details of the proposal.

14.4. The Scheme of the Regulation[21]

14.4.1. Access

Under the Regulation[22] a European Private Company can be formed by individuals or companies either by the straight registration of a new company from scratch or by way of the transformation of an existing national company into a European Private Company. Initial creation can be as a joint subsidiary or a

---

[18] Ibid. 8.

[19] Material on the whole consultation exercise, which has now closed, is available at http://europa.eu.int/comm/internal_market/en/company/company/modern/index.htm (inspected August 2003).

[20] Ibid. ch 3.6—The European Private Company, I 2.

[21] Sections 14.4 and 14.5 of this chapter are based on material that appeared in Drury (2001).

[22] See *supra* n. 16.

holding company and access is not restricted to nationals of the European Union, but is open to all. The Opinion of the European Economic and Social Committee wanted a more restrictive approach. They felt that 'the statute would be intended for activities which had a European aspect in the broad sense, i.e. either involving two partners from at least two Member States or simply an existing or planned economic activity at European level, i.e. involving more than just one Member State.'[23] If the Regulation can be used only by entities from member states it cannot play the part of a channel promoting inward investment into the EU. At a time when unemployment is again high on the political agenda, such an approach could be seen as being a trifle too protective and short-sighted.

When it comes to transformation, the draft Regulation has been a little more circumspect, and limited this to companies already formed under the law of a member state, and has prescribed a procedure for such transformations.[24] In a way this could be the most controversial aspect of the formation process because it does pave the way for companies to 'escape' from unpalatable provisions of their governing national law by a 'flight' to the European Private Company. In consequence the draft Regulation has had to ensure that companies are not tempted to transform into a European Private Company for the wrong reasons. Thus, there are provisions for a minimum capital in this draft Regulation which, compared to national private companies in Europe, are rather stringent at €25,000 fully paid up on subscription.[25] This is not because it is felt that these minimum capital provisions offer an acceptable creditor guarantee, in practical terms this simply does not work, but rather because it was felt necessary to impose an entry barrier to deter frivolous use of this form, and to give it the economic credibility that must constitute an important feature of this new creation.

14.4.2. Basic Features

The European Private Company has limited liability, with each shareholder being liable only to the extent of the contribution made for their shares. It may not issue securities to the public, in line with the conception of the private or close company form. It has legal personality from the moment of its registration.[26] To assist with overcoming potential conflict of laws problems the registered office of the European Private Company must be located in the same jurisdiction as its central administration.[27] There is considerable freedom in the choice of a name for the company, provided that the name is 'not misleading or liable to cause confusion'. The name must be preceded or followed either by the words 'European Private Company' or by the acronym 'EPC'.

---

[23] Opinion of the European Economic and Social Committee on a European Company Statute for SMEs, Brussels, 21 March 2001, para 3.2.1.

[24] See art 35 of the draft Regulation (*supra* n. 16).   [25] See art 3 of the draft Regulation.

[26] See art 2 of the draft Regulation.   [27] See art 6 of the draft Regulation.

14.4.3. Formation Procedure

The European Private Company is created by means of registration in the normal companies registry in the State where its central administration is to be located. This may be in the local Commercial Court or, as in the UK at a central Companies Registry. Certain basic information must be provided which will be put on the register and also sent on to a central EU register to be created for the purpose.[28] This will be publicized both locally and at EU level in the Official Gazette and should be readily accessible by means of public search facilities. The relevant registry will issue a Certificate of Incorporation.

The initial capital provisions[29] requiring a minimum of €25,000, reflect the need to establish economic credibility for this new form of company. To ensure that the money is forthcoming shares must be paid up in full before registration, and the company will only be registered if an official receipt for this money by a bank or a notary is submitted.

14.4.4. Organization and Operation

The basic principle that has been adopted is freedom of choice, as long as this is consistent with the adequate protection of shareholders and third parties. Thus, in the company's articles of association, the founders may set up any form of management structure that they feel comfortable with. A single manager, a one-tier board, with or without a managing director or a two-tier board are all possible. These articles too will set out the rights of the shareholders, and considerable freedom is permitted, much on the British model, and so the voting or other rights do not have to be proportionate to the nominal value of the shares. However, certain minimum rights are guaranteed to the shareholders. Although the articles will set out who does what, in the sense of allocating which matters are to be dealt with by the shareholders and which by the management body, certain matters are specifically reserved for the shareholders. These include the approval of the accounts, the allocation of the annual profits—to reserves or distribution—the appointment of auditors if necessary and the alteration of the articles.

Third-party protection is achieved in a way consistent with a lot of European legislation and will be familiar. The Regulation provides in Article 16 that 'The company shall be represented in relation to third parties by one or more individuals or legal entities having full power to act in all circumstances in the company's name.' The power allocation follows French phraseology, but is apt for its purpose. As the names of these representatives will be published, and accessible to third parties, all that they have to do is to access the right person and the deals made by them should be fully binding. This is reminiscent of the German approach.

---

[28] See art 8 of the draft Regulation.   [29] See art 3 of the draft Regulation.

The Regulation lays down certain standards for the actions of the management body.[30] Basically the company's officers on its governing body or bodies (e.g. boards of directors or management) are liable if they breach the terms of the Regulation or the company's articles or other rules applicable. It was difficult to impose universally acceptable yet realistic standards of duty, but in the end those drafting the Regulation settled for the fairly open formula of 'They shall be liable . . . for breach of their duties and the standard of diligence reasonably required in the conduct of business.' In terms of seeking a remedy for breach of these duties, individual shareholders may bring an action against the relevant officers for any losses suffered on a personal basis, as they can in France. Following the path of the majority of European jurisdictions, it was agreed that shareholders representing 10 per cent of the capital may bring an action on behalf of the company. This is less generous than French private company law but does avoid the complexities of the British rules.

14.4.5. Shareholders and Minority Protection

In this area a balancing act needed to be performed between a number of potentially conflicting forces. On the one hand, the drafting team wished to create as much freedom and flexibility as possible to encourage use of this form. On the other, they wished to provide what was felt to be as realistic a protection for the minority shareholders as possible, while not providing too many avenues, which could lead to the breakup or self-destruction of the company. Because of the essentially close company nature of the entity that they were creating they needed to make it clear that the shareholders could, if they wished, restrict the free right of a member to transfer their shares, usually by requiring the approval of some group or body within the company, e.g. management or shareholders meeting.

Minority protection can take many forms, usually in combination. There can be rules relating to the provision of information from which minority shareholders can deduce that they are being oppressed, there can be rules enabling minority shareholders to enforce directors' duties and rules giving some statutory remedy for oppression. The draft Regulation has all of these elements and more. In terms of granting shareholders access to information, they must be informed of all collective decisions taken by the general meeting and are to be allowed access to the company's principal management documents. Shareholders may also submit questions in writing that the company's officers shall be bound to answer. If no answer is forthcoming, shareholders are given the right to petition the court for the appointment of a special auditor to report on certain acts of the management. This concept of appointing an expert de minorité is found in both French and German law.[31]

---

[30] See art 17 of the draft Regulation (*supra* n. 16).

[31] For France, see art 226 of the Loi of 24 July 1966 for the SA, extended to the SARL by the Loi No 84-148 of 1 March 1984. For Germany, see art 142 of the Aktiengesetz of 1965.

As has been mentioned, shareholders holding 10 per cent of the capital or the votes may bring an action against the company's officers for recovery of damage suffered by the company because of breaches of duty by the management.[32]

A remedy may be provided in the articles themselves under which shareholders may claim to have their shares acquired in the circumstances and under the procedure specified in the articles. Another more forceful exit route is given by the Regulation,[33] which provides for any shareholder to petition the Court for the compulsory acquisition of their shares in certain defined circumstances including:

- a significant change in the articles,
- transfer of the company's assets to another company,
- a substantial change in the company's business, or
- an unjustified withholding of distributions on their shares.

The drafting team did not want to be too liberal in providing an exit route because of fears that the most timid or even prudent shareholders might use it to bale out as soon as things began to get tough and not stick with the venture that they had agreed to participate in. The boot was also put on the other foot by including provision for a majority to remove a minority shareholder who has become unacceptable because such a shareholder has seriously damaged the company's interests, or because their continuance as a shareholder is detrimental to the proper operation of the company.[34] These rules were borrowed from Dutch private company law.[35]

If a shareholder finds a potential purchaser for their shares who is unacceptable to the others, the Regulation states that the articles '*shall* determine the manner of withdrawal of a shareholder to whom approval is denied'.[36] A price-fixing mechanism must be provided that allows a disaffected member to leave the company by selling their shares at a reasonable value. Such an exit route is found in French law.[37]

14.4.6. Capital, Accounts, and Economic Credibility

These topics can be linked because they express different but possibly complementary approaches to the protection of third parties dealing with a company. Having a minimum capital is still seen by many jurisdictions as providing some assurance to potential creditors. However, the efficacy of this device is doubted by many commentators, especially this one. Having access to information on a company's accounts can help a third party to evaluate the risks associated with extending credit to that company. Having both mechanisms might help to engender confidence in the European Private Company as a serious business form.

---

[32] See art 18 of the draft Regulation.
[33] See art 21.2 of the draft Regulation.
[34] See art 21.1 of the draft Regulation.
[35] See Netherlands Civil Code, Book 2, §§ 335–43.
[36] See art 20.1 of the draft Regulation.
[37] See Code de Commerce Art L. 233–14.

The drafting team agreed to include a minimum capital because so many Civil Law systems are still wedded to the idea and would not readily accept a new company form in their territory which lacked it, and also because of the need to reassure member states that all of their companies will not flee to the European Private Company overnight to avoid this requirement. They had the *Centros* decision very much in mind. The minimum capital chosen is, as has been said, €25,000. The incorporation of a European Private Company is not something that should be undertaken lightly or frivolously, and setting the minimum capital at this level was seen as a sufficient barrier for this purpose. Despite scepticism over the ability of a minimum capital to provide an effective guarantee for the company's creditors, there was general agreement on the application of rules for the maintenance of the company's capital once it has been subscribed. This could operate to boost the confidence of third parties dealing with the European Private Company. These rules should be at least up to the standard of those set out in the Second Directive. In fact, in an effort to create an atmosphere of economic credibility and rectitude the rules in the Regulation go much further.

Bearing in mind the protection given to third parties by the publication of accounts, despite the fact that they can fall rapidly out of date, the drafting team agreed that the European Private Company must comply with the European Union's rules on the publication of the accounts for private companies.[38]

14.4.7. Employee Participation

The area of employee participation proved to be a little controversial, as might be expected given its history in the European Company Statute. It is provided in the draft Regulation that the rules relating to disclosure to and consultation of the employees should be determined by the law applicable to the registered office of the European Private Company.[39] Each state would be able to go its own way, but this could, in the author's view, lead to undesirable diversity between different jurisdictions and fifteen different types of European Private Company and perhaps to unwelcome episodes of jurisdiction shopping. An alternative would be to provide a threshold limit on the number of employees that a European Private Company can have, perhaps using the successful EEIG rules[40] as a precedent. That number is open to discussion, but it is worth noting that 99.8 per cent of the businesses in the EU have less than 250 employees.

14.4.8. Insolvency

Insolvency presented a completely different set of problems and wisely the drafting team simply referred this to the law applicable to companies of parallel type in the member states.

---

[38] See art 32 of the draft Regulation (*supra* n. 16).   [39] See art 33 of the draft Regulation.
[40] See Council Regulation (EEC) No 2137/85 of 25 July 1985 on the European Economic Interest Grouping (EEIG).

14.4.9. Governing Law

The desire of the drafting team to avoid reference to the various national company laws as subsidiary laws was very strong. The Regulation has taken a very tough line on this point and lays down a hierarchy of rules governing the European Private Company. We begin obviously with the Regulation itself and then refer to the provisions of the company's articles that are not inconsistent with the Regulation. Anything governed by the Regulation may never be subject to the application of the law of the member states, even with respect to those points that it does not settle expressly. Instead the general principles of the Regulation, the general principles of Community company law (in so far as these can be determined), and the general principles common to the national laws are then applied in turn by the judge in order to form the basis of a solution to the relevant problem. National laws, as such, can only be applied where the Regulation expressly refers to them, as it does, for example, in the case of accounting rules and insolvency provision. The thinking of the majority of the drafting group was that the danger from the reference out of key areas of European Private Company law, with the potential for the creation of fifteen types of such company, outweighed the difficulties that judges would be faced with in their search for an appropriate solution. Judges would thus be forced to come up with solutions in keeping with the concepts inherent in the European Private Company project.

14.5. THE MODEL ARTICLES OF ASSOCIATION

14.5.1. The Function of the Model Articles

In approaching the task of drafting these articles, the drafting team have borne a number of ideas in mind. If those founding a European Private Company wish to use it as a subsidiary in a group of companies or as a vehicle for a joint venture, they are very likely to have access to fairly sophisticated legal advice. Such types of European Private Company are likely to require forms of articles that have been very specifically designed to meet the particular needs of their participants. On both of these counts there seems very little utility in providing a standard format for articles, and in any event, drafting such a form catering for such a wide range of possibilities would be all but impossible. The drafting team has therefore concentrated on two broad classifications where they felt that a standard form could have a useful part to play. The first category is the small owner-managed business formed by a limited number of participants operating in many ways as a quasi-partnership. They anticipated that the owners of the enterprise would wish to have a hands-on role in its management. Those running such a business would probably not have access to sophisticated and therefore expensive legal advice. Thus, providing them with a ready-made, but still flexible form of constitution seemed to be a worthwhile objective.

The second classification is that of a business with a larger and more diverse group of participants. What is envisaged here is the possibility of at least one passive investor—a person or company who contributes to the capital, but who does not necessarily contemplate playing a major part in the day-to-day management of the business. For such an enterprise a more defined managerial structure will usually be necessary, imposing certain obligations on the managers to report to, and if desired take instructions from, the full body of shareholders. Again, this is essentially a small or medium-sized enterprise where the margins, or the initial investments may not be that great, and where expensive advice from lawyers skilled in the international corporate scene is simply either not available or is too expensive to justify. In such a case, providing a model format for the constitution could be particularly valuable.

Another thing that these models do is to demonstrate that this type of entity could actually work in practice. It will, it is hoped, give the whole project greater credibility. They will help to show the flexibility of such a legal form to lawyers in Europe who are not totally accustomed to such freedom. In many ways the draftsmen wished to convey the idea that this Regulation as a whole starts from the characteristic British approach that everything is possible unless the law prohibits it, rather than the approach that characterizes some European systems, the German AG or public company for example, which take the general line that the company's constitution can only do what the relevant law permits it to do and where flexibility is somewhat limited.

14.5.2. Common Provisions

It was very interesting to find when approaching the task of drafting a working constitution for the European Private Company that the much-vaunted British Table A model articles[41] were actually of very limited use. Both German and particularly French precedents were of considerable help, and the statute for the French Société par Actions Simplifiée,[42] the most recent legislation available, was the most use of all. The British model articles were so completely linked to and integrated with the British legislation that they did not provide particularly useful precedents for a constitution that in many ways had to stand up on its own.

The philosophy of the EPC is that it is an entity that is largely contractual in nature and the Regulation would make only a minimal provision covering the essential elements of a system of company law. Everything else is left to be regulated by the terms of the foundation contract or constitution. In consequence there was no reservoir of basic concepts to fall back on that a national system of

---

[41] Contained in The Companies (Tables A to F) Regulations 1985 (SI 1985/805).
[42] Société par Actions Simplifiée; SAS Loi of 3 Jan. 1994.

company law would provide, and therefore the contract itself had to cover many of these issues. This is a strength rather than a weakness because it enables the easy adoption of this EPC format by businesses from very diverse national backgrounds. Hence the model articles cover things like the following:

- the fiduciary duties of directors, in particular the obligation to avoid a conflict between their personal interest and their duty to the company,
- a business judgement rule providing a defence against a negligence claim where the directors acted 'honestly and reasonably having duly obtained sufficient information before making any relevant decision',
- pre-emption rights of shareholders on an increase in share capital,
- the requirement of a three-quarters majority resolution to dissolve the company or to alter those terms of the articles that do not require unanimity,
- the ability of the shareholders, by a special majority resolution, to give the directors binding instructions on the exercise of their management powers,
- relieving shareholders from the effects of any alteration in the articles requiring them to contribute further capital unless they have consented in writing,
- the ability of the shareholders to ratify a breach of the 'no conflict' rule and so on.

The articles also cover such standard matters as the company's name, objects, registered office, duration, share capital, transfer and transmission of shares, and procedures for meetings and voting, as one would expect. Because the draftsmen were envisaging a close company or a family company using the EPC form, they have provided in the articles a restriction on the free transfer of shares. In doing so, they have given two options. Basically the consent of the remaining shareholders is required for any transfer of shares, but special provision is made for alternative ways of dealing with the situation that arises when a majority shareholder wishes to transfer part only of their holding. This might happen, for example, where founders wish to bring their children into the business and the other shareholders may not approve. The draft provides alternative avenues through which either all shareholders, or a three-quarters majority of the other shareholders, must approve a transfer; the latter possibility excludes the potential transferor from this decision. The drafts also provide a realistic pro rata valuation method that comes into operation if the remaining shareholders reject the potential transferee and become entitled, or in the final analysis obliged, to buy the shares themselves.

The issue of dispute resolution provoked many stimulating discussions. On the one hand, the draftsmen were conscious of the small business nature of many of the potential users of the EPC and the need for an informal method of resolving disputes without going through an expensive process of litigation. On the other hand, they realized that because they were working in an environment where there were few legal precedents for a judge in interpreting the Regulation and any corporate constitution, it was necessary for a body of case law to emerge fairly rapidly. Hence the Community as a whole had an interest in cases going to national courts and the ECJ to provide guidelines and to facilitate the creation of a body of European company law. For this purpose litigation was an advantage. The use of arbitration as dispute resolution machinery was quickly ruled out because it can be as expensive and time-consuming as straight litigation and did not produce the precedents required. In the end, mediation was favoured as the most desirable method to incorporate in the model articles. Finding a suitable definition with sufficient certainty proved a problem and an alternative wording was incorporated in the notes that used the rules of the Centre for Dispute Resolution, which, although based in the United Kingdom, is beginning to have a much wider availability in Europe.

14.5.3. The Micro Business Model

The matters referred to above were dealt with in both of the models that were drafted. Where the models diverge is primarily in the matter of management structure and shareholders' proceedings. In the first model, where a very limited number of participants was envisaged, there is a relatively simple structure that recognizes that the owners of the business are actively involved in its management at all levels. Quite properly they do not separate out what they are doing in running the business from what they do in managing the company or in acting as its shareholders. Hence there is no need to differentiate these roles with great formality in the structure provided, and that structure should incorporate a certain amount of flexibility. In consequence the articles provide that the business is to be managed by the shareholders acting as a management board unless a unanimous decision is taken to appoint a manager.

In family companies as some members of the family get older and frailer, they may wish to leave the active day-to-day management to the younger and more dynamic elements, while still retaining some measure of control. Thus, one or more of these younger members may be appointed managers or an outsider can be appointed to fulfil this function. If a manager is appointed then certain crucial decisions are reserved for a collective decision of the shareholders. These decisions can be taken at a meeting or by way of written consultation (including electronic communication). If no manager is appointed, then the shareholders as a body run the business and make all of the management decisions.

14.5.4. The More Capacious Model

The second model contemplates a slightly larger and more diverse body of shareholders, with the possibility that one or more of them will take a passive rather than an active role in the day-to-day management of the business. Therefore, a more formal corporate structure was required that makes provision for the managing team to report back to the shareholders and that clearly puts the shareholders themselves in the driving seat as far as major decisions are concerned. In addition, the draftsmen were aware of the major differences in European private company management structures between a single or very small group of managers, as found in the SARL, the GmbH, and similar types of company, and the board of directors, which typifies the British and Irish types of private company, or both board and management as can be the case in Denmark.

In order to promote the wide acceptability of this form and to maintain some measure of familiarity for the users, it was decided to provide alternative structures in the body of the model articles. The first possibility is for a manager or managers to be responsible for the management of the company's business. These are to be natural persons because the complexity of having one company to manage another is scarcely called for in a standard model for this type of company. Some formality is required in the conduct of the business in the interests of any passive shareholders, and thus written minutes need to be kept of all formal decisions. Managers are required to devote their whole time and attention to the affairs of the company and must have their service contracts approved by the shareholders. Dismissal is by way of a simple majority collective decision of the shareholders. While the manager may be one of the shareholders, no express provision is made for this, indicating the slightly more detached and less cosy nature of the management's position in this type of company.

The alternative structure that is provided places management responsibility in the hands of a board of directors, acting essentially as a board. The board may appoint a managing director and enter into a service contract with them, as is very common practice in the United Kingdom. Removal of any director is by collective decision of the shareholders taken by simple majority. Provision is made for major decisions affecting the company to be taken not by the managing body but by the shareholders acting collectively. Because the draftsmen wished to give the maximum freedom to those running the company and because they recognized the need for some informality in the conduct of the company's affairs, they did not require these decisions to be taken at a formal shareholders general meeting, but made provisions for written consultation as well. However, to protect the passive shareholders they did require there to be at least one formal meeting each year, but enabled this to be dispensed with if the shareholders voted unanimously for it. Provisions were also made for the conduct of any meeting and alternative ways of resolving a deadlock by giving or prohibiting a casting vote by the chairman.

14.6. CONCLUSION

This chapter has briefly traced the spread of the private company form in twentieth-century Europe. It has also, equally briefly, looked at the patterns of take-up of this form in the member states of the European Union. Everywhere but

Greece we find that this form has enjoyed great popularity and thus fulfilled a need of the small business community in each country. In Greece the advantages flowing from the private company have not been found sufficient to persuade many businesses to adopt this form, especially as the public company form 'enjoys the confidence of the financial system' (Tellis 1995: 149–50). In the European Union itself, although the public company form is about to become available in the shape of the European Company Statute, the private company at a supranational level is not available. It is argued that a need exists for such a form, and that the draft Regulation prepared by the drafting team assembled by CREDA and MEDEF has given a realistic impetus to the debate on the feasibility of such a form succeeding.

This draft is unlike any of the forms that currently exist in the sense that it was not created by way of a legal transplant from another system, and equally is not an adaptation of any existing pubic company form. It is the product of the fusion of ideas from many sources, hopefully combined into a coherent whole as a supranational entity. Although drafted in France under the auspices of French organizations, it is not dominated by purely French ideas. German, British, Dutch, and EU concepts have also all played their part in its creation. With such a multinational European provenance it surely stands a better chance of being acceptable to the small business community in the European Union, especially bearing in mind the fact that this community has shown itself very willing to adopt ideas from other national sources in the past.

If these ideas are found to be sound, they could pave the way for the eventual introduction of a European Private Company structure that could offer exciting possibilities to SMEs in Europe, which are keen to expand or collaborate in ways that minimize the importance of national frontiers.

REFERENCES

Boucourechliev, J. (1973), *Pour une SARL Européenne*, Paris, PUF.

—— (ed.) (1997), *Propositions pour une Société Fermée Européenne*, Luxembourg: Office des publications officielles des Communautés européennes.

De Kluiver, H.-J. (1995), 'The European Private Company? A Dutch Perspective', in H.-J. De Kluiver and W. van Gerven (eds.), *The European Private Company?*, Antwerpen: MAKLU.

Drury, R. (2001), 'The European Private Company', in M. Neville and K. Sørensen (eds.), *The Internationalisation of Companies and Company Laws*, Copenhagen: Mette Neville & Karsten Engsig Sørensen; DJØF Publishing.

Kozyris, P. J. (1985), 'Corporate Wars and Choice of Law', *Duke Law Journal* 1985: 1.

Merle, P. (1994), *Droit Commerciale: Sociétés Commerciales*, Sirey: Dalloz.

Peltzer, M., Brooks, J., and Hopcroft, T. (1996), *GmbH-Gesetz*, Köln: Otto Schmidt.

Ripert, G., and Roblot, R. (1989), *Traité élémentaire de Droit Commercial*, Librairie générale de droit et de jurisprudence.

Schmitthoff, C. (1972), 'How the English Discovered the Private Company', in P. Zonderland (ed.), *Quo Vadis, Ius Societatum*, Deventer: Kluwer.

Tellis, N. (1995), 'The Private Company in Greece', in H.-J. De Kluiver and W. van Gerven (eds.), *The European Private Company?*, Antwerpen: MAKLU.

15

The Reform Agenda for Partnerships and Closely Held Companies in the Netherlands and the European Union

THEO RAAIJMAKERS

15.1. INTRODUCTION

Small and medium-sized enterprises (SMEs) are a crucial component of developed economic systems.[1] Their importance derives from their ability to serve as the basic engine for economic growth within individual member states.[2] Indeed, they serve as a catalyst to job creation, productivity growth, and assist in the innovation of markets, products, and services. Generally, a successful entrepreneurial system requires a conducive set of financial instruments, contract law, tax and labour law rules, and flexible institutions that can assist the development and expansion of new firms (Black and Gilson 1997). Moreover, a flexible law on business law forms is integral to the success of the EU economy (McCahery and Vermeulen, Chapter 7, this volume). It is worth noting that Europe seems to lag behind in developing a legal regime and financial infrastructure that could supply the basis for the rapid growth in the supply of entrepreneurs while protecting the interests of investors.

In this context, the March 2000 Lisbon Summit represents a crucial attempt to bridge the entrepreneurial gap between the United States and the European Union. To be sure, the task is no small matter, since there is no common view on which arrangements are necessary to create an institutional structure that supports the development of new businesses. The Lisbon recommendations require member states to take appropriate measures to improve 'entrepreneurship' in an

---

[1] Many observers have explained that the sort of infrastructure that supports high-tech start-ups includes: education and schooling in new technologies, tax incentives, modernization of civil and commercial law in respect of a variety of 'new economy' issues. The argument goes that the introduction of improved incentives in labour and social security law and a common approach to liberalization may well assist the economy environment.

[2] The 1999 Report of the Commission (Pb C 93, 28 March 1999) estimates that more than 5 million SMEs account for approximately 30 per cent of all European enterprises. The Commission expects that about 30 per cent of these firms will eventually disappear as a consequence of badly prepared transfers resulting in the loss of 6.5 million jobs.

integrated way (viz. taking all aspects of entrepreneurial activities and their organization into account). This, in turn, requires promulgating rules that enable entrepreneurs to choose from the available menu of business forms that best suits their needs at lowest initial and permanent cost, as well as proper mechanisms and enabling rules to finance the subsequent growth of flexible, low-cost mechanisms to 'upstream' reorganizations during the stages of a firm's life cycle from its start as sole proprietorship through venturing with others and/or incorporation, to going public and going private by means of conversions, mergers, acquisitions, splits, takeovers, dissociation, and dissolution. Recently, the European Commission has indeed started a few projects aimed at supporting and facilitating SMEs. For instance, the Commission has recommended the facilitation of transfers and other reorganizations of SMEs, in order to limit the downside pressures of bankruptcy.

A central aim of this chapter will be to identify possible reforms that might serve to promote the efficient conditions for entrepreneurial firms to operate in the European Union. To the extent that corporate law bears directly on SMEs, legal changes are needed to improve the affairs of investors and entrepreneurs. Some member states, such as Germany and the United Kingdom, have already undertaken to adopt reforms. In the United Kingdom, policymakers have introduced a limited liability partnership form for professional associations (Freedman, Chapter 10, this volume; Morse, Chapter 11, this volume) and are considering the introduction of a new limited liability firm for small business. The recent work by the Company Law Review Steering Group in Britain is likely to switch discussion to a policy-oriented debate about the relative merits of the respective limited liability vehicles for small firms. This should lead other member states to consider how to modernize their legal business forms menu to meet the evolving needs of their small and medium firms. Indeed, Germany, in response to the English reforms, has amended their laws resulting in a more flexible, cost-effective, and enabling regime of business reorganization law. Not all member states are responding to the demand for new business forms, however. Some member states are locked into a path-dependent statutory process, which forecloses the possibility of fundamental partnership and close corporation law reform. Attempts to alter these provisions are restrained by powerful interest groups. This appears to be the case in the Netherlands where many policymakers agree that urgent reform is needed to create favourable legal rules for SMEs. Yet, notwithstanding the introduction of a new partnership Bill, there is little prospect for fundamental structural reform permitting, for example, the introduction of a limited liability company (LLC) or limited liability partnership (LLP). Unlike the United States, the 'stable era of partnership law' prevails in the Netherlands (Ribstein, Chapter 6, this volume).

In developing the selection of topics that relate to the programme of reform for partnership and closely held business forms in Europe, we begin our discussion in Section 15.2, with a discussion of the importance of the single-person firm. The single-person firm is important because of the sheer number of such firms and the complex problems that arise when attempting to differentiate them from other enterprises. Fortunately, the evolution towards flexible rules— that allow entrepreneurs to create and tailor firms to meet their own needs—has tended to resolve many of the problems. Section 15.3 turns to focus on the importance of partnership law and asks whether the limited liability partnership form should be extended to non-professional small firms. In this subpart, we also analyze the US discussions on the development of the Limited Liability Partnership. Moreover, we focus on the proposed reform of partnership law in the Netherlands, arguing that the new Bill cannot meet the needs of various types of firms. We also discuss the structural importance of limited partnerships for investment. There are significant legal deficiencies that beset this form that makes it difficult for owners to exit or restructure the vehicle. This section concludes with a description of the crucial role of cooperative structures for some European economies. Section 15.4 provides a survey of the reform of closely held business forms. Section 15.5 concludes.

15.2. FORMS OF BUSINESS ENTERPRISES: THE SOLE PROPRIETORSHIP

Organizing economic activity through an enterprise facilitates individuals to address the complex problems of arranging contracts and making decisions about the allocation of costs/profits and provides an effective technique for creating incentives and encouraging employee cooperation in meeting the demands of the marketplace (Holmström 1999). Thus, the enterprise serves as a framework for organizing a business through a variety of contractual relations. Whilst a sole proprietor retains complete control rights over his business assets, other firms often will 'co-venture' through, for example, loan and other forms of debt finance. Equally, a business may need to allocate decision-making to professional managers and hire employees to carry out contracts. Basically, the development of relations with capital and labour providers and the sole proprietor tends to a certain degree of 'personification' of the firm. In a partnership entrepreneurship is shared and partners will share (residual) rights of control. Both sorts of enterprises tend to have similar characteristics. Unlike corporations, sole proprietorships and partnerships are generally regarded not to create a distinct legal entity (Cheffins 1997). Under standard corporate law, the question of what constitutes a company is determined by reference to legislation. But there is no common concept of an enterprise distinguished from the entrepreneur(s) whatever their business form.

The freedom to organize and reorganize requires agreement on such a basic concept of the enterprise. Accounting for the connection between companies and the distinctions between distinct legal entities (which are often quite different) involves an analysis of the different forms and nature of the business enterprise. Given the dynamics of a business enterprise, it follows that flexible reorganization mechanisms will be indispensable for providing the means to alter the form and content of the business. For instance, a company may wish to alter or change the identity of the 'owners-entrepreneurs' by resort to incorporation. Or a firm might wish to change its lines of business, which may call for a partial transfer of assets. Thus, while the common characteristics of a company may vary significantly, the solution of employing the terms entrepreneur/owner and the firm/enterprise should provide a basis for clarification and simplification of the basic elements of the business organization and its reorganization arrangements. A few examples may serve to illustrate the usefulness of this approach.

In continental legal systems, lawyers have accepted for centuries the 'saisi-ne' principle, namely that the person of the descendant is perpetuated in his heirs (Raaijmakers 2000). Does a person own a business that (by mere consensus) may be continued by his heirs? In this view, the firm does not change, but only the 'owners'. If during an interim stage a participant could trigger dissolution, it would create heavy costs on the others. Just as dissolution is important for equity investors in other firms, the European Commission recommended the introduction of a majority rule in heritage law and the possibility of an exit by 'disagreeing' heirs (against book value upon immediate retreat and against fair value upon payment in instalments). In the context when participants threaten to dissolve, it would make little sense to opt for disposal of the firm by selling it to third parties. In this setting, it is important to notice that the business persists. Given the alternative, the arrangement was crucial in avoiding threatened terminations and allowing such a firm to continue under the control of different parties. Conversely, if we accept the characteristics of the firm to be associated with ownership transfers and conversions into different legal forms (e.g. partnerships), can the basic elements also include, for example, transfers of firms as is? In other words, can the obligations of the owner be assigned by operation of law? Can it be pledged? Or must we regard the firm, as in the Netherlands, as a collection of assets and liabilities, each of which, though the firm as such may be the object of any agreement changing the control thereof, must be transferred separately in the form as required for each separate constituent part? It is submitted that this approach denies the firm's essence as a 'universitas iuris' (encompassing the goodwill as belonging to the proprietor as part of his control rights as the object he transfers).

Interestingly, the Directive on protection of employees in case of mergers (etc.) employs an exceptionally wide conception of 'enterprise', including the transfer of 'enterprises' of the government and its agencies. By its very nature, this Directive is of a narrow scope and protective nature and consequently does not cover the underlying (preceding) transactions as such. Under such conditions, it does not facilitate the transfer of a business as such. Thus, should an owner, for example, exercise his contractual freedom to sell or buy a business, the transfer itself has no impact on the range of assets and liabilities surviving such transfer, ensuring continuity. In addition, we can build on the Commission's initiatives as well as the existing legislation in some member states. For example, Belgian law facilitates the disposal (or contribution in kind) of the business by an entrepreneur by enabling such transfer to take place by operation of law. In case of contribution in kind, i.e. essentially 'incorporation', this amounts to a 'conversion', namely a transaction through which the entrepreneur is allowed to transform the form of his business organization. There are similar transfer constructions provided under German law. In this respect, the well-established HGB facilitates 'conversions' of sole proprietorships. Moreover, the Umwandlungsgesetz of 1995, in essence trespassing the border between persons and artificial persons (Raiser 1994; Schmidt 1997), is designed to facilitate the transfer (and contribution in kind) of a business into a corporation. This measure extends also to cover certain types of 'privatizations'.

Analytically, the Commission's approach, which aims at establishing a variety of rules for transfers and reorganizations of sole proprietorships and partnerships, offers a medium for parties to buy and sell ownership interests with a minimum cost. Also we should build on the achievements of some EU jurisdictions in developing rules that allow for the transfer of an interest in a partnership. Popular examples are the German 'Firmenrecht', including the Civil Code provisions, its partnership law and its recent Umwandlungsgesetz, the revised Belgian Commercial Code, French law on the 'fonds de commerce' and its revised bankruptcy law. These legal regulations also contain in part provisions for conversions, mergers, and contribution in kind of sole proprietorships.

In coming to terms with a framework to analyse the alternative types of business enterprises, abandoning the classical approach of the corporation as an artificial being should mark the beginning for the development of common EU ground for approaching the business enterprise.

15.3. PARTNERSHIPS

The foregoing discussion indicated that the demarcation between unincorporated companies and partnerships is difficult to define with precision. As a result we tend to look to the underlying dynamics to determine whether they are different from other types of firms. We now turn our attention to the significance of the partnership forms of business organizations. We begin with a general analysis of the economic significance of partnerships and then examine the recent proposals to modernize partnership law in the Netherlands.

Professional and commercial partnerships make important contributions to the economic success of countries in Western Europe. Typically multinational multidisciplinary partnerships are active in the provision of accounting, financial, and legal services. Whilst high-tech entrepreneurs are reluctant to use the partnership form (despite the apparent tax advantages), SMEs attempting to develop new products have opted for the partnership business form. The rapid uptake of the partnership form points to the attractiveness of limited liability and the advantages attached to raising new investment capital despite the limitations of the form.

Historically, partnership law focused on commercial ventures designed for the benefit of a few partners only. The form arises from the earlier developmental forms in that a businessman's heirs are entitled (as joint owners) to joint control of his firm, and agreed to continue that business, whereupon their mutual relationship was governed by severe principles of brotherhood (*fraternitas*) (Zimmermann 1996). Modern European partnership law emerged from this source and served as the basis for the organization of both the professional and business forms. Analytically, partnerships typically consist of a few partners who make investments in the business based on settled expectations that are reflected in an enforceable contract. The partnership form provides for full control over the assets of the partnership, and makes partners liable for their partnership's debts (pro rata parte in the professional partnership, jointly and several in the trading partnership).

Most jurisdictions have viewed the partnership primarily as a 'contract'. Other jurisdictions focused on the element of joint ownership and the separation of assets into the partnership's firm.[3] By the late twentieth century, it can be argued that the mega-partnerships arrangements can no longer be adequately characterized as 'contracts' in the ordinary sense of the word, although its 'membership' aspects still possess strong contractual features. It might seem that the partnership form, at least for these types of relationships, possess characteristics that are similar to those associated with the public corporation. The economic theory of the 'nexus of contracts' can assist in providing support for the apparent convergence of the partnership form and the modern corporation. Thus also here a distinction is made between the 'entrepreneur' and his/their firm. In practice, the larger the number of partners, the more a partnership will tend towards an association (*universitas personarum*), which we are inclined to define as a separate person, or at least a separate legal entity.

We should start to acknowledge that in modern Europe there are a substantial number of partnerships operating as distinct entities. Policymakers should revisit a number of issues, particularly the entity status of these establishments and the problem of membership status in a partnership. In coming to terms with the partnership form of the business association, there are a number of concerns that require legislative attention and a clear direction about: (1) the dissociation

---

[3] For a long time, UK and US partnership law endorsed the aggregate theory. German, Swiss, and Austrian law were characterized by the 'Gesamthand' element. Both groups now seem to accept the principle of the partnership constituting an entity distinct from its partners. For a long time a tension existed between the partnership being 'personified' as a separate entity distinct from its partners and the notion of the partnership as a 'mere' contract between the partners. In Roman law, as incorporated into continental law, the contractual element was dominant. For the German 'Gesamthand', the dominant element was the joint ownership ('joint ownership and tenancy'). Under French law partnerships are 'personnes morales', as are trading partnerships under Belgian and Scots law. The US UPA (1914) was based on the aggregate theory, but § 201 of the RUPA (1994) clearly chose to define the partnership as an 'entity distinct from its partners'. A similar development is taking place in the United Kingdom. The impact is important, since it provides an essential basis for 'reorganizations', such as dissociation and expulsion of partners, without dissolution of the partnership (and hence the continued existence of its business).

of partners from the association; (2) the determination of the value of the membership upon entry and exit; (3) the transfer of the partnerships' business, also in bankruptcy; and (4) adopting techniques for the limitation of liabilities for contractual and tort claims against any particular partner and which do not spread out of the present and future exposures of other partners (compare LLP and Partnerschaftgesellschaft).[4] Additionally there are some general questions concerning the mutual relationship between partners that require conclusions and recommendations.

15.3.1. Partnership Law Reform in the Netherlands

In this context, we analyse the recent attempt to modernize the Netherlands partnership law regime.

In an earlier Consultation Memorandum (Maeijer 1998),[5] the Dutch government tabled a number of comments for discussion: (1) whether the public partnership should have legal personality, (2) whether liabilities of partners in a professional partnership should be changed, and (3) whether the partnership 'on shares' should be reintroduced. After a long and substantial public debate on the direction of partnership law reform, a final Bill has emerged recently. The new Bill, which was drafted by Professor J. M. M. Maeijer, creates a hybrid partnership law.

The Bill distinguishes public partnerships without legal personality ('openbare vennootschap') and with legal personality ('openbare vennootschap met rechtspersoonlijkheid') and limited partnerships without ('commanditaire vennootschappen') and with legal personality ('commanditaire vennootschap met rechtspersoonlijkheid'). Under the Bill, legal personality is acquired by execution of the partnership agreement in the form of a notarial deed. Public partnerships are not, as Meijers and Van der Grinten had proposed in their earlier drafts, just recognized as legal persons. This is somewhat awkward, since acquisition of legal personality does not offer any advantages in terms of partners' liability, does not change tax treatment (which will continue to be based on transparency), does not—at least not in the real world in view of the restrictions of joint ownership—change the entitlement of the partnership to its enterprise (assets and liabilities) nor its right to standing in court or its ability to be declared bankrupt. The Bill explains the advantage of legal personality to be that complications with respect to transfer shares in the assets of the partnership in case of exit of a partner can be avoided, but it is difficult to ascertain the fundamental difference with present principles of joint ownership in public

---

[4] In the United States and the United Kingdom the limited liability partnership has developed. Germany in 1995 introduced its Partnerschaftsgesellschaftsgesetz. It provides for the ability to avoid liability incurred by other partners. An essential difference in this respect remains compared to the business venture where the partners control and jointly manage the business of the partnership.

[5] Professor Maeijer introduced the subject during the Congress at the Tilburg Center for Company Law on Partnerships and Close Corporations in May 2001.

partnerships in which partners jointly control a common business rather than a loose collection of assets and liabilities. It does not, however, reveal to what extent a public partnership, without legal personality, will continue to have the aforementioned features of personality. It appears that there will be no deviation from current practice, which means that acquisition of the label 'legal person' only leads to fees for the notary public and other forms of professional advice. It is worth pointing out that legal personality cannot be acquired by simply registering the firm in the Commercial register.

What's new in this legislation? The present distinction between civil (and professional) partnerships, regulated in the Civil Code, and commercial partnerships (Commercial Code) will disappear. The latter will be 'de-commercialized'. Partnership law will be concentrated into one chapter (7.13) of Book 7 of the New Civil Code (specific contracts) and encompass the 'silent' (non-public), for which the present word 'maatschap' will be used, the public professional, the public commercial and the limited partnership (commanditaire vennootschap), the public professional partnership with legal personality, the public commercial partnership with legal personality and the limited partnership with legal personality. The limited partnership on shares will not be reactivated. The Bill does not introduce an LLP/LLLP or any other form of partnership that allows partners to limit their external liability.

Remarkably the Bill does not contain any chapter on the relationship amongst the partners. The general bona fides rule for contracts is applicable, but the Bill does not indicate what particular fiduciary duties arise in a partnership. Accountability has been separately provided for, the nullity on complete exclusion from any share in profits has been maintained, separate provisions on dissociation and dissolution have been proposed, but the Bill does not contain any default rules on such matters as non-competition during the partnership or after an exit respectively. The rules on dissociation and dissolution largely follow present law, with one important exception: the default rule will be that unless the partners agreed otherwise, any dissociation of a partner will not affect the continuity of the partnership (and its business), but rather attribute that partner upon his exit the right to be paid the agreed upon value of his share. Expulsion is possible only if the partners agreed explicitly. Dissolution and dissociation may be acquired in court 'for good reason'. Liquidation of partnerships has now been framed along the framework for legal persons of Book 2 NCC. The liquidation of silent partnerships follows the rules on joint ownership.

Most remarkably the Bill is very strict on reorganizations. A public partnership may 'acquire' legal personality by agreement of the partners to be executed in the form of a notarial deed. But it does not constitute 'acquisition', since in fact a new partnership has to be created to which the business, i.e. in the set up of the Bill its separate assets and liabilities, should be transferred in the way prescribed for each thereof. This means that goodwill—as well as the consequences for the fiduciary duties of each of the partners—remains as obscure as it is now. It is somewhat astonishing that the Bill does not allow for a simple conversion, particularly since no substantial changes arise for the relationship between the partners, nor vis-à-vis third parties. Yet, conversion from a 'partnership with legal personality' into a BV is possible, but again not into an NV. Thus, the concept of 'legal personality' is overestimated and the Bill overlooks that public partnerships will continue to have the capacity to own assets and incur liabilities, which characteristics are precisely those that make 'something' a legal person under Netherlands law.

If one follows my characterization of sole proprietor firms, the step towards partnerships is a small one, since the crucial element is whether the right to a business is controlled by a single person or by more than one person under joint control. Entrepreneur A agrees to take B on board to take his business on as a partnership, i.e. under full joint control, in return for payment of half the fair value of the business. B thus acquires the agreed part of the 'right' (ownership/control) that A has in his firm. If B owns a business himself, A and B may agree to 'merge' by exchanging pro rata parte such ownership and control rights to their businesses into a partnership that will henceforth be under their joint control. A and B may be individuals as well as corporations. This analysis facilitates—at least conceptually—the regulation of reorganizations (conversions, mergers, and split-ups with or without a change of business form) to enable horizontal and vertical choices in a firm's life cycle. The entrepreneur's choice from the menu of available business forms will continue to be influenced by tax considerations (partnership providing tax transparency and a BV being taxed as a corporation), financing issues, flexibility of (re)organization, prospect of possible listing, limited liability, proper default rules, but they may also argue that with the assistance of counsel they will be able to properly draft their internal organization by themselves.

An improvement is that a public partnership (but only those with legal personality) may be converted into a BV, but the Bill is misguided by not allowing conversion into an NV or other form of legal person. Conceptually there is no reason for such limitation and it therefore recommended that conversions into a (close or public) corporation be allowed. Reforms to the tax code should be introduced to allow such reorganizations. The proposed procedure for conversion is rather cumbersome, requiring, apart from a notarial deed, judicial supervision and approval.

The Bill, furthermore, does not facilitate other reorganizations, particularly mergers and split-ups. Reorganizations of limited partnerships both into general partnerships and sole proprietorships, as well as into capital corporations, should indeed be facilitated (also taxwise). Most jurisdictions allow the former, but not the latter. Based on a review of today's partnership practice, it is submitted that a flexible law is needed to enable all reorganizations ranging from conversions to mergers, splits, and sale of assets. Here, too, the main principle should be the distinction between the firm and its owner(s), i.e. the partnership as an entity distinct from its members (i.e. partners). This should allow association and exits (dissociation) against payment of proper value.

Whilst the Netherlands reforms will introduce a number of much-needed modernizing provisions of partnership law, there are, as we have seen, a number of weaknesses that remain. Indeed, it is submitted that a wider and deeper set of proposals is needed to achieve the goal of modernizing partnership law. First, and perhaps most importantly, an entrepreneurial culture will be further strengthened by the introduction of the LLC and LLP respectively. Supplying firms with choice in business forms should lower the cost for businesses and is likely to spur more legal innovation.

15.3.2. Limited Partnerships

This section discusses general questions about the limited partnership form of business association that has changed many times over the years. The supposed advantage of the limited partnership form is that it allows parties to devise customized forms that may limit liability and economize on transaction costs. In Medieval Europe, the limited partnership created new financing and funding opportunities for businessmen through the development of the concept of 'co-entrepreneur' enabling wealthy nobles and clergymen to participate with 'risk capital' in trading ventures emerging across twelfth century's Europe, without violating the severe ecclesiastical usury rules. The 'silent' partner entrusted risk capital (not a loan) to the managing partner against becoming entitled to profit sharing (not interest); liability for the partnership's liabilities was limited to his contribution only.[6] To begin with, the degree of 'control' of the 'silent' partner has always caused problems over the deterring of misconduct. Indeed, the separation of ownership from control has meant that the 'silent' partner may not involve himself in the management of the partnership. Departure from adherence to this principle has led to limited partners having managing partners' liability imposed on them. Nevertheless, the question where to draw the line between exercising 'distant' control and being involved in 'management' remains a difficult question. Safe harbour provisions are necessary to enable involvement in general control and clear definition of what constitutes management to the extent of being directly involved in third-party relationships and representation of the partnership. This is not only important in cases where certain heirs wish to participate in the venture but not in its management. Similarly, such clarity is important in the case of venture capital participation and their need more broadly to protect themselves from opportunism by owners or their agents.

Distinguishing the limited partnership from other types of business associations remains an important task. It is crucial to recognize that limited partnerships differ from other business associations in that they are often designed to

---

[6] Conceptually this resembles the Roman law *peculium*. The picture, however, was not very clear and throughout history the nature of the limited partnership and the contribution of the 'silent' partner has been debated. See Asser (1983).

economize on a specific commercial transaction (Ribstein 1999). In general, a limited partnership consists of general partners, who are joint and severally liable for the debts of the firm, with limited partners, who possess limited liability. It is argued that the limited partnership needs to be re-evaluated in the light of the proliferation of business associations enjoying limited liability. These proposals raise a number of questions about the specific role and nature of limited partnerships. In the first place, does a separate entity emerge? If we turn to German and French law, we can see that for 'silent', i.e. undisclosed (not registered) limited partnerships, the venture idea and the profit sharing of the silent partner persists, but the contribution of the 'silent' partner is to the business (assets) of the managing partner(s).[7] At the other end of the spectrum, interests ('units') in limited partnerships are classified as tradeable securities that are subject to securities legislation in the European Union.

As discussed earlier, the limited partnership provides a strong solution in heritage cases in which some heirs want to continue the business as managing partners and others wish to remain as silent partners. It may be that principles of heritage law coincide with those of partnership law. Under heritage law, conflicts must be resolved by unanimous vote where partnership law allows majority voting. The continuation of the firm will require majority voting. The Commission rightly focused on this dilemma in its 1994 SME memorandum. In the light of the pre-eminent role of limited partnerships in the modern economy, and the special role they play, it is suggested that flexible default rules should be designed so as to: (1) define management rights; (2) determine liability of members for a debt or other contingency; (3) provide a means for members to transfer their interests; and (4) provide dissociation-at-will rules. It is important to keep in mind that there is no reason why such legal reforms should not also define a limited partnership as an entity as distinct from its members (i.e. partners) to better allow parties to avoid the limitations of the aggregate characterization of earlier precedent, and permit sufficient flexibility to avoid costly obligations. Certainly, this view is supported by some recent leading cases that confirm the view that a partnership constitutes an entity distinct from its partners.

15.3.3. Cooperative Associations and Mutual Insurance Corporations

This section discusses the nature of agricultural cooperatives and mutual insurance corporations in order to explain how this sort of enterprise differs from other business enterprises. Producer cooperatives that process farm-owned and other products for their members differ markedly in their scope from other firms. Farmers have an incentive to form cooperatives through which they

---

[7] 'Stille Gesellschaft' (paras 230–237 German HGB) and 'societe en participation' (art 1873 French CC).

can increase their bargaining power. Given the nature of farming, with its homogeneous commodities and many producers, cooperatively owned firms can sometimes exercise monopsony over markets.

It is important to note that cooperatives are the by-product of political and consumer movements. For instance, the 'Pioneers of Rochdale' combined their efforts to create economic power in the market. Essentially the cooperative formed a different mechanism to avoid their competing amongst each other. The legal history literature has given attention to the role cooperatives played in responding to the disaster in rural market development that occurred in the second half of the nineteenth century. The agricultural cooperatives and mutual associations were successful over long periods in creating a buffer against adversity. It is conventional wisdom now that some cooperatives have prospered in many industries and consequently become large and often international businesses. In the latter case, their membership often becomes depersonalized. In large firms, one of the problems facing the cooperative's delegated managers is how to finance growth (Galle 1993: 183–203; Van der Sangen 1999: 353–472). Typically, cooperatives employ a number of schemes for raising money, most of which create a tension between the total amount of capital that can be raised and the farmer's patronage dividend on capital. Perhaps the most difficult issue is the problem of issuing capital stock. In most countries cooperatives avoid issuing stock to a class of owners that have distinct interests from those of the cooperative's members. A further reason is that cooperatives do not pay out dividend interest on members' equity investment and consequently they pay out members at book or net value. It is thought that cooperatives sometimes want to pay dividends because they wish to lock-in members' invested capital and create disincentives to leave. In any event, there are a number of competing tensions in any cooperative that must balance competing considerations regarding the amount of capital required, the speed in which it may be accumulated, and the return on each member's share.

At first glance, the cooperative organization appears to consist of a number of different types of business forms: the association, corporation, and partnership. The upshot is that different jurisdictions will use their own arrangements to deal with this conceptual ambiguity. In some countries, the cooperative is treated as an association and in others as a corporation with shares. For example, this structure has become one of the many forms available in the Netherlands menu of business organizations. Again, there are strong reasons for characterizing the cooperative in terms of its underlying bargaining relationships. We noted earlier that the most important aspects of the enterprise is that it can contract with patrons, suppliers of capital and labour, and that some of the costs of market contracting can be eliminated by the optimal allocation of control. As with other forms, such as the sole proprietorship and partnership, the cooperative tends to deal with the problems it confronts by contract. As a consequence, we can ask for flexible and enabling measures to deal with some of the disadvantages of ownership. In this regard, the Commission has published a draft Statute for Cooperative Associations that cannot always be seen as taking advantage of the benefits of presumptive rules.

15.4. PRIVATE CORPORATIONS AND THE LIMITED LIABILITY COMPANY

This section will discuss the nature of the private corporation and the limited liability company (LLC). New business forms are currently popular in the United States and the European Union because of their low-cost access to limited liability. It is widely accepted that a business can be incorporated into a closely held corporation, i.e. a corporation held by one or more persons acting as co-ventures. While statutory law tends to separate the ownership and control dimensions, partners typically act as both shareholder and manager in private companies.[8]

In UK law the 'quasi partnership' has been developed to ensure that partnership agreements or bona fides rules can be upheld against the strict rules of corporate law based upon the majority rule. Correspondingly, the GmbH Act was introduced in Germany as early as 1892 to enable such a combination of contractual and 'institutional' rules so as to provide ventures with the grant of limited liability. In the United States the advent of the Close Corporation Supplement to the Model Business Corporation Act prompted the introduction of this business form in many states. This model allows promoters to organize their business internally as a partnership, e.g. by eliminating the board requirements and allowing the firms to be governed by partnership rules. The Limited Liability Company's development in the United States appears to improve the mix of business menus for small firms. Unlike the European Union, capital requirements have long been phased out of US law. The LLC brings us to the final stage in the evolution of the historical association of, on the one hand, limited liability, corporate governance norms, and two-tier tax treatment, and, on the other hand, unlimited liability, partnership governance norms, and one-tier tax treatment. The success of the LLC confirms the view that limited liability forms governed by partnership norms and one-tier tax treatment foster efficiency by lowering the cost of shareholder monitoring, reducing the risk of investment, and creating the free transferability of shares. Likewise, France has quite recently introduced the SAS (Société par Actions Simplifiée), which is designed to facilitate joint venture-like cooperation between firms. Increasingly there is pressure for jurisdictions to develop new types of limited liability forms for small firms. Interestingly, the European Commission and the Paris Chamber of Commerce have encouraged the introduction of a European close corporation (Boucourechliev 1973; Raaijmakers 1976: 116–30). Such developments

---

[8] Although we have to clearly distinguish the 'close' corporation originally held by one or a few promoters acting as a 'partners' and the second and following generations of heirs acquiring shares of the promoters that are no longer 'tied' by strict cooperation agreements. Such acquirors tend to take the position of distinct limited partners. Therefore in these cases a de facto separation of ownership and control also emerges.

must be welcomed, since they fit into an agenda for reform aimed at the efficient provision of a flexible set of 'menus' for business forms, including (cross-border) joint ventures (Drury, Chapter 14, this volume).

Statutes generally allow for the reorganization of private companies into a public corporation. However, efforts to effect the conversion of a (limited) partnership into a private corporation have been frustrated. Here, again, if we accept the partnership as an entity entitled to control its own business, then we should be able to accept that an entity can be converted by resolution of its 'members' into another (legal) entity, i.e. a close corporation. Such transactions are quite often primarily arranged for tax purposes and consequently are not aimed at all at a dissolution. Indeed, that is not what the members envisaged or intended. Such business actions reflect the members' preference to continue their business as a partnership, albeit in a form more convenient for the stage in the life cycle of the firm.

15.5. Conclusion

In the United States, there is a wide range of legal business forms that effectively permits firms to select the appropriate legal rules to satisfy their contracting needs. The emergence of these new business forms was prompted by the influence activities of interest groups. The drafters also urged policymakers to attempt to discover the basic patterns of business forms and reorganizations. It is submitted that the introduction of similar style business forms is crucial to meeting the challenges of modernizing European partnership law and providing a competitive legal infrastructure for SMEs. In this respect, it is crucial to ask whether the 'traditional' instruments of the Treaty are well suited to meet the challenges set by the Lisbon Summit. As is well known, the federalization of corporate law failed in earlier stages of US law reform, which had many of its own 'subsidiarity' problems (Romano 1996). EU policymakers are beginning to consider taking up similar initiatives. Moreover, the pressures on lawmakers at the member state level are also leading to the competition among business forms across Europe. We expect, moreover, that the legal changes taking places in ECJ case law, along with the Commission's more aggressive approach to the modernization of company law, should provide a powerful stimulus for legal change. If nothing else, such efforts could provide a common research framework for future legislative developments at the member state level.

References

Asser, A. D. H. (1983), *In solidum of pro parte*, Leiden: Leiden University Press.

Bebchuk, L. A. (1992), 'Federalism and the Corporation: The Desirable Limits on State Competition in Corporate Law', *Harvard Law Review* 105: 1435.

Black, B., and Gilson, R.J. (1997), 'Venture Capital and the Structure of Capital Markets: Banks versus Stock Markets', *Journal of Financial Economics* 47: 243.

Boucourechliev, J. (1973), *Pour une S.A.R.L. Européenne*, Presses Universitaires de France.

Cheffins, B. R. (1997), *Company Law: Theory, Structure, and Operation*, Oxford: Clarendon Press.

Coffee, Jr., J. C. (1999), 'The Future as History: The Prospects for Global Convergence in Corporate Governance and Its Implications', *Northwestern University Law Review* 93: 641.

Galle, R. C. J. (1993), *De coöperatie*, Deventer: Tjeenk Willink.

Holmström, B. (1999), 'The Firm as a Subeconomy', *Journal of Law, Economics & Organization* 15: 74.

Maeijer, J. M. M. (1998), 'Memorandum with Respect to the Bill Regarding the (Personal) Partnership ((Persoonlijke) Vennootschap): Title 7.13 of the New Civil Code (NBW)', University of Nijmegen, Mimeo.

Raaijmakers, M. J. G. C. (1976), *Joint Ventures*, Deventer: Kluwer.

—— (2000), *Pitlo/Raaijmakers, Vennootschaps- en Rechtspersonenrecht*, Deventer: Gouda Quint.

Raiser, Th. (1994), 'Gesamthand und juristische Person im Licht des neuen Umwandlungsrechts', *Archiv für juristische civilistische Praxis* 194: 495.

Ribstein, L. E. (1999), 'Limited Partnerships Revisited', *University of Cincinnati Law Review* 67: 953.

—— and Kobayashi, B. H. (2001), 'Choice of Form and Network Externalities', *William and Mary Law Review* 43: 79.

Romano, R. (1996), 'Explaining American Exceptionalism in Corporate Law', in W. W. Bratton, J. A. McCahery, S. Picciotto, and C. Scott (eds.), *International Regulatory Competition and Coordination: Perspectives on Economic Regulation in Europe and the United States*, Oxford: Clarendon Press.

Schmidt, K. (1997), *Gesellschaftsrecht*, Köln: Carl Heymanns Verlag.

Van der Sangen, G. J. H. (1999), *Rechts-karakter en financiering van de coöperatie*, Deventer: Tjeenk Willink.

Wouters, J. (2000), 'European Company Law: Quo Vadis?', *Common Market Law Review* 37: 257.

Zimmermann, R. (1996), *The Law of Obligations: Roman Foundations of the Civilian Tradition*, Oxford: Clarendon Press.

Zweigert, K., and Kötz, H. (1998), *An Introduction to Comparative Law* (translated by Tony Weir), Oxford: Oxford University Press.

16

Taxation of Partnerships/Hybrid Entities

PETER ESSERS and GERARD T. K. MEUSSEN

16.1. INTRODUCTION

The taxation of partnerships in cross-border situations has proved to be exceptionally complicated and is perhaps one of the most difficult issues in the application of rules on international tax law. Unfortunately, the OECD Model Tax Convention and many bilateral tax treaties do not address international partnership taxation considerations. However, the OECD (1999) has recently issued a Partnership Report ('Report') that exhaustively reviews double taxation issues. Despite the issuance of the Report, problems nevertheless arise if a partnership is situated in one state (the source state) while the partners are residents of another state (the resident state). Depending on the circumstances, the resident state has to make a fiscal judgement concerning the partnership, a legal form that is often alien to its own jurisdiction. When dealing with the partners, for example, the source state may treat the partnership differently from the resident state. One state may for instance treat the partnership as transparent; the other may treat it as non-transparent. In principle every state applies its own domestic rules that may lead to a different outcome. Consequently, there is no such thing as a uniform global treatment of foreign partnerships for tax purposes.

This chapter examines the main tax problems that arise when dealing with a foreign partnership and considers a range of solutions designed to resolve these problems. This chapter has three sections. In Section 16.2, we offer an overview of the fundamental conflicts involving the tax treatment of partnerships. Section 16.3 analyses initially UK and Dutch treatment in dealing with the tax position of foreign entities. We also set out our own recommendations. Section 16.4 concludes.

16.2. OVERVIEW

In general, most countries adopt the same analytic approach to foreign and domestic partnerships. They have to investigate the foreign law's legal characteristics of the entity. On the basis of these characteristics a country applies its domestic tax legislation in order to determine whom it should tax—the partnership or a separate legal entity or its partners. The Report shows that, in cross-border situations, partners face being liable for tax to the state of residence and the state of source. The risk is associated with (a) the different classification of a given entity in the state of residence and the state of source, and (b) the different tax treatment in these states, of a given entity despite common classification. These problems primarily occur when partners reside in a different state from that in which the partnership has been established.

16.2.1. Problems Regarding the Tax Treatment of Partnerships

The problems regarding the tax treatment of partnerships (and their partners) are commonly divided into three categories: (1) differences in qualification of a partnership; (2) differences in treatment of income; and (3) the entitlement to tax treaty benefits. We briefly describe these problems below.

Most countries recognize the concepts of 'company' and of 'partnership' for tax purposes. However, the definitions of these two concepts tend to vary. Yet, in most cases (OECD 1999), the similarities between the legal systems will be sufficient to ensure that if domestic law determines that an entity should be treated as a partnership for tax purposes, then other countries will be constrained to follow. But entities that are not so prevalent may easily create difficulties if they cannot be classified in one of these categories. Consequently, they may need to be classified separately. In these circumstances, it may be possible that one country will treat the entity as a partnership (i.e. transparent for tax purposes) while the other country will treat the entity as a company (i.e. non-transparent for tax purposes). In such cases, the entity is marked as being a hybrid entity, meaning that it is regarded as transparent in one country and non-transparent in another. These differences in qualification may lead to completely different tax results in the countries involved.

Even if both countries qualify a partnership in the same manner (i.e. transparent for tax purposes), there may be problems regarding the qualification and allocation of specific items of income. For example, while some countries accept that a partner may also be a creditor of the partnership and may therefore derive interest income from the partnership, other countries consider that no interest may be paid to a partner. This leads to a different tax treatment of the interest payment as the latter country classifies it as a distribution.

Problems may also arise with respect to how different countries apply the transparency principle. Some countries, for example, apply a full transparency approach. Other jurisdictions, in contrast, acknowledge the existence of the partnership to some extent by determining the results at the level of the partnership itself, followed by the allocation of these results to the individual partners. Thus, these distinct approaches may lead to different treatments regarding a specific item of income.

The conflicts described above have emerged in the application of the provisions of tax treaties. Article 1 of the OECD Model Treaty provides that only persons who are residents of the Contracting State are entitled to the benefits of the Tax Convention entered into by these states. In this context, the foregoing declaration raises several issues: (1) is a partnership a 'person' on the treaty level;[1] (2) is a partnership a 'resident of a Contracting State' on the treaty level;[2] and (3) is a partnership liable to tax?[3]

On the basis of the Report, the Commentaries to the OECD Model Treaty will be revised to clarify that a partnership is a person (company or other body of persons) within the meaning of Article 3(1) under (a) of the OECD Model Treaty (1999) and that the partnership is a resident within the meaning of Article 4 of the Convention if it is not treated as fiscally transparent in a state. If the partnership is treated as fiscally transparent, the partners may be entitled to invoke a tax treaty.

The US–Netherlands Tax Treaty (1992) recognizes the existence of a partnership for treaty purposes. Article 3(1)(g) states that the term 'nationals' means—besides individuals—all legal persons, partnerships and associations deriving their status as such from the law in force in one of the states.

Another example is found in the protocol to the new Belgium–Netherlands Treaty. Article 4(b) states that:

Where a company is not subject to tax as such in a Contracting State and is subject to tax as such in the other Contracting State, the other Contracting State shall apply, at the request of the company, the provisions of Chapters III, IV, and V of this Convention insofar as these provisions would have applied if the persons entitled to the company's capital had directly received the income or owned the capital, each according to its share in the company. The application of the preceding sentence shall not alter the base on which the tax is imposed on the company according to the internal law of the other Contracting State and shall reduce this base only insofar as such reduction results directly from the preceding sentence.

Treaty benefits primarily consist of the entitlement to a reduced 5 per cent withholding tax on dividends, which is applicable to payments, 'if the beneficial owner is a company (other than a partnership) which holds directly at least 25 per cent of the capital of the company paying the dividend'.[4] Also with respect to royalties and interest reduced withholding tax rates are possible. Paragraph 11 of the OECD Commentary on Article 10 of the OECD Model Treaty (1999) states that: 'If a partnership is treated as a body corporate under the domestic laws applying to it, the two Contracting States may agree to modify subparagraph (a) of paragraph 2 in a way to give the benefits of the reduced rate provided for parent companies also to such partnership.'

Yet, in a cross-border situation, the problems result from a difference in qualification for tax purposes of a partnership. We examine the conflict of qualification in the next section.

---

[1] OECD Model Treaty, art 3(1)(a).   [2] OECD Model Treaty, art 4(1).
[3] Ibid.   [4] OECD Model Treaty, art 10(2)(a).

16.2.2. Reasons for Categorization of a Partnership/Entity[5]

When looking at the source state, a qualification of the partnership is needed for a number of different reasons. In this way the source state can determine: (1) whether to tax the partnership or its members; (2) the applicable rate of tax; (3) the taxable income; and (4) where there is a tax treaty involved, whether the partnership is a resident of the other Contracting State for purposes of the tax treaty. But also for the resident state of the partner, a qualification of the partnership is needed namely to determine: (1) the type of income to tax (profits or a dividend); (2) the timing of taxation (when the income of the partner is earned or when it is distributed); and (3) whether a foreign tax credit is available for the underlying tax.

16.2.3. The Entitlement of a Partnership to Tax Treaty Benefits

In a cross-border situation, it is worth pointing out that the application of the domestic tax law is the necessary starting point in determining the tax treatment of partnerships. These provisions will determine who may be subjected to tax on the type of income involved.

In order to have access to a tax treaty, Article 1 of the OECD Model Treaty (1999) is of particular importance. This article states that: 'This Convention shall apply to persons who are resident of one or both of the Contracting States.' When evaluating a partnership for international tax purposes, one may make a distinction between partners and the partnership. If income is earned by the partnership itself, the issue arises whether the partnership is entitled to the benefits of the tax treaty. As a consequence, there are a number of fundamental questions that have to be answered, namely: (1) is a partnership a person on the basis of the OECD Model Treaty; and (2) is a partnership a 'resident of a Contracting State' according to the OECD Model Treaty?

We turn initially to consider the first question. In Article 3(1)(a) of the OECD Model Treaty, the term 'person' is said to include an individual, a company, and any other body of persons. The Commentary on Article 3 of the Model, however, explains that, in paragraph 2, this definition is not exhaustive and should be read as indicating that the term 'person' is used in a very wide sense. Note that Article 3(1)(b) of the OECD Model Treaty states that the term 'company' means any body corporate or any entity that is treated as a body corporate for tax purposes. It is not surprising that the Committee that drew up the OECD Partnership Report still felt uncertain of the tax position of a partnership under the OECD Model Treaty. Indeed, this is precisely why the Commentary on

---

[5] In this context, the terms 'characterization', 'categorization', and 'qualification' of a partnership have the same meaning.

Article 3 of the Model is extended in paragraph 2 to include the following sentence: 'Partnerships will also be considered to be "persons" either because they fall within the definition of "company" or, where this is not the case, because they constitute other bodies of persons.'

Having examined whether a partnership is a person under the Treaty, we turn next to consider whether a partnership is a 'resident of a Contracting State' under the OECD Model Treaty. It is clear that, according to Article 4(1) of the OECD Model Treaty, the term 'resident of a Contracting State' means any person who, under the law of that state, is liable for to tax therein by reason of his domicile, residence, place of management, or any other criterion of a similar nature. If a partnership is treated as a company or taxed in the same way, the partnership will be considered to be a resident of the Contracting State. In that case the partnership is entitled to the benefits of the treaty. And, if the state in which a partnership has been organized treats that partnership as fiscally transparent, then the partnership is not 'liable to tax' and can, in principle, not invoke the treaty. In such cases, the partners are entitled with respect to their share of income of the partnership to the benefits provided for in the tax treaty. Surely, the aspect of 'liable to tax' is not as easy as it may seem. Indeed, the Report correctly points out that, at the treaty level, it is not as simple as one might expect to qualify a partnership as transparent or non-transparent. This is because partnerships can be treated in various ways. Sometimes a partnership is partly treated as a taxable entity and partly disregarded for tax purposes.

16.3. CHARACTERIZATION CONFLICTS

This section will examine the conflicts of characterization of income or organization in international contexts. We refer to Dutch tax law to illustrate the conflicts of characterization that are likely to arise.

In the context of Dutch tax law, conflicts of characterization with regard to foreign partnerships generally arise in two situations: (1) a Dutch resident participates in a foreign partnership; and (2) a foreign partnership, established abroad, derives taxable income from a Dutch source. In the first situation, the classification of the foreign partnership as a transparent entity leads to the conclusion that the partners themselves will be taxable for the earned income. As the resident state of the partners, the Netherlands considers the income earned abroad as part of the worldwide income of the partners. Relief for double taxation may be granted unilaterally or on the basis of tax treaties. If the Netherlands considers the foreign partnership as a non-transparent entity, the Dutch partners will not be taxed directly for the profits made by the partnership. These profits will be allocated to the foreign partnership itself. Only if payments are received from the partnership that can be qualified as, e.g. interests or dividends, the partners will be taxed for these income items. If a Dutch corporation participates in such a non-transparent foreign entity, the participation exemption may be applicable to dividends and capital gains with respect to the participation in this partnership.

In the second situation, a foreign partnership deriving income from a Dutch source, the salient question is who should be regarded as taxable subject in the Netherlands: the foreign partnership or its partners? If the partnership can be characterized as an entity mentioned in Article 3 of the Dutch Corporate Income Tax Act, it will be subject to the corporate income tax for its income derived from Dutch sources. The entities mentioned in this article are, *inter alia*, open limited companies and other companies without legal personality with a capital fully or partially divided into shares.

16.3.1. Characterization Criteria

Even though most states have more or less clear rules for categorization of domestic bodies, the characterization of foreign bodies causes many problems.

Avery Jones et al. (2002: 305) make a distinction between four approaches: (1) all foreign bodies are classified as taxable corporations (e.g. Italy or Switzerland); (2) a foreign body is classified according to whether it is a legal entity (e.g. Belgium or Canada); (3) a country like the United States allows the taxpayer to choose the categorization of most bodies; and (4) the approach adopted by most countries where foreign bodies generally must be fitted into the domestic tax law categories or fitted by analogy into the list of domestic bodies subject to corporate income tax. In these countries, as a general rule the foreign general law governing the foreign partnerships is the starting point. The next step is that this general law structure has to be characterized by analogy to the closest internal law equivalent. The foreign tax characterization is not decisive in this respect. As Avery Jones et al. (2002: 289) correctly state 'this approach fails to deal with the problem that the other states' bodies may be inherently different from one's own.' Many differences exist between partnerships. Some are unique; others are typical for common law or civil law countries.

The research done by Avery Jones et al. (2002) in Germany, the Netherlands, the United Kingdom and Sweden demonstrates that no uniformity exists in the categorization criteria that are used in these countries to determine the difference between transparent and non-transparent entities. In the Netherlands, according to a Decree of 18 September 1997 (Vakstudie-Nieuws 1997: 4373, para 8) a six-factor test is applied to the foreign partnership when the Netherlands is the resident country of the partners. If all of these tests are satisfied, the foreign partnership is considered non-transparent. To achieve this, the following questions have to be answered in the affirmative: (1) is a resolution required to distribute profits; (2) is liability of the partners limited to the capital contribution; (3) is the entity the owner of the assets used for conducting the business operations; (4) are interests in the partnership freely transferable; (5) is the capital divided into shares; and (6) is the entity subject to foreign taxation?

If the answers to these questions are not in all cases 'yes', a distinction is made between limited partnerships and other entities.

A limited partnership is considered to be non-transparent if the partnership interest of the partners can be transferred without the consent of all partners. Other entities are considered to be non-transparent if they are owners of the assets unless the business is effectively carried on for the risk and account of the partners. The latter is assumed if, in combination with the full liability of the partners, no resolution is required for the distribution of partnership profits. The emphasis on the resolution to distribute profits is explained by the Dutch legislator's assumption with respect to the fiscal dichotomy between transparent and non-transparent companies. This assumption is based on the thought that the profits of a transparent partnership directly increase the ability to pay of its individual partners, whereas this is not the case for shareholders in corporations. However, this assumption proves to be based on a misunderstanding. The starting point both for partners in partnerships and for shareholders in corporations is that they only gain the right to payment of their share in the profit to which they are entitled after the determination of the company's profit and as a result of this determination. So, in principle, no separate decision is needed once this has been done (van Kempen 1999: 69) Thus, we agree with Avery Jones et al. (2002: 311) that the application of this resolution test 'is likely to depend on the terms of the partnership agreement so that the result may be similar to giving the taxpayer the choice of how to characterize the body in a way similar to the US check-the-box regulations.'

In the United Kingdom, the Inland Revenue uses the following tests: (1) does the foreign entity have a legal existence separate from that of the persons who have an interest in it; (2) does the entity issue share capital or something else that serves the same function as share capital; (3) is the business carried on by the entity itself or jointly by the persons who have an interest in it; (4) are the persons who have an interest in the entity entitled to share in its profits as they arise, or does the amount of profits to which they are entitled depend on a decision of the entity or its members, after the period in which the profits have arisen, to make a distribution of its profits (this is the same test as described under 1 in the Netherlands); (5) who is responsible for debts incurred as a result of the carrying on of the business: the entity or the persons who have an interest in it; and (6) do the assets used for carrying on the business belong beneficially to the entity or to the persons who have an interest in it? In the United Kingdom, the third and fourth tests are regarded as the most important.

16.3.2. Two Main Characterization Conflicts

A distinction can be made between two main characterization conflicts. The first is that the resident state of the partners considers a foreign partnership as transparent, whereas the resident state of the partnership taxes the partnership as a corporate body. The second characterization conflict appears when the foreign partnership is considered to be a non-transparent entity by its resident state, while the state of residence of the partners considers it to be transparent.

16.3.2.1. *Czech KS with Dutch Resident Partners/Individuals*

An example of the first characterization conflict is a situation in which Dutch resident individuals are partners of a Czech limited partnership (Komanditni Spolecnost, KS) (Stevens 2002: 201). In this situation, the Netherlands considers the KS as a transparent entity; the Czech Republic classifies the KS as a non-transparent entity. For the application of the OECD Model Treaty, the KS will be considered as a 'company' (Article 3(1)(b)) and as a 'resident' (Article 4(1)) because the KS is liable to tax in its country of residence. As a consequence, the Czech Republic will tax the entire profits of the entity according to Article 7 of the Netherlands–Czech Republic DTT (Article 7, OECD Model Treaty). In case of dividend distributions, the Czech Republic will levy a reduced dividend withholding tax according to Article 10(2) of the Netherlands–Czech Republic DTT (Article 10(2) OECD Model Treaty).

According to Dutch national tax law, the KS is considered to be transparent. As a consequence, the profits realized by the KS become an integral part of the world income of the Dutch partners. They may be exempted as profits of a foreign permanent establishment. 'Dividend' distributions are not recognized as such. For that reason, the Netherlands is not obliged to grant a credit for the Czech dividend withholding tax.

The question is whether this characterization conflict, and as a result of this, allocation conflict should be extended to the tax treaty or whether the treaty offers a solution for these conflicts. There are, however, two conflicting views. The first view states that, at treaty level, the profits of an enterprise have to be allocated to the same subject.[6] The consequences of this approach are: (1) for the application of Article 7 OECD Model Treaty, only the enterprise of the foreign state, the KS, is recognized; the Netherlands is not allowed to tax the profits of this KS as long as they are not distributed; losses are not deductible; and (2) according to Article 10 OECD Model Treaty dividend distributions are taxed in the Netherlands; the Czech Republic may levy a reduced dividend withholding tax; the Netherlands would have to give a credit for this reduced foreign source taxation (Article 23B OECD Model Treaty). The second view provides that, despite the fact that the KS is a resident for treaty purposes, the Netherlands is allowed to apply its own characterization and allocation rules. This means that the differences because of the different characterization rules are extended to the treaty. In paragraph 102 of the OECD Partnerships report it is stated that 'a useful starting point is the recognition of the principle that the

---

[6] Some commentators, like Daniels (1991), base their opinion on the first sentence of art 7 of the OECD Model Treaty ('the profits of an enterprise of a Contracting State shall be taxable only in that State'). The expression, 'an enterprise carried on' is interpreted, in art 3(1)(c) of the OECD Model Treaty, according to the law of the state of residence of the entity (i.e. Czech Republic). Others, like Vogel (1986), base their opinion on art 23B in combination with art 10 of the OECD Model Treaty.

domestic law of the State applying its tax governs all matters regarding how and in the hands of whom an item of income is taxed.' Because the Netherlands does not recognize the 'dividend' distribution, the Netherlands is not obliged to prevent double taxation on this distribution.

The Netherlands has stated that if double taxation would occur this should be avoided by means of the mutual agreement procedure of Article 25 OECD Model Treaty.[7]

16.3.2.2. *US (Limited) Partnership with Dutch Resident Partners*

The second characterization conflict arises if, for example, the Netherlands, the state in which the partners live, considers the foreign partnership as non-transparent, whereas in the other state, for example the United States, the entity is treated as transparent. Because the partnership is not liable to tax, it will not be regarded as a 'company' or 'resident' for the application of the treaty. As a consequence, the United States will tax the partnership on the basis of Article 7 OECD Model Treaty only if and in so far as a permanent establishment exists in the United States. According to its national law, the Netherlands is only entitled to tax the profits at the moment they are distributed as 'dividends' by the partnership.

The above-mentioned divergence of views with respect to the extension of the characterization conflicts to a tax treaty can also in this situation be distinguished. On the one hand, the country of residence of the partnership, the United States, has the right to tax the profits if and in so far as the enterprise is carried on by a US permanent establishment. The Netherlands should give an exemption for these profits on the basis of Article 23A OECD Model Treaty. According to this opinion, 'dividend' distributions cannot be taxed in the Netherlands. On the other hand, the Netherlands insists (which is official policy of the government) that it is allowed to apply its own characterization and allocation rules. Nevertheless, if one or more partners in the US partnership are Dutch corporations, the Netherlands, according to the Decree of 18 September 1997, will apply the participation exemption on the 'dividend' distributions, although the foreign partnership itself is not liable to a profit tax in the United States. No relief is provided for partners-individuals.

16.3.3. Possible Solutions to Mitigate Categorization Problems

Avery Jones et al. (2002: 314) have examined three possible solutions to reduce the problems of categorizing foreign entities. They are: (1) the partner's residence state is to follow the partnership state's tax categorization; (2) the use of tax treaties to determine the categorization of the other state's bodies; and (3) accept the source state's characterization, but interpret the treaty or include specific treaty provisions that require the source state to follow the

---

[7] Decree of 18 September 1997 (Vakstudie-Nieuws 1997: 4373, para 8).

categorization of the partner's residence state. We critically review the respective positions below.

16.3.3.1. *Partner's Residence State Is to Follow the Partnership State's* *Tax Categorization*

Many complications arising from characterization conflicts could be reduced if the partner's residence state would follow the partnership state's tax characterization. This could also mean that the partner's residence state would accept the choice of the partnership in its resident state to be treated as transparent or non-transparent. CFC rules would mostly prevent abuse if the choice to be treated as non-transparent entity would lead to no or a nominal corporate income tax.

This approach would confirm the opinion expressed in the OECD Partnership Report that in case of qualification conflicts due to differences in the domestic law between the state of source and the state of residence, the qualification of the income under the law of the source state should be binding upon the residence state.[8] According to the Report, this follows from the wording of Article 23 OECD Model Treaty. The Netherlands, however, has reservations about this point. That is to say, the Netherlands only accepts this opinion if this has been explicitly laid down in the text of a tax treaty, if it forms the outcome of a mutual agreement procedure, or if it has been laid down in an internal rule of policy. Portugal has expressed similar reservations.

16.3.3.2. *Use of Tax Treaties to Determine the Categorization of the Other* *State's Bodies*

The second alternative relies on the tax treaty to provide for a categorization of partnerships. On this view, it would be necessary to amend the OECD Model Treaty in order to make a clear distinction between companies (non-transparent) and partnerships (transparent), e.g. by defining that the term 'company' means any entity that is treated as a body corporate for tax purposes. It is worth pointing out that Avery Jones et al. (2002: 316) notes that this approach is not fully satisfactory, since it does not account for cases in which three countries are involved. Also, the treaty categorization needs to be sufficiently flexible towards changes in national tax laws.

16.3.3.3. *Acceptance of the Source State's Characterization, but Interpret the* *Treaty or Include Specific Treaty Provisions that Require the Source* *State to Follow the Categorization of the Partner's Residence State*

The starting point for this approach is the application of states' own characterization rules. If there are differences created by this approach, specific treaty provisions or the interpretation of the treaty should be sufficient to mitigate these differences. An example of this approach can be found in the Netherlands.

---

[8] OECD Partnership Report (1999), para 105; Commentary of the OECD Model Treaty (2000), para 32.2 of the Commentary to art 23.

A Decree of 17 March 1997 deals with the situation that a foreign body holds a substantial participation in a Dutch company (Vakstudie-Nieuws 1997: 1456). Whilst the Netherlands regards the foreign entity as non-transparent, other countries may consider it to be transparent. The Dutch Ministry of Finance is prepared, subject to a number of conditions, to apply the treaty as if the participants in the foreign body owned a proportionate share in the Dutch company directly. This is in line with the solution in the OECD Partnership Report, which holds that regardless of the source state's internal law categorization, the source state should interpret the treaty so that the treaty with the partners' residence state applies if that state treats the partnership as transparent.[9] An example of a specific treaty provision is found in paragraph 4(b) in the first Protocol to the new Belgium–Netherlands Treaty.

According to the Netherlands, the solution proposed by the OECD is only applicable to the extent that it has been explicitly laid down in a specific tax treaty provision or in an internal rule of policy (like the Decree of 17 March 1997). If this is not the case, one can only rely on the mutual agreement procedure (Engelen and Pötgens 2000: 252)

16.4. Conclusion

In this chapter we have attempted to shed some light on the very complicated issue of the fiscal treatment of partnerships in international tax law in cross-border situations. We have focused on the problems that arise from differences in qualification of a foreign partnership in the country of residence of the partners and the country of residence of the partnership. After having reviewed the three above-mentioned methods, we prefer the first proposal. Under this approach, the country where the partnership is situated is determinative. The resident country of the partners should follow this qualification. Our own view is that the country where the partnership is situated has the strongest position in determining the tax position of the partnership. This method implies, of course, that part of the tax authority of the country of residence of the partners is removed because it must follow the qualification of the state of residence of the partnership. We find this appropriate, nevertheless, in the light of the goal to prevent double taxation or double non-taxation.

Moreover, we have shown that an analysis of the OECD Partnership Report taxation of foreign partnerships reveals that a number of outstanding tax problems exist. For instance, there are significant differences that arise by qualifying type of income (dividend payment versus interest payment). Furthermore, some countries treat specific partnerships only as partly transparent and partly non-transparent. Whilst a number of these problems are mentioned in the Report, we must look outside the Report to find solutions.

[9] Commentary of the OECD Model Treaty (2000), para 6.3; para 6.4 of the Commentary on art 1 and para 8.46 of the Commentary on art 4.

REFERENCES

Avery Jones, John, et al. (2002), 'Characterization of Other States' Partnerships', *Bulletin—Tax Treaty Monitor*, IBFD (July) 288.

Daniels, R. (1991), *Issues in International Partnership Taxation*, Deventer: Kluwer.

Engelen, F., and Pötgens, F. G. (2000), 'Report on the Application of the OECD Model Tax Convention to Partnership and the Interpretation of Tax Treaties', *European Taxation* 4: 252.

OECD (1999), *The Application of the OECD Model Tax Convention to Partnerships*, Paris: OECD.

—— (2000), *OECD Model Tax Convention and Commentary*, Paris: OECD.

Stevens, A. J. A. (2002), *Fiscale aspecten van de Commanditaire Vennootschap*, Deventer: Kluwer.

van Kempen, M. L. M. (1999), *Rechtspersoonlijkheid en belastingplicht van vennootschappen*, Deventer: Tjeenk Willink.

Vogel, K. (1986), 'Double Taxation Treaties and their Interpretation', *International Tax and Business Lawyer* 4: 86.

Appendix 1
The European Private Company
Draft Regulation: The Articles

I. GENERAL PROVISIONS

Article 1 (Definition)

1. A European Private Company ('EPC') may be incorporated by one or more individuals or legal entities, nationals of a Member State or not, in the conditions and in the manner provided for under this Regulation.

2. All founding shareholders shall, personally or through agents having special authority, be joined as parties to the articles of association. The articles of association shall be a contract binding on the founding shareholders and, after registration, on the company and future shareholders.

Article 2 (Features)

1. Each shareholder shall be liable only to the extent of the contribution made.

2. The EPC may not issue securities to the public or issue bearer shares.

3. The articles of association define, within the framework of this Regulation, the rights of shareholders, the organization and operation of the company, the powers of its governing bodies and the manner of transfers of shares.

4. The EPC shall have legal personality from the time of its registration.

Article 3 (Capital)

1. The capital of the EPC shall be divided into shares of a fixed amount. It shall not be less than 25,000 Euros or an equivalent amount, at the time of registration, in another currency. It shall be subscribed for and paid in full at the time of registration.

2. Share capital may be contributed in cash or in kind, but not in work or services.

3. The funds generated by payment for the shares shall be deposited for the account of the company being incorporated by the parties who have received them, within eight days after receipt thereof, with a notary or a bank, in exchange for an acknowledgement of receipt.

The Appendix was prepared by Robert Drury (one of the primary draftsmen of the Regulation).

The funds may be withdrawn only after registration of the company in the manner provided for under Article 8 of this Regulation, by the company's agent upon submission of the certificate from the agency registering the company.

4. Contributions in kind shall be put at the disposition of the company within the same period. They shall be delivered against an acknowledgement of receipt to an agent of the company being incorporated.

Article 4 (Valuation of Contributions in Kind)

1. The articles of association shall contain a valuation of each contribution in kind.

2. Such valuation shall be performed on the basis of a report appended to the articles of association and drafted subject to his, her or its own responsibility by an expert authorized to perform the statutory review of accounts according to the legislation of each Member State, in accordance with Directive 84/253/EEC. Such expert shall be appointed by the future shareholders acting unanimously or, in default, by a Court decision at the request of the most diligent future shareholder.

3. If the company is incorporated by a single person, such expert shall be appointed by the sole shareholder.

4. If the value stated in the articles of association is different from the value returned by the expert, the founding shareholders shall be jointly liable to third parties in respect of the value attributed to the contributions in kind upon the company's incorporation, during a term of five years from the date of registration.

Article 5 (Incorporation Methods)

1. An EPC may be incorporated by means of creation or transformation, whether or not connected with a merger or division.

2. Only companies listed under Article 1 of Directive 68/151/EEC may be transformed into EPCs. Such transformation shall not entail either winding up or creation of a new legal entity.

(a) The governing, management, or administrative body or bodies of the company shall draw up a proposal for the transformation and a report explaining and justifying the legal and economic aspects of the transformation, and stating the consequences for the shareholders and employees of the adoption of the form of an EPC.

(b) The proposed transformation shall be publicized in accordance with the legislation applicable in each Member State implementing Article 3 of Directive 68/151/EEC, one month at least prior to the date of the general meeting called to resolve upon the transformation.

(c) Prior to the general meeting, one or more independent experts, appointed or approved in the manner provided for by the legislation in each Member

State implementing Article 10 of Directive 78/855/EEC, by a judicial or administrative agency of the State in which the company transforming into an EPC is established, shall attest that the company has assets valued at no less than the amount of its issued capital.

(d) The general meeting shall approve the proposed transformation and the EPC's articles of association of the EPC in the manner provided for by the legislation of each Member State implementing Article 7 of Directive 78/855/EEC.

3. If the EPC has not been incorporated within six months after the first deposit of funds performed in accordance with Article 3-3 of this Regulation, the contributors may, through an agent representing them collectively, withdraw the amount of their contributions.

Article 6 (Registered Office)

1. The registered office of the EPC shall be located within the Union. It shall correspond to the location of its central administration.

2. The registered office of the EPC may be transferred to another Member State. Such transfer shall not entail a winding up or creation of a new legal entity. The transfer plan shall be drawn up by the body or bodies designated by the articles of association. It shall be filed and publicized in the manner provided for under Articles 8 and 9 of this Regulation. No decision to approve the plan may be taken within a period of one month following its publication.

3. The shareholders and creditors of the company shall be entitled to examine at the company's registered office the transfer plan and report referred to under the foregoing paragraph not less than one month before the date scheduled for the general meeting called to resolve upon the transfer.

4. When an EPC no longer complies with the obligation of having its central administration on the territory of the Member State of the European Union where it is registered, it shall be required to rectify the position within three months. In default of rectification within the period of three months, the company shall be liable to winding up.

Article 7 (Name)

The EPC shall select a corporate name which may include the object of the company, the name of one or more shareholders, or be entirely imaginary, provided that it must not be misleading or liable to cause confusion. The company's name shall be preceded or followed immediately by the words 'European Private Company' or the acronym 'EPC'.

Article 8 (Registration)

1. The EPC shall be registered in the State of its registered office, in the register specified by the legislation in that State implementing Article 3 of Directive 68/151/EEC.

2. The registration formalities may be carried out by any person authorized by the founders for such purpose or appointed by the articles of association to represent the company in relation to third parties.

3. For registration purposes, the following information shall be provided: The company's form and name, its duration if determined, the objects of the company, the address of the company's registered office, the amount of subscribed capital and the body or bodies having authority to enter into commitments to third parties for the company and to represent it before the Courts. The names and particulars of the persons appointed to such governing body or bodies shall also be specified.

The following documents shall be provided: The articles of association, a document specifying the allotment of shares, the acknowledgement of receipt of the deposit of the capital contributions, and evidence, if appropriate, that the contributions in kind have been put at the disposition of the company, the experts' report on such contributions, and if applicable, the resolution approving the transformation, merger, or division.

4. The agency responsible for the register shall ascertain that the requirements provided for under paragraph 3 are met and that all the information required to be included in the articles of association under this Regulation is contained therein. It shall issue a certificate evidencing compliance with the registration procedure and validity of the registration. It shall transmit all such information and any amendment or striking-out to the central Community register created for such purpose.

5. An EPC's registration with, or striking-out from, the national register shall be publicized.

Article 9 (Publication)

Matters relating to the EPC and requiring publication under this Regulation shall be publicized in accordance with the legislation of each Member State implementing Article 3-4 of Directive 68/151/EEC, and shall also be publicized by means of a notice in the OJEC. Such notice shall contain in all cases the corporate name, registration number, date of registration of the action, and location of the EPC's registered office.

Article 10 (Adoption of Acts)

1. The company shall not be bound by any acts of the founders carried out in its name prior to its registration. It may, however, after registration, substitute itself for the founders, subject to the consent of the other party if the act adopted constitutes a binding agreement.

2. Unless the act is adopted by the company, the individuals or legal entities having carried it out shall be jointly and severally liable and without limitation therefor during a term of five years from the date of registration.

Article 11 (Nullity)

Nullity of a company may arise only out of an express provision of the law applicable in the State of the registered office in accordance with Article 11 of Directive 68/151/EEC.

Article 12 (Governing Law)

1. The EPC shall be governed by the provisions of this Regulation and the provisions of the EPC's articles of association which are not inconsistent therewith.
   The matters governed by this Regulation shall not be subject to application of the law of the Member States, even with respect to those points which it does not settle expressly.

2. The following shall be successively applied in the order stated below:
   The general principles of the Regulation;
   The general principles of Community company law and the general principles common to the national laws, provided that they are not inconsistent with this Regulation.

3. The provisions of national company law in the State of the registered office of the EPC shall apply only in those cases where this Regulation makes express reference thereto.

Article 13 (Contents of Schedules to the Regulation)

This Regulation includes:

   (a) as Schedule 1: Standard-form articles of association which the shareholders may expressly adopt wholly or in part;
   (b) as Schedule 2: The form of company to which the EPC shall be considered equivalent in each Member State, in particular in respect of the application of accounting, social and criminal legislation;
   (c) as Schedule 3: The corporate forms into which an EPC may be transformed.

II. Organization and Operation

Article 14 (Organization of the Company)

The articles of association shall determine the company's organization. In particular, they shall determine the manner of appointment, powers and terms of operation of the company's governing bodies, and the relationship between them.

They shall specify the terms of appointment of the statutory auditors and their function and duties in the circumstances and conditions provided for by the national law implementing Directive 78/660/EEC.

Article 15 (Rights and Powers of the Shareholders)

1. The articles of association shall determine the pecuniary and non-pecuniary rights relating to each class of shares. They need not be proportional to the fraction of the capital represented by each share.

The following matters shall be so determined, in particular:
the proportion of the distributed profits and of the surplus assets in a liquidation attributable to each share;
the number of votes granted, for decisions taken collectively by the shareholders, to each share to which a voting right attaches. Such number may vary according to the nature of the decisions.

2. The articles of association shall determine the decisions which must be taken collectively by the shareholders. They shall also provide for the required procedures and requirements, in particular as to the manner of consultation and requirements as to quorum and majority. Unless otherwise provided for by the articles of association, collective decisions shall be binding on the officers.

3. The approval of the annual accounts and the allocation of profits, the appointment of the statutory auditor provided for under Article 14, and any amendment of the articles of association, in particular as regards increase, redemption or reduction of the capital, merger, spin-off or winding up, shall require a collective decision.

One or more shareholders holding at least ten per cent of the votes may, at any time, call for a consultation of the shareholders holding voting rights, in the manner provided for by the articles of association.

4. A sole shareholder shall exercise the powers granted to the shareholders collectively.

5. The collective decisions referred to under paragraphs 2 and 3 shall be minuted. Resolutions of the sole shareholder shall be minuted or reduced to writing.

Article 16 (Representation of the Company in Relation to Third Parties)

1. The company shall be represented in relation to third parties by one or more individuals or legal entities having full powers to act in all circumstances in the company's name. They shall exercise such powers within the limits of the objects of the company, and subject to those matters in respect of which the Regulation or the articles of association require collective decisions by the shareholders.

2. In its relations with third parties, the company shall be bound even by action taken by its representatives outside the objects of the company. Provisions in the articles of association restricting the governing bodies' powers may not be relied on as against third parties.

Article 17 (Liability of Officers)

1. The officer or officers of the EPC, appointed in accordance with Article 14, shall be liable, individually or jointly, to the company for actions in breach of the rules applicable to the company by virtue of Article 12 of this Regulation. They shall be liable, in the same manner, for breach of their duties and the standard of diligence reasonably required in the conduct of business.

2. When a legal entity performs representation or management or takes part therein, its officers shall be subject to the same requirements and obligations and incur the same civil and criminal liability as if they performed management in their personal capacities, without prejudice to the liability of the legal entity which they manage.

3. De facto officers shall be treated as de jure officers as regards all obligations and liability to which the latter are subject.

Article 18 (Actions for Reparation)

1. Each shareholder may bring action against the officer or officers for reparation of the damage suffered by the shareholder personally.

2. Shareholders holding ten per cent at least of the capital or votes may, individually or together, bring action for reparation on behalf of the company against the officers. The plaintiffs may call for reparation of all the damage suffered by the company to which, if applicable, the damages shall be awarded.

3. Actions for reparation shall be time-barred three years after the event causing the damage or, if concealed, after its discovery.

Article 19 (Nullity of a Resolution)

Any resolution of the shareholders or a governing body of the company in breach of a rule or a significant formality provided for under this Regulation or

the articles of association may be annulled by the Court of competent jurisdiction. The action for annulment may be brought, within six months after the
date of such resolution, by any shareholder not having approved it, subject to
rectification by the company.

III. RULES GOVERNING SECURITIES

Article 20 (Assignment of Shares, Change in Control)

1. If a transfer of shares requires approval, the articles of association shall specify the body having competence to give it, and the applicable procedure and
timetable. They shall determine the manner of withdrawal of a shareholder to
whom approval is denied.

2. The articles of association may specify that any change in control over a
shareholder, as defined by the articles of association, shall be treated as an
assignment. It shall be notified to the company in the manner and within the
period determined by the articles of association.

3. The articles of association may provide for non-pecuniary rights attaching to
the shares of the EPC held by a non-approved shareholder or the shareholder
over which control has changed, to be held in abeyance.

Article 21 (Compulsory Assignment and Withdrawal of a Shareholder)

1. Shareholders may be required to assign their shares in the circumstances and
according to the procedure provided for under the articles of association.

In addition, at the request of one or more shareholders holding a majority of
votes, the Court of competent jurisdiction may order an assignment of a shareholder's shares, if the shareholder has seriously damaged the company's interests or if the continuation of the shareholder as a member of the company is
detrimental to its proper operation. The articles of association may also provide
for the non-pecuniary rights of such shareholder to be held in abeyance until the
assignment has been carried out.

2. Shareholders may claim acquisition of their shares in the circumstances and
in accordance with the procedure provided for under the articles of association.
In addition, any shareholder considering that their interests have been damaged
may petition the Court of competent jurisdiction for the acquisition of their
shares, in the event of a significant change in one or more of the articles of
association, assignment or contribution to another company of all or the essential assets of the EPC, substantial change in the company's business or the withholding, for several financial years, to an extent not justified by the company's
financial position of any distribution of profits relating to their shares.

Article 22 (Price for Acquisition or Assignment of Shares)

1. The manner of determination of the price for acquisition or assignment shall be determined by the articles of association in the cases referred to under Articles 20 and 21. The price may not be less than the actual value of the shares.

2. If the shares are redeemed by the EPC, it shall be bound to assign or cancel them within six months after the redemption.

Article 23 (Inalienability of Shares)

The articles of association may provide that shares shall be inalienable for a term not exceeding five years.

Article 24 (Effects of Assignment in Breach of the Articles of Association)

Any assignment in breach of the terms of the articles of association shall be void. In the event of breach of a pre-emptive right, provided for under the articles of association in favour of the company or one or more shareholders, the Court of competent jurisdiction may order, at the request of one of the parties or of the company, transfer of the benefit of the assignment to the company or one or more of the aforesaid assignees, at a price determined in the manner provided for under Article 22.

Article 25 (Change in Terms of the Articles of Association Governing the Securities)

Resolutions adding, removing or amending terms of the articles of association provided for under Articles 20, 21 and 22 may be passed only by the shareholders acting unanimously.

IV. ACTION RELATING TO THE CAPITAL

Article 26 (Capital Increase or Reduction)

1. Increases or reductions in the capital shall be resolved upon in the manner determined by the articles of association in accordance with Article 15.

2. The proposed reduction shall be notified to the statutory auditor, who shall draw up a report within one month before the date scheduled for the collective decision. Such report shall be notified immediately to the shareholders who are to take part in the collective decision and the known creditors shall be informed of the proposed reduction, their right to enter objections and the manner of the exercise thereof.

3. In the case of a capital reduction of capital, creditors whose debts antedate the resolution may enter objections within one month after publication of the reduction resolution in the manner provided for under Article 9. The Court trying the matter, if it upholds the objection, may order either reimbursement of the debts or the grant of security. Capital reduction operations may not begin during the period allowed for objections.

Article 27 (Redemption of its Own Shares by the Company)

1. Without prejudice to the effect of Article 26, the EPC may redeem its own shares in the manner and on the terms provided for under the articles of association.

2. The EPC may not, however, hold directly or indirectly through a party acting in its own name but on behalf of the company more than 25 per cent of the total of its own shares. The shares owned by the EPC shall not carry dividends and may not vote.

3. The provisions of the foregoing paragraph shall not apply in the event of a transfer of all assets and liabilities or of enforcement of a judicial decision.

4. Under penalty of nullity, an EPC may not accept a pledge of its own shares, or advance any funds or grant any loan or security interest for the purpose of acquisition of its own shares.

Article 28 (Diminution of the Company's Net Assets)

1. In the event of a diminution of the company's net assets to a level less than that of the minimum capital, the shareholders shall be consulted within one month after the losses are entered in the accounting records in order to resolve either to wind up the company or to continue its operations. In the latter case, the shareholders shall, within six months, contribute further capital such that net assets of the company are at least equal to the amount mentioned under paragraph 1 of Article 3.

2. If the company's net assets fall below half of the subscribed capital, the shareholders shall be consulted within one month in order to consider whether the company should be wound up. If winding up is not resolved upon, the company shall be bound, within six months after the losses are entered in the accounting records, and subject to the provisions of Article 3 of this Regulation, to reduce its capital by an amount at least equal to that of the losses, or to contribute further capital so as to restore the company's net assets to an amount at least equal to that of the subscribed capital.

3. In the event of breach of the foregoing provisions of this Article, the company may be wound up in accordance with the procedure applicable in the Member State of its registered office.

V. MANAGEMENT SUPERVISION

Article 29 (Agreements with the Company)

1. Under penalty of nullity of the agreement, officers or shareholders other than legal entities may not in any manner whatsoever, directly or indirectly, obtain any loans from the company, obtain any overdraft from it, as a shareholder's current account or otherwise, or obtain from it any security or any guarantee or other surety in respect of their commitments to third parties.

2. The statutory auditor referred to under Article 14 of this Regulation shall submit to the shareholders a report on agreements giving rise to conflicts of interests, made directly or indirectly between the company and one or more of its officers or shareholders. The articles of association shall determine the applicable procedure.

3. Agreements between the sole shareholder and the company represented by the sole shareholder shall be minuted or reduced to writing.

4. These provisions shall not be applicable to transactions entered into by the company in the ordinary course of its business.

Article 30 (Disclosure to Shareholders)

1. Any shareholder shall be entitled to be informed of the collective decisions referred to under Article 15, and shall be allowed access to the company's principal management documents.

2. The shareholder may submit questions in writing regarding the operation of the company, which the officers shall be bound to answer in accordance with a procedure determined by the articles of association.

Article 31 (Management Audit)

The officers shall be bound to reply, within one month, to any question relating to one or more acts of management, submitted in writing by one or more shareholders holding ten per cent or more of the capital or votes, or by any other party having such right under the articles of association. In the absence of a satisfactory reply, and if the situation is liable to be detrimental to the corporate interest, such shareholder or shareholders may petition the President of the Court of competent jurisdiction to appoint one or more auditors to report on such act or acts of management.

VI. Annual Accounts

Article 32

The EPC shall be subject to the accounting rules applicable, in each Member State, to the form of company to which it is considered equivalent for such purpose under Schedule 2.

VII. Employees' Rights

Article 33

The rules relating to disclosure to and consultation of the employees, and if applicable, their involvement in the corporate bodies, shall be determined by the law applicable to the registered office of the EPC.

VIII. Criminal Law

Article 34

The EPC, its officers and its shareholders shall be subject to the rules of criminal law applicable in each Member State to the corporate form to which it is considered equivalent for such purpose by Schedule 2, except the provisions providing for penalties relating to obligations which are not applicable to it in accordance with Article 12 of this Regulation.

IX. Transformation of the EPC

Article 35

1. The EPC may be transformed into one of the companies in the list attached as Schedule 3. Transformation shall not entail winding up or creation of a new legal entity.

2. The competent body or bodies shall draw up a transformation plan and a report presenting and justifying the legal and economic features of the plan. The report shall set out the consequences of adoption of the new corporate form for the shareholders and for the employees.

3. The transformation plan shall be notified to the employees, and publicized in the manner provided for by the legislation of each Member State implementing Article 3 of Directive 68/151/EEC, one month at least prior to the collective resolution relating to the transformation.

4. Prior to the collective resolution, one or more independent experts, appointed or approved in the manner provided for by the legislation in each Member State in accordance with Article 10-1 of Directive 78/855/EEC, shall certify that the company has assets valued at no less than the amount of its subscribed capital.

5. The transformation plan and the articles of association of the new company shall be submitted to the EPC's shareholders for approval in the manner provided for under the articles of association.

6. The transformation shall entail an amendment of the registration and a publication, in accordance with Article 9 of this Regulation.

X. Winding up, Liquidation, Insolvency and Cessation of Payments

Article 36 (Governing Law)

1. With respect to winding up, liquidation, insolvency, cessation of payments and other insolvency or similar proceedings, the EPC shall be subject to the legal rules applicable to the companies to which it is considered equivalent in each State pursuant to this Regulation. The persons referred to by national law may be held liable, individually or jointly, for all or part of the corporate liabilities, and subject to disqualifications and forfeitures, in the manner provided for by such law.

2. Without prejudice to the cases in which they may be held liable personally, initiation of proceedings against an EPC on the grounds of its insolvency or cessation of payments shall not entail initiation of such proceedings against the shareholders or officers.

3. An EPC against which proceedings have been brought for winding up, liquidation, insolvency, cessation of payments or other similar proceedings, may not transfer its registered office to another Member State.

Article 37 (Publication)

Insolvency or cessation of payments, initiation of proceedings for winding up or liquidation, and termination thereof and the resolution to continue operation, shall be publicized in accordance with Article 9 of this Regulation.

Article 38 (Action for Winding up and rectification)

In the event of an action for winding up, the Court trying the matter or the agency having authority may not order winding up if, on the date of its decision on the merits, the situation has been rectified.

4. Prior to the collective cessation, one or more independent reports appointed or approved in accordance with Article 10 of Directive shall, in each Member State, in accordance with Article 10 of Directive, report that while still the company has done all which it states that the relevant shall be fulfilled.

5. The management plan and the draft decree shall, apart of the relevant information to be taken into account for the approval of the registration, provide for made the stipulated legislation.

6. The management plan and draft approval of the registration and a putative, competent in accordance with these rules Section 9 of this Regulation.

7. In respect to cooperation, Editors shall apply ...

Article 6 ("Governing law")

1. Where registered undertaking, both immediately have presented a resolution of other undertakings within the meaning of Section 10 by virtue of the legal rules applicable to the companies involved, it is expressly conforming in each State pursuant to a registration. The measures referred to above should not also be laid upon individuals who took over, in respect of the company's obligations, concluded in dissolution situation and liabilities of the company covered for by resolution.

Without prejudice to the general terms of which there is a legal notice, measures of proceedings pursuant to a Court be brought on this basis, on the terms of execution, and the ascertainment of such prices throughout the distribution of collective.

2. An EEO cannot which the collective dissolution of principal for shall thought item distinguish between various sources. Treatment of what shall be the collective measures of one regime relating to collective Member State.

Article 7 ("Publication")

measures of registration scheme, including that relation of the registration. A liquidation, and taken in thereby, shall the resolution to continue also that shall be collected in accordance with Section 9 of this Regulation.

Article 8 ("Dissolution and rectification")

1. The resolution of a scheme to wind up the EEO shall, except for the agency being mandatory duty or commensurate, and the collected resolution from the nominee be situation in their relations.

Appendix 2
The European Private Company Draft Regulation: Schedule 1. Standard Form Articles of Association

MODEL A

Form

1. The company is a European Private Company formed pursuant to European Union Regulation number . . . ('the Regulation').

Name

2. The name of the company is '. . . European Private Company'.

Object

3. The object of the company is to . . .

Registered Office

4. The registered office of the company is at . . .

Duration

5. The duration of the company is indefinite.

Share Capital

6.1 The company's share capital is . . . divided into . . . shares of . . . each which shall be subscribed for and paid in full at the time of subscription in cash or in kind but not in work or services.

6.2 Any increase of capital shall be paid for in full at the time of subscription.

6.3 No shareholder shall be bound by any alteration to these articles requiring them to take or subscribe for more shares in the company or increasing their liability contribute to the company's share capital or otherwise pay money to the company unless such shareholder has agreed in writing to be so bound.

Contributions

7. The founding shareholders shall contribute the share capital in the following proportions:-

In cash . . .	Mr. . . .	. . . Euros
	Mr. . . .	. . . Euros
Total		. . . Euros, which amount was deposited on . . /. . /. . to the credit of an account opened in the name of the company [in formation] at . . . Bank as is proven by [receipt no. . . .].

In kind in the form of . . . which the founding shareholders value at . . . Euros, and which has been put at the disposition of the company as is proven by the receipt of . . . as agent for the company in formation. A report valuing the contribution(s) in kind is appended to these articles.

Transfer of Shares

8.1 Shares are transferred by a written form of transfer signed by or on behalf of the transferor and transferee.

8.2 Shares are freely transferable to other shareholders but shares or any interest in them may only be transferred to third parties with the written approval of [other] shareholders representing [three quarters of] the shares not subject to the proposed transfer.

Note: The words in square brackets represent alternative ways of dealing with the problem that arises where a majority shareholder wishes to transfer part of their holding to a third party of whom the remaining shareholders may not approve. Such a transfer should be subject to the approval of either all of the other shareholders (in which case all of the words in the brackets could be removed) or of a three-quarters majority of the other shareholders (in which case the brackets themselves should be removed).

8.3 Within 28 days of receiving a written request to transfer shares the company shall notify the applicant of the decision of the shareholders.

8.4 If a shareholder requests approval to transfer some or all of their shares, the continuing shareholder or shareholders who so wish are entitled to take a transfer of the shares at a fair valuation determined in accordance with article 8.6 below, and if more than one such shareholder, to take them in proportion to their existing shareholdings

8.5 If the shareholders refuse approval of a transfer of shares the shareholder requesting transfer shall make reasonable endeavours to find a transferee willing to take a transfer who is acceptable to the continuing shareholders. If such endeavours fail to find an acceptable transferee, the continuing shareholders shall at the expiration of six months from the refusal of the original transfer take the shares of the shareholder requesting transfer in proportion to their existing shareholdings at a fair valuation for an immediate or deferred payment.

Note: While it may be desirable to find an exit route for disappointed transferors, they should not have too immediate a right to offload their shares on the continuing members as a sudden withdrawal of capital would threaten the survival of many small businesses.

8.6 A fair valuation shall be found by taking the market value of all the company's shares, assuming a sale by a willing seller to a willing buyer as at the end of the six month period referred to, and by multiplying that market value by the fraction of the whole share capital of the company which the shares to be transferred represent.

8.7 Failing agreement on valuation, a fair valuation on the basis set out above shall be decided by an independent person acting as an expert valuer. The independent valuer shall be the company's statutory auditor if one is appointed, or if none, shall be nominated by agreement between the parties, or in the event that they fail to agree the valuer shall be nominated by [the President for the time being of the . . . Chamber of Commerce].

Note: This should result in a pro rata valuation rather than one discounted by reason of the shares being a minority holding nor one giving a premium for control.

8.8 Any share or shares may only be held in the name of a single shareholder and the company shall not be bound by or recognize any interest in shares except the absolute right of the holder to the whole interest therein.

Note: This provision, which is usual in English companies, is inserted to deal with the problem of shares being held by trustees, or an administratiekantoor in the Dutch system or possibly under a usufruct in this and other systems.

Management and Representation

9.1 The business of the company shall be managed by the shareholders exercising all the powers of the company as a management board unless by unanimous decision they appoint a manager or managers to act in their place for a fixed period. The manager or managers may be appointed from among the shareholders or not, as the shareholders shall decide.

9.2 If no manager or managers are appointed the members shall conduct such business by majority decision, each having one vote. The quorum required for taking such decisions shall be two. If so requested by any one member or members together holding at least 20 per cent of the shares of the company they shall vote on the basis of one vote per share. Otherwise, subject to the requirements of the Regulation and these articles, they may conduct their business as they think fit.

9.3 Any two members acting jointly shall represent the company in making commitments to third parties and before the courts. If a manager or managers are appointed, a sole manager acting alone or, if more than one manager is appointed, any two acting jointly, shall so represent the company.

Shareholders' Rights

10.1 Profits allocated for distribution and surplus assets in a liquidation shall be distributed to shareholders in the proportion in which they hold shares in the company.

10.2 Where the share capital of the company is increased the shares shall first be offered to the members of the company in proportion to their existing holdings. If any member declines to purchase any such shares they shall be offered to the other members of the company in proportion to their existing holdings. If any of the shares then remain unsold they shall be offered to any members willing to purchase them. Any remaining shares shall be issued in accordance with a collective decision of the members.

10.3 Shareholders shall be entitled to one vote per share on decisions taken collectively by them.

10.4 If a manager or managers are appointed the following decisions shall neverthless be taken collectively by the shareholders:

(i)   the dismissal or re-appointment of a manager;
(ii)   the appointment of a new manager or managers;
(iii)   the approval of the annual accounts and other documents required by the applicable national law;
(iv)   the allocation of profits;
(v)   the appointment of a statutory auditor as required by the applicable law;
(vi)   any variation of the articles of association;
(vii)   any increase, redemption or reduction of capital;
(viii) any merger or division of the company;
(ix)   the mortgaging or charging of any assets of the company;
(x)   the disposal of all or a substantial part of the company's business undertaking;
(xi)   decisions, other than those in the ordinary course of business, which may materially affect the company or its shareholders;
(xii)   that the company be dissolved or enter into insolvency proceedings.

10.5 The shareholders may at any time by unanimous resolution in writing notify the manager or managers of any further matter that is to be decided by the shareholders collectively or upon which they wish to be consulted.

10.6 One or more shareholders holding at least ten per cent (10%) of the votes may at any time call for a consultation of the shareholders holding voting rights. This consultation may either take place at a meeting in respect of which all shareholders have been given sufficient notice to enable them to attend or, if no member dissents, by written or other permanent means of communication signed or otherwise authenticated by them.

10.7 Collective decisions may either be taken at a meeting in respect of which all shareholders have been given sufficient notice to enable them to attend or, if no member dissents, by written or other permanent means of communication signed or otherwise authenticated by them and acceptable as good evidence of the decision made. Such communication shall be returned to the registered office of the company within a reasonable time of receipt of notification of the decision to be taken.

10.8 Members may vote at any meeting either in person or by proxy. Members may appoint a shareholder or a manager to act as their proxy, and the instructions in such proxies shall be binding upon the person so appointed. An instrument appointing a proxy shall be in writing, executed by the member and must be delivered to the registered office of the company at least 48 hours before the meeting in respect of which it is to be exercised.

10.9 The quorum for any meeting at which a collective decision is to be taken shall be two members present in person or by proxy.

10.10 Except as otherwise provided in these articles, collective decisions shall require the approval of shareholders holding a majority of the votes attaching to the shares of the company.

10.11 Collective decisions adding, removing or amending the terms of the articles of association provided for under Articles 20, 21 and 22 of the Regulation may only be made by the shareholders acting unanimously.

Note: A reference to the articles of association would be preferable to a reference to the Regulation once this document is printed.

10.12 A collective decision of the members to dissolve the company or to make any alteration to the articles of association other than those specified above may only be made by shareholders representing three-quarters of the shares in the company.

10.13 Minutes of the collective decisions of the shareholders shall be recorded in writing or other permanent legible form.

10.14 Collective decisions of the shareholders are binding on the manager or managers and other officers if any.

10.15 Whether a manager or managers are or are not appointed, the shareholders shall have access at all reasonable times to the company's principal management documents and to such books, accounts and other documents and records of the company as are necessary to enable them to carry out their managerial duties and to assert their rights under the Regulation and these articles.

Financial Year

11. The financial year of the company runs from . . . to . . . each year.

Transmission of Shares

12. On the death of any shareholder, the surviving shareholders may not object to the transmission of shares to a spouse, an ascendant or descendant of the deceased shareholder, but in the case of transmission to any other person they may exercise the same rights over these shares as if the personal representatives of the deceased shareholder had requested approval of a transfer of shares under Article 8 above.

Compulsory Assignment and Withdrawal of a Shareholder

13.1 If a shareholder has seriously damaged the company's interest or if the continuation of the shareholder as a member of the company is detrimental to its proper operation, the shareholder may be required to assign their shares as appears below and one or more shareholders holding a majority of voting rights in the company may apply to the Court of competent jurisdiction for an order that the offending shareholder assign their shares as directed.

13.2 The continuation of a shareholder as a member of the company shall be considered detrimental to its proper operation inter alia in the following circumstances:

    (i)   if a creditor of a shareholder becomes entitled to any interest in the shares or in their proceeds of sale by reason of a legal process for the enforcement of a debt or other obligation;

   (ii)   if any insolvency proceedings or proceedings for the realization of any security are instituted against any shareholder;

  (iii)   if a shareholder pledges all or part of their shares without the prior consent of the other shareholders;

  (iv)   if a shareholder commits a serious breach of any obligation arising under these articles;

   (v)   if there is any change in the control of any corporate shareholder, except where the new shareholders of that corporate member to whom control passes are either the spouses or descendants of the previous shareholders.

13.3 In the circumstances specified in Article 13.2 above, or in the event that an order of a competent Court under Article 21.1 of the Regulation requiring the assignment of any shares is not immediately complied with, the non-pecuniary rights attaching to those shares may immediately be suspended by a collective decision.

13.4 A shareholder who considers their interests to have been damaged may petition the Court of competent jurisdiction for the acquisition of their shares in the circumstances and in the manner appearing in Article 21.2 of the Regulation.

13.5 Where shares are assigned or acquired under this article the price shall be determined in accordance with Articles 8.6 and 8.7 above, but may not be less than the actual value of the shares.

Redemption of Shares

14. Either The shares issued by the company shall not be redeemable

or Without prejudice to Article 15 of the Regulation, the company may redeem its shares *in compliance with the laws of of the place of its registered office regulating the equivalent form of company specified in Schedule 2 of the Regulation.*

Note: See Regulation Article 12. It is suggested that the italicized words should be added to Article 27.1 of the Regulation. In the United Kingdom, for example, there are rules to protect creditors in the case of companies buying their own shares and it would be highly desirable for the EPC to comply with something resembling these.

Auditors

15.1 In the circumstances required by the legislation in force in the state of the company's registered office applicable to the equivalent form of company in that jurisdiction specified in Schedule 2 of the Regulation, the company shall appoint an auditor.

15.2 In other cases the company may appoint an auditor if the members by collective decision so decide.

15.3 Every appointment of an auditor shall be made by a collective decision of the members.

15.4 The terms of appointment, qualifications, function and duties of such auditors shall be as required by the applicable legislation.

Formation Expenses

16. The reasonable expenses of forming the company shall be borne by the company.

Dispute Resolution

17. In cases other than where a shareholder is entitled under the Regulation or these articles of association to bring a matter before a Court of competent jurisdiction, in any dispute arising between members or between members and the company the parties will use their best endeavours to settle it by voluntary mediation involving the non-binding intervention by a neutral third party who helps the disputants to negotiate an agreement [for alternative wording see below] and no party may commence any court procedings in relation to any such dispute until they have in good faith attempted to settle it by mediation and that mediation has terminated.

Note: Reference to a more precise procedure for such a mediation may be thought desirable in some cases, e.g. for a British EPC, and a clause like the following which refers to the known and established rules of the Centre for Dispute Resolution even though it is a commercial organization may be used as an alternative, e.g. 'in accordance with the Centre for Dispute Resolution (CEDR) Model Mediation Procedure or such other procedure having effect to employ the services of a suitably qualified mediator in the settlement of the dispute'.

Model B

Articles 1–8 are the same as in Model A.

Management and Representation

9.1 The first members of the management body are . . . They are appointed for a period of three years, but are eligible for re-appointment. The shareholders may remove, appoint or re-appoint any member of the management body by a simple majority of votes cast at a collective decision, each member to be voted upon individually.

Either

9.2 The management body is the manager or managers, natural persons, who is/are responsible for the management of the business of the company.

9.3 Subject to the provisions of these articles and to the matters reserved by them for the collective decision of the shareholders and to any direction given to the manager(s) by collective decision of the shareholders restricting their authority or limiting their discretion in management, each manager shall have the most extensive powers to act in all circumstances in the name of the company.

9.4 Each manager may represent the company in making commitments to third parties or before the courts.

9.5 The manager or managers may delegate any of their management functions (except those that are required to be performed by the management body as a whole either by the Regulation or by these articles) to such person or persons as they choose.

9.6 The manager(s) shall ensure that written minutes are kept of all formal decisions.

9.7 The managers shall devote their whole time and give their undivided attention to the affairs of the company.

9.8 Any decisions by the company to enter into a contract of employment with a manager and to determine the terms of such a contract shall be taken collectively by the shareholders.

9.9 The office of manager is vacated:
on removal by collective decision of the shareholders;
on being made bankrupt or otherwise entering formal insolvency proceedings;
on being prohibited by the law of any Member State from holding office as a director or manager of a company;
on suffering mental incapacity.
Or

9.2 The management body is the board of directors which is responsible for the management of the business of the company. The board of directors shall transact business as a board, the directors acting together by board resolution.

9.3 Subject to the provisions of these articles and to the matters which are reserved by them for the collective decision of the shareholders and to any direction given to the board of directors by collective decision of the shareholders restricting their authority or limiting their discretion in management, the board of directors shall have the most extensive powers to act in all circumstances in the name of the company.

9.4 The board of directors may appoint a member of the board to be chief executive on such terms as it thinks fit and may delegate any management functions to such person or persons as it chooses.

9.5 The board of directors acting as a board may represent the company in making commitments to third parties or before the courts. However, if a sole chief executive is appointed, such a person shall so represent the company. If more than one chief executive is appointed, any two acting jointly shall so represent the company.

9.6 The board of directors may regulate its proceedings as it thinks fit except that it shall ensure that written minutes are kept of all formal decisions.

9.7 The board of directors may enter into a contract of employment with a chief executive on such terms as it thinks fit.

9.8 The office and employment of a chief executive shall terminate if the chief executive ceases for any reason to be a director.

9.9 The office of director is vacated:
on removal by collective decision of the shareholders;
on being made bankrupt or otherwise entering formal insolvency proceedings;
on being prohibited by the law of any Member State from holding office as a director or manager of a company;
on suffering mental incapacity.

All

9.10 The management body and each member of it shall act in the interests of the company.

9.11 No member of the management body or any other officer of the company shall put themselves in a position where their interest may conflict materially with the interest of the company.

9.12 If any member of the management body or any other officer of the company profits from any circumstance in which their interest conflicts with that of the company they shall be liable to account to the company for all profits arising.

9.13 If any member of the management body or any other officer of the company enters into a contract or other transaction with the company whereby their interest conflicts with that of the company, the company may in its discretion affirm or avoid the contract or other transaction.

9.14 A transaction entered into by any member of the management body or any other officer with the company shall be valid and such persons may retain the benefit of any transaction notwithstanding a conflict of interest in either case if at least seven days before its conclusion they gave notice in writing to the management body, the person specified in Article 29.2 of the Regulation and the shareholders of their interest and of the nature of the transaction and no shareholder within that period of seven days requests the board to call a meeting of shareholders to resolve as a collective decision that the company shall not enter into that transaction or that such a person may not retain the benefit of the transaction.

9.15 If such a transaction referred to in Article 9.14 is not within the ordinary course of the business of the company the period of seven days in that article shall run from the time of the receipt by the shareholders of a copy of the report referred to in Article 29.2 of the Regulation.

9.16 By a resolution of shareholders representing a majority of the share capital, the liability to the company of any member of the management body or of any other officer of the company in respect of a conflict of interest may be waived and any contract with the company affirmed either prospectively or retrospectively.

9.17 The members of the management body are jointly and severally liable to the company in respect of serious management errors where they fail to exhibit the care, skill and diligence reasonably to be expected of a business person under the circumstances, except that they shall not be so liable if they acted honestly and reasonably having duly obtained sufficient information before making any relevant decision.

9.18 On any collective decision of the shareholders to exempt a member of the management body from liability for any breach of duty to the company, such a member, being a shareholder, shall be disqualified from voting and shall not be counted in the quorum present at any meeting at which they are so disqualified.

9.19 The management body is responsible for ensuring that the company complies with the accounting rules referred to in Article 32 of the Regulation and that the shareholders are consulted in the circumstances set out in Article 28 of the Regulation.

Shareholders' Rights

10.1 Profits allocated for distribution and surplus assets in a liquidation shall be distributed to shareholders in the proportion in which they hold shares in the company.

10.2 Where the share capital of the company is increased the shares shall first be offered to the members of the company in proportion to their existing holdings.

If any member declines to purchase any such shares they shall be offered to the other members of the company in proportion to their existing holdings. If any of the shares then remain unsold they shall be offered to any members willing to purchase them. Any remaining shares shall be issued in accordance with a collective decision of the members.

10.3 Shareholders shall be entitled to one vote per share on decisions taken collectively by them.

10.4 The following decisions shall be taken collectively by the shareholders and not by the management body:

(i)   the dismissal or re-appointment of a member of the managing body;

(ii)   the appointment of a new member of the managing body;

(iii) the approval of the annual accounts and other documents required by the applicable national law;

(iv)   the allocation of profits;

(v)   the appointment of a statutory auditor as required by the applicable law;

(vi)   any variation of the articles of association;

(vii) any increase, redemption or reduction of capital;

(viii) any merger or division of the company;

(ix)   the mortgaging or charging of any assets of the company;

(x)   the disposal of all or a substantial part of the company's business undertaking;

(xi)   decisions, other than those in the ordinary course of business, which may materially affect the company or its shareholders;

(xii) that the company be dissolved or enter into insolvency proceedings.

10.5 The shareholders may at any time by a three quarters majority resolution notify the management body of:

any further matter in addition to those listed in Article 10.4 that is to be decided by the shareholders collectively;

any matter, whether specific or general, about the occurrence of which they wish to be individually informed.

10.6 The shareholders may by a three-quarters majority resolution give a direction which shall be binding on the management body with regard to the exercise of its management powers or discretions.

10.7 One or more shareholders holding at least ten per cent (10%) of the votes may at any time require the management body to arrange for a meeting or other consultation of the shareholders holding voting rights, and shall have the right to propose any item to be considered. The management body shall either call a meeting in respect of which all shareholders have been given at least fourteen days notice or, if no member dissents, arrange for a consultation of all of the shareholders by written or other permanent means of communication signed or otherwise authenticated by them.

Shareholders' Proceedings

11.1 Except where procedures are specifically provided by these articles or the law applicable under the Regulation, collective decisions may either be taken at a meeting in respect of which all shareholders have been given at least fourteen days notice or, if no member dissents, at a meeting held with shorter notice or by a consultation in writing of all of the shareholders.

11.2 When a decision is taken by consultation in writing the text of the resolution proposed is sent by the managing body to each shareholder by a letter sent by recorded delivery [lettre recommandée AR]. Shareholders shall indicate their acceptance or rejection of the resolution so communicated by written or other permanent means of communication signed or otherwise authenticated by them and acceptable as good evidence of the decision made which shall be returned to the registered office of the company within fourteen days of receipt of notification of the resolution.

11.3 Shareholders may vote at any meeting either in person or by proxy. Shareholders may appoint another shareholder or a member of the managing body to act as their proxy, and the instructions in such proxies shall be binding upon the person so appointed. An instrument appointing a proxy shall be in writing, executed by the member and must be delivered to the registered office of the company at least 48 hours before the meeting in respect of which it is to be exercised.

11.4 The quorum for any meeting at which a collective decision is to be taken shall be two members present in person or by proxy.

11.5 Except as otherwise provided in these articles, collective decisions shall require the approval of shareholders holding a majority of the votes cast at that collective decision.

11.6 Collective decisions adding, removing or amending the terms of the articles of association provided for under Articles 20, 21 and 22 of the Regulation may only be made by the shareholders acting unanimously.

Note: A reference to the articles of association would be preferable to a reference to the Regulation once this document is printed.

11.7 A collective decision of the shareholders that the company be dissolved or enter into insolvency proceedings or to make any alteration to the articles of association other than those specified above requires the approval of shareholders holding a three-quarters majority of the votes cast at that collective decision.

11.8 Minutes of the proceedings including the collective decisions of the shareholders shall be recorded in writing or other permanent legible form.

11.9 Collective decisions of the shareholders are binding on the management body and on all other officers of the company.

11.10 A general meeting in respect of which all shareholders have been given at least twenty-one days notice shall be held once each year for the approval of the annual accounts and other documents required by the applicable national law unless by a unanimous collective decision the shareholders elect to dispense with holding annual general meetings for this purpose. A collective decision made by shareholders holding a majority of the votes cast may subsequently require the holding of annual general meetings for the approval of the accounts and other documents specified above.

11.11 The shareholders shall have access at all reasonable times to the company's principal management documents, including minutes of the decisions and proceedings of the management body and of the shareholders and to such books, accounts and other documents and records of the company as may be necessary to enable them to carry out their managerial duties and to assert their rights under the Regulation and these articles.

11.12 Any period of notice of any meeting or other proceeding referred to in these articles shall be exclusive of the day upon which the notice is given and of the day upon which or by which the meeting or other proceeding is to take place.

11.13 Any requirement for the giving of notice under these articles shall mean the service of notice in writing, and a notice sent by facsimile transmission to a number given by the shareholder to the company for that purpose or by any other electronic process approved for the purpose by unanimous decision of the shareholders shall be deemed to be in writing.

11.14 Where a meeting is called under these articles the chairman shall be as follows:

> a chief executive if appointed or the sole member of the management body (where there is only one), if present within fifteen minutes of the time appointed for the meeting, shall preside as chairman;
> failing which the members of the management body present at the meeting shall appoint a chairman;
> failing which the shareholders present at the meeting shall appoint a chairman.

11.15 In the case of an equality of votes at any such meeting the chairman *shall/shall not* be entitled to a casting vote in addition to any other vote that they may have.

Articles 12–17 are the same as Articles 11–16 in Model A apart from the numbering.

Dispute Resolution

18. In cases other than where a shareholder is entitled under the Regulation or these articles of association to bring a matter before a Court of competent jurisdiction, in any dispute arising between members or between members and the

company the parties will use their best endeavours to settle it by voluntary mediation involving the non-binding intervention by a neutral third party who helps the disputants to negotiate an agreement. [for alternative wording see below]

Note: Reference to a more precise procedure for such a mediation may be thought desirable in some cases, e.g. for a British EPC, and a clause like the following which refers to the known and established rules of the Centre for Dispute Resolution, even though it is a commercial organization, may be used as an alternative, e.g. 'in accordance with the Centre for Dispute Resolution (CEDR) Model Mediation Procedure or such other procedure having effect to employ the services of a suitably qualified mediator in the settlement of the dispute'.

Index